CRIMINAL LAW AND PROCEDURE

TITLES IN THE DELMAR PARALEGAL SERIES

Ransford C. Pyle, *Foundations of Law for Paralegals: Cases, Commentary, and Ethics,* 1992.

Peggy N. Kerley, Paul A. Sukys, Joanne Banker Hames, *Civil Litigation for the Paralegal,* 1992.

Jonathan Lynton, Donna Masinter, Terri Mick Lyndall, *Law Office Management for Paralegals,* 1992.

Daniel Hall, *Criminal Law and Procedure,* 1992.

CRIMINAL LAW AND PROCEDURE

Daniel Hall

LAWYERS COOPERATIVE
PUBLISHING

DELMAR
PUBLISHERS INC.

NOTICE TO THE READER

Cover photo courtesy of Eastern New York Correctional Facility.

Cover design by The Drawing Board.

Chapter opening illustrations courtesy of George B. Abbott.

Delmar Staff

Administrative Editor: Jay Whitney
Editing Supervisor: Marlene McHugh Pratt
Production Supervisor: Larry Main
Design Coordinator: Karen Kunz Kemp

For information, address

Delmar Publishers Inc.
2 Computer Drive West, Box 15-015
Albany, New York 12212

10 9 8 7 6 5 4 3 2 1

Library of Congress Cataloging-in-Publication Data

Hall, Daniel (Daniel E.)
    Criminal law and procedure for paralegals/Daniel Hall.
        p. cm.—(Delmar paralegal series)
    Includes index.
    ISBN 0-8273-4559-3 (textbook)
    1. Criminal law—United States. 2. Criminal procedure—United
States. 3. Legal assistants—United States—Handbooks, manuals,
etc. I. Title. II. Series.
KF9219.3.H32 1992
345.73—dc20
[347.305]   91-24349
                                                         CIP

CONTENTS

SECTION 1 Criminal Law

CHAPTER 1: Introduction to the Legal System of the United States   2

CHAPTER 2: Introduction to Criminal Law   24

CHAPTER 3:   **The Two Essential Elements**   **54**

CHAPTER 4:   Crimes Against the Person   100

CHAPTER 5:   Crimes Against Property and Habitation   150

CHAPTER 11: Trial, Sentencing, and Appeal   332

**CHAPTER 13:   Interrogation and Other Law-
                Enforcement Practices   418**

DEDICATION

To Stace

DELMAR PUBLISHERS INC.

 AND

LAWYERS COOPERATIVE PUBLISHING

ARE PLEASED TO ANNOUNCE THEIR PARTNERSHIP
TO CO-PUBLISH COLLEGE TEXTBOOKS FOR
PARALEGAL EDUCATION.

DELMAR, WITH OFFICES AT ALBANY, NEW YORK, IS A PROFESSIONAL EDUCATION PUBLISHER. DELMAR PUBLISHES QUALITY EDUCATIONAL TEXTBOOKS TO PREPARE AND SUPPORT INDIVIDUALS FOR LIFE SKILLS AND SPECIFIC OCCUPATIONS.

LAWYERS COOPERATIVE PUBLISHING (LCP), WITH OFFICES AT ROCHESTER, NEW YORK, HAS BEEN THE LEADING PUBLISHER OF ANALYTICAL LEGAL INFORMATION FOR OVER 100 YEARS. IT IS THE PUBLISHER OF SUCH REKNOWNED LEGAL ENCYCLOPEDIAS AS **AMERICAN LAW REPORTS, AMERICAN JURISPRUDENCE, UNITED STATES CODE SERVICE, LAWYERS EDITION,** AS WELL AS OTHER MATERIAL, AND FEDERAL- AND STATE-SPECIFIC PUBLICATIONS. THESE PUBLICATIONS HAVE BEEN DESIGNED TO WORK TOGETHER IN THE DAY-TO-DAY PRACTICE OF LAW AS AN INTEGRATED SYSTEM IN WHAT IS CALLED THE "TOTAL CLIENT-SERVICE LIBRARY®" (TCSL®). EACH LCP PUBLICATION IS COMPLETE WITHIN ITSELF AS TO SUBJECT COVERAGE, YET ALL HAVE COMMON FEATURES AND EXTENSIVE CROSS-REFERENCING TO PROVIDE LINKAGE FOR HIGHLY EFFICIENT LEGAL RESEARCH INTO VIRTUALLY ANY MATTER AN ATTORNEY MIGHT BE CALLED UPON TO HANDLE.

INFORMATION IN ALL PUBLICATIONS IS CAREFULLY AND CONSTANTLY MONITORED TO KEEP PACE WITH AND REFLECT EVENTS IN THE LAW AND IN SOCIETY. UPDATING AND SUPPLEMENTAL INFORMATION IS TIMELY AND PROVIDED CONVENIENTLY.

FOR FURTHER REFERENCE, SEE GENERALLY:

AMERICAN JURISPRUDENCE 2D: AN ENCYCLOPEDIC TEXT COVERAGE OF THE COMPLETE BODY OF STATE AND FEDERAL LAW.

AM JUR LEGAL FORMS 2D: A COMPILATION OF BUSINESS AND LEGAL FORMS DEALING WITH A VARIETY OF SUBJECT MATTERS.

AM JUR PLEADING AND PRACTICE FORMS, REV.: MODEL PRACTICE FORMS FOR EVERY STAGE OF A LEGAL PROCEEDING.

AM JUR PROOF OF FACTS: A SERIES OF ARTICLES THAT GUIDE THE READER IN DETERMINING WHICH FACTS ARE ESSENTIAL TO A CASE AND HOW TO PROVE THEM.

AM JUR TRIALS: A SERIES OF ARTICLES DISCUSSING EVERY ASPECT OF PARTICULAR SETTLEMENTS AND TRIALS WRITTEN BY 180 CONSULTING SPECIALISTS.

UNITED STATES CODE SERVICE: A COMPLETE AND AUTHORITATIVE ANNOTATED FEDERAL CODE THAT FOLLOWS THE EXACT LANGUAGE OF THE STATUTES AT LARGE AND DIRECTS YOU TO THE COURT AND AGENCY DECISIONS CONSTRUING EACH PROVISION.

ALR AND ALR FEDERAL: SERIES OF ANNOTATIONS PROVIDING IN-DEPTH ANALYSES OF ALL THE CASE LAW ON PARTICULAR LEGAL ISSUES.

U.S. SUPREME COURT REPORTS, L ED 2D: EVERY REPORTED U.S. SUPREME COURT DECISION PLUS IN-DEPTH DISCUSSIONS OF LEADING ISSUES.

FEDERAL PROCEDURE, L ED: A COMPREHENSIVE, A—Z TREATISE ON FEDERAL PROCEDURE—CIVIL, CRIMINAL, AND ADMINISTRATIVE.

FEDERAL PROCEDURAL FORMS, L ED: STEP-BY-STEP GUIDANCE FOR DRAFTING FORMS FOR FEDERAL COURT OR FEDERAL AGENCY PROCEEDINGS.

BANKRUPTCY SERVICE, L ED: A COMPLETE SERVICE FOR PRACTICE UNDER THE CURRENT BANKRUPTCY REFORM ACT.

IMMIGRATION LAW SERVICE: A PRACTICE-ORIENTED, ANALYTIC TEXT TREATMENT OF SUBSTANTIVE AND PROCEDURAL IMMIGRATION LAW, PLUS UNIQUE "HOW TO" CHAPTERS ON REPRESENTING PARTICULAR CLIENTS.

AMERICAN LAW OF PRODUCTS LIABILITY 3D: A COMPREHENSIVE PRACTICE SET, WHICH INCLUDES ANALYSIS OF GOVERNING PRINCIPLES AND ALL STATE AND FEDERAL STATUTES, RELEVANT CASELAW, FORMS, AND CHECKLISTS.

SOCIAL SECURITY LAW AND PRACTICE: ANALYSIS, FORMS, AND SOURCE MATERIAL RELATING TO THE FIELD OF SOCIAL SECURITY.

TABLE OF CASES

FOREWORD

Since my appointment to the federal bench in 1979, I have witnessed many significant changes in the fields of criminal law and criminal procedure. The 1990s are likely to prove to be more turbulent than the 1980s. It is this dynamic aspect of the law which accentuates the importance of using a thorough and up-to-date text. *Criminal Law and Procedure* is such a textbook.

The year preceding the production of this book bore witness to many events which will prove to be of great consequence in criminal law. First, the United States Supreme Court changed not only in its membership, but in ideological balance. Second, and related to the first observation, a number of important decisions were rendered by that court. Daniel Hall has incorporated many of those decisions into this book, providing not only a complete analysis of the law, but one that is current.

In addition, Daniel has made this book interesting to read. His presentation of legal terms and review questions and problems will be extremely helpful to the student.

During his tenure with my court, Daniel proved to be an effective and energetic educator, whether working with his legal studies students or the court's interns. This enthusiasm and energy are found in *Criminal Law and Procedure*, providing the student and instructor with a thorough and easy-to-read text.

Gene F. Brooks, Chief Judge
United States District Court
Southern District of Indiana

PREFACE

This text is written primarily for the paralegal and legal studies student. However, it may be used successfully in any undergraduate criminal law class.

The text has been written with an understanding that criminal law and procedure may be taught as one course or two; that both associate- and bachelor-level students will be reading it; and that some students will already have a significant exposure to the law, while others will have none. With this understanding of the diversity of the programs and students enrolled therein, this book has been organized so that any undergraduate course in substantive criminal law, criminal procedure, or a combination of the two—whether used by two-year or four-year students—may successfully use this book.

The text is broken into two sections: criminal law and criminal procedure. Section 1, criminal law, contains eight chapters. Included in Section 1 are: two introductory chapters, mens rea and actus reus, crimes against person and property, parties and inchoate crimes, and defenses. In Chapter 1 the student is exposed to basic structural information. Federalism, separation of powers, and a special examination of the judicial branch are included. Chapter 2 introduces the student to criminal law itself, including such topics as sources of criminal law, the power of government to control behavior, and purposes of punishment. These chapters will be invaluable to the student who has had little exposure to the law. For the more advanced students, the instructor may wish to omit these chapters, in whole or part, from the required readings.

Section 2, criminal procedure, begins with a discussion of the history and impact of the United States Constitution on criminal procedure. The chapters discuss the pre-trial process, trial procedure, sentencing, appeal, and habeas corpus. The right to counsel, interrogations and confessions, searches, seizures, and arrests are also examined. There are five chapters in this section. Two appendices have been included: The Constitution of the United States and selected excerpts of the Model Penal Code.

One complaint I have heard (and had) about other texts designed for paralegal students is the absence of cases. Cases serve an important function. First, they expose legal studies students to case analyses. Second, cases increase students' interest in the material because they involve real people who are involved in genuine conflicts. Most students are intrigued by this fact. Third, cases reinforce the legal principles discussed in the text. As such, well-edited case excerpts have been included. I considered many factors when determining which cases would be included, such as: how engrossing the facts were, the age of the case, readability, understandability, and clarity. In short, I selected the most recent, pedagogically valuable case I could find.

Should an instructor want to omit some, or all, of the cases from the students' readings, this may be done without loss of material, as the text stands alone. The cases simply illustrate the subject matter discussed.

I have included two question sections at the end of each chapter. For lack of better terms, one has been named "Review Questions" and the other "Review Problems." Generally, the questions sections require students to define terms or explain basic concepts discussed in the chapter. The problems sections require more of the student; that is, the student is required to apply facts to a legal problem.

The author wishes to extend his gratitude to a number of people who were helpful to him. First, to Jay Whitney of Delmar, who has been responsible for the writing of this book, from start to finish. Most of all, I appreciate the confidence he had in my ability. Thanks also to Glenna Stanfield of Delmar for her assistance in every way, especially for fielding all my calls and questions.

Thanks to the Hon. Gene E. Brooks, Chief Judge of the United States District Court for the Southern District of Indiana, for all of his assistance and for proving to me that a federal judge can be both compassionate and humorous, except while playing cards. Also, special thanks to Bob Katzmann for the encouragement and friendship he extended, and to P.T. for understanding why I had to miss the occasional film, philharmonic, or Sugar. The same is extended to Kevin for listening and to Professor Harold Norris of the Detroit College of Law for dedicating his life to the defense of civil liberties and the education of young lawyers.

Finally, for those who reviewed and commented on the manuscript:

Kathleen Reed
    University of Toledo
    Toledo, Ohio
Ralph V. Seep
    Senior Editor
    Lawyers Cooperative Publishing
    Rochester, New York
Susan H. Brewer
    J. Sargeant Reynolds Community College
    Richmond, Virginia
Clarke Wheeler
    Santa Fe Community College
    Gainesville, Florida
John L. Frank
    Chippewa Valley Technical College
    Eau Claire, Wisconsin
Michael Fitch
    Edmonds Community College
    Lynnwood, Washington

SECTION ONE

Criminal Law

...erdam man robbed of $700

...year old man was robbed of ...n Hamilton Hill early ...y morning by four men ...him, police said.

...las Kaminski of Eugene ...otterdam, told police ...ont of an Albany Street...

at 1:50 a.m. when the four knocked him to the ground, him and stole $700 from ...aker, police s...

a teen accused ...urglary

...year-old ...view Gar... ...l-degree ...urglary yest... ...he al... broke in... ...ace... ...s ... ...A... ...ce... ...king ...ed, b... ...Charles Jame... and ...d without bail, ...

Phoenix Hotel occup... jailed on ra... ge

A man w... ...re into a ...hoenix Ho... ...aped its ...5 year-old ...yesterday was ...charged ...and ba... ...s to the E... ...er o... ...lo, ... L. ...Herbert Williams... who... the hotel, 596 Se...ond ... arrested by Troy po...ce ab... ...n yesterday in the hotel... ...liams was arraigned bef... Court Judge Patrick McC... hearing on the felony ch... scheduled for 11:30 a.m. in City Court.

a. files rape

...ANA KENNEDY
Associated Press

PALM BEACH, Fla. — ...n Kennedy Smith ... was ...d with rape yesterday, nearly ...weeks after a 29-year-old ...n reported he attacked her the ... Kennedy family's seaside

...e Attorney David Bludworth ...warrant had been issued for ...'s arrest, and police said the

"I'm very confident that wh... thing is resolved that I'll be ... stand by my original statement, which was that I didn't commit an offense of any kind," Smith said in Washington.

In a statement, the woman step-daughter of ... reti... Midwest... ...sai... feel a p... ...belief ...

67-year-old man nabbed in stabbing of store clerk

A 67-year-old man is accused of stabbing a clerk who suspected him of shoplifting at the Mohawk Mall yesterday, police said.

Thomas D. Braxton, 67, of Barrett ...treet, ...nectady, was charged ...h four counts of first-degree ...bery and second-degree assault.

...misdeme... ...ounts of ...session of st... ...perty and ...sting an ...m.

...dent.

...lice said ...egan the moment ...tried to stop Braxton from ...ving ...without paying for ...chandise ... ...raxton pulled a ...ting knife ...nd allegedly stabbed

Bludworth's announcement before more than 100 reporters capped weeks of speculation and controversy in the United States and overseas. The intense interest has been driven in part by the fact that Smi... ...with... ...cle. S... ...dw... ...and ... ...and ...

Braxton ran but was c... Sgt. Darryl L. Ostrand... nearby Metro Ford pa... police said. Braxton c... struggle with officers bef... handcuffed, they said.

The clerk — who police ... identify — was taken to ... Hospital and required sti... arm.

Braxton, who suf... diabetes, also was tak... Clare's for breathing ... police said.

The knife, which ha... blade, was recovered.

Braxton was being held...

debate, in part over the decis... some news organizations to ... the woman who made ... accusation.

Providing more fuel for ... debate, Bludworth announced ... ...d misdemeanor cha... ...publishers of The ... ...The Boca Raton-b... ...tabloid was the ...
See NEPHEW, P...

Edinburg man, 2... ...sodomy of girl

An Edinburg man faces a ...re-... ...amat... ...5-year prison senten... ...pleading guilty in Saratoga C... ...ourt yesterday to attempt... ...irst-degree sodomy with ...0-year-old girl.

Jimmy L. Russell Sr., 29, o... ...inclair Drive, is expected ... ...receive the maximum sentence f... ...attempted sodomy after plead... ...uilty to a charge reduced from ...irst-degree sodomy, said District ...ttorney David A. Wait.

Russell is accused of having ...eviant sex with the girl in ...dinburg last November, said ...

...Springs, pleaded guilty to ... count of second-degree sodo... after originally being charged ... city police with five counts.

Incidents involving a 13-year... boy occured in March, according ... police.

Under a plea bargain, he is ... receive the maximum sentence of 1/3 to seven years in prison, Wa... said.

Both men will be sentence... formally by County Court Judg...

Five people who allegedly failed to make court-ordered family support payments were arrested yesterday by Rensselaer County sheriff's deputies.

Twelve deputy sheriffs searched for ... so-called "deadbeat parents" starting at 4:30 a.m. yesterday.

Besides arresting five people, deputies say they gathered information on the whereabouts of

county taxpay... the families ... mother fails t... Warren McGre...

Arrested were ... 24, of 91... Wynantskill; Nassau; and T... J. Skelton, 36 and William ... Fifth Ave., ...

CHAPTER 1
Introduction to the Legal System of the United States

"And now, a few words about Federalism . . . "

The accumulation of all power legislative, executive and judiciary in the same hands, whether hereditary, self-appointed, or elective, may justly be pronounced the very definition of tyranny.

James Madison,
Federalist Paper No. 47

OUTLINE

SECTION 1.1 FEDERALISM

Before one can undertake learning criminal law or criminal procedure, a basic understanding of the legal system of the United States is necessary. This can be a complex task, as criminal law and procedure are significantly influenced by federal and state constitutional law, the common law, and statutory law at both the federal and state levels. It will be easier to understand how these areas of law affect criminal law if we first explore the basic structure of American government.

The United States is divided into two sovereign forms of government—the government of the United States and the governments of the many states. This division of power is commonly

3

known as **federalism**. It is also common to refer to this division as the vertical division of power, as the national government rests above the state governments in hierarchy. The drafters of the Constitution of the United States established these two levels of government in an attempt to prevent the centralization of power, too much power being vested in one group. The belief that "absolute power corrupts absolutely" was the catalyst for the division of governmental power.

In theory, the national and state governments each possess authority over its citizens (dual sovereignty), as well as over particular policy areas, free from the interference of the other government. The principle of federalism is found in the Tenth Amendment to the Constitution of the United States, which reads, "The powers not delegated to the United States by the Constitution, nor prohibited to it by the States, are reserved to the States respectively, or the people." In essence, the Constitution sets up a limited national government by giving the national government only those powers expressly or implicitly reserved to it by the Constitution. On the other hand, the many state governments are not limited to those powers specifically reserved to them. States may legislate in areas not mentioned in the Constitution, provided that no other constitutional provision is violated by so doing. What this all means is that certain governmental duties are the responsibility of the national government, others are the responsibility of the many states, and some are powers that the national and state governments share **concurrently**.

However, when state and federal law directly conflict with each other, and both national and state governments possess jurisdiction over the area in question, federal law is controlling. This is due to the "Supremacy Clause" of the Constitution, which provides that the "Constitution, and the laws of the United States . . . shall be the supreme law of the land."[1] Neither state statutes nor state constitutions may conflict with the United States Constitution.

If the United States Constitution provides for exclusive state regulation of an area, then state law is controlling. If the United States Congress regulates an area that is exclusively under state control, and the federal statute conflicts with the state statute, then the national law is subordinate to the state law.

Keep in mind that the United States Constitution is the highest form of law in the land. It is the national constitution that establishes the structure of our government. You will learn later the various duties of the judicial branch of government. One duty is the interpretation (determining what written law means) of statutes and constitutions. The highest court in the United States is the United States Supreme Court, and, as such, that Court is the

SIDEBAR

At trial, a sidebar is a meeting between the judge and the attorneys, at the judge's bench, outside the hearing of the jury. Sidebars are used to discuss issues that the jury is not permitted to hear. In this text sidebars will appear periodically. These are feature boxes that contain information relevant to the subject being studied.

STATE JURISDICTION	CONCURRENT JURISDICTION	NATIONAL JURISDICTION
1. States may regulate for the health, safety, and morals of its citizens	1. Those acts that fall into both federal and state jurisdictions	1. Crimes that are interstate in character
2. Those acts that involve a state government, its officials and property		2. Crimes involving the government of the United States, including its officials and property.
Example: murder; rape; theft; driving under the influence of a drug; gambling	Example: Bank Robbery of a federally insured institution	Example: Murder of a federal official or murder on federal land; interstate transportation of illegal item; interstate flight of a felon

Federal and State Criminal Jurisdiction

final word on what powers are exclusively federal, state, or concurrently held. However, once the United States Supreme Court decides that an issue is one exclusively under the control of state governments, then each state is the final word on that issue.

An example of an area that is considered national in character and not subject to regulation by the states is the coining of a national currency. This is relevant in criminal-law context because the authority to create a national currency also involves the authority to punish those who attempt to counterfeit that currency. This is a crime that the national government may punish, while a state may not. Examples of other crimes under federal law are interstate drug trafficking, theft from a federally insured banking institution, or murder of a federal official. But remember that the national government is a limited government. For that reason

LEGAL TERMS

federalism
A system of government with two or more levels of government where each maintains a certain amount of independence over a policy area from the other levels of government.

concurrent jurisdiction
When two or more governmental units share authority over a policy area, person, or thing.

most crimes fall under the **jurisdiction** of state governments. The Constitution gives the duty of protecting the general welfare of the people to the states. Deciding what acts should be criminal and punishing individuals who take those actions is such a duty. As such, most crimes are state law crimes. Murder, rape, assault, and embezzlement are all crimes usually punished by states, not the federal government. Hence, when a person makes the statement, "Don't make a federal case out of this," implying that crimes under federal law are more serious than those under state law, he or she is exhibiting her lack of understanding of the legal system, because those crimes that are usually perceived as being serious are normally subject to state jurisdiction, not federal.

Many crimes are prohibited by both state and federal law. In these instances state and federal authorities share jurisdiction to bring charges against the accused. Drug dealers are subject to federal law if they transport or sell drugs in interstate commerce and are also subject to the laws of the states where the transactions occurred. Who will bring charges in these situations is more a political question than a legal one, but see the chapter that discusses double jeopardy for further information on two or more governmental entities charging and trying an individual for the same crime.

Note that local governments have not been mentioned so far. This is because the Constitution does not recognize the existence of local governments. However, state constitutions and laws establish local forms of government, such as counties, cities, and districts. These local entities are often empowered by state law with limited authority to create criminal law. These laws are usually in the form of ordinances and will be discussed later, in Chapter 2.

The result of this division of power is that the states (as well as other jurisdictions, such as the District of Columbia), the federal government, and local governments each have a separate set of criminal laws. For this reason you must keep in mind that the principles you will learn from this book are general in nature. It would be both impossible and pointless to teach the specific laws of each jurisdiction of the United States.

SECTION 1.2 SEPARATION OF POWERS

Another division of governmental power is known as **separation of powers**. This is the division of the power vested in the national government into three branches, the executive, legislative, and judicial, making a horizontal division of power, just as

	LEGISLATIVE BRANCH	**EXECUTIVE BRANCH**	**JUDICIAL BRANCH**
The Government of the United States (Federal Government)	United States Congress	President of the United States	Federal Courts
State Governments	State Legislatures	Governors	State Courts

The Division of Governmental Power

federalism is the vertical division. Each branch is vested with certain functions that the other two may not encroach upon. The purpose of this system of checks and balances is to prevent the centralization of power, as is the purpose for having both state and national levels of government. The executive branch consists of the president of the United States, the president's staff, and the various administrative agencies that the president oversees. Generally, it is the duty of the executive branch to enforce the laws of the national government. In criminal law, the executive branch investigates alleged violations of the law, gathers the evidence necessary to prove that a violation has occurred, and brings violators before the judicial branch for disposition. The president does this through the various federal law enforcement and administrative agencies.

The legislative branch consists of the United States Congress, which creates the laws of the United States known as **statutes**. Finally, the judicial branch is comprised of the various federal courts of the land. That branch is charged with the administration of justice. A more comprehensive discussion of the judicial branch will follow later in this book.

Keep in mind that two levels of government exist, excluding local entities. Even though the United States Constitution does not establish three branches of government for the many states (the United States Constitution only designs the structure of the federal government), all state constitutions do, in varying forms, model the federal constitution. The result is a two-tiered system with each tier split into three parts.

What should be gleaned from this is that the legislatures are responsible for defining what acts are criminal, what process must be used to assure that a wrongdoer answers for an act, and what punishment should be imposed for the act.

It is the duty of the executive branch to enforce and implement the laws created by the legislature, as well as to enforce

LEGAL TERMS

jurisdiction
1. Authority of a governmental unit over a policy area, person, or thing.
2. Authority of a court to hear a case.
3. Location where a governmental unit resides.

separation of powers
The division of governmental power into the legislative, executive, and judicial branches

statutes
The written law created by a legislature. A subject matter compilation of statutes is known as a code.

the orders of courts. For example, if a state legislature prohibits the sale of alcohol on Sundays it is the duty of the appropriate state law-enforcement agencies, such as the police or alcohol, firearm, and tobacco agents, to investigate suspected violations and to take whatever lawful action is necessary to bring violators to justice. Law enforcement, in the criminal law context, is accomplished through law-enforcement agencies and prosecutorial agencies. At the federal level there are many law-enforcement agencies. The Federal Bureau of Investigation, Drug Enforcement Administration, United States Marshal Service, and Department of the Treasury name only a few. State law-enforcement agencies include state departments of investigation, state police departments, and local police departments. These and other enforcement agencies are responsible for investigating criminal conduct and for gathering evidence to prove a criminal violation has occurred. When the law enforcement agency has completed its investigation the case is turned over to a prosecutor. The prosecutor is the attorney responsible for representing the people. The prosecutor files the formal criminal charge, or conducts a grand jury, and then conducts the prosecution through its fruition. In the federal system the prosecutor is called a United States attorney. In the states and localities prosecutors are known as district attorneys, county attorneys, city attorneys, or, simply, prosecutors.

Finally, the judicial branch is charged with the administration of justice. The courts become involved after the executive branch has arrested or accused an individual of a crime. This will be explored further in the next section of this chapter. Of the three branches, paralegal professionals are likely to have the greatest amount of contact with the judicial branch. As such, it is important to understand the structure of the judicial system.

SECTION 1.3 THE STRUCTURE OF THE COURT SYSTEM

Within the federal and state judiciaries a hierarchy of courts exists. All state court systems, as well as the federal court system, have at least two types of courts, trial courts and appellate courts. However, each state is free to structure its judiciary in any manner, and, as such, significant variation is found in the different court systems. What follows are general principles that apply to all states and the federal system.

Trial courts are what most people envision when they think of courts. Trial courts are where a case begins, where witnesses are heard and evidence presented, often to a jury, as well as to a

judge. In the federal system trial courts are known as United States District Courts. The United States is divided up into judicial districts, using state boundaries to establish district limits. Each state constitutes at least one district, while larger states are divided into several districts. For example, Kansas has only one district, and the federal trial court located in Kansas is known as the United States District Court for the District of Kansas. California, on the other hand, is made up of four districts, the Northern, Eastern, Central, and Southern Districts of California.

State trial courts are known by various names, such as district, superior, county, and circuit courts. Despite variations in name these courts are very similar.

Appellate courts review the decisions and actions of trial courts (or lower appellate courts, as discussed below) for error. These courts do not conduct trials, but review the **record** from the trial court and examine it for mistakes, known as trial court error. Usually, appellate courts will hear argument from the attorneys involved in the case under review, but witnesses are not heard or other evidence submitted. After the appellate court has reviewed the record and examined it for error an opinion of the court is rendered. An appellate court can reverse, affirm, or remand the lower court decision. To reverse is to determine that the court below has rendered a wrong decision and to change that decision. When an appellate court affirms a lower court it is approving the decision made and leaving it unchanged. In some cases an appellate court will remand the case to the lower court. A remand is an order that

SIDEBAR

The court system is actually many court systems comprised of the federal system and the many state systems. As of 1990 there were 28,658 state court judges in the United States sitting in 15,642 state courts. By 1988 there were 280 bankruptcy judges, 284 magistrates, 575 district judges, 168 circuit judges, and 9 Supreme Court justices.

Source of state statistics: Judicial Council of California, National Center for State Courts.

Source of federal statistics: R. Katzmann, Judges and Legislators (Washington, D.C.: Brookings, 1988), p.60.

LEGAL TERMS

inferior courts
 Courts with limited jurisdiction. Usually not courts of record and fall under trial courts in the hierarchy of the court system.

the case be returned to the lower court and that some action be taken by the judge when the case is returned. Often this will involve conducting a new trial. For example, if an appellate court decides that a judge took an action that prevented a criminal defendant from having a fair trial, and the defendant was convicted, an appellate court may reverse the conviction and remand the case to the trial court for a new trial with instructions that the judge not act in a similar manner.

In the federal system and many states there are two levels of appellate courts, an intermediate and highest level. The intermediate level courts in the federal system are the United States Circuit Courts of Appeal. There are thirteen circuits in the United States.[2] Appeals from the district courts are taken to the circuit courts. The highest court in the country is the United States Supreme Court. Appeals from the circuit courts are taken to the Supreme Court. While appeal to a circuit court is generally a right anyone has, the Supreme Court is not required to hear most appeals, and doesn't. In recent years the Supreme Court has denied review of approximately 97 percent of the cases appealed.[3] Therefore, the circuit courts are often a defendant's last chance to have his or her case heard.

Many states also have intermediate-level appellate courts, as well as a high court, although a few states have only one appellate court. Most states call the high court the supreme court of that state and the intermediate level court the court of appeals. An exception is New York, which has named its highest court the Court of Appeals of New York and its lower-level courts supreme courts.

In states that have only one appellate court appeals are taken directly to that court. New Hampshire is such a state, so appeals from New Hampshire's trial courts are taken directly to the Supreme Court of New Hampshire. Note that in most instances a first appeal is an appeal of right. That means that one has a right to appeal, and the appellate court is required to hear the case. However, second appeals are generally not appeals of right, unless state law has provided otherwise. To have a case heard by the United States Supreme Court and most state supreme courts the person appealing must seek *certiorari,* an order from an appellate court to the lower court requiring the record to be sent to the higher court for review. When "cert." is granted, the appellate court will hear the appeal, and when cert. is denied it will not.

Finally, be aware that a number of **inferior courts** exist. These are courts that fall under trial courts in hierarchy. As such, appeals from these courts do not go to the intermediate level appellate courts, as described above, but to the trial level court first. Municipal courts, police courts, and justices of the peace are

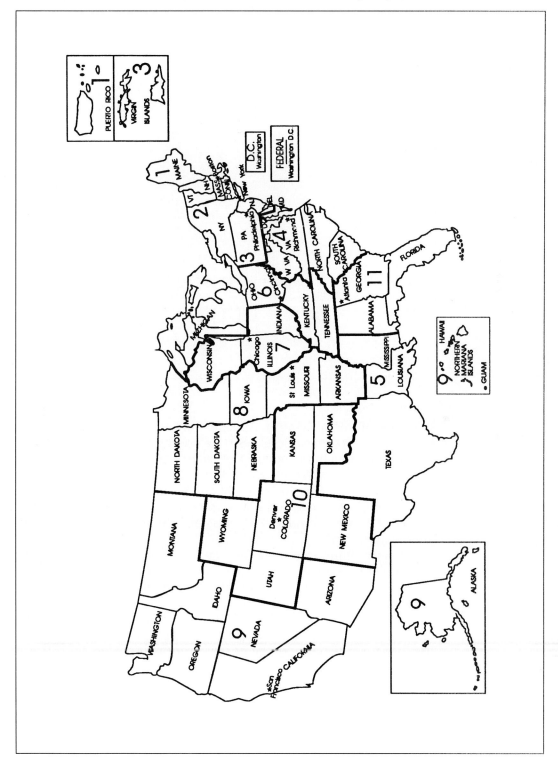

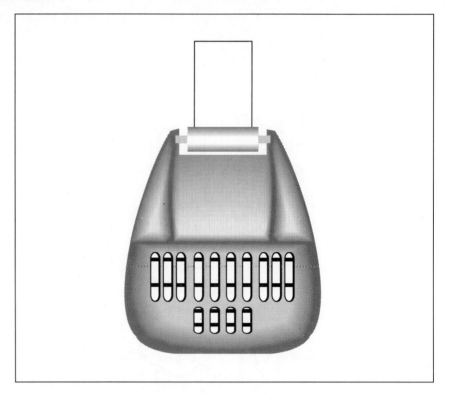

Stenographs are one method of recording hearings and trials; these are used by court reporters.

examples of inferior courts. Appeals from these courts are initially heard by the state trial level court before the appeal is taken to one of the state appellate courts. The federal system also has inferior courts. The United States Bankruptcy Courts are inferior courts, as appeals from the decisions of these courts go to the district courts, in most cases, and not to the courts of appeals. Only after the trial court has rendered its decision may an appeal be taken to an appellate court.

Bear in mind that most inferior courts in the state system are not **courts of record**. No tape recording or stenographic recording of the trial or hearing at the inferior court is made. As such, when an appeal is taken to the trial level court it is normally *de novo*. This means the trial level court conducts a new trial, rather than reviews a record, as most appellate courts do. This is necessary because there is no record to review, since the inferior court is not a court of record. Federal district courts do not conduct new trials, as all federal courts, including bankruptcy courts, are courts of record. State inferior courts have limited jurisdiction; for example, municipal courts usually hear municipal ordinance violations and only minor state law violations. The amount of money that a person may be fined and the amount of time that a defendant may be

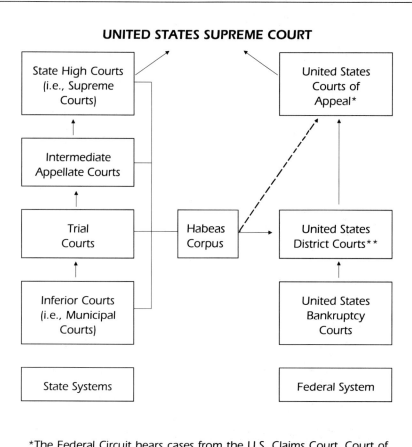

**State and Federal
Court Structures**

*The Federal Circuit hears cases from the U.S. Claims Court, Court of International Trade, Board of Patent Appeal and Interferences, and findings of various administrative agencies.

**District Courts and Circuit Courts both review Habeas Corpus petitions from those incarcerated in the state system.

sentenced to serve in jail are also limited. Generally, no juries are used at the inferior court level.

Above is a basic diagram of the federal and state court systems. You will note that the appellate routes are indicated by lines drawn from one court to another. Later in this book you will learn how the appeals process works and how the federal and state systems interact in criminal law. Make note where this diagram is located so that you may refer to it later.

Most state trial courts are known as **courts of general jurisdiction.** Courts of general jurisdiction possess the authority to

LEGAL TERMS

courts of record
are courts which maintain a verbatim record of the trials and hearings it conducts.

courts of general jurisdiction
are courts that have the authority to hear a wide variety of cases, both civil and criminal. Most state trial courts are general jurisdiction courts.

hear a broad range of cases, including civil law as well as criminal. On the other hand **courts of limited jurisdiction** only hear specific types of cases. You have already been introduced to one limited jurisdiction court, municipal courts. Inferior courts, such as municipal courts, are always courts of limited jurisdiction. Some states employ systems that have specialized trial courts to handle domestic, civil, or criminal cases. These may be in the form of a separate court, e.g., Criminal Court of Harp County, or may be a division of a trial court, e.g., Superior Court of Harp County, Criminal Division. Appellate courts may also be limited in jurisdiction to a particular area of law, such as the Oklahoma Court of Criminal Appeals.

The federal government also has special courts. As previously mentioned, a nationwide system of bankruptcy courts is administered by the national government. In addition, the United States Claims Court, Tax Court, and Court of International Trade are part of the federal judiciary, and each have a specific area of law over which they may exercise jurisdiction. Often those cases over which they have jurisdiction are exclusive of district courts. However, the jurisdiction of those courts is outside the scope of this book, as they deal only with civil law. Criminal cases in federal court are heard by district courts, and criminal appeals are heard by the circuit courts of appeals.

SECTION 1.4 THE DUTIES AND POWERS OF THE JUDICIAL BRANCH

Of the three branches of government, attorneys and paralegals have the most interaction with the judicial branch. It is for that reason that we single out the judicial branch for a more extensive examination of its functions.

First, it must be emphasized that all courts, local, state, and federal, are bound by the United States constitution. The effect of this is that all courts have a duty to apply federal constitutional law. This is important in criminal law because it allows defendants to assert their United States constitutional claims and defenses in state court, where most criminal cases are heard. Of course, defendants may also assert applicable state defenses as well.

As previously stated, the judicial branch is charged with the administration of justice. The courts administer justice by acting as the conduit for dispute resolution. The courts are the place where civil and criminal disputes are resolved, if the parties cannot reach a resolution themselves. In an effort to resolve disputes courts must apply the laws of the land. To apply the law judges

The Supreme Court 1990–1991. Top Row: Justices Kennedy, O'Connor, Scalia, and Souter. Bottom Row: Justices Blackmun, White, Rehnquist (Chief), Marshall, and Stevens.

must **interpret** legislation and the constitutions of the nation. To interpret means to read the law in an attempt to understand its meaning. This nation's courts are the final word in declaring the meaning of written law. If a court interprets a statute's meaning contrary to the intent of a legislature, then the legislature may later rewrite the statute to make its intent more clear. This has the effect of "reversing" the judicial interpretation of the statute. The process is much more difficult if a legislature desires to change a judicial interpretation of a constitution. At the national level the Constitution has been amended twenty-six times. The amendment process is found in Article V of the Constitution and requires not only action by the federal legislature but also action by the states. To amend a constitution is simply a more cumbersome and time-consuming endeavor than amending legislation.

The judicial branch is independent from the other two branches of government. Often people think of the courts as enforcers of the law. While this is true in a sense, it is untrue in that

LEGAL TERMS

courts of limited jurisdiction
are courts that have the authority to hear only specific classes of cases. Some states have family law, criminal law, probate and juvenile courts, all of which are limited jurisdiction courts.

interpret
Whenever a court reads statutes or other law and determines the meaning of that law, the court is interpreting law.

the judicial branch does not work with the executive branch in an attempt to achieve criminal convictions. It is the duty of the courts of this nation to remain neutral and apply the laws in a fair and impartial manner. The United States Constitution established a judiciary system that is shielded from interference from the other two branches. For example, the Constitution prohibits Congress from reducing the pay of federal judges after they are appointed. This prevents Congress from coercing the courts into action under the threat of no pay. The Constitution also provides for lifetime appointments of federal judges, thereby keeping the judicial branch from being influenced by political concerns, which may cause judges to ignore the law and make decisions based on what is best for their political careers. Judicial independence permits courts to make decisions that are disadvantageous to the government, but required by law, without fear of retribution from the other two branches.

The need for an independent judiciary is most important when considering the power of **judicial review**. Judicial review is a power held by the judicial branch, which permits it to review the actions of the executive and legislative branches and declare acts that are in violation of the Constitution void. Hamilton wrote of the power of judicial review, and of the importance of an independent judiciary, in the Federalist Papers, where he stated:

* * *

. . .Permanency in office frees the judges from political pressures and prevents invasions on judicial power by the president and Congress.

* * *

The Constitution imposes certain restrictions on the Congress designed to protect individual liberties, but unless the courts are independent and have the power to declare the laws in violation of the Constitution null and void these protections amount to nothing. The power of the Supreme Court to declare laws unconstitutional leads some to assume that the judicial branch will be superior to the legislative branch. Let us look at this argument.

Only the Constitution is *fundamental* law; the Constitution establishes the principles and structure of the government. Argue that the Constitution is not superior to the laws suggests that the *representatives of the people* are superior *to the people* and that the Constitution is inferior to the government it gave birth to. The courts are the arbiters between the legislative branch and the people; the courts are to interpret the laws and prevent the legislative branch from exceeding the powers granted it. The courts must not only place the Constitution higher than the laws passed by Congress, they must also place the intentions of the people ahead of the intentions of the representatives . . .

* * * [emphasis original]

The landmark case dealing with judicial review is *Marbury v. Madison,* 1 Cranch 137; 2 L.Ed. 60 (1803). Justice Marshall wrote the opinion for the Court and determined that, although the Constitution does not contain explicit language providing for the power of judicial review, Article III of the Constitution indirectly endows the power in the judiciary. It is now well-established that courts possess the authority to review the actions of the executive and legislative branches and to declare any law, command, or other action void if such violates the United States Constitution. The power is held by both state and federal courts. Any state law that violates the United States Constitution may be struck down by either federal or state courts. Of course, state laws that violate state constitutions may be stricken for the same reason.

The power to invalidate statutes is rarely used. This is true for two reasons. First, the judiciary is aware of how awesome the power is, and this causes courts to be reluctant to use it. Second, many rules of statutory constructions exist, which have the effect of preserving legislation. For example, if two possible interpretations of a statute are possible, one that violates the Constitution and one that does not, one rule of statutory construction requires that the statute be construed so that it is consistent with the Constitution. Although rarely done, statutes are occasionally determined invalid. In the chapter on defenses, you will learn many constitutional constraints on government behavior. These defenses often rely on the power of the judiciary to invalidate statutes or police conduct to give them teeth.

SECTION 1.5 COMPARING CIVIL LAW AND CRIMINAL LAW

The difference between civil law and criminal law appears obvious, and great differences do exist. Yet, most students are surprised at the similarities that can be found.

The source of most of the dissimilarities between criminal law and civil law is the differing objectives of the two. The purpose of criminal law is twofold. First, it is intended to prevent behavior that society has determined undesirable. A second purpose of criminal law is to punish those who take the acts deemed undesirable by society. Arguably, there is only one purpose, to prevent

LEGAL TERMS

judicial review
The power of the judicial branch to review the acts of the executive and legislative branches and declare any action that is in violation of the Constitution void.

antisocial behavior. Under this theory punishment is only used as a tool to achieve the primary goal of preventing antisocial behavior. In any event, prevention and punishment are essential reasons why we have criminal law and a criminal justice system.

On the other hand, civil law has as its primary purpose the compensation of those injured by someone else's behavior. It is argued that the real purpose of civil law is the same as that of criminal law. By allowing lawsuits against individuals who have behaved in a manner not consistent with society's rules, civil law actually acts to prevent nonconformity. However, prevention of bad behavior may be more the consequence of civil law than the purpose. To understand this you must know something about civil law.

Many definitions of civil law exist. The *American Heritage Dictionary of the English Language* (1980) defines it as "The body of law dealing with the rights of private citizens." *Black's Law Dictionary*, Fifth Edition (1979) defines civil law as "Laws concerned with civil or private rights and remedies, as contrasted with criminal laws." This author prefers a negative definition similar to the latter, such as, all law, except that which is criminal law. Whatever definition you accept, many areas of law fall under the umbrella of civil law. Two of the largest categories of civil law are **contract law** and **tort law**.

Contract law is a branch of civil law that deals with written agreements between two or more parties. You probably have already entered into a contract. Apartment leases, credit card agreements, and book-of-the-month club agreements are all contracts. To have a contract you must have two or more people agreeing to behave in a specific manner in the future. Both parties benefit from the contract, and both lose something. For example, when you agree to lease an apartment you gain the use of the apartment during the lease period, and your landlord loses the right to use the property. The flipside is that the landlord gets your money, in the form of rent, and you lose the value of that rent. You promise to pay rent at a specified time, and the landlord promises to give you the use of the premises during the rental period. In contract law the duties and obligations to the parties are created by the parties themselves and appear in the form of a contract. If you violate your obligation to your landlord under the contract (i.e., you move out earlier than the contract allows) you have committed a civil wrong called a breach of contract. The landlord may sue you for your breach and receive **damages**. Damages are monetary compensation for loss.

Tort law is a branch of civil law that is concerned with civil wrongs, but not contract actions. We have all seen the television ads for personal injury attorneys. These attorneys are practicing in

LEGAL TERMS

contract law
A branch of civil law concerned with written agreements between two or more persons. These written agreements are called contracts. A violation of a contract is known as a breach of contract.

tort law
A branch of civil law concerned with compensating individuals for personal injury, property damage, and other losses. The duty to not injure another in tort law is created by the law, in contrast with contract law where the duty is created by the parties themselves. Many crimes are also torts. To commit such a civil wrong is to commit a tort.

damages
1. The loss suffered by an individual due to the wrongful act of another.
2. Money received from a lawsuit to compensate for loss to property, person, or rights.

the tort law area. A civil wrong, other than a breach of contract, is known as a tort. Torts are different from contracts in that the duty owed another party in contract law is created by the written agreement. In tort law the duty is imposed by the law. For example, at a party you are struck and injured by a beer bottle that has been heaved by an intoxicated partier: a tort has been committed. The partier is known as a *tortfeasor*, which is the term used to describe one who commits a tort. Yet, why does that partier owe you a duty to not strike you with a flying beer bottle? You have not entered into a contract with the partier where he has promised not to harm you in this manner. The answer is that the law imposes the duty to act with caution when it is possible to injure another or cause injury to another's property. This duty is imposed upon all people at all times. The law requires that we all act **reasonably** when conducting our lives.

When a person fails to act reasonably and unintentionally injures another, that person is responsible for a **negligent tort**. Automobile accidents and medical malpractice are examples of negligent torts. When a person injures another intentionally, an **intentional tort** has occurred. Many intentional torts are also crimes, and this is an area where civil law and criminal law have much in common. If at that fraternity party you make a partier angry, and as a result he intentionally strikes you with the bottle, then he has committed both a crime and an intentional tort. While criminal law may impose a jail sentence (or other punitive measures), tort law normally seeks only to compensate you for your injury. So, if you suffered $1,000 in medical bills to repair your broken nose you would be entitled to that amount, but the partier cannot be sentenced to jail or otherwise be punished within the civil tort action. A separate criminal charge may be filed by the government.

The final type of tort is a **strict liability tort**. In these situations liability exists even though the tortfeasor has acted with extreme caution and intended to cause no harm. An example of a strict liability tort is blasting. Whenever a mining company or demolition company uses blasting it is liable for any injuries or damages it has caused to property, even if the company exercised extreme caution.

Damages that are awarded (won) in a lawsuit and compensate a party for actual loss are **compensatory damages**. Compensatory damages do just what the name states—compensate the injured party. However, another type of damages exists, **punitive damages**. Contrary to what you have learned so far, punitive damages are awarded in civil suits and are intended to prevent undesirable behavior by punishing those who commit outrageous acts. Punitive damages are often requested by plaintiffs in lawsuits, but are rarely awarded. Don't worry if the idea of punitive

LEGAL TERMS

reasonableness
  The standard of care expected of all people in tort law.

negligent torts
  A branch of tort law that deals with compensating individuals for the unreasonable acts of others that cause injury to property, person, or rights.

intentional torts
  A branch of tort law that deals with compensating individuals for the intended acts of others that cause injury to property, person, or rights.

strict liability torts
  A branch of tort law wherein liability exists for injuries caused by certain acts even though no intent to injure exists, and the party being sued exercised extreme care.

compensatory damages
  Damages that equal the amount of loss and nothing more.

punitive damages
  Damages that exceed the amount of actual loss and are intended to prevent future misconduct.

damages confuses you because it appears to be a criminal law concept. It isn't. In fact, many lawyers argue that punitives should not be allowed because a person can end up punished twice, once when convicted and sentenced by a criminal court and again by a civil court if punitives are awarded. Yet, punitive damages have been upheld in most instances by the Supreme Court. A note of caution: Do not get the concept of punitive damages mixed up with restitution or fines, which are discussed in the chapter on punishment.

Finally, a few other differences between criminal law and civil law should be mentioned. First, in civil law the person who brings the lawsuit (the plaintiff) is the person who was injured. Let's use an example. You go to the Piggly Wiggly (grocery store) to do your shopping and request the assistance of a checkout person who recently was divorced from a spouse who looks very much like you. The checker immediately becomes enraged and vents all of his anger for his ex-wife on you by striking you with a box of Captain Crunch, which he was checking. He has committed a possible assault and battery in both tort law (these are intentional torts) and criminal law. However, in tort law you must sue the checker yourself to recover any losses you suffer.

This is not true in criminal law. The government, whether national, state, or local, is always the party who files criminal charges. Often you will hear people say that they have filed criminal charges against someone. This is not true. What they have usually done is file a complaint, and the government has determined whether criminal charges are to be filed. This is true because a violation of criminal law is characterized as an attack on the citizens of a state (or the federal government), and, as such, a violation of public, not private, law. Since it is public, the decision to file, or not file, is made by a public official, the prosecutor. So in the example above you have to contact either the police or your local prosecutor to have a criminal action brought against the checker. In civil cases the case is entitled Citizen v. Citizen, and in criminal law it is Government (i.e., State of Montana) v. Citizen. In some jurisdictions criminal actions are brought under the name of the people. This is done in New York, and criminal cases filed there are entitled The People of the State of New York v. Citizen.

There is no difference between a criminal action brought under the name of the state and a criminal action filed under the name of the people of a state. All prosecutions at the national level are brought by the United States of America. Note that governments may become involved in civil disputes. For example, if the state of South Dakota enters into a contract with a person, and a dispute concerning that contract arises, the suit will either be Citizen v. South Dakota or South Dakota v. Citizen.

SIMPLE CAPTION—CRIMINAL CASE

IN THE UNITED STATES DISTRICT COURT FOR
THE DISTRICT OF MARYLAND
NORTHERN DIVISION

UNITED STATES OF AMERICA)
_____ Plaintiff,)
)
v.)   CASE NO. _____
)
JOHN D. CRIMINAL,)
_____ Defendant.)

SIMPLE CAPTION—CIVIL CASE

IN THE UNITED STATES DISTRICT COURT FOR
THE DISTRICT OF MARYLAND
NORTHERN DIVISION

JOHN I. CITIZEN)
_____ Plaintiff,)
)
v.)   CASE NO. _____
)
JANE Q. SMITH)
_____ Defendant.)

SIDEBAR

ABOUT CASE NAMES, TITLES, AND CAPTIONS

Cases filed with courts are given a case title, also known as a case name. The title consists of the parties to the action. In civil cases the title is citizen v. citizen, for example, Joe Smith v. Anna Smith. In criminal actions the title is the government v. citizen. For example, United States of America v. Joe Smith or State of New Mexico v. Anna Smith.

Cases also have captions. The caption appears at the top of the title page of all documents filed with a court and includes the case name, the court name, the case number, and the name of the document being filed with the court. The illustration at the left is an example of a caption.

The two fields also differ in what is required to have a successful case. In civil law one must show actual injury to win. If, from our example from above, the box of Captain Crunch missed your head and you suffered no injury (damages), you would not have a civil suit. However, a criminal action for assault or battery may still be brought since no injury is required in criminal law. This is so because the purpose of criminal law is to prevent this type of conduct, not to compensate for actual injuries. To turn this around, there are many instances where a person's negligence could be subject to a civil cause of action, but not to a criminal action. If a person accidently strikes another during a game of golf with a golf ball, causing injury, the injured party may sue for the concussion received, but no purpose would be served by prosecuting the individual who hit the ball. No deterrent effect is achieved, as there was no intent to cause the injury. In most cases, society has made the determination (through its criminal laws) that a greater amount of **culpability** should be required for criminal

LEGAL TERMS

culpability
    Blameworthiness; guilt.

liability than for civil. Criminal law is usually more concerned with the immorality of an act than is tort law. This is consistent with the goals of the two disciplines, as it is easier to prevent intentional acts than accidental ones. These concepts will be discussed later in the chapter on mens rea.

REVIEW QUESTIONS

1. What is the primary duty of the executive branch of government in criminal law?
2. Define the phrase "court of record."
3. Define jurisdiction and differentiate between a court of general jurisdiction and a court of limited jurisdiction.
4. What are the goals of criminal law? Civil law?
5. Who may file a civil suit? A criminal suit? How are these different?
6. What is a compensatory damage? A punitive?
7. Should punitive damages be permitted in civil law? Explain your position.
8. Define culpability.

REVIEW PROBLEMS

1. In 1973 the United States Supreme Court handed down the famous case, *Roe v. Wade*, 410 U.S. 113 (1973), wherein the Court determined that the decision to have an abortion is a private decision that is protected from government intervention, in some circumstances, by the United States Constitution. Suppose that a state legislature passes legislation (state statute) that attempts to reverse that decision by prohibiting all abortions in that state. Which is controlling in that state, the statute or the decision of the United States Supreme Court? Explain your answer.
2. Same facts as above, except the state supreme court has determined that the state constitution protects the life of fetuses from abortion, except when the life of the mother is endangered. Which is controlling when a mother seeks to have an abortion and her life is not endangered to any greater amount than the average pregnancy, the state constitutional provision protecting the fetuses or the decision of the United States Supreme Court? Explain your answer.

3. Assume that the United States Supreme Court has previously determined that regulation of traffic on county roads is a power reserved exclusively for the states. In reaction to this opinion the United States Congress enacts a statute providing that the regulation of county roads will be within power of the United States Congress from that date forward. Your law office represents a client who is charged with violating the federal statute that prohibits driving on all roads while intoxicated. Do you have a defense? If so, explain.

NOTES

[1] United States Constitution, Art. VI.

[2] 28 U.S.C. 41, et seq.

[3] According to the Office of the Deputy Clerk, Supreme Court of the United States, there were 4,773 petitions and appeals to the Supreme Court in 1988. Of that figure the court heard 147 cases, or slightly more than 3 percent of the total appeals and petitions for certiorari.

CHAPTER 2
Introduction to Criminal Law

"My only mistake was accepting their personal check for the ransom money."

If men were all angels, no government would be necessary.

James Madison

OUTLINE

SECTION 2.1   THE DISTINCTION BETWEEN CRIMINAL LAW AND CRIMINAL PROCEDURE

In all areas of legal study a distinction is made between substantive aspects of that study and procedural aspects. The substance of tort law tells you what a tort is and what damages an injured party is entitled to recover from a lawsuit. Substantive contract law defines what a contract is, tells us whether it must be in writing to be enforceable, who must sign it, what the penalty for breach is, and other such information. The field of civil procedure sets rules for how to bring the substance of the law before a court for resolution of a claim. To decide that a client has an injury that can be compensated under the law is a substantive decision. The question then becomes, how does this injured client get the compensation to which he or she is entitled. This is the procedural question. Procedural law tells you how to file a lawsuit, where to file, when to file, and how to prosecute the claim. Such is the case for criminal law and procedure.

Criminal law, as a field of law, defines what constitutes a crime. It establishes what conduct is prohibited and what punishment can be imposed for violating its mandates. Criminal law establishes what degree of intent is required for criminal liability. In addition, criminal law sets out the defenses to criminal charges that may be asserted. Alibi, insanity, etc., are defenses and fall under the umbrella of criminal law.

Criminal procedure puts substantive criminal law into action. It is concerned with the procedures used to bring criminals to justice, beginning with police investigation and continuing throughout the process of administering justice. When and under what conditions may a person be arrested? How and where must the criminal charge be filed? When can the police conduct a search? How does the accused assert a defense? How long can a person be held in custody by the police without charges being filed? How long after charges are filed does the accused have to wait before a trial is held? These are all examples of questions that criminal procedure deals with. Do not worry if you cannot always distinguish between a procedural question and a substantive one. There is considerable overlap between the two concepts.

The first half of this text is devoted to criminal law and the latter half to criminal procedure. During the remainder of the book the phrase "criminal law" will be used often. This, in most cases, refers to general criminal law, including both substantive criminal law and criminal procedure.

SECTION 2.2 THE POWER OF GOVERNMENT TO REGULATE BEHAVIOR

Freedom and liberty are two concepts that pervade the American political being. Most of us have learned that it was the longing for freedom of religious thought that was the cause of the English Puritan emigration from England to what was to become Plymouth, Massachusetts, in 1620. Later, the desire for freedom from the oppressive crown of England was the catalyst for the Declaration of Independence and the American Revolution. Finally, the fear that all governments tend to abuse their power led to the creation of a constitution that contains specific limits on governmental power and specific protections of individual rights. But what exactly is freedom? Liberty?

Freedom is a term that generally means the ability to act free from interference. In a political and legal sense it means the ability to act free from the interference of government. However, even in the most free societies personal behavior is limited. This is because the actions of every member of society has the potential, at times, of affecting other members. The total absence of government is anarchy, but few people believe that freedom results from anarchy. Without government there is little control over the individuals' behavior. No system would exist to punish those who intentionally injure others. No system would exist to allow someone injured by the negligence of another to recover his or her losses. There would be no deterrence to wrongful behavior, other than fear of retribution from the victim. The strong and cunning would prey on the weak and unintelligent; the licentious on the decent. While it is true that to live in such a world would be living free from government interference, it cannot be reasonably considered freedom. If women are in constant fear of sexual assault they are not free. If people are hesitant to own property for fear of it being taken by others they are not totally free. In order to prevent anarchy people establish governments. The people then vest their governments with certain authorities and powers, so that the government can control the behavior of all the people.

The forefathers of the United States did this when they met in Philadelphia to draft the Constitution of the United States. Some characterize the relationship between a democratic form of government and its people as a contract. The people give up some freedoms in an effort to secure other freedoms. The preamble to the United States Constitution recognizes this principle. It states "We, the People of the United States, in order to form a more perfect union, establish justice, insure domestic tranquility, provide for the common defense, promote the general welfare, and secure the

LEGAL TERMS

criminal law
The substantive law of crimes and punishment. Defines what conduct is criminal and what punishment may be imposed for such conduct.

criminal procedure
The law that establishes processes for putting substantive criminal law into action.

blessings of liberty to ourselves and our posterity, do ordain and establish this Constitution for the United States of America." The concept is also found in the Declaration of Independence, where Thomas Jefferson penned "that all Men are created equal, that they are endowed by their Creator with certain unalienable Rights, that among these are Life, Liberty, and the Pursuit of Happiness—That to secure these Rights, Governments are instituted among Men, deriving their just Powers from the Consent of the Governed . . . "

So the contract is formed. The people are to receive the benefits of an organized, fair government. A government is to establish laws designed to protect the people from one another and from other nations. In exchange, the people agree to comply with the laws created by their government. Some would argue that the duty extends to require the people to participate in the activities of the government. You have probably heard people speak of a "duty" to vote. Clearly, this is the rationale for requiring individuals to sit as jurors.

Every government is different. Some governments permit little or no political participation by the people. Others permit more. In those nations where the people are active participants the rights and duties of individuals can vary significantly. This is because values are very different from culture to culture. Hence, what one society believes to be an important freedom and protects from government interference may not be so valued by other societies.

However, one fact that is true of nearly all nations is that governmental involvement with the affairs of the people is continually increasing. This is due in part to the fact that people are less independent, that is, that members of society now depend on one another to provide goods and services that were once commonly self-provided. In addition, the staggering increase in world population has caused people to have much more contact with each other than they did 100 years ago. The greater the population, contact between, and dependence of people on one another, the greater the number of conflicts that will arise requiring government intervention. As the population and dependence of people increases so does the likelihood that one person's action may affect another. A person who lives alone in a forest far from other people can scream loudly in the middle of the night without bothering anyone. He or she could dispose of trash in any manner desired. If that same person lived in the middle of a city the scream could wake people, and the improper disposal of trash could cause the spread of disease, as well as create an unpleasant environment. As the number of contacts between members of a society increases, so does the number of conflicts requiring government intervention. Even if the parties involved do not desire legal intervention to resolve their conflict society will sometimes intervene through its government to prevent unacceptable behavior. For example, society has decided that duels are not an acceptable method of resolving disputes, even if two individuals wish to use this method. The government will try to prevent such behavior from occurring. If the duel isn't discovered until after-the-fact, then the parties involved may be punished for participating.

As the need for government involvement in private lives of citizens increases it becomes more difficult to protect individual rights, also known as **civil liberties**. Although we the people have bestowed upon our government certain powers which have the effect of limiting our behavior, we have also specifically created "civil rights," which the government may not encroach upon. Many of these rights are contained in the first ten amendments of our Constitution, which are commonly known as the **Bill of Rights**. As the world becomes more populated and complex the balance between permissible government involvement in the private lives of its citizens and impermissible encroachment upon those citizens' civil liberties becomes harder to maintain. As that line becomes thinner, the duty of the lawyer and legal assistant to be zealous in preparation of their defenses increases.

As previously discussed, the attempt to control people's behavior is achieved through both civil law and criminal law. Generally, society reserves only those acts that are perceived as serious moral wrongs or extremely dangerous for sanction under criminal law. Those acts that are accidental or are not serious breaches of moral duty are usually not criminal, but may lead to civil liability. Thoughts about which acts should be considered under each category are very subjective and often change because a problem may intensify or because the public perceives an increased problem, even though the situation may not be any different than years before.

For example, the 1980s saw an increased effort to stop people from driving while under the influence of alcohol. Many states enacted new laws increasing the penalty for violating their D.U.I. statutes. In addition, a few states limited police discretion by requiring that violators be arrested. The practice once exercised by many police departments of driving drunk drivers home was stopped by legislative command. At one time it can be argued that civil law was as much of a deterrent to driving under the influence as was criminal. Fear of civil liability for causing property damage or personal liability was as great as fear of criminal liability due to the inconsistent and often minor penalties which followed convictions for driving under the influence. However, as public concern over alcohol-related automobile accidents increased the focus turned to criminal law to prevent such behavior. Increased penalties, consistent arrest policies, and mandatory alcohol treatment for those convicted are now common. The

LEGAL TERMS

civil liberties
Also known as civil rights. Individual, personal rights. In the United States many of these rights are protected by the constitutions of the national government and the many state governments. The freedoms of speech and religion are examples of civil rights.

Bill of Rights
The first ten amendments to the United States Constitution. It contains certain rights that are guaranteed to the people, such as the freedom from unreasonable searches and seizures.

extensive media coverage that particular cases have received, such as the Larry Mahoney accident,[1] have gotten the word out that one who drives while intoxicated risks arrest, conviction, and punishment, as well as civil liability for injuries to property and person. What this example teaches is that society determines what acts will be treated as criminal based on public perceptions of morality, the importance of deterrence, and the danger posed to the public by the acts in question. Do not forget that criminal acts are often the subject of civil suits. This is not always true, as you learned in section 1.5, when the general purposes of civil law and criminal law were discussed.

SECTION 2.3 THE PURPOSES OF PUNISHING CRIMINAL LAW VIOLATORS

You have already learned that the general goal of criminal law is to prevent behavior determined by society to be undesirable. The criminal justice system uses punishment as a prevention tool. Many theories support punishing criminal law violators. Although some people focus on one theory and use it as the basis for punishment, a more accurate approach, in this author's opinion, is to realize that many theories have merit and that when a legislature establishes the range of punishment applicable to a particular crime many theories were involved in motivating individual legislators. It is highly unlikely that all legislators would base their decisions on one theory. Just as you will find when you read the following theories, each legislator is likely to have a particular preference, but is influenced at least to a small degree by all or many of the theories.

Section 2.3(a) Specific and General Deterrence

Specific deterrence seeks to deter individuals already convicted of crimes from committing crimes in the future. It is a negative reward theory. By punishing Mr. X for today's crime we teach him that he will be disciplined for future criminal behavior. The arrest and conviction of an individual acts to show that individual that society has the capability to detect crime and is willing to punish those who commit crimes.

General deterrence attempts to deter all members of society from engaging in criminal activity. In theory, when the public observes Mr. X being punished for his actions the public is deterred from behaving similarly for fear of the same punishment. Of course, individuals will react differently to the knowledge of

Mr. X's punishment. People will weigh the risk of being caught and the level of punishment against the benefit of committing the crime. All people do this at one time or another. Have you ever intentionally run a stoplight? Jaywalked? If so, you have made the decision to violate the law. Neither crime involves a severe penalty. That fact, in addition to the probability of not being discovered by law enforcement agents, probably affected your decision. Presumably, if conviction of either crime was punished by incarceration (time in jail), then the deterrent effect would be greater. Would you be as likely to jaywalk if you knew that you could spend time in jail for such an act? Some people would; others would not. It is safe to assume, however, that as the punishment increases so does compliance. However, one author has made the observation that it is not as effective to increase the punishment as it is to increase the likelihood of being punished.[2] It is unknown how much either of these factors influence behavior, but it is generally accepted that they both do.

Section 2.3(b)   Incapacitation

Incapacitation, also referred to as restraint, is the third purpose of criminal punishment. Incapacitation does not seek to deter criminal conduct by influencing people's choices, but prevents criminal conduct by restraining those who have committed crimes. Criminals who are restrained in jail or prison, or who are in the extreme executed, are incapable of causing harm to the general public. This theory is often the rationale for long-term imprisonment of individuals who are believed to be beyond rehabilitation. It is also promoted by those who lack faith in rehabilitation and feel as though all criminals should be removed from society to prevent the chance of repetition.

Crimes that are caused by mental disease or occur in a moment of passion are not affected by deterrence theories, because the individual does not have the opportunity to consider the punishment that will be inflicted for committing the crime before it is committed. Deterrence theories are only effective when considering individuals who are sufficiently intelligent to understand the consequences of their actions, who are sane enough to understand the consequences of their actions, and who are not laboring under such uncontrollable feelings that an understanding that they may be punished is lost.

Section 2.3(c)   Rehabilitation

Rehabilitation is another purpose for punishing criminals. The theory of rehabilitation is that if the criminal is subjected to

LEGAL TERMS

specific deterrent
A theory of punishment that states that by punishing an individual for one offense society is deterring that individual from committing future offenses.

general deterrent
A theory of punishment that states that by punishing individuals for offenses all members of a society are deterred from committing future offenses.

incapacitation
A theory of punishment where removal of an individual from society is sought so as to eliminate the danger that individual poses to other members of society. Incarceration and capital punishment are two types of incapacitation.

rehabilitation
A theory of punishment where society attempts to alter the criminal's behavior to conform to social norms. Education, training, and therapy are among the methods used to rehabilitate or correct the violator.

various educational and technical programs, treatment and counseling, and other measures, it is possible to alter the individual's behavior to conform to societal norms. Another author has noted that:

> To the extent that crime is caused by elements of the offender's personality, educational defects, lack of work skills, and the like, we should be able to prevent him from committing more crimes by training, medical and psychiatric help, and guidance into law-abiding patterns of behavior. Strictly speaking, rehabilitation is not "punishment," but help to the offender. However, since this kind of help is frequently provided while the subject is in prison or at large on probation or parole under a sentence that carries some condemnation and some restriction of freedom, it is customary to list rehabilitation as one of the objects of a sentence in a criminal case.[3]

Holding Cell

The concept of rehabilitation has come under considerable scrutiny in recent years, and the success of rehabilitative programs is questionable. However, the poor quality of prison rehabilitative programs may be the cause of the lack of success of these programs.

Section 2.3(d) Retribution

Retribution, or societal vengeance, is the fifth purpose. Simply put, punishment through the criminal justice system is society's method of avenging a wrong. The idea that one who commits a wrong must be punished is an old one. The Old Testament speaks of an "eye for an eye." However, many question the place of retribution in contemporary society. Is retribution consistent with American values? Jewish or Christian values? The question is actually moot, as there are few instances where retribution stands alone as a reason for punishing someone who doesn't comply with the law. In most instances society's desire for revenge can be satisfied while fulfilling one of the other purposes of punishment, such as rehabilitation.

It has also been asserted that public retribution prevents private retribution.[4] That is, when the victim (or anyone who might avenge a victim) of a crime knows that the offender has been punished the victim's need to seek revenge is lessened or removed.

LEGAL TERMS

retribution
  A theory of punishment that asserts that a social benefit is derived when society takes revenge on those who violate criminal laws.

Therefore, punishing those who harm others has the effect of promoting social order by preventing undesirable conduct by victims of crimes. Retribution in such instances has a deterrent effect in that victims of crimes are less likely to seek revenge. This is a good example of how the various purposes discussed are interrelated.

Finally, consider a sociological note. Do not become so focused on criminal law as a method of social control that you forget the many other methods of control that exist.

> The criminal law is not, of course, the only weapon which society uses to prevent conduct which harms or threatens to harm these important interests of the public. Education, at home and at school, as to the types of conduct that society thinks good and bad, is an important weapon; religion, with its emphasis on distinguishing between good and evil conduct, is another. The human desire to acquire and keep the affection and respect of family, friends and associates no doubt has a great influence in deterring most people from conduct which is socially unacceptable. The civil side of the law, which forces one to pay damages for the harmful results which his undesirable conduct has caused to others, or which in inappropriate situations grants injunctions against bad conduct or orders the specific performance of good conduct, also plays a part in influencing behavior along desirable lines.[5]

SECTION 2.4   SOURCES OF CRIMINAL LAW

Criminal law is actually a body of many laws emanating from many sources. Today most American criminal law is a product of legislative enactment. That has not always been the case. Further, administrative regulations now make up a much larger percentage of those laws considered criminal. It is vital to successful legal research that you understand the sources of criminal law. As you read this section you will begin to see why an understanding of the functions of the three branches of government is important to an understanding of all criminal law.

Section 2.4(a)   The Common Law

The oldest form of criminal law in the United States is the **common law**. The common law was developed in England and brought to the United States by the English colonists.

> The common law, as it exists in this country, is of English origin. Founded on ancient local rules and customs and in

feudal times, it began to evolve in the King's courts and was eventually molded into the viable principles through which it continues to operate. The common law migrated to this continent with the first English colonists, who claimed the system as their birthright; it continued in full force in the 13 original colonies until the American Revolution, at which time it was adopted by each of the states as well as the national government of the new nation.[6]

But what exactly is this common law? Simply stated, the common law is judge-made law. It is law that has been developed by the hands of the judges of both England and the United States. To comprehend how common law developed you must understand the concepts of **precedence** and **stare decisis**. Anytime a court renders a legal decision that decision becomes binding on itself and its inferior courts, whenever the same issue arises again in the future. The decision of the court is known as a precedent. The principle that inferior courts will comply with that decision when the issue is raised in the future is known as "stare decisis et non quieta movera," which is a Latin phrase meaning "stand by precedents and do not disturb settled points." The Supreme Court of Indiana has expressed its view of stare decisis:

> Under the doctrine of stare decisis, this Court adheres to a principle of law which has been firmly established. Important policy considerations militate in favor of continuity and predictability in the law. Therefore, we are reluctant to disturb long-standing precedent which involves salient issues. Precedent operates as a maxim for judicial restraint to prevent the unjustified reversal to a series of decisions merely because the composition of the court has changed. [citations omitted][7]

During the feudal years in England there were few formal criminal laws. Rather, local customs and practices developed into rules that governed the behavior of people. The concepts of fairness, justice, and equity were the guiding principles behind these rules. Eventually the courts began to recognize these rules. With that recognition came judicial decisions enforcing them. As precedent each of those decisions began to establish a body of law, both civil and criminal in nature. The whole of those decisions is known as the common law.

> The common law, as frequently defined, includes those principles, usages, and rules of action applicable to the government and security of persons and property which do not rest for their authority upon any express or positive statute or other written declaration, but upon statements of principles found in the decisions of courts. The common law is inseparably identified with the decisions of the courts and

LEGAL TERMS

common law
A body of unwritten law that develops from the customs, principles, and practices of a nation as recognized in judicial decisions. Although the common law can be found in written caselaw, it is often referred to as unwritten in the sense that the legislature has not created a written statute.

precedent
A decision or order of a court that is binding on other courts in the future. Generally, a decision of a court is binding only on itself and its lower courts. However, other courts may look to its opinion for guidance.

stare decisis
Latin for "Let the decision stand." Legal principle that requires courts to respect the previous opinions of other courts (precedent) if the facts and law are the same in both the new case and old case.

can be determined only from such decisions in former cases bearing upon the subject under inquiry. As distinguished from statutory or written law, it embraces the great body of unwritten law founded upon general custom, usage, or common consent, and based upon natural justice or reason. It may otherwise be defined as custom long acquiesced in or sanctioned by immemorial usage and judicial decision . . .

In a broader sense the common law is the system of rules and declarations of principles from which our judicial ideas and legal definitions are derived, and which are continually expanding. It is not a codification of exact or inflexible rules for human conduct, for the redress of injuries, or for protection against wrongs, but is rather the embodiment of broad and comprehensive unwritten principles, inspired by natural reason and an innate sense of justice, and adopted by common consent for the regulation and government of the affairs of men.[8]

As stated, the common law is fluid, ever changing consistent with societal values and expectations. As one court has stated "The common law of the land is based upon human experience in the unceasing effort of an enlightened people to ascertain what is right and just between men."[9]

What happened historically is that courts defined crimes, since there was usually no legislative enactment that determined what acts should be criminal. As time passed established "common-law crimes" developed. First the courts determined what acts should be criminal, and then the specifics of each crime developed. That is, what exactly had to be shown to establish guilt, what defenses were available, and what punishment was appropriate for conviction. Although there is great similarity between the common laws of the many jurisdictions, differences exist because judicial decisions of one state are not binding precedents on other states and because customs and practices vary between communities. However, often courts will look outside their jurisdictions for opinions to guide them in their decision making if no court in their jurisdiction has addressed the issue under consideration. Each state, as a separate and sovereign entity, has the power to decide whether to adopt the common law, in whole or in part, or to reject the common law.

Initially, the thirteen original states all adopted the common law. Most did so through their state constitutions. Today, only Louisiana has not adopted the common law in some form. However, for reasons you will learn below, approximately half of the states no longer recognize common-law crimes.[10] Even in those states, though, the civil common law and portions of the criminal common law (i.e., defenses to criminal charges) continue in force.

Most states have expressly adopted the common law either by statute or constitutional authority. Many states adopted only parts of the common law.

Generally, there is no federal common law, rather federal courts apply the common law of the states in which they reside. For example, a United States district court in New Jersey will apply New Jersey common law. Even though this may appear strange to you, it is common practice for federal courts to apply state law. A discussion of this topic is beyond the scope of this text, and, as such, no more will be said.

Finally, be aware that common law has been modified and even abolished in some jurisdictions. The modifications to, and nullifications of, common law have come about in many different manners. In some instances courts have decided that the common law must be changed to meet contemporary conditions. In extreme situations parts of the common law have been totally abolished. Because legislatures are charged with the duty of making the laws they have the final word, unless there is a state constitutional provision stating otherwise, on the status of the common law. Some legislatures have expressly given their judiciaries the authority to modify the common law, often with limitations. State legislatures are free to modify, partially abolish, or wholly abolish the common law as long as their own state constitution or the United States Constitution is not violated by so doing. The common law normally is inferior to legislation. This means that if a legislature acts in an area previously dealt with by common law the new statute is controlling, absent a statement by the legislature to the contrary. For example, assume that under common law adultery was a crime in State Y. The legislature of State Y can change this by simply enacting a statute that provides that adultery is not criminal. The legislature may also amend the common law by continuing to recognize common-law adultery, but change the penalty for violation. If a state constitution, statute, or judicial decision has not abrogated the common law presume it continues in effect.

Section 2.4(a.1) The Principle of Legality

The question of whether common-law crimes should continue to exist is debatable. Those who favor permitting common-law crimes claim that it permits courts to "fill in the gaps" left by the legislatures when those bodies either fail to foresee all potential crimes or simply forget to include a crime that was foreseen. You should question whether the judicial branch should be actively second-guessing or cleaning house for the legislative branch. There appears to be a separation of powers issue when the judicial branch begins to behave in such a manner. On the other hand few people want to see intentionally dangerous or disruptive behavior go uninhibited.

Those who oppose a common law of crimes point to the concept embodied in the phrase "nullum crimen sine lege," which means, "there is no crime if there is no statute." Similarly, "nulla poena sine lege" has come to mean that "there shall be no punishment if there is no statute." These concepts, when considered in concert, insist that the criminal law must be written, that the written law must exist at the time that the accused took the act in question, and that criminal laws be more precise than civil laws.[11] This is the **principle of legality**.

The legality principle is founded on the belief that all people are entitled to know, prior to taking an act, that an act is criminal and that punishment could result from such behavior. This is commonly referred to as "notice." The idea is sensible, as it appears to be a rule that is consistent with general notions of fairness and justice. Does it appear fair to you to hold an individual criminally accountable for taking an act that he or she couldn't have known was prohibited? The legality principle remedies the notice problem by requiring that written law be the basis of criminal liability, not unwritten common law. Understand that the law imposes a duty on all people to be aware of written law, and, as such, all people are presumed to be aware of criminal prohibitions. What follows is an excerpt from a case that discusses the legality principle.

KEELER V. SUPERIOR COURT

Supreme Court of California
2 Cal.3d 619, 470 P.2d 617 (1970)

LEGAL TERMS

principle of legality
A legal maxim that requires criminal laws to be written, such as statutes and administrative regulations. Additionally, the principle requires that criminal laws be more precise than civil and must have been enacted before the alleged criminal act took place.

MOSK, J. In this proceeding for writ of prohibition we are called upon to decide whether an unborn viable fetus is a "human being" within the meaning of the California statute defining murder (Pen. Code, Sec. 187). We conclude that the legislature did not intend such a meaning, and that for us to construe the statute to the contrary and apply it to this petitioner would exceed our judicial power and deny petitioner due process of law.

The evidence received at the preliminary examination may be summarized as follows: Petitioner and Teresa Keeler obtained an interlocutory decree of divorce on September 27, 1968. They had been married for sixteen years. Unknown to petitioner, Mrs. Keeler was then pregnant by one Ernest Vogt, whom she had met earlier that summer. She subsequently began living with Vogt in Stockton, but concealed the fact from petitioner. Petitioner was given custody of their two daughters, aged 12 and 13 years, and under the decree Mrs. Keeler had the right to take the girls on alternate weekends.

On February 23, 1969, Mrs. Keeler was driving on a narrow mountain road in Amador County after delivering the girls to their home. She met petitioner driving in the opposite direction; he blocked the road with his car, and she pulled over to the side. He walked to her vehicle and began speaking to her. He seemed calm, and she rolled down her window to hear him. He said, "I hear you're pregnant. If you are you had better stay away from the girls and from here." She did not reply, and he opened the car door; as she later testified, "He assisted me out of the car. . . [I]t wasn't rough at this time." Petitioner then looked at her abdomen and became "extremely upset." He said, "You sure are. I'm going to stomp it out of you." He pushed her against the car, shoved his knee into her abdomen, and struck her in the face with several blows. She fainted, and when she regained consciousness petitioner had departed.

Mrs. Keeler drove back to Stockton, and the police and medical assistance were summoned. She had suffered substantial facial injuries, as well as extensive bruising of the abdominal wall. A Caesarian section was performed, and the fetus was examined in utero. Its head was found to be severely fractured, and it was delivered stillborn. The pathologist gave as his opinion that the cause of death was skull fracture with consequent cerebral hemorrhaging, that death would be immediate, and that the injury could have been the result of force applied to the mother's abdomen. There was no air in the fetus' lungs, and the umbilical cord was intact.

. . . The evidence was in conflict as to the estimated age of the fetus; the expert testimony on the point, however,

SIDEBAR

HOW TO BRIEF
A CASE

Decisions of courts are often written and are called judicial opinions or cases. These cases are published in law reporters so they may be used as precedent. Many cases will appear in this text for your education. Your instructor may also require that you read other cases, often from your jurisdiction. The cases that have been included in your book have been edited, and those legal issues not relevant to the subject discussed have been excised.

Most judicial opinions are written using a similar format. First, the name of the case will appear with the name of the court, the cite (location where the case has been published), and the year. When the body of the case begins, the name of the judge, or judges, responsible for writing the opinion will appear directly before the first paragraph. The opinion will contain an introduction to the case, which normally gives you the procedural history of the case. This is followed by a summary of the facts that led to the dispute, the court's analysis of the law that applies to the case, and the court's conclusions and orders, if any.

Most opinions used are from appellate courts, where many judges sit at one time. After the case is over the judges vote on an outcome. The majority vote wins, and the opinion of the majority is written by one of those judges. If other judges in the majority wish to add to the majority opinion they may write what is known as a concurring opinion. Concurring opinions appear after majority opinions in the law reporters. When a judge who was not in the majority feels strongly about his or her position he or she may file a dissenting opinion, which appears after the concurring opinions, if any. Only the majority opinion is law, although concurring and dissenting opinions are often informative.

During your legal education you may be instructed to "brief" a case. Even if your instructor does not require you to brief the cases, you may want to, as many students understand a case better after they have completed a brief. What follows are my suggestions for reading and understanding cases.

1. Read the case. On your first reading do not take notes; simply attempt to get a "feel for the case." Then read the case again and use the following suggested method of briefing.

2. State the

concluded "with reasonable medical certainty" that the fetus had developed to the stage of viability, i.e., that in the event of premature birth on the date in question it would have had a 75 percent to 96 percent chance of survival.

An information was filed charging petitioner, in count I, with committing the crime of murder. . . .

Penal Code section 187 provides: "Murder is the unlawful killing of a human being, with malice aforethought." The dispositive question is whether the fetus which petitioner is accused of killing was, on February 23, 1969, a "human being" within the meaning of the statute. If it was not, petitioner cannot be charged with its "murder" . . . .

* * *

We conclude that in declaring murder to be the unlawful and malicious killing of a "human being" the Legislature of 1850 intended that term to have the settled common law meaning of a person who had been born alive, and did not intend the act of feticide—as distinguished from abortion—to be an offense under the laws of California.

* * *

The People urge, however that the sciences of obstetrics and pediatrics have greatly progressed since 1872, to the point where with proper medical care a normally developed fetus prematurely born . . . is "viable" . . . since an unborn but viable fetus is now fully capable of independent life . . . But we cannot join in the conclusion sought to be to be deduced: we cannot hold this petitioner to answer for murder by reason of his alleged act of killing an unborn—even though viable—fetus. To such a charge there are two insuperable obstacles, one "jurisdictional" and the other constitutional.

Penal Code section 6 declares in relevant part that "No act or omission" accomplished after the code has taken effect "is criminal or punishable, except as prescribed by this code. . . ." This section embodies a fundamental principle of our tripartite form of government, i.e., that subject to the constitutional prohibition against cruel and unusual punishment, the power to define crimes and fix penalties is vested exclusively in the legislative branch. Stated differently, there are no common law crimes in California. . . . In order that a public offense be committed, some statute, ordinance or regulation prior in time to the commission of the act, must denounce it. . . .

* * *

Applying these rules to the case at bar, we would undoubtedly act in excess of the judicial power if we were to adopt the People's proposed construction of section 187. As we have shown, the Legislature has defined the crime of murder in California to apply only to the unlawful and malicious killing of one who has been born alive. We recognize that the killing of an unborn but viable fetus may be deemed by some to be an offense of similar nature and gravity; but as Chief Justice Marshall warned long ago, "It would be dangerous, indeed, to carry the principle, that a case which is within the reason or mischief of a statute, because it is of equal atrocity, or of kindred character, with those which are enumerated." [cite omitted] Whether to thus extend liability for murder in California is a determination solely within the province of the Legislature. For a court to simply declare, by judicial fiat, that the time has now come to prosecute under section 187 one who kills an unborn but viable fetus would indeed be to rewrite the statute under the guise of construing it. . . . to make it "a judicial function" . . . "raises very serious questions concerning the principle of separation of powers." [cite omitted]

The second obstacle to the proposed judicial enlargement of section 187 is the guarantee of due process of law. . . .

The first essential of due process is fair warning of the act which is made punishable as a crime. "That the terms of a penal statute creating a new offense must be sufficiently explicit to inform those who are subject to it what conduct on their part will render them liable to its penalties, is a well-recognized requirement, consonant alike with ordinary notions of fair play and the settled rules of law. . . ."

relevant facts. Often cases read like little stories. You need to weed out the facts that have no bearing on the subject you are studying.

3. Identify the issues. Issues are the legal questions discussed by the court. For example, assume that your state statute requires the use of a deadly weapon before a battery charge may be elevated to aggravated battery. Also assume that John, who has been diagnosed as having AIDS, spat on Kim intending to harm her. The issue would be whether the saliva constitutes a deadly weapon under the statute and thereby permits an aggravated battery charge.

4. State the applicable rules, standards, or other law. In the example above this would include legal definitions of deadly weapon (whether statutory or from caselaw), as well as the definitions and elements of battery and aggravated battery.

5. Summarize the court's decision and analysis. Why and how did the court reach its conclusion? Note whether the court affirmed, reversed, or remanded the case.

Do not forget that this is an opinion of the California Supreme Court; therefore, it is not the law of the land. It is the law in California, and similar decisions have been made elsewhere.

Also note that the court determined that the common law violates "ordinary notions of fair play" and that no warning or notice was given to Keeler that his act could be defined as murder. As the court noted, these requirements are embodied in the **Due Process Clause** of the United States Constitution and the constitutions of the many states. Due process, in both civil and criminal law, requires that individuals be put on notice of impending government action, be given an opportunity to be heard and to present evidence, and often the right to a jury trial. The Due Process Clause is founded upon principles of fair play and justice. However, the United States Supreme Court has determined that states may, under some circumstances, use the common law to define criminal conduct. The court in *Keeler* based its decision on the California Constitution Due Process Clause. You should remember that the California Supreme Court is the final word on California law, and *Keeler* teaches you that the California Constitution provides more protection than the United States Constitution in this regard. Still, the United States Constitution places limits on the use of the common law by the states to create crimes. This is done primarily through the due process clause and the provision prohibiting ex post facto laws. You will learn more about the due process and ex post facto clauses later in this book when we examine defenses to criminal charges. If states, such as California in the *Keeler* case, want to increase a defendant's rights, beyond what the United States Constitution protects, they may through their own statutes or constitutions.

Section 2.4(a.2) Other Uses of the Common Law

Even in those jurisdictions that have abandoned the use of the common law to create crimes the common law continues to be important for many reasons.

First, many statutes mirror the common law in language. That is, legislatures often simply codify the common law criminal prohibitions. Hence, when a question arises concerning whether a particular act of a defendant is intended to fall under the intent of a criminal prohibition, the caselaw handed down prior to codification of the common law may continue to be helpful after codification. The result is that the crime remains the same, but the source of the prohibition has changed. It is also possible for a legislature to change only part of a common law definition and leave the remainder the same. If so, prior caselaw may be helpful when considering the unaltered portion of the definition.

Second, legislatures occasionally enact a criminal prohibition without establishing the potential penalty for violation. In such cases courts will often look to the penalties applied to similar common law crimes for guidance.

Third, the common law not only provided a mechanism to create new crimes, but established many procedures that were used to adjudicate criminal cases. These procedures most often dealt with criminal defenses. What defenses could be raised, as well as how and when, were often answered by the common law. For example, the various tests to use to determine if a defendant was sane when an alleged crime was committed were developed under the common law. If a legislature has not specifically changed these procedural rules they remain in effect, even if the power of courts to create common law crimes has been abolished.

Section 2.4(b) Statutory Law

As you have already learned, the legislative branch is responsible for the creation of law. You have also learned that legislatures possess the authority to modify, abolish, or adopt the common law, in whole or in part. During the nineteenth century states began a major movement away from the common law and began codifying the criminal law. Today, nearly all criminal law is found in criminal codes.

Although the power of the legislative branch to declare behavior criminal is significant, there are limits. The constitutions of the United States and of the many states contain limits on such state and federal authority. Most of these limits are found in the Bill of Rights. For example, the first amendment to the federal Constitution prohibits government from punishing an individual for exercising choice of religion. If a legislature does enact law that violates a constitutional provision it is the duty of the judicial branch to declare the law void. This is the power of judicial review, previously discussed in chapter one. For now, you need only understand that legislatures do not have an unlimited authority to create criminal law, that individual (civil) rights limit legislative power to make conduct criminal, and that the judicial branch acts to protect individuals from unconstitutional legislation.

Section 2.4(c) Ordinances

The written laws of municipalities are **ordinances**. Ordinances are enacted by city councils and commonly regulate zoning, building, construction, and related matters. Many cities have criminal ordinances that mirror state statutes, only they

LEGAL TERMS

due process
A concept embodied in the Fifth and Fourteenth Amendments to the United States Constitution. Also contained in all state constitutions. Generally held to mean that no person shall be deprived of life, liberty, or property without first being provided notice of an impending government action against the individual, the opportunity to be heard, and often the right to a jury trial. Generally, a provision requiring that individuals be given their day in court before their government can act against them.

ordinance
The written law of a municipality. Ordinances are enacted by city councils and can be civil or criminal in nature. Ordinances must be consistent with state and federal law, and in the criminal law context deal with minor offenses.

apply to those acts that occur within the jurisdiction of the city. For example, many cities have assault and battery ordinances, just as their states have assault and battery statutes. Traffic and parking violations may also be criminal, although some cities pursue these as civil violations, which permits the state to pursue the criminal charge.

Ordinances may not conflict with state or federal law. Any ordinance that is inconsistent with higher law may be invalidated by a court. States limit the power of cities to punish for ordinance violations, and most city court trials are to the bench, not to a jury.

Section 2.4(d) Administrative Law

It is likely that at some time in your life you have had to deal with an administrative agency. Agencies are governmental units, federal, state, and local, which administer the affairs of the government. Although often lumped together as administrative agencies there are actually two types of agencies, administrative and regulatory. The two names reflect the purposes behind each type. Administrative agencies put into effect government programs. For example, in Indiana the State Department of Public Welfare administers the distribution of public money to those deemed needy. On the other hand, state medical licensing boards are regulatory, because their duty is to oversee and regulate the practice of medicine in the various states. Both regulatory and administrative agencies receive their power from the legislative branch.

Because legislatures do not possess the time or the expertise to write precise statutes they often enact a statute that is very general and in that statute grant one or more administrative agencies the authority to make more precise laws. Just as legislative enactments are known as statutes (or codes), administrative laws are known as **regulations**. The extent to which a legislature may grant its law-making authority has been a continuing source of debate. It is argued that legislatures may not grant such an important legislative function to agencies. This is believed to be a violation of the principle of separation of powers, because agencies usually fall under the control of the executive branch, and the legislative branch is not permitted to delegate its powers to the executive branch, or vice versa.

Despite this, the United States Supreme Court has determined that agencies may create regulations, which have the effect of law, including criminal prohibitions. The Court's opinion on how much authority may be given administrative agencies has undergone a few changes over the years. In 1911 the United States Supreme Court handed down the case that follows.

UNITED STATES V. GRIMAUD

United States Supreme Court
220 U.S. 506 (1911)

* * *

Mr. JUSTICE LAMAR, after making the foregoing statement, delivered the opinion of the court.

The defendants were indicted for grazing sheep on the Sierra Forest Reserve without having obtained the permission required by the regulations adopted by the Secretary of Agriculture. They demurred [to admit the facts, but argue that a legal insufficiency exists] on the ground that the Forest Reserve Act of 1891 was unconstitutional, in so far as it delegated to the Secretary of Agriculture power to make rules and regulations and made a violation thereof a penal offense. . . .

* * *

From the various acts relating to the establishment and management of forest reservations it appears that they were intended "to improve and protect the forest and to secure favorable conditions to water flows." . . . It was also declared that the Secretary "may make such rules and regulations and establish such service as will insure the objects of such reservation, namely, to regulate their occupancy and use to prevent the forests thereon from destruction; *and any violation of the provisions of this act or such* rules and regulations shall be punished," as is provided in section 5388, c. 3, p. 1044 of the Revised Statutes, as amended.

Under these acts, therefore, any use of the reservations for grazing or other lawful purpose was required to be subject to the rules and regulations established by the Secretary of Agriculture. To pasture sheep and cattle on the reservation, at will and without restraint, might interfere seriously with the accomplishment of the purposes for which they were established. But a limited and regulated use for pasturage might not be inconsistent with the object sought to be attained by the statute. The determination of such questions, however, was a matter of administrative detail. What might be harmless in one forest might be harmful to another. What

LEGAL TERMS

regulations
Rules, which have the effect of law, created by administrative agencies. To be valid the legislature must have granted the agency the power to make the rule, provided at least minimal guidance and limits to the agency's authority to make law, and the agency must not have exceeded its grant of authority.

might be injurious at one stage of timber growth, or at one season of the year, might not be so at another.

In the nature of things it was impracticable for Congress to provide general regulations for these various and varying details of management. Each reservation had its peculiar and special features; and in authorizing the Secretary of Agriculture to meet these local conditions Congress was merely conferring administrative functions upon an agent, and not delegating to him legislative power. . . .

* * *

It must be admitted that it is difficult to define the line which separates legislative power to make laws, from administrative authority to make regulations. This difficulty has often been recognized, and was referred to by Chief Justice Marshall in *Wayman v. Southard*, 10 Wheat. 1, 42, where he was considering the authority of the courts to make rules. He there said: "It will not be contended that Congress can delegate to the courts, or to any other tribunals, powers which are strictly and exclusively legislative. But Congress may certainly delegate to others, powers which the legislature may rightfully exercise itself." What were these non-legislative powers which Congress could exercise but which might also be delegated to others was not determined, for he said: "The line has not been exactly drawn which separates those important subjects, which *must* be entirely regulated by the legislature itself, from those of less interest, in which a general provision may be made, and power given to those who are to act under such general provisions to fill up the details."

From the beginning of the Government various acts have been passed conferring upon the executive officers power to make rules and regulations—not for the government of their departments; but for administering the laws which did govern. None of these statutes could confer legislative power. But when Congress had legislated and indicated its will, it could give to those who were to act under such general provisions "power to fill up the details" by the establishment of administrative rules and regulations, the violation of which could be punished by fine or imprisonment fixed by Congress, or by penalties fixed by Congress or measured by the injury done.

*   *   *

It is true that there is no act of Congress which, in express terms, declares that it shall be unlawful to graze sheep on a forest reserve. But the statutes, from which we have quoted, declare, that the privilege of using reserves for "all proper and lawful purposes" is subject to the proviso that the person shall comply "with the rules and regulations covering such forest reservation." The same act makes it an offense to violate those regulations. . . .

*   *   *

The Secretary of Agriculture could not make rules and regulations for any and every purpose. [cite omitted] As to those here involved, they all regulate matters clearly indicated and authorized by Congress. . . .

The view of the court changed in the 1930s when the court began to scrutinize legislative delegations of rule-making authority to agencies, and on a few occasions found the grant to be excessive.[12] However, the court has come full circle on this issue, and today the reasoning that led to the decisions of the 1930s is no longer accepted. The law today is reflected in the case, *U.S. v. Barron*, 594 F.2d 1345, 1345 (10th Cir. 1979), wherein that court stated that the New Deal-era decisions are probably no longer viable and that what is now required is for Congress to "clearly delineate" the general policy sought to be achieved by the statute, to name the agency authorized to make the regulations, and to set the boundaries of that agency's authority. So long as Congress complies with these three requirements, the delegation is likely to be upheld. Of course, the agency must act within the limits set. Most states have interpreted their own constitutions similarly and permit a delegation with only "minimal guidelines from the legislative branch."[13]

Finally, the likelihood of such a delegation of authority being upheld increases as a legislature's control over the penalties for violation increases. Some statutes expressly set the penalty for violation. You may recall that this is what Congress had done in the Forest Reserve Act, which was in issue in the *Grimaud* case. Other statutes set a maximum penalty and permit the agency to specifically set the penalties for various agency-made violations. In the largest grant of authority some legislation permits the agency to establish the regulation and set the penalty. This final method may not be permitted in your jurisdiction, and you should research this issue if you have a client charged with violating a regulation that also sets the penalty.

At the federal level administrative regulations can be found in the Code of Federal Regulations. Also, the Federal Register, which is published daily, carries new regulations that have not yet made it into the Code of Federal Regulations. Most states also have a reporting system for regulations. As a legal professional you should be aware of what regulations are reported in your jurisdiction and where to find them. Administrative regulations can be voluminous and are becoming increasingly important as legislatures are increasingly depending on administrative agencies to make law.

Section 2.4(e) Court Rules

Just as administrative agencies need the authority to "fill in the gaps" of legislation because statutes are not specific enough to satisfy all of an agency's needs, so do courts. The United States Congress and all of the state legislatures have enacted some form of statute establishing general rules of civil and criminal procedure. However, to "fill in the gaps" left by legislatures courts adopt **court rules**, which also govern civil and criminal processes. Although court rules deal with procedural issues (such as service of process, limits on the length of briefs and memoranda, and timing of filing) and not substantive issues, they are important. Of course, court rules may not conflict with legislative mandates. If a rule does conflict with a statute, the statute is controlling. One exception to this rule may be when the statute is unconstitutional and the rule is a viable alternative, but discussion of that issue is best left to a course on constitutional law and judicial process.

Most court rules are drafted under the direction of the highest court of the state and either become effective by vote of the court or after being presented to the state legislature for ratification. In the federal system the rules are drafted by the Judicial Conference under the direction of the Supreme Court and then presented to Congress. If Congress fails to act to nullify the rules they become law. Of course, Congress may amend the rules at will. Many jurisdictions also have local rules, that is, rules created by local courts for practice in those courts. The rules cannot conflict with either statutes or higher court rules. In the federal system district courts adopt local rules. Being familiar with the rules of the courts in your jurisdiction is imperative. If you are not, you may miss important deadlines, file incomplete documents, or have your filings stricken.

Section 2.4(f) The Model Penal Code

On occasion the **Model Penal Code** will be referenced in this text. Actually entitled *Model Penal Code and Commentaries,* it was drafted by a group of individuals expert in criminal law while working for the the American Law Institute, which is a private organization. The intent of the drafters of the Code was to draft a consistent, thoughtful code that would be recommended to the states for adoption. The code itself is not law until adopted and made into law by a legislature.

According to one source, by 1985 thirty-four states had "enacted widespread criminal-law revision and codification based on its provisions; fifteen hundred courts had cited its provisions and referred to its commentary."[14]

Section 2.4(g) Constitutional Law

Finally, constitutional law is included in this list of sources of criminal law not because it defines what conduct is criminal, but because of its significant impact on criminal law generally. Particularly, the United States Constitution, primarily through the Bill of Rights, is responsible for establishing many of the rules governing criminal procedure. This has been especially true in the past few decades. You will become more aware of why this is true as you learn more about criminal law and procedure. Pay close attention to the dates of the cases that are included in this text; it is likely that many were handed down in your lifetime.

LEGAL TERMS

court rules
Rules of civil and criminal procedure established by courts. Generally these rules supplement codes of civil and criminal procedure.

Model Penal Code
A criminal code written by criminal law scholars for the American Law Institute. The Model Penal Code has greatly influenced modern criminal law.

IMPORTANT DATES IN THE HISTORY OF THE CONSTITUTION OF THE UNITED STATES

May 25, 1787	Constitutional Convention opens in Philadelphia.
September 17, 1787	Constitutional Convention closes, and Constitution is sent to the states for ratification.
December 6, 1787	Delaware is the first state to ratify the Constitution.

June 21, 1788	New Hampshire is the ninth state to ratify and thereby provides the requisite number of ratifying states to adopt the Constitution for the entire United States.
May 29, 1790	Rhode Island is the thirteenth (last) state to ratify the Constitution.
December 15, 1791	Bill of Rights is ratified.
July 28, 1968	Fourteenth Amendment is ratified.

Although it is common to associate the study of constitutional law with the study of the United States Constitution, do not forget that each state also has its own constitution with its own body of caselaw interpreting its meaning. Even though the dominate source for defending civil liberties has been the United States Constitution, it is possible that a shift to state constitutions will occur since the current Supreme Court is expected to be more conservative on criminal issues, which means less likely to extend constitutional protections. Remember, the United States Constitution is the highest form of law, and the states may not decrease the individual protections secured by it. States may, however, increase civil liberties through state law. Most state constitutions mirror the federal constitution, often verbatim. Despite this, state courts are free to interpret their constitutional provisions as providing more protection than their federal counterparts, even if identical in text.

SOURCES OF CRIMINAL LAW

SOURCE	COMMENT
CONSTITUTIONS	The United States and every state have a constitution. The United States Constitution is the supreme law of the land. Amendment of the federal constitution requires action by both the states and United States Congress.
STATUTES	The written law created by legislatures, also known as codes. State statutes may not conflict with either their own constitution or the federal constitution. State statutes are also invalid if they conflict with other federal law, and the federal government has concurrent jurisdiction with the states. Statutes of

	the United States are invalid if they conflict with the United States Constitution or if they attempt to regulate outside federal jurisdiction. Legislatures may change statutes at will.
COMMON LAW	Law which evolved, as courts, through judicial opinions, recognized customs, and practices. Legislatures may alter, amend, abolish the common law at will. In criminal law the common law is responsible for the creation of crimes and for establishing defenses to crimes.
REGULATIONS	Created by administrative agencies under a grant of authority from a legislative body. Regulations must be consistent with statutes and constitutions and may not exceed the legislative grant of power. The power to make rules and regulations is granted to "fill in the gaps" left by legislatures when drafting statutes.
ORDINANCES	Written law of local bodies, such as city councils. Must be consistent with all higher forms of law.
MODEL PENAL CODE	Written under the direction of the American Law Institute. It was drafted by experts in criminal law to be presented to the states for their adoption. It is not law until a state has adopted it, in whole or part. More than half the states have adopted at least part of the Model Penal Code.
COURT RULES	Rules created by courts to manage their cases. Court rules are procedural and commonly establish deadlines, lengths of filings, etc. Court rules may not conflict with statutes or constitutions.

REVIEW QUESTIONS

1. What are civil liberties? Give two examples of civil liberties that are protected by the Constitution of the United States.
2. What is the common law? How do the concepts of stare decisis and precedent relate to the common law?
3. The common law is different in every state. Why?
4. What does the Latin phrase "nullum crimen sine lege" translate to? Explain the significance of that phrase.

5. Explain how the common law can violate the principle of legality.
6. State three uses the common law has in criminal law in those jurisdictions that do not permit common law creation of crimes.
7. What is the source of most criminal law today? Where does that law come from?
8. What is an ordinance?
9. What is a regulation?
10. What is a court rule?
11. Place the following sources of law in order of authority, beginning with the highest form of law and ending with the lowest. Notice that both state and federal sources of law are included: United States Code, state constitutions, federal administrative regulations, ordinances, United States Constitution, state administrative regulations, and state statutes.

REVIEW PROBLEMS

1. In theory, people can increase their "freedom" by establishing a government and relinquishing freedoms (civil liberties) to that government. Explain why this paradox is true.
2. List the various purposes for punishing criminal law violators.

3–6. Using your answers from question number two, determine if the goals of punishment can be achieved if prosecution is sought for the following acts:

3. John, having always wanted a guitar, stole one from a fellow student's room while that student was out.
4. Jack suffers from a physical disease of the mind that causes him to have violent episodes. Jack has no way of knowing when the episodes will occur. However, the disease is controllable with medication. Despite this, Jack often does not take the medicine, as he finds the injections painful and inconvenient. One day, when he had not taken the medicine, Jack had an episode and struck Mike, causing him personal injury.
5. Same facts as above, except there is no treatment or medication that can control Jack's behavior. He was diagnosed as having the disease years prior to striking Mike and has caused such an injury before during a similar violent episode.

6. Unknown to Kevin he is an epileptic. One day while he was driving his automobile he suffered his first seizure. The seizure caused him to lose control of his car and strike a pedestrian, inflicting a fatal injury.

NOTES

[1] In May, 1988, Larry Mahoney, while driving under the influence of alcohol, struck a school bus, causing it to burst into flames. At the time he hit the bus he was traveling in the wrong direction on an interstate highway. Twenty-four children and three adults died in the fire. On December 22, 1989, a Kentucky jury convicted Mr. Mahoney of second-degree manslaughter, and other lesser offenses, and recommended that he be sentenced to sixteen years in prison.

[2] See Puttkammer, E., (1953), *Administration of Criminal Law*, pp. 16–17.

[3] Schwartz and Goldstein, *Police Guidance Manuals* (University of Virginia Press, 1968), Manual No. 3, pp. 21–32, reprinted in *Cases, Materials, and Problems on the Advocacy and Administration of Criminal Justice* by Harold Norris, p. 173 (unpublished manuscript available in the Detroit College of Law library).

[4] See Note, 78 Colum. L. Rev. 1249, 1247–59 (1978) and LaFave and Scott, *Criminal Law* (Hornbook Series, St. Paul: West Publishing Co., 1986), p. 26.

[5] LaFave and Scott, p. 23.

[6] 15A AM. JUR. 2d *Common Law* 6 (1976).

[7] *Marsillett v. State*, 495 N.E.2d 699, 704 (Ind. 1986).

[8] 15A AM. JUR. 2d *Common Law* 1 (1976).

[9] *Helms v. American Sec. Co. of Indiana*, 22 N.E.2d 822 (Ind. 1986).

[10] Gardner, T., *Criminal Law: Principles and Cases*, 4th Ed. (Criminal Justice Series, St. Paul: West Publishing Co., 1989).

[11] Robinson, P., *Fundamentals of Criminal Law* (Boston: Little, Brown and Co., 1988).

[12] *Schechter Poultry Corp. v. United States*, 295 U.S. 495 (1935).

[13] LaFave and Scott, p. 111.

[14] Samaha, J., *Criminal Law*, 3rd Ed. (St. Paul: West Publishing Co., 1990).

CHAPTER 3

The Two Essential Elements

"I admire a man who knows where he's going."

Even a dog distinguishes between being stumbled over and being kicked.

Oliver Wendell Holmes

OUTLINE

SECTION 3.1   MENS REA

Nearly every crime consists of two essential elements, the mental and the physical. This chapter begins by addressing the mental part and concludes by examining the physical.

It is common to distinguish between acts that are intentional and those acts that occur accidentally. Everyone has had an experience where they have caused injury to another person or another person's property accidentally. The fact that the injury was accidental and not intended often leads to a statement such as, "I'm sorry, I didn't mean to hurt you." In these situations people often feel a social obligation to pay for any injuries they have caused, or to assist the injured party in other ways, but probably do not expect to be punished criminally. As the quote by the late Supreme Court Justice Holmes states, "Even a dog distinguishes between being stumbled over and being kicked," and, as implied by this statement, to make such a distinction between accidental and intentional acts that injure others appears to be natural and consistent with common notions of fairness. The criminal law often models this theory; that is, people are often held accountable for intentional behavior and not for accidental, even though the consequences may be the same. However, this is not always the case. Under some circumstances accidental behavior (negligent or reckless) may be the basis of criminal liability.

Mens rea is the mental part, the state of mind required to be criminally liable. It is often defined as "a guilty mind" or possessing a criminal intent. It is best defined as the state of mind required to be criminally liable for a certain act. It is sometimes the case that no intent whatsoever is required to be guilty of a crime, while most criminal laws require intent of some degree before criminal liability attaches to an act. Mens rea is an important concept in criminal law. It is also a confusing one. This is in large part because of the inconsistency and lack of uniformity between criminal statutes and judicial decisions. One author found seventy-nine words and phrases in the United States Criminal Code used

to describe mens rea.[1] Often when courts or legislatures use the same term they do so assuming different meanings for the term. For this reason the drafters of the Model Penal Code attempted to establish uniform terms and definitions for those terms. The Model Penal Code approach is examined later. First, you will learn how the common law treated mens rea.

Section 3.1(a)   Mens Rea and the Common Law

One principle under the common law was that there should be no crime if there was no act accompanied by a guilty mind. The Latin phrase that states this principle is "actus non facit reum nisi mens sit rea." Today, under some statutes, no intent is required to be guilty of a crime. Despite this, the principle that "only conscious wrongdoing constitutes crime is deeply rooted in our legal system and remains the rule, rather than the exception . . . "[2]

Many terms have been used to describe a guilty mind. Malicious, mischievous, purposeful, unlawful, intentional, with specific intent, knowing, fraudulent, with an evil purpose, careless, willful, negligent and reckless, are examples of terms and phrases used to describe the requisite mental state required to prove guilt.

LEGAL TERMS

mens rea
　　Guilty mind; the state of mind required to be held criminally liable for an act.

Section 3.1(a.1)   General, Specific, and Constructive Intent

One common distinction is between **general intent** and **specific intent**. The distinction between these two terms turns on whether the defendant intended to cause the consequences of the act. If the defendant had a desire or purpose to cause the result of the act, then the defendant possessed specific intent. If the defendant only intended the act, and not the result of that act, then the defendant possessed general intent. For example, Don Defendant throws a large rock at Vern Victim, inflicting a fatal wound. If Defendant only intended to injure Victim, not kill him, then he possessed general intent. However, if Defendant threw the rock hoping it would kill Victim, then he possessed specific intent. The distinction between general and specific intent is often an important one, as statutes often require specific intent for a higher-level crime and general for a lower. In the example above, many state statutes would allow Defendant to be charged with first-degree murder if he intended to kill Victim, but only second-degree murder if he only intended to injure Victim.

If a defendant intends to cause the result, then the fact that the means used to achieve the result is likely to fail is irrelevant. For example, assume Defendant desires to cause the death of Victim. One day while walking down a street Defendant notices Victim far away. Defendant picks up a rock and hurls it toward Victim hoping it will strike Victim and kill him, although because of the distance he does not expect the rock to strike its intended target. However, all those afternoons practicing his baseball pitch payed off, and the rock hit Victim in the head, killing him instantly. The fact that Defendant threw the rock with an intent to kill is enough to establish Defendant's specific intent. The fact that the act is unlikely to be successful is no defense.

Specific intent may also be proved, in some jurisdictions, by showing that the defendant knew that by taking an act he or she would be violating the law. This requirement of knowledge is known as **scienter**. In those jurisdictions that require such knowledge, if an individual violates a criminal law while believing that the act engaged in is lawful, then specific intent is lacking, and only general intent can be proven.[3] Scienter often does not require proof of subjective knowledge (what was actually in the defendant's mind), but can be established if the prosecution can prove that the defendant should have known the fact in question.

Often without scienter no crime exists to punish. Consider the crime of receiving stolen property. If an individual received stolen property, but did so without knowledge that it was stolen, then no crime has been committed to charge. For some crimes that require scienter, the absence of scienter may leave a general intent crime. If a man strikes a person who he believes is obstructing traffic, he has committed an assault. If he knew, or should have known, that the man was a police officer attempting to direct traffic, then he may be accountable for the higher crime of assault to a police officer. However, if the policeman is not wearing his uniform and did not announce himself as an officer, then the defendant is liable only for simple assault.

Under the common law specific intent could be found in a third type of situation, that is, whenever **constructive intent** could be proven. That is, although the defendant does not intend to cause the result, it is so likely to occur that the law treats the act as one of specific intent. If John fires a handgun at close range at Sally, aiming at her torso, and kills her as a result, it is possible that he could be charged with the specific intent crime of first-degree murder, even though he only intended to injure her. This is because the possibility of killing someone under those circumstances is significant. However, this may not be true if he aimed at her leg and the weapon discharged improperly, causing the bullet to strike her in the torso. This is because the likelihood of killing someone with a gunshot to the leg is much less than with a gunshot to the upper body. The bullet entered Victim's torso as a result of the malfunction of the gun; it was not Defendant's desire to shoot her in the upper body.

As to the amount of probability necessary to prove constructive intent, only "practical or substantial" probability is required, not absolute.[4]

Specific intent can be found in a fourth situation, whenever a defendant intends a result beyond the act taken. This refers to situations where a criminal act is uncompleted. For example, if a man attacks a woman intending to rape her, but she is able to free herself and escape, he may be charged with assault with the intent to rape. To prove this charge the prosecution must show that he assaulted the victim with the specific intent of raping her. Proving that the defendant had a specific intent to assault her is not enough to sustain the intent to rape charge, although it would justify a conviction for assault, a lesser crime. Another example is the crime of breaking and entering with the intent to burglarize. Again, the prosecution must prove that the defendant intended to steal from the home after the entry and didn't complete the burglary for some reason. Proving that the defendant broke in and entered, but had no intent to steal will support a conviction for breaking and entering, but not intent to commit burglary.

General intent is much easier to define, as it is simply the desire to act. In most situations, if the prosecution can show that

LEGAL TERMS

general intent
The intent to take an act, but not necessarily to cause the results of that action.

specific intent
The intent not only to act, but to cause the precise harm that results from that act; the intent not only to act, but to cause a consequence beyond what occurred; intent to cause a result that is imputed to a defendant when the act taken is substantially likely to cause the result, even though the defendant did not possess a true desire to cause the result.

scienter
A mens rea concept that requires that a defendant knew, or should have known, that the act taken was prohibited by law.

constructive intent
Intent to cause the result of an action which is imputed to a defendant even though the defendant had no desire to cause the result. The intent may only be attributed to the defendant if the act had a substantial likelihood of causing the outcome.

a defendant intended to take the act prohibited, then general intent is proved. Generally, no desire to cause a particular consequence is required. So, if you fire a gun without a desire to kill someone, but the bullet does kill a person, you possess a general intent and may be prosecuted for a general intent homicide.

Some jurisdictions require more than simply a desire to act to prove general intent. In those states some level of negligence must be proven. Consider the following two examples: Rural Defendant has lived on a farm for over twenty years. Defendant's nearest neighbor is over three miles away, and defendant routinely target shoots in his back yard. He has never encountered anyone in the area where he shoots, and everyone who lives in the community knows of his practice. One day while target shooting he accidently shoots and kills a trespasser he didn't know was on his property. In the second example, Metro Defendant likes to hunt on weekends. One weekend Metro and his friend were hunting, and Metro lost sight of his friend. Eager to capture his first deer of the season Metro fired into a bush in which he observed some movement. It was Metro's friend that was in the bush, and Metro's gunshot inflicted a fatal wound. In both examples the defendants had no desire to harm the individuals shot, and both possessed the intent to fire the weapon. A strict construction of general and specific intents results in both committing a general intent murder, but not a specific. However, in some jurisdictions Rural may be free from liability because he appears to have been less reckless or negligent than Metro, who should have considered the possibility that it could have been his friend he was firing at.

This discussion has not exhausted the many definitions and distinctions that exist for specific and general intent. In the following case it appears than the Court of Appeals for the District of Columbia has created a hybrid general-specific intent for the crime of cruelty to children.

JANET A. CARSON, APPELLANT
V.
UNITED STATES, APPELLEE

556 A.2d 1076; 1989 D.C. App. LEXIS 57 (1989)

OPINION: Mack, Associate Judge: On June 4, 1985, Janet Carson arrived home from work at about 3:45 P.M. and was informed by one of her children that a fuse needed replacement. While looking for a fuse, appellant noticed that eight dollars were missing from her dresser drawer. She called her children—thirteen-year-old Cornell, six-year-old Everett, five-year-old Angelica and eight-year-old Charmaine Schmidt—to her bedroom; each child denied knowing anything about the missing money. At that point she went downstairs, and as she returned upstairs she picked up an electrical cord; she later testified that she routinely used the cord to discipline the children. She again asked the children about the missing money, and they again denied any knowledge of the money's disappearance. Appellant then whipped each of the children several times.

The next day at the school attended by Everett, Angelica, and Charmaine, school officials noticed marks and bruises on the children. Detective Harmon of the Metropolitan Police Department went to the school and took the three children to Children's Hospital. Everett's abrasions were cleaned and bandaged; the other two children received no treatment.

Appellant was subsequently charged with three counts of cruelty to children (one count of cruelty to Everett Carson, one count of cruelty to Angelica Carson and one count of cruelty to Charmaine Schmidt). . . . [Ms. Carson was convicted and sentenced to thirty days on each count, which was suspended to one year's probation. She appealed the conviction and this is the opinion of the appellate court. In all appeals, the person who files the appeal is known as the appellant and the responding party is known as the appellee.]

I.

Before considering appellant's claim that the evidence was insufficient to support her conviction, we must first determine the mens rea required for conviction under D.C. Code § 22–901 [cruelty to children]. We conclude that the offense is a general intent crime, which also requires a showing of malice. . . .

Section 22–901 provides in pertinent part:

Any person who shall torture, cruelly beat, abuse, or otherwise willfully maltreat any child under the age of 18 years . . . shall be deemed guilty of a misdemeanor, and, when convicted thereof, shall be subject to punishment by a fine of not more than $250, or by imprisonment for a term not exceeding 2 years, or both.

The Criminal Jury Instructions for the District of Columbia, No. 4.18 (3rd ed. 1978), define the elements of the offense as follows:

1. That the defendant tortured, cruelly beat, abused or otherwise maltreated a child;

2. That at the time of the incident, the child was under the age of 18 years; and

3. That the defendant acted willfully, that is, with an evil intent or with bad purpose to maltreat the child. It is not enough that you find that the defendant exercised bad judgment or acted unreasonably. Rather, it is necessary that you find that the defendant was motivated by an evil intent or state of mind in committing the acts which constitute the offense.

* * *

Judicial interpretation of D.C. Code § 22–901 has been limited . . . the United States Court of Appeals for the District of Columbia held that the terms "abuse" and "willfully mistreat" as sued in the statute "call for something worse than good intentions coupled with bad judgment," and incorporate "the requirement of an evil state of mind." . . . The cases would seem to teach that cruelty to children is something more than a general intent crime and something less than a specific intent crime.

* * *

In other contexts, this court has equated the terms "evil intent" and "malice." [citations omitted] This court has noted that a showing of bad or evil purpose is "necessary to distinguish the mental state required for malice-based offenses from that involved in crimes the conviction for which demands proof no more than general intent or criminal negligence." [citations omitted] Thus, if cruelty to children requires proof of something more than general intent, that something more would seem to be malice.

* * *

II.

Having determined the mens rea required for conviction of cruelty to children, we must now determine whether the government's proof was sufficient to establish the requisite mens rea in this case. Appellant concedes that the record supports the trial court's finding of general intent. However, she argues that the government failed to prove that she acted with malice. She argues that according to her undisputed testimony, she was motivated not by an evil intent, but rather by a "concern for [her] children's welfare and upbringing." At first blush, the record supports her argument as to motivation.

The government argues, however, that to find malice "all that is required [is] a conscious disregard of a known and substantial risk of the harm . . . "

Malice is a rather slippery concept, not amenable to precise definition. Authors of the Model Penal Code chose not to use the term. Perkins and Boyce in their treatise on criminal law explain that "malice in the legal sense imports (1) the absense of all elements of justification, excuse or recognized mitigation, and (2) the presence of either (a) an actual intent to cause the particular harm which is produced or harm of the same general nature, or (b) the wanton and willful doing of an act with awareness of a plain and strong likelihood that such harm may result." PERKINS AND BOYCE, CRIMINAL LAW at 860 (3rd ed. 1982). What does this mean in the context of cruelty to children? Simply put, we believe that a parent acts with malice when a parent acts out of a desire to inflict pain rather than out of genuine effort to correct the child, or when the parent, in a genuine effort to correct the child, acts with a conscious disregard that serious harm will result.

* * *

In this case, appellant's testimony regarding her motive was not directly contradicted. The government relied basically on the nature of the wounds and the manner of the punishment to establish malice. The government introduced pictures of the injuries sustained by the children and also pointed to the ages of the children, and the fact that appellant used an electrical cord to whip the children as evidence that appellant acted with evil intent, or at least as evidence that appellant acted with a conscious disregard that serious harm (of the nature which would flow from an evil intent) would result.

From our perspective in this court, we cannot conclude that the evidence justifies the inference that appellant acted out of a desire to inflict pain. . . .

. . . The trial court also noted that appellant had "high standards" for her children—"she didn't want them to steal; she didn't want them to use drugs." The court found that appellant had worked hard to make a good life for herself and her children. She had left the welfare rolls and become a policewoman, "supporting all those children on her own." We echo the trial court's sentiment that appellant had a genuine and deep-felt love and concern for her children.

Further, we do not believe that the punishment was so excessive or the manner so egregious as to lead to the conclusion that appellant acted with a conscious disregard of the serious harm which would result. The mother testified that the whippings lasted perhaps a minute. As to the manner of discipline, reasonable people might disagree as to whether whipping with an electrical cord is in itself offensive or no more offensive than the use of commonly employed devices or methods used to exact discipline. We would only note that appellant testified that because the children were jumping around and that because she was eight months pregnant and therefore awkward, the cord made contact on the children's bodies where it otherwise may not have done so.

However, when the manner of punishment, the length of punishment, the nature of the injuries and the ages of the children are viewed as a whole, we cannot say that the trial court was plainly in error in concluding that appellant acted with conscious disregard of the harm which resulted. . . .

Conviction AFFIRMED

Section 3.1(a.2) Malum In Se and Malum Prohibitum

Often crimes are characterized as either malum in se or malum prohibitum. If a crime is inherently evil it is malum in se.

If a crime is not evil in itself, but is only criminal because declared so by a legislature, then it is malum prohibitum. Murder, rape, arson, and mayhem are examples of crimes which are malum in se. Failure to file your quarterly tax report or to get the proper building permit are both crimes malum prohibitum.

The distinction between malum in se and malum prohibitum is used throughout criminal law, but the importance of the distinction is in how it affects intent. Crimes malum in se are treated as requiring an evil intent, and crimes malum prohibitum are not. Some crimes may be both malum in se and malum prohibitum, depending upon the degree of violation. For example, speeding "a little over the limit may be malum prohibitum, but speeding at high speed malum in se."[5] Whether an act is malum prohibitum or in se often determines what crime may be charged. This usually revolves around the issue of foreseeability of harm. From the example above, speeding slightly over the limit is not likely to cause another's death, while racing through a city thirty miles over the speed limit can foreseeably cause a fatal accident. If while driving four miles over the speed limit the defendant strikes and kills a pedestrian who walks into the driver's path from behind another car, the act is likely to be determined malum prohibitum, and no resulting manslaughter charge will follow. However, the same may not be true if the driver is traveling thirty miles over the speed limit at the time the accident occurs.

Although some jurisdictions no longer distinguish between crimes malum in se and malum prohibitum, many still do. What crimes fall into each category is determined by judicial decision, and, as such, the caselaw in your juridiction must be researched to determine where the crime in question falls.

Section 3.1(a.3) Transferred Intent

Whenever a person intends a harm, but because of bad aim or other cause the intended harm befalls another, the intent is transferred from the intended victim to the unintended victim. This is the doctrine of **transferred intent**. If John Defendant observes his neighbor burning the American flag and in anger shoots at him, missing him, but killing William, the doctrine of transferred intent permits prosecution of Defendant as if he intended to kill William.

There are limits on the doctrine of transferred intent. First, the harm that actually results must be similar to the intended harm. If the harms are substantially different, then the intent does not transfer. For example, if A throws a baseball at B's window hoping to break it, and the ball instead hits C in the head and kills him, it cannot be said that the intent to break the window transfers to C and that A can be punished for intentionally killing C. A may be criminally liable for a lesser crime, such as involuntary manslaughter, depending upon the amount of negligence involved, but he is not responsible for intentionally causing C's death.

A second limitation on the doctrine is that the transfer cannot increase the defendant's liability. Another way of stating this is that any defenses the defendant has against the intended victim are transferred to the unintended victim. For example, A shoots at B in self-defense, but hits C, inflicting a fatal wound. Since A had a valid defense if B had been killed by the shot, then A also has a defense as to C. In this case A has committed no crime. In some situations a defense may only limit a person's criminal liability to a lesser charge. You will learn later that certain defenses negate specific intent, but not general intent. One such defense is intoxication. Assault is a general intent crime, while assault with an intent to kill is a specific intent crime. Intoxication may be a defense to the higher assault with an intent to kill, but not assault. So, if A, while intoxicated, hurls a knife at B, but hits C, A may be charged with assault since intoxication would be no defense if he hit B. A would have a defense against the specific intent crime of assault with intent to kill, so the same defense is available for harm to C.

Section 3.1(b)   Strict Liability

At the beginning of this chapter it was noted that some acts are criminal although no guilt, fault, or negligence accompany a prohibited act. These crimes are proven simply by showing that the act was committed, and no particular mental state has to be proved at all. This is **strict liability**, or liability without fault, and is an exception to the common-law requirement that there be both an evil mind and an evil act to have a crime. The term strict liability is not used in all jurisdictions. Further, the term also has a tort meaning. Do not confuse criminal liability without fault with tort strict liability. However, for convenience, the phrase "strict liability" will be used in this text.

Strict liability crimes usually are minor violations, punished by fines and not incarceration. However, strict liability is permitted for felonies and may be punished with incarceration.

Most traffic violations, such as running a stoplight and speeding, are examples of strict liability crimes. Statutory rape is treated as a strict liability crime in most states; therefore, the accused adult cannot claim that he or she had a mistaken belief that the minor was above the statutory age when the two had sexual intercourse. There are many other strict liability crimes in every state, and legislatures are increasingly using the strict liability standard when declaring acts illegal.

It is common for crimes that are malum prohibitum to be strict liability, while crimes malum in se usually require proof of some mental state. It is also generally true that violation of crimes malum prohibitum are not punished as severely as crimes malum in se.

Crimes with strict liability are often termed "public offenses" or "regulatory offenses." This is because many of the strict liability laws deal with potential, rather than actual, harms. For example, a murder statute can only be applied after someone has been murdered. However, many strict liability offenses deal with violations and no harm. For example, running a stoplight, speeding, or failing to have adequate fire extinguishers in your business may or may not result in an injury. Regardless of whether harm results, you are liable for the offense. This is considered regulatory because the purpose is to induce compliance (using the easy proof standard) with the law, rather than punish for caused harm. The increased compliance is a result of an awareness by people that violation alone means liability, hence they are more cautious and less likely to engage in the prohibited conduct. Of course, this argument can be made to justify making all crimes strict liability. The idea of not requiring any intent for acts to be criminal is contrary to American values of fairness and justice, and this

LEGAL TERMS

transferred intent
A legal doctrine that holds that if a defendant intends to harm A, but unintentionally harms B using the means intended to harm A, the intent to harm A is transferred to B. This allows defendant to be prosecuted as if there was an intent to harm B.

strict liability
A type of criminal offense that requires no showing of mens rea. One is liable for such crimes merely by committing the prohibited act.

is probably the reason that the strict liability standard has not been extended to all crimes.

Strict liability is only available for crimes defined by legislatures. With little restriction legislatures may define an act as criminal without requiring proof of intent. However, in those jurisdictions that continue to recognize common law crimes mens rea must be an element.

Many have alleged that liability without fault is violative of the Constitution, but the United States Supreme Court has upheld strict liability statutes in most instances.[6] Despite this, if a legislature declares that a crime that has traditionally required proof of specific intent or purpose has no mens rea requirement, the due process question should be raised. This is especially true if the crime can be punished with a significant jail sentence.

In the case that follows the defendant entered federal property, a military bombing range, and collected spent bomb casings, which had been on the site for years. The casings were exposed to the weather and were rusting when the defendant removed them. The defendant was charged with converting (stealing) the casings. The defendant was convicted at the trial level, and the United States Supreme Court reversed the conviction. What follows is an excerpt of that opinion.

MORISSETTE V. UNITED STATES

342 U.S. 246 (1952)

* * *

. . . The contention that an injury can amount to a crime only when inflicted by intention is no provincial or transient notion. It is universal and persistent in mature systems of law as belief in freedom of the human will and a consequent ability and duty of the normal individual to choose between good and evil. A relation between some mental element and punishment for a harmful act is almost as instinctive as the child's familiar exculpatory "But I didn't mean to," and has afforded the rational basis for a tardy and unfinished substitution of deterrence and reformation in place of retaliation and vengeance as the motivation for public prosecution. . . .

Crime, as a compound concept, generally constituted only from concurrence of an evil-meaning mind with an evil-doing hand, was congenial to an intense individualism and took deep and early root in American soil. As the states codified the common law of crimes, even if their enactments were silent on the subject, their courts assumed that the omission did not signify disapproval of the principle but merely recognized that intent was so inherent in the idea of the offense that it required no statutory definition.

However, [some crimes fall into a] category of another character, with very different antecedents and origins. The crimes there involved depend on no mental element but consist only of forbidden acts or omissions. . . . The industrial revolution multiplied the number of workmen exposed to injury from increasingly powerful and complex mechanisms, driven by freshly discovered sources of energy, requiring higher precautions by employers. Traffic of velocities, volumes and varieties unheard of came to subject the wayfarer to intolerable casualty risks if the owners and drivers were not to observe new cares and uniformities of conduct. Congestion of cities and crowding of quarters called for health and welfare regulations undreamed of in simpler times. Wide distribution of goods became an instrument of wide distribution of harm when those who dispersed food, drink, drugs, and even securities, did not comply with reasonable standards of quality, integrity, disclosure and care. Such dangers have engendered increasingly numerous and detailed regulations which heighten the duties of those in control of particular industries, trades, properties, or activities that affect public health, safety or welfare.

. . . Many violations of such regulations result in no direct or immediate injury to person or property but merely create the danger or probability of injury which the law seeks to minimize. . . .

* * *

Stealing, larceny, and its variants and equivalents, were among the earliest offenses known to the law that existed before legislation [common law]. . . . State courts of last resort, on whom fall the heaviest burden of interpreting criminal law in this country, have consistently retained the requirement of intent in larceny-type offenses. If any state has deviated, the exception has neither been called to our attention nor disclosed by our research.

We hold that the mere omission from [the conversion statute] of any mention of intent will not be construed as eliminating that element from the crimes denounced.

Section 3.1(b.1) Strict Liability and Statutory Construction

The problem addressed by the Supreme Court in *Morissette* occurs often: What is the mens rea requirement when a statute does not provide for such? That decision depends on many factors. First, the **legislative history** of the statute may indicate whether the crime was intended to have a mens rea requirement or not. The statements of members of legislatures while debating the law (before it became law and was a bill), reports of committees of Congress, and other related materials may indicate whether the legislature intended for a mens rea requirement. Second, courts look to whether the crime existed under the common law. If so, the mens rea used under the common law may be adopted by the court. Other factors include the seriousness of the harm to the public; mens rea standards for other related crimes; the punishment that is imposed for conviction; the burden that would be placed on the prosecution if mens rea is required; and rules of statutory construction.

Generally, the greater the potential harm to the public and the more difficult it is for prosecution to prove mens rea, the more likely a court is to find that strict liability is to be imposed.[7] Although not a significant factor, the amount of penalty can play a role. The greater the penalty, the more likely that some intent will be read into the statute. Also, courts will look to other related statutes for guidance. If a state legislature has consistently required proof of intent for all crimes of larceny and theft, then if a new statute is enacted dealing with a particular theft (i.e., theft of computer information), and that law does not specify the mental state that needs to be proved, then the court will fill in the missing element with intent.

Finally, courts have rules that must be followed when interpreting a statute. These are known as **Canons of Statutory Construction**. You previously learned one of these rules; that is, whenever a statute can be construed as either constitutional or unconstitutional it must be read as constitutional. Some jurisdictions follow the rule, either by judicial rule (canon) or by statute, that if a criminal statute does not specifically impose strict liability, then the court is to impose a mens rea requirement. What follows is a case from New York, a jurisdiction where such a rule is applied.

THE PEOPLE OF THE STATE OF NEW YORK V. ALICIA TROIANO

552 N.Y.S.2d 541, 1990 N.Y. Misc. LEXIS 90 (1990)

OPINION:

[Defendant was charged with having insufficient brakes on her car and the following facts were stipulated to by the parties:]

On May 1, 1987 at approximately 11:35 P.M. the defendant was involved in a two-car accident at the intersection of Washington Avenue and Nassau Parkway in Oceanside, New York. Defendant was the owner and operator of a 1972 Oldsmobile station wagon, New York registration # UKT 792. The driver of the other vehicle died as a result of injuries suffered in that accident. The decedent failed to yield the right of way at a stop sign at that intersection. The decedent's blood alcohol level was .10%. Both vehicles were impounded. The defendant's vehicle was inspected by Al Stern of Al's Towing Corporation and as a result of that inspection the instant charge was brought.

[Mr. Stern testified that the defendant's right rear brake was insufficient under state law guidelines.]

The defendant testified that she had not experienced any problems with the braking system of the car. She did not hear any squeaks or other noises. She did not notice any leaking of brake fluid and was able to stop properly at a stop sign just minutes before the accident. Further, the car had been inspected in September, 1986 and had a proper inspection sticker affixed to the windshield.

The defense also called Mr. Troiano, defendant's husband who had been employed as an automobile mechanic until 1983. Following Stern's inspection, Mr. Troiano towed

LEGAL TERMS

legislative history
The statements of members of Congress, reports of committees, and other similar information concerning a statute before it became law are known as legislative history. Legislative history often will help judges determine what legislatures intended to accomplish by enacting the statute.

Canons of Statutory Construction
Rules that must be followed by courts when interpreting statutes. One such rule is that statutes that can be interpreted as constitutional or violative of the Constitution must be read as constitutional.

the vehicle in question back to his house. He pulled off all four wheels and examined the brake shoes and lining and found the brake lining on the right rear wheel to be a little more than 1/16 of an inch at its thinnest point and, consequently adequate.

* * *

[The statute] provides in pertinent part, "every motor vehicle, operated or driven on the highways of the State, shall be provided with adequate brakes . . . "

The court will first deal with the question of whether the statute is one of strict liability. The plain language of [the brake statute] does not require a mens rea or a culpable mental state as an element of the crime and in reliance thereon the People have made no attempt to make a prima facie showing that defendant knew or had reason to know of the defect.

"Culpable mental state" means intentional, knowing, reckless or criminally negligent conduct . . . If the commission of a particular offense or some material element thereof does not require a culpable mental state on the part of the actor, such an offense is one of "strict liability." [cite omitted]

It is a well-known principle of statutory construction that absent the legislature's clear indication of an intent to impose strict liability, a statute should be construed to require mens rea. . . .

[The court determined that the defendant had to have had knowledge of the defect to be liable and that no such showing had been made. Accordingly, defendant's motion for dismissal was granted.]

Section 3.1(c) Vicarious Liability

The term **vicarious liability** refers to situations where one person is held accountable for the actions of another. Under vicarious liability there is no requirement of mens rea, as is the case for strict liability, and, additionally, there is no requirement for an act, at least not by the defendant. The person who is liable for the actions of another need not act, encourage another to act, or intend any harm at all. As is true with vicarious liability in tort law, this situation is most common between employers and employees.

Employers may be liable for the actions of their employees when criminal laws relating to the operation of the business are violated. For example, the owner of a business may be prosecuted for failure to comply with product safety regulations, even though that was a duty delegated to an employee, and the owner had no knowledge that the products manufactured were substandard. Vicarious liability is often imposed on those who market food and drugs.[8] This is because of the significant public welfare interest in the quality of these products.

Section 3.1(c.1) Corporate Liability

Corporate liability is a form of vicarious liability. Under the common law corporations could not be convicted of crimes. However, this is no longer the law.

Corporations, partnerships, and other organizations can be held criminally accountable for the acts of their employees and agents. The agent must be working within the scope of his or her employment for the company to be liable. If an employee of Burger King strikes an enemy while on break in the parking lot of the store, the company is not liable for battery. However, if officers of a corporation send employees into a workplace knowing that it is dangerous and represent to the employees that it is safe, the company may be liable for battery to the employee, or even manslaughter, if death results.

The Model Penal Code provides for corporate liability when the agent is acting within the scope of employment. In addition, it must be shown that the corporation had a duty under the law to take some act, and the act was not done or the act taken by the agent was authorized, requested, commanded, performed, or recklessly tolerated by the board of directors or other high management.[9]

Obviously, companies cannot be incarcerated, so fines are usually imposed. In some instances, **injunctions** may be imposed. Finally, note that corporate liability does not free the agent from criminal liability. In most cases the agent or employee remains criminally liable for his or her act.

Section 3.1(d)   Current Approaches to Mens Rea

Section 3.1(d.1)   The Model Penal Code and States of Mind

The drafters of the Model Penal Code chose to reject most of the common-law terms when they addressed mens rea. The result is that the Model Penal Code recognizes four states of mind: purposeful; knowing; reckless; and negligent.[10]

LEGAL TERMS

vicarious liability
Whenever a person can be held criminally liable for the actions of another, that person is vicariously liable. No showing of mens rea has to be shown for either the person who acted or the person liable. Further, the person liable does not have to take any action to be criminally liable.

corporate liability
A form of vicarious liability. Corporations, partnerships, and other organizations may be liable for the acts of their agents when those agents are acting within the scope of employment.

injunctions
Orders issued by courts directing someone to take an act or to refrain from acting.

To act **purposely** a defendant must have a desire to cause the result. Purposely most closely equates with what the common law called specific intent.

To act **knowingly** a defendant must be aware of the nature of the act and be practically certain that his conduct will cause a particular result, which is not the defendant's objective. The difference between purposeful acts and knowing acts is that to be purposeful, one must act intending to cause the particular result. To act knowingly, the defendant must be practically certain (nearly 100 percent positive) that the result will occur, but the defendant is not taking the act to cause that result. For example, if a legitimate moving company owner leases a van to an illegal drug dealer knowing that the van will be used to transport drugs across the country, then the owner has acted knowingly. He has not acted with purpose because it is not his objective to transport the contraband.

The third state of mind recognized by the Model Penal Code is **recklessly**. A person acts recklessly when he or she consciously disregards a substantial and unjustifiable risk that the result will occur. The difference between a knowing act and a reckless act is in the degree of risk. "A person acts 'knowingly' with respect to a result if he is nearly certain that his conduct will cause the result. If he is aware only of a substantial risk, he acts 'recklessly' with respect to the result."[11] The Code says that the risk taken must be one that involves a "gross deviation from the standard of conduct that a law-abiding person would observe in the actor's situation."[12]

The final state of mind is **negligently**. The definition of negligence is similar to reckless; that is, that there must be a

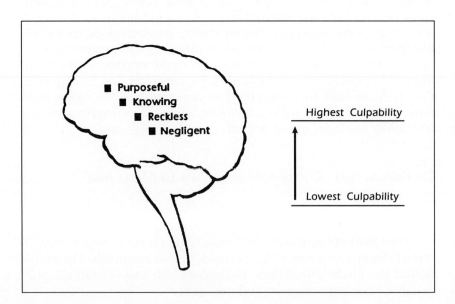

Mens Rea Under the Penal Code

"substantial and unjustifiable risk" taken by the defendant. However, a person acts negligently when there is no conscious awareness of the risk, when there should have been. To act recklessly one must take a risk that amounts to a "gross deviation from the standard of conduct that a law-abiding person would observe in the actor's situation." When a defendant has acted negligently she has failed to perceive (be aware of) the risk altogether, and that failure is a gross deviation from a law-abiding person's standard.

Section 3.1(d.2) Element Analysis

So far the discussion of culpable states of mind has been limited to one state of mind for each individual crime. For example, under the common law a specific intent to kill must be proven to establish first-degree murder. This was true of all offenses under the common law; that is, only one state of mind had to be shown. This was true even if the crime had many different elements.

Elements are the parts of a crime. The prosecution must prove all the elements of a crime to gain a conviction. For example, under the common law the elements of larceny were: 1. The taking and carrying away 2. personal property 3. of another 4. with an intent to steal. The prosecution has the burden of proving all four elements. If the prosecution fails to prove any element the defendant must be acquitted. Under the common law only one mental state had to be proved: intent to steal. Additionally, the prosecution had to show that the other four elements occurred without reference to mental state. This is known as offense analysis, as the entire offense is thought of as requiring one mental state.

The Model Penal Code, as well as some specific statutes, recognize that the various acts of a crime may involve differing mental states. As such, each element of a crime may have different mens rea.[13]

Assume state law prohibits: 1. Notary publics 2. from notarizing documents 3. of known blood relatives 4. of the third degree or closer (degrees define closeness of family relationship). Under the Code the first two elements appear to require no mental state— just the act of a notary notarizing a document. Hence, it would be no defense for the notary to claim that he was signing the document as a witness and not as a notary. The third element requires specific knowledge that the person for whom they are notarizing the document is a blood relative. If the notary can prove that there was no reason for him to have known of the relationship, then his knowledge is negated. The last element is likely to be treated as a negligence element. It would be a valid defense for the notary to show that he made a reasonable error as to

LEGAL TERMS

purposely
Under the Model Penal Code an act is purposeful when taken with an intent to cause a particular result.

knowingly
Under the Model Penal Code an act is taken knowingly when the result is practically certain to occur, although causing that result is not the purpose for taking the act.

recklessly
Under the Model Penal Code an act is reckless when it is taken in disregard of substantial risk.

negligently
Under the Model Penal Code an act is negligent when a person takes the act and fails to perceive the substantial risk of harm that may result from the act.

elements
The parts of a crime. The prosecution must prove all the elements of a crime to gain a conviction.

the degree of the relationship, but not a defense if the error was unreasonable.

Section 3.1(e) Proving Mens Rea

At trial the prosecution has the burden of establishing that the defendant possessed the required mental state when the act was committed. Proof of intent can be troublesome to prosecution, especially when the prosecution has to prove **subjective intent**. Subjective intent refers to the motives, intentions, and desires that were in the defendant's mind at the time the act took place. Subjective intent is a defendant's actual intent.

Objective intent is not the defendant's actual intent, rather it is a legal imposition upon the defendant of what he or she should have known or believed at the time that the act occurred. Generally, the law imposes a reasonable person standard. That means that the defendant is expected to have known or believed what a reasonable person would have known at the time of the act. Objective intent is easier to prove than subjective intent. This is because the prosecution does not have to probe directly into a defendant's mind to prove that an intent to harm existed; rather, all that has to be shown is that the defendant should have known that the harm would result.

In most cases defendants do not admit that they took the act in question. Even when defendants do admit to taking some acts it is common to deny intent. For those crimes that require intent, admission of the act is not enough to sustain a conviction. The question is, how does a prosecutor gain a conviction for a crime that requires a showing of intent when the defendant denies possessing the required intent? The answer is by using **inferences**.

An inference is a conclusion that a judge or jury is permitted to make after considering the facts of a case. Imagine that a man walks up to another man and strikes him in the head with a hammer, using great force in his swing. The wound is fatal, and the man is charged with first-degree murder. To sustain a first-degree murder charge in this jurisdiction it must be shown that the man intended to cause the victim's death. The defendant disavows such intent, admitting only that he intended to hit and injure the victim. In such a case the jury would be permitted to infer the defendant's intent to kill the victim from the seriousness of the act. In a jurisdiction that uses the objective standard the jury could conclude that a reasonable person would have known that the blow from a hammer would cause the victim's death, and the subjective intent of the defendant would not matter.

A **presumption** is a conclusion that must be made by a judge or jury. Most people have heard of the presumption of innocence in criminal law. This presumption is a **rebuttable presumption**. Rebuttable presumptions are conclusions that must be made by a judge or jury, unless disproven by the facts. Hence, defendants are innocent until proven guilty. **Irrebuttable presumptions** are conclusions that must be made by the judge or jury and cannot be disproved. Despite what the evidence shows, an irrebuttable presumption stands as a fact.

SECTION 3.2 ACTUS REUS

Earlier in this chapter you learned the Latin phrase "actus non facit reum nisi mens sit rea." The phrase expresses the common-law requirement that two essential elements must be present to have a crime, a guilty mind and a guilty act. **Actus reus** is the physical part of a crime; it is the act engaged in by the accused. An act is a physical movement. If Mrs. X shoots and kills Mrs. T, the act is pulling the trigger of the gun.

The Model Penal Code states that a "person is not guilty of an offense unless his liability is based on conduct that includes a voluntary act. . . ."[14]

Section 3.2(a) Voluntariness

To be held criminally liable for one's actions, those actions must be voluntary. To be voluntary an act must occur as a result of the actor's conscious choice. The person accused must have acted freely, or no liability is attached. The Model Penal Code requires that acts be voluntary and specifically lists the following as being involuntary:

1. reflexes and convulsions;
2. bodily movements during unconsciousness or sleep;
3. conduct during hypnosis or resulting from hypnotic suggestion; and
4. other movements that are not a product of the effort or determination of the actor.[15]

Do not confuse the concepts of mens rea and actus reus. All that is required to have an act is a choice by the defendant to act. No evil intent is required to have an act; that is a question of mens rea. Say that Jim chooses to swing his arm. As a result he hits Tom. What intent is required to prove battery and whether Jim possessed that intent are questions of mens rea. For actus reus all that need be known is whether Jim voluntarily chose to swing his

LEGAL TERMS

subjective intent
The desires, motives, and intentions in a defendant's mind when he or she acts. The actual intent of a defendant.

objective intent
A legal determination of what a defendant should have known or believed at the time he or she acted, regardless of the defendant's actual intent.

inference
A conclusion that a judge or jury is permitted to reach after considering the facts of a case.

presumption
A conclusion that a judge or jury is required to make.

rebuttable presumption
A conclusion that the judge or jury must make until disproved.

irrebuttable presumption
A conclusion that the judge or jury must make and cannot be disproved.

actus reus
One of two essential elements of crimes. It is the physical part, the act engaged in by the accused. Mens rea is the other essential element.

arm. His swing would be involuntary if Bill grabbed Jim's arm and moved it, causing it to strike Tom.

In the case that follows a woman was acquitted of murdering her daughter because it was determined that her acts were not voluntary.

KING V. COGDON

Supreme Court of Victoria (1950)[16]

Mrs. Cogdon was charged with the murder of her only child, a daughter called Pat, aged 19. Pat had for some time been receiving psychiatric treatment for a relatively minor neurotic condition of which, in her psychiatrist's opinion, she was now cured. Despite this, Mrs. Cogdon continued to worry unduly about her. Describing the relationship between Pat and her mother, Mr. Cogdon testified: "I don't think a mother could have thought any more of her daughter. I think she absolutely adored her." On the conscious level, there was no doubt [of] Mrs. Cogdon's deep attachment to her daughter.

To the charge of murdering Pat, Mrs. Cogdon pleaded not guilty. Her story, though somewhat bizarre, was not seriously challenged by the Crown, and led to her acquittal. She told how on the night before her daughter's death she had dreamt that their house was full of spiders and that these spiders were crawling all over Pat. In her sleep, Mrs. Cogdon left the bed she shared with her husband, went into Pat's room and awakened to find herself violently brushing at Pat's face, presumably to remove the spiders. This woke Pat. Mrs. Cogdon told her she was just tucking her in. At the trial, she testified that she still believed, as she had been told, that the occupants of a nearby house bred spiders as a hobby, preparing nests for them behind the pictures on their walls. It was these spiders that in her dreams had invaded their home and attacked Pat. There had also been a previous dream in which ghosts had sat at the end of Mrs. Cogdon's bed and she had said to them, "Well, you have come to take Pattie." It does not seem fanciful to accept the psychological explanation of these spiders and ghosts as the projections of Mrs. Cogdon's subconscious hostility towards her daughter; a hostility which was itself rooted in Mrs. Cogdon's own early life and marital relationship.

The morning after the spider dream she told her doctor of it. He gave her a sedative and, because of the dream and certain previous difficulties she had reported, discussed the possibility of psychiatric treatment. That evening Mrs. Cogdon suggested to her husband that he attend his lodge meeting, and asked Pat to come with her to the cinema. After he had gone Pat looked through the paper, not unusually found no tolerable programme, and said that as she was going out the next evening she thought she would rather go to bed early. Later while Pat was having a bath preparatory to retiring, Mrs. Cogdon went into her room, put a hot water bottle in the bed, turned back the bedclothes, and placed a glass of hot milk beside the bed ready for Pat. She then went to bed herself. There was some desultory conversation between them about the war in Korea, and just before she put out her light Pat called out to her mother, "Mum, don't be so silly worrying about the war, it's not on our front step yet."

Mrs. Cogdon went to sleep. She dreamt that "the war was all around the house," that the soldiers were in Pat's room, and that one soldier was on the bed attacking Pat. This is all of the dream that she could later recapture. Her first "waking" memory was of running from Pat's room, out of the house to the home of her sister who lived next door. When her sister opened the front door Mrs. Cogdon fell into her arms crying, "I think I've hurt Pattie."

In fact Mrs. Cogdon had, in her somnambulistic state, left her bed, fetched an axe from the woodheap, entered Pat's room, and struck her two accurate forceful blows on the head with the blade of the axe, thus killing her.

* * *

At all events the jury believed Mrs. Cogdon's story . . . [Mrs. Cogdon] was acquitted because the act of killing itself was not, in law, regarded as her act at all. . . .

There was no defense of insanity raised in this case. If there had been, the analysis would have been different. In most jurisdictions one cannot claim lack of a voluntary act if insanity is also claimed. In those situations the rules of the insanity defense apply.[17]

Section 3.2(b) Thoughts and Statements as an Act

Thoughts alone are not acts that can be made criminal. People may think evil thoughts, but if there is no act furthering such a thought, there is no crime.

Generally, people are also free to speak. The First Amendment to the United States Constitution protects freedom of speech. When the First Amendment applies, speech may not be made criminal. There are, however, limits to First Amendment protection of speech. Inciting riots, treason, solicitation, conspiracy, and causing imminent harm to others are examples of speech that may be prohibited. You will learn more about the First Amendment protection of speech later.

Section 3.2(c) Personal Status as an Act

Generally, a person's status can not be declared criminal. Illness, financial status, race, sex, and religion are examples of human conditions. Some conditions are directly related to illegal behavior. For example, being addicted to illegal narcotics is a condition that can not be punished. This is due to the fact that status is generally believed to not be an act. However, using and selling prohibited narcotics are acts and may be punished.

Vagrancy is one area over which there is a split in legal opinion. Some courts have held that vagrancy may be prohibited, while others have determined that vagrancy is a condition and does not constitute a crime. One author has noted that there is a "growing body of authority" holding such statutes unconstitutional.[18]

In *Robinson v. California*, 370 U.S. 660 (1962) the United States Supreme Court was called upon to review a California statute that made it a crime "either to use narcotics, or to be addicted to the use of narcotics." The Court reversed Robinson's conviction and in the opinion stated:

> This statute, therefore, is not one which punishes a person for the use of narcotics, for their purchase, sale or possession, or for antisocial or disorderly behavior resulting from their administration. It is not a law which even purports to provide or require medical treatment. Rather, we deal with a statute which makes the "status" of narcotic addiction a

criminal offense, for which the offender may be prosecuted "at any time before he reforms." California has said that a person can be continuously guilty of this offense, whether or not he has ever used or possessed any narcotics within the state, and whether or not he has been guilty of any antisocial behavior there.

It is unlikely that any State at this moment in history would attempt to make it a criminal offense for a person to be mentally ill, or a leper, or to be afflicted with a venereal disease. A State might determine that the general health and welfare require that the victims of these and other human afflictions be dealt with by compulsory treatment, involving quarantine, confinement, or sequestration. But, in the light of contemporary human knowledge, a law which made a criminal offense of such a disease would doubtless be universally thought of to be an infliction of cruel and unusual punishment in violation of the Eighth and Fourteenth Amendments. . . .

We cannot but consider the statute before us as of the same category. . . . We hold that a state law which imprisons a person thus afflicted as a criminal, even though he has never touched any narcotic drug within the State or been guilty of any irregular behavior there, inflicts a cruel and unusual punishment in violation of the Fourteenth Amendment. . . .

Section 3.2(d) Possession as an Act

Possession of certain items, such as narcotics, burglary tools or dangerous weapons may be made criminal. Possession is not, strictly speaking, an act. Possession does not involve an active body movement; rather, possession is a passive state of being. Even so, most possession laws have been upheld.

Jurisdictions differ in what is required to prove possession. Some require that actual possession be shown, while others allow proof of constructive possession. Constructive possession is used to extend criminal liability to those who never exercised actual possession, but had dominion and control over the contraband. A person who is the owner and driver of a car may never possess the cocaine that his passenger is using, but the law says that the driver is in constructive possession since the dominion and control over the auto belongs to the driver. In essence, the law imposes a duty on people to remove illegal items from the area over which they have dominion and control. Failure to comply with such a duty is treated as an act and can lead to criminal liability.

One problem with crimes of possession is the possibility of convicting people who had no knowledge of the existence of illegal items in an area under their dominion and control. An owner of a house has dominion and control over the guest room, but may not be aware that a guest has brought illegal items into the room. Most jurisdictions have remedied this problem by requiring knowledge of the presence of the goods. The Model Penal Code also uses such a test. The Code states that possession is an act as long as the "possessor knowingly procured or received the thing possessed or was aware of his control thereof for a sufficient period to have been able to terminate his possession."[19] Under the Code possession can be actual or constructive. However, if constructive, the possessor must have known of the items for a period of time long enough to permit the possessor to terminate possession. So, if the owner of the house only discovered the cocaine minutes before the police arrived to search the premises, no possession could be found on the owner's behalf.

Finally, one person or many people can be in possession of items. Using the example from above, assume that two or more people jointly owned the home in question. All of the owners could be liable, if it was determined that all had constructive possession and adequate time to remove the cocaine from the house. It is possible that fewer than all of the owners knew of the cocaine, and, as such, did not have constructive possession. Each person who is alleged to have dominion and control (constructive possession) must be examined individually, and separate decisions as to their individual liability must be made.

Section 3.2(e) Omissions as Acts

Generally, only acts are prohibited by criminal law. Rarely does criminal law require a person to act. However, there are some situations where people have a duty to act, and failure to act is criminal. An **omission** is a failure to act when required to do so by criminal law.

It is often the case that a person who may have a moral duty to act does not have a legal duty to act. In most instances people do not have a legal duty to assist one another in times of need. It would not be criminal in most jurisdictions for an excellent swimmer to watch another drown. Nor would it be criminal to watch another walk into a dangerous situation, such as a bank robbery in progress, if the observer had no connection with the criminal event. There are exceptions to this rule. To be liable for a failure to act a person must have a "duty" to act. The duty to act can come about in many different ways.

Section 3.2(e.1) Duty Imposed by Statute

First, criminal statutes may impose a duty to act. The following are examples of duties imposed by statutes: businesses that store or dispose of toxic materials are required to file certain documents; taxpayers are required to file tax returns; and those involved in automobile accidents are required to stop at the scene of the accident.

Under the common law, in most instances, people had no duty to assist others whose lives were in danger. Today criminal statutes may impose liability for failure to assist someone in danger. A few states have enactments that directly change the common law rule and require people to assist others who are in danger. However, even in those jurisdictions rescue need not be attempted if the rescuer's life will be endangered.[20] Imposing criminal liability for not rescuing someone in danger of losing life or limb continues to be the exception and not the rule. However, no legal reason prevents all jurisdictions from requiring people to rescue one another when there is no danger associated with the rescue.

Under the common law several exceptions to the no duty to assist people in danger rule evolved. Many of these are discussed in the following paragraphs. Bear in mind that many legislatures codified one or more of these exceptions. In those cases, the duty is imposed by statute and not the common law.

Section 3.2(e.2) Duty by Relationship

A duty to assist another can be created by the existence of a personal relationship. The most common examples are parent to

LEGAL TERMS

omission
A failure to act when required to do so by a criminal law. Failing to file a tax return is an example of an omission.

child and spouse to spouse. In such personal relationships a level of dependence exists that gives rise to criminal liability for failure to assist the party who is in danger. There is no bright line rule used for determining if a duty is owed. The more that one party becomes dependent upon another party or the parties become dependent upon one another, the more likely that a duty to assist is created.

Generally, any time a joint enterprise is undertaken by two or more parties, it can be assumed that a duty to assist one another during that enterprise is created. For example, if two people decide to go river rafting, they must rescue one another during that rafting trip, provided that that the rescuer is not endangered by attempting the rescue.

In the parent-child relationship, a parent can be guilty of manslaughter if her child dies as a result of the parent's failure to seek medical attention for the child when he or she is sick or for failing to pull his child out of a pool when the child is drowning. The same would be true of a spouse. If a wife permitted her husband to die when she could have saved his life by summoning medical attention, she could be criminally liable. In addition, it has been held that employers owe a duty to assist their employees. In the case that follows an employer was convicted of manslaughter for his failure to assist one of his employees.

UNITED STATES V. KNOWLES

26 F.Cas. 800 (N.D.CAL. 1864)

[Instructions to jury] The defendant is charged in the indictment with the crime of murder upon the high seas. The district attorney does not, however, seek from you a conviction of the defendant for this offense. He asks only a conviction for manslaughter, and the trial has been conducted as if the indictment charged only this lesser offense. . . . It alleges that the defendant was, on the first day of April, 1864, captain of the American ship Charger, belonging to citizens of the United States; that the ship had on board 10 mariners, and among them one John P. Swainson; that the ship was provided with three boats, for the protection and safety of the lives of the persons on board, in case control of accident; and that it was the duty of the defendant to manage and control the ship and boats, so as to insure such protection and safety; that on the first day of April, 1864, the said Swainson was employed as seaman upon the royal-yard-arm of the mainmast of the ship in furling the royal-sail; that whilst thus employed he accidentally fell into the sea; and that the defendant willfully omitted to stop the ship, or to lower either of the boats, or to make any attempt to rescue and save Swainson, as was his duty to do; that Swainson would have been rescued and saved had the defendant stopped his ship and lowered either of his boats, and from his negligence and omission in this respect, Swainson was drowned.

. . . In the majority of cases where manslaughter is charged, the death alleged has resulted from direct violence on the part of the accused. Here the death is charged to have been occasioned by the willful omission of the defendant to perform a plain duty.

Section 3.2(e.3) Duty by Contract

A duty to act can be created in a third way, by contract. For example, physicians are hired to care for the health of their patients. If a doctor watches as a patient slowly dies, doing nothing to save the patient's life when there were measures that could have been taken, the doctor is liable for homicide. The same is true of a lifeguard. The lifeguard is hired to save those who are drowning, and if a lifeguard sits and watches a swimmer drown when the swimmer could have been saved, the lifeguard is liable for homicide.

Remember, the general rule is that people owe no duty to rescue others. So, if an expert swimmer happens to be on the beach when another person is drowning, the expert swimmer can watch the person drown without risking criminal liability.

Section 3.2(e.4) Assumption of Duty

Even though the general rule is that people do not have a duty to rescue strangers, it is possible, either expressly or by one's actions, to make an **assumption of duty**. The assumption is express if it is stated orally or in writing. Assumption is different from duty premised on contract, in that assumptions are gratuitous. If Sidney is at a pool and agrees to care for another's child,

LEGAL TERMS

assumption of duty
When a person begins a rescue attempt, that rescuer has a duty to complete the rescue, if possible. The rescuer is said to have assumed the duty of rescuing the person in danger.

then Sidney has assumed the duty expressly. If the child falls into the pool, and Sidney takes no action to save the child, Sidney is liable for murder if the child drowns.

It is possible through one's actions to assume the duty to rescue someone. Let's assume Sidney is now at a lake. One person, David, is swimming, and three other people are relaxing on the beach. David begins to scream for help. Sidney jumps up and dives into the water to rescue David. Halfway out to David he changes his mind, and returns to shore. By the time he returns to shore it is too late for someone else to make the swim to David, and he dies. In this case, Sidney assumed the duty of the rescue by beginning the rescue attempt. However, whether Sidney is liable for murder depends on what condition the drowning person is left in after Sidney changed his mind. If Sidney's actions caused the other three people on the beach to fail to attempt a rescue, then Sidney's actions left David in a worse condition than he would have been in had Sidney not begun the rescue. However, if Sidney's actions did not prevent anyone else from attempting a rescue, then Sidney's action did not put David in a worse situation, and Sidney is not liable for murder, even if the other person fails in the rescue attempt.

Finally, note that we can easily change this last example into an express assumption. All that has to be added is a statement by Sidney to the others on the beach that he will swim out and rescue David. Such a statement, if it caused others to forego a rescue attempt, is an express assumption of duty.

Section 3.2(e.5) Creating Danger

Any time a person creates the circumstance that endangers a stranger, a duty to save the stranger is created. This is true whether the danger was caused intentionally or negligently. So, if an arsonist sets fire to a house that is believed to be empty and is discovered not to be, the arsonist must attempt to save anyone inside. If not, the arsonist is also a murderer. The same would be true of a negligently caused fire. If an electrician begins a fire in a home and does nothing to warn the inhabitants, the electrician is also liable for murder.

Section 3.2(f) Causation

Some acts are criminal even though the prohibited result does not occur. For example, it is a crime to lie when testifying in court (the crime of perjury). Assume that the purpose of the lie is to deceive the jury and change the outcome of the case. Even if no juror, or anyone else for that matter, believes the lie, and the purpose is not achieved, it is a crime. Causation is not an issue for such crimes.

For those crimes that do require a particular result, the act must be the "cause" of the result. In criminal law two forms of causation exist, factual and legal. If either of these "causes" are missing, then a defense as to the intent of the crime exists. Even if so, the actor may be convicted of a lower, non-intent crime.

An act is the **cause in fact** of the result if the result would not have occurred unless the act occurred. This is known as the *sine qua non* test, which means "but for" the conduct the harm would not have resulted.

Legal cause must also be proved. Legal causation focuses on the degree of similarity between the defendant's intended result and the actual result. It also examines the similarity between the intended manner used to bring about a result and the actual manner that caused the result. Generally, the greater the similarity between the purpose and the result, and the manner intended and the manner that actually caused the result, the more likely that the defendant is the legal cause. Legal cause is also commonly referred to as **proximate cause**. Proximate means nearly, next to, or close. In the context of criminal causation it refers to the relationship between the act and the result. The result must be a consequence of the act, not a coincidence. A happening is proximately caused by an act if a reasonable person would have foreseen and expected the result. This is called **foreseeability**.

Most problems raised in this area involve legal causation, not factual causation. This is because to prove factual causation it must be shown that the defendant took an act which set into motion the events that led to the prohibited result. The question that should be asked is, had the defendant not taken the act or acts in question would the result have happened? If the answer is no, then the defendant is the factual cause. On the other hand, determining legal causation is more troublesome.

Let's examine a few examples. Hank shoots Mark intending to kill him. Mark dies from the gunshot wound. Hank is the factual cause of the murder because it was his conduct that caused Mark to die. To state it another way, "but for" Hank's act Mark would not have died. Hank is also the legal cause of Mark's death because the resulting death is identical to Hank's intention.

Now assume that Hank intended only to injure Mark, not kill him. Accordingly, he shot Mark in the arm. Mark then contacted a hospital, which dispatched an ambulance. The paramedics who arrived to assist Mark negligently administered a dangerous medication, which caused his death. Hank continues to be the factual cause of Mark's death because if he had not injured

LEGAL TERMS

cause in fact
To prove some crimes, particularly those that require behavior amounting to purposeful under the Model Penal Code, it must be shown that the defendant's behavior was the cause of the resulting harm. This is also known as the "but for" or *sine qua non* test. This is because "but for" the defendant's behavior the harm would not have happened.

legal cause
In addition to proving cause in fact, it must also be shown that defendant's actions were the legal cause or proximate cause of the harm. To do this it must be shown that the harm that resulted was similar to the harm intended by the defendant.

proximate cause
Nearness; closeness. In criminal law the prohibited result must be proximately caused by criminal act. That is, the result must be a consequence of the act, not coincidence.

foreseeability
A causation concept, specifically a test to determine proximate cause. People are liable for their actions if the consequences are foreseeable. Results are foreseeable if a reasonable person would have known that the result was probable.

Mark the medical attention that ended Mark's life would not have been necessary. However, Hank is not the legal cause of Mark's death. This is because the result greatly differs from Hank's intent. There is not enough similarity between Hank's purpose when he shot Mark (to cause an injury) and the resulting harm (Mark's death).

Note that it is common for legal cause to be lacking when an **intervening cause** exists, as it does in this example. An intervening cause is a happening that occurs after the initial act and changes the outcome stemming from that act. Intervening causes act to block the connection between an act and the result, because the intervening cause changes what would have been the result if the result would have flowed freely from the act. Intervening causes can negate or lower criminal liability for the particular result. However, lower crimes may continue to be punishable. In the example the intervening cause is the negligent medical care of the paramedics. Hank's intent was not to cause Mark's death, and, as such, he was not the legal cause of his death. Of course, Hank may also have a mens rea defense.

Assume Hank shot Mark intending to kill him, but because Hank is a poor shot he only injured Mark. As above, the paramedics who treat Mark negligently administer the wrong medication and cause his death. Again, Hank is the factual cause of Mark's death. Whether he is the legal cause is debatable. Even though the intended result occurred, it occurred in a manner entirely unintended. If the manner in which the result occurs differs significantly from the manner that was intended, the defendant may not be liable. This appears consistent with common notions of fairness—why should Hank be liable for murder when at least part of the blame belongs to the paramedics? Courts are split on this issue, and some would find that Hank is liable for intent murder, while others would hold Hank liable for a lower murder.

Let's change the facts again. Hank intends to kill Mark while on a hunting trip. Hank's plan was to shoot Mark during the trip and claim that it was an accidental shooting. Hank takes Mark to a desolate area, and they begin hunting. During the trip Mark becomes lost and eventually dies from hunger. In this case Hank is not the factual cause of Mark's death, even though he is the legal cause.

If a victim suffers the intended injury while attempting to avoid the injury, the defendant is liable for the crime, even though the manner is entirely different than intended. So if Mark is struck and killed by a bus while running from Hank, who intends to stab Mark to death, Hank is considered both the legal and factual cause of Mark's death. There is a limit to this theory; that is, there must be some proximity between the unintended manner and the act. If a reasonable person would not have expected the result to occur, the defendant is not liable. So, if Mark was not killed by a passing bus, but rather by a hit on the head by a piano, which was accidentally dropped by movers, Hank is not the legal cause of his death. This is true even though Mark would not have happened to be under the piano if he wasn't running from Hank.

In the rare instance where two events happen at the same time (simultaneously), and both could be the legal cause of the outcome, then both are treated as the legal cause. This is true even if only one event was the actual cause. For example, if two people shoot a victim at the same moment, then both are liable for murder. However, it is possible that only one actually caused the death. If it is not possible to determine which bullet was the actual cause of death, then both people are liable. If it can be determined which bullet was responsible for killing the victim, then the other party is relieved of responsibility for murder (although not attempted murder).

Even though the examples above dealt with purposeful crimes, remember that the principle applies to all crimes that require a particular result. The result need not be one that comes about purposefully or intentionally. Crimes of recklessness and negligence may require a specific result to be criminal. Reckless homicide requires that the behavior that is reckless actually causes a death. What follows is an excerpt of an appeal wherein the defendant successfully argued that causation was an element of driving-under-the-influence-of-alcohol manslaughter. The state of Florida contended that no causation had to be found, that all that had to be proved was that the defendant was in operation of a vehicle while under the influence of alcohol, an accident occurred, and someone died as a result of that accident. The Supreme Court of Florida found that the Florida legislature intended that causation be an element. In the excerpt, the Court refers to a dissenting opinion from another case that explains how the absence of a causation requirement can sometimes lead to an absurd result.

BARBARA ANN MAGAW V. STATE OF FLORIDA

SUPREME COURT OF FLORIDA
537 So.2d 564 (1989)

* * *

Not surprisingly, Magaw contends that the amended statute [D.U.I. manslaughter statute] has added an element

LEGAL TERMS

intervening cause
  An independent happening that occurs after an act and affects the outcome of an act. Intervening causes can act to lower or eliminate criminal liability as to a particular result.

of causation to the crime, whereas the state suggests that the amendment was merely cosmetic and made no substantive changes. There is some merit in both arguments because the meaning of the statute both before and after the amendment has not been entirely clear. In order to convict under the new statute, it is necessary to prove that the operation of a vehicle by a person under the influence caused the death of another, thereby suggesting the requirement of causation. On the other hand, the old statute which provided for conviction if the death of any human being was caused by the operation of a motor vehicle by an intoxicated person has been consistently construed as not requiring proof of causation. . . .

. . . Since *Canon v. State* was decided in 1926 the Florida Supreme Court has consistently held the offense of DWI manslaughter to be a strict liability crime. In *Baker v. State,* 377 So.2d 17 (1979) the Florida Supreme Court stated "statutes which impose strict criminal liability, although not favored, are nonetheless constitutional." However, as Justice Boyd pointed out in his dissenting opinion in that case, "Under this law as construed by the Court today, the following application is possible. An intoxicated person drives an automobile to an intersection and properly stops at a stop light. While there in a stationary position, the vehicle is struck from behind by another automobile due to negligent operation by the driver. The negligent driver dies from injuries received in the collision. The completely passive, non-negligent but intoxicated motorist can be convicted of DWI manslaughter and imprisoned for fifteen years."

This bill would insert the element of causation into the definitions of DUI crimes which call for increased penalties due to accidents involving serious bodily injury or death.

* * *

In view of the history of [the new DUI manslaughter law], the legislative intent is clear. We conclude that the [new DUI manslaughter law] introduced causation as an element. . . . We caution, however, that the statute does not say that the operator of the vehicle must be the sole cause of the fatal accident. Moreover, the state is not required to prove that the operator's drinking caused the accident. The statute requires only that the operation of the vehicle should have caused the accident. Therefore, any deviation or lack of care on the part of a driver under the influence to which the fatal accident can be attributed will suffice.

* * *

[Although Magaw convinced the Court that causation was a requirement under the new statute she lost the appeal because her accident occurred three months prior to the new law taking effect.]

The Model Penal Code also requires that the conduct in question be the actual result or cause of the result. Also, under the Model Penal Code if a particular result is necessary to prove a crime, then the "element is not established unless the actual result is a probable consequence of the actor's conduct." Further, the Code states that the crime is not proven if the actual result is different from the defendant's purpose, unless:

1. The resulting harm is the same, however it occurred to the wrong person or thing (transferred intent).
2. The actual harm is not as great or serious as intended.
3. The actual harm involves the same kind of injury or harm as intended and is not *too remote or accidental* in its occurrence to have a bearing on the actor's liability.

These apply to all levels of culpability under the Code, that is, purposeful, knowing, reckless, and negligent and must be adjusted accordingly. So, if the crime is one of recklessness or negligence, then the above should be viewed in light of risks and probable results and not purpose.[21]

The phrase "too remote or accidental" is the Code's proximate cause requirement. It is the same as discussed above, only the drafters of the Code chose not to use the phrase "proximate cause." In *People v. Warner-Lambert Company, et al.,* a company and some of its officers were indicted for manslaughter and negligent homicide. The charges stemmed from an industrial accident that occurred at one of Warner-Lambert's plants. The high court of New York dismissed the indictments, finding that the defendants were not the proximate cause of the deaths of the employees of the plant because the explosion that caused their deaths was not foreseeable.

PEOPLE V. WARNER-LAMBERT COMPANY, ET AL.

51 N.Y.2d 295, 414 N.E.2d 660 (N.Y. 1980),
cert. denied, *450 U.S. 1031 (1981)*

* * *

On the day on which the explosion occurred, Freshen-Up gum, which is retailed in the shape of a square tablet with a jelly-like center, was being produced at the Warner-Lambert plant by a process in which filled ropes of the gum were passed through a bed of magnesium stearate (MS), a dry, dustlike lubricant which was applied by hand, then into a die-cut punch (a Uniplast machine) which was sprayed with a cooling agent (liquid nitrogen), where the gum was formed into the square tablets. Both the MS (normally an inert, organic compound) and the liquid nitrogen were employed to prevent the chicle from adhering to the sizing and cutting machinery, the tendency to adhere being less if a dry lubricant was used and the punch was kept at a low temperature. The process produced a dispersal of MS dust in the air and an accumulation of it at the base of the Uniplast machine and on overhead pipes; some also remained ambient in the atmosphere in the surrounding area.

Both MS and liquid nitrogen are considered safe and are widely used in the industry. In bulk, MS will only burn or smoulder if ignited; however, like many substances, if suspended in the air in sufficient concentration the dust poses a substantial risk of explosion if ignited. . . . Liquid nitrogen is highly volatile, is easily ignited and, if ignited, will explode. Among possible causes of such ignition of either liquid oxygen or ambient MS are electrical or mechanical sparks.

* * *

. . . There was proof that an inspection of the plant by Warner-Lambert's insurance carrier in February, 1976, had resulted in advice to the insured that the dust condition in the Freshen-Up gum production area presented an explosion hazard and that the MS concentration was above the [low point where explosion could occur], together with recommendations for installation of a dust exhaust system and modification of electrical equipment to meet standards for dust areas.

Although a variety of proposals for altering the dust condition were considered by the individual defendants in consultations and communications with each other and some alterations in the MS application were made, both ambient and settled MS dust were still present on November 21, 1976. . . .

* * *

. . . The issue before us, however, is whether defendants could be held criminally liable for what actually occurred, on theories of reckless or negligent conduct, based on the evidence submitted to this Grand Jury, viewed in the light most favorable to the People. The focus of our attention must be on the issue of culpability, taking into account the conduct of the defendants and the factors of foreseeability and of causation, all of which in combination constitute the ultimate amalgam on which criminal liability may or may not be predicated.

First, we look at the evidence as to the actual event or chain of events which triggered the explosion—evidence which may only be characterized as hypothetical and speculative. . . . The prosecution hypothesizes that under what it describes as "the most plausible of theories" the initial detonation was attributable to mechanical sparking. . . .

Another explanation for the initial explosion was offered by an expert called by the prosecution who hypothesized that liquid oxygen . . . dripped onto settled MS dust at the base of the Uniplast, became trapped there and then, when subjected to the impact caused by a moving metal part, reacted violently, causing ignition of already dispersed MS.

Viewed most favorably to the People, the proof with respect to the actual cause of the explosion is speculative only, and as to at least one of the major hypotheses—that involving oxygen liquefaction—there was no evidence that the process was foreseeable or known to any of the defendants. In sum, there was no proof sufficient to support a finding that defendants foresaw or should have foreseen the physical cause of the explosion. This being so there was not legally sufficient evidence to establish the offenses charged or any lesser included offense.

* * *

Section 3.2(f.1) The "Year and a Day Rule"

Under the common law a person could not be charged with murder if the victim did not die within one year and one day after the act took place. The rule was one of causation. It was developed to prevent a conviction for murder at a time in history when medical science was not precise enough to determine the actual cause of a person's death. If a person lived for over a year and a day after injured by a defendant's acts and then died, it was assumed that medical science could not pinpoint the exact cause of death and that to hold the defendant liable would be unjust. It is questionable, in light of the advances in medicine, whether the rule should continue to exist.[22]

LEGAL TERMS

concurrence
For those crimes that consist of both a mental and physical part it must be shown that the mens rea and the act were joined to cause the result.

Section 3.2(g) Concurrence

In this chapter you have learned that there are two primary components of crimes, the mental and the physical. Although a showing of mens rea is not required for every crime, there must be a showing of some act or omission for all crimes.

For those crimes that have both a mental and physical element, an additional requirement of **concurrence** must be proved. Concurrence is the joining of mens rea and the act. The mens rea must be the reason that the act was taken. Stated another way, the mental state must occur first and set into motion the act. For example, Doug hates Andy and desires to see him dead. Because of this feeling Doug waits for Andy to leave his house one night and runs him down with his car. In such a case Doug's mens rea set into motion the act that caused Andy's death. Now imagine that Doug accidentally kills Andy in an auto accident. After the accident Doug exclaims his happiness over Andy's demise. In this case the mens rea occurred after the act. It was not the catalyst for the act which killed Andy, and, as such, there was no concurrence.

The mere fact that the mental state happens before the act does not mean that there is concurrence. There must be a connection between the intent and the act; the mens rea must set the act into motion. So if Doug were to form the desire to kill Andy today, but takes no action to further the desire, he cannot be charged with murder a year later when he accidentally shoots Andy while hunting.

As stated by the Court of Appeals of Indiana:

> Unless statutorily stated otherwise, it is black letter law that in order to constitute a crime "criminal intent" . . . must unite with an overt act, and they must concur in point of time. There must be a criminal act or omission as well as criminal intent. A felonious intent unconnected with an unlawful act constitutes no crime. . . . A person can only be punished for an offense he has committed and never for an offense he may commit in the future. A crime cannot be predicated upon future acts or upon contingencies or the taking effect of some future event. [cites omitted][23]

SIDEBAR

AVOIDING PROSECUTION
"Common law rule may shield Georgia man from murder charges"
    As David Lebron Cross sits in a Cobb County, Ga., jail, he has developed a great appreciation for common law. And well he should because it may be England's creation of the "year-and-a-day rule" that will keep him from going to trial for murder.
    Cross was charged with child abuse in August 1987 after he allegedly shook his 4-month-old daughter, Sala, so hard she incurred brain damage and became comatose. Doctors determined that the baby would not recover and recommended she be taken off life support. Cross, however, fought attempts by his wife, Linda Lawson Cross, to let Sala die.

REVIEW QUESTIONS

1. In criminal law "causation" is broken down into two forms. Name and briefly describe each.
2. Can a person be prosecuted for failing to save a stranger from danger? Why or why not?
3. What is concurrence?
4. What is an omission?
5. The Model Penal Code recognizes four types of mens rea. Name and briefly describe each.
6. What is vicarious liability?
7. What is a rebuttable presumption? An irrebuttable presumption?
8. Can corporations and other associations be guilty of crimes?

Finally in December 1988, Fulton County, Ga., Superior Court Judge Don Langham ruled that keeping Sala alive by artificial means was "cruel and inhumane." The infant was taken off life support and died within a few weeks, 17 months after she was first hospitalized.

Cross was indicted for homicide. Prosecutor Fonda Clay said Cross admitted shaking the baby, but said he did it because Sala was choking on her bottle. Prosecutors claim, though, that Cross had abused the child before, breaking one of her legs and two ribs just two weeks before the alleged shaking.

Murder Charges Dismissed

But on Aug. 2, Cobb County Superior Court Judge Watson White granted a defense motion to throw out the murder indictment because the infant's death occurred more than a year and a day after the alleged incident.

"After reviewing the law, I don't see anywhere in any cases or statutes where the year-and-a-day rule has been revoked," White said. "Therefore, it must still be in effect."

Child-abuse prosecutor Bruce Hornbuckle, who is handling the case, plans an appeal directly to the Georgia Supreme Court.

"The year-and-a-day rule is archaic

REVIEW PROBLEMS

1–6. Many prisoners in the state and federal correctional systems are held at minimum-security "farms." Only those inmates considered not to be dangerous are housed at these facilities because of the minimal security. In fact, in many cases it is possible for inmates to simply walk off. Of course, most do not leave the premises, because to do so results in an increased sentence (either due to a conviction for escape or a decrease in "good time") and a likelihood that the sentence will be spent in prison, rather than the more desirable farm. Despite this, prisoners of these facilities do escape. What follows are several different sets of facts involving a ficticious inmate, Spike Vincelli. Read each and discuss the defenses, if any, that Spike may have against a charge of escape. Discuss each in light of the following two statutes:

STATUTE ONE:

IT SHALL BE UNLAWFUL FOR ANY PERSON COMMITTED TO ANY CORRECTIONAL FACILITY TO ESCAPE FROM THAT FACILITY. ESCAPE IS DEFINED AS PASSING BEYOND THE BORDERS OF A FACILITY WITH AN INTENT TO NEVER RETURN OR BEING LAWFULLY BEYOND THE BORDERS OF THE FACILITY AND NOT RETURNING WHEN REQUIRED TO DO SO WITH AN INTENT TO NEVER RETURN. VIOLATION OF THIS STATUTE CONSTITUTES A FELONY.

STATUTE TWO:

IT SHALL BE UNLAWFUL FOR ANY PERSON COMMITTED TO ANY CORRECTIONAL FACILITY TO LEAVE THE PREMISES OF THE FACILITY. LEAVING IS DEFINED AS PASSING OVER THE BOUNDARY LINES OF THE FACILITY. VIOLATION OF THIS STATUTE CONSTITUTES A MISDEMEANOR.

1. On June 21 Spike Vincelli received a telephone call from a hospital informing him that his mother was involved in a serious accident. That evening Spike left to see his mother, intending to return in the morning.
2. On June 21 Spike Vincelli had his first epileptic seizure. The seizure caused Spike to fall outside the boundary line surrounding the facility.
3. On June 21 Spike Vincelli decided that he was bored with living on the farm. That night he walked off the premises and

fled for a friend's house three hundred miles away, intending never to return.

4. On June 21 Spike Vincelli became involved in a fight with Ben Ichabod. In a fit of rage Ben picked Spike up and threw him over the fence surrounding the farm. Spike was caught outside the fence by a guard before he had an opportunity to return.

5. In early April Spike Vincelli decided that he was going to escape. He developed a plan that called for him to leave in July and meet his brother, who was passing through the area. As part of the plan Ben Ichabod, a fellow inmate, was enlisted to pick Spike up off the ground and throw him over the fence that surrounded the facility. However, Ben, who is not very bright, threw Spike over the fence on June 21.

6. On June 21 Spike Vincelli became involved in a fight with Ben Ichabod. Ben, in a fit of rage, picked Spike up and threw him over the fence surrounding the facility. While outside the fence Spike became overcome with a sense of freedom and ran from the facility.

7. Fred failed to show for a date he had made with Penni. Penni, who was angered by Fred's actions, decided to vent her anger by cutting the tires of Fred's automobile. However, Penni did not know what make of automobile Fred drove and mistakenly cut the tires of a car owned by Fred's neighbor, Stacey. Penni is now charged with the "purposeful destruction of personal property." Penni claims that her act was not purposeful because she did not intend to cut the tires of Stacey's car. Discuss this defense.

8. William, an experienced canoeist, was hired by a Boy Scout troop to supervise a canoe trip. While on the trip two boys fell out of their canoe and began to drown. William watched as the boys drowned. Is William criminally liable for the deaths?

9. Sherri, who was near bankruptcy, decided to burn her house down and make claim on her insurance carrier for the loss. Sherri started the fire, which spread to a neighbor's house, located twenty feet from Sherri's home. Unknown to Sherri her neighbor was storing massive quantities of dynamite in the home. The fire at the neighbor's house spread to the room where the explosives were being stored, and the resulting explosion caused such vibrations that a construction worker one block away fell off a ladder and subsequently died from the fall. Sherri is charged with arson and murder. She has pled guilty to arson, but maintains that she is not liable for the death of the worker. Is she correct?

and out of date with today's medical technology," he said. "In the year 1200, when a guy died two years after getting hit in the head with a brick, this was probably a good law."

Now, he said, the law "opens the door for murderers to use advances in medical technology to . . . beat the murder rap."

Bert Cohen, Cross' attorney, said there was no intentional plan to keep Sala alive long enough to invoke the year-and-a-day rule. "Is the rule open to abuse? Yes," Cohen said. "Is it still the law in Georgia? Yes. Should David Cross be charged with murder? No."

Hornbuckle plans to argue on appeal that when the Georgia legislature rewrote the criminal code in 1968 and did not include the year-and-a-day rule, it in effect voided it.

According to briefs filed by Hornbuckle, courts in Michigan, New Jersey, Ohio, Oklahoma, Pennsylvania, and Rhode Island have abolished the rule, while only Maryland and Missouri have upheld it.

Of the 13 states that had enacted the rule by statute, only four retained it as of 1986. New York and Oregon courts held that the rule was abrogated when the legislature failed to include it in comprehensive criminal code revisions.

Also, California and Washington have revised their rules to prohibit murder charges when the victim's death occurs *three years* and a day after the assault.

"Authorities across Georgia have frequently chosen not to try cases because of the year-and-a-day rule," said Joseph Chambers, executive director of the Prosecuting Attorneys Council in Georgia.

"The common-law rule was never designed to allow child abusers to avoid a murder conviction through advances in medical technology, and every state legislature should consider revising it. But on the other hand, it's also unfair for defendants to have such serious charges hanging over their heads all their lives. At some point there has to be an end to when you hold a person responsible for an act that occurred years earlier."

In a similar case in Warren County, Pa., near Pittsburgh, Tracey Crane is expected to stand trial this winter for the murder of her

10. The following statute was enacted by State Legislature:

> IT SHALL BE UNLAWFUL FOR ANY PERSON TO BE A PEDOPHILE. PEDOPHILIA IS DEFINED AS A CONDITION WHERE A PERSON OVER THE AGE OF SEVENTEEN YEARS POSSESSES A SEXUAL DESIRE FOR A PERSON UNDER THE AGE OF EIGHT YEARS.

While attending a group therapy session, Jane admitted that she had sexual interest in boys under eight years of age. A member of the group contacted the local police and reported Jane's statement. She was subsequently arrested and charged with violating the above statute. Discuss her defenses, if any.

11. Ashley, Amy, and Karen are roommates in college. They occupy a four-bedroom apartment, and all share in the bills and household duties. One weekend a friend of Karen's, Janice, came to visit. Janice arrived on Thursday and was scheduled to stay until Monday. She stayed in the extra bedroom. On Thursday evening Ashley discovered, while she was watching Janice unpack, that Janice had a significant amount of cocaine in one suitcase. Later that night, Ashley discussed this matter with Karen, who stated, "I'm sure she does—why does it matter to you?" Ashley immediately confronted Janice and told her that she would have to remove the cocaine from the premises or she would call the police. Janice picked up the suitcase, carried it to her car and placed it in the trunk. The next morning, when Karen learned what Ashley had done, she encouraged Janice to bring the suitcase back into the apartment.

On Sunday morning the police arrived with a warrant to search the apartment. The search uncovered the suitcase in the extra bedroom. Later, at the police station, the suitcase was opened, and the drugs were discovered. All four women were charged with possession. Do Amy, Ashley, or Karen have a defense? The jurisdiction where they live applies the Model Penal Code.

NOTES

[1] Goldstein, J., et al., *Criminal Law: Theory and Process* (New York: Free Press, 1974).

[2] 21 AM. JUR. 2d *Criminal Law* 129 (1981).

[3] See *U.S. v. Birkenstock*, 823 F.2d 1026 (7th Cir. 1987) and *U.S. v. Pompanio*, 429 U.S. 10 (1976).

[4] LaFave and Scott, *Criminal Law* (Hornbook Series, St. Paul: West Publishing Co., 1986), p. 217.

[5] LaFave and Scott, p. 34.

[6] See *Lambert v. California*, 355 U.S. 225 (1957) for a case where the United States Supreme Court found that a strict liability statute was violative of the due process clause of the United States Constitution.

[7] LaFave and Scott, pp. 244–245.

[8] See *United States v. Dotterweich, 320 U.S. 277 (1943).*

[9] Model Penal Code §2.07 deals with liability of corporations and unincorporated associations.

[10] Model Penal Code §2.02, General Requirements of Culpability.

[11] Kaplan and Weisberg, *Criminal Law* (Boston: Little, Brown and Co., 1986).

[12] Model Penal Code §2.02(2)(c).

[13] The Model Penal Code actually recognizes three "objective elements" that may have differing culpability levels. Those are circumstance, result, and conduct. Also, the Code provides at §2.02(4) that one mental state shall apply to an entire offense, unless a contrary intent is plain.

[14] Model Penal Code §2.01.

[15] Id.

[16] From N. Morris, *Somnambulistic Homicide: Ghosts, Spiders, and North Koreans,* 5 Res Judicata 29 (1951).

[17] Loewy, A., *Criminal Law,* 2nd Ed. (Nutshell Series, St. Paul: West Publishing Co., 1987).

[18] LaFave and Scott, p. 200.

[19] Model Penal Code §2.01(4).

[20] Vermont and Rhode Island are states that impose a duty to rescue. See 12 Vt.Gen.Stat. §519 and R.I.Gen.Laws §11–56–1.

[21] Model Penal Code §2.03

[22] Loewy, p. 55.

[23] *Gebhard v. State of Indiana*, 484 N.E.2d 45, 48 (Ind. App. 1 Dist. 1985).

daughter, Leslie. Crane and her husband, David, had opposed the removal of life-support systems that were keeping their daughter alive.

Reprinted from the October, 1990, issue of the ABA Journal, the Lawyer's Magazine, *published by the American Bar Association.*

CHAPTER 4
Crimes Against the Person

"I'm not surprised. Look how he's dotted his 'I's' with those little circles."

The state without law would be like the human body without mind.

Cicero

OUTLINE

SECTION 4.1   STUDYING CRIMES

In the next three chapters you will learn about many crimes. It would be impossible to include a discussion of all crimes. Each city and state has its own unique laws. What follows is a discussion of the major crimes recognized, in some form, in most jurisdictions. The crimes have been catagorized as crimes against the person, crimes against property, and crimes against the public. Although it is common to make these distinctions, do not become involved with understanding why these classifications have been made, as they are used only for organizational purposes. In a sense, all crimes are offenses against the public. That is why the public prosecutes crimes, and private individuals may not. Also, any offense "against property" is actually injuring a person, not the property. A stolen television set does not long to be returned to its rightful owner. However, the rightful owner does feel wronged and desires the return of the stolen item. In a sense the classifications are often accurate in that they describe the focus of the criminal conduct. The focus of a thief's act is property; hence, a crime against property. The focus of a rapist's attack is a human; hence, a crime against a person.

All of the following crimes have been broken into parts. Each part of a crime is an **element** of that crime. At trial, every element of a crime must be proven beyond a reasonable doubt by the prosecution. If any element is not proven beyond a reasonable doubt, the accused must be found not-guilty. The rule requires that each element be proved individually. That is, if a crime consists of six elements, and a jury is convinced that five have been proven, but cannot say that the sixth has been proven beyond a reasonable doubt, then there must be a not-guilty verdict. This is true even if the jury was solidly convinced that all the other elements were true and generally believed that the defendant committed the

LEGAL TERMS

element
   Each crime consists of many parts. Each part of a crime is known as an element. Each element of a crime must be proven beyond a reasonable doubt by the prosecution to support a conviction.

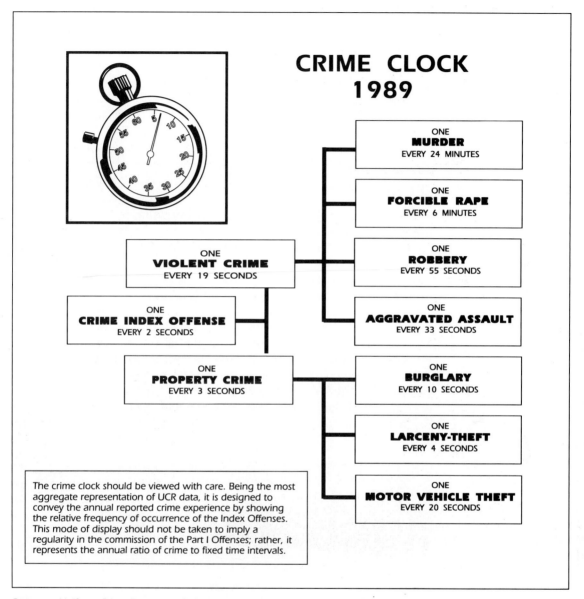

CRIME CLOCK
1989

ONE
VIOLENT CRIME
EVERY 19 SECONDS

ONE
CRIME INDEX OFFENSE
EVERY 2 SECONDS

ONE
PROPERTY CRIME
EVERY 3 SECONDS

ONE
MURDER
EVERY 24 MINUTES

ONE
FORCIBLE RAPE
EVERY 6 MINUTES

ONE
ROBBERY
EVERY 55 SECONDS

ONE
AGGRAVATED ASSAULT
EVERY 33 SECONDS

ONE
BURGLARY
EVERY 10 SECONDS

ONE
LARCENY-THEFT
EVERY 4 SECONDS

ONE
MOTOR VEHICLE THEFT
EVERY 20 SECONDS

The crime clock should be viewed with care. Being the most aggregate representation of UCR data, it is designed to convey the annual reported crime experience by showing the relative frequency of occurrence of the Index Offenses. This mode of display should not be taken to imply a regularity in the commission of the Part I Offenses; rather, it represents the annual ratio of crime to fixed time intervals.

Source: Uniform Crime Reports, U.S. Dept. Justice, FBI, August 5, 1990.

crime. Later you will learn more about the "beyond a reasonable doubt" standard.

Finally, you may notice that it is often the case that if one crime has been proven all the elements of a related lesser crime can also be proved. For example, if a defendant is convicted of murdering someone with a hammer, he has also committed a battery of the victim. In such circumstances, the lesser offense merges into the greater offense. This is the Merger Doctrine. Under this doctrine both crimes may be charged, but if the defendant is convicted of the more serious crime the lesser is absorbed by the greater, and the defendant is not punished for both. If acquitted of the greater charge, the defendant may be convicted of the lesser.

SECTION 4.2 HOMICIDE

Homicide is the killing of one human being by another. Not all homicides are crimes. It is possible to cause another person's death accidentally, that is, accompanied by no mens rea, which gives rise to criminal liability.

Criminal homicide occurs when a person takes another's life in a manner proscribed by law. The law proscribes more than intentional killings. Under the Model Penal Code purposeful, knowing, negligent, and reckless homicides may be punished.

The mens rea part of homicide is important. The determination of what mens rea was possessed by the defendant (actually, what mens rea can be proven by the prosecution) will usually determine what crime may be punished. Under the common law various forms of murder were developed. This is where we will begin.

Section 4.2(a) Homicide and the Common Law

Initially under the common law all murders were punished equally: the murderer was executed.[1] Over time judges realized that the rule was harsh, and the belief that not all homicides should be punished equally developed. As a result, homicides were divided into murder and manslaughter. Manslaughter was punished by incarceration, not death.

Murder, under the common law, was defined as: 1. The unlawful killing of a 2. human being with 3. malice aforethought. It was the requirement of malice aforethought that distinguished murder from manslaughter. Although malice aforethought was defined differently among the states, the following types of homicide became recognized as murder under the common law:

1. When the defendant intended to cause the death of the victim.
2. When the defendant intended to cause serious bodily harm, and death resulted.
3. When the defendant created an unreasonably high risk of death that caused the victim's death, regardless of the defendant's mens rea. This was known as "depraved-heart murder."
4. When the doctrine of felony-murder was applicable.

All criminal homicides that did not constitute murder were treated as manslaughter. Today, nearly every jurisdiction further divides murder into degrees, and most divide manslaughter into voluntary and involuntary. Few jurisdictions rely on the common-law definition of malice aforethought. However, many states continue to recognize felony-murder.

Section 4.2(a.1) The Felony-Murder Doctrine

Under the common law one who caused an unintended death during the commission (or attempted commission) of any felony was guilty of murder. This became known as **felony-murder.** Under the early common law all felonies were punished by death. Generally, most of the crimes that were felonies under the common law involved a threat to human life. This threat was one justification for the harshness of the rule. However, as the common law developed, many new crimes were created, many of which did not pose a serious threat to human life. For this reason the felony-murder doctrine was very harsh, as it applied to all felonies despite their relative dangerousness to human life. Over time courts began to limit the application of the rule to specified felonies; specifically, those perceived as posing the largest threat to human life.

LEGAL TERMS

felony-murder doctrine
  If one causes the unintended death of another during the commission, or attempted commission, of a felony, that person is guilty of murder. The rule imputes the mens rea required to establish murder to the defendant.

It was common to apply the rule to rape, mayhem, arson, kidnapping, and robbery.

For example, Andy and Gene decide to rob the First National Bank of Owensville. They agreed to use whatever amount of violence necessary to carry out the robbery. During the robbery a bank teller summoned the police by use of a silent alarm. As Andy and Gene were leaving the bank the police shouted to them ordering their surrender. Andy then fired a shot from his gun and fatally wounded a police officer. Using the felony-murder rule both Gene and Andy are criminally liable for the death of the police officer, even though Gene did not fire the weapon or conspire with Andy to kill the officer.

The felony-murder rule acts to impute the required mens rea to the defendant and to create a form of vicarious liability between co-felons. The rule imputes mens rea because it applies in situations of unintended death; however, murder in the first degree is a specific intent crime. The rationale is that one who engages in inherently dangerous crimes should be aware of the high risk to human life that is created by the crime. Vicarious liability is also imposed in some states; that is, all the individuals involved in the perpetration of the crime may be criminally liable for the resulting death.

Today, most states have felony-murder statutes. Generally, the following must be shown to establish a felony-murder:

1. The defendant must have been engaged in the commission, or attempted commission, of a named felony, and
2. during the commission, or attempted commission, of that felony a death occurred, and
3. there is a causal connection between the crime and the death.

In most jurisdictions the legislature has specified the crimes that must be committed, or attempted, for the rule to apply. A few jurisdictions have limited the application of the rule to those crimes that were felonies under the common law, and others have limited the rule to those felonies that involve a threat to human life.

To satisfy the second requirement it must be determined when the commission of the crime began and when it concluded. This appears to be an easy task, and is in most cases, but there are instances when it is not clear. Suppose that a robber knew that a large sum of money was being transferred between a bank and an armored car at a particular time and intended to steal the money during that transfer. Also assume that the traffic was heavier than anticipated by the robber on the day of the planned robbery, and in an effort to arrive at the bank on time, the robber ran a stop sign. While passing through the intersection the robber struck another vehicle, killing the driver. Was this death during the commission, or attempted commission, of the robbery? What if a police officer were to chase an individual from the scene of the commission of one of the named felonies and is shot fifteen minutes and one mile away from the scene of the crime? Is this during the commission, or attempted commission, of the felony? It is likely that no felony-murder would be found in the first example, because the death was too far removed from the actual commission of the crime. The result would be different if the robber struck and killed the motorist while fleeing from the police immediately after the commission of the holdup. This answers the second question. Courts have generally held that deaths that occur during the flight of a felon are "during the commission of the felony." However, the chase must be immediate, and the rule does not apply if there is a gap between the time the crime occurred, or was attempted, and the time the chase begins.

Requirement number three can be a troublesome requirement. In many ways this requirement is similar to the causation requirement discussed in the chapter on actus reus. That is, the commission, or attempted commission, of the felony must be the legal cause (proximate cause) of the death. The death must be a "consequence, not coincidence" of the act; the resulting death must have been a foreseeable consequence of the act. So, if a patron of a store suffers a heart attack during a robbery, which was precipitated by the crime, the robbers are guilty of felony-murder if the patron dies. However, if a patron who is unaware of an ongoing robbery suffers a heart attack and dies, the robbers are not liable for the death. The mere fact that the death and the crime occurred simultaneously does not mean that the robbers were the legal cause of the death.

In some states the act that causes the death of the victim need not be taken by one of the perpetrators of the crime. For example, if Gene and Andy become involved in a shoot-out with the police after they robbed the First National Bank of Owensville, Wyoming, and the police accidentally shoot an innocent bystander, then Gene and Andy are guilty of felony-murder. This is because they began the series of events which led to the death of the bystander. However, if a police officer (or another) kills one of many felons who are jointly involved in the commission of the crime, it is generally held that the other felons are not guilty of felony murder.[2]

Although the felony-murder rule does impose vicarious liability between co-felons, this aspect is limited. If a defendant can prove that he did not take the act which caused the death; did not authorize, plan, or encourage the act of his co-felon; and had no reason to believe that his cohort would take the act, he has a defense to felony-murder in some jurisdictions. Note that the rules concerning parties (principals and accomplices) to crimes may create liability independent of the felony-murder rule.

Finally, note that in most jurisdictions that continue to recognize felony-murder, the murder is treated as first-degree murder for the purpose of sentencing. Other statutes provide that felony-murders that occur during named felonies are to be treated as first-degree murder and that murders during "all other felonies" are to be treated as second-degree murder. Even if the statute which creates this "all other felony" category does not expressly state that the felony must involve a danger to human life, it is common for courts to impose the requirement.

In the case that follows a defendant appealed his conviction at the trial level of involuntary manslaughter and aggravated burglary. The Ohio Court of Appeals applied a statute which read, "No person shall cause the death of another as a proximate result of the offender's committing or attempting to commit a felony." The statute named the crime involuntary manslaughter. The case is interesting from a causation perspective. Read the case and decide for yourself if the defendant should be punished for the death that occurred.

THE STATE OF OHIO V. LOSEY

23 Ohio App.3d 93, 491 N.E.2d 379 (1985)

* * *

Defendant testified that he approached a house located at 616 Whitehorne Avenue shortly after 11:00 P.M. on November 25, 1983; that he knocked at the front door and, upon receiving no response, forced open the door and proceeded to attempt to remove a bicycle. His friend, who had been waiting outside, yelled that a car was slowly approaching. The defendant then placed the bicycle beside the front door and departed, leaving the front door open behind him. James Harper, the owner of 616 Whitehorne Avenue, testified that he heard a noise at approximately 1:00 A.M. Shortly thereafter, his mother, with whom he resided, appeared at his bedroom door inquiring about the noise. They proceeded together to the living room, whereupon they discovered the open front door and the bicycle standing near the door.

James Harper stated that he told his mother to go back to her bedroom while he went to check the rest of the house. After so checking, he returned to the living room and was calling the police when his mother appeared in the hallway looking very upset and then collapsed. He called an emergency squad, which attempted to revive Mrs. Harper for almost an hour when the squadmen pronounced her dead. Prior to the burglary, Mrs. Harper had returned from bingo at approximately 10:00 P.M. that evening and had gone to bed. Based on these facts, the trial court found defendant guilty of aggravated burglary and involuntary manslaughter.

* * *

The doctor's testimony established that defendant's conduct was a cause of Mrs. Harper's death in the sense that it set in motion events which culminated in her death. However, it still must be determined whether defendant was legally responsible for her death—whether the death was the proximate result of his conduct. It is not necessary that the accused be in a position to foresee the precise consequence of his conduct; only that the consequence be foreseeable in the sense that what actually transpired was natural and logical in that it was within the scope of the risk created by his conduct . . .

By the same token, in this case, the causal relationship between defendant's criminal conduct and Mrs. Harper's death was not too improbable, remote, or speculative to form a basis for criminal responsibility. Although the defendant did not engage in loud or violent conduct calculated to frighten or shock, his presence was nevertheless detected by Mrs. Harper . . .

[Conviction Affirmed.]

Section 4.2(a.2) Misdemeanor Manslaughter

Similar to the felony-murder rule, one may be guilty of misdemeanor manslaughter if a death results from the commission of a misdemeanor, not a felony. Conviction of misdemeanor manslaughter results in liability for manslaughter, often involuntary manslaughter, and not murder.

Just as the felony-murder doctrine has been limited in recent years, so has the crime of misdemeanor manslaughter. This is due in large part to the significant increase in the creation of non-violent crimes by legislatures and administrative bodies. Many states require that the misdemeanor be *malum in se,* and crimes that are *malum prohibitum* can not be a basis for misdemeanor manslaughter. Requiring that the misdemeanor have a mens rea element is another limitation; that is, strict liability crimes may not be the basis for misdemeanor manslaughter. There is a trend to reject the misdemeanor manslaughter rule (as there is with the felony-murder rule) and require that one of the four types of culpability recognized by the Model Penal Code (purposeful, knowing, negligent, or reckless) be present before imposing liability.

Section 4.2(b)   Statutory Approaches to Homicide

Although the common law only recognized one form of murder, most states now divide murder into degrees; most often into first and second degrees. **First-degree murder** is the highest form of murder and is punished more severely than second-degree murder. **Second-degree murder** is a higher crime than manslaughter.

Section 4.2(b.1)   First- and Second-Degree Murder

For a murder to be of the first degree, the highest crime, it must be shown that the homicide was willful, deliberate, and premeditated. Generally, first-degree murder applies whenever the murderer has as a goal the death of the victim. "Willful," as used in first-degree murder, is a specific intent concept. To be willful the defendant must have specifically intended to cause the death.

"Deliberate" usually is defined as a cool mind, not acting out of an immediate passion, fear, or rage. The term "premeditated" means to think beforehand. Similar to deliberate, it eliminates impulsive acts from the grasp of first-degree murder. It is commonly said that there must be a gap in time between the decision to kill and the actual act. Of course, the length of the gap is the critical issue. Most courts hold that the gap in time must be "appreciable." Again, this term describes little. The fact is that courts differ greatly in how they define appreciable. There are many reported cases where a lapse of only seconds was sufficient.[3] Some courts have held that all that need be shown is that the defendant had adequate time to form the intention before taking the act, and the length of time is not determinative of the question.[4]

In *State v. Snowden*, the defendant appealed his conviction of first-degree murder, claiming that he lacked premeditation, and, as such, he should have been convicted of second-degree murder, not first.

STATE V. SNOWDEN

79 Idaho 266, 313 P.2d 706 (1957)

* * *

Defendant Snowden had been playing pool and drinking in a Boise pool room early in the evening. With a companion, one Carrier, he visited a club near Boise, then went to nearby Garden City. There the two men visited a number of bars, and defendant had several drinks. Their last stop was the HiHo Club.

Witnesses related that while defendant was in the HiHo Club he met and talked to Cora Lucyle Dean. The defendant himself said he hadn't been acquainted with Mrs. Dean prior to that time, but he had "seen her in a couple of the joints up town." He danced with Mrs. Dean while at the HiHo Club. Upon departing from the tavern, the two left together.

In statements to police officers, that were admitted in evidence, defendant Snowden said after they left the club Mrs. Dean wanted him to find a cab and take her back to Boise, and he refused because he didn't feel he should pay her fare. After some words, he related:

> She got mad at me so I got pretty hot and I don't know whether I back handed her there or not. And, we got calmed down and decided to walk across to the gas station and call a cab.

They crossed the street, and began arguing again. Defendant said: "She swung and at the same time she kneed me again. I blew my top."

Defendant said he pushed the woman over beside a pickup truck which was standing near a business building. There he pulled his knife—a pocket knife with a two-inch blade—and cut her throat.

LEGAL TERMS

first-degree murder
A homicide that is willful, premeditated, and deliberate. Generally, a purposeful murder under the Model Penal Code. The highest form of murder and is punished the most severely.

second-degree murder
All homicides that are murder, not manslaughter, but do not rise to the level of first-degree murder. Punished less severely than first-degree murder, but more than manslaughter.

The body, which was found the next morning, was viciously and sadistically cut and mutilated. An autopsy surgeon testified the voice box had been cut, and that this would have prevented the victim from making any intelligible cry. There were other wounds inflicted while she was still alive—one in her neck, one in her abdomen, two in the face, and two on the back of the neck. The second neck wound severed the spinal cord and caused her death. There were other wounds all over the body, and her clothing had been cut away. The nipple of her right breast was missing. There was no evidence of sexual attack on the victim; however, some of the lacerations were around the breasts and vagina of the deceased . . .

. . . murder is defined by statute as follows:

> All murder which is perpetrated by means of poison, or lying in wait, torture, or by any other kind of willful, deliberate and premeditated killing, or which is committed in the perpetration of, or attempt to perpetrate arson, rape, robbery, burglary, kidnapping, or mayhem, is murder in the first degree. All other murders are of the second degree.

The defendant admitted taking the life of the deceased.

The principal argument of the defendant pertaining to [the charge of premeditated murder] is that the defendant did not have sufficient time to develop a desire to take the life of the deceased, but rather his action was instantaneous and a normal reaction to the physical injury which she dealt him. . . .

> There need be no appreciable space of time between the intention to kill and the act of killing. They may be as instantaneous as successive thoughts of the mind. It is only necessary that the act of killing be preceded by a concurrence of will, deliberation, and premeditation on the part of the slayer, and, if such is the case, the killing is murder in the first degree.

In the present case, the trial court had no other alternative than to find the defendant guilty of willful, deliberate, and premeditated killing with malice aforethought in view of the defendant's acts in deliberately opening up a pocket knife, next cutting the victim's throat, and then hacking and cutting until he had killed Cora Lucyle Dean . . .

Decisions such as this obscure the difference between first- and second-degree murder. Do you agree with the Idaho Court that there can be premeditation even if there is "no appreciable space of time between the intention to kill and the act of killing?" Note that the facts of this case did not require mention of the prior case where it was held that "no appreciable" time has to be shown. The fact that the autopsy evidenced that the murder occurred after the victim suffered torture would justify a murder conviction under the statute.

Note that the statute mentioned in *Snowden* to describe first-degree murder is used by many jurisdictions. Those murders that result from poisoning, follow torture, or are traditional felony-murders are often designated first-degree murder. Second-degree murder is commonly given the negative definition "all murders that are not of the first degree are of the second." Second-degree murders differ from first in that the defendant lacked the specific intent to kill or lacked the premeditation and deliberation element of first-degree murder.

Section 4.2(b.2) Intent to Do Serious Bodily Harm and the Deadly Weapon Doctrine

One method of reducing a murder from the first degree to the second is by proving that the defendant did not intend to kill, but only intended to cause the victim serious bodily harm. Note that if the defendant intended less than serious bodily harm the crime is either manslaughter or a form of reckless or negligent homicide.

This is an area where inferences are important. Juries (or judges, if the court is acting as the finder of fact) are permitted to view the facts surrounding the murder and determine what the defendant's state of mind was at the time the act occurred. A jury may conclude from the facts that the defendant did intend to cause the death of the victim and convict of first-degree murder. If a jury concludes that the defendant did not intend to cause the death of the victim, but that the defendant did intend to cause serious bodily injury, then the crime is second-degree murder.

A related inference used in murder cases is the **Deadly Weapon Doctrine**. This is a rule that permits juries to infer that a defendant intended to kill his or her victim if a **deadly weapon** was used in the killing. Being an inference, this conclusion does not have to be drawn; this is a decision for the fact finder. If a jury were to conclude that a defendant's use of a deadly weapon indicated that murder was intended, then a first-degree murder conviction would be warranted. So, if Gwen intended only to injure Fred by shooting him, but Fred died as a result of the wound, then a jury could convict Gwen of first-degree murder. Of course, the

LEGAL TERMS

Deadly Weapon Doctrine
A rule that states that juries may infer that a defendant intended to murder if a deadly weapon was used to kill the victim.

deadly weapon
Any item, which from the manner used is calculated or likely to cause death or serious bodily injury.

jury could reject the inference if they believed that Gwen did not intend to kill Fred, and in that case either second-degree murder would be appropriate (if her intent was to inflict serious bodily injury) or manslaughter.

Any device or item may be a deadly weapon if, from the manner used, it is calculated or likely to produce death or serious bodily injury.[5] The Model Penal Code defines a deadly weapon as "any firearm, or other weapon, device, instrument, material, or substance, whether animate or inanimate, which in the manner it is used or is intended to be used is known to be capable of producing death or serious bodily injury."[6] Under these definitions some items that are not normally considered deadly may be deadly weapons if their use is calculated to cause serious bodily injury or death. The opposite is also true; some items that are normally considered deadly may not be, if used in a manner that does not pose a threat of serious harm or death. Hence, a bowling ball may be transformed from a recreational device to a deadly weapon when it is used to crush a person's skull. A gun, probably the most obvious example of a deadly device, when used for its designed purpose, may not be deemed deadly if used to hit someone over the head. A person's hands and feet are not normally deadly weapons. However, if it can be shown that the victim was significantly smaller than the defendant or that the defendant was especially expert in the use of his or her hands to cause injury, then they may constitute deadly weapons.

What follows is a case where the inference created by the deadly weapon doctrine is used to affirm a trial court conviction of attempted murder.

DAVID LABELLE V. STATE OF INDIANA

550 N.E.2d 752 (Ind. 1990)

Appellant waived his right to a jury trial and was tried to the court and found guilty of attempted murder . . . and carrying a handgun without a license . . .

The evidence produced at trial which tended to support the determination of guilt shows that members of the Outlaws motorcycle gang, who refer to themselves as "brothers," sometimes frequent the Beehive Tavern in Indianapolis. On February 2, 1987, appellant was a patron of the Beehive. He asked Oliphant, the bartender and co-owner of the bar, whether the Outlaws had come into the bar before, and Oliphant informed him that they had. Appellant remained at the Beehive until closing time and returned the next night. By 11:00 P.M., at least three employees and several patrons were in the bar. Three members of the Outlaws, including the victim, Allen Mayes, were there shooting pool. Sometime after 11:00, appellant threw a beer can at the stage, whereupon Oliphant asked him to leave, and appellant spat in his face. Oliphant testified, "[appellant said] that we're going to a funeral[,] to get my brothers together because we were going to a funeral. . . . [Appellant] told me I wasn't worth killing but a few of them—a few people in here were. And he proceeded to walk out the door." Oliphant stated that the three Outlaws were standing by the bar about ten feet from the door as he followed appellant out and that they were in roughly the same place when he came back in. Two or three minutes later, a shot rang out and Mayes was struck in the neck by a bullet and fell to the floor.

Fifteen to twenty minutes after the shooting, appellant was found under a truck which was parked across the street from the Beehive. A crowd which included the victim's two companions stood outside the bar and watched as appellant was being placed under arrest, and one of the Beehive's managers testified that appellant shouted at the two men, "Scumbags, you tell your brothers the angels are on their way[.] I got your brother."

The door to the bar has a diamond-shaped window, which is taped to leave unobstructed only a two- or three-inch peephole. Looking into the bar from the outside, the peephole is approximately five feet, seven inches off the ground. Police found a bullet hole in the taped area to the right of the peephole. . . .[the police] searched the underneath side of the truck and found a .38 caliber revolver on the transmission brace, above the approximate spot appellant's head had been when he was under the truck. . . .[The medical expert] testified that, based on test results, it was his opinion that the bullet in Mayes's neck was from a .38 caliber weapon. . . .

Appellant also claims that there was insufficient evidence of intent to kill to support a conviction for attempted murder. . . . This court held there [in a previous case] that intent may be inferred from the use of a deadly weapon in a manner likely to cause injury or death and upheld the conviction. This Court has repeatedly upheld convictions for murder and attempted murder where the State sought to carry its burden of proof on the issue of intent by producing evidence that the defendant fired a gun in a crowd or at a group of people. [cites omitted]

Appellant conceded in his testimony that he did fire a shot at the Beehive, but maintained that he was trying to hit a light over the door to the bar. He testified that he could not see into the bar because of the tape on the window and his distance from the door and that he had no intention of shooting any person, but intended only to aggravate Oliphant. . . .

State of mind can be established by the circumstances surrounding an incident. [cite omitted] Appellant questioned the bartender the night before the shooting as to whether the Outlaws frequented the Beehive. . . .The eye-level location of the peephole and the proximity of the bullet hole to it would support an inference that the shot was fired into this inhabited barroom in a manner calculated to strike anyone standing at the bar in the upper body or head. This constitutes utilization of a deadly weapon in a manner likely to cause injury or death. There was sufficient evidence to support the trial court's verdict.

The judgment of the trial court is affirmed.

Section 4.2(c) Manslaughter

Under the common law murder was an unlawful killing with malice aforethought. **Manslaughter** was an unlawful killing without malice aforethought. Just as was the case with murder, the common law did not divide manslaughter into degrees. Whenever the states began codifying homicides it was common for manslaughter to be divided into degress, commonly referred to as voluntary and involuntary, although a few jurisdictions used first- and second-degree language. Today, many jurisdictions continue to recognize two forms of manslaughter. However, many states now have only one degree of manslaughter.

The important fact is that manslaughter is a lesser crime than murder, and, accordingly, is punished less severely. It is a lesser crime because some fact or facts exist that make the defendant less culpable than a murderer in the eyes of the law. The most common fact that mitigates a defendant's culpability is the absense of a state of mind that society has decided should be punished as murder. Even though society has decided that because of such extenuating circumstances a defendant should not be punished as a murderer, it has also decided that some punishment should be inflicted.

Section 4.2(c.1) Provocation

Provocation of the defendant by the victim can reduce a homicide from murder to manslaughter. In those jurisdictions that grade manslaughter, a provoked killing is treated as the higher manslaughter, whether that be called first-degree or voluntary.

The theory of provocation, also known as "heat of passion manslaughter," is that a defendant was operating under such an anger or passion that it was impossible for the defendant to have formed the desire to kill, which is required for both first- and second-degree murder. The defense of provocation applies to those instances where people act without thinking; the impulsive act being the result of victim's behavior.

Again, an objective test is used when examining the defense of provocation. To prove provocation it must be shown that the provoking act was so severe that a reasonable person may have also killed. It does not require that a reasonable person would have killed; only that a reasonable person would have been so affected by the act that homicide was possible. A few states have enumerated the acts that may act to negate intent to kill (and reduce the homicide to manslaughter) in their manslaughter statutes. Any act not included may not be used by a defendant to reduce a murder charge.

Catching one's spouse in the act of adultery is an example of an act that is considered as adequate provocation to reduce any resulting homicide to manslaughter. This rule applies only to marriages and not to other romantic relationships. Generally, serious assaults (batteries) may constitute adequate provocation.

If two people are engaged in "mutual combat," then any resulting death may be reduced from murder to voluntary manslaughter. The key to this defense is mutuality. If it can be shown that the victim did not voluntarily engage in the fight, then the defense of mutual combat is not applicable, and the defendant is responsible for murder.

LEGAL TERMS

manslaughter
An unlawful homicide that is punished less severely than murder. Manslaughter is commonly divided into voluntary and involuntary, the former being the higher crime. Manslaughter is often distinguished from murder by the absense of culpable mens rea.

provocation
A defense that does not excuse a crime, but causes it to be reduced to a lesser crime. If a reasonable person would have been so enraged by the acts of the victim that the act of the defendant is not beyond what a reasonable person would consider normal, then the defendant may have the defense of provocation. In cases of homicide a legitimate defense of provocation reduces the crime from murder to manslaughter.

It is widely held that words and gestures are never adequate provocation. This is true regardless of how vile or vicious a statement or gesture is to the defendant. However, some recent cases have distinguished between statements that are informational and those that are not. In such situations, if a statement provides information of an act, and that act would be sufficient provocation, if witnessed, then the statement may also be provocation.

In the case that follows the trial judge refused to instruct the jury on the alternative of manslaughter, as opposed to murder. The trial judge followed the rule that statements are never adequate provocation. The appellate court reversed the judge, holding that the statements made by the defendant's wife directly before he killed her may have been adequate provocation for a jury to find voluntary manslaughter and not murder.

COMMONWEALTH V. SCHNOPPS

383 Mass. 178, 417 N.E.2d 1213 (1981)

* * *

Schnopps testified that his wife had left him three weeks prior to the slaying. He claims that he first became aware of the problems in his fourteen-year marriage at a point about six months before the slaying. According to the defendant, on that occasion he took his wife to a club to dance, and she spent the evening dancing with a co-worker. On arriving home, the defendant and his wife argued over her conduct. She told him that she no longer loved him and that she wanted a divorce. Schnopps became very upset. He admitted that he took out his shotgun during the course of this argument, but he denied that he intended to use it. . . . [The defendant and his wife continued to have marital problems for the next few months.]

On the day of the killing, Schnopps had asked his wife to come to their home and talk over their marital difficulties. Schnopps told his wife that he wanted his children at home, and that he wanted the family to remain intact. Schnopps cried during the conversation and begged his wife to let the children live with him and to keep their family together. His wife replied, "No, I am going to court, you are going to give me all the furniture, you are going to get the Hell out of here, and you won't have nothing." Then, pointing to her crotch, she said, "You will never touch this again, because I have got something bigger and better for it."

On hearing those words, Schnopps claims that his mind went blank, and that he went "berserk." He went to a cabinet and got out a pistol he had bought the day before, and he shot his wife and himself. . . .[Schopps lived and his wife died.]

Schnopps argues that "[t]he existence of sufficient provocation is not foreclosed absolutely because a defendant learns of a fact from oral statements rather than from personal observation," and that a sudden admission of adultery is equivalent to a discovery of the act itself, and is sufficient evidence of provocation.

Schnopps asserts that his wife's statements constituted a "peculiarly immediate and intense offense to a spouse's sensitivities." He concedes that the words at issue are indicative of past as well as present adultery. Schnopps claims, however, that his wife's admission of adultery was made for the first time on the day of the killing. . . .
Reversed and remanded for new trial on the manslaughter issue.

Usually, when claiming adultery as provocation, one must have actually caught his or her spouse in the act. Also, the general rule is that words are not adequate provocation. What has the Court done in this case? It appears that the Court attempted to sidestep those rules, in a manner that would permit the benefit of the defense without changing the rules. It did this by holding that in adulterous situations an admission of adultery to one's spouse, when uttered for the first time, is as shocking as finding one's spouse engaged in the act.

Finally, the defense will not be available if there was a sufficient "cooling off" period. That is, if the time between the provocation and the homicide was long enough for a defendant to regain self-control, then the homicide will be treated as murder and not manslaughter.

Section 4.2(c.2) Imperfect Self-Defense and Defense of Others

If Gwen harms Sue while defending herself from Sue's attack, Gwen is said to have acted in self-defense. Self-defense, when valid, normally works to negate criminal liability entirely. So, if Gwen kills Sue to avoid serious bodily harm or death, she has committed an excused homicide. What happens if Gwen was incorrect in her belief that her life was endangered by Sue? This is known as an imperfect self-defense and does not negate culpability entirely. It may, however, reduce liability. So, Gwen may be liable only for voluntary manslaughter and not murder. For Gwen to be successful in her claim she must prove that she had a good faith belief that her life was in danger and that the killing appeared to be necessary to protect herself.

A person may also have an imperfect self-defense when an excessive amount of force is used as protection. So, if Gwen was correct in her belief that she needed to use force for her protection, but used excessive force, she receives the benefit of reduced liability. Again, there must be a reasonable, although incorrect, belief that the amount of force used was necessary.

The concept of self-defense is extended to the defense of others. In such situations, one may be privileged to harm another to prevent that person from injuring or killing someone else. Just as with an imperfect self-defense, if one has a mistaken, but reasonable, belief that another is in danger, and kills as a result of that belief, then he or she is responsible for voluntary manslaughter and not murder. Also, if one uses deadly force when a lesser amount of force would have been sufficient to stay the attack, liability is limited to manslaughter, provided the belief that deadly force was necessary was reasonable under the circumstances.

Section 4.2(c.3) Involuntary Manslaughter

The lowest form of criminal homicide in most jurisdictions is involuntary manslaughter; sometimes named second-degree manslaughter. In most instances involuntary manslaughter is a form of negligent or reckless manslaughter.

You have already learned the misdemeanor manslaughter rule. In those jurisdictions that recognize the rule, the person who commits the misdemeanor that results in an unintended death is responsible for the lowest form of criminal homicide.

Involuntary manslaughter also refers to negligent homicide, vehicular homicide, and similar statutes that punish for unintended, accidental deaths. The classic vehicular homicide is when a motorist runs a red light, strikes another car, and causes the death of the driver or passenger of that automobile. Some states, such as Illinois, make vehicular homicide a separate crime from involuntary manslaughter and impose a lesser punishment for vehicular homicide.[7]

Be aware that many states now have specific statutes dealing with deaths caused by intoxicated drivers. Often the punishment is greater if the death is the result of a drunk or otherwise impaired driver.

The term "negligent" has a different meaning in criminal law than in civil law. In tort law any act that causes another harm that a reasonable person would not have taken leads to liability. In criminal law more must be shown. The risk taken by the defendant must be high and pose a threat of death or serious bodily injury to the victim. In addition, some jurisdictions require that the defendant be aware of the risk before liability can be imposed. Of course, knowledge can be inferred from the defendant's actions. Some jurisdictions do not require knowledge of the risk (scienter).

Section 4.2(d)   The Model Penal Code Approach to Homicide

The Model Penal Code states that "A person is guilty of criminal homicide if he purposely, knowingly, recklessly, or negligently causes the death of another human being."[8] The Code then classifies all criminal homicides as murder, manslaughter, or negligent homicide. This is done by taking the four mens rea (purposeful, knowing, reckless, and negligent) and setting them into one of the classifications. There is some overlap; for example, under some conditions a reckless homicide is murder, and under other conditions it is manslaughter. Let's look at the specifics of the Code.

As you would guess, all purposeful and knowing homicides are murder under the Model Penal Code. Additionally, a reckless homicide is murder when committed "under circumstances manifesting extreme indifference to the value of human life." The Code then incorporates a "felony-murder" type rule, by stating that recklessness and indifference to human life are presumed if the accused was engaged in the commission or attempted commission of robbery, rape, arson, burglary, kidnapping, or felonious escape. So, if an accused is involved in one of those crimes, and a death results, then he may be charged with murder under the Code. Note that the Code only creates a presumption of recklessness and indifference, which may be overcome at trial. Murder is the highest form of homicide, and the Code declares it to be a felony of the first degree.

Manslaughters are felonies of the second degree under the Code. All reckless homicides, except those described above, are manslaughters. Just as was true under the common law, the Code contains a provision that reduces heat-of-passion murders to manslaughter. Specifically, the Code states that a homicide, which would normally be murder, is manslaughter when it is "committed under the influence of extreme mental or emotional disturbance for which there is reasonable explanation or excuse. The reasonableness of such explanation or excuse shall be determined from the viewpoint of a person in the actor's situation under the circumstances he believes them to be."

Last, negligent homicides are entitled just that and are felonies of the third degree.

Section 4.2(e) Life, Death, and Homicide

The actus reus of murder and manslaughter is the taking of a human life. Determining when life begins and ends can be a problem in criminal law, especially when dealing with fetuses.

At common law it was not a crime to destroy a fetus, unless it was "born alive." To be born alive the fetus must leave its mother's body and exhibit some ability to live independently. Some courts required that the umbilical cord be cut and that the fetus show its independence thereafter before it was considered a human life. Breathing and crying are both proof of the viability of the child.

Today, many states have enacted feticide statutes. Those statutes focus on the viability of the fetus. Once it can be shown that the fetus is viable, that is, could live independently if it were born, then anyone who causes its death has committed feticide. Of course, this does not apply to abortion. Since the United States Supreme Court decision *Roe v. Wade,* 410 U.S. 113 (1973), a woman possesses a limited right to abort a fetus she carries. As such, states may not prohibit abortions that are protected under that decision. The primary purpose of feticide statutes is to punish those individuals who kill fetuses without the mother's approval, as occurred in the *Keeler* case found in Chapter 2.

At the other end of the spectrum is death. Medical advances have made the determination of when death occurs more complex than it was only years ago. For a long period of time a person was dead when there was no heartbeat and no breathing. Today, artificial means can be used to sustain both heart action and respiration. That being so, should one be free of criminal homicide in cases where the victim is being kept "alive" by artificial means and there is no reasonable hope of recovery? Should a physician be charged with murder for "pulling the plug" on a patient who has irreversible brain damage and is in a coma? Using the respiration and heart function test it would be criminal homicide to end such a treatment. However, many states now use brain death, rather than respiration and heartbeat, to determine when life has ended. In those states that employ a brain death definition it must be shown that there is a total cessation of brain function before legal death exists. The importance of defining death is illustrated by the following case.

STATE OF ARIZONA
V.
DAVID FIERRO

124 Ariz. 182, 603 P.2d 74 (1979)

* * *

The facts necessary for a resolution of this matter on appeal are as follows. Between 8 and 9 o'clock on the evening of 18 August 1977, Victor Corella was given a ride by Ray Montez and his wife Sandra as they were attempting to locate some marijuana. In the vicinity of 12th Street and Pima, Ray Montez heard his name called from another car. He stopped his car, walked over to the other car and saw that the passenger who had called his name was the defendant Fierro. Defendant told Ray Montez that his brother in the "M," or "Mexican Mafia," had instructed the defendant to kill Corella. Ray Montez told defendant to do it outside the car because he and his wife "did not want to see anything."

Montez returned to his car. Defendant followed and began talking with Corella. Corella got out of the car. Montez started to drive away when defendant began shooting Corella. Corella was shot once in the chest and four times in the head. . . .Corella was maintained on support systems for the next three days while follow-up studies were completed which confirmed the occurrence [sic] of brain death. The supportive measures were terminated and he was pronounced dead on 22 August 1977. . . .

CAUSE OF DEATH
At the trial, Dr. Hugh McGill, a surgical resident at the Maricopa County Hospital, testified that:

"After surgery he was taken to the intensive-care unit. He was evaluated by a neurosurgeon who felt there was nothing we could do for his brain, he had brain death. He remained somewhat stable over the next two or three days. We had follow-up studies that confirmed our impression of brain death and because of that supportive measures were terminated and he was pronounced dead, I believe, on the 22nd. . . ."

Defendant initially argues that the termination of support systems by attendant doctors three days after Corella suffered "brain death" was the cause of Corella's death [and as such, he could not be responsible for Corella's death]. . . .

In the instant case, the body of the victim was breathing, though not spontaneously, and blood was pulsating through his body before the life support mechanisms were withdrawn. Because there was an absence of cardiac and circulatory arrest, under the common-law rule he would not have been legally dead. Under the Harvard Medical School test and Proposal of the National Conference of Commissioners on Uniform State Laws he was, in fact, dead before the life supports were withdrawn as he had become "brain" or "neurologically" dead prior to that time. We believe that while the common-law definition of death is still sufficient to establish death, the [brain death test] is also a valid test for death in Arizona. . . .

Section 4.2(f) Suicide

Successful suicide was a crime under the common law of England. The property owned by the one who committed suicide was forfeited to (taken by) the Crown. In early American common law attempted suicide was a crime, usually punished as a misdemeanor. Today suicide is not treated as a crime. However, it is possible to restrain and examine individuals who have attempted to commit suicide under civil psychiatric commitment laws.

It continues to be criminal to encourage or aid another to commit suicide. In most situations such a commission is treated as murder.

Section 4.2(g) Corpus Delicti

Corpus delicti is a Latin phrase that translates, "the body of a crime." Prosecutors have the burden of proving the corpus delecti of crimes at trial. Every crime has a corpus delicti. It refers to the substance of the crime. For example, in murder cases the corpus delicti is the death of a victim and the act that caused the death. In arson, the corpus delicti is a burned structure and the cause of the fire.

A confession of an accused is never enough to prove corpus delicti. There must be either direct proof or evidence supporting a confession.

In murder cases the corpus delicti can usually be proved by an examination of the victim's corpse. After an autopsy a physician will usually be prepared to testify that the alleged act either did, or could have, caused the death. In some instances, the body of a victim cannot be located. Such "no body" cases make the job of the prosecution harder. Even so, if there is evidence that establishes that the person is dead, such as blood stains and discovered personal affects, then murder may be proven. Of course, the prosecution must also show that the defendant caused the death. So, if a defendant confesses to a murder, or makes other incriminating statements, and no other evidence is found, no corpus delicti exists, and the defendant cannot be convicted. However, if blood matching the victim's is discovered where the defendant stated the murder occurred, then a murder conviction can be sustained.

SECTION 4.3 ASSAULT AND BATTERY

Assault and **battery** are two different crimes, although they commonly occur together. As with homicide, all states have made assaults and batteries criminal by statute.

A battery is an intentional touching of another that is either offensive or harmful. The mens rea element varies between the states; however, most now provide for both intentional and negligent battery. Of course, negligence in criminal law involves a greater risk than in civil law. To be negligent in criminal law there must be a disregard of a high risk of injury to another; in tort law one need only show a disregard of an ordinary risk. The Model Penal Code provides for purposeful, knowing, and reckless batteries. In addition, if one uses a deadly weapon, negligence may give rise to a battery charge. Otherwise, negligence may not provide the basis for a battery conviction.

LEGAL TERMS

corpus delicti
Latin phrase meaning "the body of the crime." Refers to the substance of the crime. In murder, the corpus delicti is the death of the victim and the act of the defendant which caused the death. A burned structure and the act that caused the fire are the corpus delicti of arson.

assault
1. To put another in fear or apprehension of an imminent battery.
2. An attempted battery.

battery
An intentional (or reckless) touching of another that is harmful or offensive.

The actus reus of battery is a touching. An individual need not touch someone with his or her actual person to commit a battery. Objects that are held are considered extensions of the body. If Sherry strikes Doug with an iron, she has battered him regardless of the fact that her person never came into contact with his. Likewise, items thrown at another are extensions of the person who took the act of propelling them into the air. If Doug were to injure Sherry with a knife he threw at her, then he has battered her.

A touching must be either offensive or harmful to be a battery. Of course, any resulting physical injury is proof of harm. The problem arises when one touches another in a manner found offensive to the person being touched, but there is no apparent physical injury. For example, a man who touches a woman's breast without her consent has committed a battery because the touching is offensive. If a person touches another in an angry manner a battery has been committed, even though the touching was not intended to injure the party and in fact does no harm.

There are two breeds of assault. First, when a person puts another in fear or apprehension of an imminent battery an assault has been committed. For example, if Gary attempts to strike Terry, but Terry evades the swing by ducking, Gary has committed an assault. The rule does not require that the victim actually experience fear; apprehension of an impending battery is sufficient. Apprehension is simply an expectation of an unwanted event. Also, the threat must be imminent to rise to the level of an assault. A threat that one will be battered in the future is not sufficient. So, if Terry told Gary that he was "going to kick the shit out of him in one hour," there is no assault.

Since an apprehension by the victim is required, there is no assault under this theory if the victim was not aware of the assault. For example, if X swings his arm at Y intending to scare Y, but Y has her back turned and does not see X's behavior, then there is no assault. This is not true of batteries. If X strikes Y a battery has been committed, regardless of whether Y saw the punch coming.

The second type of assault is an attempted battery. This definition remedies the problem just discussed. Any unsuccessful battery is an assault, regardless of the victim's knowledge of the act. Of course, it must be determined that the act in question would have been a battery if it had been completed.

To prove battery it must be shown that a contact was made. This is not necessary to prove an assault. However, it is possible to have both an assault and battery. If John sees Henry swing the baseball bat that strikes him, there has been an assault and battery. However, due to the doctrine of merger the defendant will only be punished for the higher crime of battery.

Section 4.3(a) Aggravated Assault and Battery

Under special circumstances an assault or battery can be classified as aggravated. If aggravated, a higher penalty is imposed. The process of defining such crimes as more serious than simple assaults and batteries varies. Statutes may call such crimes aggravated assault or battery; or may refer to specific crimes under a special name, such as assault with intent to kill; or may simply use the facts at the sentencing stage to enhance (increase) the sentence; or may refer to such as a higher assault, such as felony assault rather than misdemeanor assault. In any event, the following facts commonly aggravate an assault or battery.

The assault is aggravated if the assault or battery is committed while the actor is engaged in the commission of another crime. So, if a man batters a woman while possessing the specific intent to rape her, he has committed an aggravated battery. This is true regardless of whether the rape was completed. If a defendant is stopped before he has committed the rape, but after he has assaulted or battered the victim, there has been an aggravated battery. Hence the crime may be titled "assault with an intent to commit rape" or "assault with intent to murder."

It is also common to make assault and battery committed on persons of some special status more serious. Law enforcement officers or other public officials often fall into this category. Of course, the crime must relate to the performance or status of the officer to be aggravated. For example, if an off-duty police officer is struck by an angry neighbor over a boundary dispute, the battery is not aggravated. Examples of other protected classes of individuals are minors and the mentally disabled.

The extent of injury to the victim may also lead to an increased charge. Usually a battery may be aggravated if the harm rises to the level of "serious bodily injury." Some states specifically state that certain injuries aggravate the crime of battery, such as the loss of an eye. Mayhem, a related crime, is discussed next.

SECTION 4.4 MAYHEM

Mayhem was a common-law crime. Mayhem is the crime of intentionally dismembering or disfiguring a person. The crime has an interesting origin. In England all men were to be available to fight for the king. It was a serious crime to injure a man in such a manner as to make him unable to fight for the king. Early punishments for mayhem were incarceration, death, and the imposition

LEGAL TERMS

mayhem
The crime of intentionally dismembering or disfiguring another.

of the same injury that was inflicted on the victim. Originally, only dismemberment that could prevent a man from fighting for the king was punished as mayhem. As such, cutting off a man's leg or arm was punishable, while cutting off an ear was not. Of course, causing a disfigurement was not mayhem.

Today, both disfigurement and dismemberment fall under mayhem statutes. Many jurisdictions specifically state what injuries must be sustained for a charge of mayhem. Causing another to lose an eye, ear, or limb are examples, as is castration.

Some states no longer have mayhem statutes, but have chosen to treat such crimes as aggravated batteries.

SECTION 4.5 SEX CRIMES

This section deals with crimes that involve sex. Keep in mind that crimes such as assault and battery may be sexually motivated. For example, if a man touches a woman's breast he has committed a battery (provided that the touching was unwelcome).

The phrase "sex crimes" actually encompasses a variety of sexually motivated crimes. Rape, sodomy, incest, and sexually motivated batteries and murders are included. Obscenity, prostitution, abortion, distribution of child pornography, and public nudity are examples of other sex-related offenses.

While certain offenses are universally prohibited, other offenses vary between the states. For example, rape is criminal in all states, while prostitution is not.

Section 4.5(a) Rape

Under the common law the elements of **rape** were 1. Sexual intercourse with 2. a woman, not the man's wife 3. committed without the victim's consent and by using force. Many problems were encountered with this definition. First, the common-law definition required that the rapist be a man. Hence, women and male minors could not be convicted of rape. Also, the **marital rape exception** provided that men could not be convicted of raping their wives. Similarly, a man could not be charged with battering his wife if the battery was inflicted in an effort to force sex. This exception was founded upon the theory that when women married they consented to sex with their husbands upon demand. Additionally, many courts wrote that to permit a woman to charge her husband with such a crime would lead to a destruction of the family unit. Finally, the last requirement, with force and without consent, led

LEGAL TERMS

rape
Sexual intercourse with another without that person's consent. Additionally, it is sometimes unlawful to engage in sexual relations with consenting parties, such as minors and incompetents.

marital rape exception
A common-law rule that held that a husband could not be charged with the rape of his wife. The rule no longer exists, in its original form, in any state.

many courts to require victims to resist the attack to the utmost and to continue to resist during the rape.

States have changed the common-law definition of rape to remedy the problems discussed above. First, most states have worded their statutes to permit minors and women to be charged with rape. While there are few cases of women actually raping men, or other women, there are several cases where women have been convicted as principals to the crime.[9] The Model Penal Code is gender-neutral as to all sex crimes, except rape.[10]

The marital rape exception has been abolished in most states. A few states have retained the rule in modified form, such as Ohio, which provides immunity to a husband, except when he is separated from his wife.[11]

Finally, the last requirement has changed significantly. A person need not resist to the extent required under the common law. What is required now is proof that the victim did resist. However, a victim need not risk life or serious bodily injury in an attempt to prevent the rape. So if a woman simply tells a man on a date "I don't want to," there has been inadequate resistance. The result would be different if the man produced a gun and told the woman he would kill her if she resisted.

So, the elements of rape, under new statutes, are: 1. Sexual intercourse 2. with another against that person's will or without that person's consent and 3. by the use of force or under such a threat of force that a reasonable person would have believed that resistence would have resulted in serious bodily harm or death.

Note that one element has not changed, the definition of sexual intercourse. Generally, the contact must be penis-vagina; anal sex, fellatio, and other acts are usually punished under sodomy statutes. The requirement is the same today as it was under the common law. The "slightest penetration" of the woman's vulva is sufficient. The man need not ejaculate.

Some states grade rape according to the extent of injuries that the victim received and whether the victim knew the rapist. The Model Penal Code punishes rape as a felony in the second degree, unless serious bodily injury occurs or the victim was not a social companion of the rapist, in which case the rape is of the first degree.

Section 4.5(b) Nonforcible Rape

Under some circumstances, one may commit a rape even though the other party consented to the sexual contact. So-called **statutory rape** is such a crime. The actus reus of statutory rape is sexual intercourse with someone under a specified age, commonly sixteen. The purpose of the law is to protect those the law

SIDEBAR

RAPE IN THE UNITED STATES
In 1989 there were 94,504 reported forcible rapes in the United States. This number includes attempted rapes and assaults with intent to rape; however, nonforcible rapes, such as statutory rape, are not included. In total, 75 out of every 100,000 women were subjected to a rape or attempted rape. Since 1985 the female rape rate has increased by 3 percent. The actual number of rapes is likely much higher, as rape is believed to be one of the most under-reported crimes.

Source: Uniform Crime Reports, U.S. Department of Justice, Federal Bureau of Investigation, August 5, 1990 at pp. 14–15.

LEGAL TERMS

statutory rape
The act of sexual intercourse with another who is under a specified age. Whether the victim consented is not relevant. In most states the crime is one of strict liability. There are a few states that recognize an exception in those instances where the defendant possessed a "good faith" or reasonable belief that the victim was of lawful age to engage in sexual activity.

presumes are too young to make a mature decision concerning sex. Hence, consent is not relevant. So, a rape has occurred when a girl under sixteen consents to sexual intercourse with an eighteen-year-old male.

In most states statutory rape is a strict liability crime. The act of having sex with someone below the specified age is proof alone of guilt. No showing of mens rea is required. A few states impose a knowledge requirement. In those states, if the accused can convince the jury that there was reason to believe that the other party was "of age," then the accused is acquitted. For example, if a fifteen-year-old girl tells a boy that she is seventeen, she indeed looks seventeen, and she shows the boy a falsified identification bearing that age, he would have a defense to statutory rape. Alaska is one of the states that recognizes the reasonable belief exception due to that state's Supreme Court decision *State v. Guest*.

STATE V. GUEST

583 P.2d 836 (Alaska 1978)

Matthews, Justice.

The question presented in the State's petition for review is whether an honest and reasonable mistake of fact regarding a victim's age may serve as a defense to a charge of statutory rape. . . .

. . . The parties entered into a stipulation that "the evidence expected to be presented at trial will support a reasonable belief on the part of each defendant that the alleged victim, age 15, was sixteen years of age or older at the time of the alleged act of intercourse." In light of that stipulation, the [trial] court ordered that it would instruct the jurors as follows:

It is a defense to a charge of statutory rape that the defendant reasonably and in good faith believed that the female person was of the age of sixteen years or older even though, in fact, she was under the age of sixteen years. If from all the evidence you have a reasonable doubt as to the question whether defendant reasonably and in good faith believed that she was sixteen years of age or older, you must give the defendant the benefit of that doubt and find him not guilty.

The state brings a petition for review from that order.

* * *

. . . It is a serious felony. If the offender is less than nineteen years of age, he may be imprisoned for up to twenty years. If he is nineteen years of age or older, he may be punished by imprisonment for any term of years.

. . . To refuse such a defense [reasonable belief] would be to impose criminal liability without any criminal mental element. The defense of reasonable mistake of fact is generally allowed in criminal cases to permit the defendant to show that he lacked criminal intent. When that opportunity is foreclosed the result is strict criminal liability.

* * *

For the foregoing reasons, we hold that a charge of statutory rape is defensible where an honest and reasonable mistake of fact as to the victim's age is shown. . . .

In many states only females are protected by statutory rape laws. If a boy of fifteen years has sex with a girl of seventeen years the law will not punish her as they would the boy if the ages were turned around. It has been alleged that such treatment is violative of the Equal Protection Clause of the United States Constitution. The United States Supreme Court has rejected that claim by reasoning that one of the goals of such statutes is the prevention of teenage pregnancy. Since females can be impregnated, states have a legitimate interest in prosecuting males who have sex with females who are under the age of consent.[12] Using this analysis a state may prosecute males only, since females cannot impregnate young men or women. However, many acts by adult females (or adult males to young males) may be prosecuted under another law, such as child molestation or criminal deviate conduct.

Similar to statutory rape, having sex with those who are incapable of consenting due to mental or emotional disability is also rape.

BOZARTH
V.
STATE OF INDIANA

520 N.E.2d 460 (Ind. App. 1988)

* * *

The facts most favorable to the judgment reveal that on the evening of January 30, 1986, Bozarth went to the Goodwill Industries dormitory in Indianapolis and was introduced to A.N., the victim. A.N. was born deaf and legally blind. Although she was 21 years of age, she was mildly retarded with a mental age of approximately 10 years old and an I.Q. of between 50 to 70.

Bozarth was deaf, 24 years old and known to be a quick learner. The Goodwill Vocational Counselor assigned him to the commercial baking training program because he demonstrated the higher functioning capabilities that the program required. The training program exposed him to other students with varying degrees of disabilities and he often explained lessons to those students.

After visiting with another acquaintance at the dormitory, Bozarth went to A.N.'s room and was invited in by A.N. Bozarth communicated with A.N. by sign language and by writing notes. They viewed photographs together, exchanged addresses, and began kissing. Bozarth indicated he wanted sex and asked A.N. to go into her restroom with him. Bozarth took their clothes off. They engaged in sexual intercourse on the floor and while seated on the toilet seat. As Bozarth was leaving, he told a resident of the dormitory that he had sex with A.N. and that her virginity was now gone.

At trial, Mary Stewart, a social worker and employee of Midtown Mental Health Center, testified that A.N. was unable to give consent to sexual intercourse at the time of the incident. A.N.'s understanding of physiology and reproduction was rudimentary and her ability to interpret the knowledge and make choices was the same as a child of 6 or 7 years of age. Even though she had two sex education discussions previous to this incident, A.N.'s evaluation indicated she did not understand the ramifications and nature of sexual conduct.

Evidence of A.N.'s inability to consent to sexual intercourse was corroborated by Dr. Alan Schetzer.

The jury returned a verdict of guilty on the rape charge and Bozarth received the presumptive sentence of ten years. His sentence, however, was later reduced to six years, upon Bozarth's motion for a modification of sentence.

* * *

. . .The factfinder could have reasonably concluded that A.N. was incapable of giving consent to sexual intercourse with Bozarth. . .

[Judgment Affirmed.]

Section 4.5(c) Sodomy

Sodomy is defined by *Webster's New World Dictionary* (3rd Ed., 1988) as "any sexual intercourse held to be abnormal, esp. bestiality or anal intercourse between two male persons." Many statutes now include sodomy in "criminal deviate conduct" statutes. Sodomy is prohibited in most states, and in most jurisdictions fellatio, cunnilingus, bestiality, homosexual activity, anal sex, and sometimes masturbation are included. There is substantial disagreement concerning whether such acts should be prohibited between consenting adults. Those who support sodomy laws usually do so for religious reasons. Those who oppose such laws contend that two adults should be permitted to engage in any sexual conduct they desire, provided that no one is injured. In any event, one practical problem exists; enforcement of sodomy laws is nearly impossible. Determining what sexual acts people engage in privately is not an easy task. Additionally, law enforcement appears to have no incentive to enforce such laws when there appears to be no resulting injury, and there is substantial noncompliance with many sodomy laws, such as fellatio and cunnilingus.

Those who oppose enforcement of sodomy laws between consenting adults do not oppose punishment of those who force acts of sodomy on others. Under the common law a man had to have penile-vulva contact to commit rape. If a man forced oral or anal sex on a woman he committed sodomy. Sodomy was also punished severely. Many states continue to prohibit sodomy, even in marriage. Some prosecutors are using sodomy laws to punish

LEGAL TERMS

sodomy
  A sexual act against nature. A prohibited sex act. Fellatio, cunnilingus, bestiality, homosexual behavior, and anal sex are commonly included in sodomy statutes.

homosexuals for their sexual activity, and the United States Supreme Court has upheld such applications of sodomy laws.[13]

Section 4.5(d) Rape Shield Laws

So-called "**rape shield laws**" were enacted in the 1970s and 1980s in an effort to protect rape victims from harrassment by defense attorneys at trial. Prior to such laws defense attorneys often would use evidence of a victim's prior sexual conduct to infer that the victim consented to the act. It is thought that the humiliation of the rape itself matched with this treatment at trial accounted for many unreported rapes.

In an effort to protect victims from unwarranted abuse at trial, rape shield laws are enacted. Evidence of prior sexual conduct, except with the defendant, is not permitted at trial. Also, evidence of a victim's reputation in the community is inadmissible.

Section 4.5(e) Incest

Sex between family members is incest. Incest is a crime. Generally, law enforcement is concerned with abuse of children, although it is also a crime for two consenting adult family members to engage in sex. Often, when an adult family member is involved with a child, other statutes, such as child molestation laws, will also apply.

The actus reus of incest is intercourse, or other sexual conduct, between family members. Normally, incest laws parallel marriage laws for a definition of family. That is, if two people are permitted to marry under state law, then they are also permitted to engage in sex, regardless of marriage. It is common for states to prohibit marriage of individuals of first cousin affinity and closer.

If the incestuous party is a parent, courts often attempt to seek family counseling and therapy, rather than incarceration. However, in extreme situations criminal penalties can be severe, civil remedies exist to remove the child from the home, as well as to terminate parental rights.

Section 4.5(f) Sex Offenses Against Children

Most states have a number of statutes specifically aimed at protecting children from sexual abuse and exploitation. Indiana has five statutes that directly pertain to sexual activity with children. Those statutes are:

Oral Sex with Father This four-year-old girl's favorite pastime was drawing pictures, and she often drew people with large heads and mouths. Authorities informed her teacher that the child had been sexually abused. The child's father had forced and bribed her to perform oral sex on him. This began when she was three and ended when the father was removed from the home when the child was four years old. *Courtesy Lively, Sexual Development of Young Children (Albany, NY: Delmar Publishers Inc., 1991).*

INDIANA CODE §35–42–4–3 Child Molesting

(a) A person who, with a child under twelve (12) years of age, performs or submits to sexual intercourse or deviate sexual conduct commits child molesting, a Class B felony. However, the offense is a Class A felony if it is committed by using or threatening the use of deadly force, or while armed with a deadly weapon, or if it results in serious bodily injury.

(b) A person who, with a child under twelve (12) years of age, performs or submits to any fondling or touching, of either the child or the older person, with intent to arouse or to satisfy the

LEGAL TERMS

rape shield laws
Statutes that prohibit evidence concerning a victim's sexual history and reputation in the community to be admitted at trial. However, evidence of a sexual history with the defendant is admitted.

sexual desire of either the child or the older person, commits child molesting, a Class C felony. However, the offense is a Class A felony if it is committed by using or threatening the use of deadly force, or while armed with a deadly weapon.

(c) A person sixteen (16) years of age or older who, with a child of twelve (12) years of age or older but under sixteen (16) years of age, performs or submits to sexual intercourse or deviate sexual conduct commits child molesting, a Class C felony. However, the offense is a Class A felony if it is committed by using or threatening the use of deadly force, or while armed with a deadly weapon.

(d) A person sixteen (16) years of age, or older who, with a child twelve (12) years of age or older but under sixteen (16) years of age, performs or submits to any fondling or touching, of either the child or the older person, with intent to arouse or to satisfy the sexual desires of either the child or the older person, commits child molesting, a Class D felony. However, the offense is a Class B felony if it is committed by using or threatening the use of deadly force, or while armed with a deadly weapon.

(e) It is a defense that the accused person reasonably believed that the child was sixteen (16) years of age or older at the time of the conduct.

(f) It is a defense that the child is or has ever been married.

INDIANA CODE §35–42–4–4 Child Exploitation

(b) Any person who knowingly or intentionally:
   (1) manages, produces, sponsors, presents, exhibits, photographs, films, or videotapes any peformance or incident that includes sexual conduct by a child under sixteen (16) years of age; or
   (2) disseminates, exhibits to another person, offers to disseminate or exhibit to another person, or sends or brings into Indiana for dissemination or exhibition matter that depicts or describes sexual conduct by a child under sixteen (16) years of age; commits child exploitation. . . .

(c) A person who knowingly or intentionally possess:
   (1) a picture;
   (2) a drawing;
   (3) a photograph;
   (4) a negative image;
   (5) undeveloped film;

(6) a motion picture;

(7) a videotape; or

(8) any pictorial representation;

that depicts sexual conduct by a child who is, or appears to be, less than sixteen (16) years of age and that lacks serious literary, artistic, political or scientific value commits possession of child pornography. . . .

INDIANA CODE §35–42–4–5 Vicarious Sexual Gratification

(a) A person eighteen (18) years of age or older who knowingly or intentionally directs, aids, induces, or causes a child under the age of sixteen (16) to touch or fondle himself or another child under the age of sixteen (16) with intent to arouse or satisfy the sexual desires of a child or the older person commits vicarious sexual gratification. . . .

(b) A person eighteen (18) years of age or older who knowingly or intentionally directs, aids, induces, or causes a child under the age of sixteen (16) to:

(1) engage in sexual intercourse with another child under sixteen (16) years of age.

(2) engage in sexual conduct with an animal other than a human being; or

(3) engage in deviate sexual conduct with another person . . . commits vicarious sexual gratification. . . .

INDIANA CODE §35–42–4–6 Child Solicitation

A person eighteen (18) years of age or older who knowingly or intentionally solicits a child under twelve (12) years of age to engage in:

(1) sexual intercourse;

(2) deviate sexual conduct; or

(3) any fondling or touching intended to arouse or satisfy the sexual desires of either the child or the older person; commits child solicitation. . . .

INDIANA CODE §35–42–4–7 Child Seduction

(e) If a person who is:

(1) at least eighteen (18) years of age; and

(2) the guardian, adoptive parent, adoptive grandparent, custodian . . . of a child at least sixteen (16) years of age but less than
eighteen (18) years of age; engages in sexual intercourse or deviate sexual conduct with the child, the person commits child
seduction. . . .

Note that statutory rape falls under the child molestation
statute in Indiana. Also, the defense of a good faith and reasonable
belief that a child is of statutory age is recognized by statute.

Man with Penis
This five-year-old
girl told her
babysitter that
this was a picture
of her grand-
father. She added,
"Grandpa,
another man, and
I took off our
clothes and
played games and
took pictures."
The babysitter
repeated the
conversation and
gave the pictures
to the child's
mother.
Courtesy Lively,
Sexual Develop-
ment of Young
Children *(Albany,
NY: Delmar
Publishers Inc.,
1991).*

Sex crimes against children are often committed by people a child knows and trusts.
Courtesy Committee for Children.

The number of people charged with committing sex crimes against children is increasing. Many of those charged are non-biological guardians. This has led to statutes such as I.C. 35–42–4–7, "Child seduction," which was added to Indiana's sex offenses statutes in 1987.

SECTION 4.6   KIDNAPPING AND FALSE IMPRISONMENT

Section 4.6(a)   Kidnapping

Kidnapping was a misdemeanor in common law, although it was regarded as a very serious crime, often resulting in life

LEGAL TERMS

kidnapping
    The 1. unlawful 2. taking and confinement and 3. asportation (carrying away) of 4. another person 5. by force, threat, fraud, or deception. All kidnappings involve a false imprisonment.

During investigations and trials, anatomically correct dolls are used with children who are victims of sex offenders.
Courtesy June Hornest, Teach A Bodies Co.

imprisonment. Felonies were often punished by death at the early common law. Today kidnapping is a felony and carries a harsh penalty in most states. Additionally, if the kidnapping takes the victim across state lines, the crime is a violation of the Federal Kidnapping Act.[14] The federal government, usually the Federal Bureau of Investigation, may become involved in any kidnapping twenty-four hours after the victim has been seized by virtue of the Federal Kidnapping Act, which creates a presumption that the victim has been transported across state lines after that period of time.[15]

The elements of kidnapping are 1. The unlawful 2. taking and confinement and 3. asportation of 4. another person 5. by use of force, threat, fraud, or deception.

The taking of the victim must be unlawful. As such, arrests made by police officers while engaged in their lawful duties are not kidnappings. Neither is it kidnapping for a guardian to take a ward from one place to another, so long as the action is lawful. However, when an officer, or other, acts completely without legal authority, he or she may not be shielded from liability.

There must be a taking and confinement. Confinement is broadly construed. If Pat puts a gun to Craig's back and orders him to walk a half-a-mile to Pat's home, there has been a confinement. Generally, there must be a restriction of the victim's freedom to take alternative action.

This taking and confinement must occur as a result of threat, force, fraud, or deception. Of course, Pat's gun in the above example is ample threat to satisfy this requirement. Deception may also be used to gain control over the victim. For example, if Jon convinces his estranged wife to enter a house under the pretense of discussing their marital difficulties and then locks the door, he has fraudulently gained control over her.

Finally, there must be an asportation of the victim. Asportation means movement. The issue of the amount of movement necessary to meet this requirement is the most controversial question concerning kidnapping as a crime. The Model Penal Code and most states now hold that if the kidnapping is incidental to the commission of another crime, there is insufficient asportation; some courts speak in terms of a movement of a "substantial distance."[16] To be incidental a kidnapping must simply be a product of an intent to commit another crime. If a bank robber orders a teller to move from her window to the safe to fill a bag with money, the first four elements of kidnapping are present; however, the fourth element, asportation, has not been established since the movement was only incidental to the robbery. The result may be different if the teller was ordered to move to the safe for the purpose of raping her. The issue of substantial distance was raised in the following case, *Commonwealth v. Hughes.* In this case the court focused on whether the movement substantially increased the risk of harm to victim.

COMMONWEALTH
V.
HUGHES

399 A.2d 694 (Pa. Super. 1979)

[The appellant approached the victim, Ms. Helfrich, who was seated on a park bench.] Appellant asked Ms. Helfrich if she wanted to go for a ride or smoke some marijuana with him. When Ms. Helfrich refused, appellant left. Minutes later, the appellant returned, placed a sharp kitchen knife to her throat, and stated, "I think you are going for a ride." Appellant forced Ms. Helfrich to walk to his car one and one-half blocks away and threatened to kill her if she resisted. Once in the car, he drove around the Media area in a reckless manner for approximately two miles and stopped his car in an abandoned lot surrounded by trees. He then forced Ms. Helfrich into the wooded area where he raped her. . . .

. . . "A person is guilty of kidnapping if he unlawfully removes another a substantial distance, under the circumstances, from the place where he is found or if he unlawfully confines another for a substantial period in a place of isolation. . . .

The framers of the Model Penal Code were aware of the experience of other jurisdictions when they drafted the model kidnapping statute. They recognized that "[w]hen an especially outrageous crime is committed there will be a public clamor for the extreme penalty and it is asking too much of public officials and juries to resist such pressures. . . . To combat the undesirable situation of charging kidnapping to obtain a higher permissible sentence, the framers of the Model Penal Code drafted the kidnapping statute restrictively. . . . The drafters made explicit their "purpose to preclude kidnapping convictions based on trivial changes of location having no bearing on the evil at hand." Model Penal Code §212.1, Comment (Tent. Draft No.11, p.16, 1960).

Drawing from the experience of other jurisdictions, the comments to the Model Code, and the fact that the Pennsylvania statute is similar to the Model Penal Code Statute of kidnapping, it is clear to us that the legislature intended to exclude from kidnapping the incidental movement of a victim during the commission of a crime which does not substantially increase the risk of harm to the victim.

Turning to the case at hand, we find that the movement of the victim was not a trivial incident to the other crime charged. Although the victim was removed only a distance of two miles, the wooded area to which she was brought was in an isolated area, seemingly beyond the aid of her friends and police. Under the circumstances, two miles is a substantial enough distance to place the victim in a completely different environmental setting removed from the security of familiar surroundings. (In addition, the movement itself seriously endangered the victim as she was subject to a knife poised at her throat and to the reckless driving of appellant. At one point, appellant drove onto a one-way street in the wrong direction.) . . . Accordingly, the conviction is sustained.

Many statutes specifically state that if the act of asportation and confinement occurs in furtherance of named crimes, then there is a kidnapping. Such statutes commonly include kidnapping for ransom, political reasons, rape, and murder. It is also common to upgrade kidnappings for these reasons. One type of kidnapping that is usually graded low is the taking of a child by a parent in violation of a court order.

Section 4.6(b) Parental Kidnapping

With a dissolution of marriage comes the separation of property owned by the couple, as well as a custody order if the couple has children. Often, costly and bitter custody disputes are also the result of divorce. In recent years "childnapping," or kidnapping of one's own child in violation of a custody order, has received much public attention.

Due to the rise in the number of such acts, new statutes specifically aimed at parental kidnapping have been adopted. The federal government entered this arena in 1980 by enacting the Parental Kidnapping Prevention Act.[17] While this statute does not concern itself with criminal sanctions for childnapping, it does require that all states respect child-custody orders of other states. That is, a person cannot escape a court order concerning custody of the child by kidnapping the child and fleeing to another jurisdiction. Interestingly, the federal government has left the actual punishment of parental kidnapping to the states. The Federal Kidnapping Act specifically excludes such acts from its reach. So, kidnapping by a parent must be punished in a state court. This may occur in the state from which the child is taken or in any state where the parent takes the child.

Kidnapping of one's own child is normally punished less severely than other kidnappings. This is sensible since many "child-nappings" do not create a risk to the child's welfare; rather, they are the result of an overzealous, loving parent. Obviously, the crime should be punished because of the harm to the custodial parent, but the crime does not have the same evil spirit a kidnapping with an intent to rape or murder does. Regretfully, not all parents have innocent motives, as evidenced by the *Siemer* case. Read this case carefully and look for the interesting twist of law.

STATE OF IOWA
V.
LARRY THOMAS SIEMER

454 N.W.2d 857 (1990)

* * *

I. Background facts and proceedings.

Defendant Larry Siemer is the live-in boyfriend of Donna Simmons, and together they were charged in June 1988 with the kidnapping of Donna's seven-year-old son, Tracey. The charge arose out of events beginning in December 1987 and continuing until April 1988 when Tracey was rescued by Des Moines police and child protection workers. The unspeakable horror of the case is revealed through the testimony of the young victim, his ten-year-old sister April, and the authorities who finally came to Tracey's aid.

The evidence discloses that Siemer began physically abusing Tracey in the fall of 1987. The abuse escalated after Christmas, at which time Tracey was banished to the furnace room of the basement. The room's entrance was covered with a dirty blanket, its windows were boarded over, and there was no light. There Siemer handcuffed Tracey to the rusty box springs that served as his bed. Tracey had no access to a toilet and was forced to lie in his own waste. A makeshift toilet made of a bucket and chair was eventually placed next to the bed so that Tracey could relieve himself without being freed from the handcuffs.

Siemer instructed April to handcuff Tracey to his bed every day after school. On Siemer's orders she also released him every morning at 6:30 A.M. to attend school. Tracey spent the weekends locked to his bed in the basement. Siemer told April to feed Tracey "a little food" each day but otherwise to "forget about him."

Tracey testified that from January through April Siemer beat him with a board and belt, hung him naked from a pipe in the ceiling, submerged him in ice water, cut him with a knife across his buttocks, fed him cat food, poured scalding hot water over his lower abdomen and genitals, and threatened him with further abuse if he dared reveal his plight. Medical experts testified that Tracey suffered permanent injuries from the scalding. . . .

III. Kidnapping.

Siemer's challenge to his kidnapping conviction is two-pronged. First, he claims that because an absence of authority to confine is one of the essential elements of the crime, no parent (or person acting on a parent's authority or in loco parentis) could be found guilty of such crime because the authority to confine inheres in the parent/child relationship. . . .

A. Authority. Under Iowa law, the crime of kidnapping charged in this case contains the following elements:
  (1) confinement of the victim;
  (2) without authority or consent;
  (3) with the intent to inflict serious injury or secretly confine.

Iowa Code §710.1 (1989). First-degree kidnapping is established by proof that the person kidnapped (or, in this case, *confined*) was intentionally subjected to torture. Iowa Code §710.2.

The only element in dispute is the one relating to authority. The trial court ruled that the authority of a parent is limited by "the bounds of moderation." Accordingly, the court instructed the jury to determine whether Siemer's conduct "constituted proper discipline, within reason and the bounds of moderation for the best interests of the child, or whether it was conduct of such undue severity or cruelty that it did not constitute proper discipline." Siemer objected to this instruction and proposed the following alternative: "If you find . . . that the defendant was acting as a parent, then you must find the defendant not guilty of kidnapping."

The trial court rejected this instruction.

Siemer contended at trial, and urges on appeal, that the legislature included an "authority" exception within section 710.1 to immunize parents from the crime of kidnapping. He buttresses his argument by reference to the common-law rule developed in child-custody disputes that a parent with lawful custody cannot be found guilty of kidnapping for taking and concealing his or her own child. [cites ommitted]

Like the district court, however, we are unwilling to accept the proposition that concealing a child in the context of a custody dispute is equivalent to concealing a child with the intent to abuse and torture. A parent's right to custody and control of a child is not absolute. . . . Moreover, we have long held in this state that a parent's right to chastise a child does not extend to "cruelty or inhumanity," for if punishment "goes beyond the line of reasonable correction," [the parent's] conduct becomes more or less criminal. . . . Abusive punishment "annuls the parental privilege and subjects the parent to applicable criminal statutes." . . .

Because of the disparate objectives which kidnapping and custodial interference statutes seek to accomplish, we reject Siemer's argument that the limited immunity granted parents in the custody context applies to the case before us. The harm the kidnapping statute addresses is unlawful confinement or asportation which increases the potential or actual injury to the victim. . . . While a parent has the authority to confine or remove a child under reasonable circumstances, we can conceive of no circumstances under which a parent could lawfully exercise such authority while harboring the intent to sexually abuse or subject the child to serious bodily injury. We thus hold that parents, or persons standing *in loco parentis*, are not beyond the reach of the kidnapping statutes as a matter of law. We find no error in the trial court so ruling.

Section 4.6(c) False Imprisonment

The crime of **false imprisonment** is similar to kidnapping, and in fact all kidnappings involve a false imprisonment. The opposite is not true. Not all false imprisonments are kidnappings. A false imprisonment occurs when 1. one person 2. interferes 3. with another's liberty 4. by use of threat or force 5. without authority. The primary distinction between the two crimes is the absense of asportation as an element of false imprisonment.

Today, some states have one statute that encompasses both false imprisonment and kidnapping. Such statutes are drafted so that the crime is graded, often elevating the crime if the motive is ransom, rape, serious bodily injury, or murder.

LEGAL TERMS

false imprisonment
  The 1. intentional 2. interference with 3. another person's liberty 4. by use of threat or force 5. without authority.

REVIEW QUESTIONS

1. What is the primary distinction between first- and second-degree murder?
2. What is felony-murder?
3. What is the difference between an assault and a battery?
4. What is the marital rape exception?
5. John caught his wife having sex with another man. In a fit of rage he killed his wife. What crime has been committed?
6. What is meant by the phrase "imperfect self-defense"?
7. What is the primary distinction between false imprisonment and kidnapping?
8. Under the common law, if a person cut another's limb off, what crime was committed?
9. Give an example of a nonforcible rape.
10. What was the common law definition of murder?

REVIEW PROBLEMS

1. State statute reads: Any act of 1. sexual intercourse 2. with another person 3. against that person's will and 4. by use of force or under such a threat of force that resistance would result in serious bodily injury or death, is rape. Explain how this statutory definition of rape differs from the common law definition.
2. On May 5 Mark and Sam, who had been neighbors for three years, argued over Sam's construction of a ditch, which diverted water onto Mark's property. Mark told Sam to stop

construction of the ditch or he "would pay with his life." The following day, Mark and Sam met again in Sam's garage. Within minutes Mark became very angry and cut Sam's leg with an axe he found in Sam's garage. After cutting Sam he panicked and ran home. Sam attempted to reach a telephone to call for help, but the cut proved fatal.

Mark has been charged with first-degree murder. He claims that he had no intent to kill Sam, rather he only intended to hit him on the leg with the dull, flat side of the axe in an effort to scare Sam. Discuss the facts and explain what crimes could be proved and why.

3. Explain the twist to the kidnapping case, *State v. Siemer,* 454 N.W.2d 857 (Iowa 1990). Was it a traditional kidnapping case?

4. On July 1, 1990, Jeff shot Megan during a bank robbery. Megan remained on life-support systems until September 4, 1991. At that time the systems were disconnected, and she ceased breathing. On June 15, 1991, her physician declared her brain dead. It was not until September 4, 1991, that her family decided to stop the life-support system. Jeff is charged with murder. Discuss any defenses he may have.

5. Penelope and Brenda had been enemies for years. One evening Penelope discovered that Brenda had attempted on many occasions to "pick up" Penelope's boyfriend. Penelope told a friend that she was "going to fix Brenda once and for all—that she was going to mess her face up bad." That evening Penelope waited for Brenda outside of her home and attacked her with a knife. She slashed her in the face four times and cut off one ear. Brenda reported the event to the police, who have turned it over to the county prosecutor's office. As the office legal assistant you have been assigned the task of determining what crime can be charged.

6. State statute reads: "It shall be a felony for any person to purposefully, knowingly, or recklessly cause the death of another person by the use of poison or other toxins." Eddie Farmer spread a toxic insecticide on his crops, which eventually mixed with rainwater and made its way into his neighbor's well. The insecticide was new, but recommended by other farmers who had used it successfully. His neighbor's seven-year-old son, Mikie, died from the poisons in the water. Eddie has been charged with violating the above statute. Is he liable?

7. One evening after a play Tracy was approached by a woman who pointed a pistol at her and ordered her to "give her all her money and jewelry." Tracy removed her jewels and handed them to her, but told her that her money was in her

purse, which was in the trunk of her car. The robber asked her where her car was parked, and Tracy pointed to a car thirty feet away. Tracy was then ordered to go to the automobile, remove the purse, and give it to the robber. She complied, and the woman ran off. The thief was eventually captured and tried for aggravated robbery and kidnapping. She was convicted of both and has appealed the kidnapping conviction. What do you think her argument would be to reverse the kidnapping conviction?

NOTES

[1] Loewy, A., *Criminal Law*, 2nd Ed. (Nutshell Series, St. Paul: West Publishing Co., 1987).

[2] See *Commonwealth v. Redline*, 391 Pa. 486, 137 A.2d 472 (1958).

[3] See LaFave and Scott, *Criminal Law* (Hornbook Series, St. Paul: West Publishing Co., 1986), §7.7.

[4] *State v. Corn*, 278 S.E.2d 221 (N.C. 1981).

[5] *Labelle v. State of Indiana*, 550 N.E.2d 752 (Ind. 1990); see also LaFave and Scott, §7.2(b).

[6] Model Penal Code §210.0(4).

[7] See Ill. Rev. Stat. ch.38 §9–3.

[8] The Model Penal Code addresses homicide at §210.0, et seq.

[9] See 65 Am.Jur.2d *Rape* 28 (1976).

[10] Model Penal Code §213.

[11] Ohio Rev. Code §2907.

[12] *Michael M. v. Superior Court of Sonoma County*, 450 U.S. 464 (1981).

[13] See *Bowers v. Hardwick*, 478 U.S. 186 (1986).

[14] 18 U.S.C §1201.

[15] 18 U.S.C. §1201(b).

[16] Model Penal Code §212.1.

[17] 28 U.S.C. §1738A.

CHAPTER 5
Crimes Against Property and Habitation

Four things belong to a judge: to hear courteously; to answer wisely; to consider soberly; and to decide impartially.

Socrates

OUTLINE

SECTION 5.1 ARSON

Arson is a crime against property. In addition, it is a crime against habitation. Crimes against habitation developed because of importance of peoples' homes. In England and the United States the concept that a "man's home is his castle" is one with great influence. A home is not merely property, but a refuge from the rest of the world. As such, special crimes developed under the common law that sought to protect this important sanctuary. Arson and burglary are such crimes.

In the common law arson was defined very narrowly. It was the 1. malicious 2. burning of a 3. dwelling house of 4. another.

This definition was so narrowly construed that an owner could burn her own property with an intent to defraud her insurer and not be guilty of arson, because she did not burn the dwelling of another.[1] In addition, the structure burned had to be a dwelling, which was defined as a structure which was inhabited by people. This definition did include outhouses and the area directly around the home (curtilage), so long as the area was used frequently by people. However, the burning of businesses and other structures was not arson.

To be a burning the dwelling must actually sustain some damage, although slight damage was sufficient. If the structure was simply charred by the fire, there had been a burning. However, if the structure was only smoke-damaged or discolored by the heat of a fire, which never touched the building, there was no arson. Finally, causing a dwelling to explode was not arson, unless some of the dwelling was left standing after the explosion and was then burned by a fire caused by the explosion.

Under the common law malice was the mens rea of arson. As was true of murder under the common law, malice meant evil intent. However, an intentional or extremely reckless burning would suffice.

Today, the definition of arson has been broadened by statute in most, if not all, states. It is now common to prosecute an owner of property for burning his own building, if the purpose was to defraud an insurer or to cause another injury. Be aware that the fraud may constitute a separate offense: defrauding an insurance carrier. Also, the structure burned need not be a dwelling under most statutes, although most statutes aggravate the crime if a dwelling is burned. While the common law did not recognize explosions as a burning, the Model Penal Code and most statutes do.[2]

The mens rea for arson under the Model Penal Code is purposeful and reckless. If a person starts a fire or causes an

LEGAL TERMS

arson
In the common law arson was the 1. malicious 2. burning 3. of a dwelling 4. of another person. Most states have expanded the definition of arson by statute to include the burning of one's own property and to include any property.

explosion with the purpose of destroying the building or defrauding an insurer, a felony of the second degree has been committed. It is a felony of the third degree to purposely start a fire or cause an explosion and thereby recklessly endanger person or structure.[3] Note that under the Code the fire need not touch the structure, as was required by the common law. Setting the fire is enough to satisfy the burning requirement.

Arson is often graded. The burning of dwellings is usually the highest form of the crime. The burning of uninhabited structures is usually the next highest form of arson, and arson of personal property, if treated as arson, is the lowest.

SECTION 5.2 BURGLARY

The 1. breaking and entering 2. of another's dwelling 3. at night 4. for the purpose of committing a felony once inside, was **burglary** under the common law. A burglary, or entry of a dwelling, may be for the purpose of theft, rape, murder, or another felony. For that reason, burglary is a crime against habitation, as well as against property and person.

The first element, the actus reus, a breaking, can be satisfied by either an actual break-in or by a constructive breaking. If one enters a dwelling by simply passing through an open door or window (a trespass), there is no breaking. Generally, there has to be some act on the part of the defendant to change the condition of the house so as to gain entry. For example, opening an unlocked door or window is a breaking, while passing through an open door or window is not a breaking. Of course, picking a lock and breaking a window or door are breakings.

SIDEBAR

BURGLARY IN THE UNITED STATES
A burglary is committed every ten seconds in the United States. In 1989 there were a total of 3,218,077 burglaries and attempted forcible entries to structures in the United States. Over 1,300 people in every 100,000 were burglarized in 1989.

Source: Uniform Crime Report, U.S. Department of Justice, Federal Bureau of Investigation, August 5, 1990.

LEGAL TERMS

burglary
In the common law the elements of burglary were: 1. the breaking and entering 2. of another's dwelling 3. at night 4. with the intent of committing a felony. By statute, burglaries now include most structures and can be committed at either day or night.

Increased crime matched with public dissatisfaction with law enforcement has led to increased citizen participation in crime prevention.

A burglar may also gain entry by a constructive breaking. A constructive breaking occurs when one uses fraud or force to gain entry. So, if a burglar poses as a telephone repairman to gain entry, then the breaking element has been satisfied. The same is true if the owner consents to the burglar's entry under threat or the use of force.

Once the breaking occurs there must be an entry of the home. The burglar does not need to fully enter the structure; an entry occurs if any part of the burglar's body enters the house. So, the individual who breaks a window and reaches in to grab an item has entered the house.

Modern statutes have eliminated the breaking requirement, although most still require some form of "unlawful entry." Since trespasses, frauds, and breakings are unlawful they would satisfy modern statutory requirements.

The second element required that the breaking and entry be of another person's dwelling. As with arson, under the common law the structure had to be a dwelling. The person who lives in the dwelling does not have to be the owner, only an occupant. As such, rental property is included. Interestingly, at least one court has held that churches are dwellings, regardless of whether a person actually resides in the church, premised on the theory that churches are God's dwellings.[4] The dwelling had to belong to another person, so one could not burglarize his own property. No jurisdiction continues to require that the structure be a dwelling. Most statutes now refer to all buildings or other structures.[5] However, if the structure burglarized is a dwelling, most states punish the crime more severely than if it was another type of building.

The third requirement was that the burglary occur at night. Although this is no longer an element of burglary, many states do aggravate the crime if it happened at night.

The fourth element is that the person entering must have as a purpose the commission of a felony once inside. This is the mens rea of the crime. If the person's intent is only to commit a misdemeanor, there is no burglary. If Jay's intent is to murder Mark, there is a burglary. It is not a burglary if Jay's intent is to punch Mark in the nose.

Of course, many breaking and enterings with an intent to commit a burglary are not completed. A burglar may be caught by surprise by someone who was not known to be inside and flee from the property. It also happens that burglars are caught in the act by occupants who return to the building. In any event, what is important to remember is that the intended felony need not be completed. All that need be proven is that the accused entered with an intent to commit a felony. As is always true, proving a person's subjective mental state is nearly impossible. As such, juries are permitted to infer intent from the actions of the defendant. A jury did just that in the following case.

THE STATE OF ILLINOIS
V.
GERRY LOCKETT

196 Ill.App.3d 981, 554 N.E.2d 566 (1990)

Justice O'CONNOR delivered the opinion of the court:

Gerry Lockett was charged with residential burglary, (Ill. Rev. Stat. 1985, ch. 38, par. 19–3), convicted after a jury trial, and sentenced to 8 years imprisonment. . . .

At about 3:00 A.M. on November 27, 1987, Allan Cannon entered his apartment, which he shared with his sister, at 1057 West Berwyn in Chicago. Cannon noticed a broken window in his sister's bedroom. He then saw a man, whom he did not know, standing about six feet away from him in the apartment hallway. The only light came from the bathroom off the hallway. The man said to Cannon, "I know your sister." Cannon fled the apartment to call the police from the nearby El station. Outside his apartment, Cannon saw the man running down an alley. Cannon described the man to police as a dark black man with curly hair, about 5'5", weighing about 200 pounds.

Cannon returned to his apartment and noticed that his bicycle had been placed on his bed, and that his sister's baby clothes, which had been packed in bags, had been thrown all over. Although the apartment was in a general state of disarray, which Cannon admitted was not uncommon, nothing had been taken. . . .

Lockett also argues, without merit, that the evidence could not support an inference of his intent to commit a theft. But when Cannon entered his apartment, he found a broken window and later noticed a rock and broken glass on the floor, indicating that the window had been broken from outside. Cannon also discovered contents of the apartment had been rearranged and thrown about. Even assuming that Lockett was, as he said, an acquaintance of Cannon's sister, and that the Cannons, as defense counsel implied, were less than diligent housekeepers, Lockett's presence, without permission, in the dark, empty apartment, at 3 A.M., supported the jury's inference of intent to commit a theft. . . .

Some statutes now provide that intent to commit any crime is sufficient, whether misdemeanor or felony. However, many continue to require an intent to commit either a felony or any theft.

In summary, most jurisdictions have changed burglary in such a way that the following elements are common: 1. an unlawful entry 2. of any structure or building 3. for the purpose of committing a felony or stealing from the premises 4. once inside.

As mentioned, burglary may be graded and higher penalties imposed if the act occurred at night; involved a dwelling, or was perpetrated at a dwelling that was actually inhabited at the time of the crime; or was committed by a burglar with a weapon.

SECTION 5.3 THEFT CRIMES

Section 5.3(a) Introduction to Theft Crimes

There are many types of theft. It is theft to take a pack of gum from a grocery store and not pay for it; for a lawyer to take a client's trust fund and spend it on personal items; for a bank officer to use a computer to make a paper transfer of funds from a patron's account to the officer's with an intent to later withdraw the money and abscond; and to hold a gun on a person and demand that property and money be surrendered. However, they are all fundamentally different crimes.

Some thefts are more violative of the person, such as robbery, and others are more violative of a trust relationship, such as an attorney absconding with a client's money. The crimes are also different in the method they are committed. A robbery involves an unlawful taking. Embezzlement, however, involves a lawful taking with a subsequent unlawful conversion.

Larceny was the first theft crime. It was created by judges under the common law. The elements of larceny were very narrow and did not cover most thefts. Larceny began as one crime, but developed into many different crimes. This was not a fluid, orderly development. This was true for two reasons. First, when larceny was first created, well over six hundred years ago, the purpose of making larceny criminal was more to prevent breaches of the peace (fights over possession of property) than to protect ownership of property. Larceny did not prohibit fraudulent takings of another's property. The theory was that an embezzlement or other theft by trick was less likely to result in an altercation (breach of the peace) between the owner and the thief, because the owner would not be aware of the theft until after it was completed. Using this theory many courts were reluctant to expand the scope of larceny. Second, in early common law, larceny was punishable by death. For this reason some judges were reluctant to expand its reach.[6]

Eventually, two other theft crimes were created, embezzlement and false pretenses. Despite the creation of these crimes, many theft acts continued to go unpunished because they fell into the cracks that separated the elements of the three common-law theft crimes. Some courts attempted to remedy this problem by broadening the definitions of the three crimes. However, computers, electronic banking, and other technological advances have led to new methods of stealing money and property, posing problems not anticipated by the judges who created the common law theft crimes. Some states have changed their definitions of larceny, false pretenses, and embezzlement to meet society's changes. Other states have simply abandoned the common law crimes and have enacted consolidated theft statutes. The common-law theft crimes, modern consolidated theft statutes, and the Model Penal Code approach to theft will be discussed below.

Section 5.3(b) Larceny

At common law the elements of **larceny** were: 1. the trespassory taking 2. and carrying away (asportation) 3. of personal property 4. of another 5. with an intent to permanently deprive the owner of possession. The actus reus of larceny was the taking and carrying away of personal property of another. The mens rea was the intent to permanently deprive the owner of possession.

To prove larceny it is necessary to "take" the property in question. A taking alone would not suffice; the taking must have been unlawful or trespassory. That is, the property must be taken by the defendant without the owner's consent. This element is only concerned with the method that the defendant used in acquiring

SIDEBAR

THEFT IN THE UNITED STATES
    The United States Department of Justice includes shoplifting, pocket-picking, purse-snatching, thefts from automobiles, thefts of motor vehicles, and all other thefts of personal property, which occur without the use of force, as larceny for the purpose of the Uniform Crime Reporting Program. That program shows that there were nearly eight million reported larcenies in the United States in 1989. That is one larceny every four seconds, an increase of over 2 percent from 1988.

Source: Uniform Crime Reports, United States Department of Justice, Federal Bureau of Investigation, August 5, 1990.

LEGAL TERMS

larceny
    The 1. trespassory taking and 2. carrying away asportation) 3. of personal property 4. of another 5. with an intent to permanently deprive the owner of possession.

possession. For example, if Mandy were to take Sean's wallet from his hand, she has committed a taking. However, if Sean were to give Mandy his wallet with the understanding that she is to return it at a specified time, there is no unlawful taking when she does not return it; she lawfully acquired possession of the wallet. Taking property from another without that person's consent was

CRIME	ELEMENTS	EXAMPLE	
LARCENY	1. The Trespassory Taking and 2. carrying away of . . . 3. Personal Property . . . 4. Belonging to another . . . 5. with an intent to steal	1. Shoplifting	
EMBEZZLEMENT	1. Conversion of . . . 2. personal property . . . 3. belonging to another . . . 4. which was lawfully acquired . . . 5. with an intent to steal	1. Attorney stealing a client's trust account	
FALSE PRETENSES	1. A false representation . . . 2. of a material fact . . . 3. made with knowledge . . . 4. with an intent to defraud . . . 5. causing the owner to transfer title	1. Seller of artwork convinces buyer that it was painted by a famous artist when it was not	

Summary of Common Law Theft Crimes

not a trespass under the common law, while failing to return property was not.

In an effort to protect employers (masters) from the theft of their employees (servants) the theory of "constructive possession" was created. This theory held that when an employee received actual possession of his employer's property as part of the job, that the employer maintained "constructive possession," while the employee had custody of the property. If this theory had not been developed, employees would have been free to steal property entrusted to them, since larceny required a trespassory taking. Of course, if an employee took property that was not under his care, then there was a trespassory taking.

Interestingly, the theory of constructive possession was never extended to other relationships. This led to the creation of a new crime, embezzlement.

Once the taking has been effected the defendant must carry away the property. This carrying away is called asportation. Generally, any asportation, even slight movement, will satisfy this requirement. The term asportation is deceiving, as not all property has to be "carried away" to satisfy this requirement. Riding a horse away will satisfy the requirement, as will driving another's automobile. Most states have done away with the asportation requirement by statute.

Third, the item stolen must be personal property. Land and items attached to land, i.e., houses, are considered real property. Theft of such property was not larceny. All other property is personal property. Objects that are movable property are personal property. In the early years of larceny there was a further requirement that the item stolen be tangible personal property. Tangible personal property includes most items, such as automobiles, books, electronic equipment, etc. Documents, such as stocks, bonds, and promissory notes, which represent ownership of something, are considered intangible property. It was not larceny to steal intangible personal property. Under modern statutes, most states have broadened theft to include all types of property.

The fourth element is that the personal property taken and carried away must be owned by another. One cannot steal from oneself. However, the rule has been extended to prohibit prosecution of a partner for taking partnership assets, joint tenants from taking each other's things, and since husband and wife were one person under the common law it was not possible for spouses to steal from one another.

Finally, the mens rea element: It is required that the defendant intend to permanently deprive the owner of possession of the property. In short, to be a thief one must have an intent to steal. If Jack takes Eddie's lawn mower intending to return the mower when he has completed his mowing, he has not committed larceny, as he did not possess an intent to permanently deprive Eddie of his possession of the mower. Also, the accused must intend to deprive an owner (or possessor) of property to be guilty of larceny. If an accused had a good faith belief that he had lawful right to the property, the requisite mens rea did not exist, and there was no larceny.

While proving "an intent to permanently deprive the owner of possession" is the common method of proving the mens rea of larceny, it is not the only method. Courts have held that if the property is held so long that it causes the owner to lose a significant portion of its value, a larceny has occurred. Some cases have held that if the property is taken with an intent to subject the property to substantial risk there is a larceny. Of course, the intent must exist at the time of taking. To illustrate this last method, imagine a thief who steals a plane intending to use the plane in a daredevil show. In such a case the thief is subjecting the property to a substantial risk, and even though the intent was to return the plane when the show was over, there is a larceny.

Section 5.3(c) Embezzlement

The definition of larceny left a large gap that permitted people in some circumstances to steal from others. That gap was caused by requiring a trespassory taking of the property. For various reasons people entrust money and property to others. The intent is not to tranfer ownership (title), only possession. A depositor of a bank gives possession of money to the bank; a client may give an attorney money to hold in a trust account; a stockbroker may keep an account with a client-investor's money in it. In all of these situations the money is taken lawfully; there is no trespassory taking. So, what happens if the person entrusted with the money converts (steals) it after taking lawful possession? At the early common law it was not a crime. However, the thief could have been sued for recovery of the money stolen.

This theory was carried to an extreme in a case where a bank teller converted money handed to him by a depositor to himself, by placing the money in his own pocket. It was held that there was no larceny, because the teller acquired the money lawfully. The court also determined that there was no larceny under the theory of "constructive possession," because the employer (bank) never had possession of the money. If the teller had put the money in the drawer and then taken it, the bank would have had constructive possession, and he would have committed larceny. The result was that the teller was guilty of no crime.[7] Unsatisfied with this situation, the English Parliament created a new crime: **embezzlement**.

The elements of embezzlement are 1. conversion 2. of personal property 3. of another 4. by one who has acquired lawful possession 5. with an intent to defraud the owner.

To prove embezzlement the prosecution must first show that an act of **conversion** occurred. Conversion is the unauthorized control over property with an intent to permanently deprive the owner of its possession or which substantially interferes with the rights of the owner.

As was the case with larceny, only tangible personal property was included. Today, nearly all forms of personal property may be embezzled. Also, the property had to belong to another. One could not embezzle her own property.

The element that distinguished embezzlement from larceny was the taking requirement. While larceny required a trespassory taking, embezzlement required lawful acquisition. As such, lawyers, bailees, executors of estates, and trustees are examples of those who can commit embezzlement.

To satisfy the mens rea requirement of embezzlement it must be shown that the defendant possessed an "intent to defraud." Mere negligent conversion of another's property is not embezzlement. Since the mens rea requirement is so high, bona fide claims of mistake of fact and law are valid defenses. If an accountant makes an accounting error and converts a client's money, there is no embezzlement. This is a mistake of fact. If a friend you loaned money to keeps the money with the mistaken belief that he is allowed to in order to offset damage you caused to his property last year (when the law requires that he sue you for the damage), there is no embezzlement. This is a mistake of law and negates the intent required, as does a mistake of fact.

Embezzlement is prohibited in all states. Some states have retained the name embezzlement; others have named it theft and included it in a consolidated theft statute. Embezzlement, which occurs in interstate commerce, federally insured banks, and lending institutions, or involves officers and agents of the federal government, is also made criminal by the statutes of the United States.[8] 18 U.S.C. §641 is the embezzlement of public monies, property, and records statute. Violation of that provision, if the property embezzled has a value of $100 or greater, results in a fine of up to $10,000 and ten years in prison. The remainder of that statute deals with embezzlement of nonpublic property that occurs in interstate commerce or by federal officials. The penalties vary for each provision. In the following case a military officer was charged with violation of section 641.

LEGAL TERMS

embezzlement
The 1. conversion of 2. personal property of 3. another 4. after acquiring lawful acquisition 5. with an intent to defraud the owner.

conversion
An unauthorized control over property intending to permanently deprive the owner of its possession.

UNITED STATES
V.
JOSEPH GALE MAY
625 F.2d 186 (8th Cir. 1980)

Joseph Gale May, Adjutant General of the Iowa National Guard, appeals from his conviction on fifteen counts of an eighteen count indictment. We hold that the trial court erred in not instructing the jury that May could only be convicted for using military aircraft for his personal use if the jury found that his use seriously violated the government's right to use of the aircraft. . . .

. . . The evidence showed that General May, who was a passenger on the questioned flights, had a nonbusiness purpose in arranging them. On all but one occasion, May directed the flights to destinations allowing him to visit his fiancée, Ms. Gwen Applequist. Seven of the flights for which General May was convicted delivered him to and/or returned him from airfields in Florida, the former home state of Ms. Applequist; one flight was made to visit her in New Orleans; two others enable May to be with her when she attended a conference in Chicago; and a final flight enabled May to spend Thanksgiving weekend with other friends in Las Vegas, Nevada. As a result of these flights, General May was charged with embezzlement and conversion of government property in violation of 18 U.S.C. §641. . . .

* * *

More serious is May's argument that he was tried on a theory of conversion so novel and expansive as to be beyond the purview of section 641. Specifically, he alleges that the district court erred in holding that the use of property, as opposed to the property itself, is subject to conversion under the new statute. He also contends that the district court erred in instructing the jury on the standard by which conversion is to be judged.

Title 18 U.S.C. §641 applies to:
Whoever embezzles, steals, purloins, or knowingly converts

to his use or the use of another * * * any record, voucher, money or thing of value of the United States * * *.

The first prong of May's argument is that the government has impermissibly expanded the statutory concept of conversion.

At common law, only chattels or tangible property were subject to the tort of conversion. . . . The question at issue here is whether section 641 applies only to conduct involving property which would be the subject of traditional tort law analysis or whether the statutory phrase "money or other thing of value" broadened the application of the statute to conduct involving different types of valuables.

May contends that the only things which could have been converted by his allegedly unauthorized trips are the aircraft and the gasoline used to fly them. The government and the district court took the view that the subject of conversion was the flight time in government aircraft. Consistent with that theory, the government introduced evidence of the cost per hour of operation for each airplane, which included the salaries of the pilots and the mechanics who serviced the planes.

* * *

We agree with the views of [other] courts and hold that "valuables" not ordinarily subject to tort conversion may nevertheless be subject to criminal conversion under section 641. It is clear that the "thing of value" which was involved in these flights was the flight time itself. . . .

May's final contention with respect to the flight counts is that the district court erred by failing to instruct the jury that conversion requires a serious violation of the owner's right to control the use of its property. May's theory is that since the flights partially satisfied the training and flight time requirements of the National Guard pilots who flew them, the government's right to use its airplane and gasoline was not seriously violated. . . .

* * *

The touchstone of conversion is the exercise of such control over property that serious interference with the rights of the owner result, making it just that the actor pay the owner full value of the object. . . .

The problem with the district court's instruction is that it assumes that any misuse or unauthorized use of property is a conversion. . . .

* * *

We are unable to find any case using this admittedly novel standard. Determining whether the benefits from a use were incidental, as opposed to determining whether one use seriously violated the owner's rights of control, requires a primary focus on the intent of the actor rather than on the nature of the use. It is, of course, possible that the government's benefits from the flights may have been only incidental to May's purposes, but the government's right to control the use of the flight time may nevertheless have been complete. Indeed, this appears to have been the thrust of General May's defense. The failure to properly instruct the jury as to the meaning of conversion was, therefore, fatal to the flight count convictions. The government may, of course, retry May on these counts.

* * *

Section 5.3(d) False Pretenses

At common law it was not larcenous to use lies (false representations) to gain ownership of property. For example, if Brogan were to sell Sean a ring containing glass, and Brogan had represented to Sean that the ring contained a diamond, it was not larceny under the early common law, even though Brogan knew that the ring contained glass. The early judges believed strongly in the the concept of *caveat emptor*, which translates to "let the buyer beware."

As it had done with embezzlement, Parliament decided to make such acts criminal. It did so by creating the crime of **false pretenses**. The elements of false pretenses are 1. a false representation of 2. a material present or past fact 3. made with knowledge that the fact is false 4. and with an intent to defraud the victim 5. thereby causing the victim to pass title to property to the actor.

To prove the first element, it must be shown that the actor made a false representation. This representation may be made orally, by writing, or may be implied by one's actions. The law does not require that people disclose all relevant information during a business transaction. *Cavaet emptor* still exists in that regard. The law does, however, require that any affirmative statements (or implications from actions) be true. So, if a buyer fails to ask if property has a lien against it, there is no false pretense if the seller does not inform the buyer of such. The opposite it true if the buyer inquires about existing liens and encumberances and is told there are none.

The false representation must be important to the transaction. If the statement is important, the law says that it is material. Generally, a representation is material if it would have had an impact on the victim's decision-making had the victim known the truth at the time the transaction took place. For example, if Connie represents to Pam that the lighter to a used car she is selling works, when it does not, she has not committed false pretenses. However, if she states to Pam that the automobile recently had its engine replaced, that would be material and she would be liable for false pretenses if she knew that the statement was untrue.

The fact conveyed by the actor must not only be material, but it must concern a present fact or past fact. In this context, "present" refers to the time of the transaction. Statements of expected facts, promises, predictions, and expectations cannot be the basis of false pretenses. So, if Aaron buys an automobile from Kathy and promises to pay her in six months, it is no crime if he fails to pay because he loses his source of income during that period. To permit breaches of such promises to be criminal would be the same as having a debtor's prison, which is not recognized in the United States. The same is not always true if Aaron made the promise and his intent was never to pay the debt. Some states treat this as false pretenses under the theory that his state of mind at the time of the sale was fraudulent. Some states do not treat his action as criminal and place the burden on Kathy to seek her own remedy in a civil cause of action. It is also necessary that the representation be one of fact. Accordingly, opinions are not included. Of course, the line between fact and opinion is often not clear.

It must also be proved that the defendant knew the statement was false. An unintentional misrepresentation is not sufficient to establish this element in most juridictions, although most jurisdictions will find knowledge if the lower mens rea standard, reckless, is proved.

The defendant must have the additional mens rea of "intent to defraud." As with other theft crimes, if one has a bona fide belief that the property belongs to him or her, there is a defense. In addition to intending to defraud the victim, it must also be shown that the victim was defrauded. Hence, if the victim was aware of the falsity of the statement and entered into the bargain anyway, there has been no crime.

LEGAL TERMS

false pretenses
1. False representations
2. of material present or past fact
3. made with knowledge that the fact is false
4. and an intent to defraud the owner of property
5. thereby causing the owner to transfer title to the actor.

Finally, the misrepresentation must be the cause of the victim passing title to property to the defendant. Title is ownership. Tranferring possession to the defendant is not adequate. However, causing one to transfer possession of property by use of fraud was a type of larceny, known as larceny by trick. Just as with larceny and embezzlement, only tangible personal property was included within the grasp of the prohibition at early common law. Today, false pretenses usually includes all property that is subject to the protection of larceny—in most instances, this includes all personal property.

Section 5.3(d.1) Fraudulent Checks

Related to the crime of false pretenses is the crime of acquiring property or money by writing a check (draft) from an account that has insufficient funds to cover the draft. The act appears to fall into the category of false pretenses. Some theorize that when a check is written it is a promise of future payment, and, accordingly, the check does not meet the "representation of present or past fact" requirement of false pretenses. Courts have rejected that view and held that at the time one drafts a check a representation is made that there are adequate funds in the account to pay the amount drafted.

Today, most states have bad check statutes. Conviction of these laws, for the most part, results in a less serious punishment than conviction on false pretenses.[9] Three common material elements are found in bad check statutes. First, the mens rea may be proven by showing either an intent to defraud the payee or knowledge that there were insufficient funds in the account. Second, the check must be taken in exchange for something of value, and, third, there must have been insufficient funds in the account.

Section 5.3(d.2) Mail Fraud

Another crime related to false pretenses is mail fraud.[10] Mail fraud is a crime against the United States, since the mail system is run by a federal agency. Using the United States mail system with an intent to defraud another of money or property is mail fraud. The intended victim need not be defrauded; the act of sending such mails with the intent to defraud is criminal alone.

Mail fraud has become increasingly important in recent years, because it often is the foundation of a RICO count.

Section 5.3(d.3) Racketeer Influenced and Corrupt Organizations Act (RICO)

Another federal statute that deals with fraud is the Racketeer Influenced and Corrupt Organizations Act, commonly known as **RICO**.[11] The United States Congress enacted RICO in the early 1970s in an attempt to curb organized crime.

Judicial interpretation of RICO has led to much controversy in recent years. Some people contend that the effect of court opinions has been to extend the prohibition of RICO beyond Congress's original intent. Today, all businesses, not just traditional organized crime, are subject to RICO.

To establish a RICO violation the United States must prove that the 1. defendant received money or income 2. from a pattern of racketeering activity and 3. invested that money in an enterprise (business), 4. which is in interstate commerce or affects interstate commerce.

The second element is the key to proving a RICO violation. The term "pattern" means two or more acts, referred to as the predicate acts. Those acts must fall into the definition of a "racketeering activity." The statute provides a list of state and federal crimes that are considered to be racketeering. Murder, kidnapping, extortion, and drug sales and transportation are examples of the state crimes included in the list. Mail fraud, wire fraud, white slave traffic, securities fraud, and bribery are a few examples of the federal crimes included. Mail fraud is often the basis of a RICO violation, since the mails are often used by such enterprises.

Violation of RICO can result in serious criminal penalties. In addition, victims of such activity may sue and receive treble damages, costs, and attorneys' fees. RICO also provides for **forfeiture** of property in criminal proceedings. Forfeiture is the taking of property and money of a defendant by the government. Many crimes have forfeiture provisions. A forfeiture is not the same as a fine. Both forfeitures and fines are levied as punishment, but the focus of a fine is to generally hurt a defendant's pocketbook. Forfeitures are specifically aimed at getting the property or money connected to the crime for which the individual was convicted. So, in a RICO situation, a convicted party could stand to lose the enterprise itself, as well as all profits from that activity.

The following case is a civil case. However, many aspects of civil RICO are identical to criminal RICO. One such aspect is the pattern requirement. Whether the case is civil or criminal, a "pattern of racketeering" must be proven. The United States Supreme Court addressed the pattern question because the various appellate courts of the United States were divided on how to define that phrase. This case is also a good illustration of how "legitimate businesses" are subject to RICO.

H.J. INC.
V.
NORTHWESTERN BELL TELEPHONE CO.

492 U.S. ___ (1989)

* * *

Petitioners, customers of respondent Northwestern Bell Telephone Co., filed this putative class action in 1986 in the District Court for the District of Minnesota. Petitioners alleged violations of 18 U.S.C. §§1962(a), (b), (c), and (d) by Northwestern Bell and other respondents—some of the telephone company's officers and employees, various members of the Minnesota Public Utilities Commission (MPUC), and other unnamed individuals and corporations—and sought an injunction and treble damages under RICO's civil liability provisions, §§1964(a) and (c).

The MPUC is the state body responsibe for determining the rates that Northwestern Bell may charge. Petitioners' 5-count complaint alleged that between 1980 and 1986 Northwestern Bell sought to influence members of the MPUC in the performance of their duties—and in fact caused them to approve rates for the company in excess of a fair and reasonable amount—by making cash payments to commissioners, negotiating with them regarding future employment, and paying for meals, for tickets to sporting events and the like, and for airline tickets. . . .

* * *

. . . Our guides in the endeavor must be the text of the statute and its legislative history. We find no support in those sources for the proposition, espoused by the Court of Appeals for the Eighth Circuit in this case, that predicate acts of racketeering may form a pattern; only then they are part of separate illegal schemes. Nor can we agree with those courts that have suggested that a pattern is established merely by proving two predicate acts . . .

* * *

The legislative history, which we discussed in [another case] shows that Congress indeed had a fairly flexible concept of a pattern in mind. A pattern is not formed by "sporadic activity," S. Rep. No. 91–617, p. 158 (1969), and a person cannot "be subjected to the sanctions of [RICO] simply by committing two widely separated and isolated criminal offenses. . . . Instead, "[t]he term 'pattern' itself requires the showing of a relationship" between the predicates and of "the threat of continuing activity. . . ." It is this factor of *continuity plus relationship* which combines to produce a pattern." RICO's legislative history reveals Congress's intent that to prove a pattern of racketeering activity a plaintiff or prosecutor must show that the racketeering predicates are related, *and* that they amount to or pose a threat of continued criminal activity.

* * *

Section 5.3(d.4) Forgery

Another crime related to fraud is **forgery**. Forgery is the 1. making of 2. false documents (or the alteration of existing documents making them false) 3. and passing the document 4. to another 5. with an intent to defraud.

The purpose of forgery statutes is to both prevent fraud and to preserve the value of written instruments. This is important because if forgery were to become common, people would no longer trust commercial documents, such as checks and contracts. The effect that would have on commerce is obvious.

The actus reus of forgery is the making of the document. That involves the actual writing and drafting of the document, as well as passing the document (uttering) to a potential victim. The mens rea of forgery is that the actor know of the falsity of the document and have an intent to defraud.

In many jurisdictions forgery and uttering are separate crimes. In those states one must only make the false instrument and possess an intent to defraud. The defendant need not present the document (utter) to the victim. That act, when accompanied with an intent to defraud, is the crime of uttering.

Section 5.3(e) Receiving Stolen Property

Not only is it a crime to steal another's property, but it is also a crime to receive property that one knows is stolen, if the intent is to keep that property. In essence, one who buys or receives as a gift property that is known to be stolen is an accessory (after the fact) to the theft. While the law applies to anyone who violates its prohibitions, the primary focus of law enforcement is fences. Fences are people who purchase stolen property with the intent of reselling the property for a profit. They act as the retailers of stolen property with the thieves acting as suppliers.

The elements of **receiving stolen property** are 1. receiving property 2. that has been stolen 3. with knowledge of its stolen character 4. with an intent to deprive the owner of the property.

Receipt of the property may be shown either by showing actual possession or constructive possession of the property. Constructive possession occurs any time the defendant has control over the property, even though the defendant does not have actual possession. For example, if one makes arrangements for stolen property to be delivered to his home, there is receipt once the property is in the defendant's house, even if the defendant was not present when the property was delivered. Receiving not only includes purchases of stolen property, but other transfers, such as gifts.

The property in question must have been stolen. In this context, stolen property includes that property acquired from larcenies, robberies, embezzlement, extortion, false pretenses, and similar crimes.

The final two elements deal with the mens rea of the crime of receiving stolen property. It is necessary that the defendant knew of the property's stolen character at the time of acquiring the property. Actual knowledge that the property was stolen is required. However, if it can be proven that the defendant had a subjective belief that the goods were stolen, but lacked absolute proof of that fact, the crime has been committed. The fact that a reasonable person would have known that the property was stolen is not enough to convict for receiving stolen property. If one receives property under a bona fide belief that he or she has claim to the property, he or she is not guilty of receiving stolen property, even though that belief was unfounded.

The last element requires that the receiver of the property intend to deprive the owner of the property. Of course, if a defendant intends to keep the property for herself, then this requirement is met. The language of the crime is broader, however, and includes any intent to deprive the owner of the use, ownership, or possession of the property. So, if one receives the property intending to destroy it or to give it as a gift, this element has been satisfied.

Not only do the states prohibit receiving stolen property, but the federal government also makes it a crime to receive stolen property that has traveled in interstate commerce or to receive stolen property while on lands controlled by the United States.[12]

Section 5.3(f) Robbery

The material elements of **robbery** are 1. a trespassory taking 2. and carrying away (asportation) 3. of personal property 4. from another's person or presence 5. using either force or threat 6. with an intent to steal the property.

Robbery is actually a type of assault mixed with a type of larceny. Because of the immediate danger created by the crime of robbery, it is punished more severely than either larceny or simple assault. Robbery was a crime under the common law and is a statutory crime in all states today.

The elements of trespassory taking, asportation, intent to steal, and that the property belong to another, are the same as for larceny. However, robbery also requires that the property be taken from the victim's person or presence. So property taken from another's hands, off another's body, or from another's clothing is taken from the person. Property that is taken from another's presence, but not from their person, also qualifies. For example, if a bank robber orders a teller to stand back while the thief empties the cash drawer, there has been a robbery. The states differ in their definitions of "from another's presence," but it is generally held that property is in a victim's presence any time the victim is in control of the property. This is true in the bank robbery example, as the teller was exercising control over the cash drawer at the time of the robbery.

It is also necessary that the crime be committed with the use of force or threat. This element is the feature that most distinguishes robbery from larceny. As far as force is concerned, if any force is used beyond what is necessary to simply take the property, there is robbery. For example, it is larceny, not robbery, if a pickpocket steals a wallet free of the owner's knowledge. Only the force necessary to take the wallet was used. It is robbery, however, if the victim catches the pickpocket, and an altercation ensues over possession of the wallet. The same result is true when dealing with purse snatchers. If the snatcher makes a clean grab and gets away without an altercation, it is larceny from the person. If the victim grabs the bag and fights to keep it, then it is robbery. A threat of force may also satisfy this requirement. So, if the robber states to the victim, "Give me your wallet or I'll

SIDEBAR

CRIME IN THE UNITED STATES
Robbery is defined as the "taking or attempting to take anything of value from the care, custody, or control of a person or persons by force or threat of force or violence and/or by putting the victim in fear. During 1989 there were a total of 578,326 reported robberies under this definition. This represented an increase of 6.5 percent over 1988. There is one reported robbery every 55 seconds in the United States.

Source: Uniform Crime Reports, U.S. Department of Justice, Federal Bureau of Investigation, August 5, 1990.

LEGAL TERMS

receiving stolen property
1. Receiving property 2. that has been stolen 3. with knowledge of its stolen character 4. with an intent to deprive the owner of the property.

robbery
The 1. trespassory taking 2. and carrying away (asportation) 3. of personal property 4. from another's person or presence 5. using force or threats 6. with an intent to deprive the owner of the property.

U.S. Department of Justice
United States Marshals Service

WANTED
BY U.S. MARSHALS

NOTICE TO ARRESTING AGENCY: Before arrest, validate warrant through National Crime Information Center (NCIC).

United States Marshals Service NCIC entry number: (NIC/ W482873894).

NAME: JULIANO, Anthony Michael

ALIAS: "ZOO"

DESCRIPTION:

Sex: ....MALE
Race: ....WHITE
Place of Birth:..................NEWARK, NEW JERSEY
Date(s) of Birth: ....SEPTEMBER 24, 1922
Height: ....5'1"
Weight:.........................145 LBS
Eyes: ....BROWN
Hair: ....GRAY (BALDING)
Skintone: ....MEDIUM
Scars, Marks, Tattoos: ....NONE
Social Security Number: 145-16-4245
NCIC Fingerprint Classification:..17 14 14 17 19 17 PO 14 14 16

SHOULD BE CONSIDERED ARMED AND DANGEROUS
  JULIANO has a long criminal history of violent crimes including armed
  robberies and assault and battery with a weapon.

WANTED FOR: PAROLE VIOLATION

Warrant Issued: District of Connecticut
Warrant Number: 8814-0321-0157-C

DATE WARRANT ISSUED: March 21, 1988

MISCELLANEOUS INFORMATION: JULIANO has been arrested twenty-three times
  for armed bank robbery.

If arrested or whereabouts known, notify the local United States Marshals Office, (Telephone: _____).

If no answer, call United States Marshals Service Communications Center in McLean, Virginia.
   Telephone (800)336-0102: (24 hour telephone contact) NLETS access code is VAUSMOOOO.
        (800) 423-0719 (TDD)

PRIOR EDITIONS ARE OBSOLETE AND NOT TO BE USED

Form USM-132
(Rev. 2/84)

blow your head off," there is a robbery, even though there was no physical contact.

In most jurisdictions the threatened harm must be immediate; threats of future harm are not adequate. It is also possible that the threat will be to someone else, such as a family member. The thief who holds a man's wife and threatens to harm her if the man does not give up his money is not free from the charge of robbery because the person giving up the money is not the one threatened.

The mens rea of robbery is the specific intent to take the property and deprive the owner of it. As was true of the other theft crimes, a good faith, but incorrect, claim of right to the property is a defense. In *Richardson v. United States,* 403 F.2d 574 (D.C. Cir. 1968) a defendant's claim of right to money was a gambling debt. The trial court did not permit the illegal debt to be used as a defense, but the appellate court reversed. It stated in its opinion that:

> The government's position seems to be that no instruction on a claim of right is necessary unless the defendant had a legally enforceable right to the property he took. But specific intent depends upon a state of mind, not upon a legal fact. If the jury finds that the defendant believed himself entitled to the money, it cannot properly find that he had the requisite specific intent for robbery.

Not only is robbery a crime pursuant to state law, but the United States also has prohibited certain robberies. Robbery of a federally insured bank is an example.[13]

Robbery is usually, if not always, graded. Robbery is graded higher if it results in serious injury to the victim or is committed using a deadly weapon.

Section 5.3(g) Extortion

Extortion is more commonly known as blackmail. Extortion is similar to robbery because both involve stealing money under threat. However, the threat in a robbery must be of immediate harm. Extortion involves a threat of future harm. In the common law extortion applied only against public officers. Today, extortion is much broader. The elements of extortion are 1. the taking or acquisition of property 2. of another 3. using a threat 4. with an intent to steal the property. In a few jurisdictions the extortionist must actually receive the property, while others only require that the threat be made.

A threat of future physical harm will do, as will threats to injure another's reputation, business, financial status, or family relationship. As was the case with robbery, the threat may be directed at one person, and the demand for property may be made on another. For example, if a thief states to John, "Give me $100,000 or I will kill your wife," he is an extortionist, even though he has not threatened John.

The threatened conduct itself need not be illegal to be extortion. For example, if Stacey tells Lisa that she is going to inform the authorities of Lisa's involvement in illegal drug trade unless she pays her $10,000, she is an extortionist, even though telling the police of the activity is not only legal, but encouraged by society.

The federal government has made it a crime for federal officers to extort the public, to be involved in an extortion that interferes with interstate commerce, and to extort another by threatening to expose a violation of federal law.

The following case deals with extortion in the labor relations area. In most situations it is proper for unions and employees to threaten to picket an employer. In this case the threats were not part of usual labor-management relations; they were made with the purpose of extorting corporate money. Accordingly, the threats were found to be extortion, not protected labor activity.

PEOPLE
V.
DIOGUARDI

8 N.Y.2d 260, 203 N.Y.S.2d 870 (1960)

The Appellate Division has reversed defendants' convictions for extortion and conspiracy to commit extortion, dismissed the indictment, and discharged them from custody. In addition to the conspiracy count, the indictment charged defendants with extorting $4,700 from the officers of two corporations. Said corporations were non-union, conducted a wholesale stationery and office supply business in Manhattan, did an annual business of several million dollars, and their stock was wholly owned by a family named Kerin. Anthony Kerin, Sr., president and "boss" of the Kerin companies, made all the important corporate decisions. The other two corporate officers were his son Kerin, Jr., and one Jack Shumann.

Defendant McNamara, the alleged "front man" in the extortive scheme, was an official of Teamster's Local 295 and 808, as well as a member of the Teamster's Joint Council. Defendant Dioguardi, the immediate beneficiary of the payments and the alleged power behind the scene, was sole officer of Equitable Research Associates, Inc.—a *publishing house*, according to its certificate of incorporation, a *public relations concern*, according to its bank account and the Yellow Pages of the telephone directory, a *labor statistics concern*, according to its office secretary and sole employee, and a *firm of labor consultants,* according to its business card. . . .

[During late 1955 and early 1956 various unions were attempting to unionize Kerin's business. The two primary unions involved in this attempt were both locals of the Teamsters. Eventually, one union began picketing the business while the other was on the premises handing out literature.]

The appearance of the picket line—which truck drivers from two companies refused to cross—thoroughly alarmed the Kerin officers, since they were in an "extremely competitive business," and a cessation of incoming or outgoing truck deliveries for as short a period as two weeks would effectively force them out of business. . . .

* * *

. . . McNamara assured Kerin, Sr., that his troubles could be ended, and *would be,* if he did three things: (1) "joined up" with McNamara's local 295, (2) paid $3,500 to Equitable to defray the "out-of-pocket" expenses incurred by the various unions that had sought to organize the companies, and (3) retained Equitable as labor consultant at $100 per month for each company for the period of the collective bargaining contract. . . . McNamara repeatedly assured Kerin, Sr., that the picketing would stop immediately and the companies would be guaranteed labor peace if his program were accepted.

Kerin, Sr., stated that he was not adverse to having his employees organized by local 295, if it was a good honest union, and that he could "accept the idea of a hundred dollars a month as a retainer fee for labor counsel and advise." He protested against the proposed payment of $3,500, however, as an "extraordinary charge" that sounded "like a hold-up," to which McNamara replied: "It may seem that way to you, Mr. Kerin, but that is the amount of money that these unions that have sought to organize you . . . have expended, and *if we are going to avoid further trouble and further difficulties, it is my suggestion that you pay that to the Equitable Associates.* . . .

* * *

Upon the proof in this record, a jury could properly conclude that defendants were guilty of extortion—cleverly

> conceived and subtly executed, but extortion nonetheless. The essence of the crime is obtaining property by a wrongful use of fear, induced by a threat to do an unlawful injury [cite omitted]. It is well-settled law in this State that fear of economic loss or harm satisfies the ingredient of fear necessary to the crime.
>
> * * *

Section 5.3(h) Consolidated Theft Statutes

The distinctions between the three common-law crimes of theft, larceny, embezzlement, and false pretenses, are often hard to draw. This fact matched with the belief that there is no substantive difference between stealing by fraud or by quick use of the hands has led many jurisdictions to do away with the common law crimes of larceny, false pretenses, and embezzlement, and replace them with a single crime named theft. Exactly what crimes are included in such statutes differs, but larceny, false pretenses, and embezzlement are always included. Many jurisdictions also add one or more of the following: fraudulent checks; receiving stolen property; and extortion.

These statutes often use the language of the common law in defining theft. For example, Florida's statute reads:

> A person is guilty of theft if he knowingly obtains or uses, or endeavors to obtain or to use, the property of another with intent to, either temporarily or permanently: (a) Deprive the other person of a right to the property or a benefit therefrom or Appropriate the property to his own use or to the use of any person not entitled thereto.[14]

This statute includes the three common-law theft crimes. The primary change of consolidated theft statutes is that prosecutors no longer need to charge which specific crime has occurred. At trial, if the jury decides that a defendant has committed a larceny and not an embezzlement, they can convict. Under the common law if the defendant was charged with embezzlement, not larceny, the jury would be forced to acquit if they determined that he committed larceny and not embezzlement.

Robbery is usually not included in consolidated theft statutes because of its significant threat of harm. Consolidation usually includes only misappropriations of property that do not pose serious risks to life.

Of course, those crimes that are included in consolidation statutes are not always punished equally. Grading of such offenses based on the amount of property appropriated and the type of property stolen is common.

Section 5.3(i) The Model Penal Code Consolidation

The Model Penal Code contains a comprehensive consolidation of theft offenses.[15] Provided that a defendant is not prejudiced by doing so, the specification of one theft crime by the prosecution does not prohibit a conviction for another. So if the defendant is specifically charged with larceny, he may be convicted of false pretenses or embezzlement by a jury.

The Code recognizes the following forms of theft:

1. Theft by taking (includes common-law larceny and embezzlement).
2. Theft by deception (includes common-law false pretenses).
3. Theft by extortion.
4. Theft of property known to be mislaid, misdelivered, or lost, and no reasonable attempt to find the rightful owner is made.
5. Receiving stolen property.
6. Theft of professional services by deception or threat.
7. Conversion of entrusted funds.
8. Unauthorized use of another's automobile.

The Code declares that thefts are felonies of the third degree if the amount stolen exceeds $500 or if the property stolen is a firearm, automobile, airplane, motorcycle, motorboat, or other vehicle, and in cases of receiving stolen property, if the receiver of the property is a fence, then it is a felony of the third degree regardless of the value of the property. The Code makes all unauthorized uses of automobiles misdemeanors.

Because the crime of robbery involves a danger to people it is treated as a separate crime.[16] If during the commission of a theft the defendant inflicts serious bodily injury upon another, threatens serious bodily injury, or threatens to commit a felony of the first or second degree, there is a robbery. It is a felony of the second degree unless the defendant attempts to kill or cause serious bodily injury, in which case it is a felony of the first degree.

Forgery is also treated as a separate offense.[17] Forgery is treated as a felony of the second degree if money, securities, postage stamps, stock, or other documents issued by the government are involved. It is a felony of the third degree if the forged document affects legal relationships, such as wills and contracts. All other forgeries are misdemeanors.

Section 5.3(j) Destruction of Property

Every year a significant amount of financial loss is the result of destruction of property. Arson accounts for much of this total, but not all. Most, if not all, states have statutes making the destruction of another's property criminal. These laws may be part of the statute covering arson or may be a separate section of the criminal code.

Destruction of property, commonly called **criminal mischief**, is normally a specific intent crime and includes all types of destruction that affect the value or dignity of the property. For example, defacing the tombstone of a Jew by painting a swastika on it would be criminal mischief, even though the paint can be removed, and the tombstone is left physically unharmed.

Mischief is often graded so that offenses against public property, which result damage in excess of a stated dollar amount, or which involve a danger to human life, are penalized more heavily than others. The most serious mischiefs are usually low-grade felonies, and the remainder misdemeanors. The Kentucky mischief statutes read:

KENTUCKY REVISED STATUTE §512.020

(1) A person is guilty of criminal mischief in the first degree when, having no right to do so or any reasonable ground to believe that he has such right, he intentionally or wantonly defaces, destroys, or damages any property causing pecuniary loss of $1,000 or more.

(2) Criminal mischief in the first degree is a Class D felony.

KENTUCKY REVISED STATUTE §512.030

(1) A person is guilty of criminal mischief in the second degree when, having no right to do so or any reasonable ground to believe that he has such a right, he intentionally or wantonly defaces, destroys, or damages any property causing pecuniary loss of $500 or more.

(2) Criminal mischief in the second degree is a Class A misdemeanor.

KENTUCKY REVISED STATUTE §512.040

(1) A person is guilty of criminal mischief in the third degree when:

(a) Having no right to do so or any reasonable ground to believe that he has such right, he intentionally or wantonly defaces, destroys or damages any property; or

(b) He tampers with property so as knowingly to endanger the person or property of another. (2) Criminal mischief in the third degree is a Class B misdemeanor.

At common law hairline distinctions existed between the three crimes against property: larceny, embezzlement, and false pretenses. Today, statutes in most states have consolidated theft crimes so that the focus is now on whether a theft occurred, not whether the correct crime has been charged. These consolidation statutes include larceny, false pretenses, and embezzlement. Although it varies, often such statutes will also include receiving stolen property, various forms of fraud, and extortion. Robbery and forgery are treated as separate crimes.

Arson and burglary are also separate crimes because they involve more than a threat to property. Under the common law only residences were protected by arson and burglary laws. Because of the sanctity that our culture attaches to dwellings and because of the danger to human life created by arson and burglary, these crimes received special attention. Today, arson and burglary have been broadened to include more than just dwellings.

In addition to criminal remedies for these crimes, victims will often have civil remedies available. As previously discussed, the victim is responsible for filing and proving such a civil case. However, a prior admission of guilt (or conviction) may prevent the defendant from relitigating his innocence in a civil trial.

LEGAL TERMS

criminal mischief
The destruction or damaging of another's property is commonly known as mischief.

REVIEW QUESTIONS

1. What is "constructive breaking," when referring to the crime of burglary?
2. Define larceny.
3. What is criminal mischief?
4. Embezzlement is often punished more severely than simple larceny. Why?

5. What does the acronym RICO represent? What are the basic elements of RICO?
6. What are "fences"? Under the common law what crime do fences commit?
7. How is destruction of a building by explosion treated by the Model Penal Code? At common law?
8. Brogan runs by a woman on the street and grabs her purse as he passes her. The purse is easily pulled from her arm, and Brogan's intent is to keep the contents. What crime has been committed?
9. Brogan runs by a woman on the street and grabs her purse as he passes her. The woman catches the strap and fights to keep the purse; however, the strap breaks, and Brogan is successful. He keeps the contents of the purse. What crime has been committed?
10. What is the difference between forgery and uttering?

REVIEW PROBLEMS

1. Arson is quite different today then it was under the common law. What are the major differences?
2. Burglary is quite different today then it was under the common law. What are the major differences?
3. Doug and Sherri are an elderly couple who are retired and residing in Florida. Both have suffered a substantial physical deterioration, including vision loss and poor memory. Ned, who had coveted their 1962 Corvette for years, told the couple that they should trust him with their financial affairs, including giving him title to their vehicle. He told the two that he would drive them to the places they needed to go, but that state law required that his name appear on the title of the car, since he would be the sole driver. Doug and Sherri complied with his request, believing that his statement concerning Florida law was correct.

   Subsequently, the couple created a trust account and named Ned as trustee. The purpose of the account was to provide Ned with a general fund from which he was to pay the household bills. Ned withdrew all the money and placed it into his personal account. When this occurred the couple contacted Ned who claimed to know nothing of the account. Sherri contacted the local prosecutor who conducted an investigation. Through that investigation it was discovered that Ned held title to the Corvette.

You work for the prosecutor. Your assignment is to determine what crimes have been committed, if any. Your state has no theft statute, but recognizes common law theft crimes.

4.   Gary and Paige were friends until they discovered that they shared an interest in Tracy. After Paige won her affection, Gary became enraged and took a key and ran it down the side of Paige's car. He then poured gasoline over the car and set it on fire. Gary has been arrested. What crimes should be charged?

5.   Kevin was walking down the sidewalk that passed in front of Sean's home. As he passed Sean's house he looked in a front window and noticed a carton of soft drinks sitting in the kitchen. As he was thirsty, Kevin broke the front window and crawled into Kevin's house. Once inside he poured himself a glass of cola and sat down at the dining room table. While seated at the table he picked up a ring with a value in excess of $1,000, and put it into his pocket. When he finished his drink he placed the empty glass in the sink and left. He later sold the ring and bought a stereo with the proceeds. What crimes have been committed, using common law theft crimes?

6.   Brogan has an affair with Janice, who is married. After Janice ends the affair Brogan threatens to tell Janice's husband about their sexual involvement unless Janice pays Brogan $5,000. Janice complies. What crime has been committed?

7.   Penni is working the night shift at a local convenience store when Craig and Guido come in. Craig states to Penni, "Give us all the money in the register and we will not hurt you. Give us any trouble and we will knock the #?!@ out of you!" Penni complied. What crime has been committed? What if they had been brandishing weapons?

8.   Discuss what crimes you think should be included in consolidated theft statutes and why. Explain why particular crimes should be left out of such a statute.

NOTES

[1] 5 Am.Jur.2d *Arson* 2 (1962).
[2] Model Penal Code §220.1.
[3] Model Penal Code §220.1(1) and (2).

[4] *People v. Richards,* 108 N.Y. 137, 15 N.E. 371.

[5] LaFave and Scott, *Criminal Law* (Hornbook Series, St. Paul: West Publishing Co., 1986), p. 797.

[6] Loewy, A., *Criminal Law,* 2nd Ed. (Nutshell Series, St. Paul, West Publishing Co., 1987).

[7] Bazeley's Case, 2 East P.C. 571 (Cr.Cas.Res.1799); see LaFave and Scott, *Criminal Law* (Hornbook Series, St. Paul: West Publishing Co., 1986), §8.1.

[8] 18 U.S.C. §641, et seq.

[9] LaFave and Scott, *Criminal Law* (Hornbook Series, St. Paul: West Publishing Co., 1986), §8.9.

[10] 18 U.S.C. §1341.

[11] 18 U.S.C. §1961 et seq.

[12] 18 U.S.C. §2311 et seq.

[13] 18 U.S.C. §2113.

[14] Fla. Stat. Ann. §812.012, et seq.

[15] Model Penal Code §223 et seq. deals with theft offenses.

[16] Id at §222.1.

[17] Id at §224.1.

CHAPTER 6
Crimes Against the Public

*I shall not today attempt further to define [obscenity];
and perhaps I could never succeed in intelligibly
doing so. But I know it when I see it. . . .*

**Justice Stewart,
concurring in *Jacobellis v. Ohio*, 378 U.S. 184 (1964).**

OUTLINE

SECTION 6.1 DEFINING A "CRIME AGAINST THE PUBLIC"

The two previous chapters were concerned with crimes that involve the victimization of individuals or entities, such as corporations and other business organizations. This chapter examines those crimes that do not have individual victims. These are crimes involving the public welfare, social order, and society's morals. In one sense, the victims of these crimes is the public as a whole; although, in this sense, all crimes injure society as a whole.

Religion has played a strong role in determining what acts, which do not harm anyone, should be illegal. Of course, religious groups do not dictate such policy—this would violate the First Amendment's prohibition of mixing church and state. Religion does, however, influence the moral values of the members of a society. In the United States this influence is predominately Christian. This is the reason that some acts, which directly harm no one, are prohibited.

Some critics call for an end to "victimless crimes." Despite this, many victimless crimes exist and are likely to continue to be prohibited. However, in a democracy such as the United States it is important to examine such crimes carefully to avoid an unwarranted infringement of civil liberties. The more a law is premised upon a moral judgment, the greater the scrutiny should be.

Some of the crimes that follow bear directly upon the administration of government and justice and less upon moral determinations. For example, contempt of court is a crime against the public, and the premise of its prohibition is the theory that if society punishes offenders, others will comply with court orders, and the administration of justice will be enhanced. Prostitution is an example of a crime that is prohibited more for moral reasons than any other.

The crimes included in this chapter have been divided into three subsections: crimes against public morality; crimes against the public order; and crimes against the administration of government.

SECTION 6.2 CRIMES AGAINST PUBLIC MORALITY

Section 6.2(a) Prostitution and Solicitation

Often said to be the oldest profession, **prostitution** is prohibited in every state except Nevada, where each county is given the authority to determine whether to make it criminal.

Prostitution is defined as 1. providing 2. sexual services 3. in exchange for compensation. In a few states only intercourse is included in the defintion of sexual services. In most states, however, sexual services include sodomy, fellatio, cunnilingus, and the touching of another's genitals. The Model Penal Code includes homosexual and other deviate sexual conduct in its definition of sexual activity.[1]

The service must be provided in exchange for compensation. The person who is sexually promiscuous, but unpaid, goes unpunished. Compensation normally means money, but it can come in any form. So the prostitute who accepts legal services from a lawyer in exchange for sexual services has received compensation.

Where prostitution is illegal it is common for prostitutes to use businesses, such as massage parlors and escort services, as a front.

COMMONWEALTH
V.
WALTER

388 Mass. 460, 446 N.E.2d 707 (1983)

[Detectives of the Cambridge Police Department responded to an advertisement which read: "Swedish and Shiatsu Massage in Harvard Square. . . . "]

Officer Walsh went to the address in an unmarked police car with Detective Bombino and two other policemen. He pressed the buzzer for apartment 24, and a woman, whom he later identified as the defendant, came to the door. He asked if she were the "Chris," with whom he had just spoken, and she said, "Yes. Why don't you come up?" He followed her to apartment 24, where he saw a man sitting in the bedroom clothed only in pants. After a brief conversation with

LEGAL TERMS

prostitution
The crime of
1. providing
2. sexual services
3. in exchange for compensation.

the defendant, the man put on the rest of his clothing and left.

The defendant invited Officer Walsh into the bedroom, and told him to get undressed. She asked him for $30, which he gave to her. She massaged his body generally, using her hands and some oil. During the course of the massage she removed her shirt and was naked from the waist up. She then massaged his genitals, in an act of masturbation, for about forty-five seconds. Officer Walsh then got off the bed and said he was a police officer, and that she was under arrest. . . .

The defendant argues that a full body massage which includes the genitals, by use of the hands only, for a fee, is not prostitution within the meaning of the statute. . . . She argues that "sexual activity" is confined to coitus or oral-genital contact.

We conclude that prostitution includes performing masturbation upon a person's genitals by another's hands, for a fee. The term "sexual activity," resting as it does on the common understanding of the meaning of prostitution. . . .

The defendant next argues that prohibition of her activities interferes with her constitutional right to privacy. . . .

The scope of the right to privacy under the United States Constitution is not well defined. However, whatever protection it affords to the private, sexual activity of consenting adults, we conclude that the defendant's activities were not protected, because they were performed for a fee. We will not extend a constitutional right to privacy to one who indiscriminately performs sexual acts for hire. . . .

Solicitation is a related crime. Any person who engages in selling sex, buying sex, or attempting to buy sex is guilty of solicitation. Note that a prostitute may be guilty of both solicitation and prostitution, if the prostitute make the first contact with the buyer. There need not be the actual sale of sex for solicitation—only an attempt to sell sexual services. The clients of prostitutes, when prosecuted, are charged with solicitation.

The Model Penal Code states that "A person commits a violation if he hires a prostitute to engage in sexual activity with him, or if he enters or remains in a house of prostitution for the purpose of engaging in sexual activity."[2]

Those who promote prostitution ("pimps") are usually punished more severely than prostitutes and customers. The Model Penal Code makes knowingly promoting prostitution a felony of the third degree if a child under sixteen years of age is prostituted; the defendant's wife, child, or other ward is prostituted; the defendant forces or encourages another to engage in prostitution; or the defendant owns, controls, or manages a house of prostitution. In all other cases promotion is a misdemeanor.

Nearly all sex for hire cases fall under state jurisdiction. However, the federal government may be involved in prosecution when a prostitute is transported in interstate commerce, or any other person is transported in interstate commerce for an immoral purpose.[3]

Section 6.2(b) Deviate Sexual Conduct

Rape and related crimes were discussed in an earlier chapter. That chapter focused on sexual behavior that results in harm to a victim. This discussion is different, as there is usually no victim, other than society as a whole. Deviate sexual conduct has many definitions, but most states include fellatio, cunnilingus, anal sex, and all homosexual activity, within the grasp of their deviate sexual statutes. So, consenting adults, married or not, may be prosecuted for participating in such sexual activity.

The foundation of the prohibition of sodomy and related acts is morality. Many religions, including Christianity, believe that all sex other than vaginal intercourse between a man and woman is deviate. The reality is that many, if not most, people engage in sex that falls into the definition of deviate sex. For this reason, many contend that such acts are normal and should not be prohibited. Others argue that it does not matter if the behavior is normal or deviate—that sex between two consenting adults is private and involves no victims and, as such, is of no concern of the government. However, such laws continue to exist. Further, they have survived constitutional challenges in most instances.

BOWERS
V.
HARDWICK

478 U.S. 186 (1986)

MAJORITY OPINION BY JUSTICE WHITE

In August 1982, respondent was charged with violating the Georgia statute criminalizing sodomy by committing that act with another adult male in the bedroom of respondent's home. After a preliminary hearing, the District Attorney decided not to present the matter to the grand jury unless further evidence developed.

Respondent then brought suit in the Federal District Court, challenging the constitutionality of the statute insofar as it criminalized sodomy. He asserted that he was a practicing homosexual, that the Georgia sodomy statute, as administered by the defendants, placed him in imminent danger of arrest, and that the statute for several reasons violates the Federal Constitution. . . .

This case does not require a judgment on whether laws against sodomy between consenting adults in general, or between homosexuals in particular, are wise or desirable. It raises no question about the right or propriety of state legislative decisions to repeal their laws that criminalize homosexual sodomy, or of state court decisions invalidating those laws on state constitutional grounds. The issue presented is whether the Federal Constitution confers a fundamental right upon homosexuals to engage in sodomy and hence invalidates the laws of the many States that still make such conduct illegal. . . .

. . . Respondent, however, asserts that the result should be different where the homosexual conduct occurs in the privacy of the home. He relies on *Stanley v. Georgia*, 394 U.S. 557 (1969), where the Court held that the First Amendment prevents convicting for possessing and reading obscene material in the privacy of his home: "If the First Amendment means anything, it means that a State has no business telling a man, sitting alone at his house, what books he may read or what films he may watch."

Stanley did protect conduct that would not have been protected outside the home, and it partially prevented the enforcement of state obscenity laws; but the decision was firmly gounded in the First Amendment. The right pressed upon us here has no similar support in the text of the Constitution, and it does not qualify for recognition under the prevailing principles for construing the Fourteenth Amendment. . . .

[The vote of the Court was 5–4. Justice White wrote the majority opinion. Chief Justice Burger and Justices Powell, O'Connor, and Rehnquist joined in that opinion. Burger and Powell also filed concurring opinions. Justice Stevens filed a dissenting opinion, which Justices Brennan and Marshall joined. Justice Blackmum also filed a dissent and Justices Marshall, Brennan, and Stevens joined.]

DISSENTING OPINION BY JUSTICE BLACKMUN

This case is no more about a "fundamental right to engage in homosexual sodomy," than *Stanley v. Georgia* was about a fundamental right to watch obscene movies. . . . Rather, this case is about "the most comprehensive of rights and the most valued by civilized men," namely, "the right to be left alone." . . . "

. . . . Like Justice Holmes, I believe that "[i]t is revolting to have no better reason for a rule of law than that so it was laid down in the time of Henry IV. It is still more revolting if the grounds upon which it was laid down have vanished long since, and the rule simply persists from blind imitation of the past." I believe we must analyze respondent's claim in light of the values that underlie the constitutional right to privacy. If that right means anything, it means that, before Georgia can prosecute its citizens for making choices about the most intimate aspects of their lives, it must do more than assert that the choice they have made is an "abominable crime not fit to be named among Christians." . . .

"Our cases long have recognized that the Constitution embodies a promise that a certain private sphere of individual liberty will be kept largely beyond the reach of government" . . .

In construing the right to privacy, the Court has proceeded along two somewhat distinct, albeit complementary, lines. First, it has recognized a privacy interest with reference to certain decisions that are properly for the individual to make. . . . Second, it has recognized a privacy interest with reference to certain places without regard for the particular activities in which the individuals who occupy them are engaged. . . .

Only the most willful blindness could obscure the fact that sexual intimacy is a "sensitive, key relationship of human existence, central to family life, community welfare, and the development of human personality." The fact that individuals define themselves in a significant way through their intimate sexual relationships with others suggests, in a Nation as diverse as ours, that there may be many "right" ways of conducting those relationships, and that much of the richness of a relationship will come from the freedom an individual has to choose the form and nature of these intensely personal bonds. . . .

The behavior for which Hardwick faces prosecution occurred in his own home, a place to which the Fourth Amendment attaches special significance. . . . Just as the right to privacy is more than the mere aggregation of a number of entitlements to engage in specific behavior, so too, protecting the physical integrity of the home is more than merely a means of protecting specific activities that often take place there. . . .

. . . I can only hope . . . the Court soon will reconsider its analysis and conclude that depriving individuals of the right to choose for themselves how to conduct their intimate relationships poses a far greater threat to the values most deeply rooted in our Nation's history than tolerance of nonconformity could ever do. Because I think the Court today betrays those values, I dissent.

Despite continued prohibition of sodomy, and related acts, in many states, the laws are seldom enforced. One reason is that law enforcement officials have shown a reluctance to enforce such laws, often because crimes perceived as more serious are time demanding and leave little manpower and resources to enforce victimless crimes. In addition, there simply is the problem of discovering violations. Most sexual conduct occurs privately, and, as such, police rarely discover violations independently. Of course, those who participate in prohibited sexual conduct are not likely to report their sex partners' acts to law enforcement.

Section 6.2(c) Indecent Exposure and Lewdness

Indecent exposure, or the exposure of one's "private parts" in public, was a common-law misdemeanor. Today, the crime is usually criminalized by state statute or by local ordinance.

Most indecent exposure laws require 1. an intentional exposure 2. of one's private parts 3. in a public place. In some jurisdictions it is required that the exposure be done in an "offensive manner."

In 1991, the United States Supreme Court examined a public nudity statute in the context of nude barroom dancing. In *Barnes v. Glen Theater, Inc.*, 1991 U.S. Lexis 3633 (June 21, 1991), the Court upheld an Indiana statute that requires dancers to wear pasties and g-strings. While the court found that nude dancing was expressive conduct, it determined that states may require the dancers to cover their genitals. The court did say that erotic performances were protected by the First Amendment, provided the dancers wear a scant amount of clothing.

The Model Penal Code prohibits public indecency. The Code goes further and has a provision which proscribes all lewd acts that the defendant knows is likely to be observed by others who would be "affronted or alarmed" by the act.[4]

Section 6.2(d) Obscenity

Congress shall make no law respecting the establishment of religion, or prohibiting the free exercise thereof; *or abridging the freedom of speech,* or of the press; or the right of the people peaceably to assemble, and to petition the Government for a redress of grievances.

This is the First Amendment to the United States Constitution. Most, if not all, states have a similar provision in their constitutions. The italicized portion represents the only protection of speech in the Constitution. Because it is brief and broad, it is dependent upon a great amount of interpretation to give it meaning. Also, because of its brevity and broadness, courts often interpret it differently. Even the Supreme Court has changed its interpretation of the clause, in particular areas, on several occasions. Freedom of speech encompasses far more than will be examined in this chapter. What will be discussed in this chapter is the extent of governmental power to regulate conduct that it deems to be indecent. Specifically, this section will address sexually explicit materials, including films, books, and erotic dancing.

It is well-established that the term "speech," as it is used in the First Amendment, means more than spoken utterances. It includes all forms of expression.

Both the federal and state governments regulate conduct, speech, books, movies, and other forms of expression that are believed to be "obscene." State governments are the most involved with regulating obscenity due to general police power (the power to regulate for the health, welfare, and safety of its citizens). However, the federal government is involved; for example, it has criminalized sending obscene materials through the mail.[5]

Not all indecencies may be criminalized. Simply because something strikes one person as indecent does not mean that it should be prohibited. People have differing values, and to allow governments to prohibit all conduct (or other things) that is found offensive by some member of society would be to allow our government to criminalize all aspects of life. In addition, people perceive things differently. For example, in 1990 the Cincinnati Arts Center was charged with obscenity for displaying photographs taken by a respected artist, Robert Mapplethorpe. Included in the photos were depictions of nude children. The prosecutor contended that the pictures were obscene. A jury did not agree. The Arts Center and its director were acquitted, and many of the jurors commented that the testimony of art experts convinced them that the pictures had serious artistic value and were not obscene.[6]

It is important that the First Amendment be flexible and tolerant of new ideas and methods of expression. Simply because the majority of citizens would not see value in a form of expression does not mean it has no value. If the opposite were true, then expression aimed at particular minority groups could be censored. This is not to say that there is no limit on the freedom of expression. When considering sexually oriented expression, that line is drawn where the expression becomes obscene.[7]

Obscenity has proven to be an elusive concept for the Supreme Court. Through a series of decisions, from 1957 to the present, the Court has attempted to define obscenity. The quote by Justice Potter Stewart, which opened this chapter, is a testament to the difficulty in defining such a concept. It also reflects what many people believe, that they may not be able to define obscenity, but they recognize it when they see it.

In *Roth v. United States,* 354 U.S. 476 (1957), it was held that obscenity is not protected by the First Amendment because it lacks redeeming social importance. The Court then established a test for determining whether something was obscene, and, as such, not protected by the First Amendment. That test was "whether to the average person, applying contemporary community standards, the dominant theme of the material taken as a whole appeals to prurient interest." In addition, the material had to be "utterly without redeeming social value." Simply because "literature is dismally unpleasant, uncouth, and tawdry is not enough to make it obscene."[8]

In 1973 the Supreme Court reexamined the *Roth* obscenity test in *Miller v. California*, 413 U.S. 15 (1973). In *Miller* the Court rejected the requirement that the material be "utterly without redeeming social value," and lowered the standard to lacking "serious literary, artistic, political, or scientific value." The test under *Miller* has three parts:

1. The average person, applying contemporary community standards, would find that the work, taken as a whole, appeals to the prurient interest and
2. the work must depict or describe, in a patently offensive manner, sexual conduct specifically defined by the applicable state law, and
3. the work, when taken as a whole, must lack serious literary, artistic, political, or scientific value.

The *Miller* test makes it easier for states to regulate sexual materials. An "average person" has been equated with a reasonable person, as used in tort law.[9] The material must appeal to "prurient interest." Materials that have a tendency to excite a lustful, "shameful or morbid interest in nudity, sex or excretion" meet the prurient interest element.[10] Material that provokes normal, healthy, sexual desires is not obscene because it does not appeal to prurient interest.[11]

The Court gave examples in *Miller* of "patently offensive" materials that included depictions or descriptions of "ultimate sex acts, normal or perverted, actual or simulated . . . of masturbation, excretory functions, and lewd exhibition of the genitals."

One area where the states have substantially more power to regulate obscenity is when minors are involved. The Court has held that all child pornography is unprotected because of the special protection that is necessary to protect children from exploitation. See *New York v. Ferber*, 458 U.S. 747 (1982). Similarly, governments may prohibit the distribution and sale of erotic materials to minors, even if such materials are not obscene. See *Capitol News Co. v. Metropolitan Government of Nashville and Davidson County*, 562 S.W.3d 430 (Tenn. 1978). Also, in *Osborne v. Ohio*, ___ U.S. ___, 110 S.Ct. 1691 (1990), the Supreme Court held that a person may be convicted for possession of child pornography in the home. This is an exception to the general rule that a person may possess obscene material in the home.

As mentioned in *Miller v. South Bend* governments may control the time, place, and manner of expression. Accordingly, certain restrictions may be valid that deal with expression in certain places, such as establishments that sell alcohol. Later, in the chapter that addresses constitutional defenses to criminal accusations, other time, place, and manner issues will be addressed.

One place where the power of the government to regulate sexually explicit materials is lessened is in homes. In many respects, the law reflects the attitude that a "man's home is his castle," and deserves special protection. As such, the United States Supreme Court struck down the conviction of a man for possession of obscene materials in his home.[12] However, as previously mentioned, a person is not privileged to possess child pornography in the home.

The Model Penal Code makes it a misdemeanor to knowingly or recklessly do any of the following:[13]

1. Sell, deliver, or provide (or offer to do one of the three) any obscene writing, picture, record, or other obscene representation.
2. Present or perform in an obscene play, dance, or other performance.
3. Publish or exhibit obscene materials.
4. Possess obscene materials for commercial purposes.
5. Sell or otherwise commercially distribute materials represented as obscene.

The Code presumes that anyone who distributes obscene materials in the course of their business has done so knowingly or recklessly.

Material is considered obscene under the code if "considered as a whole, its predominant appeal is to prurient interest, that is, a shameful or morbid interest, in nudity, sex, or excretion, and if in addition it goes substantially beyond customary limits of candor in describing or representing such matter." Note that the Code's definition is similar to the constitional definition. The Code does add the requirement that the material go beyond "customary limits of candor." The Code makes it an affirmative defense that the obscene material was possessed for governmental, scientific, educational or other justified causes. It also is not a crime for a person to give such materials to personal associates in noncommercial situations. The Code focuses on punishing commercial dissemination of obscene material.

Obscenity is a complex area of law. Many different criminal prohibitions exist throughout the states and federal government that focus on the sale, distribution, and possession of sexually oriented materials, performance of erotic dance, and public nudity. So long as minors are not involved, the activity is protected unless it is obscene. To determine whether pornography is obscene (hardcore) one must apply the *three-part Miller* test. The states are free to regulate if children are involved, either as a participant in the erotic materials (or performance) or as a buyer of erotic materials, even if the material is not obscene.

Because of the plethora of cases in this area, it is strongly recommended that thorough research be conducted. There is a good chance that precedent with similar facts may be found. Beware, however, that this is an issue that often leaves courts split. Be sure that the opinions you find reflect the law of your jurisdiction.

SECTION 6.3 CRIMES AGAINST THE PUBLIC ORDER

Section 6.3(a) Introduction

Crimes against the public order are crimes that involve **breaches of the peace**. The phrase breaches of the peace refers to all crimes that involve disturbing the tranquility or order of society. Making breaches of the peace criminal has its roots in early English common law. In England, breaches of the peace by individuals were criminal, as were breaches by groups.

Three groups of breaches were recognized; all were punished as misdemeanors. If three or more people met with an intention of causing a disturbance they committed the common law offense of unlawful assembly. If the group took some action in an attempt to breach the peace they were guilty of rout, and if they were successful the crime was riot.

Today, all jurisdictions prohibit breaches of the peace in some form by statute. The names of statutory crimes include disorderly conduct, unlawful assembly, riot, inciting violence, unlawful threat, and vagrancy.

Section 6.3(b) Riot and Unlawful Assembly

Most states now have legislation that prohibits groups of people from meeting with the purpose of committing an unlawful act or committing a lawful act in an unlawful manner. This crime may be named unlawful assembly or riot. A group, or "assembly," is a specified minimum number of people, often three or five. Some

LEGAL TERMS

breaches of the peace
  Crimes that involve disturbing the tranquility or order of society. Disturbing the peace, rioting, inciting violence, and vagrancy are examples of crimes that are categorized as breaches of the peace.

jurisdictions continue to recognize the distinctions between unlawful assembly, rout, and riot.

The Model Penal Code recognizes two related crimes: riot and failure to disperse. Both crimes require an assembly of two or more persons who are behaving disorderly. If the purpose of the assembly is to commit a crime (felony or misdemeanor), to coerce public officials to act or not act, or if a deadly weapon is used, then the crime is riot.[14]

Failure to disperse occurs when a law-enforcement officer, or other official, orders the members of a group of three or more to disperse, and someone refuses. The disorderly conduct that the assembly is engaged in must be "likely to cause substantial harm or serious inconvenience, annoyance, or alarm," before an officer may order the group to disperse. This provision is included because the freedoms to associate and assemble are protected by the First Amendment to the United States Constitution, and such activity may be regulated only when it poses a threat to person, property, or society.

Most jurisdictions punish these crimes as misdemeanors. However, they may be elevated to felony if committed with a dangerous weapon, if someone is injured as a result of the activity, or if law enforcement officers are obstructed from performing their duties. The Model Penal Code makes rioting a felony of the third degree and failure to disperse a misdemeanor.

Section 6.3(c) Disturbing the Peace

As mentioned, individuals may also commit crimes against the public order. Disturbing the peace is such a crime. This crime is also known as disorderly conduct, threat, excessive noise, and affray. In essence, any time the public order or tranquility is unreasonably interrupted by an individual, disturbance of the peace has occurred. States may have one law that encompasses all such acts or separate statutes for each.

Disturbances may occur in hundreds of forms. One may disturb the peace by making loud noises in a residential area at midnight, by attempting to cause fights with others, or by encouraging others to engage in similar conduct. Statutes often also prohibit indecent language and gestures.

These statutes are often broadly worded and are vague. As such, they are often attacked as being unconstitutional. The defenses of overbreadth and vagueness are discussed in the chapter on defenses and will not be covered here. One defense that will be examined is the First Amendment right to free speech and its relationship to offensive words and gestures.

As you have learned, the First Amendment protects all forms of expression. This protection prohibits government from making expression criminal. However, exceptions to the First Amendment have been created. Words that have a likelihood of causing a riot are such an exception. That is, even though the words are expression, they may be punished. The reason is obvious: riots lead to property damage, personal injuries, and sometimes death. As such, the interest of the government to control such behavior outweighs the First Amendment interest.

The **fighting words Doctrine** is another exception. The Supreme Court has defined fighting words as those that inflict injury, tend to incite an immediate breach of the peace, or by their nature will cause a violent reaction by a person who hears them.[15] Laws that regulate speech that is allowed to be regulated, such as fighting words, must be drafted narrowly; that is, only the conduct intended must be prohibited. If a law is drawn which has the effect of making fighting words and legitimate speech illegal, it is unconstitutional and void.

The defendant in the following case was convicted of disorderly conduct. The Court found that his speech was unprotected because he used fighting words.

CITY OF LITTLE FALLS V. EDWIN GEORGE WITUCKI

295 N.W.2d 243 (Minn. 1980)

On December 11, 1978, a Morrison County Court jury found defendant guilty of disorderly conduct in violation of Little Falls, Minnesota, Ordinances. . . .

At approximately 11:00 P.M. on September 19, 1978, defendant Edwin George Witucki and a few of his friends entered the West Side Bar in Little Falls, Minnesota. Just outside the building defendant found a cat which he carried into the building and placed on the bar. Pursuant to defendant's request, one bartender served the cat some beef jerky and a shotglass of cream and served defendant a drink.

About five minutes later, the other bartender, Paula Erwin, told defendant to take the cat outside. He refused. She told him he was cut-off from being served until the cat

LEGAL TERMS

fighting words Doctrine
Words that cause injury or tend to cause immediate breaches of the peace are fighting words. Such expression is not protected by the First Amendment to the United States Constitution.

was removed. He responded, "I let you slip once too many times, I'm not going to let you slip again." Erwin, for the third time, told defendant to remove the cat. He responded by saying, "Hey, Butch [defendant], I don't have to take any of your crap." She then turned to return to the other end of the bar, and Witucki called her a "black-haired witch," a "cock-sucker," and a "son-of-a-bitch."

When asked at trial about her reaction to the words, Erwin testified, "I didn't care for them very well. It scared me. There was nothing I could do about it. There were no guys around so I thought the best thing for me to do, because I was really mad at the time, was just to walk away from him." She also testified that calling the police or any sort of violent action on her part would not be wise or safe because he might wait for her outside after hours and because he was much larger than she and there were no men around to help her.

* * *

The question is, did defendant's words in the circumstances in which they were uttered constitute "those personally abusive epithets which, when addressed to the ordinary citizen, are as a matter of common knowledge, inherently likely to provoke violent reaction." . . .

In *In re* S.L.J. the appellant was a fourteen-year-old girl who yelled "fuck you pigs" at two police officers. . . . The court noted that although "no ordered society would condone the vulgar language" and although "her words were intended to, and did, arouse resentment in the officers, the constitution requires more before a person can be convicted for mere speech." The court held that where the words were spoken in retreat by a small teenage girl who was between fifteen and thirty feet from the two police officers sitting in their squad car, "there was no reasonable likelihood that [the words] would tend to incite an immediate breach of the peace or to provoke violent reaction by an ordinary, reasonable person.

In *Cohen v. California*, 403 U.S. 15, 91 S.Ct. 1780, 29 L. Ed.2d 284 (1971), the defendant wore a jacket on which the words "Fuck the Draft" were plainly visible. The words were not directed against the person of any possibly offended person; they were directed against the draft.

The instant case is readily distinguishable from both *In re S.L.J.* and *Cohen v. California.* Unlike the defendant's language in *Cohen,* Witucki's language was directed at and was intended to be about a person, namely Erwin. The abusive language hurled by defendant at Erwin could readily be found by a jury to be inherently likely to incite violence. Defendant was not, as in *Cohen,* merely expressing a controversial political opinion in a vulgar way; he was directly insulting and intimidating an innocent person.

* * *

The fact that the words used by appellant are vulgar, offensive, and insulting, and that their use is condemned by an overwhelming majority of citizens does not make them punishable under the criminal statutes of this state unless they fall outside the protection afforded to speech by the First Amendment.

* * *

Defendant's speech in this case is not a "trifling and annoying instance of individual distasteful abuse of a privilege." He addressed such abusive, vulgar, insulting and obscene language toward the bartender that his language was properly found to be within the fighting words category of unprotected speech. . . .

[Conviction Affirmed]

Section 6.3(d) Incitement/Advocacy of Unlawful Conduct

Whenever one person, acting independently, encourages another to commit an unlawful act or intends to cause a riot, the crimes of incitement of lawful behavior or incitement of riot may be charged. Unlike riot, which requires a group, one person may commit this crime. Unlike disturbing the peace, it may be committed in a peaceful manner.

However, since the First Amendment applies, such statutes must be narrow. In fact, only speech which creates a **clear and present danger** may be controlled. The United States Supreme Court has said that "incitement of imminent lawless action" may be regulated.[16] Anything less may not be regulated. Hence, merely

LEGAL TERMS

clear and present danger doctrine
Words that create a clear and present danger are not protected by the First Amendment and may be regulated by government.

advocating unlawful conduct in the abstract is protected. Advocating future unlawful conduct is also protected, as it poses no imminent threat.

Section 6.3(e) Threats

Finally, in the speech arena, threats are addressed. Threat statutes may make threatening individuals, groups, or even property criminal. Threats to harm people are similar to assaults. However, threat is broader, as it often protects property and the people at large. The purpose of threat statutes is to preserve public order, and the purpose of assault statutes is to protect individuals.

For example, if a defendant were to call in a bomb threat to a public office there would be no assault, but there is a threat. A person may be guilty of threat by making the prohibited statements, even if untrue. So, if a defendant makes a bomb threat, but has placed no bomb in the building, a crime has been committed. Threats are misdemeanors in most jurisdictions and are punished less severely than assaults. In the following case the defendant was convicted under the Kentucky threat statute.

THOMAS
V.
THE COMMONWEALTH OF KENTUCKY

574 S.W.2d 903 (Ky. App. 1978)

The case for the Commonwealth was based solely on the testimony of Gladys Thomas. Mrs. Thomas on direct examination stated that on the Friday before she went to swear out the warrant that she was in her front yard cutting weeds with a butcher knife when appellant came out of the house, hit her across the back with his hand, laughed and ran into a barber shop next door. Appellant then came back laughing and hit her across the back with a belt and then ran into a liquor store about three doors down from the house. Appellant continued to aggravate Mrs. Thomas until she asked him to go and get her a coke. Mrs. Thomas then testified thusly:

So, we went about an hour, an hour and a half after my mom left and he came in and said, "I told you to get ready to go," and I said, "I'm not going," and he grabbed me by the hair of the head and threw me against the refrigerator and said, "you are going to I will kill you and prove self-defense. This is one time everything is on my side. So, just get dressed and let's go somewhere and show everybody what a happy family we are."

Next, Mrs. Thomas gave testimony concerning the circumstances surrounding the threat which is the basis for the charge against appellant:

So, on Wednesday, he came in and he said, "I will come home. I'm coming home." I said, "you can't. You absolutely cannot. I went and applied for welfare," and he said, "I have to tell the man, Mr. Clark, that I'm here or I'll be in trouble." One thing led to another and he jumped in the middle of the floor and said, "you and Brenda have got me against the wall. You're going to get me in trouble. I will cut both your heads off before I go back." Those are almost the exact words. And I looked around and the little girl was standing right in the screen door.

On cross examination, Mrs. Thomas testified that this threat was made in the late afternoon and that on the next morning, on July 15, 1976, she sent and got a warrant.

[The applicable Kentucky statute] provides thusly:

A person is guilty of terroristic threatening when:

(a) He threatens to commit any crime likely to result in death or serious bodily injury to another person or likely to result in substantial property damage to another person; or
(b) He intentionally makes false statements for the purpose of causing evacuation of a building, place of assembly, or facility of public transportation.
(c) Terroristic threatening is a Class A misdemeanor. [cite ommitted].

This court believes that [the above statute] is not unconstitutionally vague and overbroad since the conduct proscribed, "threaten[ing] to commit a crime likely to result in death or serious physical injury" is not protected under either the Kentucky or United States Constitutions. Further, the language of the statute is sufficiently explicit to put the average citizen on notice as to the nature of the conduct so proscribed.

This court is aware of the recent decision in *U.S. v. Sturgill*, 563 F.2d 307 (6th Cir. 1977), which invalidated [another Kentucky statute] on the basis that it was unconstitutionally overbroad. [The invalidated statute] provides: "A person is guilty of harassment when with intent to harass, annoy or alarm another person he: (b) In a public place, makes an offensively coarse utterance, gesture, or display, or addresses abusive language to any person present."

In *Sturgill*, the court, citing *Gooding v. Wilson*, 405 U.S. 518, 92 S.Ct. 1103, 31 L.Ed.2d 408 (1972), held that in order for a statute, which punishes spoken words only, to withstand an attack on its constitutionality; it must be first authoritatively interpreted by the state courts as not interfering with speech protected by the First Amendment.

This case can be distinguished from *Sturgill*, in that the language so proscribed under [the terroristic threatening statute] is clearly without constitutional protection under the First Amendment. . . .

Certainly, [the terroristic threat statute] does not apply in the case of idle talk or jesting. The defendant's intent to commit the crime of "terroristic threatening" can be plainly inferred from the defendant's own words and the circumstances surrounding them. All the statute requires is that the defendant threaten "to commit any crime likely to result in death or serious physical injury to another person or likely to result in substantial property damage to another person." [conviction] Affirmed.

Section 6.3(f) Vagrancy and Panhandling

Vagrancy, as a criminal law issue, has received considerable attention. Most states and municipalities have statutes that forbid vagrancy. At common law a vagrant was one who wandered from place to place with no means of support, except the charity of others. At one time, in early English law, vagrancy applied to disorderly persons, rogues (a dishonest wanderer), and vagabonds (a homeless person with no means of support).

Beginning in the 1880s it was common in the United States for statutes to prohibit a wide range of behavior as vagrancy.

These statutes were drafted broadly to permit law enforcement great discretion in their enforcement. This discretion was used to control the "undesirables" of society. Many statutes made the status of being homeless, a gambler, and a drug addict a crime.

Today, states may not make personal status, such as drug addiction or alcoholism, a crime. The United States Supreme Court has held that doing so violates the Eight Amendment's prohibition of cruel and unusual punishment.[17] However, until 1972, people found undesirable by the police could be arrested under broadly worded vagrancy statutes for "wandering," or walking around a city, because this was an act, not a status. This ended in 1972 when the United States Supreme Court handed down *Papachristou v. City of Jacksonville.*

PAPACHRISTOU
V.
CITY OF JACKSONVILLE

405 U.S. 156 (1972)

This case involves eight defendants who were convicted in a Florida municipal court of violating a Jacksonville, Florida, vagrancy ordinance. . . .

[The ordinance was very broad in its scope, prohibiting many acts, including: Rogues and vagabonds, or dissolute persons who go about begging, common gamblers, juggling and other unlawful games and plays, common drunkards, common night walkers, wandering from place to place without lawful purpose or object, men who are able to work but live upon the earnings of their wife or children, habitual loafers, persons who are not working and spend too much time near houses where liquor is sold, and many other acts.]

The facts are stipulated. Papachristou and Calloway are white females. Melton and Johnson are black males. Papachristou was enrolled in a job-training program sponsored by the State Employment Service at Florida Junior College in Jacksonville. Calloway was a typing and shorthand teacher at a state mental institution located near Jacksonville. She was the owner of the automobile in which the four defendants were arrested. Melton was a Vietnam war veteran who had been released from the Navy after nine months in a veterans' hospital. On the date of his arrest he was a part-time computer helper while attending college as a full-time student in Jacksonville. Johnson was a tow-motor operator in a grocery chain warehouse and was a lifelong resident of Jacksonville.

At the time of their arrest the four of them were riding in Calloway's car on the main thoroughfare in Jacksonville. They had left a restaurant owned by Johnson's uncle where they had eaten and were on their way to a nightclub. The arresting officers denied that the racial mixture in the car played any part in the decision to make the arrest. The arrest, they said, was made because the defendants had stopped near a used-car lot which had been broken into several times. There was, however, no evidence of any breaking and entering on the night in question.

Of these four charged with "prowling by auto" none had been previously arrested except Papachristou who had once been convicted of a municipal offense.

Jimmy Lee Smith and Milton Henry (who is not a petitioner) were arrested between 9 and 10 A.M. on a weekday in downtown Jacksonville, while waiting for a friend who was to lend them a car so they could apply for a job at a produce company. Smith was a part-time produce worker and part-time organizer for a Negro political group. He has a common-law wife and three children supported by him and his wife. He had been arrested several times but convicted only once. Smith's companion, Henry, was an 18-year-old high school student with no previous record of arrest.

This morning was cold, and Smith has no jacket, so they went briefly into a dry cleaning shop to wait, but left when requested to do so. They thereafter walked back and forth two or three times over a two-block stretch looking for their friend. The store owners, who apparently were wary of Smith and his companion, summoned two police officers who searched the men and found neither had a weapon. But they were arrested because the officers said they had no identification and because the officers did not believe their story. . . .

This ordinance is void for vagueness, both in the sense that it "fails to give a person of ordinary intelligence fair notice that his contemplated conduct is forbidden by statute," . . . and because it encourages arbitrary and erratic arrests and convictions. . . .

Living under a rule of law entails various suppositions, one of which is that "[all persons] are entitled to be informed as to what the State commands or forbids " . . .

The Jacksonville ordinance makes criminal activities which by modern standards are normally innocent. "Nightwalking" is one. Florida construes the ordinance not to make criminal one night's wandering, on the "habitual" wanderer or, as the ordinance describes it, "common night walkers." We know, however, from experience that sleepless people often walk at night, perhaps hopeful that sleep-inducing relaxation will result. . . .

. . . Here the net cast is large, not to give the courts the power to pick and choose but to increase the arsenal of the police. . . .

Another aspect of the ordinance's vagueness appears when we focus, not on the lack of notice given a potential offender, but on the effect of the unfettered discretion it places in the hands of the Jacksonville police. Caleb Foote, an early student of this subject, has called the vagrancy-type as offering "punishment by analogy." Such crimes, though long common in Russia, are not compatible with our constitutional system. We allow our police to make arrests only on "probable cause," a Fourth Amendment and Fourteenth Amendment standard applicable to the States as well as to the Federal Government. Arresting a person on suspicion, like arresting a person for investigation, is foreign to our system, even when the arrest is for past criminality. Future criminality, however, is the common justification for the presence of vagrancy statutes. . . .

A direction by a legislature to police to arrest all "suspicious" persons would not pass constitutional muster. A vagrancy prosecution may be merely the cloak for a conviction which could not be obtained on the real but undisclosed grounds for the arrest. . . .

Those generally implicated by the imprecise terms of the ordinance—poor people, nonconformists, dissenters, idlers—may be required to comport themselves according to the lifestyle deemed appropriate by the Jacksonville police and the courts. Where, as here, there are no standards governing the exercise of the discretion granted by the ordinance, the scheme permits and encourages an arbitrary and discriminatory enforcement of the law. It furnishes a convenient tool for "harsh and discriminatory enforcement by local prosecuting officials, against particular groups deemed to merit their displeasure" . . . . It results in a regime in which the poor and the unpopular are permitted to "stand on a public sidewalk . . . only at the whim of any police officer." . . .

A presumption that people who might walk or loaf or loiter or stroll or frequent houses where liquor is sold, or who are supported by their wives or who look suspicious to the police are to become future criminals is too precarious for a rule of law. . . .

The Jacksonville ordinance cannot be squared with our constitutional standards and is plainly unconstitutional.

The result of *Papachristou* has been more narrowly drawn vagrancy statutes. Today such laws focus on more particularized behavior, and in many instances, a mens rea element has been added. This prevents simple acts, such as walking at night, from being criminal. For example, a vagrancy law may prohibit "loitering or standing around with an intent to gamble," or "loitering or standing in a transportation facility (e.g., bus station) with the intent of soliciting charities."

In recent years panhandling (begging) has increasingly become a problem for most cities. Panhandlers often choose to congregate in and near public transportation egresses and ingresses due to the large number of people who use such facilities. Because panhandlers are sometimes aggressive and intimidating to patrons of such facilities, some jurisdictions have chosen to prohibit begging at public transportation sites. New York City has such a regulation. That regulation was challenged as unconstitutional in 1990 by a group of homeless persons. They contend that panhandling is protected expression under the First Amendment.

The Second Circuit Court of Appeals rejected that claim in *Young, et al. v. New York Transit Authority, et al.* Note that at the time this book went to production the United States Supreme Court had granted certiorari, and the case was awaiting decision.

YOUNG, ET AL.
V.
NEW YORK CITY TRANSIT AUTHORITY, ET AL.

903 F.2d 146 (2nd Cir. 1990)

The central issue on this appeal is whether the prohibition of begging and panhandling in the New York City subway system violates the First Amendment of the United States Constitution. . . . [The transit authority implemented regulations which prohibit all panhandling and begging, however, solicitation for religious, charitable, and other causes, is permitted with certain restrictions.]

Before the district court was the following additional evidence. The New York City Subway System transports approximately 3,500,000 passengers on an average workday, operates twenty-four hours a day, seven days a week, and consists of 648 miles of track, 468 subway stations and over 6,000 subway cars. Many parts of the subway system are almost one hundred years old. In a timeworn routine of New York life, each day a multitude descends the steep and long staircases and mechanical escalators to wait on narrow and crowded platforms bounded by dark tunnels and high power electrical rails.

In 1988, the [Transit Authority] initiated a lengthy study-process concerning the "quality of life problems" experienced by riders in their use of the subway system. The study-process disclosed the fact that begging contributes to a public perception that the subway is fraught with danger. A research survey conducted by Peter Harris revealed that, in fact, two-thirds of the subway ridership have been intimidated into giving money to beggars. . . .

During the course of the study-process, [Transit Authority] concerns were not limited to the safety of the ridership. . . . Moreover, the sad statistics reveal that during a ten-month period in 1989, an average of six homeless persons per month died in the subway, including fifteen persons who were struck by trains. . . .

A. Speech v. Conduct

On this appeal the plaintiffs contend that "begging is pure speech fully protected by the First Amendment." Recently, the Supreme Court once again admonished against adopting the "view that an apparently limitless variety of conduct can be labeled 'speech' whenever the person engaging in the conduct intends thereby to express an idea." . . .

Common sense tells us that begging is much more "conduct" than it is speech. . . .

In determining "whether particular conduct possesses sufficient communicative elements to bring the First Amendment into play," the Supreme Court asks "whether an intent to convey a particularized message was present, and [whether] the *likelihood was great* that the message would be understood by those who viewed it." . . . For example, the Supreme Court has recognized the "expressive nature" in the burning of a United States flag by a protestor during a political march . . . in the wearing of black arm-bands by school students on particular days in protest of the Vietnam War . . . in the peaceful picketing by union members of a supermarket in a large shopping center to protest unfair labor practices . . . and in conducting a silent sit-in by black persons against a library's segregation policy. . . . We note that in all of these cases there was little doubt from the circumstances of the conduct that it formed a clear and particularized political or social message very much understood by those who viewed it. . . .

Pursuant to the [caselaw] begging is not inseparably intertwined with a "particularized message." It seems fair to say that most individuals who beg are not doing so to convey any social or political message. Rather, they beg to collect money. Arguably, any given beggar may have "[a]n intent to convey a particularized message," e.g.: "I am homeless;" or "There is a living to be made in panhandling." To be sure, the possibilities are myriad. However, despite the intent of an individual beggar, there hardly seems to be a "great likelihood" that the subway passengers who witness the conduct are able to discern what the particularized message might be. . . .

B. The "Schaumburg" Trilogy

On this appeal the plaintiffs also argue that there is no meaningful distinction between begging and other types of charitable solicitation. . . .

. . . Before the district court was evidence that subway passengers experience begging as intimidating, harassing and threatening. Moreoever, the passengers perceive that beggars and panhandlers pervade the system. Indeed, such conduct has been reported in virtually every part of the system. Nowhere in the record is there any indication that passengers felt intimidated by organized charities. . . . In amending the regulation based on its experience, the [Transit Authority] drew a distinction between the harmful effects caused by individual begging and the First Amendment interests associated with solicitation by organized charities. Further, the [Transit Authority] obviously made a judgment that while solicitation by organized charities could be contained to certain areas of the system, the problems posed by begging and panhandling could be addressed by nothing less than the enforcement of the total ban. . . .

We hold that the [regulation] does not violate the First Amendment. . . .

DISSENTING OPINION BY JUDGE MESKILL

* * *

According to the majority, common sense tells us that begging enjoys no First Amendment protection because it is conduct unassociated with any particularized message and because begging, unlike "charitable solicitation," is mere solicitation for money with a diminished communicative content. I agree that common sense and everyday experience should inform our decision. Their true teaching, however, is that both beggars and organized charities who send representatives into the subway have one primary goal: in the words of the majority, "the transfer of money." . . .

As the number of homeless persons grows in the United States, so will the problems associated with vagrancy and panhandling. Examine statutes and ordinances that prohibit such activities with an awareness that they must be drawn carefully to avoid a First Amendment speech problem. Also be aware that other constitutional provisions may be implicated, such as the First Amendment's freedom of association and the Due Process and Equal Protection Clauses of the Fifth and Fourteenth Amendments.

Section 6.3(g)   Drug and Alcohol Crimes

Section 6.3(g.1)   Introduction

Crimes that involve the use or sale of narcotics and alcohol may be classified in many ways. In one sense, such activity offends many people in society and appears to be an offense against the public morality. Whenever a pimp uses a young woman's drug addiction to induce her to become involved in prostitution, it appears to be a crime against an individual.

Despite this, drug and alcohol crimes have been included in this section due to their impact on the order of society. Alcohol-related driving accidents are the cause of many fatalities. Drug addiction often is the cause of other crimes, such as theft, assaults, and prostitution. Police report that a number of domestic problems are caused by alcohol and drugs and that much of the violence directed toward law-enforcement officers is drug-related. Large cities, such as Detroit and Washington, D.C., have experienced a virtual drug boom, which has led to increased assaults, batteries, and drug-related homicides. Many addicts, desperate for a "fix," steal for drug money.

Drug and alcohol use are also expensive. Business America has recently awakened to the expenses associated with employee drug use. Employees who use drugs have a high frequency of absenteeism and low productivity. Decreased performance caused by drug use can be costly, in both human and dollar terms. This is true especially in positions that require great concentration or pose risks to others, such as that of commercial pilots. In addition to business expenses, the high cost of rehabilitation can disable a family financially, and the costs of drug-abuse detection and prosecution can be taxing on a government.

All of this led the federal government to increase its role in drug-law enforcement during the Reagan and Bush administrations. The national government has made money available to localities for increased drug-related law enforcement, as well as intensified its own law-enforcement effort.

Section 6.3(g.2) Alcohol Crimes

Let it not be mistaken, alcohol is a drug. However, the law treats alcohol differently than it does other drugs. Alcohol may be legally possessed, consumed, and sold, subject only to a few restrictions. Narcotics, on the other hand, are significantly restricted. Their sale, possession, and consumption are limited to specific instances, such as for medical use. The federal government, as well as every state, has statutes that spell out what drugs are regulated.

There are many alcohol-related crimes. Public drunkenness laws make it criminal for a person to be intoxicated in a public place. This crime is a minor misdemeanor and rarely prosecuted, as many law-enforcement agencies have a policy of allowing such persons to "sleep it of" and then releasing them.

All states have a minimum age requirement for the sale or consumption of alcohol. Those below the minimum age are minors. Any minor who purchases or consumes alcohol is violating the law. Additionally, any adult who knowingly provides alcohol to a minor is also guilty of a crime, commonly known as contributing to the delinquency of a minor.

Merchants holding liquor licenses may be subject to criminal penalties for not complying with liquor laws, such as selling alcohol on holidays, Sundays, or election day, as well as for selling alcohol to minors. A merchant who violates liquor laws may also suffer the civil penalty of revocation of liquor license.

Alcohol and automobiles have proven to be a deadly and expensive combination. All states have laws that criminalize driving while under the influence of alcohol or drugs. Driving while under the influence of alcohol or drugs, driving while intoxicated, and driving with an unlawful blood-alcohol level are the names of these crimes.

These statutes are generally of two genres. One type of law generally prohibits the operation of a motor vehicle while under the influence of any drug, including alcohol. To prove this charge the quantity of the drug or alcohol in the defendant's system is not at issue; the defendant's ability to operate the vehicle safely is. In such cases, field sobriety tests are often required of the suspect. These are tests that the suspect usually performs at the location where the police made the stop. Coordination, spatial relations, and other driving-related skills are tested by field sobriety tests.

The second type of law prohibits driving a motor vehicle any time a person's blood-alcohol level is above a stated amount. The states vary in the quantity required, although, 10 percent (.10) is common. The effect of these laws is that an irrebuttable presumption is created. The law presumes that anyone with the stated blood-alcohol level or above cannot safely operate a motor vehicle. Under such statutes, evidence that a person can safely operate a motor vehicle with a blood-alcohol level greater than the maximum allowed is not permitted.

In recent years drunk driving has received considerable public and legislative attention. The result has been stricter laws and greater punishment for offenders. The once common police practice of driving drunk drivers home is virtually nonexistent today.

First offenses are usually misdemeanors. Second or third offenses are felonies. In many jurisdictions there has been a move toward alcohol treatment, rather than incarceration. This often involves house arrest, alcohol treatment, and defensive driving education. Also while in these programs convicted persons are commonly required to submit to periodic blood or urine screening.

For first-time offenders these programs have many advantages over prison. First, the focus is on curing the alcohol problem. If successful, the possibility of repetition is eliminated. Second, convicted persons are often permitted to continue to work and maintain family relationships. Finally, the cost of administration of alcohol programs is lower than the cost of incarceration. The

Drug Dealer Testifying Before the U.S. Congress The hood is used to conceal the identity of the witness. *Courtesy C-Span.*

value of such programs for repeat offenders is questionable, and in many jurisdictions jail time is required as early as a second conviction.

Section 6.3(g.3)   Drug Crimes

Unlike alcohol, possession of other drugs is a crime. Every state and the federal government have enacted some variation of the Uniform Controlled Substance Act, a model act (similar to the Model Penal Code) drafted by the Commissioners on Uniform Laws. These statutes establish schedules of drugs. They categorize drugs, based on their danger, potential for abuse, and medical benefits. These factors then determine a drug's allowed useage. For example, one schedule exists for drugs that may not be used under any condition, and another schedule permits use for medical and research purposes only. There are three basic drug crimes: possession, sales/distribution, and use.

Possession of prohibited drugs is a crime. Of course, actual possession is sufficient actus reus, but some jurisdictions also make constructive possession criminal. Constructive possession permits conviction of those people who exercise dominion and control over property where the illegal drug is located, even though the person has no "actual physical possession" of the prohibited narcotic. However, the Model Penal Code[18] and most jurisdictions require knowledge that the drug was present before culpability is imposed. As such, if a guest stays in Robert's home, Robert is not criminally liable for any drugs the guest has stowed away, unless Robert is aware of their presense. Once Robert becomes aware he must see that the drugs are removed within a reasonable time or risk a possession charge.

First-time conviction of possession, if the quantity is small, is a misdemeanor and normally results in probation. In many states, if a person pleads guilty, submits to a term of probation, and successfully completes the probation, then no adjudgment of guilt is entered. So, no record of conviction exists. Probation terms usually include drug counseling, periodic drug testing, and no other arrests during the period.

The sale or distribution of prohibited drugs is the second primary drug offense. Generally, it is punished more severely than possession. Not only are sales prohibited, but any "delivery" or "distribution" of drugs is illegal. "Possession with an intent to deliver or sell" is similar to simple possession, except a mens rea of intending to sell must be proven. Possession with an intent to sell or deliver is punished more severely than possession, often punished equally with actual sale or delivery.

This sign, found in a federal prosecutor's office, reflects the attitude of many Americans and the policies of the Reagan and Bush administrations.

The quantity of the drug involved affects the level of punishment for both possession and sale/distribution offenses. Other factors, such as selling to minors, may aggravate the sentence.

Unauthorized use of a controlled substance is also a crime. The user must be knowing. So, if a person takes a pill containing a controlled substance that someone gives him or her, who represented it to be an aspirin, there is no crime. Of course, the taking must be voluntary. So if a person is forced down and injected with an illegal drug, he or she has committed no crime.

Recall from the earlier discussion of actus reus that addiction to controlled substances may not be made criminal. The United States Supreme Court has held that criminalizing a person's status as an addict is cruel and unusual punishment, as prohibited by the Eight Amendment to the United States Constitution.[19] It is permitted, however, to punish a person for the act of taking a controlled substance.

Section 6.3(g.4) RICO and CCE

You have already learned that the Racketeer Influenced and Corrupt Organizations Act (RICO) was enacted to fight organized crime in all its forms. Another federal statute, **Continuing**

Criminal Enterprise (CCE),[20] was enacted specifically to combat drug trafficking. The statute is aimed at prosecuting the people at the top of the drug dealing and smuggling pyramid, and, accordingly, it has become known as the "Drug Kingpin Statute."

A person engages in a criminal enterprise if 1. he is an administrator, organizer, or other leader 2. of a group of five or more people 3. who are involved in series of drug violations. A series of violations means three or more drug convictions.[21]

Conviction of CCE results in stern punishment. A general violation receives twenty years to life in prison. Second convictions carry thirty years to life. If a person is determined to be a "principal leader," the amount of drugs involved was enormous, or the enterprise made $10 million or more in one year from drugs, then life imprisonment is mandatory. Fines may also be imposed. Also, the statute provides for imprisonment or death in cases where murder results from the enterprise.[22]

Finally, the Comprehensive Forfeiture Act of 1984[23] applies to both RICO and CCE violations. This statute permits the government to seize property and money that is used in the commission of the crimes and that is a product of the crimes. So, if a drug dealer uses a boat to smuggle drugs, the boat can be seized, even though it may have been purchased with "honest" money. Any items acquired with drug money may be seized, as can bank accounts and trusts.

SECTION 6.4 CRIMES AGAINST THE ADMINISTRATION OF GOVERNMENT

Section 6.4(a) Perjury

Perjury was a crime at common law and continues to be prohibited by statute in all states.

The basic elements of perjury are: 1. The making of a 2. false statement 3. with knowledge that it is false 4. while under oath. To gain a conviction the prosecution has the tough burden of proving the mens rea: that the person who made the statement knew that it was false. As with other crimes, juries are permitted to infer a defendant's knowledge from surrounding facts.

In addition, the statement must be made while under oath. Be aware that this includes far more than testifying in court. Most laws provide for all statements made before one authorized to administer oaths. So, perjury laws apply to people who sign affidavits

LEGAL TERMS

Continuing Criminal Enterprise (CCE)
   A federal statute, commonly known as the "Drug Kingpin Statute," because its aim is at high-level drug dealers and smugglers. To prove a CCE violation it must be shown that:
   1. the defendant was an administrator, organizer or other leader
   2. of a group of five or more people
   3. who have engaged in a series of drug violations.

perjury
   The 1. making of a 2. false statement 3. with knowledge of its falsity 4. while under oath.

before notary publics, appear as a witness before a court reporter (i.e. deposition) or a grand jury, and before all others who have the authority to administer oaths. For those individuals who have a religious objection to "swearing," the law permits an affirmation. This is simply an acknowledgment by the witness that the testimony he or she renders is truthful. The law treats an affirmation in the same manner as it does an oath.

Some jurisdictions require that the false statement be "material," or important to the matter. This prevents prosecutions for trivial matters. Some jurisdictions have defined materiality as any matter that may affect the outcome of a case. If a statement is not material, even if untrue, then a perjury conviction is not permitted.

A related crime is **subornation of perjury**. This occurs when one convinces or procures another to commit perjury. One who commits subornation is treated as a perjurer for the purpose of sentencing.

In addition to being a crime in every state, the United States has also made perjury criminal by statute. 18 U.S.C. §1621 reads:

> Whoever (1) having taken an oath before a competent tribunal, officer, or person, in any case in which a law of the United States authorizes an oath to be administered, that he will testify, declare, depose, or certify truly . . . is true, willfully and contrary to such oath states or subscribes any material matter which he does not believe to be true. . . .

Of course, truth is a complete defense to a charge of perjury. What is truthful is not always easy to determine, and in most questionable cases prosecutors choose not to pursue the matter. This is in large part due to the mens rea element.

Section 6.4(b) Bribery

As is true of perjury, **bribery** was a crime at English common law. Actually, bribery was initially a violation of biblical law, because it was wrong to attempt to influence judges, who were considered to be God's earthly representatives. Eventually, the crime was recognized by the courts of England.

Today, bribery is a statutory crime in the states and in the United States. The essential elements of the crime are 1. to solicit or accept 2. anything of value 3. with the purpose of 4. violating a duty or trust. Two primary forms of bribery are that of a public official and commercial bribery.

As mentioned, bribery began as a prohibition of influencing a judge. The crime was eventually extended to include bribery of all public officials and public servants. Statutes make it bribery to be the one accepting or giving the "thing of value." Hence, if a corporate official gives a public official money in exchange for awarding a contract to the company, both the corporate officer and the public official have committed bribery.

Most bribery statutes declare that unsuccessful offers are bribes. So, if the public official rejects the offer of the corporate officer, there is still a bribery violation. The offer need not be of money in exchange for a favor; anything of value is sufficient. Automobiles, tickets to a St. Louis Cardinal's game, and a promise of sexual favors all will satisfy this requirement.

The offer must be made to a public official or servant. Both terms are defined broadly. Further, the person offering must be seeking to influence the official in a matter over which the official has authority. Most courts have held that whether the officer actually had the authority to carry out the requested act is not dispositive; the issue is whether the offeror believes that the official possesses the authority. Awarding of government contracts, setting favorable tax assessments, and overlooking civil and criminal violations are examples of corrupt acts.

The offer alone makes the offerer guilty of bribery. For the public official to be convicted there must be an acceptance. This usually means that the official has done the requested act; however, it is widely held that an acceptance is all that is necessary to support a conviction.

Bribery has been extended beyond the public affairs realm to commercial life. Whenever a person who is engaged in business activities breaches a duty or trust owed to someone (or something, such as a business organization) in exchange for something of value, bribery has been committed.

The Model Penal Code declares that commercial bribery is a misdemeanor. The Code applies to people in specific positions, such as lawyers, accountants, trustees, and officers of corporations.[24] Anyone who makes an offer to someone in one of these positions to violate the trust or duty created by the position is guilty of bribery. Of course, any person holding such a position who accepts such an offer is also guilty of bribery. The Code specifically states that any person who holds himself out to the public to be in the business of appraising the value of services or commodities is guilty of bribery if he accepts a benefit to influence his decision or appraisal. Knowing that one is violating the trust is the mens rea under the Code.

If a seller for the company, Widgcom Inc., were to offer the purchasing agent of Retailers, Inc., money in exchange for receiving the contract to supply Retailers with Widgets for the next year, commercial bribery has occurred. A corporate officer who accepts

LEGAL TERMS

subornation of perjury
The 1. act of convincing or procuring another 2. to commit perjury.

bribery
1. Soliciting or accepting 2. anything of value 3. with the purpose of violating a duty or trust. Common classifications of bribery are commercial and of a public official.

free personal air travel in exchange for buying all corporate airline tickets from the same airline has committed bribery.

Finally, note that there are statutes that prohibit "throwing" athletic contests for pay. That is, any player, coach, owner, or official who accepts a benefit to cause one participant to win or lose commits bribery. These laws often apply to both professional and amateur sports.

Section 6.4(c) Tax Crimes

We have all heard the quip, "In life, only two things are certain, death and taxes." Tax revenues are the lifeblood of government. In the United States people are taxed at the federal level, state level, and local level (county, municipal, and school district taxes). These taxes come in many forms, including income tax, gift and estate tax, sales tax, and excise taxes. Tax laws apply to individuals, estates, and business entities (i.e., corporations).

All taxing authorities have statutes that impose both civil and criminal penalties for violation of tax laws. Common violations of tax laws are tax evasion, failing to file a required tax return, filing a fraudulent return, and unlawful disclosure of tax information. These are not the only crimes related to taxes, however, as shown by the applicable federal statutes, which embody sixteen tax-related crimes.[25]

Tax evasion involves paying less tax than required or under-reporting one's income with the intent of paying less tax. The federal statute covering tax evasion reads:

---

26 U.S.C. §7201 Attempt to evade or defeat tax

Any person who willfully attempts in any manner to evade or defeat any tax imposed by this title or the payment thereof shall, in addition to other penalties provided by law, be guilty of a felony and, upon conviction thereof, shall be fined not more than $100,000 ($500,000 in the case of a corporation), or imprisoned not more than 5 years, or both, together with the costs of prosecution.

Tax fraud, a crime closely related to evasion, involves using fraud or false statements to avoid a tax obligation. This may occur in many ways, including falsifying statements that are provided to a revenue agency, such as fraudulent receipts used for deductions. Filing false tax returns is also a form of tax fraud.

Failure to file a required tax return is also criminal. The relevant federal statute reads:

26 U.S.C. §7203 Willful failure to file return, supply information, or pay tax

Any person required under this title to pay any estimated tax or tax, or required by this title or by regulations made under authority thereof to make a return, keep any records, or suppy any information, who willfully fails to pay such estimated tax or tax, make such return, keep such records, or supply such information . . . be guilty of a misdemeanor and, upon conviction thereof, shall be fined not more than $25,000 ($100,000 in the case of a corporation), or imprisoned not more than 1 year, or both, together with the costs of prosecution. . . .

Note that section 7203 applies to anyone who is required to file a tax return, pay a tax, or supply information. As such, this provision can be the basis of a prosecution of an employer who pays her employees in cash and makes no report to the Internal Revenue Service. Likewise, although some entities are not taxed, such as partnerships, they are required to file informational returns, and failure to do so violates this provision.

Tax evasion, filing fraudulent tax returns, and the unauthorized disclosure of information are crimes of commission. That is, an affirmative act is required to commit these crimes.

Failing to file a required return, or other information, is an act of omission. Proving such crimes requires not proof of an illegal act, but that a required act was not taken. The above statutes require willful violations. Negligence in preparing a tax return or in filing the return are not criminal. However, such errors may lead to civil penalties.

The "willfulness" requirement was recently considered by the Supreme Court in *Cheek v. United States*.

LEGAL TERMS

tax evasion
The 1. willful 2. underpaying (or under-reporting) 3. of a tax.

tax fraud
The use of fraud or false documents to avoid a tax obligation.

failure to file
Failing to file a required return, or other information, is a crime of omission.

CHEEK
V.
UNITED STATES

No. 89-658, slip op. (U.S. Jan. 8, 1991)

* * *

Willfulness, as construed by our prior decisions in criminal tax cases, requires the Government to prove that the law imposed a duty on the defendant, that the defendant knew of this duty, and that he voluntarily and intentionally violated this duty. We deal first with the case where the issue is whether the defendant knew of the duty purportedly imposed by the provision of the statute or regulation he is accused of violating, a case in which there is no claim that the provision at issue is invalid. In such a case, if the Government proves actual knowledge of the pertinent legal duty, the prosecution, without more, has satisfied the knowledge component of the willfulness requirement. But carrying this burden requires negating a defendant's claim of ignorance of the law or a claim that because of a misunderstanding of the law, he had a good-faith belief that he was not violating any of the provisions of the tax laws. This is so because one cannot be aware that the law imposes a duty upon him and yet be ignorant of it, misunderstand the law, or believe that the duty does not exist. In the end, the issue is whether, based on all the evidence, the Government has proved that the defendant was aware of the duty at issue, which cannot be true if the jury credits a good-faith misunderstanding and belief submission, whether or not the claimed belief or misunderstanding is objectively reasonable.

In this case, if Cheek asserted that he truly believed that the Internal Revenue Code did not purport to treat wages as income, and the jury believed him, the Government would not have carried its burden to prove willfulness, however unreasonable a court might deem such a belief. . . .

We thus disagree with the Court of Appeals' requirement that a claimed good-faith belief must be objectively reasonable if it is to be considered as possibly negating the Government's evidence purporting to show a defendant's awareness of the legal duty at issue. Knowledge and belief are characteristically questions for the fact-finder. . . .

Tax laws require the disclosure of all income and profits. This includes income from illegal sources. Gamblers are required to report their winnings; prostitutes their income; and drug dealers the profits derived from their sales. Failure to report income from illegal acts is prosecuted the same as failure to report legally earned income. Because requiring people to report income from illegal activities raises a self-incrimination problem, tax laws require that all information obtained be kept confidential. Tax officials are not permitted to disclose such information to law-enforcement authorities, and to do so is **unlawful disclosure**. The privilege against self-incrimination will be discussed more thoroughly in the chapter on defenses to criminal accusations.

In the case that follows, the tax evasion and fraud conviction of Reverend Sun Myung Moon, father of the "Moonies," was upheld by the Second Circuit Court of Appeals.

UNITED STATES
V.
SUN MYUNG MOON

718 F.2d 1210 (2nd Cir. 1983)

* * *

Defendants argue that the evidence presented was insufficient to find them guilty beyond a reasonable doubt on the substantive tax offenses charged in Counts Two through Six. To find defendants guilty of fraud in the filing of Moon's income tax returns, the jury had to find that statements contained in the returns which were verified as true were in fact false, and that these false statements were willfully made. . . .

Under the government's theory of the case, Moon failed to report interest income earned on the Chase Manhattan Bank accounts that he purportedly owned and income recognized as a result of distribution of Tong Il stock to him at no cost. Appellants' principal contentions at trial were that the Chase accounts and Tong Il stock belonged to the Church,

LEGAL TERMS

unlawful disclosure
Information contained in tax returns is confidential. Any revenue official or employee who discloses such information, even to law enforcement, is guilty of unlawful disclosure.

that Moon merely held these assets as the nominee, agent, and/or trustee of the Church, and that therefore he was not taxable on either the Chase interest or Tong Il stock distribution.

In concluding that the jury properly found the Chase accounts and Tong Il stock to be Moon's personal property, we start first with the fact that the Chase accounts and Tong Il securities were maintained in Moon's name and controlled by him. Second, some funds clearly destined for Church entities were put in existing Church bank accounts which were owned and controlled by Church operations. Third, from his handling of the Chase accounts and Tong Il stock Moon seemingly regarded them as his own, not belonging to the Church. Fourth, high-ranking members of the Church were told that the Chase funds belonged to "Father," not to the Church. . . .

We turn to the evidence that Moon willfully filed income tax returns for the 1973–75 tax years knowing that these returns contained false information. . . . Willfulness in tax fraud cases has become equated with bad faith, want of justification, or knowledge that the taxpayer should have reported more income than he did. . . .

The evidence presented on this issue, although circumstantial, was sufficient to sustain the jury's verdict. The salient points follow. Moon signed his 1974 and 1975 returns, acknowledging that he had read them and that they were accurate, and he signed an RSC–12 form giving similar assurances as to his 1973 return; Moon and Kamiyama both knew of Moon's interest income at Chase and income from the distribution of Tong Il stock; Moon actively supervised all of his personal financial matters and never signed anything until he understood it. . . .

[Conviction affirmed]

Section 6.4(d) Obstruction of Justice

Obstruction of justice refers to any number of unlawful acts. As a general proposition, any act which interferes with the performance of a public official's duties is obstructing justice. However,

Oliver North Testifying Before the U.S. Congress He had been charged with obstruction of justice, destroying and altering National Security Council documents, and accepting illegal gratuities. His first conviction was reversed on appeal. See *United States v. Oliver North*, 910 F.2d 843 (D.C. Cir. 1990). *Courtesy C-Span.*

the crime is most commonly associated with law enforcement and judicial officials.

The types of acts that fall under such statutes include tampering with witnesses or jurors, interfering with police officers, destroying evidence needed for a court proceeding, and intentionally giving false information to a prosecutor in an effort to hinder a prosecutorial effort. However, obstruction statutes are drafted broadly, thereby permitting unique prosecutions. For example, it is common for women who are physically abused by their husbands to contact the police during a violent episode and demand their husbands' arrests, usually in an effort to get the man out of the house. Once they are arrested, many women lose interest in prosecuting their husbands and often refuse to testify against them in court. In such a case, a prosecutor could charge the wife with obstruction of justice because of her refusal to testify.

Resisting arrest is a similar crime. At common law, one could resist an unlawful arrest. While a few jurisdictions have retained this rule, this is not presently the law in most jurisdictions. Most states have followed the Model Penal Code approach, which prohibits even moderate resistence to any arrest.[26] It is a wise rule, considering the remedies that are available if a police officer makes an unlawful arrest. If the arrest is unlawful, but in good faith, the arrestee will be released either at the police station or after the first judicial hearing. If the arrest was unlawful and made maliciously,

SIDEBAR

TWO CASES OF
CONTEMPT
    Contempt of court
orders are common
in domestic law
cases. One case,
which received con-
siderable media atten-
tion, involved Dr.
Elizabeth Morgan.
Dr. Morgan refused
to obey a court order
to disclose the loca-
tion of her child,
Heather, claiming
that her ex-husband
had molested their
child. The judge
ordered that she dis-
close the location of
the child so her ex-
husband could exer-
cise his court-ordered
visitation rights. She
refused, and the
judge ordered that
she be incarcerated
until she disclosed
the child's where-
abouts. Dr. Morgan
spent a total of 759
days in jail and was
released only after an
act of Congress
limited the amount of
time a civil contem-
nor could spend in
jail to one year.
    A case that comes
from Houston, Texas,
teaches that the con-
tempt power of
judges is powerful.
Houston attorney
John O'Quinn was
found in criminal con-
tempt by a federal
district judge for
sleeping in a jury
room. The basis for
the contempt citation
was an order from
the judge that
O'Quinn (and others)
"stay out of the facili-
ties up here on this
floor unless you get
prior permission."
The Fifth Circuit

then the arrestee will not only be released, but has a civil cause of action for false imprisonment.

Section 6.4(e) Contempt

Failure to comply with a court order is contemptuous, as is taking any act with the purpose of undermining a court's authority or intending to interfere with its administration and process. While statutes provide for contempt, it is widely accepted that the contempt power is inherent.

Contempt is broken down into direct and indirect criminal contempt and direct and indirect civil contempt. Direct contempt refers to those acts that occur in the presence of the judge. Although usually in the courtroom, the judges' chambers and office area are included. Indirect contempt refers to actions taken outside the presence of a court, but are violative of a court order.

Criminal contempt is levied to punish a person for violating a court order. Civil contempt, on the other hand, does not have punishment as its purpose. It is intended to coerce a person into complying with a court order. For example, if Mary refuses to testify at a trial despite an order to testify, the judge may order her confined until she complies. Once she testifies, she is free. It is often said that those guilty of civil contempt hold the keys to their jail cells, while criminal contemnors do not. In theory, one who has been held in civil contempt can be punished for criminal contempt after complying with the court order. In practice this seldom occurs, presumably because judges feel that the civil punishment imposed is adequate.

The contempt power is significant. Indirect criminal contemnors are entitled to all the protections that others charged with crimes receive. That is, a right to a trial, assistance of counsel, and proof beyond a reasonable doubt. Direct criminal contemnors have no such rights, since the act took place in the presence of a judge. However, any sentence imposed may be appealed and reviewed for fairness.

Civil contemnors have few rights. They do not possess the rights of those accused of crimes, because civil contempt is not considered a criminal action. In most instances they enjoy no right to appeal. A civil contemnor holds her own key; she must comply with the court's order. Of course, if an appellate court determines that the underlying order is unlawful, the civil contemnor is released. However, they may be charged with criminal contempt for failure to comply with the order before it was held unlawful by an appellate court. The fact that a court order may be nullified at some future date does not justify noncompliance. Court orders must be obeyed to assure the orderly administration of justice.

Legislatures also have the power to cite for contempt. Legislatures, usually through committees, conduct hearings and other proceedings when considering bills and amendments to statutes. The contempt power serves the same function for legislatures that it does for courts. It furthers the orderly performance of legislative duties. Refusal to testify before a legislative body (usually a committee), to produce documents or other items, and disrupting a proceeding are examples of legislative contempt. Persons charged with legislative contempt possess the same rights as those charged with other crimes, such as the Fifth and Fourteenth Amendments guarantee. In most instances, legislative bodies refer contempt cases to prosecutors, rather than adjudicate such cases themselves.

Court of Appeals reversed the conviction, finding that the judge's order was too vague. However, this is a good example of the breadth of the contempt power; had the judge's order been more specific, it would have been upheld.

Sources for story one: Time, *"A Hard Case of Contempt,"* September 18, 1989 and U.S. News and World Report, *"A Mother's 759 Days of Defiance,"* October 9, 1989.

REVIEW QUESTIONS

1. Andy approaches Roberta, who is standing on a street corner, and offers her $50 for sex. Roberta, an undercover vice officer, arrests Andy. What crime should he be charged with?

2. Is there a constitutional right to engage in homosexual conduct between mature, consenting adults?

3. When may a state regulate material that is thought to be sexually repulsive? What constitutional provision hinders governments from regulating such expression?

4. What are fighting words? Are they protected by the First Amendment?

5. Is proof that a driver's blood-alcohol level exceeded the statutory maximum the only way to prove that a driver was under the influence? Is is a valid defense for a driver-defendant to claim that she could drive safely, even though her blood-alcohol level exceeded the amount allowed by statute?

6. What are the elements of Continuing Criminal Enterprise, and who is the statute aimed at?

7. What are the basic elements of bribery? The Model Penal Code recognizes two types of bribery. Name the two.

8. Distinguish criminal contempt from civil contempt. Do the same for direct contempt and indirect contempt.

9. Is this statement true? "Perjury is a law that applies only to judicial proceedings." Explain your answer.

10. What are the elements of indecent exposure?

LEGAL TERMS

contempt
Failing to comply with a court order or interfering with the administration of a court is contemptuous. Contempt has many forms. Civil contempt is used to coerce persons into complying with court orders. Criminal contempt is levied as a punishment for violating court orders. Violations that occur in the presence of a court are referred to as direct, and those outside the presence of a court are indirect. Legislative bodies also possess contempt power.

REVIEW PROBLEMS

1. Are the following statutes constitutional? Explain, if not.

   STATUTE ONE: LOITERING

   Any person who loiters in a place in an unusual manner for longer than fifteen minutes and reasonably causes a person to be concerned for their safety must identify himself to police when requested. Any person who refuses to identify himself under these circumstances or takes flight when approached by a police officer is guilty of loitering.

   STATUTE TWO: LOITERING

   Any person who continually loiters in public parks without apparent employment or who lives off the handouts of others is guilty of loitering.

2. State law prohibits "hardcore pornography." Among the many prohibitions of the law is a provision making it a felony to possess or sell materials that are known to depict bestiality (sex between a human and an animal). Sam, a local adult bookstore owner, sold a magazine to Herb entitled "Wild on the Farm." The magazine was sealed, and its contents were not visible. The magazine was delivered to Sam in error, part of a large shipment of magazines and books.

   During a raid on Sam's establishment the local police discovered the sales ticket reflecting Herb's purchase, his name, and his address. The police then obtained a search warrant for Herb's home and found the magazine during their search. Sam and Herb have both been charged with violating the state's obscenity law. Should they be convicted? Explain your answer.

3. Do you believe that acts that harm no one, but that most members of society find immoral, should be criminalized? Explain your position.

4. How has bribery been changed since it has become a statutory crime?

   5–7. Classify each of the following as direct or indirect contempt and civil or criminal contempt.

5. During a personal injury trial Noah told the judge to "kiss his ass" and then threw an apple, striking the judge in the head.

6. During a union dispute a judge ordered striking employees back to work. They refused to comply with the order and the

judge ordered that each employee pay $50 per day until he or she returned to work.

7. Jon received a court order to tear down a fence he had constructed. The order was served by a sheriff. Immediately after the sheriff handed the order to him, Jon screamed "Forget that idiot judge, I'm not tearing down the fence!" Jon never removed the fence, and the judge had him arrested, and ordered him to remain in jail until he agreed to comply with the order.

8. Consider and discuss this statement: Possession and use of drugs or alcohol should not be a crime. The only dangers presented from these substances arise when a person works, drives, or conducts some activity that requires the full use of the senses, while under their influence. Criminal statutes should be narrow and proscribe only the harm sought to be prevented. No harm is created by use in controlled environments, such as in the home. Accordingly, statutes should only proscribe engaging in certain undertakings while under the influence of alcohol or drugs.

NOTES

[1] Model Penal Code §251.2(1).

[2] Model Penal Code §251.2(5).

[3] 18 U.S.C. §2421.

[4] Model Penal Code §251.1

[5] 18 U.S.C. §1461.

[6] Anderson, "Mapplethorpe Photos on Trial," *A.B.A. Journal*, December 1990, p. 28.

[7] There are other limits on First Amendment freedoms. Some of these are discussed in the defenses chapter, under the constitutional defenses section.

[8] *Manual Enterprises, Inc. v. Day*, 370 U.S. 478, opinion by Justice Harlan.

[9] 50 AM. JUR. 2d *Lewdness, Indecency, etc.* 7 (1970).

[10] See *Roth v. United States*, 354 U.S. 476, 487, note 20 (1957).

[11] *United States v. Guglielmi*, 819 F.2d 451 (4th Cir. 1987).

[12] *Stanley v. Georgia*, 394 U.S. 557 (1969).

[13] Model Penal Code §251.4.

[14] Model Penal Code §250.1.

[15] *Champlinsky v. New Hampshire*, 315 U.S. 568 (1942).

[16] *Brandenburg v. Ohio*, 395 U.S. 444 (1969).

[17] See Chapter Three, supra, "Personal Status as an Act."

[18] Model Penal Code §2.01(4).

[19] *Robinson v. California,* 370 U.S. 660 (1962)
[20] 21 U.S.C. §848
[21] *United States v. Brantley,* 733 F.2d 1429 (11th Cir. 1984)
[22] 21 U.S.C. §848(e)
[23] 21 U.S.C. §853(a)
[24] Model Penal Code §224.8
[25] 26 U.S.C. §7201, et seq
[26] Model Penal Code §3.04(2)(a)(i)

CHAPTER 7
Parties and Inchoate Offenses

"Hold out your wallet and repeat after me, 'Help yourself' . . . "

No man is above the law and no man is below it; nor do we ask any man's permission when we require him to obey it. Obedience to the law is demanded as a right, not asked as a favor.

President Theodore Roosevelt

OUTLINE

SECTION 7.1   PARTIES TO CRIMES

Not all crimes are committed by individuals. Not all planned crimes are completed. This chapter examines those two issues, group criminal responsibility and uncompleted crimes. Those who participate in a crime are referred to as parties. Uncompleted crimes are referred to as inchoate crimes.

At common law there were four parties to crimes: principals in the first degree; principals in the second degree; accessories before the fact; and accessories after the fact.

A **principal** in the first degree is the participant who actually took the proscribed act. For example, three people (A, B, and C) agree to rob a grocery store. A enters the store and points a gun at

LEGAL TERMS

principals
   Participants in a crime who are present during the criminal act. A principal in the first degree is the party who actually takes the prohibited act, while a principal in the second degree aids, counsels, assists, or encourages the principal in the first degree.

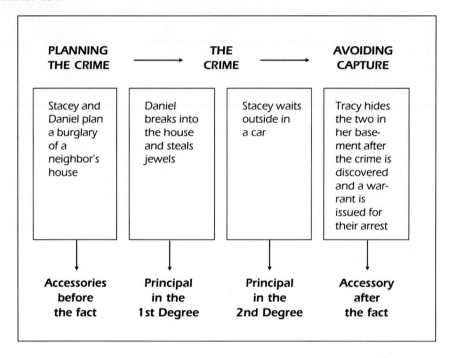

PLANNING THE CRIME →	THE CRIME →		AVOIDING CAPTURE
Stacey and Daniel plan a burglary of a neighbor's house	Daniel breaks into the house and steals jewels	Stacey waits outside in a car	Tracy hides the two in her basement after the crime is discovered and a warrant is issued for their arrest
Accessories before the fact	**Principal in the 1st Degree**	**Principal in the 2nd Degree**	**Accessory after the fact**

Parties to a Burglary

a checker and demands that money be placed in a bag. A is a principal in the first degree.

A principal in the second degree is a party who aids, counsels, assists, or encourages the principal in the first degree during the commission of the crime. This requires that a party must be present during a crime to be a principal in the second degree. However, constructive presence is sufficient. Whenever a party is physically absent from the location of the crime, but aids from a distance, that party is a principal in the second degree. So, if B, from the above hypothetical case, waits in the getaway car outside the bank, B is a principal in the second degree. First-degree and second-degree principals are punished equally. Principals in the second degree are also referred to as accomplices, as are accessories before the fact.

Anyone who aids, counsels, encourages, or assists in the preparation of a crime, but is not physically present during the crime, is an **accessory** before the fact. If C is an expert in bank security and assisted in the planning of the robbery, then C is an accessory before the fact. The primary distinction between a principal in the second degree and an accessory before the fact is the lack of presence during the crime of an accessory before the fact.

At common law accessories could not be convicted until the principals were convicted. In addition, procedural rules made it more difficult to convict accessories than principals. These rules are no longer the law. Statutes group principals in the first and second degree together with accessories before the fact and punish all equally.

The mens rea of an accomplice (before and during a crime) is usually intentional (specific) in common-law terms, or knowing or purposeful in Model Penal Code language. Negligent and reckless acts do not make a person a principal in the second degree or an accessory.

Accessories after the fact continue to be treated differently. A person is an accessory after the fact if: 1. aid, comfort, or shelter is provided to a criminal 2. with the purpose of assisting the criminal in avoiding arrest or prosecution 3. after the crime is committed 4. and the accessory was not present during the commission of the crime. D is an accessory after the fact, if A and B flee to D's house, who hides A and B from the police. It is possible to be an accessory both before and after the fact. Hence, if C were to hide A and B from the police, C would be both an accessory before and after the fact. Accessories after the fact are not punished as severely as the other three classifications of parties.

The mental state required to prove that a person was an accessory after the fact is twofold: first, it must be shown that the defendant was aware of the person's criminal status (scienter) and second, that the defendant intended to hinder attempts to arrest or prosecute the criminal.

SECTION 7.2 INCHOATE CRIMES

Not all planned crimes are completed. Because of the danger posed by substantial planning, accompanied by an intent to carry out a plan, some uncompleted crimes may be punished.

By punishing inchoate acts, the deterrent purpose of the criminal justice system is furthered. If the rule were otherwise, law-enforcement officials would have no incentive to intervene in a criminal enterprise before it is completed. By punishing attempt, conspiracy, and solicitation, an officer may prevent a planned criminal act from occurring without risking losing a criminal conviction.

Section 7.2(a) Attempt

The reasons planned crimes are not always successful are numerous. In some instances, law-enforcement intervention

LEGAL TERMS

accessories
Parties who are not present during a crime, but who assist the principals in some manner. An accessory before the fact aids, counsels, assists, or encourages before the act takes place, and accessories after the fact assist the criminal in avoiding arrest or prosecution after the crime.

prevents the completion of a crime. If a police officer stops Penny from shooting Tom moments before she would take the act, should she be free from criminal liability because she wasn't successful? The law answers that question in the negative, calling such uncompleted crimes attempt.

Attempt was not a crime at early common law; however, attempt cases do appear later in English common law. The first cases began to appear in the late 1700s and early 1800s.[1] Many of the early cases have been traced to an English court that is no longer in existence, the Star Chamber. Today, attempt is recognized in the United States by all states.

The purpose of attempt laws is to deter people from planning to commit crimes, to punish those who intended to commit a crime, but were unsuccessful, and to encourage law-enforcement officers to prevent unlawful activity. The last may appear obvious, however, if it were not for making attempts illegal, police would have an incentive to permit illegal acts, so as to be able to punish the wrongdoer.

There are essentially three elements to all attempts. One, the defendant must intend to commit a crime. Two, the defendant must take some act in furtherance of that intent. Three, the crime is not completed.

First, the mens rea element: The defendant must intend to take some act that amounts to a crime; in common-law language, specific intent, and under the Model Penal Code, knowingly or purposefully. Some statutes specifically identify what crime must be intended, while others simply refer to an intent to commit any felony. In any event, the accused must intend to commit some specific crime, such as murder, rape, or theft.

The second element, the actus reus of attempt, can be problematic. The problem revolves around this question: how close to completion of the intended crime must a defendant come to be guilty of attempt? It is well-established that thoughts alone do not establish a crime; mere preparation without anything further does not amount to the crime of attempt. The failing student who sits at home and contemplates how to "do in" his criminal law instructor commits no crime. It is not until the student goes further that he can be liable for attempt.

Various tests are used to determine if an act is close enough to completion to permit an attempt conviction. The four commonly used tests are proximity, res ipsa loquitor, probable desistance, and the Model Penal Code's "substantial steps" test.

The **proximity** test examines what acts have been taken and what acts are left to be taken in order to complete the crime. Justice Holmes has said that there "must be a dangerous proximity to success."[2]

The **res ipsa loquitor** test (also called the unequivocality test) looks at crimes individually and finds an act, a certain point in time, which indicates that the defendant has "no other purpose than the commission of that specific crime."[3] For example, most courts have held that once a defendant hires another to commit a crime, attempt has been committed. The step of hiring the person who will complete the crime crosses the line between mere preparation and illegal act.

The third test, **probable desistance**, focuses on the likelihood that the defendant would have followed through with the crime had the opportunity existed. The foundation of the theory is that all people may plan illegal acts at some time in life, but that there is a point where most stop. Any person who passes this line of demarcation has exhibited that the crime would have been completed, had the situation permitted. Critics have attacked this test, claiming that the determination of such a line, if it exists, is arbitrary.

The Model Penal Code uses a "**substantial step**" to completion test.[4] That is, one is guilty of attempt if substantial steps have been taken toward the commission of a crime. The Code specifically states that the conduct in question must "strongly corroborate" the actor's criminal purpose. The Code goes further and lists acts that may constitute attempts, provided that they "strongly corroborate" an intent to commit a crime. That list includes:

1. Lying in wait or searching for the intended victim.
2. Enticing or seeking to entice the intended victim to go to the place where the crime will be committed.
3. Investigating the location where the crime is to be committed.
4. Unlawfully entering a structure where the crime is to be committed.
5. Possession of materials necessary to complete the crime, provided that the tools are specially designed for the commission of the crime.
6. Possession, collection, or fabrication of materials to be used in the crime, near the scene of the crime, where the materials serve no lawful purpose.
7. Soliciting someone to commit a crime.

Keep in mind that different results are possible if the tests above are applied to the same facts. In the following case the line between preparation and attempt is examined. Do you agree with the Court?

LEGAL TERMS

attempt
When a person 1. has an intent to commit some crime, 2. takes some act beyond mere preparation in furtherance of that crime, 3. but the crime is not completed, attempt has been committed.

proximity
A test used to determine if a person's actions rise to the level of attempting a crime. Proximity focuses on the acts taken in furtherance of the intended crime and what acts remain to be taken to complete the crime.

res ipsa loquitor
A second test that looks to crimes individually for a specific act that indicates that the defendant has no other purpose than the commission of some specific crime.

probable desistance
A third test that states that if the defendant had passed the point in preparation where he is unlikely to quit, he is guilty of attempt.

substantial steps
A fourth test, from the Model Penal Code. If a defendant has taken substantial steps toward completion of a crime, and the steps strongly corroborate her intent to commit the crime, then he or she is guilty of attempt.

PEOPLE
V.
MURRAY

15 Cal. 160 (1859)

The evidence in this case entirely fails to sustain the charge against the defendant of an attempt to contract an incestuous marriage with his niece. It only discloses declarations of his determination to contract the marriage, his elopement with the niece for that avowed purpose, and his request to one of the witnesses to go for a magistrate to perform the ceremony. It shows very clearly the intention of the defendant, but something more than mere intention is necessary to constitute the offense charged. Between preparation for the attempt and the attempt itself, there is a wide difference. The preparation consists of devising or arranging the means or measures necessary for the commission of the offense; the attempt is the direct movement toward the commission after the preparation is made. To illustrate: a party may purchase and load a gun, with the declared intention to shoot his neighbor; but until some movement is made to use the weapon upon the person of his intended victim, there is only preparation and not attempt. For the preparation, he may be held to keep the peace; but he is not chargeable with any attempt to kill. So in the present case, the declarations, and elopement, and request for a magistrate, were preparatory to the marriage; but until the officer was engaged, and the parties stood before him, ready to take the vows appropriate to the contract of marriage, it cannot be said, in strictness, that the attempt was made. The attempt contemplated by the statute must be manifested by acts that would end in the consummation of the particular offence, but for the intervention of circumstances independent of the will of the party. [Conviction reversed]

Despite which test is applied, if a defendant has a change of heart and does not complete the crime, even after crossing the line, then abandonment may be available as a defense.

Of course, the abandonment must be voluntary. Generally, any reason which causes a defendant to desist, other than the defendant's independent decision not to complete the crime, falls outside the defense. A criminal who chooses to not rob a store because a police officer arrives at the scene moments before the planned act was to occur is not entitled to the defense of abandonment.

Two other defenses which arise in the context of attempt are **legal and factual impossibility**. Legal impossibility refers to this situation: when a defendant believes her acts are illegal when they are not.

If a defendant takes an act believing it illegal, when it is actually lawful, she is not liable. The law of attempt does not punish one for attempting to do a lawful thing, even if the person had an evil mind.

Factual possibility refers to situations when people attempt to commit a crime, but it is impossible to do so. For example, John breaks into his friend's school locker to steal property, but discovers that the locker is empty. Distraught by the situation, John decides to relax by smoking marijuana. Unknown to John, the cigarette contains no marijuana or other illegal drug. John has made two factual errors. In both instances John could be convicted because factual impossibility is not a defense. This rule is justified by the fact that the defendant possessed the required mens rea and took all the acts necessary to commit the offense. The only reason the crime was not fully completed was because of an extraneous fact that was unknown to the defendant.

Section 7.2(b) Conspiracy

Conspiracy is 1. an agreement 2. between two or more persons 3. to commit an unlawful act or a lawful act in an unlawful manner. The agreement is the actus reus of the crime, and the intent to commit an unlawful act or a lawful act in an unlawful manner is the mens rea.

In some jurisdictions, the agreement alone satisfies the actus reus. In others, some act must be taken in furtherance of the objective of the agreement. Although at least one jurisdiction requires the conspirators to take "substantial steps" to be liable for conspiracy, most require less; often proof of an "overt act" will sustain a conviction. Hence, while mere preparation is not sufficient to impose liability for attempt, it is sufficient in many jurisdictions to prove conspiracy.

LEGAL TERMS

legal impossibility
  A defense to criminal accusations. A person who takes an act, believing it illegal when it is not, is not liable for attempt.

factual impossibility
  It is not a defense to a criminal accusation for a person to claim that it was impossible for the crime to be completed.

conspiracy
  A crime. The elements are 1. an agreement 2. between two or more people 3. to do something unlawful or to do something lawful in an unlawful manner.

At least two people must join in the agreement. One limitation on this rule is the **Wharton's Rule**. Under this rule, two people cannot be charged with conspiracy when the underlying offense itself requires two people. For example, gambling is a crime that requires the acts of at least two people. The Wharton's Rule prohibits convictions of both gambling and conspiracy. This is not true of murder, since murder can be committed by one person. The Wharton's Rule is limited, however, to two people. So if three people agree to gamble, a conviction of gambling and conspiracy to commit gambling is permitted.

The mens rea of conspiracy has two aspects. First, conspirators must have an intent to enter into an agreement. Second, conspirators must possess a specific intent to commit some unlawful objective. That objective must be to commit an unlawful act or a lawful act in an unlawful manner. The language of conspiracy speaks of doing unlawful acts, not necessarily criminal. This is important because some acts, when taken by an individual, may lead to civil, but not criminal, liability. However, when the same acts are taken by a group, the law of conspiracy makes them criminal. This is common in the area of fraud.

The mens rea requirement of conspiracy is strict. Contrary to the general rule, mistake of law and fact are often accepted defenses. It is a defense for a party to have been under the mistaken belief that the group's actions and objectives were legal. This is because the conspiracy must be corrupt; the parties must have had an evil purpose for their union.

What if a party withdraws from the conspiracy while it is ongoing? As a general rule, withdrawal is not a defense, because the crime was complete when the parties entered into the agreement. However, if the jurisdiction requires an agreement plus an overt act or substantial steps, then withdrawal before those acts occur is valid. To determine when withdrawal occurred, courts look to the defendant's actions. Withdrawal is effective at the time his acts would have conveyed to a reasonable person, standing in his co-conspirator's shoes, that he was abandoning the conspiracy. Additionally, the withdrawal must occur within a time that permits the other parties to abandon the objective. A last-second withdrawal, when it is too late to stop the wheels from turning, is not a defense. The Model Penal Code recognizes voluntary withdrawal as an affirmative defense.[5]

A few procedural issues are unique to conspiracy. As a whole, these rules favor prosecution. First, conspiracy is considered a crime, independent of any crime that is the objective of the conspiracy. If Amy and Ashley conspire to murder Elsa, they have committed two offenses: murder and conspiracy to murder. It is not a violation of the Fifth Amendment's double jeopardy prohibition to punish both crimes (cumulative punishment). Conspiracy to commit a crime and the commission of that crime do not merge into one. This is why conspiracy can be inchoate; it can be charged in those cases where the objective is not met. If Amy and Ashley are not successful in their murderous plot, they are still liable for conspiracy to murder. One exception to the general rule of cumulative punishments is Wharton's Rule, discussed above.

Prosecutors must show an agreement between two or more parties to prove conspiracy. This creates some difficulties at trial. One difficulty concerns whether alleged co-conspirators should be tried together or separately. Because the United States Supreme Court has approved trial of all parties either at the location where the agreement was entered into or at any location where an act in furtherance of the conspiracy occurred, defendants are usually tried together.[6] It is possible for a defendant to be tried in a location where he has never been, and some argue that this is unconstitutional. In addition, critics argue that trying defendants together creates an increased likelihood of conviction because a form of "guilt by association" occurs in juror's minds.

Another procedural irregularity is the **co-conspirator hearsay rule**. **Hearsay** is an out-of-court statement. While hearsay evidence is normally inadmissible at trial, the co-conspirator exception permits the statements of one party that are made out of court to be admitted. The rule is limited to statements made during the planning and commission of the conspiracy, and statements made after it is completed are inadmissible.

Because two people (or more) are required to have a conspiracy, if only two people are charged, and one is acquitted, then the other cannot be punished. For example, Edgar and Robert are charged and tried together for conspiring to rob a bank. If the jury acquits one, the other must also be acquitted. At least two people must be convicted. So, if a group of people are charged, and the jury acquits all but two, the convictions stand.

Finally, be aware that many statutes deal with conspiracies, even though they are not named so. You have already examined two federal conspiracy statutes, the Racketeer Influenced and Corrupt Organizations Act and Continuing Criminal Enterprise. In recent years there has been a rise in the number of conspiracy filings. This is largely the result of RICO and related statutes and because of the procedural advantages that prosecutors have, as discussed above.

Section 7.2(c)   Solicitation

You have already encountered **solicitation** in the discussion of prostitution. But solicitation is much broader than attempting

LEGAL TERMS

Wharton's Rule
A legal doctrine that prohibits cumulative punishment in cases where two parties are necessary for the underlying offense, such as bigamy, gambling, and bribery.

co-conspirator hearsay rule
An exception to the hearsay rule, which permits the hearsay statements of co-conspirators to be admitted at trial, provided such statements are made during the conspiracy.

hearsay
An out-of-court statement. The general rule of evidence makes hearsay inadmissible. There are many exceptions to this rule.

solicitation
The crime of
1. encouraging, requesting, or commanding
2. another 3. to commit a crime.

to engage someone in prostitution. Solicitation is the 1. encouraging, requesting, or commanding 2. of another 3. to commit a crime.

Solicitation is a specific intent crime: The person must intend to convince another to commit an offense. While the crime may be prostitution, it can be any crime in most jurisdictions. A few states limit the pool to felonies. The actus reus of the crime is the solicitation.

The crime is different than attempt, because the solicitation itself is a crime, and no act to further the crime need be taken. Of course, if Gwen asks Tracey to kill Jeff, and the deed is completed, then Gwen is an accessory before the fact of murder, as well as a solicitor.

In *State v. Furr*, the Supreme Court of North Carolina decided that it is solicitation for one person to engage another to find someone to commit a crime.

STATE
V.
FURR

292 N.C. 711, 235 S.E.2d 193 (1977)

The defendant and his wife had been married about 21 years and had four children when they separated in 1973. After the separation, Furr moved his real estate office from their home to a nearby location near the square in Locust, North Carolina. His wife, Earlene, continued to live at the house on Willow Drive and Furr moved into Western Hills Mobile Home Park. The couple's relationship was apparently quite volatile, and Furr exhibited increasing hostility towards Earlene after the separation.

In April, 1973, Earlene filed a civil action against the defendant resulting in a judgment against him in October, 1973. A year later, on his wife's motion, defendant was adjudged to be in contempt and was committed to jail. While in Stanley County jail, Furr met Raymond Clontz and Donald Owens, drove them by Earlene's home and explained how to get into the house. He offered Owens $3,000.00 to kill

Earlene and offered to give Clontz a lot which the latter wanted to store cars on if Clontz would do the job. Neither man accepted the offer.

In October, 1974, defendant asked "Buck" Baker if he knew a "hit man." At the time Furr was angry because Earlene had disposed of some racing equipment. Furr also approached Donald Eugene Huneycutt on several occasions to ask whether Huneycutt knew a "hit man." In the initial encounters, Furr wanted Johny Jhue Laney killed because Laney had murdered his own wife, Doris, who was defendant's girl friend. By early 1975, however, Furr's plans extended as well to Earlene and her attorney, Charles Brown. Huneycutt told him killing women and lawyers would create "too much heat," but defendant responded that he could stand the heat and had his mother for an alibi.

Defendant also asked George Arnold Black, Jr., to kill Earlene, and drove him by the house in the fall of 1974. Like the others, Black declined the offer.

Solicitation of another to commit a felony is a crime in North Carolina, even though the solicitation is of no effect and the crime solicited is never committed. The gravamen of the offense of soliciting lies in counseling, enticing or inducing another to commit a crime.

Defendant argues that the evidence shows only that the defendant requested that Huneycutt find someone else to murder each of the three intended victims, and not that Huneycutt himself commit the crime. . . . Accepting for the moment defendant's argument that defendant solicited Huneycutt only to find another "hit man," we hold that such a request constitutes the crime of solicitation to commit a felony. . . .

Defendant further contends that there was no evidence to support three indictments alleging solicitation. . . . The evidence is that during that month, shortly after both men were released from jail where defendant had been quite talkative about his marital problems, Clontz and Furr met to discuss a lot which Clontz wished to purchase. Furr said he wanted $3,000.00 for the lot and Clontz agreed to take it. Then, as Clontz related at trial, Furr told him not to be so hasty, that "he would make some arrangements about the payment for the lot in another way; that he wanted me to do a job for him." Clontz told Furr that he "knew what he was talking about, but that [he] wasn't interested in it." Defendant then told him he had to go to court with his wife in a few weeks and "that he had to have something done before court time or he was going to be in serious trouble. He said his wife was already getting $250.00 a week from him, and she had possession of the house, and had his property tied up and that he had to have something done." In this context, we find no other reasonable interpretation of defendant's words on this occasion than that he was requesting Clontz to kill his wife. [Conviction affirmed]

REVIEW QUESTIONS

1. Distinguish a principal in the first degree from a principal in the second degree. Which is punished more severely?
2. A person who helps principals prepare to commit a crime, but is not present during the commission, is called what?
3. Has Jan committed attempted murder if she decides to kill her sister and mentally works out the details of when, how, and where?
4. What are the elements of conspiracy?
5. What is hearsay? What is the co-conspirator hearsay rule?
6. What is meant by the phrase "inchoate crimes."
7. What is the difference between solicitation and attempt?

REVIEW PROBLEMS

1-3. Use the following facts to answer questions one through three.

Abel and Baker were inmates sharing a cell in state prison. During their stay they planned a post-release convenience store robbery. They decided which store to rob, when they would rob it, and what method they would use. Having frequented the store on many occasions, Abel knew the store had a safe and that the employees did not have access to its contents. Neither Abel or Baker had any experience with breaking into safes and decided to seek help.

Accordingly, they sought out "Nitro," a fellow inmate who was a known explosives expert. They requested his assistance and promised to pay him one-third of the total recovery. He agreed. However, he would only be able to teach the two how to gain entry to the safe, because he was not scheduled for release until after the day they had planned for the robbery. He added that he owned a house in the area and that it would be available for them to use as a "hide-out until the heat was off."

The two were released as planned and drove to the town where the store was located. As instructed by Nitro, the two went to a store and purchased the materials necessary to construct an explosive which was to be used to gain entry to the safe. That evening Abel and Baker went to the store with their homemade explosive. They left the car they were traveling in and went to the rear of the store to gain entry through a back door. However, as they entered the alley behind the store they encountered a police officer. The officer, suspicious of them, examined their bag and discovered the bomb. Abel and Baker escaped from the officer and stayed in Nitro's house for three days before being discovered and arrested.

1. What crimes has Abel committed?
2. What crimes has Baker committed?
3. What crimes has Nitro committed?

NOTES

[1] See *Rex v. Scofield*, Cald. 397 (1784) and *Rex v. Higgins*, 2 East 5 (1801).

[2] *Hyde v. United States*, 225 U.S. 347 (1912).

[3] Turner, *Attempts to Commit Crimes*, 5 Cambridge L.J. 230, 236 (1934).

[4] Model Penal Code §5.01.

[5] Model Penal Code §5.03.

[6] *Hyde v. U.S.*, 225 U.S. 347 (1912)

CHAPTER 8
Defenses to Criminal Accusations

"We'll have to let him go. He wasn't burning leaves, he was burning a flag."

It is contrary to the laws of God, nature, and the kingdom, for any man to be his own accuser.

John Bradshaw, 1640

OUTLINE

SECTION 8.1 "DEFENSE" DEFINED

Criminal defendants usually claim that they are innocent of the charges raised against them. A defendant's reason for asserting that he is innocent is called a defense. Defenses can be factual: "I didn't do it!" They can also be legal: "I did it, but the case was filed after the statute of limitation had run." Many defenses have been developed under the common law; however, many others have been created by legislation. Finally, some defenses find their origin in the constitutions of the states and federal government. The basic purpose of all defenses is to avoid liability. Some defenses are complete (perfect); that is, if successful, the defendant goes free. Other defenses are partial; the defendant avoids liability on one charge, but may be convicted of a lesser offense.

SECTION 8.2 AFFIRMATIVE DEFENSES

There is a special class of defenses known as **affirmative defenses**. Affirmative defenses go beyond a simple denial; they raise special issues. Defenses that raise the question of a defendant's mental state to commit a crime (i.e., insanity and intoxication) and whether justification or excuse existed to commit the crime (i.e., self-defense) fall into the affirmative defenses class.

As a general rule, criminal defendants may sit passively during trial, as the prosecution bears the burden of proving the allegations. In all instances, **burden of proof** refers to two burdens, the burden of production and the burden of persuasion.

Because it is not practical to require prosecutors to prove that every defendant was sane, wasn't intoxicated, or didn't have justification to use force, the burdens for affirmative defenses are different than for other defenses. First, defendants have the duty of raising all affirmative defenses. At trial this means that defendants must produce some evidence to support the defense. This is known as the **burden of production**. Defendants do not have to convince the fact-finder that the defense is valid. They are only required to bring forth enough evidence to establish the defense.

After defendants have met the burden of production, the **burden of persuasion** then must be met. There is a split among the states; some require the defendant to carry this burden, while others require it of the prosecution. If the defendant has the burden, then she must convince the fact-finder that the defense is true. Defendants must prove this by a preponderance of evidence. In those jurisdictions that require prosecutors to disprove an affirmative defense, there is again a split as to the standard of proof required. Some require proof by a preponderance and others require proof beyond a reasonable doubt.

Some of the defenses that will be covered in this chapter are affirmative defenses. It is necessary to research local law to determine which procedure is followed in a particular jurisdiction and what defenses are considered "affirmative defenses."

SECTION 8.3 INSANITY

Few aspects of criminal law have received as much public attention as the insanity defense. The defense has also been the subject of considerable scholastic research and discussion. Some critics charge that the defense should not be available. Others criticize not the availability of such a defense, but the particular tests that are employed to determine sanity. Despite its critics, insanity is recognized by nearly all jurisdictions as a defense.

In reality, insanity is a mens rea defense. If a defendant was insane at the time of the crime it is unlikely that the requisite mens rea existed. It is generally held that one who is insane is incapable of forming a rational purpose or intent. In fact, in most jurisdictions defendants may put on evidence to establish that insanity prevented the requisite mens rea from being formed. This is the defense of **diminished capacity**. It is a direct attack on the mens rea element of the crime, separate from the defense of insanity. If successful, the result could be conviction of a lesser,

LEGAL TERMS

affirmative defenses
A special defense, such as insanity or self-defense. Contrary to the general rule, defendants have the burden of production concerning affirmative defenses in all jurisdictions, as well as the burden of persuasion in many.

burden of proof
The duty of a party to raise legal issues or introduce facts to support a position. Burden of proof involves two concepts: burden of production and burden of persuasion.

burden of production
The duty of a party to raise an issue and introduce some evidence in its support. It is unnecessary to convince the fact-finder that the contention is true.

burden of persuasion
The duty of a party to convince the fact-finder that something is true.

diminished capacity
A defense. Whenever a defendant's mental condition does not meet the test of insanity, but the defendant's mental state prevented the forming of the requisite mens rea, most states allow the defendant to introduce evidence of her mental state in an attempt to be convicted of a lesser crime. Some states do not permit this, as they treat the defense of insanity as "all or nothing."

Parties approach the bench to discuss insanity of the defendant at the time of trial.

general intent crime. However, a few states have made defendants choose between the insanity defense and no assertion of lack of mens rea due to insanity.

The theory underlying the defense of insanity is that no purpose of criminal law is served by subjecting insane persons to the criminal justice system. Since they have no control over their behavior, they cannot be deterred from similar future behavior. Similarly, no general deterrence will occur, as others suffering from a mental or physical disease of the mind cannot alter their behavior. The one purpose that may be served, incapacitation, is inappropriate if the defendant no longer suffers from a mental disease, or if the disease is now controlled. In those cases where the defendant continues to be dangerous, there is no need to use the criminal justice system to remove them from society, because this can be accomplished using civil commitment.

Something that must be remembered is that criminal law has its own definition of insanity. Other areas of law (i.e., civil commitment) use different tests, as do other professions (i.e., psychiatry). Each jurisdiction is free to use whatever test it wishes to determine insanity. Three tests are used to determine sanity in the criminal law context: M'Naghten; Irresistible Impulse; and the Model Penal Code. A fourth test, the Durham, is no longer used in any jurisdiction, but is mentioned because of its historical significance.

Section 8.3(a) M'Naghten

In 1843 Daniel M'Naghten was tried for killing the British prime minister's secretary. M'Naghten was laboring under the paranoid delusion that the prime minister was planning to kill him, and he killed the minister's secretary, believing him to be the prime minister. The jury found M'Naghten not guilty by reason of insanity.[1] The decision created controversy, and the House of Lords asked the justice of the Queens Bench to state what the standards for acquittal on the grounds of insanity were.[2] Those standards were attached to the decision and set forth the following standard, known as the **M'Naghten** test.

1. At the time that the act was committed
2. the defendant was suffering from a defect of reason, from a disease of the mind, which caused
3. the defendant to not know
   a. the nature and quality of the act taken or
   b. that the act was wrong.

This test has become known as the M'Naghten, or the right-wrong test. It is the test used by most jurisdictions today. First, the defendant must have suffered from a disease of the mind at the time the act occurred. Disease of the mind is not clearly defined, but it appears that any condition that causes one of the two events from the third part of the test is sufficient. That is, any disease of the mind that causes a defendant to not know the quality of an act or that an act is wrong is sufficient. In at least one case extremely low intelligence was found adequate.[3]

The phrase "the defendant must not know the nature and quality of the act" simply means that the defendant did not understand the consequences of his physical act. The drafters of the Model Penal Code gave the following illustration: a man who squeezes his wife's neck, believing it to be a lemon, does not know the nature and quality of his actions.[4]

What is meant by "wrong," as used in the M'Naghten test? Courts have defined it two ways. One asks whether the defendant knew that the act was legally wrong, and the other asks whether the defendant knew that the act was morally wrong.

Section 8.3(b) Irresistible Impulse

Under the M'Naghten test, a defendant who knew that his actions were wrong, but could not control his behavior because of a disease of the mind, is not insane. This has led a few jurisdictions, which follow M'Naghten, to supplement the rule. These states continue to follow the basic rule, but add that a defendant

LEGAL TERMS

M'Naghten test
A test used to determine insanity. Generally, it must be shown that a disease of the mind caused the defendant to not know either the nature and quality of the act or that the act was wrong.

is not guilty by reason of insanity if a disease of the mind caused the defendant to be unable to control her behavior. This is true even if the defendant understood the nature and quality of the act or knew that the behavior was wrong. This is known as **irresistible impulse**.

Irresistible impulse-type tests actually predate M'Naghten and can be found in American cases as far back as 1863.[5] Of course, the largest problem with implementing the irresistible impulse test is distinguishing acts that can be resisted from those that cannot.

Section 8.3(c) Durham

In 1871 the New Hampshire Supeme Court rejected the M'Naghten test and held that a defendant was not guilty because of insanity if the crime was the "product of mental disease." No other jurisdictions followed New Hampshire's lead until 1954, when the District of Columbia Court of Appeals handed down *Durham v. United States*, 214 F.2d 862 (D.C. Cir. 1954). Generally, the **Durham test** requires an acquittal if the defendant would not have committed the crime if he had not been suffering from a mental disease or mental defect.

Durham was overturned in 1972 by the District of Columbia Court of Appeals in favor of a modified version of the Model Penal Code test.[6] Today, Durham is not used by any jurisdiction.

Section 8.3(d) The Model Penal Code Test

The Model Penal Code contains a definition of insanity similar to, but broader than, the M'Naghten and irresistible impulse tests. This test is also referred to as the **substantial capacity** test. The relevant section of the Code reads:[7]

> A person is not responsible for criminal conduct if at the time of such conduct as a result of mental disease or defect he lacks substantial capacity either to appreciate the criminality [wrongfulness] of his conduct or to conform his conduct to the requirements of law.

The Code is similar to M'Naghten in that it requires that mental disease or defect impair a defendant's ability to appreciate the wrongfulness of his act. The final line, "conform his conduct to the requirements of law," is the section that incorporates the irresistible impulse concept.

The Code's approach differs from the M'Naghten and irresistible impulse test in two important regards. First, the Code requires only substantial impairment, while M'Naghten requires total impairment of the ability to know the nature or wrongfulness of the act. Second, the Code uses the term "appreciate," rather than "know." The drafters of the Code clearly intended more than knowledge, and, as such, evidence concerning the defendant's personality and emotional state are relevant.

The Model Penal Code test has been adopted by a few jurisdictions. The federal courts used the test until Congress enacted a statute that established a test similar to the M'Naghten test.[8] That statute places the burden of proving insanity, by clear and convincing evidence, on the defendant.

Section 8.3(e) Procedures of the Insanity Defense

Insanity is an affirmative defense. In the federal system and in many states, defendants must provide notice to the court and government that insanity will be used as a defense at trial. These statutes usually require that the notice be filed a certain number of days prior to trial. This notice provides the prosecution with an opportunity to prepare to rebut the defense prior to trial.

In most instances, lay testimony is not adequate to prove insanity. As such, psychiatric examination of defendants is necessary. The judge presiding over the case will appoint a psychiatrist, who will conduct the exam and make the findings available to the judge. Often defendants wish to have a psychiatrist of their own choosing perform the examination. This is not a problem if the defendant can afford to pay for the service. In the case of indigent defendants who desire an independent mental examination, statutes often provide reimbursement from the government for independent mental examinations up to a stated maximum. In the federal system, trial courts may approve up to $1,000 in defense-related services. Defendants who seek reimbursement for greater expenses must receive approval from the chief judge of the circuit.[9]

As with all affirmative defenses, the defendant bears the burden of production at trial. Generally, the defendant must present enough evidence to create some doubt of sanity. The states are split on the issue of persuasion. Some require that the prosecution disprove the insanity claim, usually beyond a reasonable doubt. In other jurisdictions the defendant bears the burden of persuasion, usually by preponderance of the evidence. One exception is federal law, which requires the defendant to prove insanity by the higher standard—clear and convincing evidence.[10]

Section 8.3(f) Disposition of the Criminally Insane

Contrary to popular belief, those adjudged insane by a criminal proceeding are not immediately and automatically released. In

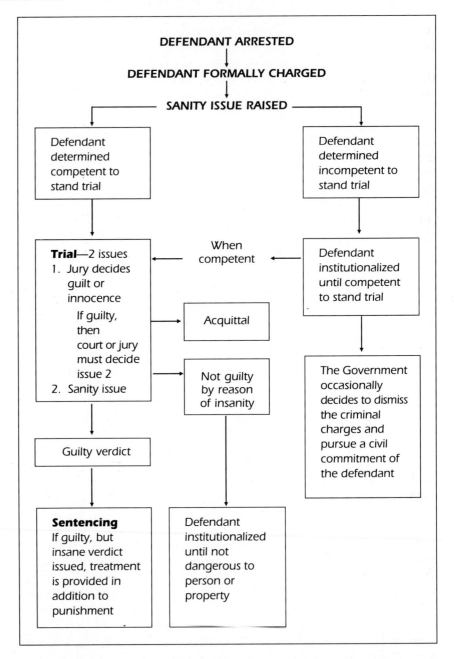

DEFENDANT ARRESTED

DEFENDANT FORMALLY CHARGED

SANITY ISSUE RAISED

Defendant determined competent to stand trial

Defendant determined incompetent to stand trial

Trial—2 issues
1. Jury decides guilt or innocence
   If guilty, then court or jury must decide issue 2
2. Sanity issue

When competent

Defendant institutionalized until competent to stand trial

Acquittal

Not guilty by reason of insanity

The Government occasionally decides to dismiss the criminal charges and pursue a civil commitment of the defendant

Guilty verdict

Sentencing
If guilty, but insane verdict issued, treatment is provided in addition to punishment

Defendant institutionalized until not dangerous to person or property

Insanity and Criminal Procedure

most jurisdictions, after a defendant has been determined "not guilty by reason of insanity," the court (the jury in a few states) must then make a determination of whether the person continues to be dangerous. If so, commitment is to be ordered. If the defendant is determined not to be dangerous, then release follows. A few jurisdictions have followed the Model Penal Code approach,[11] which requires automatic commitment following a finding of not guilty by reason of insanity. This is the rule in the federal system.[12]

In theory, those committed have a right to be treated for their mental disease. In fact, because of lack of funds, security concerns, and overcrowding problems in facilities, adequate treatment is often not provided.

Once a committed person has been successfully treated and is no longer a danger, release is granted. The determination of dangerousness is left to the judge, not hospital administrators or mental health professionals—an often-criticized practice. Patients, doctors, government officials, and even the judge can begin the process of release. Some states provide for periodic reviews of the patient's status in order to determine the propriety of release. The relevant federal statute reads, in part:[13]

> When the director of the facility in which an acquitted person is hospitalized . . . determines that the person has recovered from his mental disease or defect to such an extent that his release, or his conditional release under a prescribed regimen of medical, psychiatric, or psychological care or treatment, would no longer create a substantial risk of bodily injury to another person or serious damage to property of another, he shall promptly file a certificate to that effect with the clerk of the court that ordered the commitment . . . The court shall order a discharge of the acquitted person or, on the motion of the attorney for the government or on its own motion, shall hold a hearing [to determine if the patient is dangerous]. . . .

At that hearing the defendant has the burden of proving by clear and convincing evidence that a risk to people or property is not created by release.

Finally, some states have a "guilty, but mentally ill" verdict. Juries may return such a verdict when the defendant's illness does not rise to the level of negating culpability, but when treatment should be provided in addition to incarceration.

Section 8.3(g)   Insanity at the Time of Trial

The United States Supreme Court has held that a defendant who is insane at the time of trial may not be tried.[14] The Court found that the Due Process Clauses of the Fifth and Fourteenth Amendments require that a defendant be able to assist in his defense and understand the proceeding against him.

The test for determining insanity in this context is different than discussed above. Insanity exists when a defendant lacks the capacity to understand the proceedings or assist in his defense. This simply means that defendants must be rational, possess the ability to testify coherently, and be able to meaningfully discuss the case with his lawyer.

If a defendant is unable to stand trial because he is insane, he is usually committed until he is competent. Many statutes have mandatory commitment of defendants determined incompetent to stand trial. However, indefinite confinement is unconstitutional, based solely upon a finding of incompetence to stand trial. Generally, the Supreme Court has held that a lengthy (eighteen months or longer) detention (awaiting competence to stand trial) is tantamount to punishment and violative of the Due Process Clause.[15] In such cases, there must be a separate finding of dangerousness to continue to hold such persons.

A mistrial is to be declared in the event that a defendant becomes incompetent during a trial, and defendants who are sane at trial but become insane before sentencing should be sentenced to a psychiatric facility.

Last, the Supreme Court has held that a person who has become insane after being sentenced to death may not be executed until his or her sanity is regained.[16] The constitutional basis of the Court's decision was the Eighth Amendment's prohibition of cruel and unusual punishment. Justice Marshall has stated that "It is no less abhorrent today than it has been for centuries to exact in penance the life of one whose mental illness prevents him from comprehending the reasons for the penalty or its implications.[17]

SECTION 8.4 DURESS AND NECESSITY

Consider these facts: Terry Teller is ordered by bank robber, who is brandishing a gun, to place the money in her drawer in a bag and to give it to bank robber or "she will be planted six feet under." Has Terry committed theft? Although the elements of theft may be satisfied, she has the defense of **duress**. To prove duress, one must show 1. that he was threatened 2. and that the threat caused a reasonable belief 3. that the only way of avoiding serious personal injury or death to himself or others 4. was to commit the crime. Duress was recognized at common law and continues to be a statutory defense today.

First, it must be shown that a threat was made. Second, the threat must create a reasonable fear of immediate serious bodily harm or death. This fear must be reasonable; that is, even if the person making the threat had no intention of following through, the defense is still valid if a reasonable person would have thought the threat was real. Hence, even if bank robber never intended to kill Terry, she has the defense of duress. Terry need not be the one threatened for her to be able to claim duress. So if bank robber threatened to kill a customer unless she complied, Terry could claim duress. The fear must not only be reasonable, but it must be of serious bodily injury or death. If bank robber exclaims, "Put the money in the bag or I'll smack you across the face," the threatened danger is not sufficient to support the defense of duress. In addition, the threat of harm must be imminent or immediate. Threats of future harms are not adquate duress.

One limitation that is recognized nearly everywhere is that murder is not justified by duress. This rule is criticized, rightfully so, because it does not account for those situations where taking one life may save many more.

It is no defense to a crime to claim that one was only carrying out the orders of a superior, such as an employer or military superior. This issue was addressed in *United States v. Calley*.

UNITED STATES V. CALLEY

46 C.M.R. 1131 (1975)

[D]uring midmorning on 16 March 1968 a large number of unresisting Vietnamese were placed in a ditch on the eastern side of My Lai and summarily executed by American soldiers.

[PFC] Meadlo gave the most graphic and damning evidence. He had wandered back into the village alone after the trial incident. Eventually, he met his fire team leader, Specialist Four Grzesik. They took seven or eight Vietnamese to what he labeled a "ravine," where Lieutenants Calley, Sledge, and Dursi and a few other Americans were located with what he estimated as seventy-five to a hundred Vietnamese. Meadlo remembered also that Lieutenant Calley told him, "We got another job to do, Meadlo," and that the appellant started shoving people into the ravine and shooting them. Meadlo, in contrast to Dursi, followed the directions of his leader and himself fired into the people at the bottom of the "ravine." Meadlo then drifted away from the area but he doesn't remember where.

Specialist Four Grzesik found PFC Meadlo, crying and distraught, sitting on a small dike on the eastern edge of the

LEGAL TERMS

duress
A defense applicable when a person commits a crime under threat of serious bodily harm or death.

village. He and Meadlo moved through the village, and came to the ditch, in which Grzesik thought were thirty-five dead bodies. Lieutenant Calley walked past and ordered Grzesik to take his fire team back into the village and help the following platoon in their search. He also remembered that Calley asked him to "finish them off," but he refused.

Specialist Four Turner saw Lieutenant Calley for the first time that day as Turner walked out of the village near the ditch. Meadlo and a few other soldiers were also present. Turner passed within fifteen feet of the area, looked into the ditch and saw a pile of approximately twenty bodies covered with blood. He saw Lieutenant Calley and Meadlo firing from a distance of five feet into another group of people who were kneeling and squatting in the ditch. . . .

Of the several bases for his argument that he committed no murder at My Lai because he was void of mens rea, appellant emphasized most of all that he acted in obedience to orders. . . .

An order of the type appellant says he received is illegal. Its illegality is apparent upon even cursory evaluation by a man of ordinary sense and understanding. . . .

We find no impediment to the findings that appellant acted with murderous mens rea, including premeditation. . . .

The Court mentioned that the order's illegality was "apparent upon even cursory evaluation by a man of ordinary sense and understanding." What if an order appears to be legal and the person who follows it has a reasonable belief of its legality? In such cases, the defense of duress does apply.[18]

Necessity is similar to duress. However, while duress is created by human pressures, necessity comes about by natural forces. When a person is confronted with two choices, both causing harm, he is to choose the lesser harm. If he does, he may have the defense of necessity to the act taken. For example, a person may be justified in breaking into someone's cabin in order to avoid freezing to death. Or a captain of a ship may be justified in a trespassory use of another's dock, if setting ashore is necessary to save the ship and its passengers.

Necessity is a broad and amorphous concept. As a general proposition it applies any time a person is confronted with the task of choosing between two or more evils. The harm avoided need not be bodily injury; it can also be harm to property. Of course, choosing property over life is never justified. Finally, if an alternative existed that involved less harm than the chosen act, the defense is invalid.

Duress and necessity are complete defenses. When valid, they result in acquittal on all related charges.

SECTION 8.5 USE OF FORCE DEFENSES

In some situations, the law permits actors to use physical force against others. Self-defense, defense of others, defense of property, and use of force to makes arrests fall into this area. Self-defense, defense of others, and defense of property, when successful, are complete defenses. Imperfect self-defense (including defense of another) does not lead to acquittal; however, it does reduce murder to manslaughter.

Section 8.5(a) Self-Defense

To prove **self-defense** it must be shown that the actor 1. was confronted with an unprovoked, 2. immediate threat of bodily harm, 3. that force was necessary to avoid the harm, 4. and that the amount of force used was reasonable.

One who initiates an attack on another can not claim self-defense as a general proposition. There are two exceptions to this rule. First, if an attacker is met with excessive force in return, then he may defend himself. For example, Mike attacks Norm with his fists, and in defense Norm uses a deadly weapon. In such a circumstance, Mike may also use deadly force to protect himself. Second, if an attacker withdraws from the attack and is pursued by the intended victim, then he may claim self-defense. Suppose Randy attacks Sue with an intent to sexually assault her. After he grabs her, she displays a gun, and he runs. If Sue follows after him, intending to cause him harm, then he would be privileged to use force to defend himself.

The threat of harm must be immediate in most jurisdictions. Threat of future harm does not justify using force against another. To satisfy this requirement the harm must be one that will occur unless force is used, and no other means of avoiding the harm exists. However, this principle is occasionally stretched. For example, some jurisdictions have permitted a jury to be instructed on the "battered wife defense." Under this defense a woman who is constantly abused by her husband may be justified in using force at a time when there is not strictly "immediate danger." The theory

LEGAL TERMS

necessity
A defense applicable when a person commits a crime in order to avoid a more serious harm from happening.

self-defense
A defense that justifies the use of force against another to avoid personal injury or death. The defense is extended to defending others.

is that women in such circumstances have two choices: either waiting for their husbands to kill them or striking first in a form of offensive self-defense. Critics of this defense contend that since other remedies are available, such as leaving the husband and obtaining a court order restraining him from bothering her, there is no "immediate danger."

Finally, the force used to defend oneself must be reasonable. It would be unreasonable to knife a person who is attempting to slap one's hand. Deadly force may be used to defend against an attack that threatens serious bodily injury or death. Deadly force may not be used to defend against other attacks.

All jurisdictions require that a person retreat from an attack, if posssible, before using deadly force. This is known as the **retreat doctrine**. There are many exceptions to the doctrine. Retreat is not required whenever it poses a danger to the party, nor is retreat expected from one's home. Police officers are not required to retreat when performing their lawful duties. The Model Penal Code has a retreat provision that recognizes these exceptions.[19]

> The use of deadly force is not justifiable . . . [if] the actor knows that he can avoid the necessity of using such force without complete safety by retreating or by surrendering possession of a thing to a person asserting a claim of right thereto or by complying with a demand that he abstain from any action which he has no duty to take, except that (1) the actor is not obliged to retreat from his dwelling or place of work, unless he was the initial aggressor. . . .

The Code provides that public officials need not retreat during the performance of their duties. There is no duty to retreat rather than using non-deadly force.

Also, notice that the Code requires not only retreat, but that "thing[s]" be surrendered and one comply with another's demands before deadly force is used. Of course, one can later use civil law to recover unlawfully taken items or to recover for complying with a demand that caused damage. The aggressor will be liable both civilly and criminally for such unlawful demands.

Section 8.5(b)   Defense of Others

It is also a justified use of force to defend another. The rules are similar to that of self-defense: there must be a threat of immediate danger to the other person; the perception of threat must be reasonable; the amount of force used must be reasonable; and deadly force may only be used to repel a deadly attack.

At common law one was only privileged to defend those with whom a special relationship existed, such as parent and child.

Today, most jurisdictions permit any person to use force to protect another.

What happens when a person uses force to defend another who is not privileged to use force himself? For example, Perry is an undercover police officer attempting to arrest Norm, who is resisting. Randa observes what is happening and comes to Norm's defense, believing that Norm was being unlawfully attacked. There is a split of authority concerning this problem. Some jurisdictions limit the authority of the defender to use force to the privilege held by the person being attacked. Since Norm was not privileged to use force against the police officer, Randa is guilty of assault. Other states, however, use an objective test. Under such a test, if a reasonable person standing in Randa's shoes would have believed that force was justified, then she would be acquitted.

Section 8.5(c) Defense of Property and Habitation

At common law and by legislative enactment today, one may use force to defend property. As with defending oneself, only reasonable force may be used. Because property is not as valuable as life, deadly force may not be used to protect property. As such, one must allow another to take or destroy property before killing to defend it. No force is reasonable if other methods of protecting the property were available. So, if one has ample time to seek assistance from the police or the courts, force would be unreasonable. On the other hand, if an enemy appears at one's house and begins to destroy a car in the driveway, force would be permitted to protect the vehicle. The actor must have a reasonable belief that his or her property is in danger of trespass or destruction and that the force used was necessary to defend the property.

The basic rules concerning defense of property also apply to defense of habitation: one must have a reasonable belief that the property is threatened; only reasonable force may be used to protect the property; and other nonviolent remedies must be utilized before resorting to force. However, one difference between dwellings and other property is that deadly force may be used, under some circumstances, to protect one's home.

In early common law the security of the home was as important as life itself. As such, people were permitted to use deadly force against any forcible intruder after warning the person not to enter. Today the rule has been narrowed, and statutes now commonly require that the occupant must believe that the intruder intends to commit a felony once inside before deadly force may be used.

The Model Penal Code allows the use of deadly force if either
1. the intruder is attempting to take the dwelling (with no legal

LEGAL TERMS

retreat doctrine
   If it is possible to safely do so, one must retreat before using deadly force to repel an attack.

claim to do so) or 2. the intruder is there to commit a crime (arson, burglary, theft) and has threatened deadly force or poses a substantial risk to those inside.[20]

This provision of the Code incorporates a self-defense concept. Remember, the rules of self-defense apply in the home also. So, any time a person's life (or another's) is threatened, deadly force may be used.

Some people choose to protect their property with man-made devices, such as electric fences and spring guns. Others have used natural protection, such as dogs and snakes. Despite which is used, the rules are the same. If the device employs non-deadly force, it is likely to be lawful. An electric fence, which does not have sufficient electric current to kill, is a justified use of force.

However, the result is often different when one uses deadly force. There are two perspectives on the use of deadly traps to protect property. One permits the use of deadly force so long as the person who set the trap would have been permitted to use such force himself, if he had been present. So, if a murderer gains entry to a house and is killed by a spring gun, the occupant is not criminally liable since he would have been privileged to use deadly force against the murderer. The second perspective, adopted by the drafters of the Model Penal Code, rejects the use of deadly traps in all instances.[21] This position is sound, as deadly traps do not discriminate between the dangerous and the non-dangerous. The occupant who sets such a trap is simply lucky if the intruder is a criminal and not a fireman responding to a blaze in the home.

Section 8.5(d) Imperfect Self-Defense

The so-called "imperfect self-defense" is actually a mens rea defense. It applies to those situations when a person cannot make a successful self-defense (or defense of another) claim, but because he lacked malice aforethought (or purpose), his crime should not be murder, but manslaughter. The defense only applies to homicides and is not recognized everywhere.

As stated above, a person must have a reasonable belief that he or another is in danger of serious bodily injury or death before deadly force may be used. What if a person possesses a good faith, but unreasonable belief? Self-defense is unavailable, but since there is no malicious intent, purpose, or malice aforethought (depending on the jurisdiction's definition of murder), the crime is reduced to manslaughter. The defense is available in a second situation: whenever a person who initiates an attack using non-deadly force later justifiably uses deadly force to defend himself.

Section 8.5(e) Arrests

Sometimes it is necessary for law enforcement officers to use force to execute their duties and to defend themselves. When a police officer uses force in defense of another's attack, the rules of self-defense that you have already learned apply. In addition, because the use of force is an integral part of law enforcement, it is often justified. However, a person making an arrest does not have an unlimited right to use force against an arrestee. This section examines a person's right to resist an unlawful arrest, the so-called "citizen's arrest," and arrests by law-enforcement officers.

Section 8.5(e.1) Resisting Unlawful Arrests

In some states, people may use force to resist an unlawful arrest. The amount of force is usually limited to non-deadly, although some jurisdictions permit one to use deadly force. Of course, if a person uses force against a lawful arrest, he is fully liable for whatever crime results (assault, battery, or murder), as well as for resisting a lawful arrest.

The rule permitting force to resist a lawful arrest evolved during a time when arrestees were detained for long periods before appearing before a court, jail conditions were extremely poor, and no civil remedies existed for unlawful arrests. In light of these harsh facts, public policy was best served by permitting people to resist unlawful arrests.

Today, many jurisdictions have adopted an approach closer to the Model Penal Code's, which prohibits any resistance to an arrest by a law-enforcement officer. This is the sensible approach, as the reasons for permitting resistance no longer exist: arrestees must be promptly brought before judges and released if there is no probable cause. When available, bail is set immediately. Also, federal law now permits civil suits against law-enforcement officers for violation of a person's civil rights. Prohibiting resistance advances two important public policy objectives: first, it fosters obedience to police, and, second, it reduces violence.

Section 8.5(e.2) Arrests by Law-Enforcement Officers

A law-enforcement officer is privileged to use reasonable force to apprehend criminals and to prevent those incarcerated from escaping. At common law police could use all but deadly force to arrest misdemeanants and deadly force to arrest felons. This latter rule was justified by the fact that all felons were put to death at early common law.

In 1974 a Memphis, Tennessee, police officer shot and killed a fifteen-year-old male who was fleeing a burglary. The boy had stolen forty dollars. The family of the deceased boy sued the police department in federal court for violating his constitutional rights. The case ended up before the United States Supreme Court.

In Tennessee v. Garner, 471 U.S. 1 (1985), the Court held that the use of deadly force by a police officer was a "seizure," under the Fourth Amendment. Accordingly, the test used to determine whether the use of deadly force is proper is the Fourth Amendment's test: reasonability. The Court then held that the use of deadly force is only reasonable when the person fleeing is a dangerous felon. The Court did not state what standard must be applied in cases of non-deadly force.

In 1989 the Court handed down *Graham v. Connor*, where the standard was set for all preconviction arrests. In that opinion, which follows, the Court held that all seizures are to be evaluated under the Fourth Amendment reasonableness standard.

GRAHAM V. CONNOR

_____ U.S. _____ (1989)

This case requires us to decide what constitutional standard governs a free citizen's claim that law-enforcement officials used excessive force in the course of making an arrest, investigatory stop, or other "seizure" of his person. We hold that such claims are properly analyzed under the Fourth Amendment's "objective reasonableness" standard. . . .

. . . . On November 12, 1984, Graham, a diabetic, felt the onset of an insulin reaction. He asked a friend, William Berry, to drive him to a nearby convenience store so he could purchase some orange juice to counteract the reaction. Berry agreed, but when Graham entered the store, he saw a number of people ahead of him in the checkout line. Concerned about the delay, he hurried out of the store and asked Berry to drive him to a friend's house instead.

Respondent Connor, an officer of the Charlotte, North Carolina, Police Department, saw Graham hastily enter and leave the store. The officer became suspicious that something was amiss and followed Berry's car. About one-half mile from the store, he made an investigatory stop. Although Berry told Connor that Graham was simply suffering from a "sugar reaction," the officer ordered Berry and Graham to wait while he found out what, if anything, had happened at the convenience store. When Officer Connor returned to his patrol car to call for backup assistance, Graham got out of the car, ran around it twice, and finally sat down on the curb, where he passed out briefly.

In the ensuing confusion, a number of other Charlotte police officers arrived on the scene in response to Officer Connor's request for backup. One of the officers rolled Graham over on the sidewalk and cuffed his hands tightly behind his back, ignoring Berry's pleas to get him some sugar. Another officer said: "I've seen a lot of people with sugar diabetes that never acted like this. Ain't nothing wrong with the M.F. but drunk. Lock the S.B. up." App. 42. Several officers then lifted Graham up from behind, carried him over to Berry's car, and placed him face down on the hood. Regaining consciousness, Graham asked the officers to check in his wallet for a diabetic decal that he carried. In response, one of the officers told him to "shut up" and shoved his face down against the hood of the car. Four officers grabbed Graham and threw him head-first into the police car. A friend of Graham's brought some orange juice to the car, but the officers refused to let him have it. Finally, Officer Connor received a report that Graham had done nothing wrong at the convenience store, and the officers drove him home and released him.

At some point during the encounter with the police, Graham sustained a broken foot, cuts on his wrists, a bruised forehead, and an injured shoulder; he also claims to have developed a loud ringing in his right ear that continues to this day. . . .
[The Court then discussed previous cases which held that a due process standard should be applied in all cases of excessive force. To be successful using the due process standard, a plaintiff had to prove the actions of the police were "sadistic and malicious."]

We reject this notion that all excessive force claims brought under §1983 [A federal statute permitting cases against government officials to be brought in federal court] are governed by a single generic standard. As we have said many times, §1983 "is not itself a source of substantive rights," but merely provides "a method for vindication of federal rights elsewhere conferred. . . . In addressing an excessive force claim brought under §1983, analysis begins by identifying the specific constitutional right allegedly infringed by the challeged application of force. . . . In most instances, that will be either the Fourth Amendment's prohibition against unreasonable seizures of the person, or the Eighth Amendment's ban on cruel and unusual punishments, which are the two primary sources of constitutional protection against physically abusive governmental conduct. . . .

. . . Today we make explicit what is implicit in *Garner's* analysis, and hold that *all* claims that law-enforcement officers have used excessive force—deadly or not—in the course of an arrest, investigatory stop, or other "seizure" of a free citizen should be analyzed under the Fourth Amendment and its "reasonableness" standard. . . .

The "reasonableness" of a particular use of force must be judged from the perspective of a reasonable officer on the scene, rather than with the 20/20 vision of hindsight. . . . The calculus of reasonableness must embody allowance for the fact that police officers are often forced to make split-second judgments—in circumstances that are tense, uncertain, and rapidly evolving—about the amount of force that is necessary in a particular situation.

As in other Fourth Amendment contexts, however, the "reasonableness" inquiry in an excessive force case is an objective one: the question is whether the officer's actions are "objectively reasonable" in light of the facts and circumstances confronting them, without regard to their underlying intent or motivation. . . .

Exactly how *Tennessee v. Garner* is affected by *Graham* remains to be seen. There are two theories. First, some contend that *Graham* emasculates *Tennessee v. Garner* by overruling the dangerousness standard. That is, in cases where deadly force is used it need not be shown that the person posed a danger to the police or another—it only has to be proved that the use of the force was reasonable. The second theory, similar to the first, contends that all claims of excessive force are to be judged under the reasonableness standard, but that *Tennessee v. Garner* sets a threshold: that the use of deadly force on a nondangerous fleeing suspect is *per se* unreasonable. Under the first theory, a jury would be permitted to determine whether the use of deadly force on a nondangerous fleeing felon was reasonable. Using the second theory, if a jury decided that the victim of deadly force did not pose a danger they would not be permitted to return a finding that the officer's actions were reasonable.

Finally, note that police officers are often put into positions when they must defend themselves, such as during an arrest. The same rules discussed earlier concerning self-defense apply in these situations, with one exception: Police officers are not required to retreat. As such, if a police officer is involved in an arrest that involves escalating violence, it is possible that the police officer may have to use deadly force to defend against the criminal's attack.

Section 8.5(e.3) Arrests by Citizens

At common law a private citizen was privileged to arrest those who committed a felony or misdemeanor (which amounted to a breach of the peace) in his presence. Some jurisdictions have retained this rule, and others have changed it by statute.

In those jurisdictions that have changed the rule, it is common to permit so-called citizens' arrests any time probable cause exists to believe that the person has committed a felony. In most jurisdictions a citizen may not arrest a misdemeanant unless the person making the arrest witnessed the crime. Even in such cases, only certain misdemeanors may lead to such an arrest.

The reason for these rules is to provide citizens who make such arrests with immunity from civil and criminal prosecution. However, the citizen must be privileged to make the arrest and, even when privleged, a reasonable amount of force must be used.

In some jurisdictions, a private person making an arrest may use deadly force only when the person is in fact a felon. The jurisdictions employing this rule are split: some permit the use of deadly force by private citizens to arrest for any felony and others only for specific felonies (i.e., murder and rape). These jurisdictions are similar in one important regard. The person against whom the deadly force is used must have *in fact* committed the crime. A reasonable, but incorrect, belief that the person has committed a crime is not a defense. So, if Pat kills Sam while attempting to arrest him for a crime he did not commit, Pat is liable for manslaughter, even though she had a reasonable belief that he committed the crime. Some states have followed the Model Penal Code approach, which prohibits the use of deadly force by private persons in all circumstances.[22]

The results are different if a private person is assisting a law-enforcement officer. In fact, many states have statutes that require citizens to assist police officers upon order. In such cases, the private party is privileged to use whatever force is reasonable. In addition, a private person responding to a police officer's order to assist him in an arrest, is privileged, even if the police officer was exceeding her authority and had no cause to make the arrest. In such instances, the police officer may be liable for both her actions and the actions of the private party summoned. Of course, there are limits to the rule. For example, a private person who obeys a police officer's order to strike an already apprehended and subdued criminal would not be privileged.

Section 8.5(f)   Infancy

At common law it was a complete defense to a charge that the accused was a child under the age of seven at the time the crime was committed. It was irrebuttably presumed that children under seven were incapable of forming the requisite mens rea to commit a crime. A rebuttable presumption of incapacity existed for those between seven and fourteen years-of-age. The presumption could be overcome for those between seven and fourteen if the prosecution could prove that the defendant understood that the criminal act was wrong.

Few minors are charged with crimes today. This is the result of the advent of the juvenile court systems in the United States. Currently all states have a juvenile court system that deals with juvenile delinquency and neglected children.

Statutes vary, but it is common for juvenile courts to be given exclusive jurisdiction over criminal behavior of juveniles. However, some states give concurrent jurisdiction to criminal courts and juvenile courts. If concurrent, the juvenile court usually must waive jurisdiction before the criminal court can hear the case. Determining who is a juvenile also differs, with some jurisdictions utilizing a method similar to the common law (irrebuttable and rebuttable presumptions) and others simply setting an age cutoff, such as fourteen or sixteen.

The purpose of the juvenile justice system differs from that of the criminal justice system. While criminal law has punishment as one of its major purposes, the purpose of the juvenile system is not to punish, but to reform the delinquent child.

Section 8.5(g) Intoxication

In this context, intoxication refers to all situations where a person's mental or physical abilities are impaired by drugs or alcohol. It is generally said that voluntary intoxication is a defense if it has the effect of negating the required mens rea. In common-law language this means that if intoxication prevents a defendant from being able to form a specific intent, then the crime is reduced to a similar general intent crime. For the crime of murder, intoxication is a defense if it prevents the defendant from forming the premeditation, deliberation, or purposeful element. In such cases the charge is reduced from first-degree to second-degree murder. Not all states recognize voluntary intoxication as a defense.

In the rare case of involuntary intoxication the defendant is relieved of liability entirely. To be successful with such a claim, the defendant is required to show that the intoxication had the same affect as insanity. In jurisdictions using the M'Naghten test for insanity, a defendant is required to prove that the intoxication prevented him from knowing right from wrong.

Section 8.5(h) Mistake

People may be mistaken in two ways. First, one may believe that some act is legal when it is not. This is a mistake of law. Second, a person may not understand all the facts of a given situation. This is a mistake of fact. As a general proposition, mistake of fact is a defense, and mistake of law is not. However, many exceptions to each rule have been developed. A few of these exceptions are noted below.

Mistake of fact is a defense whenever it negates the mens rea aspect of a crime. For example, an intent to steal another's property is an element of theft. If an attorney picks up a briefcase believing it to be his when it is actually someone else's, it is not theft. The mistake negates the intent to steal. To be valid, mistakes must be made honestly and in good faith.

While honest mistakes of fact usually constitute a defense, there are exceptions. One exception is obvious: strict liability crimes, as there is no requirement of mens rea to negate.

In some instances an honest but unreasonable mistake of fact may not eliminate culpability entirely; however, it may reduce the crime. The imperfect self-defense previously discussed falls into this category.

We have all heard, if not quipped, "Ignorance of the law is no excuse." As a general rule this statement is true. There are two situations where a person can make a mistake of law. The first occurs when an individual is unaware that his or her actions are prohibited by statute: "I didn't know it was against the law not to file a tax return!" The second occurs when a person takes an act, under the color of a legal right and in good faith, only to find out later that the act was illegal. For example, a landlord may have a reasonable, but mistaken, belief that she has a right to take possessions from a tenant's house to satisfy a delinquent rent debt.

For the most part unawareness that an act is illegal is not a defense. The law presumes that everyone knows what is legal and what is not. Mistakes that fall into the second group act to negate mens rea and are more likely to be successful. The landlord in the example would not be guilty of larceny because of the mistake. Another example of such a defense is when a person has a reasonable, but mistaken, belief that she has the authority to take a person into custody. So, officers who arrest people in good faith, but without probable cause, are not guilty of kidnapping or criminal confinement.

Another exception to the mistake of law rule is no defense exists when a person relies on statutes, judicial opinions, or certain administrative decisions that later turn out to be wrong. The rule is sound for two reasons. First, as a matter of public policy it is not wise to prosecute people for acting in conformity with the law. The result would be individual interpretation of all laws and disregard for those statutes, regulations, or judicial decisions believed incorrect. Second, as a matter of due process, it appears that no notice has been provided that compliance with the law will be punished.

Finally, one defense that is not accepted is reliance on the advice of counsel. If a lawyer advises a client that a particular act is legal when it is not, the client will be liable for the crime if the act is taken.

Section 8.5(i) Entrapment

To what extent should police officers be permitted to encourage someone to commit a crime? This is the question which is underlying the defense of **entrapment**. Entrapment occurs when law-enforcement officers encourage another to commit a crime with the intent of arresting and prosecuting that person for the commission of that crime.

Entrapment is a defense of recent development, although all states and the federal government recognize some form of the defense today. There is no constitutional basis for the entrapment defense, so each jurisdiction is free to structure the defense in any manner. Of course, a state may also do away with the defense, although none have done so. This is a sound policy decision, as most people would agree that there must be some limit on police conduct. Not everyone agrees where the line should be drawn. Currently two tests are used to determine whether a defendant was entrapped: the subjective and objective tests.

The test used in the federal system and most widely used by the states is the subjective test. The test attempts to distinguish between those who are predisposed to commit crime from those who are not. The test is subjective; the defendant's mental state at the time of the encouragement is imperative. A defendant is predisposed if he is ready to commit the crime and is only awaiting the opportunity. The Supreme Court has said that the subjective test is designed to draw a line between the "unwary innocent and the unwary criminal."[23]

Under the subjective approach evidence of the defendant's criminal record may be relevant to show predisposition. For example, recent drug convictions may evidence a predisposition to enter into future drug purchases or sales.

The second method of determining whether a person was entrapped is objective. The Model Penal Code[24] adopts this approach, as do a minority of states. The objective approach does not focus on the particular defendant's predisposition, but asks whether the police conduct creates a "substantial risk that an offense will be committed by persons other than those who are ready to commit it."[25]

The defendant's actual state of mind is not relevant to this inquiry, and, accordingly, evidence of a defendant's criminal history is irrelevant. Under this approach, a defendant may be acquitted even though he was predisposed to commit the crime. Suppose a police officer offers a prostitute $150,000 for sex. The prostitute would have agreed had the officer offered $50. Using the subjective approach the prostitute would be convicted because she was predisposed to engage in prostitution. However, in jurisdictions using the objective test she may have been entrapped, as women who do not normally sell sex might be encouraged to do so for $150,000.

In many states entrapment may not be used to defend against crimes involving violence to people, such as battery and murder. The Model Penal Code also takes this view.

Section 8.5(j) Alibi and Consent

Alibi and consent are two factual defenses. An **alibi** is a claim by a defendant that she was not present at the scene of the crime at the time it was committed. Whenever a defendant asserts an alibi she is simply refuting the government's claim of facts. Defendants are usually required to give the government notice that

LEGAL TERMS

entrapment
A defense. Under some circumstances it is entrapment for law enforcement officers to encourage a person to engage in criminal conduct for the purpose of arresting and prosecuting that person for committing the crime encouraged. There are two tests used to determine if entrapment exists. One test focuses on whether defendants are predisposed to engage in criminal behavior (subjective), and the other focuses on the propriety of the police conduct (objective).

alibi
A defense. A claim by a defendant that she was not present at the scene of a crime at the time it was committed.

alibi is claimed prior to trial. Of course, the government must prove the elements of the crime (i.e., present at the crime) beyond a reasonable doubt. This means that the defendant bears no burden in an alibi defense.

Victim **consent** is a defense to some crimes, such as rape or larceny. That is, if a person consents to sex or to give you his property, there is no crime. Consent is, however, not a defense to many crimes, such as statutory rape, incest, child molestation, battery, and murder.

Section 8.5(k) Statutes of Limitation

Many crimes must be prosecuted within a specified time after being committed. A **statute of limitation** sets the time limit. If prosecution is initiated after the applicable statute has expired, the defendant is entitled to a dismissal.

Statutes vary in length, and serious crimes, such as murder, have no limitation. Generally, the higher the crime the longer the statute. Statutes begin running when the crime occurs; however, statutes may be tolled in some situations. Tolling refers to stopping the clock. The time that a defendant is a fugitive is commonly tolled. For example, assume that the limitation on felony assault is six years. The assault was committed on June 1, 1991. Normally, prosecution would have to be started by June 1, 1997. However, if the defendant was fugitive from June 1, 1991 to June 1, 1993, then the statute would be tolled, and the new date of limitation would be June 1, 1998.

At common law there were no limitations. Statutes of limitation are legislative creations. There is no constitutional basis for limiting the time in which to prosecute someone for criminal behavior. This being so, legislatures are free to alter or abolish statutes of limitation. If there is no limitation fixed, prosecution may occur any time after the crime.

Sometimes a prosecution for a serious crime may begin after the statute on the lesser included crime has expired. For example, battery is a lesser included crime of aggravated battery. Assume that aggravated battery has a six-year statute and battery three. In most jurisdictions, a prosecutor may not circumvent the three-year statute by charging aggravated battery and including the lesser battery offense in the information or indictment. After the time has run out on the lesser offense, but not on the more serious offense, the defendant is either convicted of the greater offense or acquitted, but can no longer be convicted on the lesser offense. However, at least one jurisdiction does not follow this rule.[26]

Section 8.5(I)   Constitutional Defenses

A variety of defenses arise from the United States Constitution. Most of these rights are found in the first nine amendments. You have already learned a few constitutional defenses, such as the protection of expression by the First Amendment. In addition, many rights that are procedural, such as the right to a speedy trial, will be discussed later. A few critical defenses have been chosen for discussion below.

Bear in mind that each state has its own constitution, which may provide greater protection than the United States Constitution. During this discussion you may want to refer to the United States Constitution, which is an appendix to this text.

Section 8.5(I.1)   Double Jeopardy

The Fifth Amendment to the United States Constitution provides that "no person shall be subject for the same offense to be twice put in jeopardy of life or limb." The principle of not punishing someone twice for the same act can be found back as far as Blackstone's Commentaries.[27] The **Double Jeopardy Clause** applies only to criminal proceedings.

There are actually two prohibitions in the Double Jeopardy Clause. The clause prevents: 1. a second prosecution for the same offense and 2. a second punishment for the same offense.

Often the question is whether a prior "jeopardy" occurred. It is generally held that a person has been put in jeopardy once a plea of guilty has been entered and accepted by a court. An unapproved plea will not suffice, and a subsequent prosecution will not be prohibited by the double jeopardy clause. In jury trials jeopardy attaches once a jury has been selected and sworn. States treat bench trials differently, although the prevailing view is that jeopardy attaches once the first witness has been sworn.

Once jeopardy attaches the defendant may not be tried again. However, there are a few exceptions. A defendant may be retried if the first trial was terminated by a properly declared mistrial. Mistrials may be declared for a variety of reasons. Death of the trial judge or one of the participating attorneys would likely result in a mistrial. If a witness blurts out an answer to a question before the judge has an opportunity to sustain an objection to the question, and the answer is extremely prejudicial, a mistrial may be declared. The causes of a mistrial are endless. Note that the mistrial must be proper. That is, if an appellate court later determines that a mistrial should not have been declared, the defendant has been put into jeopardy. It is always proper to retry a defendant whose prior trial was declared a mistrial upon the

LEGAL TERMS

consent
 A claim by a defendant that a victim agreed to the acts. A defense to some crimes, such as larceny and rape. Consent, even if true, is not a defense to some crimes, such as statutory rape and murder.

statute of limitation
 Legislative enactments that establish a time limit for the prosecution of certain offenses.

Double Jeopardy Clause
 The Fifth Amendment to the United States Constitution prohibits prosecuting or punishing a person twice for the same act. The double jeopardy clause does not prohibit two sovereign entities from punishing a person for the same act.

defendant's motion. If a defendant objects to a government motion for a mistrial, there must be a "manifest necessity" (damn good reason) for the mistrial.[28]

It is also not a violation of the Fifth Amendment to prosecute a defendant who was previously charged, but whose charges were dismissed prior to jeopardy attaching. Additionally, if a defendant appeals a conviction and prevails, the defendant may be retried, unless the appellate court finds that insufficient evidence exists to retry the defendant. However, if a defendant is acquitted on a serious charge and convicted on a lesser and then prevails on appeal, he may only be retried on the lesser. It is violative of the Fifth Amendment to retry him on the more serious offense.

The Fifth Amendment only forbids retrial for the same offense. Determining whether two acts constitute the same offense is not always an easy task. Two offenses are the same unless one requires proof of a fact that the other does not.[29] This is the "same evidence test."

The Double Jeopardy Clause is fully applicable to the states through the Fourteenth Amendment. However, the clause does not prevent second punishments for the same offense by different jurisdictions. For example, a person who robs a federally insured bank may be prosecuted by both the state where the bank resides and the United States. This is true even though the offenses are the same. Municipalities are not independent beings; they owe their existence not to the Constitution of the United States, but to a state. Accordingly, prosecutions by cities are treated as being brought by the state, and it is a violation of the Double Jeopardy Clause for a state and city to punish one for the same offense.

Section 8.5(I.2) Self-Incrimination and Immunity

The Fifth Amendment also states that no person "shall be compelled in any criminal case to be a witness against himself." The following passage explains why the framers of the Constitution included a privilege against self-incrimination.

> Perhaps the best-known provision of the Fifth Amendment is the clause against forced "self-incrimination," whose origin goes back to England where persons accused of crimes before ecclesiastical courts were forced to take an ex officio oath. That is, they had to swear to answer all questions even if the questions did not apply to the case at trial. This requirement was later adopted by the Court of Star Chamber. One of the victims of the Court was a printer and book distributor named John Lilburne, charged in 1637

with treason for importing books "that promoted Puritan dissent." Lilburne told his accusers, "I am not willing to answer you to any more of these questions because I see you go about by this examination to ensnare me. For seeing the things for which I am imprisoned cannot be proved against me, you will get other material out of my examination; and therefore if you will not ask me about the thing laid to my charge, I shall answer no more. . . . I think by the law of the land, that I may stand upon my just defense." Lilburne was convicted, fined, whipped, pilloried, and gagged, and imprisoned until he agreed to take the oath. . . .

One notorious instance of forced self-incrimination in the American colonies occurred in the Salem witch trials. In 1692, Giles Corey, an elderly Massachusetts farmer, was accused of witchcraft. He knew whether he pleaded guilty or not guilty he would be convicted, executed and his property confiscated. So to assure that his heirs inherited his property, he refused to plead and thus could not be convicted. The judges ordered him strapped to a table, and stones were loaded upon his chest to force the plea out of him. Corey's final words were "more weight." Then his chest caved in.[30]

John Bradshaw, John Lilburne's attorney, stated it best when he said that "It is contrary to the laws of God, nature and the kingdom for any man to be his own accuser."

Generally, the amendment prohibits the government from compelling people to testify when such testimony will incriminate the witness. Most people have heard of "pleading the Fifth." However, if immunity from prosecution is granted to a witness she may be compelled to testify. If a witness refuses to testify because of the fear of self-incrimination the government may offer the witness immunity from prosecution so that the testimony may be compelled. There are two types of immunity: transactional and derivative use.

Transactional immunity shields the witness from prosecution for all offenses related to his testimony. For example, if a witness testifies concerning a robbery, the government may not prosecute the witness for that robbery, even though the government may have evidence of guilt independent from the witness's testimony. Transactional immunity gives more protection to the witness than required by the Constitution, and, as such, when it is granted a witness may be ordered to testify.

For a witness to be compelled to testify **derivative use immunity** must be provided. This prohibits the government from using the witness' testimony or any evidence derived from that testimony to prosecute the witness. However, all evidence that is independently obtained may be used against the witness.

LEGAL TERMS

transactional immunity
This occurs whenever a witness is given full immunity from prosecution on all charges that were testified to.

derivative use immunity
A witness's compelled testimony may not be used against him, nor may any fruits of that testimony. However, the immunity is not complete. If the government obtains independent evidence it may be used against the witness.

Use immunity only prohibits the government from using the witness' testimony against her. Statutes that provide only for use immunity are unconstitutional, as derivative use is the minimum protection required by the Fifth Amendment.

States vary in how immunity is granted. Some permit the prosecutor to give the immunity, while others require both the request of the prosecutor and the approval of the trial judge.

A person may also waive the Fifth Amendment privilege against self-incrimination. Generally, once a person testifies freely the privilege is waived, as to the subject discussed, during the same proceeding. A witness (or defendant) may not testify selectively concerning a subject. It is often said that testifying to a fact waives to the details. This prevents a witness from testifying only to the information beneficial to one party and then refusing to testify further, even though he may have omitted important facts. However, a witness may not be compelled to testify if there is a chance he will be incriminating himself beyond the original testimony.

The fact that a witness may waive the Fifth Amendment privilege against self-incrimination on one occasion does not mean it is waived forever. First, a defendant (or witness) may speak to the police during the investigative stage and later refuse to testify at trial, provided such testimony may be incriminating. Second, it is generally held that a person who testifies before a grand jury without claiming the Fifth does not waive the right to raise the issue at trial. Third, even within the same proceeding a person may invoke the Fifth Amendment privilege against self-incrimination if the two hearings are separate and distinct. For example, a defendant may testify at a suppression hearing without waiving the privilege not to testify at trial.

Finally, the Fifth Amendment applies to all proceedings, whether civil or criminal. Therefore, a person called to testify in a civil proceeding may invoke the Fifth Amendment's privilege and refuse to testify.

Section 8.5(I.3) Vagueness and Overbreadth

It is a defense to a charge that the statute one is charged under is unconstitutionally vague or overbroad. The Due Process Clauses of the Fifth and Fourteen Amendments to the United States Constitution are the foundation of the void for vagueness and overbreadth doctrines.

A statute is void for **vagueness** whenever "men of common intelligence must necessarily guess at its meaning and differ as to its application."[31] The Supreme Court has held that uncertain statutes do not provide notice of what conduct is forbidden and are violative of due process. The Court has also found statutes that permit arbitrary or discriminatory enforcement void. That is, if the police or courts are given unlimited authority to decide who will be prosecuted the statute is invalid.

It was under the void for vagueness doctrine that many vagrancy laws have been attacked. If it were not for the doctrine, legislatures could draft statutes so that nearly everyone would be engaged in criminal activity at one time or another, and police would have unfettered discretion to decide who would be arrested.

A closely related doctrine is **overbreadth**. A statute is overbroad if it includes within its grasp not only unprotected activity, but activity protected by the Constitution. For example, in one case a city ordinance made it illegal for "one or more persons to assemble" on a sidewalk and conduct themselves in an annoying manner. The United States Supreme Court found that the law was unconstitutional not only because it made unprotected activity illegal (fighting words or riotous activity), but it also included activity that is protected by the First Amendment's free assembly and association provisions.[32] It is possible for a statute to be clear and precise (not vague), but overbroad.

Section 8.5(I.4)   Ex Post Facto and Bills of Attainder

Article I of the United States Constitution prohibits the state and federal governments from enacting both ex post facto laws and bills of attainder.

An **ex post facto** law is one that 1. makes an act illegal after the act was taken, 2. increases the punishment or severity of a crime after it occurred, 3. changes the procedural rules so as to increase the chances of conviction after the crime occurs. In short, a government may not make criminal law retroactive, if doing so is detrimental to the defendant. However, changes that benefit a defendant may be applied retroactively. So, if a legislature increases the prosecution's burden of proof after a defendant has committed a crime, but before trial, the legislature may make the change applicable to the defendant. The clause advances the notice theory (due process) and also prevents malicious legislative action from being taken against a particular person.

A **bill of attainder** is a legislative act punishing a person without a judicial trial. This provision reinforces the concept of separation of powers. It is the duty of the legislative branch to make the laws, and it is the duty of the judicial branch to determine who has violated those laws.

In a few instances, however, Congress may act in a judicial role. Congress may punish those who disrupt its functions for

LEGAL TERMS

vagueness
A statute is void if it is so vague that a person of common intelligence can not determine what conduct is proscribed.

overbreadth
A statute is overbroad and invalid if it includes within its prohibition protected activity, as well as unprotected activity.

ex post facto law
A law that declares an act illegal after it has been taken, increases the punishment or severity of a crime after it has occurred, or changes the procedural rules of a case to a defendant's detriment after the defendant has committed the illegal act. Article I of the Constitution prohibits both the federal and state governments from enacting ex post facto laws.

bill of attainder
An act of a legislature punishing a person without the benefit of a judicial trial. Article I of the Constitution prohibits both the federal and state governments from enacting bills of attainder.

contempt. In addition, Congress is authorized by the Constitution to conduct impeachment hearings of the President and federal judges and to discipline its own members.

Section 8.5(I.5) First Amendment and Religion

The First Amendment contains a large number of protections, including freedom of the press; to choose and practice a religion of choice; freedom of speech; and freedom to peaceably assemble.

Although the First Amendment is only directly applicable against the national government, the Fourteenth Amendment extends its prohibitions to the states.

Concerning freedom of religion, the First Amendment states that "Congress shall make no law respecting an establishment of religion, or prohibiting the free exercise thereof." The free exercise clause is of the most importance in criminal law. The freedom to believe is, of course, absolute. Any law prohibiting a certain religious belief is void. However, the Supreme Court has held that some religious acts may be regulated.

To determine whether a specific religious act may be criminalized, the governmental interest in regulating the behavior is balanced against the First Amendment infringement. If the governmental interest is greater than the infringement, then a state may regulate the conduct. For example, it has been held that the Mormon practice of polygamy may be regulated. Also, a parent who depends upon prayer to save a dying child may be charged with manslaughter for failing to seek competent medical care. In this instance the state's interest in protecting the child's life outweighs the parent's interest in practicing her religion in such a mannner.

On the other side, the California Supreme Court disallowed the conviction of a member of the Native American Church for possession of peyote, a drug made from cactus. The Court found that peyote was an important part of worship in the Native American Church, and, as such, California's interest in regulating the use of the drug was outweighed by the drug's religious significance.[33] Note that the United States Supreme Court took the opposite view concerning the use of peyote in *Department of Human Resources of Oregon v. Smith*, 490 U.S. _____ (1990), where the Court stated that

> [T]he right of free exercise does not relieve an individual of the obligation to comply with a valid and neutral law of general applicability on the ground that the law proscribes (or prescribes) conduct that his religion prescribes (or proscribes).

Section 8.5(I.6)   First Amendment and Speech

The First Amendment also protects speech. Not all speech is protected. You have already learned that fighting words and those words which create a "clear and present danger" may be regulated. Slanderous and libelous statements also fall outside the protection of the First Amendment. Fighting words, dangerous words, slanderous and libelous words, are all content-based doctrines; that is, it is the substance of what is being said that is regulated.

In some instances, a state may regulate speech, not because of its content, but by its time, place, and manner of being expressed. Here, a balancing of interests is conducted: does the government's interest in enforcing the statute outweigh the First Amendment interest? For example, it is unlawful to stand in the middle of the street to make a speech. The interest in maintaining a safe, consistent flow of traffic outweighs the First Amendment interest. However, the result would be different if a state attempted to prohibit all speeches made in a public place. Such a statute would be overbroad, as it includes not only activity which the state may regulate (standing in traffic), but also lawful activity. Commercial speech is subject to greater control than other speech.

Not only is the actual spoken word protected: Expression of ideas through acts are also protected, although to a lesser degree than pure speech. Picketing is an example of protected expression, as is flag burning.

TEXAS V. GREGORY LEE JOHNSON

491 U.S. _____ (1989)

Justice Brennan delivered the opinion of the Court.

After publicly burning the American flag as a means of political protest, Gregory Lee Johnson was convicted of desecrating a flag in violation of Texas law. This case presents the question whether his conviction is consistent with the First Amendment. We hold that it is not.

While the Republican National Convention was taking place in Dallas in 1984, respondent Johnson participated in a political demonstration dubbed the "Republican War Chest Tour." As explained in literature distributed by the demonstrators and in speeches made by them, the purpose of this event was to protest the policies of the Reagan administration and of certain Dallas-based corporations. The demonstrators marched through the Dallas streets, chanting political slogans and stopping at several corporate locations to stage "die-ins" intended to dramatize the consequences of nuclear war. On several occasions they spray-painted the walls of buildings and overturned potted plants, but Johnson himself took no part in such activities. He did, however, accept an American flag handed to him by a fellow protestor who had taken it from a flag pole outside one of the targeted buildings.

The demonstration ended in front of Dallas City Hall, where Johnson unfurled the American flag, doused it with kerosene, and set it on fire. While the flag burned, the protestors chanted, "America, the red, white, and blue, we spit on you." After the demonstrators dispersed, a witness to the flag-burning collected the flag's remains and buried them in his backyard. No one was physically injured or threatened with injury, though several witnesses testified that they had been seriously offended by the flag-burning. . . .

Johnson was convicted of flag desecration for burning the flag rather than for uttering insulting words. That fact somewhat complicates our consideration of his conviction under the First Amendment. We must first determine whether Johnson's burning of the flag constituted expressive conduct, permitting him to invoke the First Amendment. . . . If his conduct was expressive, we next decide whether the State's regulation is related to the suppression of free expression. See e.g., *United States v. O'Brien*, 391 U.S. 367, 377, 20 L.Ed.2d 672, 88 S.Ct. 1673 (1968). . . . If the State's regulation is not related to expression, then the less stringent standard we announced in *United States v. O'Brien* for regulations of noncommunicative conduct controls. . . . If it is, then we are outside of the O'Brien test, and we must ask whether this interest justifies Johnson's conviction under a more demanding standard. . . .

The First Amendment literally forbids the abridgement only of "speech," but we have long recognized that its protection does not end at the spoken or written word. While we have rejected "the view that an apparently limitless variety of conduct can be labeled 'speech' whenever the person engaging in the conduct intends thereby to express an idea," [in] *United States v. O'Brien* . . . we have acknowledged that conduct may be "sufficiently imbued with elements of communication to fall within the scope of the First and Fourteenth Amendments. . . .

In deciding whether particular conduct possesses sufficient communicative elements to bring the First Amendment into play, we have asked whether "[a]n intent to convey a particularized message was present, and [whether] the likelihood was great that the message would be understood by those who viewed it." . . . Hence, we have recognized the expressive nature of student's wearing of black armbands to protest American military involvement in Vietnam . . . of a sit-in by blacks in a "whites only" area to protest segregation. . . .

. . .The expressive, overtly political nature of this conduct was both intentional and overwhelmingly apparent. At his trial, Johnson explained his reasons for burning the flag as follows: "The American Flag was burned as Ronald Reagan was being nominated as President. And a more powerful statement of symbolic speech, whether you agree with it or not, couldn't have been made at that time. It's quite a just position [juxtaposition]. We had new patriotism and no patriotism." In these circumstances, Johnson's burning of the flag was conduct "sufficiently embued with elements of communication." . . .

In order to decide whether O'Brien test applies here, therefore, we must decide whether Texas has asserted an interest in support of Johnson's conviction that is unrelated to the suppression of expression. If we find that an interest asserted by the State is simply not implicated on the facts before us, we need not ask whether O'Brien test applies. . . .The State offers two separate interests to justify his conviction: preventing breaches of the peace, and preserving the flag as a symbol of nationhood and national unity. We hold that the first interest is not implicated on this record and that the second is related to the suppression of expression. . . .

The State's position, therefore, amounts to a claim that an audience that takes serious offense at particular expression is necessarily likely to disturb the peace and that the expression may be prohibited on this basis. Our precedents do not countenance such a presumption. On the contrary, they recognize that a principal "function of free speech under our system of government is to invite dispute. It may indeed best serve its high purpose when it induces a condition of unrest, creates dissatisfaction with conditions as they are, or even stirs people to anger. . . .

The State also asserts an interest in preserving the flag as a symbol of nationhood and national unity. . . .

. . .Johnson was not, we add, prosecuted for the expression of just any idea; he was prosecuted for his expression of dissatisfaction with the policies of this country, expression situated at the core of our First Amendment values. . . .

Moreover, Johnson was prosecuted because he knew that his politically charged expression would cause "serious offense." If he had burned the flag as a means of disposing of it because it was dirty or torn, he would not have been convicted of flag desecration under the Texas law; federal law designates burning as the preferred means of disposing of a flag "when it is in such condition that it is no longer a fitting emblem for display." . . .

If there is a bedrock principle underlying the First Amendment, it is that the Government may not prohibit the expression of an idea simply because society finds the idea itself offensive or disagreeble. . . .

We are tempted to say, in fact, that the flag's deservedly cherished place in our community will be strengthened, not weakened, by our holding today. Our decision is a reaffirmation of the principles of freedom and inclusiveness that the flag best reflects, and of the conviction that our toleration of criticism such as Johnson's is a sign and source of our strength. . . .

The way to preserve the flag's special role is not to punish those who feel differently about these matters. It is to persuade them that they are wrong. . . . And, precisely because it is our flag that is involved, one's response to the flag-burner may exploit the uniquely persuasive power of the flag itself. We can imagine no more appropriate response to burning a flag than waving one's own, no better way to counter a flag-burner's message than by saluting the flag that burns, no surer means of preserving the dignity even of the flag that burned than by—as one witness here did—according its remains a respectful burial. We do not consecrate the flag by punishing its desecration, for in doing so we dilute the freedom that this cherished emblem represents. . . .

Justice Kennedy, concurring.

I write not to qualify the words Justice Brennan chooses so well, for he says with power all that is necessary to explain our ruling. I join his opinion without reservation, but with a keen sense that his case, like others before us from time to time, exacts its personal toll. This prompts me to add to our pages these few remarks.

The case before us illustrates better than most that the judicial power is often difficult in its exercise. We cannot here ask another branch to share responsibility, as when the argument is made that a statute is flawed or incomplete. For we are presented with a clear and simple statute to be judged against a pure command of the Constitution. The outcome can be laid at no door but ours.

The hard fact is that sometimes we must make decisions we do not like. We make them because they are right, right in the sense that the law and the Constitution, as we see them, compel the result. And so great is our commitment to the process that, except in the rare case, we do not pause to express distaste for the result, perhaps for fear of undermining a valued principle that dictates decision. This is one of those rare cases.

Our colleagues in dissent advance powerful arguments why respondent may be convicted for his expression, reminding us that among those who will be dismayed by our holding will be some who have had the singular honor of carrying the flag into battle. And I agree that the flag holds a lonely place of honor in an age when absolutes are distrusted and simple truths are burdened by unneeded apologetics.

With respect to those views, I do not believe the Constitution gives us the right to rule as the dissenting members of the Court urge, however painful this judgment is to

> announce. . . . It is poignant but fundamental that the flag protects those who hold it in contempt . . .

Any time a statute conflicts with a constitutionally protected activity, the statute may fail. The defenses discussed above are only a few of the many constitutional defenses. Not all, but most criminal constitional defenses appear in the Bill of Rights.

Nor does this chapter exhaust all the nonconstitutional defenses that may be asserted. Do not forget that each state is free to design its criminal law in any manner it wishes, so long as it is constitutional. The most common factual, legislative, and constitutional substantive law defenses have been discussed. Many procedural defenses will be examined in the next section of this text.

REVIEW QUESTIONS

1. What are affirmative defenses? How do affirmative defenses differ from other defenses?
2. What are the elements of the M'Naghten test for insanity? Irresistable impulse? Model Penal Code?
3. What must be proven to support a claim of self-defense?
4. What is the retreat doctrine?
5. What is imperfect self-defense? When is it applicable?
6. When may a law-enforcement officer use deadly force to stop a fleeing suspect?
7. What is entrapment? What are the two tests used to determine if a defendant was entrapped?
8. May an insane defendant be tried? If not, what standard is used to determine whether the defendant is insane?
9. Differentiate overbreadth from vagueness. Give an example of each.
10. Differentiate a bill of attainder from an ex post facto law.

REVIEW PROBLEMS

1. Senator Bob Kerry of Nebraska was initially outraged by the *Texas v. Johnson* flag-burning decision. However he later

stated, "I was surprised to discover. . . [that the decision was] reasonable, understandable and consistent with those values which I believe have made America wonderful." Do you agree with Senator Kerry? Explain your position.

2. Should law enforcement be permitted to encourage children to engage in criminal activity with the purpose of arresting and prosecuting the child? Should law enforcement be permitted to use family and friend relationships to induce another to engage in criminal activity with the purpose of arresting and prosecuting the family member or friend? How about preying on another's drug or alcohol addiction?

3. Ira stabbed his good friend, inflicting a fatal wound. At trial a psychiatrist testified that Ira could not control his behavior, as he has a brain tumor that caused him to act violently. The doctor also testified that the condition did not impair Ira's ability to know what he was doing or that it was wrong. Assume that the jury believes the psychiatrist's explanation. Would Ira be convicted in a jurisdiction which uses the M'Naghten test? The irresistible impulse test? The Model Penal Code?

4. Jane was attacked by an unknown man. She was able to free herself and ran to a nearby house with the man chasing close behind. She screamed and knocked at the door of the house. The occupants of the house opened the door, and she requested refuge. The occupant refused, and she forced her way into the house. In order to gain entry Jane had to strike the occupant. Once inside she used the telephone to contact the police who responded within minutes. At the insistence of the occupants of the house, Jane has been charged with trespass and battery. Does she have a defense?

5. Gary and Gene were both drinking at a bar. Gary became angered after Gene asked Gary's wife to dance. Gary walked up to Gene and struck him in the face. Gene fell to the floor, and as he was returning to his feet Gary hit him again. In response, Gene took a knife out of his pocket and attacked Gary with it. Gary then shot Gene with a gun he had hidden in his coat. The injury proved fatal. What crime has Gary committed?

6. State law requires that all children between five years and sixteen years attend an approved school. Defendants have been charged with violating the statute, as they do not permit their children to attend school. The defendants are Mennonites and claim that it would violate their First Amendment right to freely exercise their religion. The defendants teach their children consistent with their religious teachings. Should they be convicted?

NOTES

[1] M'Naghten's Case, 8 Eng.Rep. 718 (H.L. 1843).

[2] LaFave and Scott, *Criminal Law* (Hornbook Series, St. Paul: West Publishing Co., 1986), §4.2A(a).

[3] *State v. Johnson*, 290 N.W. 159 (Wis. 1940).

[4] Model Penal Code, Tent. Draft 4, p. 156.

[5] LaFave and Scott, §4.2(d).

[6] *United States v. Brawner*, 471 F.2d 969 (D.C. Cir. 1972).

[7] Model Penal Code §4.01(1).

[8] 18 U.S.C. §17.

[9] 18 U.S.C. §3006A(e)(3).

[10] 18 U.S.C. §17.

[11] Model Penal Code §4.08.

[12] 18 U.S.C. §4243(a).

[13] 18 U.S.C. §4243(f).

[14] *Dusky v. United States*, 362 U.S. 402 (1960).

[15] *Jackson v. Indiana*, 406 U.S. 715 (1972).

[16] *Ford v. Wainwright*, 477 U.S. 399 (1986).

[17] Id at 417.

[18] See LaFave and Scott, §5.3(g).

[19] Model Penal Code §3.04(2)(b)(ii).

[20] Model Penal Code §3.06(d).

[21] Model Penal Code §3.06(5).

[22] Model Penal Code §3.07(2)(b)(ii).

[23] *Sherman v. United States*, 356 U.S. 369 (1958).

[24] Model Penal Code §2.13.

[25] Model Penal Code §2.13(2).

[26] 21 Am. Jur. 2d 225 (1990); *State v. Borucki*, 505 A.2d 89 (Me. 1986).

[27] 21 Am. Jur. *Criminal Law* 243 (1978).

[28] *Arizona v. Washington*, 434 U.S. 497 (1978).

[29] *Blockburger v. United States*, 284 U.S. 299 (1932).

[30] Passage taken from a 1991 Calendar prepared by the Commission on the Bicentennial of the United States Constitution, Washington, D.C .

[31] *Connally v. General Constr. Co.*, 269 U.S. 385 (1926).

[32] *Coates v. Cincinnatt*, 402 U.S. 611 (1971).

[33] *People v. Woody*, 61 Cal. 2d 716, 394 P.2d 813 (1965).

SECTION TWO

Criminal Procedure

CHAPTER 9
Introduction and Constitutional Aspects of Criminal Procedure

"That's all well and good Michael, but consider Whaley v. Small 172 U.S. 1,465 (1916)."

"The adminstration of criminal law must always be handicapped by consideration for personal liberty."

Harold Norris[1]

OUTLINE

SECTION 9.1 CRIMINAL PROCEDURE DEFINED

The second section of this text addresses criminal procedure. Criminal procedure is a phrase used to describe the method of enforcing substantive criminal law. To state it another way, criminal procedure puts substantive criminal law into action.

Each state and the federal government has its own procedural rules. In some instances, the variation is significant. For the purpose of this text, most references will be to federal procedure.

Many federal procedural rules can be found in the *United States Code*. A good number of procedures are judicially created (and approved by Congress) and are found in the *Federal Rules of Criminal Procedure* (F. R. Crim. P.).

What follows is a discussion of the constitutional aspects of criminal procedure; the process, from investigation to appeal; searches and seizures; arrests; confessions and admissions; and the right to counsel.

SECTION 9.2 THE CONSTITUTIONAL ASPECTS OF CRIMINAL PROCEDURE

Criminal justice is an area that belongs largely to the states. Nearly 95 percent of all criminal prosecutions occur in state courts. Not only do the states conduct most of the prosecutions, but each state is free, with few limitations, to design its criminal justice system in any manner it choses. This was especially true in the early years of the United States. For the most part, the national government did not involve itself in state criminal law for 150 years.

This began to change in the 1950s and today the United States plays a major role in defining the rights of criminal defendants in state prosecutions, as well as federal. The source of federal involvement is the United States Constitution, and two developments account for its increased role in state criminal law. First, the reach of the Constitution has been extended to the states through what is known as "incorporation." Second, the rights found in the Bill of Rights have been significantly expanded.

Section 9.2(a) Incorporation

Prior to the adoption of the Fourteenth Amendment the Bill of Rights guarantees were interpreted by the Supreme Court as only restricting the power of the national government. That meant that rights such as the right to counsel or the right to be free from unreasonable searches and seizures were only guaranteed to a defendant when prosecuted in federal court. If a state did not have a constitutional or statutory provision granting the right, then the defendant was not entitled to its protection when prosecuted in state court.

In 1868 the Fourteenth Amendment to the United States Constitution was adopted. One goal of the Fourteenth Amendment was to extend constitutional protections to the states. Section One of that amendment reads:

All persons born or naturalized in the United States, and subject to the jurisdiction thereof, are citizens of the United States and of the State wherein they reside. No State shall make or enforce any law which shall abridge the privileges or immunities of citizens of the United States; nor shall any State deprive any person of life, liberty, or property, without due process of law; nor deny to any person within its jurisdiction the equal protection of the laws.

The language of the Fourteenth Amendment is similar to that found in the Fifth Amendment insofar as they both contain a Due Process Clause. It is through the due process and equal protection clauses that the powers of the states are limited. However, what is meant by due process has been the subject of great debate among jurists.

At one extreme is a small group that contend that the Fourteenth's Due Process Clause is limited to the reach of the Fifth's Due Process Clause. They further assert that the due process guarantee does not include any right found in the Bill of Rights, or, to state it another way: due process does not overlap with other enumerated rights. As such, the due process guarantee of the Fourteenth Amendment does not extend to any of the rights found in the first ten amendments to the states. This position has never been adopted by the Supreme Court.

At the other extreme is "total incorporation." Proponents of total incorporation, who included United States Supreme Court Justice Black, argue that the entire Bill of Rights is incorporated by the Fourteenth Amendment and that all the rights contained therein may be claimed by both defendants in federal and state courts. This position has never been adopted by the Supreme Court.

Another position, which was held by the Supreme Court until the 1960s, is known as fundamental fairness. Those rights that are "fundamental" and "essential to an ordered liberty," are incorporated by the Fourteenth Amendment. The fundamental fairness doctrine held that no relationship existed between the Bill of Rights and those rights deemed fundamental, although the rights recognized under the fundamental fairness doctrine might parallel a right found in the Bill of Rights.

The Supreme Court rejected the fundamental rights doctrine in the 1960s and replaced it with a similar doctrine, the **selective incorporation doctrine**. Similar to the fundamental fairness doctrine, a right is incorporated under this doctrine if it is 1. a fundamental right and 2. essential to the concept of ordered liberty.

However, the two approaches differ in two major respects. First, under the fundamental fairness approach cases were analyzed case-by-case. That is, it was possible to have essentially

LEGAL TERMS

selective incorporation doctrine Those rights contained in the Bill of Rights that are both fundamental and essential to an ordered liberty are incorporated by the Fourteenth Amendment and applied against the states. Nearly all of the Bill of Rights has been incorporated.

the same facts with different outcomes under the fundamental fairness doctrine. Critics charged the approach was too subjective. Second, selective incorporation gives special attention to those rights contained in the Bill of Rights. Those rights found in the Bill of Rights are more likely to be incorporated than those not found in the Bill of Rights. Selective incorporation continues to be the law today.

Nearly the entire Bill of Rights has been incorporated under this doctrine. The right to grand jury indictment and the requirement of a twelve person jury are two rights that have not been incorporated. There is some debate currently concerning the right to be free from excessive bail.[2] Once incorporated, a right applies against the states to the extent and in the same manner as it does against the United States.

Section 9.2(b)   Expansion of Rights

Another major development in the area of constitutional criminal procedure has been the expansion of many rights. The language of the Constitution is concise. It refers to "unreasonable searches and seizures," "due process," "equal protection," "speedy and public trial," etc. No further definition or explanation of the meaning of these provisions is provided. The process of determining the meaning of such phrases is known as constitutional interpretation. It is possible to make each right ineffective by reading it narrowly. The opposite is also true.

During the 1960s many rights found in the Bill of Rights were "expanded" by court decisions. Expansion refers to extending a right beyond its most narrow reading. The effect of expansive interpretation is to increase defendants' rights. An example of an expansive interpretation is the *Miranda v. Arizona* decision. Although the language of the Fifth Amendment does not explicitly state that a defendant must be advised of the right to remain silent, to have the assistance of counsel, etc., the Court now requires such admonishments be given because of an expanded interpretation of the Fifth Amendment.

Another example of expanded individual rights is the right to privacy. No explicit constitutional language provides for a right to privacy. However, the Supreme Court has found a right to privacy to be implicit in the Constitution. The Court has held that the right to privacy protects a woman's right to abortion, in some circumstances, in *Roe v. Wade*, 410 U.S. 113 (1973), and a couple's right to use contraceptives in *Griswold v. Connecticut*, 381 U.S. 479 (1965), amongst many others. Many more "expansions" will be discussed later.

Section 9.2(c) Exclusionary Rule

Another important constitutional development is the creation of the **exclusionary rule**. The rule is simple: Evidence that is obtained by an unconstitutional search or seizure is inadmissible at trial.

The rule was first announced by the Supreme Court in 1914.[3] However, at that time the rule had not been incorporated. As such, the exclusionary rule did not apply to state court proceedings. This was changed in 1961 when the Supreme Court declared that evidence obtained in violation of the Constitution could not be used in state or federal criminal proceedings. The case was *Mapp v. Ohio*.

MAPP V. OHIO

367 U.S. 643 (1961)

Appellant stands convicted of knowingly having had in her possession and under her control certain lewd and lascivious books, pictures, and photographs in violation [of Ohio law]. . . .

On May 23, 1957, three Cleveland police officers arrived at appellant's residence in that city pursuant to information that "a person [was] hiding out in the home, who was wanted for questioning in connection with a recent bombing." . . .

. . . Upon their arrival at that house, the officers knocked on the door and demanded entrance but appellant, after telephoning her attorney, refused to admit them without a search warrant. They advised their headquarters of the situation and undertook a surveillance of the house.

The officers again sought entrance some three hours later when four or more additional officers arrived on the scene. When Miss Mapp did not come to the door immediately, at least one of the several doors to the house was forcibly opened and the policemen gained admittance. Meanwhile Miss Mapp's attorney arrived, but the officers, having secured their own entry, and continuing in their defiance of the law, would permit him neither to see Miss Mapp nor to enter the house. It appears that Miss Mapp was halfway down the

LEGAL TERMS

exclusionary rule
Evidence that is obtained by law enforcement in an unconstitutional manner may not be used at trial to prove a defendant's guilt.

stairs from the upper floor to the front door when the officers, in this highhanded manner, broke into the hall. She demanded to see the search warrant. A paper, claimed to be a warrant, was held up by one of the officers. She grabbed the "warrant" and placed it in her bosom. A struggle ensued in which the officers recovered the piece of paper and as a result of which they handcuffed appellant because she had been "belligerent" in resisting their official rescue of the "warrant" from her person. Running roughshod over appellant, a policeman "grabbed" her, "twisted [her] hand," and she "yelled [and] pleaded with him" because "it was hurting." Appellant, in handcuffs, was then forcibly taken upstairs to her bedroom where the officers searched a dresser, a chest of drawers, a closet and some suitcases. They also looked into a photo album and through personal papers belonging to the appellant. The search spread . . . The obscene materials for possession of which she was ultimately convicted were discovered in the course of that widespread search.

At the trial no search warrant was produced by the prosecution, nor was the failure to produce one explained or accounted for. At best, "There is, in the record, considerable doubt as to whether there ever was any warrant for the search." . . .

. . . We hold that all evidence obtained by searches and seizures in violation of the Constitution is, by that same authority, inadmissible in a state court.

Since the Fourth Amendment's right of privacy has been declared enforceable against the States through the Due Process Clause of the Fourteenth, it is enforceable against them by the same sanction of exclusion as it used against the Federal Government. . . .

Moreover, our holding that the exclusionary rule is an essential part of both the Fourth and Fourteenth Amendments is not only the logical dictate of prior cases, but it also makes very good sense. There is no war between the Constitution and common sense. Presently, a federal prosecutor may make no use of evidence illegally seized, but a State's attorney across the street may, although he supposedly is operating under the enforceable prohibitions of the same

Amendment. Thus the State, by admitting evidence unlawfully seized, serves to encourage disobedience to the Federal Constitution which it is bound to uphold. . . .

The exclusionary rule has been the subject of intense debate. There is no explicit textual language establishing the rule in the Constitution. For that reason, many contend that the Supreme Court has exceeded its authority by creating it; that it is the responsibility of the legislative branch to make such laws.

On the other side is the argument that without the exclusionary rule the Bill of Rights is ineffective. Why have constitutional standards if there is no method to enforce them? For example, why require that the officers in the *Mapp* case have a search warrant, yet permit them to conduct a warrantless search and use the evidence obtained against the defendant? These questions go to the purpose of the exclusionary rule: it discourages law enforcement from engaging in unconstitutional conduct.

The exclusionary rule works to prevent the admission into evidence any item, confession, or other thing that was obtained by law-enforcement officers in an unconstitutional manner.

The evidence must be obtained by the police in an unlawful manner. However, if a private citizen working on her own obtains evidence illegally and then turns it over to the police, it may be admitted.[4] People hired to assist the police are agents of law enforcement and are treated as police officers for this purpose.

The exclusionary rule does not apply to pretrial matters. A defendant may not challenge a grand jury indictment because the grand jury considered illegally obtained evidence. The defendant's remedy is at trial. In addition, a defendant may not refuse to answer questions before a grand jury concerning illegally obtained evidence. In most cases, but not all, evidence obtained illegally may be used at sentencing.

Most exclusionary rule issues are resolved prior to trial by way of a motion to suppress. In some instances the motion may be made at the moment the prosecutor attempts to introduce such evidence at trial. This is known as a contemporaneous objection.

Section 9.2(d) Fruit of the Poisonous Tree

The exclusionary rule applies to "primary" evidence. That is evidence that is the direct result of an illegal search or seizure. It is possible that such primary evidence may lead the police to other evidence. Suppose that police officers beat a confession out of a bank robber. In that confession the defendant tells the police where he has hidden the stolen money. The confession is the primary evidence and is inadmissible under the exclusionary rule. The money (after it is retrieved by the police) is secondary, or "derivative," evidence. Such evidence is known as **fruit of the poisonous tree** and is also inadmissible evidence. Generally, evidence that is "tainted" by the prior illegal conduct is inadmissible. The rule does not make all evidence later obtained by law enforcement inadmissible. In some instances evidence may be admissible because the connection between the illegally seized evidence and the subsequently obtained evidence is marginal, or as the Supreme Court has stated it, "the causal connection . . . may have become so attenuated as to dissipate the taint." [5]

Another situation where such evidence may be admitted is when an independant source exists. An **independent source** must be an unconnected and legal method of obtaining evidence. Consider the bank robbery example above. If a co-conspirator in the robbery also told the police where the money is, it is admissible despite the illegal confession, so long as the co-consirator's admission was lawful.

Finally, evidence that would be inevitably discovered by law enforcement may be admitted. This doctrine is similar to the independent source doctrine. However, police must actually obtain evidence from an untainted, lawful source to invoke the independent source doctrine. The **inevitable discovery doctrine** holds that evidence that is the fruit of an illegal search, seizure, or arrest may be admitted if it is probable that the evidence would have been obtained lawfully at a later date.

Section 9.2(e) Standing

A defendant must have **standing** before he may successfully have evidence suppressed. There are two aspects to standing. First, the person challenging the evidence must have an adversarial interest in the proceeding. Basically, only defendants in criminal cases may challenge evidence as seized in violation of the Fourth Amendment. A defendant's mother may not intervene in his criminal case and attempt to have evidence suppressed because her Fourth Amendment rights were violated by an illegal search and seizure—even if the claim is true. A mother lacks standing to make the claim.

The second aspect concerns the defendant's interest in the area searched or thing seized. A defendant must have a reasonable expectation of privacy to a place or thing before he can have it excluded at trial. To say it another way, the defendant's constitutional rights must be violated before evidence will be suppressed.

Therefore, the defendant may not assert his mother's right to be free from illegal searches and seizures.

Note that in *Simmons v. United States,* 390 U.S. 377 (1968), the Supreme Court held that a defendant may testify at a suppression hearing without waiving the right to not testify at trial and that any testimony given at a suppression hearing by a defendant may not be used against him at trial.

Simmons eliminated the quandary many defendants had: should they give incriminating evidence during a suppression hearing in hopes of having the evidence excluded? Of course, if a suppression claim was unsuccessful, then a defendant faced the incriminating testimony at trial. This put many defendants in a position of having to choose one right or another: the right to be free from self-incrimination versus the right to have illegally seized evidence excluded from trial. The Supreme Court held that defendants should be free from such dilemmas.

During the 1960s and early 1970s many jurists predicted that the Supreme Court would become so involved with criminal procedure that it would, in effect, write its own "constitutional criminal procedure code." This has not proven to be true; however, many areas of criminal procedure are greatly influenced by Supreme Court decisions. It is common to refer to the expansion of individual rights and the extension of those rights to the states as the "constitutionalization" of criminal procedure.

However, in recent years there appears to be a trend away from expansive interpretation. This is in large part because the composition of the Supreme Court is more conservative than it was during the 1960s. Some believe that the trend of increasing individual rights was hindering law enforcement and welcome regression. Those who believe strongly in the rights of the individual proclaim that it is better to free ten guilty persons than to imprison one innocent person. In any event, it is probable that the Supreme Court's policy of favoring expansive interpretation of individual rights is likely to cease.

Finally, do not forget that each state has its own constitution. Traditionally, state constitutional interpretation has paralleled federal constitutional interpretation; that is, state constitutions are commonly interpreted as providing no more, or less, protection than the federal constitution.

This is not always true. While a state may not use its own constitution to lessen a defendant's rights, it may increase a defendant's protections beyond that provided for in the United States Constitution. Despite the fact that it is common for a state to use identical language in its constitution to describe a right, it is free to interpret that right to be greater under state law than under federal.

LEGAL TERMS

fruit of the poisonous tree
Evidence that is derivative or tainted by a prior unconstitutional search, seizure, or arrest is inadmissible at trial.

independent source
An exception to the Fruit of the Poisonous Tree Doctrine. Evidence that is obtained unlawfully, but is also obtained from an independent source, is admissible at trial.

inevitable discovery doctrine
An exception to the Fruit of the Poisonous Tree Doctrine. Evidence that is obtained unlawfully, but would be inevitably discovered by the police, is admissible at trial.

standing
Without standing, a person may not assert a constitutional right. There are two aspects of standing. First, a person must have an interest in a proceeding before he may assert a consitutional privilege therein. Second, the defendant's right must be asserted. For Fourth Amendment issues this means that the defendant must have a privacy interest in the place searched or thing seized.

For example, you will later learn of a "good faith exception" to the warrant requirement. This exception was recognized by the United States Supreme Court in *United States v. Leon* (see Chapter 12) and is the law in the federal courts. However, at least one state (Pennsylvania) has refused to read this exception into its own constitution.

REVIEW QUESTIONS

1. What is selective incorporation? Total incorporation? Which reflects current law?
2. Name three rights that have been incorporated and one that has not.
3. What is the exclusionary rule?
4. Give an example of when evidence would be Fruit of the Poisonous Tree.
5. Name three exceptions to the Fruit of the Poisonous Tree doctrine.

REVIEW PROBLEMS

1. The Constitution of the United States significantly affects all criminal law. Why is that so when over 95 percent of all prosecutions occur in state courts?
2. Do you believe that evidence that has been obtained by law enforcement in an unconstitutional manner should be inadmissible at trial? Explain your position.

NOTES

[1] Professor of Criminal and Constitutional Law at Detroit College of Law since 1961.
[2] The Seventh Amendment's guarantee of a jury trial in civil cases also has not been incorporated.
[3] The rule, as it applied in federal courts, was announced in *Weeks v. United States*, 232 U.S. 383 (1914). However, it appears that the rule was applied in at least one case prior to that date. See LaFave and Israel, *Criminal Procedure* (Hornbook Series, St. Paul: West Publishing Co., 1985), p. 78.
[4] *Burdeau v. McDowell*, 256 U.S. 465 (1921).
[5] *Nardone v. United States*, 308 U.S. 338 (1939).

CHAPTER 10
The Pretrial Process

*When the reason of a rule ceases,
so should the rule itself.*

Legal Principle

OUTLINE

What follows is an outline of the basic process a case goes through, from pre-arrest to post-trial. As previously mentioned, the federal process is used for illustration and individual states vary somewhat.

SECTION 10.1 DISCOVERY AND INVESTIGATION OF CRIMINAL ACTIVITY

The process begins when law enforcement learns of a crime that has been committed (or is to be committed). Police learn of criminal activity in two ways. They may discover it themselves, or a citizen may report such activity.

Once police are aware of criminal activity the pre-arrest investigation begins. There are two objectives to this stage. First, police must determine whether a crime has been committed. Second, if a crime has been committed, police attempt to gather sufficient evidence to charge and convict the person believed to be guilty.

SECTION 10.2 ARREST

Once adequate evidence exists an arrest is made in most cases. However, in some misdemeanor cases a defendant is asked to come to the police station, and an arrest is not made unless the defendant refuses. The arrest may be made without an arrest

Police learn of criminal activity by themselves, or a citizen may report such activity.

warrant in some situations. In others, an *ex parte* hearing may be held to determine if probable cause exists to believe that the person under investigation committed the crime. If so, the judge may issue an arrest warrant.

At the time of arrest police ordinarily search the defendant. Once at the police station the defendant is "booked." Booking consists of obtaining biographical information about the defendant (name, address, etc.), fingerprinting the defendant, and taking his photo, commonly known as a "mug shot." The defendant is usually permitted to make a telephone call at this stage.

The defendant is then searched (sometimes deloused and showered) and held in jail until further arrangements are made. For minor offenses, the defendant may be able to post bail prior to appearing before a judge. In such cases, defendants are out of jail within hours. All others will have to wait for a judge to set a bail amount at an initial appearance. During and after this stage law-enforcement investigation and gathering of evidence may continue.

SECTION 10.3 THE COMPLAINT

The prosecutor must then review the evidence gathered by law enforcement and decide whether to charge the person held. If

AO 91 (Rev. 5/85) Criminal Complaint ●

United States District Court

_____ DISTRICT OF _____

UNITED STATES OF AMERICA
V.

CRIMINAL COMPLAINT

CASE NUMBER:

(Name and Address of Defendant)

I, the undersigned complainant being duly sworn state the following is true and correct to the best of my

knowledge and belief. On or about _____ in _____ county, in the

_____ District of _____ defendant(s) did, (Track Statutory Language of Offense)

in violation of Title _____ United States Code, Section(s) _____.

I further state that I am a(n) _____ and that this complaint is based on the following
                                            Official Title

facts:

Continued on the attached sheet and made a part hereof: ☐ Yes   ☐ No

_____
Signature of Complainant

Sworn to before me and subscribed in my presence,

_____ at _____
Date   City and State

_____   _____
Name & Title of Judicial Officer   Signature of Judicial Officer

Criminal Complaint

the prosecutor decides affirmatively she will file a **complaint**. The complaint is the first document filed with a court and acts as the initial charging instrument. F. R. Crim. P. 3 states: "The complaint is a written statement of the essential facts constituting an offense charged. It shall be made upon oath before a magistrate." The complaint need not be written upon personal knowledge. That is, an officer may use hearsay and circumstantial

AO 83 (Rev. 5/85) Summons in a Criminal Case ●

United States District Court

_____ DISTRICT OF _____

UNITED STATES OF AMERICA V.	SUMMONS IN A CRIMINAL CASE
	CASE NUMBER:

(Name and Address of Defendant)

YOU ARE HEREBY SUMMONED to appear before the United States District Court at the place, date and time set forth below.

Place		Room
		Date and Time
Before:		

To answer a(n)
☐ Indictment ☐ Information ☐ Complaint ☐ Violation Notice ☐ Probation Violation Petition

Charging you with a violation of Title _____ United States Code, Section _____ .

Brief description of offense:

_____   _____
Signature of Issuing Officer   Date

_____
Name and Title of Issuing Officer

LEGAL TERMS

complaint
A written statement containing the essential facts and law under which a defendant is charged. Used to obtain an arrest warrant (or summons) or to establish probable cause at a preliminary hearing.

evidence in a complaint. Affidavits from those who have personal knowledge, such as witnesses and victims, are often attached to the complaint.

In cases where a warrant is sought to arrest a defendant it is the complaint that is often produced in support of the request for a warrant. This occurs at the _ex parte_ hearing mentioned earlier. Federal law requires that a warrant be issued if probable cause

AO 83 (Rev. 5/85) Summons in a Criminal Case

RETURN OF SERVICE

Service was made by me on:[1]	Date

Check one box below to indicate appropriate method of service

☐ Served personally upon the defendant at:_____
_____

☐ Left summons at the defendant's dwelling house or usual place of abode with a person of suitable age and discretion then residing therein and mailed a copy of the summons to the defendant's last known address. Name of person with whom the summons was left:_____
_____

☐ Returned unexecuted:_____
_____
_____
_____

I declare under penalty of perjury under the laws of the United States of America that the foregoing information contained in the Return of Service is true and correct.

Returned on _____   _____
               Date   Name of United States Marshal

                                                    _____
                                                    (by) Deputy United States Marshal

[1] As to who may serve a summons see Rule 4 of the Federal Rules of Criminal Procedure

**Summons in a
Criminal Case**
(continued)

is established by the complaint and its accompanying affidavits. Upon the request of the government a summons (an order to appear) may be issued rather than an arrest warrant.[1]

If the defendant was arrested without a warrant the complaint serves as the charging document at the initial appearance or preliminary hearing.

For traffic violations and some lesser misdemeanors the complaint acts as both a summons to appear in court and the charging document. In such cases, the defendant only appears in court on one occasion and the ticket is used in place of an information or indictment.

SECTION 10.4 INITIAL APPEARANCE

After arrest the defendant is taken "without unnessary delay" before the nearest available federal magistrate.[2] In most cases this means that a defendant will be brought before the judge within twenty-four hours. However, if a defendant is arrested on a weekend it may be the following Monday before the defendant has his intitial appearance, unless a weekend session of court is held.

The first appearance is brief. It is the duty of the presiding judge to make sure that the person arrested is the person named in the complaint. The defendant is also informed of various rights, such as the rights to remain silent and to have the assistance of counsel. If the defendant is indigent the court will appoint counsel. The right to counsel will be discussed more fully later.

Finally, a preliminary hearing date is set and if the defendant is in jail the court determines whether he or she should be released prior to trial.

SECTION 10.5 PRETRIAL RELEASE AND DETENTION

In many cases defendants are released prior to trial. A court may order many types of releases, but the predominantly used methods are: cash bail; surety bond; property bond; and personal recognizance.

Section 10.5(a) Types of Release

The most obvious method of gaining release is to post bail. A defendant who has the resources may simply pay into the court the amount of the bail.

Whenever a third party, usually a professional bondsman, agrees to pay the bond for a defendant a surety bond is created. The common practice is for the defendant to pay the surety 10 percent or more of the bond amount in exchange for the bondsman making the defendant's bail. The 10 percent is not refunded to the defendant after the case is concluded.

Some sureties require security (collateral) before a bond will be issued. Defendants may pledge cars, houses, or other property in order to obtain release. This is a property bond.

For many misdemeanors and a few felonies a defendant may be released on personal recognizance. To gain such a release a defendant only needs to promise to appear.

Despite the method used courts frequently impose conditions upon the defendant. Defendants who are arrested, caught intimidating witnesses, or interfering with the judicial process may be jailed until trial.

Section 10.5(b) Eighth Amendment

The Eighth Amendment proscribes the imposition of "excessive bail." This provision is applicable to the states through the Fourteenth Amendment. The purpose of imposing money bail is to assure the defendant's appearance at trial, not to inflict punishment. Bail set higher than necessary to accomplish this purpose is deemed excessive.[3] In practice, courts have significant discretion in setting bail and are rarely reversed.

The Supreme Court has held that the mere fact that a defendant cannot pay the amount set by a court does not make it excessive. Additionally, the Court has stated that not all defendants have a right to bail. Defendants who are a danger to the community or are unlikely to appear for trial may be held without bail.

The exact meaning of the Eighth Amendment has not been spelled out by the Supreme Court. Whether pretrial detention laws, especially those that create a presumption of detention, are constitutional remains to be seen.

Section 10.5(c) Detention

The federal government (and presumably most states, if not all) provides for detention of some defendants prior to trial.

Pretrial detention may not be used to punish a person. To do so violates a person's due process right to be free from punishment without a fair trial. However, a defendant may be detained if there is reason to believe that he will not appear for trial or if he poses a threat to others.

In the federal system the defendant is entitled to an adversary hearing concerning pretrial detention, and the government must prove by clear and convincing evidence that the defendant is either dangerous or unlikely to appear for trial.[4] The adversary hearing must be held at the initial appearance, or upon the motion of the defendant or the government it may be continued.

While the general rule is that the government bears the burden of proving that a defendant must be detained, there are exceptions. There are two classes of presumptions in the federal statute. One presumes that certain defendants will not appear for trial, and another presumes that certain defendants are a danger to the community. For example, defendants charged with crimes of

violence who have a prior conviction for a crime of violence, which was committed while the defendant was released pending trial, are presumed to be dangerous to the community. It is also presumed that those defendants charged with drug crimes that carry ten years or more imprisonment will flee. These presumptions apply to many other defendants.[5] The presumption is rebuttable, and the defendant has the burden of disproving it. Some question the constitutionality of such presumptions, and it remains to be seen whether the statute will be reversed or upheld.

Many states have statutes that require detention of people charged with crimes punishable by life imprisonment or death, provided that the proof of guilt is great.

SECTION 10.6 PRELIMINARY HEARING

The defendant's second appearance before a judge is the **preliminary hearing**. How this stage is handled by the states varies significantly. At the preliminary hearing the court determines if probable cause to believe the accused committed the crime exists. If probable cause is found the defendant is "bound over" to the next stage of the process. The next stage is either trial or review by grand jury. If probable cause is not established the defendant is released.

If indictment by grand jury is required the case is bound over to the grand jury. The grand jury is not bound by the judge's decision that probable cause exists. It makes an independent decision whether to charge the defendant. If grand jury review is not required, the defendant is bound over for trial.

The purpose of the preliminary hearing is to have an impartial third party review the facts to be sure that probable cause exists. There is no constitutional requirement for a preliminary hearing.[6] However, many states do provide for preliminary hearings.

It is common to permit prosecutors to bypass the preliminary hearing by either submitting the case to a grand jury or by directly filing an information. Defendants often waive having a preliminary hearing. In some states prosecutors may demand a preliminary hearing over the objection of the defendant.

The preliminary hearing can be quite lengthy compared to a defendant's initial appearance. The hearing is adversarial. Witnesses are called, and the attorneys are allowed to make arguments. Rules of evidence are applied in modified form, so that hearsay and illegally obtained evidence are often considered. Defendants have a right to counsel, to cross examine the prosecution witnesses, and to present defense witnesses. The right to counsel is a matter of federal constitutional law. The other two rights are granted by state laws. The preliminary hearing can be an important asset to both the prosecution and defense, as it can serve as a source of discovery.

F. R. Crim. P. 5 requires that the date for "preliminary examination" be scheduled at the defendant's initial appearance. It shall be held within ten days of the initial appearance if the defendant is in custody and within twenty if the defendant has been released.

In 1991, the United States Supreme Court examined the need for prompt, probable-cause determinations in warrantless-arrest situations. In *County of Riverside v. McLaughlin*, no. 89-1817, slip op. (U.S. May 13, 1991), the Court held that persons arrested without a warrant must have a probable-cause determination within 48 hours after arrest or quicker if reasonable. The burden of proving a delay, which is less than 48 hours, unreasonable under the Fourth Amendment is on the defendant. If a defendant is held longer than 48 hours without a probable-cause hearing, then the burden of showing a bona fide emergency or other extraordinary circumstance falls on the government.

Time to gather additional evidence, ill will, or the fact that the defendant was arrested on a weekend are not sufficient to delay the probable-cause determination longer than 48 hours.

Similar to the rule in many states, probable cause may be founded upon hearsay evidence.[7] Motions to suppress illegally seized evidence are made after the time of the preliminary hearing, so such evidence may be considered at the preliminary examination stage. If a grand jury has issued an indictment the preliminary hearing may be dispensed within the federal system.[8]

SECTION 10.7 THE FORMAL CHARGE

There are two formal charges: the **information** and **indictment**. Informations are charges filed by prosecutors. Indictments are charges issued by grand juries. Once filed, an information or indictment replaces the complaint and becomes the formal charging instrument.

Section 10.7(a) Indictment and Grand Jury

Section 10.7(a.1) Purpose of the Grand Jury

In early American history **grand juries** were used to guard against unfair and arbitrary government prosecutions. The

LEGAL TERMS

preliminary hearing
A defendant's second appearance before a court. The purpose of the preliminary hearing is to have a neutral party review the evidence to be sure probable cause exists.

information
One of two formal methods of charging a person with a crime. Informations are filed by prosecutors.

indictment
One of two formal methods of charging a person with a crime. Indictments are issued by grand juries.

grand jury
A body of citizens numbering from twelve to twenty-three that investigates alleged criminal conduct and issues indictments.

drafters of the United States Constitution believed grand jury review so important they stated in the Fifth Amendment that "no person shall be held to answer for a capital, or otherwise infamous, crime, unless on a presentment or indictment of a Grand Jury."

Grand juries consist of twelve to twenty-three persons who are usually selected in the same method as petit juries (juries which determine guilt or innocence). Grand juries sit for longer periods of time and are called to hear cases as needed.

The purpose of grand jury review is the same as preliminary hearing: to determine whether there is probable cause to believe the defendant committed the alleged crime. However, the process used by a grand jury is quite different from that of the preliminary hearing.

Section 10.7(a.2) Procedures of the Grand Jury

First, grand juries are closed. The public, including the defendant, are not entitled to attend. Second, the prosecutor runs the show before the grand jury, and the defendant has no right to present evidence or to make a statement. Third, the actions of grand juries are secret. Those who attend are not permitted to disclose what transpires. Defendants have no right to know what evidence is presented to a grand jury, unless it is exculpatory (tends to prove the defendant's innocence). Fourth, those who testify before the grand jury are not entitled to have counsel in the jury room.[9] In most states witnesses are permitted to leave the proceeding to confer with counsel waiting directly outside. Because statements made to a grand jury can be used later, the Fifth Amendment right to be free from self-incrimination is available to witnesses. Grand juries can overcome Fifth Amendment claims (refusals to testify) by granting witnesses immunity from prosecution.

Grand juries possess the power to order people to appear, to subpoena documents, to hold people in contempt, and to grant immunity in order to procure testimony.

As a general proposition prosecutors control grand juries. For the most part grand juries convene only when called by the prosecutor. The prosecutor decides what witnesses need to be called and who should be given immunity. Nearly all people targeted (the person the prosecutor believes guilty) by prosecutors are indicted. Many criticize the grand jury system for this reason: the government has too much control over the grand juries. The argument is reasonable when one considers the historical purpose of grand jury review.

The proponents of abolishing the grand jury system argue that not only have grand juries lost their independence, but they

AO 110 (Rev. 5/85) Subpoena to Testify Before Grand Jury

United States District Court

DISTRICT OF

TO:

SUBPOENA TO TESTIFY
BEFORE GRAND JURY

SUBPOENA FOR:

☐ PERSON   ☐ DOCUMENT(S) OR OBJECT(S)

YOU ARE HEREBY COMMANDED to appear and testify before the Grand Jury of the United States District Court at the place, date, and time specified below.

PLACE	COURTROOM
	DATE AND TIME

YOU ARE ALSO COMMANDED to bring with you the following document(s) or object(s):*

☐ *Please see additional information on reverse*

This subpoena shall remain in effect until you are granted leave to depart by the court or by an officer acting on behalf of the court.

CLERK	DATE
(BY) DEPUTY CLERK	

This subpoena is issued on application of the United States of America	NAME, ADDRESS AND PHONE NUMBER OF ASSISTANT U.S. ATTORNEY

*If not applicable, enter "none"

**Subpoena to Testify
Before Grand Jury**

now act to the benefit of the prosecutors by allowing discovery of information that may have otherwise been unavailable.

Section 10.7(a.3) The Indictment

After a grand jury has completed its investigation a vote on whether to charge is taken. In the federal system grand juries

AO 110 (Rev. 5/85) Subpoena to Testify Before Grand Jury

RETURN OF SERVICE (1)

	DATE	PLACE
RECEIVED BY SERVER		
SERVED	DATE	PLACE

SERVED ON (NAME)

SERVED BY	TITLE

STATEMENT OF SERVICE FEES

TRAVEL	SERVICES	TOTAL

DECLARATION OF SERVER(2)

I declare under penalty of perjury under the laws of the United States of America that the foregoing information contained in the Return of Service and Statement of Service Fees is true and correct.

Executed on_____   _____
                    Date   *Signature of Server*

                                      _____
                                                Address of Server

ADDITIONAL INFORMATION

(1) As to who may serve a subpoena and the manner of its service see Rule 17(d), Federal Rules of Criminal Procedure, or Rule 45(c), Federal Rules of Civil Procedure.

(2) "Fees and mileage need not be tendered to the witness upon service of a subpoena issued on behalf of the United States or an officer or agency thereof (Rule 45(c), Federal Rules of Civil Procedure; Rule 17(d), Federal Rules of Criminal Procedure) or on behalf of certain indigent parties and criminal defendants who are unable to pay such costs (28 USC 1825, Rule 17(b) Federal Rules of Criminal Procedure)".

Subpoena to Testify Before Grand Jury (continued)

consist of sixteen to twenty-three people. At least twelve must vote for indictment.[10] In many cases indictments are sealed until the indicted defendant is arrested.

The Constitution requires that all federal prosecutions for capital and infamous crimes be by indictment. However, if a defendant waives her right to grand jury review she may be charged by information. The waiver of indictment form used in federal court is shown on page 315. Crimes punishable by one year or

```
AO 455 (Rev. 5/85)   Waiver of Indictment  ●
```

United States District Court

—————————————— DISTRICT OF ——————————————

UNITED STATES OF AMERICA
V.

WAIVER OF INDICTMENT

CASE NUMBER:

I, _____, the above named defendant, who is accused of

being advised of the nature of the charge(s), the proposed information, and of my rights, hereby waive

in open court on _____ prosecution by indictment and consent that the
Date

proceeding may be by information rather than by indictment.

_____
Defendant

_____
Counsel for Defendant

Before_____
Judicial Officer

Waiver of Indictment

longer in prison are "infamous."[11] A defendant may not waive indictment in federal capital cases. It is always proper to charge corporations by information since imprisonment is not possible.

The United States Supreme Court has ruled that grand jury review is not a fundamental right, and, as such, the Fifth Amendment requirement for indictment is not applicable against the states. However, many states have grand juries and require that serious charges be brought by indictment.

Indictments must be written and state in "plain and concise" terms the essential facts constituting the offense charged.[12] Indictments are liberally read, and technical errors do not make them invalid. However, an indictment must contain all the essential elements of the crime charged. If an indictment charges more than one crime, each crime must be made a separate count.[13] Jurisdiction must be noted, and the law upon which the charge is made must be cited. The indictment filed against Ted Bundy is shown below. It was upon this indictment that Ted Bundy was prosecuted, convicted, and executed.

IN THE CIRCUIT COURT OF THE SECOND JUDICIAL CIRCUIT, IN AND FOR LEON COUNTY, FLORIDA.

CASE NO. 78-670

THE STATE OF FLORIDA,

-vs-

THEODORE ROBERT BUNDY,

Defendant,
_____

) INDICTMENT FOR:

) BURGLARY OF DWELLING
) MURDER IN THE FIRST DEGREE
) MURDER IN THE FIRST DEGREE
) ATTEMPTED MURDER IN THE
)   FIRST DEGREE
) ATTEMPTED MURDER IN THE
)   FIRST DEGREE
) BURGLARY OF DWELLING
) ATTEMPTED MURDER IN THE
)   FIRST DEGREE
_____

IN THE NAME OF AND BY THE AUTHORITY OF THE
STATE OF FLORIDA:

The Grand Jurors of the State of Florida, empaneled and sworn to inquire and true presentment made in and for the County of Leon, upon their oaths, do present that

THEODORE ROBERT BUNDY

on the 15th day of January, 1978, in Leon County, Florida, did then and there unlawfully enter or remain in a structure located at 661 West Jefferson Street, the dwelling of Karen Chandler and/or Kathy Kleiner, with the intent to commit the offense of Battery therein, and in the course of committing such burglary the said THEODORE ROBERT

**Ted Bundy
Indictment**

BUNDY did make an assault upon Karen Chandler and/or Kathy Kleiner, contrary to Section 810.02, Florida Statutes;

And Your Grand Jurors being present in said Court further gives the Court to be informed and understand that THEODORE ROBERT BUNDY on the 15th day of January, 1978, in Leon County, Florida, did then and there unlawfully kill a human being, to-wit: Margaret Bowman, by strangling and/or beating her, and said killing was perpetrated by said THEODORE ROBERT BUNDY from, or with a premeditated design or intent to effect the death of said Margaret Bowman, contrary to Section 782.04, Florida Statutes;

And Your Grand Jurors being present in said Court further gives the Court to be informed and understand that THEODORE ROBERT BUNDY on the 15th day of January, 1978, in Leon County, Florida, did then and there unlawfully kill a human being, to-wit: Lisa Levy, by strangling and/or beating her, and said killing was perpetrated by said THEODORE ROBERT BUNDY from, or with a premeditated design or intent to effect the death of said Lisa Levy, contrary to Section 782.04, Florida Statutes;

And Your Grand Jurors being present in said Court further gives the Court to be informed and understand that THEODORE ROBERT BUNDY on the 15th day of January, 1978, in Leon County, Florida, did then and there unlawfully attempt to kill a human being, to-wit: Karen Chandler, by beating her about the head and knowingly or intentionally causing great bodily harm, and said attempt was perpetrated by said THEODORE ROBERT BUNDY from, or with a premeditated design or intent to effect the death of said Karen Chandler, contrary to Sections 777.04 and 782.04, Florida Statutes;

And Your Grand Jurors being present in said Court further gives the Court to be informed and understand that THEODORE ROBERT BUNDY on the 15th day of January, 1978, in Leon County, Florida, did then and there unlawfully attempt to kill a human being, to-wit: Kathy Kleiner, by beating her about the head and knowingly or intentionally causing great bodily harm, and said attempt was perpetrated by said THEODORE ROBERT BUNDY from, or with a premeditated design or intent to effect the death of said Kathy Kleiner, contrary to Sections 777.04 and 782.04, Florida Statutes;

And Your Grand Jurors being present in said Court further gives the Court to be informed and understand that THEODORE ROBERT BUNDY on the 15th day of January, 1978, in Leon County, Florida, did

Ted Bundy Indictment
(continued)

then and there unlawfully enter or remain in a structure located at 431-A Dunwoody, the dwelling of Cheryl Thomas, with the intent to commit the offense of Battery therein, and in the course of committing such burglary the said THEODORE ROBERT BUNDY did make an assault upon Cheryl Thomas, contrary to Section 810.02, Florida Statutes;

And Your Grand Jurors being present in said Court further gives the court to be informed and understand that THEODORE ROBERT BUNDY on the 15th day of January, 1978, in Leon County, Florida, did then and there unlawfully attempt to kill a human being, to-wit: Cheryl Thomas, by beating her about the head and knowingly or intentionally causing great bodily harm, and said attempt was perpetrated by said THEODORE ROBERT BUNDY from, or with a premeditated design or intent to effect the death of said Cheryl Thomas, contrary to Sections 777.04 and 782.04, Florida Statutes; and

Contrary to the form of the Statute in such case made and provided and against the peace and dignity of the State of Florida.

Harry Morrison

AS STATE ATTORNEY, SECOND JUDICIAL CIRCUIT OF FLORIDA, IN AND FOR LEON COUNTY; PROSECUTING FOR SAID STATE.

Ted Bundy Indictment (continued)

If a defendant believes that an indictment is fatally deficient it may be attacked by a motion to quash. Indictments are not quashed because of technical errors. An example of a valid reason to quash is failure to allege an essential element of the crime charged. It is not violative of the Fifth Amendment's Double Jeopardy Clause for a grand jury to issue a second indictment after the first has been quashed or dismissed.

LEGAL TERMS

arraignment
The hearing at which the formal charge is read to the defendant and he is required to enter a plea.

plea
The defendant's response to the formal charge. There are three pleas: guilty; not guilty; and nolo contendere.

Section 10.7(b)   Information

The second formal method of charging one with a crime is by information. Informations are filed by prosecutors without grand jury review. The trend is away from indictments and toward charging by information.

Informations serve the same function as indictments. Under the federal rules informations must take the same form as indictments. They must be plain, concise, and in writing. All essential elements, as well as the statute relied upon by the government, must be included.[14] As is true of indictments, informations must be filed with the appropriate court.

SECTION 10.8 ARRAIGNMENT

After the formal charge has been filed the defendant is brought to the trial court for **arraignment**. This is the hearing at which the defendant is read the formal charge and is asked to enter a **plea**.

Defendants may plead guilty, not guilty, or *nolo contendere.* By pleading guilty a defendant admits all the charges contained in the charging document, unless a plea agreement has been reached with the government. A **plea agreement**, also known as a plea bargain, is the product of negotiations between the prosecutor and the defendant. It is common for the prosecution to dismiss one or more charges of a multicount charge or to reduce a charge in exchange for a defendant's plea of guilty.

Plea bargaining is an important aspect of criminal procedure. Over 90 percent of all felony cases are disposed of by pleas of guilty. Most guilty pleas are the result of plea bargaining.

By pleading guilty defendants waive a host of rights. The right to a jury trial and to be proven guilty beyond a reasonable doubt are two rights waived by a guilty plea. Because of the significance of such waivers courts must be sure that guilty pleas are given knowingly and voluntarily. To be knowing a defendant must understand her rights and that she is waiving them by making her plea. The plea must be free of coercion or duress to be voluntary. Of course, the inducement of a plea bargain is not coercion.

The court must also find that a **factual basis** exists before a plea of guilty can be accepted. This means that there must be sufficient facts in the record to support the conclusion that the defendant committed the crime. A defendant has no right to plead guilty to a crime he did not commit. The factual basis may be established by the testimony of the investigating officer or by the defendant recounting what transpired. Once the plea is taken the court will either impose sentence or set a future date for sentencing.

If a defendant enters a not guilty plea the court will set a trial date. In some instances, courts will set a pretrial schedule, which will include a pretrial conference date and a deadline for filing pretrial motions.

plea agreement
An agreement reached between the prosecution and defense concerning the disposition of the case. It is common for the prosecution to dismiss or reduce charges in exchange for a plea of guilty.

factual basis
Before a court may accept a plea of guilty a factual basis to believe the defendant committed the crime must be established.

SIDEBAR

PLEA BARGAINING
Statistics vary, but it is widely accepted that approximately 90 percent of all felony cases are disposed of by pleas of guilty. The number is probably higher for misdemeanors. There is no question that plea bargaining greatly reduces the amount of time expended on trials. Warren Burger, past Chief Justice of the United States Supreme Court, estimated that judicial resources in the United States would have to be doubled if only 20 percent of all criminal cases would go to trial. This conclusion was in large part a matter of simple math and has been criticized. In any event, plea bargaining is an important part of the criminal justice system. It is so important that the Supreme Court has

stated that it "is not only an essential part of the process but a highly desirable part," in *Santobello v. New York*, 404 U.S. 257, 261 (1971).

In *Boykin v. Alabama*, 395 U.S. 238 (1969), it was announced that all defendants who plead guilty do so voluntarily and knowingly, the latter meaning that the defendant understands the rights that are waived by entering a plea of guilty. The right to a trial, to confront one's accusers, and the right to make the government prove guilt are among the rights waived.

The plea negotiation involves the defendant and the prosecutor. Judges do not participate in plea negotiations. After a bargain is reached it is presented to the trial court. The court may then accept the agreement and sentence the defendant accordingly. With good cause the court may also reject the agreement. Some states permit defendants to withdraw their guilty pleas if the judge rejects the bargain. In others the judge has the discretion of allowing the defendant to withdraw the guilty plea or sentencing the defendant contrary to the bargain.

Sources: Burger, The State of the Judiciary, *56 A.B.A. J. 929 (1970) and Note,* Is Plea Bargaining Inevitable?, *97 Harv. L. Rev. 1037 (1984).*

Finally, a plea of nolo contendere may be entered. Nolo contendere is a Latin phrase that translates to "I do not contest it." The defendant who pleads nolo contendere neither admits nor denies the charges and has no intent of defending himself.

Nolo contendere is treated as a plea of guilty. That is, the government must establish that a factual basis exists to believe the defendant committed the offense, and the court accepting the plea must be sure that the plea is made voluntarily and knowingly. In most jurisdictions a defendant may plead nolo contendere only with the approval of the court. This is true in the courts of the United States.[15]

The advantage of a no contest plea over a guilty plea is that the no contest plea cannot be used in a later civil proceeding against the defendant, while a guilty plea may be used. If the case has not been disposed of by a plea of guilty or nolo contendere the parties will begin preparing for trial.

SECTION 10.9 PRETRIAL ACTIVITY

Section 10.9(a) Discovery

Discovery refers to a process of exchanging information between the prosecution and defense. Discovery is not as broad in criminal cases as in civil.

The amount of discovery that should be allowed is heavily debated. Those favoring broad discovery contend that limited discovery leads to "trial by ambush," which is not in the best interests of justice. The purpose of a trial is to discover the truth and achieve justice, not to award the better gamesman. Proponents of this position claim that unexpected evidence at trial is inefficient, costly, and unfair. It is inefficient because trials will have to often be delayed to give one party time to prepare a response to the unexpected evidence. Such tactics lead to time problems for the parties, as well as the trial court. They may also be unfair. It is possible that evidence that was once available may not be at trial. If the party surprised at trial had known about the unexpected evidence a proper defense or response could have been prepared.

Finally, it appears unfair to subject defendants to the possibility of surprise when the government is insulated from certain surprises. For example, affirmative defenses must be specially pled. Intent to rely on alibi and insanity defenses must be provided to the government in most jurisdictions, often with strict enforcement of time requirements. The purpose of these rules is to prevent surprises to the government at trial. Those who support expanded discovery feel that it is unfair to place such requirement upon defendants, but not upon the government.

Those opposed contend that expansive discovery increases the likelihood that defendants will manipulate the system. In particular, defendants might intimidate government witnesses. Additionally, opponents contend that it is easier for a defendant to skillfully plan his testimony, even if false, if a defendant knows the government's entire case. For example, if a defendant originally planned to assert an alibi and found out through discovery that the government has a witness placing him at the location of the crime, he has been provided an opportunity to change his defense. Today, discovery in criminal proceedings is quite limited in many jurisdictions. A few states have enlarged what information may be obtained prior to trial.

What follows is an examination of the federal rules, as well as constitutional requirements for discovery.

Section 10.9(a.1) Bill of Particulars

One method that defendants have to obtain information about the governments case is through a **bill of particulars**. The purpose of bills of particulars is to make general indictments and informations more specific. F. R. Crim. P. 7(f) allows district courts to order prosecutors to file a bill of particulars.

Bills of particulars are not true discovery devices. If the charging instrument is sufficiently clear and detailed, the court will not grant a defense motion for particularization of the charge. A bill of particulars is intended to provide a defendant with the details about the charges against him that are necessary for the preparation of a defense and to avoid prejudicial surprise at trial.[16] The test is not whether the indictment is sufficiently drawn; the question is whether the information is necessary to avoid prejudice to the defendant.

Section 10.9(a.2) Statements of the Defendant

F. R. Crim. P. 16(a)(1)(A) states that upon request the government must allow the defendant to inspect, copy, or photograph all prior relevant written and recorded statements made by the defendant. This includes testimony that defendants give before grand juries—an exception to the rule of secrecy of grand jury proceedings.

Prosecutors are required to allow inspection of all statements made by the defendant, which are in the possession of the prosecution or which may be discovered through due diligence. Hence,

LEGAL TERMS

discovery
The pretrial process whereby the defense and prosecution exchange information about a case.

bill of particulars
A document filed by prosecutors that provides details concerning the charges against a defendant.

if a defendant makes a statement to an arresting officer, which is recorded or reduced to writing, the prosecutor must allow defense inspection even though the statement may be in the possession of the officer and not the prosecutor.

In addition to recorded statements and writings the government is required to inform the defendant of "the substance of any oral statement that the government intends to offer in evidence. . . ." This means that statements made by a defendant that are summarized by the police (or other government agent), but not verbatim or signed by the defendant, are also discoverable. However, such evidence is only discoverable if the prosecution intends to use it at trial. This is not true of written and recorded statements of a defendant.

Section 10.9(a.3) Criminal Record of the Defendant

F. R. Crim. P. 16 also requires prosecutors to furnish a copy of the defendant's criminal record to the defendant. This includes not only the records known to the prosecutor, but those that can be discovered through due diligence.

Section 10.9(a.4) Documents and Tangible Objects

Under Rule 16 defendants are also entitled to inspect and copy photographs, books, tangible objects, papers, and buildings and places that are in the possession of the government if:

1. The item is material to the preparation of the defendant's defense, or
2. The item is going to be used by the government at trial, or
3. The item was obtained from, or belongs to, the defendant.

The situations where this would apply are countless. Here are two examples. 1. If the police take pictures of the scene of a crime this provision allows the defendant to view and copy those pictures prior to trial. 2. If the police seize a building that was used to manufacture drugs the defendant can invoke this rule to gain access to the premises.

This section of Rule 16 has a reciprocal provision. That is, defendants must allow the government to inspect and copy defense items. However, the rule is not as broad for government discovery. Defendants only have to permit inspection and copy of those items intended to be used at trial.

Section 10.9(a.5) Scientific Reports and Tests

All scientific reports and tests in the possession of the government (or which can be discovered through due diligence) must be turned over to the defendant, if requested.

This provision includes reports and conclusions of mental examinations of the defendant, autopsy reports, drug tests, fingerprint analysis, blood tests, DNA (gene) tests, ballistic tests, and other related tests and examinations.

The defendant must accord the government reciprocity, if requested. For example, if a defendant undergoes an independent mental examination the government is entitled to review the report of the evaluator prior to trial.

Section 10.9(a.6) Statements of Witnesses/Jencks Act

In the federal system defendants are not entitled to inspect or copy statements of prosecution witnesses prior to trial.

However, federal statute 18 U.S.C. §3500 permits a defendant to review a prior written or recorded statement after the witness has testified for the government. This statute is commonly known as the Jencks Act. Reviewing such statements may prove important to show that a witness is inconsistent, biased, or has a bad memory.

This procedure often causes trial delay, as defendants usually request time between direct examination and cross examination to review such statements. For this reason some federal prosecutors provide this information prior to trial. The Jencks Act is a matter of federal statutory law and does not apply in state criminal prosecutions.

Section 10.9(a.7) Depositions

A deposition is oral testimony given under oath, not in a court. In civil procedure depositions are freely conducted. Upon notice to a party or subpoena to a witness an attorney can call a person to his office to testify prior to trial. This is not the case in criminal practice.

F. R. Crim. P. 15 allows depositions only when "exceptional circumstances" exist. Expected absence of a witness at trial is an example of an exceptional circumstance. If such a circumstance is shown, the deposition may be ordered by the trial court, and the deposition may be used at trial. Of course, both the defendant and government have the opportunity to question the witness at the deposition.

Section 10.9(a.8) Brady Doctrine

While most discovery occurs under the authority of statutes and court rules, the Constitution also requires disclosure of information by the government in some situations. In the following case the Supreme Court announced what is now referred to as the Brady Doctrine.

BRADY V. MARYLAND

373 U.S. 83 (1962)

Petitioner and companion, Boblit, were found guilty of murder in the first degree and were sentenced to death. . . . Their trials were separate, petitioner being tried first. At his trial Brady took the stand and admitted his participation in the crime, but he claimed that Boblit did the actual killing. And, in his summation to the jury, Brady's counsel conceded that Brady was guilty of murder in the first degree, asking only that the jury return that verdict "without capital punishment." Prior to the trial petitioner's counsel had requested the prosecution to allow him to examine Boblit's extrajudicial statements. Several of those statements were shown to him; but one dated July 9, 1958, in which Boblit admitted the actual homicide, was withheld by the prosecution and did not come to petitioner's notice until after he had been tried, convicted, and sentenced, and after his conviction had been affirmed.

Petitioner moved the trial court for a new trial based on the newly discovered evidence that had been suppressed by the prosecution. Petitioner's appeal from a denial of that motion was dismissed by the Court of Appeals without prejudice to relief under the Maryland Post Conviction Procedures Act. . . . The petition for post-conviction relief was dismissed by the trial court; and on appeal the Court of Appeals held that suppression of the evidence by the prosecution denied petitioner due process of law and remanded the case for a retrial of the question of punishment, not the question of guilt. . . .

We now hold that the suppression by the prosecution of evidence favorable to an accused upon request violates due process where the evidence is material either to guilt or to punishment, irrespective of the good faith or bad faith of the prosecution.

[This principle] is not punishment of society for misdeeds of a prosecutor but avoidance of an unfair trial to the accused. Society wins not only when the guilty are convicted but when criminal trials are fair; our system of the administration of justice suffers when any accused is treated unfairly. An inscription on the walls of the Department of Justice states the proposition candidly for the federal domain: "The United States wins its point whenever justice is done its citizens in the courts." A prosecution that withholds evidence on demand of an accused which, if made available, would tend to exculpate him or reduce the penalty helps shape a trial that bears heavily on the defendant. That casts the prosecutor in the role of an architect of a proceeding that does not comport with standards of justice. . . .

Obviously, Brady applies to both state and federal prosecutions. Note that only exculpatory evidence must be provided. Evidence that tends to prove a defendant's innocence is exculpatory. Brady does stand for the proposition that prosecutors must reveal incriminating evidence to defendants.

In most situations disclosure at trial will satisfy Brady. However, if disclosure at trial would prejudice a defendant, pretrial disclosure may be constitutionally required. As is sometimes the case with Jencks materials, prosecutors may provide such information prior to trial as a courtesy.

In a related case the Supreme Court found that it is violative of due process for prosecutors to use perjured testimony or to deceive juries. This is true even if the perjury was unsolicited by the prosecuting attorney. As such, a prosecutor has a duty to correct any testimony of her witness that she knows is false.[17]

While Brady and related cases are law in both state and federal prosecutions, the other discovery rules differ. Be sure to check local law to determine what your client has a right to discover.

Section 10.9(b)   Motion Practice

In both civil and criminal practice a **motion** is a request made to a court for it to do something. In most cases a party who files a motion is seeking an order from the court. Any time a person desires something from a court a formal motion must be filed and copies sent to the opposing counsel. Some of the most common motions follow.

Section 10.9(b.1)   Motion to Dismiss

If a defendant believes that the indictment or information are fatally flawed the appropriate remedy is a motion to dismiss. In some jurisdictions this would be a motion to quash. Examples of fatal flaws in the charging instrument are: the court lacks jurisdiction; the facts alleged do not amount to a crime; and the defendant has a legal defense, such as double jeopardy.

If it is the form of the charging instrument that is attacked courts will often permit prosecutors to amend the charge, rather than to dismiss it entirely. Dismissal of an indictment or information does mean that the defendant cannot be recharged. A person is not in "jeopardy" under the Fifth Amendment until later in the proceeding.

Section 10.9(b.2)   Motion to Suppress

You have already learned that evidence obtained in an unconstitutional manner may not be used at trial. Objection at trial to the admission of such evidence is one method of excluding such evidence. Another is by way of a motion to suppress prior to trial.

A separate hearing is conducted prior to trial to determine whether the motion to suppress should be granted. Defendants may testify at suppression hearings, and their testimony may not be used against them at trial.[18] To allow a defendant's testimony from a suppression hearing to be used at trial would place the defendant in a position of choosing between his right to suppress evidence and his right to be free from self-incrimination. The best alternative is to allow the defendant to testify and to not allow that testimony to be used later.

Who has the burden of proof in suppression hearings varies by jurisdiction and what it is the defendant wishes to be suppressed. For example, most jurisdictions place the burden of proving that a search pursuant to a warrant was unconstitutional on the defendant. The opposite is true if there was no warrant;

the government bears the burden of proving the propriety of the search. Most jurisdictions also place the burden of proving that a confession was voluntary upon the prosecution.

Section 10.9(b.3) Motion for Change of Venue

Venue means place for trial. In state criminal proceedings venue usually lies in the county where the crime occurred. In federal proceedings venue lies in the district where the crime occurred. Most federal crimes are interstate in character, and the charges may be filed in any district where the crime took place.

F. R. Crim. P. 21 permits transfer of a case from one district to another if "the defendant cannot obtain a fair and impartial trial" at the location where the case is pending. In addition, a district judge may transfer a case if it is most convenient for the defendant and witnesses.

Pretrial publicity of criminal matters may be cause to tranfer a case (change venue in state proceedings). If a defendant receives considerable negative media coverage, it may be necessary to try the defendant in another location.

Because of the First Amendment free press issue judges are generally prohibited from excluding the press or public from hearings.[19] In some instances judges may order the attorneys involved in a case from providing information to anyone not involved in the proceeding.

Section 10.9(b.4) Motion for Severance

F. R. Crim. P. 8 permits two or more defendants to be charged in the same information or indictment if they were involved in the same crime. That rule also permits joinder of two offenses by the same person in one charging instrument, provided they are similar in character or arise out of the same set of facts.

In some situations severance of the two defendants may be necessary to assure fair trials. For example, if two defendants have "antagonistic defenses," severance must be granted. Defenses are antagonistic if the jury must disbelieve one by believing the other. For example, if Defendant A denies being at the scene of a crime, and Defendant B claims that they were both there, but also claims that A forced him to commit the crime, their defenses are antagonistic.

If a defendant is charged with two or more offenses it may be necessary to sever them to have a fair trial. For example, if a

LEGAL TERMS

motion
A formal request made to a court that it do something, usually to issue an order.

defendant plans to testify concerning one charge and not the other, severance is necessary.

Section 10.9(b.5) Motion In Limine

Prior to trial both the defendant and the prosecution may file motions in limine. This is a request that the court order the other party not to mention or attempt to question a witness about some matter. A motion in limine is similar to a motion to suppress, except that it encompasses more than admission of illegally seized evidence.

For example, if one anticipates that the opposing counsel will attempt to question a witness about evidence that is inadmissible under the rules of evidence (i.e., hearsay), a motion in limine may be filed to avoid having to object at trial. This is important, as often a witness may blurt out the answer before an attorney has had an opportunity to object. In addition, knowing whether the judge will permit the admission of evidence prior to trial helps plan an attorney's case.

Section 10.9(b.6) Other Motions

A variety of other motions may be filed. If the prosecution fears that revealing information required under a discovery rule will endanger the case or a person's life, a motion for a protective order may be filed. In such cases the trial court reviews the evidence *in camera* and decides if it is necessary to keep it from the defendant. If so, the judge will enter a protective order so stating.

Motions for continuance of hearings and trial dates are common. In criminal cases courts must be careful to not violate speedy trial requirements.

If two defendants have been charged jointly, one or both may file a motion for severance of trial. If defense counsel believes that the defendant is not competent to stand trial, a motion for mental examination may be filed.

Section 10.9(c) Pretrial Conference

Sometime prior to trial the court will hold a pretrial conference. This may be weeks or only days before trial.

At this conference the court will address any remaining motions and discuss any problems that the parties have. In addition, the judge will explain her method of trying a case, such as how the jury will be selected. The next stage is trial.

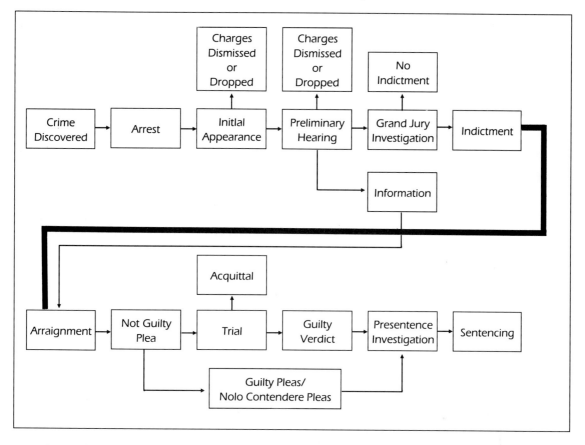

The Basic Criminal Process This charts the basic process of felony criminal cases from detection to sentencing. Misdemeanor cases normally progress through the system faster, as many stages are omitted. For example, misdemeanors are commonly prosecuted by information rather than indictment, and pre-sentence reports are often not prepared in misdeameanor cases.

REVIEW QUESTIONS

1. For what two reasons may a defendant be detained prior to trial?
2. What is the difference between an indictment and an information?
3. What are the purposes of indictments and informations?
4. If a defendant needs more information than appears in his indictment in order to prepare his defense, what should be done?
5. What advantage does a plea of nolo contendere have over a guilty plea?

6. Kevin has been charged with murder. He believes a weapon that the prosecutor plans on using at trial was unconstitutionally seized from his home. How can he raise this issue prior to trial?

7. Place the following in the proper order of occurance: preliminary hearing; formal charge; initial appearance; arraignment; trial; and complaint.

8. What is the Brady Doctrine?

REVIEW PROBLEMS

1. What is the historical purpose of the grand jury? Many feel as though grand juries should be abolished. Why?

2. Discovery in civil cases is very broad. F. R. Civ. P. 26 permits discovery of anything "reasonably calculated to lead to the discovery of admissible evidence." Should discovery in criminal cases be broader? Explain your position.

3. Do you believe that indictment by grand jury should be incorporated? Explain your position.

NOTES

[1] F. R. Crim. P. 4.

[2] F. R. Crim. P. 5.

[3] *Stack v. Boyle,* 342 U.S. 1 (1951).

[4] 18 U.S.C. §3142(f).

[5] 18 U.S.C. §3142(e) and (f).

[6] *Gerstein v. Pugh,* 420 U.S. 103 (1975).

[7] F. R. Crim. P. 5.1 and 18 U.S.C. §3060.

[8] 18 U.S.C. 3060(e).

[9] *United States v. Mandujano,* 425 U.S. 564 (1976).

[10] F. R. Crim. P. 6.

[11] *Ex parte Wilson,* 114 U.S. 417 (1884). See also F. R. Crim. P. 7.

[12] F. R. Crim. P. 7(c).

[13] F. R. Crim. P. 8(a).

[14] F. R. Crim. P. 7(c).

[15] F. R. Crim. P. 11.

[16] *United States v. Diecidue,* 603 F.2d 535 (5th Cir. 1979), cert. denied, 445 U.S. 946 (1979).

[17] *Mooney v. Holohan,* 294 U.S. 103 (1935).

[18] *Simmons v. United States,* 390 U.S. 377 (1968).

[19] *Richmond Newspapers, Inc. v. Virginia,* 448 U.S. 555 (1980).

CHAPTER 11
Trial, Sentencing, and Appeal

"We're expecting a speedy trial."

A plague on you if you don't stop arguing like lawyers.

**The Queen of Beggars speaking to the King of Beggars
in the film *Hunchback of Notre Dame*.**

OUTLINE

SECTION 11.1   TRIAL RIGHTS OF DEFENDANTS

Section 11.1(a) The Right to a Jury Trial

A trial is a method of determining guilt or innocence. In medieval England trial by ordeal, combat, and compurgation were used. Trial by ordeal was considered trial by God; that is, God determined the person's guilt or innocence.

To demonstrate how trials have changed, consider trial by ordeal. There were two ordeals; by water and fire. Two water ordeals were used. In the first the accused was thrown into a body of water. If he sank he was adjudged innocent, and if he floated he was guilty. In the second water ordeal the accused's arm was submerged in boiling water. The defendant had to survive this un-hurt to be proven innocent. The fire ordeal was similar, the ac-cused having to walk over or grasp hot irons.

Trial as we know it today finds its roots in the Magna Carta (1215), which guaranteed freemen trial by their peers. Even then the juries were comprised of people who knew the facts of the case. The concept of trial by a jury of one's peers was of great impor-tance to the colonists of the United States and made its way into the Constitution of the United States.

The Sixth Amendment to the United States Constitution reads, in part, "[i]n all criminal prosecutions, the accused shall enjoy the right to a speedy and public trial, by an impartial jury of the State and district wherein the crime shall have been com-mitted. . . . " The Sixth Amendment is fully applicable against the states via the Fourteenth Amendment.

The Sixth Amendment has been interpreted to mean that de-fendants have a right to a jury trial for all offenses that may be punished with more than six-months' imprisonment. Most crimes that have as their maximum punishment less than six months are "petty offenses," and there is no right to trial by jury.[1]

Note that the term "most" is used. Some argue that when fines become large enough, one is entitled to a jury trial, despite the amount of time one is sentenced to spend in jail. In addition, it is argued that crimes that are moral in nature and subject the defen-dant to ridicule and embarrassment justify trial by jury, even when the punishment is less than six months' imprisonment. The same question is raised concerning crimes that were indictable under the common law. The Supreme Court has not answered these questions, and the lower courts that have addressed these issues are split.

The maximum penalty allowed determines if a crime is petty, not the actual sentence. For example, if a crime is punishable by from three months to one year in jail the defendant is entitled to a jury, even if the trial judge routinely sentences those convicted to three months for the offense. Some crimes do not have a legisla-tively established punishment, such as contempt. In such cases the issue is whether the defendant is sentenced to more than six months in jail. If so, the defendant was entitled to a jury.

While the right to a jury trial for non-petty offenses is nearly always true, there are a few exceptions. There is no right to a jury in military trials. In addition, those appearing in juvenile court (delinquency proceedings) are not entitled to a jury trial.[2] Of course, juveniles who are tried as adults are entitled to the same rights as adults, including the right to have a jury trial.

Juries sit as fact-finders. A defendant may be entitled to have a jury decide guilt or innocence, but there is no right to have a jury decide other matters, such as the proper sentence or what law to apply. Some jurisdictions have juries impose sentence, or make a sentence recommendation to the trial court; however, this is not usually the practice and there is no federal constitutional reason for it.

The Supreme Court has held that there is no constitutional requirement for twelve jurors.[3] Nor does the Constitution require juror unanimity. There is a limit to how small a jury may be and how few jurors must concur in a verdict. In one case the Supreme Court found a law unconstitutional that required trial by six jurors and permitted conviction with a vote of five to one.[4]

It is common for six-person juries to be used for misdemeanors. However, a unanimous verdict is constitutionally required for conviction. If a twelve member jury is used it is constitutional to permit conviction upon a concurrence of nine or more jurors.

Finally, a defendant cannot be penalized for choosing to proceed to trial, rather than pleading guilty. In *United States v. Jackson,* 390 U.S. 570 (1968), the Supreme Court found a statute that made the death penalty available for those who were tried and not for those who pled guilty violative of the Sixth Amendment.

Section 11.1(b) The Right to a Public Trial

The Sixth Amendment also guarantees the right to a public trial. This applies throughout the trial, from openings to return of the verdict, and also applies to many pretrial hearings, such as suppression hearings. The presence of the public is intended to keep prosecutions "honest." As the Supreme Court stated in *Estes v. Texas,* 381 U.S. 532 (1965): "History has proven that secret tribunals were effective instruments of oppression."

The right to a public hearing does not mean that everyone who wishes to attend has to be permitted in. The trial judge is responsible for maintaining order in the courtroom and may require the doors be shut once all seats have been filled. Also, the disruptive citizen may be removed.

The defendant's right to a public trial is not absolute. Trial judges, acting with extreme caution, may order that a hearing be conducted in private. Facts that support excluding the public are rare. An example of when exclusion of the public may be justified is when an undercover law-enforcement agent testifies, and public exposure would put the officer's life in jeopardy.

If a court closes a hearing (or trial) without justification the defendant is entitled to a new hearing, regardless of whether the defendant was actually harmed.

Generally the press has no greater right to attend a hearing than do other members of the public. However, many judges provide special seating for members of the press.

Section 11.1(c) The Right to Confrontation and Cross Examination

The Sixth Amendment also contains a right to confront one's accusers. This means that a defendant has the right to cross examine the witnesses of the prosecution. Each state drafts its own rules of evidence, however, it may not enact a rule of evidence that conflicts with a defendant's right to confrontation.

For example, a state procedure permiting government witnesses to refuse to identify themselves was found violative of the Sixth Amendment.[5] The Supreme Court reasoned that the procedure was invalid because it did not permit the defendant to conduct his own investigation into the credibility of government witnesses.

This does not mean that defendants may probe any area on cross examination. If a state can show a compelling reason it may prohibit cross examination of a subject. For example, rape shield laws prohibit defendants from inquiring into a rape victim's sexual background in most cases. Courts have affirmed such laws, finding that the protection of the rape victims from unwarranted personal attacks is a legitimate reason to limit defense cross examination.

The confrontation clause also restricts the government's use of hearsay evidence. Hearsay is a statement made by a person out of court. The Federal Rules of Evidence prohibit hearsay, unless it falls into a recognized exception. For the prosecution to use hearsay it must be shown that 1. the witness is unavailable at trial through no fault of the government and 2. the statement was made in a situation wherein it appears reliable.

The confrontation clause implicitly includes a right of a defendant to be at his trial. This right includes the entire trial, from the selection of the jury to return of the verdict. It also includes many pretrial matters, such as exclusion hearings. Of course, defendants have a right to be present at both sentencing and probation revocation hearings. While the right to be present during one's trial is fundamental, it may be lost by disruptive behavior.

Section 11.1(d) The Presumption of Innocence/Burden of Proof

One of the most basic rights underlying the right to a fair trial is the presumption of innocence. All those accused must be proven guilty by the government. A criminal defendant has no duty to defend himself and may remain silent throughout the trial. In fact, the government is prohibited from calling the defendant to testify, and the defendant cannot be made to decide whether he will testify at the start of the trial.[6] The fact that a defendant chooses not to testify may not be mentioned by the prosecutor to the jury. A defendant may testify in his own behalf. If so, he is subject to full cross examination by the prosecutor. The Fifth Amendment right to be free from self-incrimination is discussed more fully in the defenses chapter.

The standard imposed upon the government in criminal cases is to prove guilt **beyond a reasonable doubt**. A doubt which would cause a reasonable or prudent person to question the guilt of the accused is a reasonable doubt. Although not precisely quantified, beyond a reasonable doubt is greater than the civil preponderance (51 percent likely) and less than absolute (100 percent confidence of guilt). The prosecution must prove every element of the charged crime beyond a reasonable doubt. A juror must vote for acquittal if she harbors a reasonable doubt.

To further the presumption of innocence judges must be careful not to behave in such a manner that implies to a jury that a defendant is guilty.

The Supreme Court has stated that the presense of a defendant at a jury trial in prison clothing is prejudicial.[7] In the case that follows a federal appellate court reviewed the use of "prisoner docks" for a Sixth Amendment violation.

YOUNG V. CALLAHAN

700 F.2D 32 (1st Cir. 1983)

[The Court included a footnote which stated that a prisoner dock is "a box approximately four feet square and four feet high. It is open at the top so that the defendant's head and shoulders can be seen when he or she is seated. The dock is placed typically at the center of the bar enclosure which separates the spectator's section from that portion of the courtroom reserved for trial principals. The dock is usually fifteen to twenty feet behind counsel table, and is sometimes on a raised platform."]

In January of 1979 appellant was tried in Massachusetts Superior Court on one count of assault and battery with a dangerous weapon and two counts of murder. The jury returned a guilty verdict on the assault and battery but was unable to reach a verdict on the two murder indictments. In a new trial in February of 1979, appellant was found guilty of second-degree murder on both counts. These convictions were affirmed by the Massachusetts Supreme Judicial Court. . . .

Prior to appellant's second trial, counsel moved that he be allowed to sit at counsel table rather than in the prisoner's dock on the grounds that "forcing him to sit in the prisoner's dock would deprive him of his constitutional rights to a fair trial, to the presumption of innocence, to access to counsel, non-suggestive eyewitness identifications, and due process of law." That motion was accompanied by an affidavit from appellant's trial counsel averring, based on his own observations and those of corrections officers during appellant's two years of incarceration and on appellant's conduct at the first trial, that "allowing [appellant] to sit at counsel table will not present any hazards to the orderly judicial process or to the security of its personnel," and that the trial of the case would involve a substantial amount of testimony concerning acts and conduct of the appellant over a several day period and would thus "require consultation with the defendant." . . .

In once again evaluating for constitutional error the confinement of an accused to the prisoner's box, we reiterate . . . that such confinement, like appearance in prison attire, is a "constant reminder of the accused's condition" which "may affect a juror's judgment", eroding the presumption of innocence which the accused is due. . . .

The prisoner's dock, like other physical restraints, should thus be employed only when "the trial judge has found such restraint reasonably necessary to maintain order" and when cured by an instruction to the "jurors that such restraint is not to be considered in assessing the proof and determining guilty." . . .

A criminal defendant also has a right to be free from appearing before his jury in handcuffs or shackles.

LEGAL TERMS

beyond a reasonable doubt
The standard of proof in criminal cases. The prosecution must prove every element of the charged offense beyond a reasonable doubt to obtain a conviction.

This right to be free of restraint is not absolute. Judges have the authority to take whatever measures are necessary to assure safety in the courtroom and to advance the administration of justice. Accordingly, a defendant who is disorderly may be expelled from his trial. However, before exclusion is ordered the court should consider other alternatives. Defendants who are threatening may be restrained, and those who verbally interfere with the proceeding may be gagged.[8]

Section 11.1(e) The Right to Speedy Trial

All criminal defendants have a right to a speedy trial. It is the Sixth Amendment, as extended by the Fourteenth Amendment to the states, that guarantees speedy trial. This right finds its roots as far back as the Magna Carta.

To date, the United States Supreme Court has not set a specific number of days within which trial must be conducted. Rather, the Court has said that four factors must be considered when determining if a defendant has enjoyed a speedy trial. First, the length of the delay. Second, the reason for the delay. Third, whether the defendant has asserted the right to a speedy trial. Fourth, how seriously the defendant was prejudiced.[9]

Time for speedy trial begins once the defendant is arrested or formally charged.[10] If a defendant is charged by sealed indictment, speedy trial does not start until the indictment has been opened.

Dismissal with prejudice is the remedy for violation of speedy trial. That is, the charge is dismissed and may not be refiled by the prosecutor.

All the states and the national government have enacted speedy trial acts. The Speedy Trial Act of 1974[11] is the federal statute. That act requires that individuals are to be formally charged within thirty days from the date of arrest and tried within seventy days of the date of the filing of the information or indictment or from the date the defendant had his initial appearance before the court that will try him, whichever is later.

To avoid prejudice by having a trial before a defendant has had an opportunity to prepare a defense the statute provides that trial shall not occur for thirty days, unless the defendant consents to an earlier date.

The statute specifies certain delays that are excluded from computing time for purpose of speedy trial. A few of the periods that are excluded by the Speedy Trial Act of 1974 are when the defendant is a fugitive; when trial is delayed because an issue is on appeal; time delays caused by motions of the parties; and delays resulting from mental examinations of the defendant.

The Speedy Trial Act of 1974 gives the trial court the discretion to decide whether violation of its provisions justifies a dismissal with or without prejudice. Factors that must be considered are the seriousness of the offense, the reason for delay, other facts of the case, and the impact of reprosecution on the administration of justice.[12]

Since the United States Supreme Court has not established specific time requirements for speedy trial, each state has its own time requirements. Of course, states must comply with the requirements of *Barker v. Wingo.*[13] Most states have a speedy trial provision in their constitution, which is similar, if not identical, to the Sixth Amendment. Other states set their speedy trial requirements out in statute or court rules. Time requirements differ, but trial within three months is common.

Section 11.1(f) The Right to Counsel

The Sixth Amendment to the United States Constitution provides that "in all criminal prosecutions, the accused shall enjoy the right . . . to have the Assistance of Counsel for his defense." The right to counsel is one of the most fundamental rights guaranteed criminal defendants and is fully applicable to the states.

The right to the assistance of counsel is not only found in the Sixth Amendment, but in the Fifth and Fourteenth Amendments. These alternative sources will be discussed later in the particular context within which they exist.

Section 11.1(f.1) Indigency

It has always been clear that criminal defendants are entitled to retain the attorney of their choice. It was not until 1923 that the United States Supreme Court recognized a constitutional right to appointed counsel for indigent defendants in *Powell v. Alabama*, 287 U.S. 45 (1923).

In the *Powell* case (commonly known as the Scottsboro case) nine young black males were charged with the rape of two white girls. Within one week of arrest the defendants were tried. Eight of the "Scottsboro boys" were convicted and sentenced to death. The defendants appealed, claiming that they should have been provided counsel. The Supreme Court agreed.

However, the right to appointed counsel in *Powell* was not founded upon the Sixth Amendment, but upon the Fourteenth. The Court reasoned that the absence of counsel deprived the defendants of a fair trial, and, accordingly, violated the defendant's due process rights. This decision was narrow: it applied only to capital cases where the defendant was incapable of preparing an adequate defense and did not have the resources to hire an attorney.

The due process right to counsel was subsequently extended to all situations where a defendant would not have a fair trial in the absence of defense counsel. Whether counsel was required depended on each particular case's "totality of facts." If denial of counsel was "shocking to the universal sense of justice," then the defendant's right to a fair trial, as guaranteed by the Fourteenth Amendment, was violated [*Betts v. Brady,* 316 U.S. 455 (1942)]. The Court refused to extend the right to counsel to all state criminal proceedings. Cases that involved complex legal issues or had a defendant of low intelligence were the types of situation that required the appointment of counsel under the (*Betts*) due process standard.

In 1938 the Court decided *Johnson v. Zerbst,* 304 U.S. 458 (1938), which held that the Sixth Amendment guarantees a right to counsel. The Sixth Amendment right to counsel was found to be broader than the right to counsel announced in *Powell,* as it applied to all criminal prosecutions. However, *Zerbst* did not apply to state proceedings.

Eventually, the Sixth Amendment right to counsel was extended to all state felony proceedings in *Gideon v. Wainwright,* 372 U.S. 335 (1963).

GIDEON
V.
WAINWRIGHT

372 U.S. 335 (1963)

Petitioner was charged in Florida state court with having broken and entered a poolroom with intent to commit a misdemeanor. This offense is a felony under Florida law. Appearing in court without funds and without a lawyer, petitioner asked the court to appoint counsel for him, whereupon the following colloquy took place:

THE COURT: Mr. Gideon, I am sorry, but I cannot appoint Counsel to represent you in this case. Under the laws of the State of Florida, the only time the Court can appoint Counsel to represent a defendant is when that person is charged with a capital offense. I am sorry, but I will have to deny your request to appoint Counsel to defend you in this case.

THE DEFENDANT: The United States Supreme Court says I am entitled to be represented by Counsel.

Put to trial before a jury, Gideon conducted his defense about as well as could be expected from a layman. He made an opening statement to the jury, cross examined the State's witnesses, presented witnesses in his own defense, declined to testify himself, and made a short argument "emphasizing his innocence to the charge contained in the Information filed in this case." The jury returned a verdict of guilty, and petitioner was sentenced to five years in the state prison. Since 1942, when *Betts v. Brady,* 316 U.S. 455, was decided by a divided Court, the problem of a defendant's federal constitutional right to counsel in a state court has been a continuing source of controversy and litigation in both state and federal courts. . . . Since Gideon was proceeding in forma pauperis, we appointed counsel to represent him and requested both sides to discuss in their briefs and oral arguments the following: "Should this Court's holding in Betts v. Brady . . . be reconsidered? . . . .

. . . Governments, both state and federal, quite properly spend vast sums of money to establish machinery to try defendants accused of crime. Lawyers to prosecute are everywhere deemed essential to protect the public's interest in an orderly society. Similarly, there are few defendants charged with crime, few indeed, who fail to hire the best lawyers they can get to prepare and present their defenses. That government hires lawyers to prosecute and defendants who have the money to hire lawyers to defend are the strongest indications of the widespread belief that lawyers in criminal courts are necessities, not luxuries. The right of one charged with crime to counsel may not be deemed fundamental and essential to fair trials in some countries, but it is in ours. From the very beginning, our state and national constitutions and laws have laid great emphasis on procedural and substantive safeguards designed to assure fair trials before impartial tribunals in which every defendant stands equal before the law.

This noble idea cannot be realized if the poor man charged with crime has to face his accusers without a lawyer to represent him. . . . The Court in *Betts v. Brady* departed from sound wisdom upon which the Court's holding in *Powell v. Alabama* rested. Florida, supported by two other States, has asked that *Betts v. Brady* be left intact. Twenty-two states, as friends of the Court, argue that Betts was "an anachronism when handed down" and that it should now be overruled. We agree. . . . Reversed.

Subsequently, the right to counsel was again extended to encompass all criminal cases punished with a jail term. Whether the crime is labeled a misdemeanor or felony is not dispositive of the right to counsel issue [*Argersinger v. Hamlin,* 407 U.S. 25 (1972)].

In some cases it may be to the prosecution's advantage for a defendant to have counsel, even though a sentence of imprisonment is not available for a first conviction, but is for subsequent convictions. This is because a sentence may not be enhanced to include jail time based on a prior conviction where the defendant did not have counsel. For example, the penalty for first-offense drunk driving is not punished by a term in jail; however, subsequent violations are. If Jack is arrested and convicted without counsel for his first offense, he may not be sentenced to jail time for his second drunk driving conviction because he did not have counsel during his first trial.

To qualify for an appointed counsel the defendant does not have to be financially destitute. It only need be shown that the defendant's financial situation will prevent him from being able to retain an attorney. An indigent defendant does not have a right to choose his appointed attorney; this decision falls within the discretion of the trial court.

Section 11.1(f.2) Effective Assistance of Counsel

Defendants are not only entitled to have an attorney, but to the "effective assistance of counsel." On appeal, a defendant may challenge his conviction claiming that at a lower level (trial or appellate) he did not have effective counsel.

To be successful with such a claim two facts must be shown. First, the representation must be extremely inadequate. Second, the defendant must show that he was actually harmed by the lack of adequate counsel. So, if an appellate court determines that a defendant would have been convicted with the best of attorneys, the defendant's claim of inadequate counsel fails.

A Sixth Amendment claim of ineffective assistance of counsel can take many forms. Incompetence of counsel is often claimed, but rarely successful. Attorneys are expected to make the legal and tactical decisions of the defense. The fact that defense counsel rendered incorrect legal advice is not determinative. The issue is whether the defendant's representation was shockingly substandard.

A defendant has a right to the "undivided loyalty" of defense counsel. So, it is common to have ineffective assistance of counsel claims where one attorney is representing co-defendants. In *Cuyler v. Sullivan*, 446 U.S. 335 (1980) it was held that an ineffective assistance of counsel claim based upon an alleged conflict of interest will be successful only if the defendant can show that the conflict "adversely affected" his rights.

Also, the accused has a right to confer with counsel to prepare a defense. If a court denies a defendant access to her counsel a Sixth Amendment claim may be made.

Eavesdropping on a defendant's conversation with his counsel is also improper and violative of the Sixth Amendment.

Section 11.1(f.3) The Right to Self-Representation

In *Faretta v. California*, 422 U.S. 806 (1975), the right to self-representation was established. The Supreme Court recognized that the assistance of trained legal counsel was essential to preparing and presenting a defense. However, in balance, the Court found that a defendant's right of choice was of greater importance. As such, defendants may choose to act as their own counsel (pro se), even though the decision increases the probability of a conviction.

The record must clearly show that a defendant who has chosen to proceed pro se has done so voluntarily and knowingly. The defendant "must be made aware of the dangers and disadvantages of self-representation." Whether the defendant possesses any legal training or education is not relevant.

Trial judges are permitted to appoint "standby counsel" for trial. This attorney attends the trial and is available to counsel the defendant or take over the defense, if necessary. The Court later approved the practice of appointing standby counsel over the objection of the defendant. This is routinely done in felony cases where the defendant has opted to proceed pro se.

The right to self-representation is not absolute. A defendant who engages in disruptive behavior during the proceeding may be relieved of his pro se status. Standby counsel, if appointed, may be ordered to complete the trial.

Section 11.1(f.4) The Scope of the Right

Through *Gideon* the right to counsel in criminal prosecutions was extended to the states. *Argersinger* made it clear that counsel must be provided in all cases where the defendant is sentenced to actual imprisonment. But when does the right begin?

United States Supreme Court has stated that the Sixth Amendment right to counsel applies to all critical stages of a criminal prosecution. This definition requires that a "prosecution" be initiated before the right to counsel, under the Sixth Amendment, attaches. Accordingly, the Sixth Amendment does not apply to juvenile proceedings, nor to administrative hearings such as parole determination and revocation.

The right starts whenever the "adversary judicial proceeding" is initiated. Police contacts prior to the initiation of an adversary judicial proceeding are not covered by the Sixth Amendment.

In determining what constitutes a critical stage courts focus on "whether substantial rights of the defendant may be affected." The greater the contact between the prosecutor and the defendant, the more likely the event is at a critical stage.

The first critical stage is normally the initial appearance or the arraignment. Courts have also determined that a defendant may be entitled to counsel at a police lineup, sentencing, preliminary hearing, and during a probation revocation hearing. Once charges are filed all interrogations of the defendant by the government are critical stages.

The Sixth Amendment is not the only constitutional provision assuring counsel. The Fifth Amendment's right to be free from self-incrimination also guarantees counsel in some instances, as does the Fourteenth Amendment's Equal Protection and Due Process Clauses.

SECTION 11.2 TRIAL PROCEDURE

Section 11.2(a) Voir Dire

The first stage of trial is the **voir dire**. This is a French phrase that translates "to speak the truth." Voir dire is also known as jury selection.

The process of selecting a jury differs among the jurisdictions. In all jurisdictions, prospective jurors are asked questions bearing upon their individual ability to serve as fair and impartial jurors. Each state differs in how this information is obtained. In many, the judge is responsible for asking most of the questions. In others

LEGAL TERMS

voir dire
  French. Translates "to speak the truth." The stage of trial also known as jury selection.

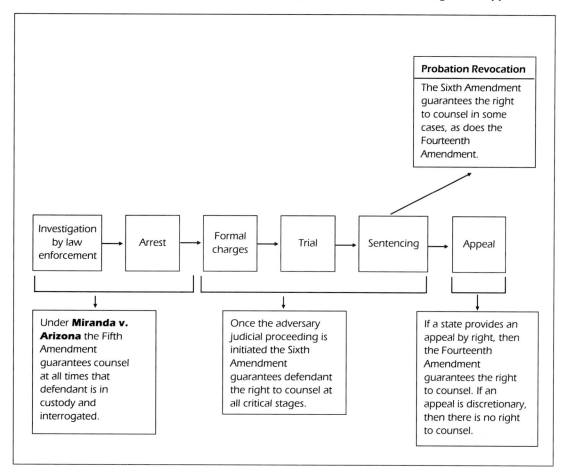

Probation Revocation

The Sixth Amendment guarantees the right to counsel in some cases, as does the Fourteenth Amendment.

Investigation by law enforcement → Arrest → Formal charges → Trial → Sentencing → Appeal

Under **Miranda v. Arizona** the Fifth Amendment guarantees counsel at all times that defendant is in custody and interrogated.

Once the adversary judicial proceeding is initiated the Sixth Amendment guarantees defendant the right to counsel at all critical stages.

If a state provides an appeal by right, then the Fourteenth Amendment guarantees the right to counsel. If an appeal is discretionary, then there is no right to counsel.

The Right to Counsel

the judge only makes a few brief inquiries, and the lawyers do most of the questioning.

There are two ways of eliminating a juror. First, if one of the attorneys believes that a juror could not be fair and impartial, then the juror will be **challenged for cause**. If the judge agrees, the juror is released. An unlimited number of jurors may be eliminated for cause.

In addition to challenges for cause, a juror may be eliminated by a party using a **peremptory challenge**. Each party is given a specific number of peremptory challenges at the start of the trial and may strike jurors until that number is exhausted. A party is free to eliminate, without stating a reason, any potential juror. However, a juror may not be eliminated because of his race.[14]

In the federal system both the defendant and prosecutor have twenty peremptory strikes in death cases, three in misdemeanors,

LEGAL TERMS

challenge for cause
    To request that a potential juror be removed because the juror has exhibited an inability to be fair and impartial.

peremptory challenge
    When a party removes a juror without giving a reason. Both the defendant and the government are given a stated number of peremptory challenges.

and in non-capital felony cases the defendant gets ten and the government six.[15] States have similar rules.

Section 11.2(b) Preliminary Instructions

The next stage in the trial proceeding is for the judge to give preliminary instructions to the jury. The trial judge will explain to the jury what its obligation is and give a brief introduction to the law and facts of the case. The judge may read the formal charge verbatim to the jury or may summarize its contents.

The presumption of innocence is explained, and the judge will admonish the jury to not discuss the case prior to deliberating. Jurors are told not to read newspaper articles or watch television reports concerning the trial.

Section 11.2(c) Opening Statements

After the judge has given the preliminary instructions the parties will address the jury. These statements are commonly known as opening statements. The purpose of opening statements is to acquaint the jury with the basic facts of the case. Opening statements is not the time for counsel to argue the law; only the facts expected to be presented should be mentioned.

In some cases the defense attorney may be permitted to wait until after the prosecution has put on its case before giving an opening. Since the purpose of opening statements is to present the facts surrounding the charge to the jury, opening statements are often waived in bench trials.

Section 11.2(d) The Prosecution's Case in Chief

Since the government has brought the charges, it puts its case on first. This will consist of calling witnesses to testify and producing exhibits.

All jurisdictions have rules of evidence that govern the procedure and admissibility of evidence. The Federal Rules of Evidence are used in the federal courts, and many states have modeled their rules after them.

Many evidentiary questions can be resolved prior to trial through a motion in limine. Those arising during trial are handled through "objections." Any time an attorney believes that a question, statement, or action of the opposing lawyer is improper he may object. The Court will then rule on the objection, and the trial will continue. In some instances the attorneys will want to argue the objection outside the hearing of the jury. In such cases a sidebar may be held, or the judge may order that the jury be removed until the matter is resolved.

The confrontation clause assures the defendant the right to cross examine the prosecution's witnesses. Normally, cross examination is limited to matters raised during the prosecution's direct examination. The defense also has the right to review an exhibit before it is shown to the jury.

Section 11.2(d.1) Directed Verdict

After the government has rested (finished its case) the defendant may move for a directed verdict or, as it is also known, a judgment of acquittal. Upon such motion the trial judge reviews the evidence presented by the government. If the evidence to support a conviction is insufficient the judge will enter a directed verdict favoring the defendant. A directed verdict may never be entered favoring the government.

The prosecution's evidence is insufficient if reasonable men could not conclude that the defendant is guilty. If the trial court grants a motion for directed verdict the jury never deliberates and is discharged. Directed verdicts are rarely granted, as most judges prefer to have the jury return a verdict.

Section 11.2(e) The Defense Case

If the motion for directed verdict is denied the defense may put on its case. The defendant is not required to put on a defense, and juries are instructed to not infer guilt by the absence of a defense.

If a defendant chooses to present a defense, the rules are the same as for the prosecution. The defendant may call witnesses and introduce exhibits, as limited by the rules of evidence. Defense witnesses are subject to cross examination by the prosecutor. Defendants do not have to testify, but may choose to do so. If a defendant does testify he is subject to cross examination by the prosecutor.

Section 11.2(f) Rebuttal

After the defense has concluded the prosecution may call rebuttal witnesses in an effort to disprove the evidence of the defense. No new issues may be raised during rebuttal. The defense is then permitted to rebut the prosecution's rebuttal evidence.

Section 11.2(g) Closing Arguments

After the evidentiary stage of the trial has concluded the parties will present their closing arguments. The length of closing arguments is left to the discretion of the trial judge.

Attorneys may argue both the facts and the law during closing arguments. However, an attorney may not argue law different from that the judge will express to the jury as controlling in the case. Closing arguments give the parties an opportunity to summarize the evidence and explain their positions to the jury.

Attorneys must not make incorrect factual or legal statements to the jury. Objections to such statements may be made. If sustained the jury will be instructed by the judge to disregard the statement. Prosecutors must be especially careful not to make inflammatory remarks about the defendant or defense counsel. Such remarks, if extreme, can lead to mistrial.

Section 11.2(h) Final Instructions

After closing arguments are completed, the judge will instruct the jury. Through these instructions the judge explains the law to the jury. The information contained in the judge's instructions includes the prosecutorial burden; the standard of proof; the elements of the charged crime; how to weigh and value evidence; and rules for reaching a verdict.

Section 11.2(i) Jury Deliberations and Verdict

After instructions the jury goes into deliberations. If necessary, because the court fears contamination of the jury, it may order the jury sequestered. In all cases jury deliberations are secret.

Generally, no person has contact with the jury when it is deliberating. If the jury has a question for the judge, it is escorted into the courtroom where all the parties may hear the question. Some judges, but not all, permit juries to take the exhibits and instructions with them into the jury room.

On occasion a jury may communicate to the judge that a verdict cannot be reached. Some courts will then give the jury an "Allen Charge." This is an instruction encouraging those jurors in the minority to re-examine their position. The charge gets its name from *Allen v. United States*, 164 U.S. 492 (1896), wherein the Supreme Court approved its use. While courts must be careful with such charges they are not violative of the United States Constitution. However, some states have banned the Allen Charge.

Whenever a jury is "hung" the court will declare a mistrial and set a new trial date. Because of the expense and inconvenience of trying cases a second time plea bargains are often reached.

If a verdict is reached the parties are summoned to the courtroom, and the jury verdict is read. The parties may request that the jury be "polled." To poll a jury each juror is asked what her verdict was. If there has been an error the judge may order the jury to return to deliberations or may declare a mistrial.

Section 11.2(j) JNOV/New Trial

If the jury returns a verdict of guilty the defendant may move for a judgment notwithstanding the verdict or JNOV. This is similar to a directed verdict, in that the defendant is asserting that the evidence is insufficient to support a guilty verdict.

In addition to JNOV a defendant may file a motion for a new trial. The common-law equivalent of a motion for a new trial was the *writ of error coram nobis. Coram nobis* is still recognized in a few states.

This motion is different than the JNOV because the defendant is not claiming that the evidence was insufficient, rather, that the trial was flawed. For example, if a defendant believes that evidence was admitted that should have been excluded and that he was denied a fair trial because of the admission of the evidence, he may file a motion for new trial. A motion for new trial may also be made because of new evidence, discovered after trial.

SECTION 11.3 SENTENCING

After conviction sentence must be imposed. For many misdemeanors and nearly all infractions, sentence is imposed immediately. For felonies and some misdemeanors a future sentencing date is set.

In most cases sentence is imposed by the trial judge. A few jurisdictions provide for a jury sentence recommendation, and an even fewer number actually permit the jury to impose sentence. The jury always plays a role in deciding whether death should be imposed.

The legislature determines how a crime should be punished. Legislatures normally set ranges within which judges may punish violators. In recent years there has been a substantial movement to limit the discretion of judges. This has been done in the federal system and many states.

A Defendant at Sentencing

The right of the legislative branch in this area is curbed by the Eighth Amendment, which prohibits "cruel and unusual punishment." The protection of the Eighth Amendment has been extended to state proceedings through the Fourteenth Amendment. However, legislatures enjoy wide discretion in deciding how to punish criminals.

Section 11.3(a) Sentencing Procedure

Section 11.3(a.1) The Pre-Sentence Investigation/ No Right to Counsel

After a defendant is determined guilty a sentencing date is set. For most felonies and misdemeanors the date will be set far enough in the future to permit the probation officer to complete a pre-sentence investigation.

The investigation typically begins with an interview of the defendant. Information concerning the defendant's drug habits, criminal history, employment history, education, medical and psychological problems, and personal finances is obtained. The defendant is also permitted to give his version of the facts surrounding the offense. There appears to be no right to counsel during this interview, although most courts and probation officers permit attorneys to attend. The right to counsel at such interviews was addressed by the Seventh Circuit Court of Appeals in the following case.

UNITED STATES V. JACKSON

886 F.2d 838 (7th Cir. 1989)

* * *

Jackson challenges the sentencing judge's use of statements he made to a federal probation officer in the course of a pre-sentence interview. Jackson argues that his Sixth Amendment right to assistance of counsel was violated. Consistent with Jackson's assertion, there is no indication in the record before us that Jackson's counsel was informed of the date and time of the interview or that he was present when the interview was conducted. . . .

The Sixth Amendment right to counsel provides every defendant with the right to have representation during a "critical stage" of the adversarial proceedings. . . . Whether a pretrial interview by a federal probation officer is a critical stage of criminal proceedings depends upon the nature of the probation officer's role in the sentence determination. . . .

A district judge's use of a defendant's statement to a probation officer in applying the Sentencing Guidelines is markedly unlike the prosecutor's adversarial use of a defendant's pretrial statement to a psychiatrist to carry the state's burden of proof before a jury. A federal probation officer is an extension of the court and not an agent of the government. The probation officer does not have an adversarial role in the sentencing proceedings. In interviewing a defendant as part of the pre-sentence investigation, the probation officer serves as a neutral information gatherer for the sentencing judge. . . .

We conclude that the Sixth Amendment right to assistance of counsel did not extend to Jackson's pre-sentence interview by the federal probation officer.

* * *

In addition to conducting an interview of the defendant the probation officer will obtain copies of vital documents, such as the defendant's "rap sheet" and relevant medical records. The probation officer will attempt to verify the information provided by the defendant through these documents and other investigatory processes.

When the probation officer has completed the investigation a pre-sentence report is prepared. This report reflects the information discovered during the investigation and is used by the court in determining what sentence should be imposed. Often, the prosecutor and law-enforcement officers involved in prosecuting the defendant, family members of the defendant, and the victim of the crime are permitted to make a statements that are incorporated into the report.

There is no constitutional right to the preparation of a pre-sentence report; however, most jurisdictions have followed the lead of the federal government, which requires a pre-sentence report unless "there is in the record information sufficient to enable the meaningful exercise of sentencing discretion."[16]

In the federal system the defendant is entitled to review the pre-sentence report prior to sentencing. This is true in most states. The right is not absolute. For example, the recommendation of the probation officer is kept confidential.[17]

At the sentencing hearing the defendant may disprove factual statements contained in the report. To this end witnesses may be called and exhibits introduced.

Section 11.3(a.2) The New Federal Guidelines

In November 1987, the new Federal Sentencing Guidelines became effective. The guidelines are a milestone in federal criminal law. Their purpose is twofold: 1. to reduce sentencing disparity and 2. to achieve "honesty in sentencing."[18] Prior to the guidelines judges were given a large penalty range from which a defendant could be sentenced. The result of this discretion was that defendants similarly situated were often sentenced very differently. As such, one goal of the new guidelines is to reduce disparity in sentencing.

The second goal, honesty in sentencing, concerns parole. Prior to the guidelines defendants could be released on parole, in some cases, after only one-third of the imposed sentence was served. In addition, prisoners complained that parole was arbitrarily and inconsistently applied. Accordingly, Congress eliminated parole, and the guidelines now reflect the time that will be served, less fifty-four days of good time that may be earned yearly (after the first year).

To achieve the first goal—the reduction of sentencing disparity—the guidelines greatly reduce the discretion of the judge in sentencing. To determine what sentence should be imposed the offender's criminal history category and offense level must be determined. The criminal history category is simply determined by the number of prior convictions of the offender.

To find an offender's offense level is more complex. First, the crime is assigned a base offense number. That number is then increased by "specific offense characteristics." Adjustments to this figure are then made for mitigating or aggravating circumstances. This final figure is the offense level.

Once the criminal history category and offense level are determined, the court looks to the sentencing table. This table provides a small range (the top figure never exceeds 25 percent of the bottom figure) from which the judge is to sentence the defendant. Only in rare instances may a judge deviate from the proscribed sentencing range.

The guidelines continue to permit judges to suspend sentences to probation for offenses at the low end of the sentencing table. For those offenses just above the probation cutoff judges may sentence an offender to probation, provided some form of confinement is ordered, such as house arrest or community confinement. There is also a third layer of offenses where the judge may order a "split sentence." This is where one-half or more of the sentence must be served in prison, and the remaining amount may be served in another form of confinement.

The new guidelines have been the subject of much controversy. Federal judges themselves have been very critical of the guidelines. Many contend the reason that judges are complaining is simply their loss of authority. While this may be true, there also appear to be problems caused by the rigidity of the guidelines.

The drafters of the guidelines knew that all factors which should be considered in sentencing could not be anticipated (or quantified). As such, provisions are made permitting deviation from the guidelines. However, deviation is rarely permitted. This has lead to some absurd results. For example, one twenty-one-year-old honor student, with no prior record, was sentenced to ten years in prison for his involvement in one drug transaction.[19] At least one federal district judge has resigned because of his dissatisfaction with the guidelines. Whether the guidelines will become more flexible remains to be seen.

The federal government was not the first to enact guideline sentencing. At least two states, Minnesota and Washington, were using guidelines when the federal version became law. It is probable that more jurisdictions will contemplate similar reform in the future.

Section 11.3(b) Forms of Punishment

Section 11.3(b.1) Capital Punishment

Clearly the most controversial punishment is the death penalty. In early American history capital punishment was commonly used. During the nineteenth century use of the death penalty greatly declined. Today, over half the states provide for the death penalty, and its use has regained popular support. Although the number of inmates actually executed every year is small, the number is increasing.

The contention that imposing death is inherently cruel and violative of the Eighth Amendment was rejected in *Gregg v. Georgia*, 428 U.S. 153 (1976). While the imposition of death is not inherently cruel, the Court has stated that each defendant must be examined individually, and all mitigating factors must be considered.[20] Hence, any statute that mandates death for the violation of its prohibition is unconstitutional.

On the other side of the spectrum is *Furman v. Georgia*, 408 U.S. 238 (1972), where it was held that the death penalty cannot be imposed under a sentencing procedure that creates a substantial risk of being implemented in an arbitrary manner. Hence, a statute cannot totally eliminate discretion, nor grant so much discretion that the death penalty could be imposed arbitrarily.

The definition of cruelty is an evolving concept. Electrocution, lethal injection, hanging, and shooting are all approved methods of executing a prisoner. Other methods, such as starvation, would not pass constitutional muster.

The Eighth Amendment has been interpreted to prohibit sentences that are disproportionate to the crime committed. In this vein the Supreme Court has held that capital punishment may not be imposed for the crime of raping an adult woman.[21] While death can be imposed for the crime of murder, it is questionable under *Coker* whether capital punishment can be imposed for any other crime.

Finally, the Court has stated that a defendant who is incapable of understanding why he is being executed because of insanity may not be executed until he regains his faculties.[22]

Section 11.3(b.2) Incarceration

Restraint is an effective method of dealing with dangerous persons. Incarceration serves this purpose, and in some cases the offender is also rehabilitated. Regretfully, because rehabilitation is rare, and, contrary to popular belief, prison conditions are often

glad but you. You won't be here to enjoy it because I command the sheriff or some other officer or officers of this country to lead you out to some remote spot, swing you by the neck from a nodding bough of some sturdy oak, and let you hang until you are dead.

"And then, Jose Manuel Miguel Xavier Gonzales, I further command that such officer or officers retire quickly from your dangling corpse, that the vultures may descend from the heavens upon your filthy body, until nothing shall remain but the bare, bleaching bones of a cold-blooded, copper-colored, bloodthirsty, throat-cutting, sheep-herding, murdering son of a bitch."

A Holding Cell

bad, many leave prison angry, no more educated or employable, and occasionally more dangerous.

However, incarceration continues to be the most common method of punishing violent offenders. Offenders may be committed to prisons, camps, or local jails. Those sentenced to short terms (one year or less) are usually housed in a local jail. Those with longer terms usually are committed to a prison.

For those crimes with incarceration as their punishment the sentencing judge is usually given a range of time from which to sentence the defendant. For example, assault may be punished by one to three years in prison. The judge is vested with the discretion to decide what amount of time within that range best suits the particular facts of the case.

In many instances a **presumptive sentence** is set by the legislature, and the judge must enumerate **aggravating** and **mitigating circumstances** when deviating from the presumptive sentence. Even then the judge must remain within the statutory limits for the crime. For example, an assault statute may call for one to three years' punishment with a presumptive sentence of eighteen months. If the judge sentences the defendant to more or less than eighteen months the reasons must be made a part of the record.

Those circumstances upon which the judge relies to increase the presumptive sentence are aggravating, and those that the judge uses to justify sentencing below the presumption are

LEGAL TERMS

presumptive sentence
A precise sentence within a range of possible penalties that must be the sentence imposed by a court in the absence of aggravating or mitigating circumstances.

aggravating circumstance
A factual reason justifying sentencing a defendant more harshly than the applicable presumptive sentence.

mitigating circumstance
A factual reason justifying sentencing a defendant below the applicable presumptive sentence.

mitigating. However, the judge may not sentence the defendant to less than one year or more than three, despite the facts of the case.

What constitutes an aggravating or mitigating circumstance is often expressly written into the statute. Examples of aggravating circumstances are: injury, torture, or death of the victim; the use of a weapon; whether the crime involved a child; and whether a trust was violated. Examples of mitigating circumstances are: physical disability of the defendant; the defendant has dependents; the crime was committed in a nonviolent manner; and the defendant was acting in good faith.

If a defendant is already serving a sentence on another crime or is convicted of two related crimes the sentencing judge may impose **concurrent** or **consecutive sentences**. If two sentences are concurrent it is said that "they run together." That is, if a defendant receives two five-year sentences he will actually spend five years incarcerated. If the sentences are consecutive the defendant will spend a total of ten years incarcerated.

After committing the defendant to a correctional institution, the judge loses responsibility for and control over him, unless a state statute provides otherwise. In many states **parole** is available to prison inmates. Parole is an early release from prison and is used to encourage inmates to stay out of trouble while in prison. Parole decisions are made by state corrections officials, i.e., a parole board. Similar to probation, an offender must comply with certain conditions while on parole. Conditions routinely include not possessing a gun, not contacting the witnesses, judge, jurors, or prosecutor involved with the offender's conviction, and not becoming involved in further criminal activity. Violation of a condition of parole may result in recommitment to prison.

Parole has fallen into public disfavor in recent years. The result has been to limit the availability of parole in many situations. Parole has been eliminated for those convicted of crimes against the United States.

Section 11.3(b.3) Probation and Revocation

A popular alternative to incarceration is probation (also known as a "suspended sentence"). Probation is not always an alternative and is rarely available for crimes that are punished with life imprisonment or death. While on probation the defendant is released from custody, but must comply with conditions imposed by the court during the probationary period. Each defendant is placed under the supervision of a probation officer during this period. The probation officer is an officer of the court, not of the corrections system.

LEGAL TERMS

concurrent sentence
Whenever two sentences run together, so that the actual sentence time equals the greater of the two sentences, they are concurrent.

consecutive sentence
Whenever one sentence follows another it is consecutive. The actual sentence time equals the sum of the two sentences.

parole
An early release from prison. An offender must comply with a number of conditions while on parole. Violation of a condition of parole may result in recommitment to prison.

revocation hearing
A court proceeding wherein it is determined if a defendant violated a condition of probation and, if so, whether the defendant should be incarcerated.

Typical conditions of probation include a requirement of steady employment, refraining from other unlawful conduct, not carrying a firearm or other weapon, and not leaving the jurisdiction of the court. A judge may tailor conditions to fit the circumstances of each case. For example, a child molester may be prohibited from obtaining employment that requires working around children. Special types of probation will be discussed below.

A defendant who violates a condition of probation may be disciplined. Generally, the decision about whether any action should be taken for a violation is made by the probation officer. If a violation is extreme the probation officer may file a petition to revoke probation. The sentencing court then holds a **revocation hearing**. If granted, the defendant is taken off probation and incarcerated.

At the revocation hearing the defendant may be entitled to counsel. As a general rule, the right is not found in the Sixth Amendment, as the "critical states" of trial have passed. In one rare case the Supreme Court has held that a Sixth Amendment right to counsel does exist at a revocation hearing. In *Mempa v. Rhay*, 389 U.S. 128 (1967), the trial judge withheld sentencing, placed the defendant on probation, and did not pronounce sentence until after the defendant violated his probation and was revoked. Since the revocation hearing turned out to be the defendant's sentencing hearing, where there is a right to counsel under the Sixth Amendment, the Court found that the Sixth Amendment applied.

The Due Process Clauses of the Fifth and Fourteenth Amendments may also provide a right to counsel at a revocation hearing. If there is a substantial question of law or fact that must be resolved at the hearing, counsel must be appointed for the indigent defendant so that the issues can be fully explored and developed. Although, if revocation is obvious, then counsel need not be allowed.

Section 11.3(b.4) Community Service

One alternative to incarceration for nonviolent offenders is community service. In such a program a defendant's sentence is suspended and the completion of a stated number of community service hours is a condition of the defendant's probation.

In most instances the probation officer will work with the probationer to find an appropriate job. However, the judge may require that a specific job be performed.

The requirements of community service range from unskilled to professional. For example, a judge may require that a professional, such as a physician or attorney, work in a clinic that provides services to the poor. The same person may be expected to pick up trash from local roads. Clearly, the former makes best use of the defendant's skills and benefits the community the most.

Section 11.3(b.5) Restitution and Fines

The purpose of restitution is to compensate the victim, not punish the offender. As such, restitution is not a substitute for other forms of punishment. Any amount of ordered restitution must, of course, be related to actual loses sustained by the victim.

Different than restitution, the purpose of a fine is to punish the offender. Fines are a very common method of punishing misdemeanants. Serious crimes are often punished with both a fine and incarceration. Any fine imposed must be reasonable; that is, the amount must be within the financial means of the offender.

Section 11.3(b.6) Modern Sentencing Alternatives

In recent years many new alternatives to incarceration have been developed. Such alternatives are actually forms of probation, and, as such, are administered by courts and probation officers.

For the nonviolent criminal work release is an alternative. While in these programs the offender lives in a jail, but is permitted to leave jail to work. Work release has many advantages. The defendant continues to earn a living. This is particularly important if the defendant has dependents. Also, it is good for the self-esteem of the offender; he continues to feel a useful part of the community. The final advantage is true of many sentencing alternatives: the cost to the public is lower because the offender is often required to pay, in whole or part, for his participation in the program.

For those convicted of some alcohol and drug offenses, courts have turned to alcohol and drug treatment over imprisonment. These programs vary greatly. For first-time drunk driving convictions offenders may be required to submit to one or more of the following, in addition to traditional conditions of probation:

1. Participation in an alcohol treatment program, such as Alcoholics Anonymous.
2. Report for periodic urine or blood tests to detect the presence of alcohol.
3. Take antabuse, a drug which makes a person ill if alcohol is ingested.
4. Participation in a defensive/safe-driving school.

If a defendant has a previous drunk driving conviction he is likely to receive some "executed time" or jail time, in addition to some or all of the above. A few courts have tried a form of shock treatment. For example, a defendant may be required to meet with drunk drivers who are responsible for killing someone and discuss that experience. In another example, at least one judge has required that a drunk driver work in a hospital emergency room so that the defendant would be exposed to alcohol-related injuries and deaths.

First time drug users may also be placed on probation, subject to conditions similar to those listed above: periodic urinalysis or blood screening and drug counseling and treatment. This form of probation is not available to drug dealers.

Two other forms of probation that may be used independently or mixed with one or more of the above are house arrest and halfway houses. If a defendant is sentenced to house arrest he or she may not leave the home without prior permission of the probation officer. Of course, in emergencies the defendant may leave the home.

Today, the use of "electronic shackles" makes enforcement of house arrests easier. These devices are attached to the probationer's leg, and through the transmission of a radio signal it can be determined if the defendant is at home.

Halfway houses are minimum security homes located in the community. Generally they serve two groups of offenders: those making the transition from prison to the community and those who need some confinement, but not jail or prison.

Halfway houses are commonly used in conjunction with work release programs. The residents are given some freedom to leave the home, but are restricted in their travel. Often such homes provide drug and alcohol counseling and treatment and vocational training.

This is not by any means an exhaustive list of alternative punishments. The list is limited only by the Constitution and the imagination of judges. For example, one Florida judge required those convicted of drunk driving to place a bumper sticker on their cars warning of their conviction. This requirement was upheld by the Florida Court of Appeals.[23]

Section 11.3(b.7) Habitual Offender Statutes

The career criminal or repeat offender is now subject to extreme penalty in most jurisdictions. These statutes are referred to as "recidivist" or **habitual offender laws**.

Most statutes provide for an increased penalty if a defendant has been convicted of a stated number of felonies, often three, within a certain period of time, such as ten years.

To prevent unfair prejudice to the defendant the jury usually does not know about the habitual charge until it has reached a verdict in the underlying charge. So, if Pam is charged with murder and of being a habitual criminal the jury would initially know only of the murder charge. If the jury comes back with an acquittal the habitual charge is dismissed. If the verdict is "guilty" the jury is then told that they must also determine if the defendant is an habitual criminal. This is a known as a bifurcated procedure.

To prove the habitual charge the prosecutor will introduce court records reflecting the prior convictions, and, in some instances call the prosecutors involved in the prior convictions to attest that the defendant was indeed convicted.

Habitual criminal laws have been attacked as violative of the Double Jeopardy Clause. Such claims have not been successful, as they are not considered a second punishment of one of the earlier offenses. Rather, evidence of a criminal record provides a reason to increase the penalty for the most recent offense.

SECTION 11.4 POST-CONVICTION REMEDIES

Technically, motions for new trials are post-conviction remedies. Other than such motions there are two major methods of attacking a conviction or other decision at the trial level: appeal and habeas corpus.

Section 11.4(a) Appeal

The Constitution of the United States does not confer a right to appeal.[24] Regardless, every state provides for appeal either through statute or constitution. Once a state establishes a right to appeal the United States Constitution requires that appellate procedure not violate the Fourteenth Amendment's Due Process or Equal Protection Clauses.

Appeals from federal district courts go to the United States Courts of Appeals (Circuit Courts). From there appeal is taken to the Supreme Court of the United States. In state cases appeal is taken to the state intermediate appellate court, if any. Appeal from that court is taken to the state high court, usually named the Supreme Court of State. All issues, federal and state, are heard by those courts. Issues of state law may not be appealed any further. If the defendant wishes to appeal a decision of the state high court concerning an issue of federal law the appeal is taken to the United States Supreme Court.

Section 11.4(a.1) Filing the Appeal

Since the right to appeal is purely statutory, it may be lost if it is not timely filed. The federal rules require that appeals be filed within ten days of the date of judgment.[25] The government is given thirty days in those instances where it may appeal. Appeals from state courts to the United States Supreme Court must be filed within ninety days of the entry of judgment.[26]

Procedures vary, but it is common to require the appellant to file a number of documents to begin the appeal. The first document is a notice or petition of appeal. This simply informs all the parties, as well as the trial judge, that the case is being appealed. A designation of record will also be filed by the parties. Through this document the parties select the portions of the trial record that they desire to be sent to the appellate court. A statement of issues that need to be resolved on appeal may also be filed by the appellant. Finally, a filing fee must be paid. People who cannot afford it may seek relief from the filing fee requirement.

After the necessary documents are filed the parties brief the issues for the appellate court. The appellate court, in its discretion, may hear oral arguments.

Because the penalty for untimely filings (dismissal of the appeal) is harsh, most courts recognize constructive filings. This is particularly true for incarcerated defendants who rely on counsel or prison officials in preparing or filing an appeal.

Note that most jurisdictions provide for the possibility of bail pending appeal. This is most often available in misdemeanor cases; however, it may be granted in felony cases also.

Section 11.4(a.2) The Scope of Review

To avoid unnecessary delay only **final orders** may be appealed. So, pretrial decisions that are erroneous are not corrected until appeal is taken after the case is completed. Orders that may not be reviewed until after final judgment are those relating to the suppression of evidence, discovery, and the sufficiency of the charging instruments.

There are a few exceptions to the final judgment rule. The most prominent exception is the collateral order doctrine. Under this doctrine, orders, which are independent of the criminal case, may be immediately appealed. The appeal proceeds concurrently with the underlying criminal case.

Appeals taken from ongoing litigation (where no final order has been issued) are called **interlocutory appeals**. Orders holding a defendant incompetent to stand trial, denying bail, and denying a defendant's double jeopardy claim have been held collateral and

LEGAL TERMS

final order
  The order or judgment ending the case. Generally, no part of a case may be appealed until a final order is issued.

interlocutory appeal
  An exception to the final judgment rule. Appeal of an order taken prior to final judgment, and, accordingly, running concurrently with the ongoing litigation.

immediately appealable.[27] Certain orders that occur after judgment, such as revocation of probation, are also immediately appealable.

Remember, cases are not retried on appeal. Appellate courts review the record for errors of law, not fact. That means the appellate court will not examine the evidence and substitute its judgment for that of the trial court (or jury). However, the court will examine the record to make sure that sufficient evidence exists to support the judgment. So long as sufficient evidence can be found the appellate court will not reverse, even if it would have decided the case differently. Issues of law are reviewed anew (de novo).

Not every error warrants reversing the trial court. Only when an error prejudices the defendant is reversal required. An error is prejudicial if there is a possibility that it changed the outcome of the case. If not, it was **harmless error**. The appellant bears the burden of proving that he was prejudiced by the error of the trial court.

Some error is so violative of the Constitution that it is irrebutably presumed prejudicial, and as such, reversal is automatic. An order denying defense counsel at trial is never harmless error.[28]

Section 11.4(a.3) Prosecution/Defense Appeals

Because of the Double Jeopardy Clause defendants have a broader right to appeal than does the government. A defendant who is tried and convicted is free to appeal any factual or legal error. However, this right may be limited by a requirement of **preservation**. To satisfy this rule the defendant must raise the issue at the trial level. This gives the trial judge an opportunity to avoid error.

Failure to raise the issue results in a waiver. For example, a defendant who does not challenge the sufficiency of an indictment at the trial level may not raise the issue for the first time before the appellate court. The same is true of evidentiary matters. The defendant must object to the admission of evidence she believes should be excluded so as to preserve the issue for appeal.

The prosecution has a limited right to appeal. Because of the prohibition of trying a person twice for the same offense the government has no right to appeal acquittals. However, most states permit the government to appeal certain orders that are issued prior to jeopardy attaching. Orders dismissing charging instruments, suppressing evidence prior to trial, and releasing the defendant before trial may be appealed. These interlocutory appeals do not violate the Fifth Amendment's Double Jeopardy Clause because jeopardy does not attach until a jury has been impaneled or the first witness is sworn in a nonjury trial.

Section 11.4(a.4) The Right to Counsel on Appeal

There is no Sixth Amendment right to counsel on appeal. The Sixth Amendment right begins once a defendant is charged and continues through, at all critical stages, trial and sentencing. In some instances, it is in effect at probation revocation. It does not ever include appeals.

The right to counsel on appeal can be found, however, in the Equal Protection Clause of the Fourteenth Amendment. The Supreme Court said, in *Douglas v. California,* 372 U.S. 353 (1963), that indigent defendants convicted of a felony have a right to appointed counsel on appeal, provided that the appeal is by right. By right means that the defendant's appeal must be heard by the appellate court. Most, if not all, states have provided for appeal by right.

If an appeal is discretionary, the Equal Protection Clause of the Fourteenth Amendment does not compel the state to provide counsel.

As is true at trial, the defendant is entitled to "effective counsel." The appointed attorney has an ethical obligation to zealously pursue the defendant's appeal. Because of the large number of frivolous appeals, the Supreme Court has stated that an appointed attorney may be allowed to withdraw; however, the following must be done: first, the attorney must request withdrawal from the appellate court; second, a brief must be filed explaining why the attorney believes the appeal to be wholly without merit. In that brief all potential issues must be outlined for the court's review. If the appellate court agrees that there are no valid issues, the attorney may be withdrawn. If the court finds an issue that has some merit, the lawyer must continue to represent the defendant.

Section 11.4(b) Habeas Corpus

Both the states and federal governments have habeas corpus relief. Discussed below is federal habeas corpus relief, particularly, federal habeas corpus in state criminal proceedings. While habeas corpus relief is available at any stage of a criminal proceeding, most habeas corpus petitions are filed after conviction. The discussion below is limited to such post-conviction petitions.

LEGAL TERMS

harmless error
Not all errors at the trial level justify a reversal. If an error is harmless, the judgment is affirmed.

preservation
Some legal issues must be raised at the trial level, or they may not be raised on appeal.

Section 11.4(b.1) History

Translated, habeas corpus means "you have the body." In action the writ is used to order someone who has custody of another to bring that person before the court. Any person who believes that he is being detained illegally may use the writ to gain his freedom. Because of the significant power of the writ it has become known as the "Great Writ of Liberty."

The writ has ancient origin, dating back as far as the twelfth century. Habeas corpus was often used to enforce provisions of the Magna Carta. The success of the writ in protecting liberty in England influenced the drafters of the American Constitution. The result is Article I, §9, clause 2, which states: "The Privilege of the Writ of Habeas Corpus shall not be suspended unless when in Cases or Rebellion or Invasion the Public Safety may require it."

Federal habeas corpus is important in criminal law because it is used to challenge state court convictions. That is, if a defendant believes that his federal constitutional rights were violated in a state court, he may attack his conviction through federal habeas corpus.

Habeas corpus has had congressional authorization since 1789. The first statute made habeas corpus available only to federal prisoners. This was changed by the Habeas Corpus Act of 1867, which extended habeas corpus to all people "restrained of his or her liberty in violation of the constitution, or of any treaty or law of the United States." The 1867 act continues to be in effect, with some modifications.

Section 11.4(b.2) Scope of Review

The current habeas corpus statutes are found at 28 U.S.C. §§2241–55. Section 2254 provides habeas corpus relief to state prisoners. Under section 2255 federal prisoners are to move to vacate or set aside their sentences, in a procedure nearly identical to section 2254. Relief under this section must be sought before a federal prisoner can bring habeas corpus. Even then, the statute states that habeas corpus shall not be issued if the prisoner was unsuccessful with a section 2255 claim, unless that proceeding was "inadequate or ineffective." A biased judge is an example of when habeas corpus may be issued after a section 2255 motion has been denied.

The federal courts continued to have little involvement with state proceedings, even after the 1867 act extended the reach of federal habeas corpus to state prisoners. This was in large part due to Supreme Court decisions limiting the review of federal habeas corpus to questions of jurisdiction.

The scope of review was enlarged in *Brown v. Allen,* 344 U.S. 443 (1953) where it was held that federal habeas corpus could be used to relitigate all issues of federal law. This decision significantly increased the power of federal habeas corpus and resulted in increased intervention of federal courts in state criminal proceedings.

The Supreme Court has since narrowed habeas corpus relief in one regard: a state prisoner may not use federal habeas corpus to relitigate Fourth Amendment claims (search and seizure), provided the defendant was provided a "full and fair litigation" in state court. Even with this exception federal habeas corpus remains a powerful remedy for state prisoners.

Section 11.4(b.3) Exhaustion of Remedies

Before a state prisoner can seek the aid of a federal court he must satisfy certain procedural requirements. First, the defendant must use all means available in the state system to correct the alleged error. This is the doctrine of exhaustion of remedies. Section 2254(b) states:

> An application for a writ of habeas corpus in behalf of a person in custody pursuant to the judgment of a State court shall not be granted unless it appears that the applicant has exhausted the remedies available in the courts of the State, or that there is either an absence of available corrective process or the existence of circumstances rendering such process ineffective to protect the rights of the prisoner.

The remedies that must be exhausted depend on what is available in the state system, such as motions for new trial, state habeas corpus relief, and appeals. Of course, if there is no remedy available, the defendant may immediately petition for habeas corpus relief.

If there is a remedy available, but it would be futile to exhaust it, habeas corpus may be brought without it. For example, assume State Supreme Court has previously addressed the legal issue raised by the defendant, and its decision is contrary to the defendant's claim. Unless there is reason to believe that the court will reconsider its decision there is no need to exhaust this remedy. Excessive delay in the state proceedings may also be a basis for bringing habeas corpus before the state remedies have been exhausted, provided the state doesn't have a remedy for such delays (i.e., mandamus).

The fact that a defendant has failed to timely appeal (or file a motion for new trial, etc.) does not mean that habeas corpus is unavailable. The question is: are state remedies available? If a defendant has missed his right to appeal under state law, and no other remedy is available, then habeas corpus may be used to resolve his federal constitutional claims.

Section 11.4(b.4) The Custody Requirement

The Habeas Corpus Act speaks of prisoners "in custody." However, this has been interpreted to include all wrongful restraints of liberty. The Supreme Court has said those people who are subject to "restraints not shared by the public generally" are entitled to habeas corpus protection, even though they may not be in the physical custody of the government.

Under this interpretation persons placed on probation and parole have been held to be in custody, as have defendants released on bail.[29] Habeas corpus protection is also available to a defendant who has served his entire sentence, because the restraint of liberty includes not only incarceration but collateral loss of civil liberties (i.e., right to carry a weapon), injury to reputation, and the possibility of an increased penalty for a later conviction.

A defendant who is lawfully detained may use habeas corpus to challenge her sentence if she believes it is excessive. Also, if she is convicted of several crimes and was sentenced to consecutive sentences, she need not wait until the lawful sentence expires before petitioning for habeas corpus. It appears that an invalid sentence may be attacked, even though it runs concurrently with a valid sentence. Again, the collateral affects of the conviction are the rationale.

Section 11.4(b.5) Procedure

The following rules were established by the United States Supreme Court to implement 22 U.S.C. §2254.[30] The petition for habeas corpus relief is filed in the federal district within which the prisoner is being held. The petition shall name the person who has custody of the applicant as the respondent. Indigent persons may file a motion to proceed in forma pauperis, which relieves such persons from paying the filing fee.

Immediately after the petition is filed the district judge will examine the petition. If the petition is "plainly" invalid the court will dismiss the petition. If not, the court will direct the respondent to answer the petition.

Counsel may be appointed and discovery is available, with leave of the district court. After the petition has been answered and appropriate discovery conducted, the district court may hold an evidentiary hearing and issue an opinion or rule from the record without a hearing. Habeas corpus decisions may be appealed.

Section 11.4(b.6)   The Right to Counsel

To date, the Supreme Court has not found a constitutional right to the assistance of counsel in preparing and presenting a petition for habeas corpus.

In some instances the district court may have to hold an evidentiary hearing. It is possible that in such instances a due process right to counsel exists to assure that the hearing is fair. The issue is not of critical importance presently, because federal habeas corpus rules require the appointment of counsel for such hearings. Additionally, the rules give the district court the discretion to appoint counsel earlier, if necessary.

While there may be no right to counsel, there is a right to "access to the courts." As such prisoners must be furnished with paper, pens, stamps, and access to a law library. Further, unless a prison provides adequate legal assistance to its prisoners, so-called "jailhouse lawyers" may not be prohibited from assisting other inmates in the preparation of legal documents.

REVIEW QUESTIONS

1. What rights are encompassed by the "Confrontation Clause"?
2. What is the standard of proof in criminal cases? Define that standard.
3. How soon after arrest must a defendant be tried to comply with the Sixth Amendment's speedy trial clause?
4. What is a pre-sentence investigation? Who conducts the investigation, and what is its purpose?
5. What are aggravating and mitigating circumstances in sentencing?
6. When does the Sixth Amendment right to counsel begin? When does it attach during the prosecution?
7. What is the final judgment rule?
8. Does a defendant have a right to appointed counsel on appeal?
9. What is habeas corpus?
10. Distinguish harmless from prejudicial error.

REVIEW PROBLEMS

1–4. Do each of the following defendants have a right to a jury trial? Explain your answer.

1. A juvenile delinquency proceeding has been initiated against John because of his involvement with drugs. For over a year he has been dealing drugs, a crime punishable by as much as five years in prison in his state.
2. Jane is charged with simple assault. In her state that crime is punishable by a maximum fine of $2,500 and twelve months imprisonment. However, the judge assigned to her case has never sentenced a person to more than four months and customarily suspends that sentence to probation.
3. Nick is sixteen years old. He is charged with murder in state trial court. Murder in his state is punished with life imprisonment or death.
4. Norm, an officer in the military, has been charged with raping a female officer. Rape is punished with ten years to life imprisonment in the military.

5–8. Kevin, an attorney, has been indicted for embezzlement. After his preliminary hearing he filed a motion to suppress a confession he believes was illegally obtained. A hearing was conducted, and the trial court granted his motion. The evidence was vital to the prosecution.

Kevin's attorney has also requested that the trial be continued, because he claims that Kevin is not competent to stand trial. The judge ordered a mental evaluation, held a hearing, and found Kevin competent to stand trial.

The defense also requested that the court order a number of police officers to submit to depositions prior to trial. The court denied the motion.

At trial, the defendant objected to the introduction of a document that he believes was unconstitutionally obtained during a search of his office. The judge overruled the objection and admitted the confession into evidence.

Answer the following questions using the facts above:

5. The prosecution strongly believes that the documents that were suppressed are admissible. The prosecutor objects on the record to the judge's order and then appeals the issue after Kevin is acquitted. What should be the outcome on appeal?
6. Kevin disagrees with the trial court finding of competency. What is his remedy?

7. Believing that Kevin cannot have a fair trial without the depositions, his attorney filed an interlocutory appeal seeking an order from the appellate court requiring the trial judge to provide for the depositions. What should be the outcome?
8. Kevin appealed the decision of trial court that denied his motion to suppress the document. The appellate court affirmed the trial court, and Kevin filed a habeas corpus petition in federal court claiming that his federal constitutional rights were violated by the admission of the evidence. What should be the outcome?

NOTES

[1] *Baldwin v. New York*, 399 U.S. 66 (1970).
[2] *McKeiver v. Pennsylvania*, 403 U.S. 528 (1971).
[3] *Williams v. Florida*, 399 U.S. 78 (1970).
[4] *Burch v. Louisiana*, 441 U.S. 130 (1979).
[5] *Smith v. Illinois*, 390 U.S. 129 (1968).
[6] *Brooks v. Tennessee*, 406 U.S. 605 (1972).
[7] *Estelle v. Williams*, 425 U.S. 501 (1976).
[8] *Stewart v. Corbin*, 850 F.2d 492 (9th Cir. 1988).
[9] *Barker v. Wingo*, 407 U.S. 514 (1972).
[10] *United States v. Marion*, 404 U.S. 307 (1971).
[11] 18 U.S.C. §3161.
[12] 18 U.S.C. §3162.
[13] See footnote number 9 infra.
[14] *Batson v. Kentucky*, 476 U.S. 79 (1986).
[15] F. R. Crim. P. 24(b).
[16] F. R. Crim. P. 32(c)(1).
[17] F. R. Crim. P. 32(c)(3).
[18] Breyer, *The Federal Sentencing Guidelines and the Key Compromises Upon Which They Rest*, 17 Hofstra L. Rev. 4 (1988).
[19] Federal Judges Association, *In Camera*, December, 1990.
[20] *Lockett v. Ohio*, 438 U.S. 586 (1978).
[21] *Coker v. Georgia*, 433 U.S. 584 (1977).
[22] *Ford v. Wainwright*, 477 U.S. 399 (1986).
[23] *Goldschmitt v. State of Florida*, 490 So.2d 123 (Fla. Dist. Ct. App. 1986), *rev. denied*, 496 So.2d 142 (1986).
[24] *McKane v. Durston*, 153 U.S. 684 (1894).
[25] F. R. Crim. P. 37.
[26] Supreme Court Rule 11.1.
[27] LaFave and Israel, *Criminal Procedure* (Hornbook Series, West: St. Paul, 1985) §26.2(c).

[28] *Gideon v. Wainwright,* 373 U.S. 335 (1963).

[29] *Jones v. Cunningham,* 371 U.S. 236 (1963) and *Hensley v. Municipal Court,* 411 U.S. 345 (1973).

[30] See *Rules Governing Section 2254 Cases in The United States District Courts* (Feb. 1989). These rules also contain the forms necessary to petition for habeas corpus relief in the district courts of the United States.

CHAPTER 12
Searches, Seizures, and Arrests

Constitutional law enforcement is effective law enforcement.

Harold Norris

OUTLINE

SECTION 12.1   THE FOURTH AMENDMENT

Searches, seizures, and arrests are vital aspects of law enforcement. Because they involve significant invasions of individual liberties, limits on their use can be found in the constitutions, statutes, and other laws of the states and federal government.

The most important limitation is the Fourth Amendment of the United States Constitution, which reads:

> The right of the people to be secure in their persons, papers and effects, against unreasonable searches and seizures, shall not be violated, and no warrants shall issue but upon probable cause, supported by oath or affirmation, and particularly describing the place to be searched and the persons or things to be seized.

There are two remedies available to the defendant whose Fourth Amendment rights have been violated by the government. First, in his criminal prosecution he may invoke the exclusionary rule. Second, he may have a civil cause of action against the offending officer under a civil rights statute or for a "constitutional tort."[1]

Note that the protections in the Bill of Rights only apply against the government. Evidence obtained by a private citizen, acting on her own, is not subject to the exclusionary rule. So, if Ira's neighbor illegally enters and searches his house, discovers evidence of a crime, and turns that evidence over to law enforcement, it may be used at trial. Of course, the result would be different if the neighbor was working under the direction of a government official.

The concepts of "reasonable expectation of privacy" and "probable cause" are important throughout the law of searches, seizures, and arrests. Accordingly, they will be examined first.

Section 12.1(a)   Privacy

Until 1967 the Fourth Amendment had been interpreted to protect "areas." For a violation of the Fourth Amendment to occur law-enforcement officers had to physically trespass upon the property of the defendant. This standard was changed in *Katz v. United States*, 389 U.S. 347 (1967).

KATZ V. UNITED STATES

389 U.S. 347 (1967)

The petitioner was convicted in the District Court for the Southern District of California under an eight-count indictment charging him with transmitting wagering information by telephone from Los Angeles to Miami and Boston, in violation of a federal statute. At trial the Government was permitted, over the petitioner's objection, to introduce evidence of the petitioner's end of telephone conversations, overheard by FBI agents who had attached an electronic listening and recording device to the outside of the public telephone booth from which he had placed his calls. In affirming his conviction, the Court of Appeals rejected the contention that the recordings had been obtained in violation of the Fourth Amendment, because "[t]here was no physical entrance into the area occupied by [the petitioner]." We granted certiorari in order to consider the constitutional questions thus presented.

The petitioner has phrased those questions as follows:

A. Whether a public telephone booth is a constitutionally protected area so that evidence obtained by attaching an electronic listening recording device to the top of such booth is obtained in violation of the right to privacy of the user of the booth.

B. Whether physical penetration of a constitutionally protected area is necessary before a search and seizure can be said to be violative of the Fourth Amendment to the United States Constitution.

We decline to adopt this formulation of the issues. In the first place, the correct solution of Fourth Amendment problems is not necessarily promoted by incantation of the phrase "constitutionally protected area." Secondly, the Fourth

Amendment cannot be translated into a general constitutional "right to privacy." That Amendment protects individual privacy against certain kinds of governmental intrusion, but its protections go further, and often have nothing to do with privacy at all. Other provisions of the Constitution protect personal privacy from other forms of governmental invasion. But the protection of a person's *general* right to privacy—his right to be left alone by other people—is, like the protection of property and of his very life, left largely to the law of the individual States.

Because of the misleading way the issues have been formulated, the parties have attached great significance to the charterization of the telephone booth from which the petitioner placed his calls. The petitioner has strenuously argued that the booth was a "constitutionally protected area." The Government has maintained with equal vigor that is was not. But this effort to decide whether or not a given "area," viewed in the abstract, is "constitutionally protected" deflects attention from the problem presented by this case. For the Fourth Amendment protects people, not places. What a person knowingly exposes to the public, even in his own home or office, is not a subject of Fourth Amendment protection. . . . But what he seeks to preserve as private, even in an area accessible to the public, may be constitutionally protected. . . .

The Government stresses the fact that the telephone booth from which the petitioner made his calls was constructed partly of glass, so that he was as visible after he entered it as he would have been if he had remained outside. But what he sought to exclude when he entered the booth was not the intruding eye—it was the uninvited ear. He did not shed his right to do so simply because he made his calls from a place where he might be seen. No less than an individual in a business office, in a friend's apartment, or in a taxicab, a person in a telephone booth may rely upon the protection of the Fourth Amendment. One who occupies it, shuts the door behind him, and pays the toll that permits him to place a call is surely entitled to assume that the words he utters into the mouthpiece will not be broadcast to the world. To read the Constitution more narrowly is to ignore the vital role that the public telephone has come to play in private communication.

The Government contends, however, that the activities of its agents in this case should not be tested by Fourth Amendment requirements, for the surveillance technique they employed involved no physical penetration of the telephone booth from which the petitioner placed his calls. It is true that the absence of such penetration was at one time thought to foreclose further Fourth Amendment inquiry . . . for that Amendment was thought to limit only searches and seizures of tangible property . . . we have since departed from the narrow view on which that decision rested. Indeed, we have expressly held that the Fourth Amendment governs not only the seizure of tangible items, but extends as well to the recording of oral statements, overheard without any "technical trespass under . . . local property law." *Silverman v. United States*, 365 U.S. 505, 511. Once this much is acknowledged, and once it is recognized that the Fourth Amendment protects people—and not simply "areas"—against unreasonable searches and seizures, it becomes clear that the reach of that Amendment cannot turn upon the presence or absence of a physical intrusion into any given enclosure.

We conclude that the underpinnings of [prior decisions] have been so eroded by our subsequent decisions that the "trespass" doctrine there enunciated can no longer be regarded as controlling. . . .
[The Court then held that the warrantless search was conducted in violation of the Fourth Amendment.]

The *Katz* **reasonable expectation of privacy** test continues to be the method of determining whether a search or seizure has occurred. Consistent with *Katz* the Supreme Court has defined a search as "when an expectation of privacy that society is prepared to consider reasonable is infringed." In the same opinion the Court defined a seizure as a "meaningful interference with an individual's possessory interest" in property.[2]

LEGAL TERMS

reasonable expectation of privacy
The legal standard for determining whether the Fourth Amendment comes into play. Government action that encroaches upon a person's reasonable expectation of privacy amounts to a search under the Fourth Amendment.

Section 12.1(b) Probable Cause

Section 12.1(b.1) Probable Cause Defined

The Fourth Amendment requires the existence of **probable cause** before warrants are to be issued. When a warrant is first obtained the probable cause determination is made by a judge. In those cases where a police officer acts without a warrant, it is the officer which makes that determination. In both cases, as you will see, probable cause is required.

Probable cause is a phrase describing the minimum amount of evidence necessary before a search, seizure, or arrest is proper. Whether the issue concerns a search and seizure or arrest, the same quantity of evidence is necessary to establish probable cause.

There is no one universal definition of probable cause. In fact, the definition of probable cause differs depending on the context. In all situations, it is more than mere suspicion and less than the standard required to prove a defendant guilty at trial (beyond a reasonable doubt). As the Supreme Court has expressed, probable cause is present when the trustworthy facts within the officer's knowledge are sufficient in themselves to justify a "person of reasonable caution" in the belief that seizable property would be found or that the person to be arrested committed the crime in question.[3]

Section 12.1(b.2) Sources Used to Establish Probable Cause

When making the probable cause determination an officer may rely on his own observations, hearsay evidence, and statements of witnesses, victims, and other law-enforcement officers. The act that evidence will be inadmissible at trial does not make it an improper source of information when considering probable cause.

However, innuendo or conjecture that is not supported by facts may not be considered. While the evidence does not have to rise to the level of being admissible at trial, it must have some credibility.

It is common for the police to depend on information from "informants" to obtain a search warrant. An informant is a person who has knowledge concerning a crime because of his involvement in crime. The reliability of such information (and whether it should be the basis of a warrant) is hotly debated.

In *Aguilar v. Texas,* 378 U.S. 108 (1964), the Supreme Court established a two-prong test for the use of such information (usually hearsay) when making a warrant determination. First, the affidavit had to contain information about the basis for the informant's information. This permitted the issuing judge to determine whether the informant's allegations were well founded.

Second, the officer had to provide the judge with his reasons for believing that the informant was reliable. This could be done, for example, by showing that the informant had been truthful in the past.

In *Illinois v. Gates,* 462 U.S. 213 (1983) the Court reversed position and adopted a "totality of the circumstances" test, thereby overruling *Aguilar.* However, the Court did not abandon the two prongs of *Aguilar.* While the two prongs are no longer determinative, they continue to be important factors when examining the "totality of the circumstances." The Court stated that:

> The task of the issuing magistrate is simply to make a practical, common-sense decision whether, given all the circumstances set forth in the affidavit before him, including the "veracity" and the "basis of knowledge" of persons supplying hearsay information, there is a fair probability that contraband or evidence of a crime will be found in a particular place.

Gates at 233. This test does not require that the officer name the informant in the application for warrant. All that is required is that the magistrate be given enough information to make his own determination concerning the credibility and reliability of the informant.

SECTION 12.2   SEARCHES AND SEIZURES

Section 12.2(a)   The Warrant Requirement

Depending upon the circumstances, a search may be conducted with or without a warrant. The Supreme Court has expressed that there is a strong preference for the use of warrants, when possible, over warrantless actions.[4] The warrant preference serves an important purpose: it protects citizens from overzealous law-enforcement practices.

> The presence of a search warrant serves a high function. Absent some grave emergency, the Fourth Amendment has interposed a magistrate between the citizen and police.

LEGAL TERMS

probable cause
The Fourth Amendment requires the existence of probable cause before a warrant for a search, seizure, or arrest may be issued. Warrantless arrests must also be supported by probable cause. Probable cause is a phrase describing a quantity of evidence greater than mere suspicion, but less than beyond a reasonable doubt.

This was done not to shield criminals nor to make the home a safe haven for illegal activities. It was done so that an objective mind might weigh the need to invade the privacy in order to enforce the law. The right of privacy was deemed too precious to entrust to the discretion of those whose job is the detection of crime and the arrest of criminals.

McDonald v. United States, 335 U.S. 451, 455–456 (1948). Accordingly, a search conducted pursuant to a valid search warrant is per se reasonable. Warrantless searches are permitted only in special circumstances, and it is the responsibility of the government to prove that the facts of the case fit into one of the exceptions to the warrant requirement.

In order to give this preference some "teeth," the Supreme Court, in *Aguilar v. Texas,* 378 U.S. 108, 111 (1964), announced that "when a search is based upon a magistrate's, rather than a police officer's determination of probable cause," reviewing courts are to accept lesser competent evidence than if the officer made the determination herself, so long as there was a "substantial basis" for the magistrate's decision. To say it another way: less evidence is required to sustain a search if a warrant was obtained prior to the search.

"Reviewing courts" are referred to because the determination that probable cause exists by a magistrate when issuing a warrant is not final. A defendant may later attack any evidence seized pursuant to a warrant through a motion to suppress. As stated, determinations by a magistrate are less likely to be overturned than those made by police officers.

The Supreme Court created an exception to the rule that evidence must be suppressed if seized pursuant to an invalid warrant in *United States v. Leon,* 468 U.S. 897 (1984), wherein it held that evidence seized by an officer who executed a search warrant with a good faith belief that the warrant was valid will not be excluded, even though the warrant is later determined invalid. If a warrant is facially invalid, then any fruits of a search thereof must be excluded, because an officer cannot in good faith believe that such a warrant is valid. Of course, if an officer uses false information to convince the magistrate that probable cause exists, the good faith exception does not apply. The same is true if an officer knows that the magistrate issuing the warrant is not neutral and detached.

Section 12.2(a.1) Requirements for Obtaining a Warrant

The Fourth Amendment enumerates the requirements that must be met before a warrant can be issued. It is the responsibility

AO 106 (Rev. 5/85) Affidavit for Search Warrant

United States District Court

_____ DISTRICT OF _____

In the Matter of the Search of
(Name, address or brief description of person or property to be searched)

**APPLICATION AND AFFIDAVIT
FOR SEARCH WARRANT**

CASE NUMBER:

I _____ being duly sworn depose and say:

I am a(n) _____ and have reason to believe
                              Official Title

that ☐ on the person of or ☐ on the premises known as (name, description and/or location)

In the _____ District of _____
there is now concealed a certain person or property, namely (describe the person or property)

which is (give alleged grounds for search and seizure under Rule 41(b) of the Federal Rules of Criminal Procedure)

in violation of Title _____ United States Code, Section(s) _____
The facts to support the issuance of a Search Warrant are as follows:

Continued on the attached sheet and made a part hereof.   ☐ Yes   ☐ No

_____
Signature of Affiant

Sworn to before me, and subscribed in my presence

_____ at _____
Date   City and State

_____   _____
Name and Title of Judicial Officer   Signature of Judicial Officer

**Application and
Affidavit for
Search Warrant**

of the law-enforcement officer requesting the warrant to establish these elements to the judge making the warrant determination. The form application for search warrant used in the federal courts appears above.

First, the evidence presented must establish probable cause to believe that within the area to be searched the items sought will be found. Second, there must be probable cause to believe that the items sought are connected to criminal activity.

Third, the area to be searched and any item to be seized must be described with particularity. The amount of specificity required varies from case to case. A warrant that authorizes a police officer to search a particular home for unauthorized contraband clearly violates the Fourth Amendment, while a warrant authorizing a search of the same home for a "nine-inch knife with an ivory handle" is valid, provided the warrant is valid in all other respects (probable cause, etc.).

Warrants issued for the seizure of items that are illegal in themselves do not need to be as particular as others. For example, a warrant to search for a book must be more specific than one for drugs. The description "book" is clearly insufficient, while a warrant to search for "cocaine" probably is not.

As to location, a street address is normally sufficient. If there is no street address, the warrant should describe the location, owner, color, and architectural style of the property. Of course, any additional information that aids in describing property should be included. If the building to be searched is an apartment building or similar multi-unit structure, the specific subunit to be searched must be stated in the warrant.

Fourth, the facts that are alleged to establish probable cause must be "supported by Oath or affirmation." In the typical case this means that the government will produce one or more affidavits to prove that a warrant is justified. Note that the example of an application for a search warrant provides space for a supporting affidavit.

Finally, the warrant must be issued by a neutral and detached magistrate. While judges are most commonly given the authority to issue warrants, a state may grant this authority to others. However, the Supreme Court has stated that the person authorized must be neutral and detached and be capable of determining whether probable cause exists.

Thus, a state law permitting a state's attorney general, who had investigated the crime and would later be responsible for its prosecution, to issue a warrant, was invalid.[5] In another case, a court clerk was found sufficiently detached, neutral, and capable to issue a warrant, since the clerk worked for a court and was under the supervision of a judge.[6]

Section 12.2(a.2) Scope of Warrants

Warrants may be issued to search and seize any item that constitutes evidence of a crime, is the fruit of a crime, is contraband, or is used to commit a crime.[7] A warrant may be issued to search or seize any place or property, whether belonging to a suspected criminal or an innocent third party.

The particularity requirement acts to limit the breadth of a search. If an officer searches beyond the scope of a warrant the exclusionary rule will make the fruits from the forbidden area inadmissible at trial.

In some circumstances the particularity requirement is heightened. For example, because of the importance of protecting the press from government intrusion, warrants to search newsrooms or similar areas must be drafted with "particular exactitude."[8] The same is true if a search will probe into confidential information, such as client records of attorneys and physicians.

As a general proposition, a warrant to search premises does not authorize the police to search the occupants of the premises.[9] Of course, a search may be conducted if an independent basis exists justifying the action. It is generally true that the occupants of an area to be searched may be detained until the search is complete.

Section 12.2(a.3) Executing the Warrant

The warrant may direct a particular officer or an entire unit of police officers to conduct the search. The language of the warrant itself contains the duties of the officers executing the warrant, as well as their limitations.

As a general proposition, warrants are to be executed during the day. This is because a nighttime search is considered to be more intrusive than a daytime search[10] and because the probability of resistance is greater at night.

To conduct a nighttime search a specific request for a warrant authorizing such must be made. To receive a warrant permitting a nighttime search an officer must present the magistrate with facts evidencing the necessity for a nighttime search; proof that a daytime search will not be successful. An anticipated nighttime delivery of illegal goods justifies a nighttime warrant, as does a concern that evidence of a crime is to be destroyed in the night.

Most states have statutes requiring that warrants be executed within a specific amount of time after issuance. Warrants issued under federal law must be executed within ten days of issuance.[11]

In all cases the search must be conducted when there is probable cause. If an officer fails to execute a warrant before probable cause has dissipated, then any resulting search is violative of the Fourth Amendment, and the fruits thereof are subject to the exclusionary rule. This is true even if the search is conducted within the period of time set by law.

At the premises of a search the police must announce their purpose and provide the warrant to the owner or occupant for review. This is true whether entry is gained through the use of

AO 93A (Rev. 5/85) Search Warrant Upon Oral Testimony ●

United States District Court

_____ DISTRICT OF _____

In the Matter of the Search of

(Name, address or brief description of person or property to be searched)

SEARCH WARRANT UPON ORAL TESTIMONY

CASE NUMBER:

TO: _____ and any Authorized Officer of the United States

Sworn oral testimony has been communicated to me by _____

                                                              Affiant

that ☐ on the person of or ☐ on the premises known as (name, description and/or location)

in the _____ District of _____ there is now
concealed a certain person or property, namely (describe the person or property)

I am satisfied that the circumstances are such as to make it reasonable to dispense with a written affidavit and that there is probable cause to believe that the property or person so described is concealed on the person or premises above described and that grounds for application for issuance of the search warrant exist as communicated orally to me in a sworn statement which has been recorded electronically, stenographically, or in long-hand and upon the return of the warrant, will be transcribed, certified as accurate and attached hereto.

YOU ARE HEREBY COMMANDED to search on or before _____

                                                                          Date

the person or place named above for the person or property specified, serving this warrant and making the search (in the daytime — 6:00 AM to 10:00 PM) (at anytime in the day or night as I find reasonable cause has been established) and if the person or property be found there to seize same, leaving a copy of this warrant and receipt for the person or property taken, and prepare a written inventory of the person or property seized and promptly return this warrant to _____
as required by law.   U.S. Judge or Magistrate

_____   at   _____
Date and Time Issued   City and State

_____   _____
Name and Title of Judicial Officer   Signature of Judicial Officer

I certify that on _____   at _____
                            Date   Time

_____ orally authorized the
              U.S. Judge or Magistrate

issuance and execution of a search warrant conforming to all the foregoing terms.

_____   _____   _____
Name of affiant   Signature of affiant   Exact time warrant executed

Search Warrant Upon Oral Testimony

force or not. However, to prevent the destruction of evidence or injury to the officers, judges may issue "no-knock" warrants if the facts indicate that one or the other is likely to occur.

After a search is completed the officers are required to inventory items seized. Federal rules require that the owner of the property be given a receipt for the goods taken.[12] Property unlawfully taken must be returned to the owner, unless it is unlawful in itself, such as drugs.

AO 93A (Rev. 5/85)   Search Warrant Upon Oral Testimony

RETURN

DATE WARRANT RECEIVED	DATE AND TIME WARRANT EXECUTED	COPY OF WARRANT AND RECEIPT FOR ITEMS LEFT WITH

INVENTORY MADE IN THE PRESENCE OF

INVENTORY OF PERSON OR PROPERTY TAKEN PURSUANT TO THE WARRANT

CERTIFICATION

I swear that this inventory is a true and detailed account of the person or property taken by me on the warrant.

_____

Subscribed, sworn to, and returned before me this date.

_____   _____
U.S. Judge or Magistrate   Date

Search Warrant Upon Oral Testimony
(continued)

Section 12.2(b) Exceptions to the Search Warrant Requirement

While the general rule is that a warrant must be obtained before a search may be undertaken, there are many exceptions. The exceptions to the warrant requirement are sometimes referred to as exigent circumstances.

Section 12.2(b.1) Consent Searches

A voluntary **consent** to a search obviates the warrant requirement. A person may consent to a search of their person or property. The scope of the search is limited by the person consenting. Absent special circumstances, a consent to search may be terminated at any time by the person giving consent.

A person's consent must be voluntary. All of the circumstances surrounding the consent are examined to determine whether the consent was voluntary. There is no requirement that police officers inform a person that he may refuse to consent.[13]

Of course, a defendant who is threatened or coerced into consenting has not voluntarily consented. It is not coercion for a person to be told that if he does not consent that a warrant will be obtained authorizing the desired search. It is coercion for officers to tell a person that if he does not consent to a search that a warrant will be obtained and the officers will ransack his home.[14]

Consent is invalid if it is obtained by a mistaken belief that the officer had a legal right to conduct the search. For example, if Officer Frisk tells Patty Patdown that he has a warrant, or that the law does not require that he have one, and she acquiesces, the search is invalid if he had no warrant or legal right to conduct the search.

The same is true when officers use fraud or deceit to obtain consent. For example, in one case a defendant was arrested and interrogated. He gave no incriminating information during the questioning. The following day the officers went to the home of the defendant and told his wife that he had confessed to the crime and had sent the police to seize the contraband. Based upon these statements the defendant's wife consented to a search by the officers. The state court found that this tactic led to an involuntary consent and that the evidence seized was inadmissible at trial.[15]

The facts of that case raise another issue: third-party consent. This arises often in cases where many people share a single dwelling or room, such as families, fraternities, and dorms. In *United States v. Matlock*, 415 U.S. 164 (1974), the Supreme Court found that a third party may consent as long as the parties share access, control, and use of the property. If co-inhabitants section off a dwelling, each tenant having exclusive control over a specific area, then only the tenant using an area may consent. If there are closets, desks, or similar areas which are reserved for one person's private use, only that person may consent.

Having a property interest in property does not give one a right to consent to a search of the property. The Supreme Court has said that neither landlords nor hotel managers may consent to the search of their tenants' rooms.[16] They may have a property interest, but the privacy interest rests with the tenants.

Section 12.2(b.2) Plain View

Another exception to the warrant requirement is the **plain view doctrine**. Under this rule, a warrantless seizure of evidence by an officer who is lawfully in a position to see the evidence is valid.

COOLIDGE V. NEW HAMPSHIRE

403 U.S. 443 (1971)

* * *

It is well established that under certain circumstances the police may seize evidence in plain view without a warrant. But it is important to keep in mind that, in the vast majority of cases, *any* evidence seized by the police will be in plain view, at least at the moment of seizure. The problem with the "plain view" doctrine has been to identify the circumstances in which plain view has legal significance rather than being simply the normal concomitant of any search, legal or illegal.

An example of the applicability of the "plain view" doctrine is the situation in which the police have a warrant to search a given area for specified objects, and in the course of the search come across some other article of incriminating character. . . . Where the initial intrusion that brings the police within plain view of such an article is supported, not by a warrant, but by one of the recognized exceptions to the warrant requirement, the seizure is also legitimate. Thus, the police may inadvertently come across evidence while in "hot pursuit" of a fleeing suspect. . . . And an object that comes into view during a search incident to arrest that is appropriately limited in scope under existing law may be seized without a warrant. . . . Finally, the "plain view" doctrine has been applied where a police officer is not searching for evidence against the accused, but nonetheless inadvertently comes across incriminating evidence. . . .

LEGAL TERMS

consent searches
A person may waive her Fourth Amendment right to a search warrant. The consent must be voluntary, and the person consenting must have an interest in the property for the consent to be valid. There must be more than a mere property interest; the consenting party must have rights of control and use of the property.

plain view
An officer, who is in a location where he has a right to be, may seize evidence which falls into his plain view.

What the "plain view" cases have in common is that the police officer in each of them had a prior justification for an intrusion in the course of which he came inadvertently across a piece of evidence incriminating the accused. . . . Of course, the extension of the original justification is legitimate only where it is immediately apparent to the police that they have evidence before them; the "plain view" doctrine may not be used to extend a general exploratory search from one object to another until something incriminating at last emerges. . . .

A large body of cases discuss the plain view doctrine. From those cases it can be gleaned that for a seizure to be lawful under the doctrine, the following must be shown: 1. The officer must lawfully be in an area 2. from which the object to be seized is in plain view 3. and the officer does in fact, but inadvertently, see the item 4. and there must be probable cause to believe the object is connected to a crime.

First, the officer must be in a place where he has a right to be. An officer, as is true of anyone, has a right to be in public places. So, evidence seen in a public park, on the street, or in a business open to the public may be seized without a warrant.

Evidence located on private property is different. As a general rule, the police have no right to enter private property to seize evidence which was in plain view from a public area. In such cases the officer is expected to obtain a warrant; the officer's observation providing the requisite probable cause. However, if an exception exists, i.e., to prevent the destruction of the evidence, the officer may immediately seize the evidence.

If an officer is on private property for a lawful reason, then the officer may seize evidence in plain view without first obtaining a warrant. There are many reasons that an officer may be in a position to see evidence. Many of these were discussed in *Coolidge*. An officer who has to enter a home to execute an arrest warrant is not expected to overlook illegal objects in plain sight. The same is true if the officer is executing a search warrant, is in hot pursuit, is responding to an emergency, or is conducting a stop and frisk.

An officer who sees evidence because he has gone beyond the scope of his right violates the Fourth Amendment, and the plain view doctrine will not support a seizure. For example, if an officer has a warrant to search a defendant's garage, any evidence obtained, even if in plain view, from the defendant's home may not be used at trial.

Second, the evidence seized must be in plain sight or plain view. Only the sense of sight may be used to establish plain view. Of course, whether an item is in plain sight depends on the scope of the officer's authority. An officer who has a search warrant authorizing the search of a closet for a gun may seize cocaine lying on the floor of the closet. The same is not true if the warrant did not authorize a search of the closet. In any case, the item must be plainly visible from a place where the officer has a right to be.

If an officer moves something with the intent of gaining a better vantage of the item, it is not in plain view. In one case, the movement of a stereo to record its serial number was considered an illegal search, since the officers were on the premises for another reason. The Court noted in that case that merely observing the stereo, which was in plain view, was legal. If the serial number had been visible without moving the stereo, then recording its number would not have been violative of the Fourth Amendment. But moving the stereo constituted a "new invasion" of the defendant's rights.[17]

Officers may use mechanical or electrical aids in seeing evidence, so long as they are in a place they have a right to be and they are not conducting a search (encroaching on someone's right to privacy). Flashlights and binoculars are examples of such aids.

Third, the discovery must be inadvertent. If an officer has probable cause to believe that evidence will be found, a warrant must be obtained or a warrant exception must exist before a seizure will be upheld. In *Coolidge,* at 470–471, the Court stated that:

> [T]he discovery of evidence in plain view must be inadvertant. The rationale of the exception to the warrant requirement, as just stated, is that a plain-view seizure will not turn an initially valid (and therefore limited) search into a "general" one, while the inconvenience of procuring a warrant to cover an inadvertent discovery is great. But where the discovery is anticipated, where the police know in advance that location of the evidence and intend to seize it, the situation is altogether different. The requirement of a warrant imposes no inconvenience whatever. . . .

Finally, the officer must have probable cause to believe that the object is subject to seizure. Contraband (an item which is illegal itself, such as drugs) can be seized, as can property used to commit crimes, which has been used in a crime, or which has been stolen.

Section 12.2(b.3) Motor Vehicles

Automobiles are protected by the Fourth Amendment. However, the Supreme Court has refused to extend full Fourth Amendment protection to people in automobiles. The Court's rationale for decreased protection is twofold. First, because of the mobile nature of vehicles, they can be moved quickly. Second, they are used on the public roads where they and their occupants are visible to the public; as such, a person has a lesser expectation of privacy.

In *Carroll v. United States,* 267 U.S. 132 (1925), it was announced that a warrantless search of a vehicle stopped on a public road is reasonable, provided that the officer has probable cause to believe that an object subject to seizure will be found in the vehicle. The existence of probable cause is the key to such a search. This authority has been extended to permit the search to continue after the vehicle has been impounded.[18]

The sticky question in this area is: what is the scope of this right to search? Generally, the officer is given the scope that a magistrate would have if a warrant were sought. So, if an officer has probable cause to believe that a shotgun used in a crime will be found in the car, a search of the glove box is improper. The opposite would be true if the item sought was a piece of jewelry, such as a ring.

Officers may also search closed items found in the vehicle, provided that probable cause exists to believe that the item sought may be contained therein. The same rules apply as above. Rifling through a suitcase found in a car in search of a stolen painting, which is larger than the suitcase, is unreasonable and violative of the Fourth Amendment. Once the sought-after evidence is found the search must cease.

Section 12.2(b.4) Inventory Searches

Police officers may impound vehicles whenever the driver or owner is arrested. Impoundment means towing the vehicle to a garage or parking lot for storage.

While the decision to impound a vehicle is generally left to the discretion of the police officer, an officer may not refuse a less-intrusive manner of caring for the vehicle. For example, if a husband and wife are riding together, and the husband is arrested for drunk driving, the wife is to be permitted to drive the vehicle home, provided she is capable.

Once impounded, an inventory search may be conducted. The purpose of an inventory search is to protect the owner of the vehicle from vandalism, protect the safety of the officers and others, and to protect the police department from claims of theft.

Since inventory searches are not conducted with an intent to discover evidence, there is no requirement of probable cause. If the facts of a case show that the police impounded a vehicle for the purpose of searching it, the search is improper.

Inventory searches are limited in scope. While it is reasonable to search unlocked glove compartments and trunks, it is unreasonable under the Fourth Amendment if they are locked. A search of a vehicle's seats, floor area, and dashboard are routine. The Supreme Court has also stated that closed items found in impounded vehicles are subject to inventory searches in *Colorado v. Bertine*, 479 U.S. 367 (1986).

To avoid arbitrary inventory searches police departments are expected, if not required, to establish an inventory search policy and procedure. All items discovered during an inventory search are to be recorded.

Section 12.2(b.5) Border Searches

Unlike ordinary searches, searches at the border of the United States do not require probable cause. Border searches must, however, comply with the reasonableness requirement of the Fourth Amendment.[19]

Searches of luggage and other items never require suspicion, nor do general searches of the person. However, more intrusive seaches, i.e., strip and bodily cavity searches, do require some suspicion before they may be conducted.

Federal statute permits border patrol officers to search vehicles at or near the borders of the United States that are believed to be transporting illegal aliens. 8 U.S.C. §1357(a).

Section 12.2(b.6) Search Incident to Arrest

Two search issues arise during and immediately following an arrest. First, may officers search the arrestee's person without first obtaining a warrant? Second, may officers search the arrestee's home, apartment, or other structure where the defendant is arrested?

The issue of searching the defendant's person was addressed in *United States v. Robinson*, 414 U.S. 260 (1973), where the Court held that after a lawful arrest, the defendant's person may be fully searched without first obtaining a warrant. The Court held that to require officers to obtain a warrant would needlessly endanger their lives and would increase the possibility of evidence being destroyed by the defendant. Search incident to arrest includes a search of the defendant's clothing. There is no probable cause requirement for a search incident to arrest.

The second issue concerns searching the area where the defendant is arrested. The premier case in this area is *Chimel v. California*, 395 U.S. 752 (1969).

CHIMEL V. CALIFORNIA

395 U.S. 752 (1969)

This case raises basic questions concerning the permissible scope under the Fourth Amendment of a search incident to a lawful arrest.

The relevant facts are essentially undisputed. Late in the afternoon of September 13, 1965, three police officers arrived at the Santa Ana, California, home of the petitioner with a warrant authorizing his arrest for the burglary of a coin shop. The officers knocked on the door, identified themselves to the petitioner's wife, and asked if they might come inside. She ushered them into the house, where they waited 10 to 15 minutes until the petitioner returned home from work. When the petitioner entered the house, one of the officers handed him the arrest warrant and asked for permission to "look around." The petitioner objected, but was advised that "on the basis of the lawful arrest," the officers would nonetheless conduct the search. No search warrant had been issued.

Accompanied by the petitioner's wife, the officers then looked through the entire three-bedroom house, including the attic, the garage, and a small workshop. In some rooms the search was relatively cursory. In the master bedroom and sewing room, however, the officers directed the petitioner's wife to open drawers and "to physically remove contents of the drawers from side to side so that [they] might view items that would have come from [the] burglary." After completing the search, they seized numerous items—primarily coins, but also several medals, tokens, and a few other objects. The entire search took between 45 minutes and an hour. . . .

. . . When an arrest is made, it is reasonable for the arresting officer to search the person arrested in order to remove any weapons that the latter might seek to use in order to resist arrest or effect his escape. Otherwise, the officer's safety might well be endangered, and the arrest itself frustrated. In addition, it is entirely reasonable for the arresting officer to search for and seize any evidence on the arrestee's person in order to prevent its concealment or destruction. And the area into which an arrestee might reach in order to grab a weapon or evidentiary items must, of course, be governed by a like rule. A gun on a table or in a drawer in front of one who is arrested can be as dangerous to the arresting officer as one concealed in the clothing of the person arrested. There is ample justification, therefore, for a search of the arrestee's person and the area "within his immediate control"—construing that phrase to mean the area from within which he might gain possession of a weapon or destructible evidence.

There is no comparable justification, however, for routinely searching any room other than that in which an arrest occurs—or, for that matter, for searching through all the desk drawers or other closed or concealed areas in the room itself. Such searches, in the absense of well-recognized exceptions, may be made only under the authority of a search warrant. . . .

Application of sound Fourth Amendment principles to the facts of this case produces a clear result. . . . The scope of the search was . . . "unreasonable" under the Fourth and Fourteenth Amendments, and the petitioner's conviction cannot stand.

Reversed.

Chimel significantly changed the law, as before *Chimel* was decided officers had the authority to search a much greater area as incident to arrest. The "within the defendant's immediate control" test continues to be the governing law. As with any other lawful search and seizure, any evidence obtained may be used to prosecute the defendant.

A related concept, the protective sweep, was given constitutional recognition in *Maryland v. Buie,* 494 U.S.____ (1990). A protective sweep is a brief and limited warrantless search of an arrestee's home, which is permitted if the defendant is arrested therein. The purpose of the protective sweep is to check the house for other persons who may pose a danger to the arresting officers.

Section 12.2(b.7) Preservation of Evidence

In some instances evidence may be destroyed before a warrant can be obtained. In such cases an officer may make a warrantless search and seizure.

While the typical case involves the destruction of evidence, the preservation of evidence theory also has been applied to evanescent evidence (evidence that may vanish on its own). For example, in *Schmerber v. California*, 384 U.S. 757 (1966), a defendant, who was arrested for drunk driving, was subjected to a warrantless blood alcohol test. The Court concluded that the warrantless test was reasonable under the Fourth Amendment.

> The officer in the present case, however, might reasonably have believed that he was confronted with an emergency, in which the delay necessary to obtain a warrant, under the circumstances, threatened "the destruction of evidence.". . . We are told that the percentage of alcohol in the blood begins to diminsh shortly after drinking stops, as the body functions to eliminate it from the system. Particularly in a case such as this, where time had to be taken to bring the accused to the hospital and to investigate the scene of the accident, there was no time to seek out a magistrate and secure a warrant. Given these special facts, we conclude that the attempt to secure evidence of blood-alcohol content in this case was an appropriate incident to petitioner's arrest.

Schmerber at 770–71. So, any evidence that may be destroyed, intentionally or not, before a warrant can be obtained, can be the foundation of a warrantless search and seizure under the preservation of evidence exception to the Fourth Amendment's warrant requirement.

Section 12.2(b.8) Emergency Searches and Hot Pursuit

One of the many responsibilities of being a police officer is to respond to emergencies and to assist those in danger. Police officers are permitted to enter areas protected by the Fourth Amendment without a warrant if there is an emergency.

An officer may respond to cries for help from within a home or may enter a building that is on fire to assist fire-fighters. The possibilities are endless. Provided the officer has a genuine and reasonable belief that there is an emergency, the entry does not violate the Fourth Amendment. Of course, once inside any evidence in plain view may be seized.

Similar to the emergency exception is the hot pursuit exception. An officer who is chasing a suspect does not have to end the pursuit at the door of a home or business. The normally unlawful entry into the structure is permitted to catch the defendant. Again, once inside the plain view exception applies.

Section 12.2(b.9) Open Fields

The Open Fields Doctrine is not, technically, an exception to the search warrant requirement. That is because to be an exception to the Fourth Amendment warrant requirement, the Fourth Amendment must apply to the conduct of the officers. The Supreme Court has held that the "open fields" around one's home are not protected by the Fourth Amendment, so officers are free to intrude upon such areas without first obtaining a warrant. In addition, officers will not be liable for trespass if they make such an intrusion while performing a lawful duty.[20]

The reason that open fields are not protected is because of the language of the Fourth Amendment itself: "The right of the people to be secure in their house, papers, and effects. . . ." The Supreme Court has found that this extends the Fourth Amendment's protection only to a person's home and the curtilage of that home.

Curtilage is the area directly around one's home. It is treated as part of the home, as the Court has recognized that a person's privacy interest does not end at the front door of the home. Determining whether an area is curtilage, and protected, or an open field, and unprotected, can be troublesome. In *United States v. Dunn*, 480 U.S. 294 (1987), the High Court held that a barn that was located sixty yards from a house was not within the curtilage, even though a fence enclosed the barn. In that opinion the Court stated four factors that should be considered when making an open fields determination. Those are:

1. The proximity of the area claimed to be curtilage from the home.
2. Whether the area enclosed is enclosed with the home.
3. The nature of the use of the area.
4. The attempts of the residents to keep the area private.

The closer the area in question is to the home, the fact that it is enclosed by fencing, that it is commonly used by the residents, and that the residents have taken measures to assure privacy in the area, all increase the probability that the area will be determined to be curtilage. The issue is whether the residents have a reasonable expectation of privacy in the area.

The advent of aerial surveillance has made it possible for law-enforcement officers to see what were once remote areas. The question in the Fourth Amendment context is, do people have a reasonable expectation of privacy in areas observable from aircraft?

One federal district court outlined five factors to be considered when examining the validity of aerial surveillance:

1. The height of the aircraft.
2. The size of the objects viewed.
3. The nature of the use of the area.
4. The number of flights over the area.
5. The frequency and duration of the aerial surveillance.

United States v. Bassford, 601 F.Supp. 1324, 1330 (D.Ma. 1985). Structures, even though in an open field, may be protected if it appears that one took measures to assure privacy.[21] However, the fact that an area is curtilage does not mean that a warrantless aerial observation is unreasonable. In *California v. Ciraolo*, 476 U.S. 207 (1986) the Supreme Court upheld an aerial observation of a backyard that was surrounded by a fence and not visible from the street.

Finally, although the Fourth Amendment speaks of "houses," its protection extends to businesses and other structures as well. However, it is likely that the expectation of privacy will be less in a business than in a dwelling.

Section 12.2(b.10) Stop and Frisk

On October 31, 1963, a Cleveland, Ohio, police detective observed three men standing on a street corner. Suspicious of the men, the detective positioned himself in order to watch their behavior. After some time the officer concluded that the men were "casing a job, a stick-up."

The officer approached the men, identified himself, and asked them to identify themselves. After the men "mumbled something," the officer grabbed one of the men and conducted a frisk, or a pat-down, of the man's clothing. The officer felt a pistol in the man's coat pocket. He removed the gun from his coat and then "patted down" the other two men. Another gun was discovered during those frisks.

The officer testified that he conducted the frisks because he believed the men were carrying weapons. The first man frisked was defendant Terry. At trial he was convicted of carrying a concealed weapon and was subsequently sentenced to one to three years in prison. His appeal made it to the United States Supreme Court.

In *Terry v. Ohio*, 392 U.S. 1 (1968) the Supreme Court was confronted with these issues: Did the officer's behavior amount to a search or seizure under the Fourth Amendment? If so, was the search or seizure of the officer reasonable?

The Court decided that defendant Terry had been seized under the Fourth Amendment. "It must be recognized that whenever a police officer accosts an individual and restrains his freedom to walk away, he has 'seized' that person." As to the frisk the Court stated that "it is nothing less than sheer torture of the English language to suggest that a careful exploration of the outer surfaces of a person's clothing all over his or her body in an attempt to find weapons is not a search."

With these statements the Court made it clear that the police practice of stopping and frisking people is one governed by the Fourth Amendment. However, the Court then concluded that an exception to the probable cause requirement was justified because the intrusion upon a person's privacy is limited in a stop and frisk, as opposed to an arrest and full search.

Officers are not given carte blanche to stop and frisk. Although probable suspicion is not required, officers must have a "reasonable suspicion" that the person to be stopped has committed, is committing, or is about to commit a crime. The officer's suspicion must be supported by "specific and articulable facts which, taken together with rational inferences from those facts, reasonably warrant that intrusion." *Terry* at 21. An officer's intuition alone is not enough suspicion to support a *Terry* seizure.

Not all contacts between an officer and a citizen amount to a seizure. In *United States v. Mendenhall*, 446 U.S. 544 (1980), it was stated that a seizure occurs anytime a reasonable person believes that she is not free to leave. There need not be an attempt to leave. A person may feel restrained by physical contact from a police officer, tone of voice, threatening language, or the threatening presence of many officers.

Mere questioning of a citizen by a police officer does not rise to the level of a detention. However, if the interrogation becomes accusatory or its duration lengthy, the Fourth Amendment may come into play. A Texas statute that required an individual to comply with a police officer's order to identify himself, even though there was no basis to believe criminal activity was afoot, was found unconstitutional in the following case.

BROWN V. TEXAS

443 U.S. 47 (1979)

This appeal presents the question whether appellant was validly convicted for refusing to comply with a policeman's demand that he identify himself pursuant to a provision of the Texas Penal Code which makes it a crime to refuse such identification on request.

I

At 12:45 in the afternoon of December 9, 1977, Officers Venegas and Sotelo of the El Paso Police Department were cruising in a patrol car. They observed appellant and another man walking in opposite directions away from one another in an alley. Although the two men were a few feet apart when they first were seen, Officer Venegas later testified that both officers believed the two had been together or were about to meet until the patrol car appeared.

The car entered the alley, and Officer Venegas got out and asked appellant to identify himself and explain what he was doing there. The other man was not questioned or detained. The officer testified that he stopped the appellant because the situation "looked suspicious and we had never seen the subject in that area before." The area of El Paso where appellant was stopped has a high incidence of drug traffic. However, the officers did not claim to suspect appellant of any specific misconduct, nor did they have any reason to believe that he was armed.

Appellant refused to identify himself and angrily asserted that the officers had no right to stop him. Officer Venegas replied that he was in a "high drug problem area"; Officer Sotelo then "frisked" appellant, but found nothing.

When appellant continued to refuse to identify himself, he was arrested for violation of Tex. Penal Code Ann. . . .

In the absence of any basis for suspecting appellant of misconduct, the balance between the public interest and appellant's right to personal security and privacy tilts in favor of freedom from police interference. The Texas statute under which appellant was stopped and required to identify himself is designed to advance weighty social objectives in large metropolitan centers: prevention of crime. But even assuming that purpose is served to some degree by stopping and demanding identification from an individual without any specific basis for believing he is involved in criminal activity, the guarantees of the Fourth Amendment do not allow it. When such a stop is not based on objective criteria, the risk of arbitrary and abusive police practices exceeds tolerable limits. . .

The application of [the Texas law] to detain appellant and require him to identify himself violated the Fourth Amendment because officers lacked any reasonable suspicion to believe appellant was engaged or had engaged in criminal conduct. Accordingly, appellant may not be punished for refusing to identify himself, and the conviction is reversed.

The stopping of a vehicle does fall within the reach of the Fourth Amendment. However, the Supreme Court has said that once a person is lawfully pulled over he or she may be ordered out of the vehicle, even though there is no reason to believe that the driver is a threat.

In addition to requiring reasonable suspicion, the *Terry* Court also stated that stops are to "last no longer than is necessary," and the investigative methods employed during the stop should be the "least intrusive means reasonably available to verify or dispel the officer's suspicion in a short period of time." If an officer detains a person longer than necessary, the investigatory detention turns into a full seizure (arrest), and the probable cause requirement of the Fourth Amendment commences.

Florida v. Royer, 460 U.S. 491 (1983) provides an example of the distinction between an investigatory detention and an arrest. The defendant, a suspected drug dealer, was questioned in a public area of an airport. After a few minutes he was taken forty feet to a small police office, where he consented to a search of his luggage. The Court concluded that the search was the product of an illegal arrest, as less-intrusive methods of investigation were available. As alternatives, the Court mentioned that the officers could have used narcotics dogs to inspect the luggage or could have immediately requested consent to search the defendant's luggage. The act of requiring the defendant to accompany the officers to a small room forty feet away transformed the detention from a *Terry* stop to an arrest, which was violative of the Fourth Amendment because it was not supported by probable cause.

The fact that there has been a lawful stop does not itself justify a frisk. The purpose behind permitting investigatory stops is the advancement of crime detection and prevention. Frisks, on the other hand, are permitted to protect officers and others from the person stopped.

To conduct a frisk an officer must have a reasonable belief that the person is armed and dangerous. Again, the officer must be able to point to facts to support this conclusion. An officer may draw on his experience as a police officer in making the decision. Again, however, intuition (suspicion not supported by any facts) alone is not adequate.

Full searches require probable cause. A *Terry* frisk requires less, and, accordingly, the permitted intrusion is less. The search must be limited to the outer clothing. A search of interior clothing or pockets is improper.

If the defendant is in an automobile, the officer may search those areas within the person's immediate control.[22] Once any lawful stop of a vehicle is made the driver may be ordered out of the vehicle. However, to frisk an occupant of a vehicle, the *Terry* standard must be met.

If during a pat-down an officer feels an item that may be a weapon, then the officer may reach into the clothing of the citizen to seize the item. Any item seized, whether a weapon, contraband, or other item associated with a crime, may be used as evidence.

If the officer does not feel an item that may be a weapon, the search can go no further. This is true even if the officer feels what is possibly evidence of another crime, such as feeling a bag that contains marijuana.

SECTION 12.3 ARREST

One of the most serious interferences with a person's liberty is to be physically seized by a government. Equally, arrest plays an important role in effective law enforcement.

Because of the significant impact arrest has on a person's life, the right to arrest is limited by the Fourth Amendment.

Section 12.3(a) Defining Arrest

Generally, an arrest is a deprivation of freedom by a legal authority. As you have already learned, seizures by the police take on two primary forms. First, at the lower end of the spectrum is the *Terry v. Ohio* seizure. Such seizures occur whenever a person reasonably believes that he is not free to leave. In addition, the seizure must be as brief as possible and be of limited intrusion to the person detained.

Any seizure that goes beyond the *Terry* standard is an arrest. A *Terry* investigatory detention may be transformed into an arrest if the person is detained for an unreasonable length of time or the police use intrusive investigatory tactics. Whether an officer intends to arrest is not dispositive, nor is an announcement to the citizen that he is or is not under arrest. The totality of the facts will determine whether the intrusion amounts to an arrest under the Fourth Amendment.

The requirements for a *Terry* stop were discussed previously in this chapter. Below is a discussion of the Fourth Amendment requirements for arrest.

Section 12.3(b) The Warrant Preference

Searches must be conducted pursuant to a valid warrant, unless an exception to the warrant requirement can be shown. Arrests are quite different. Rather than a requirement for a warrant, in most instances, there is simply a preference for one. The "informed and deliberate determinations of magistrates empowered to issue warrants . . . are to be preferred over the hurried action of officers."[23] As is the case with warrantless searches, probable cause determinations by magistrates will be supported on appeal with less evidence than those made by police officers.

Despite the preference, most arrests are made without first obtaining a warrant. The authority to make warrantless arrests has a long history. Under the common law, a law officer could arrest whenever he had reasonable grounds to believe that a defendant committed a felony. Misdemeanants who breached the peace could be arrested without warrant if the crime was committed in the presence of an officer.

It was in *United States v. Watson*, 423 U.S. 411 (1976), where the Supreme Court recognized that warrantless arrests in public places, based upon probable cause, did not violate the Fourth Amendment. There is no constitutional requirement that an officer obtain a warrant to effect an arrest in a public place—even if the officer has adequate time to get the warrant prior to making the arrest. However, the Fourth Amendment does require that probable cause exist before an arrest can be made.

For a warrantless arrest in a public place to be upheld it must be shown that the officer who made the arrest had: 1. probable cause to believe that a crime was committed and 2. that the

AO 442 (Rev. 5/85) Warrant for Arrest

United States District Court

_____ DISTRICT OF _____

UNITED STATES OF AMERICA
V.

WARRANT FOR ARREST

CASE NUMBER:

To: The United States Marshal
   and any Authorized United States Officer

YOU ARE HEREBY COMMANDED to arrest _____
Name

and bring him or her forthwith to the nearest magistrate to answer a(n)

☐ Indictment ☐ Information ☐ Complaint ☐ Order of court ☐ Violation Notice ☐ Probation Violation Petition

charging him or her with (brief description of offense)

in violation of Title _____ United States Code, Section(s) _____

Name of Issuing Officer   Title of Issuing Officer

Signature of Issuing Officer   Date and Location

(By) Deputy Clerk

Bail fixed at $ _____ by _____
                                              Name of Judicial Officer

RETURN
This warrant was received and executed with the arrest of the above-named defendant at _____

DATE RECEIVED	NAME AND TITLE OF ARRESTING OFFICER	SIGNATURE OF ARRESTING OFFICER
DATE OF ARREST		

Warrant for Arrest

person arrested committed that crime. As with searches and seizures, probable cause can be established in a number of ways: statements from victims and witnesses; personal knowledge and observations of the officer; reliable hearsay; and informant tips.

Most, if not all, states permit officers to arrest without a warrant if there is probable cause to believe that the suspect committed a felony. States vary in their treatment of misdemeanors, but most only permit warrantless arrest for a misdemeanor

AO 442 (Rev. 5/85) Warrant for Arrest

THE FOLLOWING IS FURNISHED FOR INFORMATION ONLY:

DEFENDANT'S NAME:_____

ALIAS: _____

LAST KNOWN RESIDENCE: _____

LAST KNOWN EMPLOYMENT: _____

PLACE OF BIRTH: _____

DATE OF BIRTH: _____

SOCIAL SECURITY NUMBER: _____

HEIGHT: _____   WEIGHT: _____

SEX: _____   RACE: _____

HAIR: _____   EYES: _____

SCARS, TATTOOS, OTHER DISTINGUISHING MARKS: _____

_____

_____

FBI NUMBER: _____

COMPLETE DESCRIPTION OF AUTO: _____

_____

INVESTIGATIVE AGENCY AND ADDRESS: _____

_____

_____

_____

Warrant for Arrest (continued)

committed in an officer's presence. Some states have a broader rule which permits the arrest of a misdemeanant, even if the crime was not committed in the presence of an officer, provided there is both probable cause and an exigent circumstance.

An officer's determination of probable cause may later be attacked by the defendant. If the officer was wrong, then the defendant may be successful in obtaining his freedom or suppressing any evidence which is the fruit of the illegal arrest.

In those cases when an officer does seek an arrest warrant, the requirements previously discussed concerning search warrants apply. That is, the warrant must be issued by a neutral and detached magistrate upon a finding of probable cause, supported by oath or affirmation.

Section 12.3(c) Arrests in Protected Areas

So far the discussion of arrests has been confined to arrests made in public. If the arrest is to be made in an area protected by the Fourth Amendment, such as a person's home, a warrant must be obtained, unless an exception exists.

In *Payton v. New York*, 445 U.S. 573 (1980), it was held that a valid arrest warrant implicitly carries with it a limited right to enter the suspect's home to effect the arrest, provided there is reason to believe the suspect is within. Under *Payton*, the search must be limited to those areas where the suspect may be hiding. Since the entry is lawful, any evidence discovered in plain view may be seized.

Arrest warrants do not authorize the entry into the private property of third persons. In the absence of consent or exigent circumstances, a search warrant must be obtained before a search of a third person's home or property may be conducted.[24]

The warrant requirement is obviated if the occupant gives her consent to the search. Exigent circumstances, such as hot pursuit, also justify warrantless entries into homes to effect an arrest.

Section 12.3(d) Search Incident to Arrest and the Protective Sweep

As you learned earlier in this chapter, an officer may search an arrestee fully as incident to arrest. In addition, the area within the arrestee's immediate control may also be searched. The scope of a search incident to arrest, however, is limited to those areas where a weapon may be obtained by the person arrested. Clearly, a search of any room other than the one where a defendant is being held is not supported by the search incident to arrest doctrine.

The search incident to arrest doctrine does not consider the possibility that other potentially dangerous people may be present, but out of sight, when an arrest is made. Must police take the risk that no other dangerous people are on the premises when making a lawful arrest? This question was answered by the Supreme Court in *Maryland v. Buie*, 494 U.S. _____ (1990).

MARYLAND V. BUIE

494 U.S. ___ (1990)

A "protective sweep" is a quick and limited search of a premises, incident to an arrest and conducted to protect the safey of police officers or others. It is narrowly confined to a cursory visual inspection of those places in which a person might be hiding. In this case we must decide what level of justification is required by the Fourth and Fourteenth Amendments before police officers, while effecting the arrest of a suspect in his home pursuant to an arrest warrant, may conduct a warrantless protective sweep of all or part of the premises. . . .

On February 3, 1986, two men committed an armed robbery of a Godfather's Pizza restaurant in Prince George's County, Maryland. One of the robbers was wearing a red running suit. The same day, Prince George's County police obtained arrest warrants for respondent Jerome Edward Buie and his suspected accomplice in the robbery, Lloyd Allen. Buie's house was placed under police surveillance.

On February 5, the police executed the arrest warrant for Buie. They first had a police department secretary telephone Buie's house to verify that he was home. The secretary spoke to a female first, then to Buie himself. Six or seven officers proceeded to Buie's house. Once inside, the officers fanned out through the first and second floors. Corporal James Rozar announced that he would "freeze" the basement so that no one could come up and surprise the officers. With his service revolver drawn, Rozar twice shouted into the basement, ordering anyone down there to come out. When a voice asked who was calling, Rozar announced three times: "this is the police, show me your hands." App. 5. Eventually, a pair of hands appeared around the bottom of the stairwell and Buie emerged from the basement. He was arrested, searched, and handcuffed by Rozar. Thereafter, Detective Joseph Frolich entered the basement "in case there was someone else" down there. . . . He noticed a red running suit lying in plain view on a stack of clothing and seized it.

The trial court denied Buie's motion to suppress the running suit, stating in part: "The man comes out from a basement, the police don't know how many other people are down there." . . .

It goes without saying that the Fourth Amendment bars only unreasonable searches and seizures. . . .our cases show that in determining reasonableness, we have balanced the intrusion on the individual's Fourth Amendment interests against its promotion of legitimate governmental interests. . . . Under this test, a search of the house or office is generally not reasonable without a warrant issued on probable cause. There are other contexts, however, where the public interest is such that neither a warrant nor probable cause is required. . . .

The *Terry* case is most instructive for present purposes. There we held that an on-the-street "frisk" for weapons must be tested by the Fourth Amendment's general proscription against unreasonable searches because such a frisk involves "an entire rubric of police conduct—necessarily swift action predicated upon the on-the-spot observations of the officer on the beat—which historically has not been, and as a practical matter could not be, subjected to the warrant procedure.". . .

The ingredients to apply the balance struck in *Terry* and *Long* are present in this case. Possessing an arrest warrant and probable cause to believe Buie was in his home, the officers were entitled to enter and to search anywhere in the house in which Buie might be found. Once he was found, however, the search for him was over, and there was no longer that particular justification for entering any rooms that had not yet been searched.

That Buie had an expectation of privacy in those remaining areas of his house, however, does not mean such rooms were immune from entry. In *Terry* and *Long* we were concerned with the immediate interest of the police officers in taking steps to assure themselves that the persons with whom they were dealing were not armed with or able to gain immediate control of a weapon that could unexpectedly and fatally be used against them. In the instant case, there is an analogous interest of the officers in taking steps to assure themselves that the house in which the suspect is being or has just been arrested is not harboring other persons who are dangerous and who could unexpectedly launch an attack. The risk of danger in the context of an arrest in the home is as great as, if not greater than, it is in the on-the-street or roadside investigatory encounter. . . .

We should emphasize that such a protective sweep, aimed at protecting the arresting officers, if justified by the circumstances, is nevertheless not a full search of the premises, but may extend only to a cursory inspection of those spaces where a person may be found. The sweep lasts no longer than is necessary to dispel the reasonable suspicion of danger and in any event no longer than it takes to complete the arrest and depart from the premises.

. . . The Fourth Amendment permits a properly limited protective sweep in conjunction with an in-home arrest when the searching officer possesses a reasonable belief based on specific and articulable facts that the area to be swept harbors an individual posing a danger to those on the arrest scene. . . .

It is important to note that the "protective sweep" may not be automatically conducted by the police, unlike a search incident to arrest. An officer must have a reasonable belief, supported by specific and articulable facts, that a dangerous person may be hiding in the home, before a protective sweep may be conducted. There need not be a belief of dangerousness to conduct a search incident to arrest.

A protective sweep must be limited to searching those areas where a person might be hiding. How far this will be permitted to go remains to be seen. Justice Brennan, dissenting in *Buie*, made this statement:

> . . . Police officers searching for potential ambushers might enter every room including basements and attics, open up closets, lockers, chests, wardrobes, and cars; and peer under beds and behind furniture. The officers will view letters, documents and personal effects that are on tables or desks or are visible inside open drawers; books, records, tapes, and pictures on shelves; and clothing, medicines, toiletries and other paraphernalia not carefully stored in dresser drawers or bathroom cupboards. While perhaps not

After arrest and prior to being placed with other inmates, arrestees are often "deloused," or cleaned and treated for lice and other contractibles.

a "full-blown" or "top-to-bottom" search . . . a protective sweep is much closer to it than to a "limited patdown for weapons" or a "frisk" [as authorized by *Terry v. Ohio*].

Section 12.3(e) Executing Arrest Warrants

Arrest warrants may be executed at the officer's discretion, whether day or night. However, common sense dictates that warrants be served at a reasonable hour, unless an exigency exists.

In *Ker v. California*, 374 U.S. 23 (1963), an unannounced entry into a person's home was found to be violative of the Fourth Amendment. Therefore, the general rule is that an officer must knock and announce his reason for being there. A number of exceptions to this rule have been recognized, including:

1. When the safety of the police or others will be endangered by the announcement.
2. When the announcement will allow those inside to destroy evidence or escape.
3. When the occupants know the purpose of the officers.

The Court has said that the knock and announcement requirement applies whether the police gain entry by force or not. The use of a key, opening an unlocked door, smashing a window, or breaking a door down, all must be preceded by a knock and announcement by the police, unless one of the exceptions noted above justifies otherwise.

Section 12.3(f) Illegal Arrests

Does the exclusionary rule apply to people as it does to things? That is, should a defendant be excluded from trial because he has been arrested unlawfully? Generally, the Supreme Court has answered no. *Frisbie v. Collins*, 342 U.S. 519 (1952). Therefore, the fact that a defendant is kidnapped has no bearing on whether the criminal proceeding will continue.

There may be an exception to this rule. If the conduct of the government is outrageous, shocking, and a gross invasion of a defendant's constitutional rights, he may be set free. This is known as a *Toscanino* claim, named after the defendant in the following case.

UNITED STATES V. TOSCANINO

500 F.2d 267 (2nd Cir. 1974)

Francisco Toscanino appeals from a narcotics conviction entered against him in the Eastern District of New York. . . .

Toscanino does not question the sufficiency of the evidence or claim any error with respect to the conduct of the trial itself. His principal argument . . . is that the entire proceedings in the district court against him were void because his presence within the territorial jurisdiction of the court had been illegally obtained. . . . He offered to prove the following:

"On or about January 6, 1973 Francisco Toscanino was lured from his home in Montevideo, Uruguay by a telephone call. This call has been placed by or at the direction of Hugo Campos Hermedia. Hermedia was at that time and still is a member of the police in Montevideo, Uruguay. . . .

". . . The telephone call ruse succeeded in bringing Toscanino and his wife, seven months pregnant at the time, to an area near a deserted bowling alley in the City of Montevideo. Upon their arrival there Hermedia together with six associates abducted Toscanino. This was accomplished in full view of Toscanino's terrified wife by knocking him unconscious with a gun. . . .

"At no time had there been any formal or informal request on the part of the United States of the government of Uruguay for the extradition of Francisco Toscanino nor was there any legal basis to justify this rank criminal enterprise. . . .

"Later that same day Toscanino was brought to Brasilia. . . . For seventeen days Toscanino was incessantly tortured and interrogated. Throughout this entire period the United States government and the United States Attorney for the Eastern District of New York . . . did in fact receive reports as to its progress. . . . [Toscanino's] captors denied him sleep and all forms of nourishment for days at a time. Nourishment was provided intravenously in a manner precisely equal to an amount necessary to keep him alive. Reminiscent of the horror stories told by our military men who returned from Korea and China, Toscanino was forced to walk up and down a hallway for seven or eight hours at a time. When he could no longer stand he was kicked and beaten but all in a manner contrived to punish without scarring. When he could not answer, his fingers were pinched with metal pliers. Alcohol was flushed into his eyes and nose and other fluids . . . were forced up his anal passage. Incredibly, these agents of the United States government attached electrodes to Toscanino's earlobes, toes, and genitals. Jarring jolts of electricity were shot throughout his body, rendering him unconscious for indeterminate periods of time but again leaving no physical scars. . . .

[Toscanino was eventually drugged and brought to the United States to stand trial.]

Since *Frisbie*, the Supreme Court in what one distinguished legal luminary describes as a "constitutional revolution," . . . has expanded the interpretation of "due process." No longer is it limited to the guarantee of "fair" procedure at trial. In an effort to deter police misconduct, the term has been extended to bar the government from realizing directly the fruits of its own deliberate and unnecessary lawlessness in bringing the accused to trial. . . .

> . . . Accordingly, we view due process as now requiring a court to divest itself of jurisdiction over the person of a defendant where it has been acquired as the result of the government's deliberate, unnecessary and unreasonable invasion of the accused's constitutional rights. . . .

Later, the Second Circuit Court of Appeals reiterated that the *Toscanino* reasoning only applies to situations where the government's conduct is both shocking and outrageous, as was true of the allegations in *Toscanino. United States ex rel. Lujan v. Gengler,* 510 F.2d 62 (2nd Cir. 1975), *cert. denied* 421 U.S. 1001 (1975). Be aware that not all courts have followed the Second Circuit's lead. Rather than deal with the thorny legal issue, most courts have factually distinguished their cases from *Toscanino.* The Supreme Court has not yet addressed the issue.

Even though a defendant's person may not be excluded because of an illegal arrest, the evidence obtained pursuant to that arrest may be. For example, if there is a causal connection between an illegal arrest and a subsequent confession, then the statement must be excluded. *Taylor v. Alabama,* 457 U.S. 687 (1982). Or, if evidence is obtained through a search incident to an illegal arrest, it must also be suppressed. In short, any evidence obtained as a result of an illegal arrest must be excluded, unless an independent basis for its discovery can be shown by the government.

Section 12.3(g) Considering Fourth Amendment Problems

Search and seizure problems can be complex. It is an area of the law that is highly fact-sensitive. It is also an area where one must be careful and precise in analysis. Often search and seizure issues will be numerous in a single case, each issue interrelated and interdependent.

In many instances, the validity of a search or seizure will depend on the validity of an earlier search or seizure. Therefore, if the government fails at an earlier stage, it is probable it may fail again later. For example, the police arrest Barry Burglar and conduct a search incident to arrest. During that search they discover burglar tools and other evidence of the alleged burglary. If it is determined that the arrest was invalid, then the fruits of the search incident to arrest must be suppressed. If the evidence discovered from the search led to other evidence, it may also be excluded.

Often officers obtain evidence in stages—each stage increasing the governmental interest in crime prevention, and concurrently increasing the officer's suspicion—thereby permitting a greater invasion of a person's privacy.

Even though search and seizure laws can be complex, don't forget to use common sense when analyzing Fourth Amendment issues. The exceptions to the search warrant requirement are not surprising; common sense tells a person that an officer may continue to pursue a fleeing murderer into his home without first obtaining a warrant. Similarly, it is not shocking that illegally obtained evidence may not be used to convict a defendant.

Two very strong policies are at battle in Fourth Amendment issues: crime detection and prevention versus the citizens' right to be free from intrusive government behavior. Consider these concerns when contemplating Fourth Amendment problems.

REVIEW QUESTIONS

1. In what way did *Katz v. United States* change Fourth Amendment law?
2. What are the basic requirements of obtaining a search warrant?
3. Stacey is a suspect in an embezzlement investigation. The police believe that she has hidden evidence in her neighbor's house, without the neighbor's consent. The neighbor will not consent to a search. Can the police obtain a search warrant for the non-suspect's home?
4. What is the plain view doctrine?
5. What is curtilage? Open fields? Why are the concepts important in criminal law?
6. Distinguish a stop from an arrest; a frisk from a search.
7. A police officer is approached by a man on the street who tells him that he was just robbed. The man points out the robber, who is standing in a park just across the street. Must the officer obtain a warrant to make the arrest?
8. A police officer is approached by a man on the street who tells him that he was just robbed. Although he did not see where the robber fled, he knew the assailant's name and address, as the two men "grew up together." The officer and the victim went to the police station and completed an incident report. After a phone call to one of suspect's neighbors they learned

that he was at home. Must the officer obtain a warrant to make the arrest?

9. Same facts as in question number seven, except the victim points to a fleeing suspect. The officer chases the suspect to a house, where the officer sees the suspect enter through the use of a key. Must the officer end the chase and obtain a warrant?

10. What is a protective sweep?

REVIEW PROBLEMS

1. Tommy Transmitter planned to burglarize a local audio/visual dealer. On the night he intended to commit the burglary, Tommy was observed standing in an alley behind the shop by a police officer. It was 11:50 P.M., June, and Tommy was wearing a pair of jeans, tennis shoes, and a shirt.

   After five minutes the officer approached Tommy and asked him "what he was doing in the alley at such a late hour." Tommy responded that he lived only a few blocks away, was suffering from insomnia, and decided to take a walk. He produced identification that confirmed that he lived a short distance from the store. The officer then grabbed Tommy, swung him around, pushed him against the wall of the store, and "frisked him." After feeling a hard object in his back pocket the officer reached in and discovered a small 3″ × 3″ container full of locksmith tools. He then arrested Tommy for possession of burglary tools and conducted a search incident to arrest. During that search he discovered a diagram of the audio/visual store hidden in Tommy's pants.

   Tommy was subsequently charged with attempted burglary and possession of burglary tools. He has filed a motion to suppress the tools and diagram, as well as a motion to dismiss. Should the motions be granted? Discuss.

   2–5. Assume that officers have a valid search warrant for defendant's apartment. The warrant specifies that the officers may search for stolen stereos. May the officers do the following?

2. Search the defendant's desk drawers in his study?
3. Search the defendant's closets in his bedroom?
4. Search the defendant's body?
5. Seize a transparent bag of cocaine that is found lying on the defendant's dining room table.

6. Do you agree with Justice Brennan that the protective sweep goes beyond the *Terry v. Ohio* decision? Explain your position.

7. In *United States v. Leon* the Supreme Court created a "good-faith" exception to the probable cause requirement of the Fourth Amendment. Under *Leon*, evidence seized in good faith pursuant to a search warrant is admissible at trial, even though it is later determined that probable cause was lacking. Should this exception be extended to warrantless searches where an officer has a good-faith belief that probable cause exists?

8. Do you believe that the exclusionary rule is required under the Fourth Amendment? Can you think of any alternatives to the rule?

NOTES

[1] *Biven v. Six Unknown Named Agents*, 403 U.S. 388 (1971).

[2] *United States v. Jacobsen*, 466 U.S. 109, 113 (1984).

[3] *Carroll v. United States*, 267 U.S. 132 (1934).

[4] *Beck v. Ohio*, 379 U.S. 89 (1964).

[5] *Coolidge v. New Hampshire*, 403 U.S. 443 (1971).

[6] *Shadwick v. Tampa*, 407 U.S. 345 (1972).

[7] F. R. Crim. P. 41(b).

[8] *Zurcher v. Stanford Daily*, 436 U.S. 547 (1978).

[9] *Ybarra v. Illinois*, 444 U.S. 85 (1979).

[10] *Jones v. United States*, 357 U.S. 493 (1958).

[11] F. R. Crim. P. 41(c)(1).

[12] F. R. Crim. P. 41(d).

[13] *Schneckloth v. Bustamonte*, 412 U.S. 218 (1973).

[14] *United States v. Kampbell*, 574 F.2d 962 (8th Cir. 1978).

[15] *Commonwealth v. Wright*, 190 A.2d 709 (Pa. 1963).

[16] For a discussion of landlord-tenant situations, see *Stoner v. California*, 376 U.S. 483 (1964).

[17] *Arizona v. Hicks*, 480 U.S. 321 (1987).

[18] *Chambers v. Mahoney*, 399 U.S. 42 (1970).

[19] See Torcia, *Wharton's Criminal Evidence*, 13th Ed. (New York: Lawyers Co-operative, 1986 Supp.) §733.

[20] *Oliver v. United States*, 466 U.S. 170 (1984).

[21] *United States v. Broadhurst*, 612 F.Supp. 777 (D.C. Cal. 1985).

[22] *Michigan v. Long*, 463 U.S. 1032 (1983).

[23] *Aguilar v. Texas*, 378 U.S. 108, 110–111 (1964).

[24] *Stealgald v. United States*, 451 U.S. 204 (1981).

CHAPTER 13
Interrogation and Other Law-Enforcement Practices

"Have we grilled you before?"

The drug kingpin may know not to use his cordless telephone if he wants privacy, but the ordinary, ill-informed citizen does not.

Laurence H. Tribe[1]

OUTLINE

SECTION 13.1 INTERROGATIONS, CONFESSIONS, AND ADMISSIONS

Questioning by police officers is a commonly used law-enforcement tool. An **interrogation** occurs whenever an officer questions a person he suspects has committed a crime. A **confession** is a statement made by a person claiming that she has committed a crime. If a person asserts certain facts to be true, which are inculpatory, but do not amount to a confession, she has made an **admission**.

The use of interrogations, confessions, and admissions to prove guilt is controversial. The United States Supreme Court has recognized that admissions are highly suspect when relied upon alone to obtain a confession. The Court stated in *Escobedo v. Illinois*, 378 U.S. 478 (1964), that a "system of criminal law enforcement which comes to depend on the 'confession' will, in the long run, be less reliable and more subject to abuses than a system which depends on extrinsic evidence independently" obtained through other law-enforcement practices.

At common law, confessions and admissions could be used freely, as long as they were made voluntarily. The early basis to exclude involuntary confessions was the Due Process Clauses of the Fifth and Fourteenth Amendments.[2] Eventually, a federal defendant could seek to have a confession suppressed if he was not taken before a magistrate promptly after his arrest. This was known as the McNabb-Mallory rule.

Today, interrogations, confessions, and admissions are governed by these rules, as well as two broader rights: the Fifth Amendment right to be free from self-incrimination and the Sixth Amendment right to counsel.

Section 13.1(a) Miranda

Contrary to popular belief, the famous *Miranda v. Arizona* case is not a Sixth Amendment right to counsel cases; rather, it is a Fifth Amendment right to be free from self-incrimination cases.

MIRANDA
V.
ARIZONA

384 U.S. 436 (1966)

The cases before us raise questions that go to the roots of our concepts of American criminal jurisprudence: the restraints society must observe consistent with the Federal Constitution in prosecuting individuals for crime. More specifically, we deal with the admissibility of statements obtained from an individual who is subjected to custodial police interrogation and the necessity for procedures which assure that the individual is accorded his privilege under the Fifth Amendment to the Constitution not to be compelled to incriminate himself. . . .

Our holding will be spelled out with some specificity in the pages which follow but briefly stated it is this: the prosecution may not use statements, whether exculpatory or inculpatory, stemming from custodial interrogation of the defendant unless it demonstrates the use of procedural safeguards effective to secure the privilege against self-incrimination. By custodial interrogation, we mean questioning initiated by law-enforcement officers after a person has been taken into custody or otherwise deprived of his freedom of action in any significant way. As for the procedural safeguards to be employed, unless other fully effective means are devised to inform accused persons of their right of silence and to assure a continuous opportunity to exercise it, the following measures are required. Prior to any questioning, the person must be warned that he has a right to remain silent, that any statement he does make may be used as evidence against him, and that he has a right to the presense of an attorney, either retained or appointed. The defendant may waive effectuation of these rights, provided the waiver is made voluntarity, knowingly, and intelligently. If, however, he indicates in any manner and at any stage of the process that he wishes to consult with an attorney before speaking there can be no questioning. Likewise, if the individual is alone and indicates

LEGAL TERMS

interrogation
The questioning of a person suspected of committing a crime by the police.

confession
A statement claiming that one has committed a crime.

admission
A statement which is inculpatory, but not a confession.

in any manner that he does not wish to be interrogated, the police may not question him. The mere fact that he may have answered some questions or volunteered some statements on his own does not deprive him of the right to refrain from answering any further inquiries until he has consulted with an attorney and thereafter consents to be questioned.

The constitutional issue we decide in each of these cases is the admissibility of statements obtained from a defendant questioned while in custody or otherwise deprived of his freedom of action in any significant way. In each, the defendant was questioned by police officers, detectives, or a prosecuting attorney in a room in which he was cut off from the outside world. In none of these cases was the defendant given a full and effective warning of his rights at the outset of the interrogation process. In all of the cases, the questioning elicited oral admissions, and in three of them, signed statements as well which were admitted at their trials. They all thus share salient features—incommunicado interrogation of individuals in a police-dominated atmosphere, resulting in self-incriminating statements without full warnings of constitutional rights.

An understanding of the nature and setting of this in-custody interrogation is essential to our decisions today. The difficulty in depicting what transpires at such interrogations stems from the fact that in this country they have largely taken place incommunicado. From extensive factual studies undertaken in the early 1930s . . . it is clear that police violence and the "third degree" flourished at that time. In a series of cases decided by the Court long after those studies, the police resulted to physical brutality—beating, hanging, whipping—and to sustained and protracted questioning incommunicado in order to extort confessions. . . .

Again we stress that the modern practice of in-custody interrogation is psychologically rather than physically oriented. As we have stated before " . . . this court has recognized that coercion can be mental as well as physical, and that the blood of the accused is not the only hallmark of an unconstitutional inquisition. . . .

The circumstances surrounding in-custody interrogation can operate very quickly to verbear the will of one merely made aware of his privilege [against self-incrimination] by his interrogators. Therefore, the right to have counsel present at the interrogation is indispensable to the protection of the Fifth Amendment privilege under the system we delineate today. Our aim is to assure that the individual's right to choose between silence and speech remains unfettered throughout the interrogation process. A once-stated warning, delivered by those who will conduct the interrogation, cannot itself suffice to that end among those who most require knowledge of their rights. A mere warning given by the interrogators is not alone sufficient to accomplish that end. Prosecutors themselves claim that the admonishment of the right to remain silent without more "will benefit only the recidivist and the professional." Even preliminary advice given to the accused by his own attorney can be swiftly overcome by the secret interrogation process. . . . Thus, the need for counsel to protect the Fifth Amendment privilege comprehends not merely a right to consult with counsel prior to questioning, but also to have counsel present during any questioning if the defendant so desires.

The presense of counsel at the interrogation may serve several significant subsidiary functions as well. If the accused decides to talk to his interrogators, the assistance of counsel can mitigate the dangers of trustworthiness. With a lawyer present the likelihood that the police will practice coercion is reduced, and if coercion is nevertheless exercised the lawyer can testify to it in court. The presense of a lawyer can also help to guarantee that the accused gives a fully accurate statement to the police and that the statement is rightly reported to the prosecution. . . .

Section 13.1(a.1) Custodial Interrogation

Not all questioning by law-enforcement officers must be preceded by the Miranda warnings. A defendant must be "in custody" and "interrogated" by police before *Miranda* has effect. This is known as the "custodial interrogation" requirement.

The Court used the phrase "taken into custody or otherwise deprived of his freedom of action in any significant way" to define the custody element of *Miranda*. While a statement by a police officer to a suspect that he is not under arrest is not dispositive, it may be considered. Of course, a person is in-custody if an officer announces that an arrest is being made or that the person is not free to leave. The Court made is clear that the in-custody element may be satisfied anywhere—it is not required that the defendant be at the police station to be in-custody.

All of the surrounding facts must be considered in making the custody determination. The location of the interrogation is very important. There is a greater chance of finding a person in-custody if the questioning took place in a police station or prosecutor's office over the suspect's home or in public. The presence of other persons during the interrogation decreases the odds of the suspect being in-custody. The Court found the fact that the suspects in *Miranda* were "cut off from the outside world" troubling. The length and intensity of the questioning is also relevant. A brief encounter between a citizen and a police officer is generally not a custodial situation.

In addition to being in-custody, a defendant must be subjected to an interrogation before *Miranda* applies. Clearly, interrogation includes questioning by law-enforcement officers. But this is not all. In *Rhode Island v. Innis*, 446 U.S. 291 (1980), the Supreme Court held that any "functional equivalent" to express questioning is also interrogation. That is, all actions or words by police officers that can reasonably be expected to elicit an incriminating response are interrogation.

The nature of the information elicited is not relevant; the *Miranda* court stated that the decision applies to both inculpatory and exculpatory statements. Accordingly, *Miranda* is effective whether a defendant confesses or simply makes an admission.

Section 13.1(a.2) Exceptions to Miranda

Not every communication between a police officer and a suspect amounts to an interrogation under *Miranda*. First, volunteered statements are not the product of interrogation. The *Miranda* decision explicitly states that officers are under no duty to interrupt a volunteered confession in order to read a confessor his Miranda rights.

Second, routine questions that are purely informational normally do not lead to incriminating responses and need not be preceded by a reading of the Miranda warnings. Questions about one's name, age, address, and employment are not treated as interrogation.

Third, questions made by officers in the interest of public safety do not have to follow a Miranda warning. In one case a woman told two police officers that she had just been raped by a man carrying a gun and that the rapist had gone into a nearby grocery. The officers went to the store and arrested the man. However, he did not have the gun on his person. One of the police officers asked the arrestee where the gun was, and the arrestee responded by indicating the location where the gun was hidden in the store. The Supreme Court decided that despite the fact that the question was interrogation and the defendant had not been mirandized, the evidence could be used at trial. The Court recognized that in such situations, when there is a danger to the officers or the public, officers must be permitted to extinguish the public threat. To accomplish this purpose the relatively rigid rules of *Miranda* are relaxed when there is a public safety exigency.[3]

Related to the public safety exception is spontaneous questioning by police. If a question is asked spontaneously, such as in response to an emergency, there is no interrogation. For example, if an officer were to return to a room where he has placed two arrestees to find one dead, it would not be an interrogation if the officer were to excitedly utter, "Who killed this man?"

Section 13.1(a.3) Multiple Interrogations and Reinterrogation

Miranda clearly stated that once a defendant invokes his right to remain silent, whether before or during questioning, the interrogation must stop. The same is true once a defendant states that he wants counsel present; the interrogation must cease until the defendant's attorney is available. If the defendant's attorney is not available, the police are to respect his right to remain silent and not question him until the attorney arrives.

Under very limited circumstances police officers may reattempt to interrogate a defendant who has invoked his right to remain silent. While multiple attempts to interrogate an arrestee about the same crime are not permitted, it has been determined that a second interrogation about a separate and unrelated crime may be valid.[4]

Miranda clearly stated that once an accused has invoked the right to counsel, the police are prohibited from interrogating him until he has conferred with counsel. *Miranda* did not answer this question: may police reinterrogate a defendant without his counsel present once he has consulted with his lawyer? The answer is found in the following decision.

MINNICK
V.
MISSISSIPPI

____ U.S.____ (1990)

To protect the privilege against self-incrimination guaranteed by the Fifth Amendment, we have held that the police must terminate interrogation of an accused in custody if the accused requests the assistance of counsel. *Miranda v. Arizona,* 384 U.S. 436, 474 (1966). We reinforced the protections of *Miranda* in *Edwards v. Arizona,* 451 U.S. 477, 484–485 (1981), which held that once the accused requests counsel, officials may not reinitiate questioning "until counsel has been made available" to him. The issue in the case before us is whether *Edwards'* protection ceases once the suspect has consulted with an attorney.

Petitioner Robert Minnick and fellow prisoner James Dyess escaped from a county jail in Mississippi and, a day later, broke into a mobile home in search of weapons. In the course of the burglary they were interrupted by the arrival of the trailer's owner, Ellis Thomas, accompanied by Lamar Lafferty and Lafferty's infant son. Dyess and Minnick used the stolen weapons to kill Thomas and the senior Lafferty. Minnick's story is that Dyess murdered one victim and then forced Minnick to shoot the other. Before the escapees could get away, two young women arrived at the mobile home. They were held at gunpoint, then bound by hand and foot. Dyess and Minnick fled in Thomas' truck, abandoning the vehicle in New Orleans. The fugitives continued to Mexico, where they fought, and Minnick then proceeded alone to California. Minnick was arrested in Lemon Grove, California, on a Mississippi warrant, some four months after the murders.

The confession at issue here resulted from the last interrogation of Minnick while he was held in the San Diego jail, but we first recount the events which preceded it. Minnick was arrested on Friday, August 22, 1986. Petitioner testified that he was mistreated by local police during and after the arrest. The day following the arrest, Saturday, two FBI agents came to the jail to interview him. Petitioner testified that he refused to go to the interview, but was told he would "have to go down or else" . . . . The FBI report indicates that the agents read petitioner his *Miranda* warnings, and that he acknowledged he understood his rights. He refused to sign a rights waiver form, however, and said he would not answer "very many" questions. Minnick told the agents about the jail break and the flight, and described how Dyess threatened and beat him. Early in the interview, he sobbed "[i]t was my life or theirs," but otherwise he hesitated to tell what happened at the trailer. The agents reminded him he did not have to answer questions without a lawyer present. According to the report, "Minnick stated 'Come back Monday when I have a lawyer,' and stated that he would make a more complete statement then with his lawyer present." . . .

After the FBI interview, an appointed attorney met with petitioner. Petitioner spoke with the lawyer on two or three occasions, though it is not clear from the record whether all of these conferences were in person.

On Monday, August 25, Deputy Sheriff J.C. Denham of Clarke County, Mississippi, came to the San Diego jail to question Minnick. Minnick testified that his jailers again told him he would "have to talk" to Denham and that he "could not refuse." . . . Denham advised petitioner of his rights, and petitioner again declined to sign a rights waiver form. Petitioner told Denham about the escape and then proceeded to describe the events at the mobile home. . . .

Minnick was tried for murder in Mississippi. He moved to suppress all statements given to the FBI or other police officers, including Denham. The trial court denied the motion with respect to petitioner's statements to Denham, but suppressed his other statements. Petitioner was convicted on two counts of capital murder and sentenced to death.

On appeal, petitioner argued that the confession to Denham was taken in violation of his rights to counsel under the Fifth and Sixth Amendments. The Mississippi Supreme Court rejected the claims. . . .

The Mississippi Supreme Court relied on our statement in *Edwards* that an accused who invokes his right to counsel "is not subject to further interrogation by the authorities until counsel has been made available to him. . . . " 451 U.S., at 484–485. We do not interpret this language to mean, as the Mississippi court thought, that the protection of *Edwards* terminates once counsel has consulted with the suspect. In context, the requirement that counsel be "made available" to the accused refers to more than an opportunity to consult with an attorney outside the interrogation room.

In *Edwards,* we focused on *Miranda's* instruction that when the accused invokes his right to counsel, the "interrogation must cease until an attorney is *present* during custodial interrogation." 451 U.S., at 482 (emphasis added). In the sentence preceding the language quoted by the Mississippi Supreme Court, we referred to the "right to have counsel *present* during custodial interrogation." . . .

. . . In our view, a fair reading of *Edwards* and subsequent cases demonstrates that we have interpreted the rule to bar police-initiated interrogation unless the accused has counsel with him at the time of questioning. Whatever the ambiguities of our earlier cases on this point, we now hold that when counsel is requested, interrogation must cease, and officials may not reinitiate interrogation without counsel present, whether or not the accused has consulted with his attorney.

* * *

Minnick makes it clear that once an accused has asserted a right to counsel that all police-initiated interrogations must occur with counsel present.

Section 13.1(a.4) The Warnings

Before a person in custody may be interrogated, the required warning must be recited to the arrestee. Specific language does not have to be used, as long as the defendant is fully and effectively apprised of each right.

The Supreme Court stated, in *Miranda*, that the following rights must be conveyed to the defendant:

1. The right to remain silent.
2. Any statements made may be used against the defendant to gain a conviction.
3. The right to consult with a lawyer and to have a lawyer present during questioning.
4. For the indigent, a lawyer will be provided without cost.

The warnings are to be read to all persons in custody who are to be interrogated. The law does not presume that any person, including an attorney, knows her rights. The warnings should be presented in a timely manner and read at a speed that the arrestee can gain a full understanding of their import.

Many law-enforcement agencies have made it a policy to record (video/audio or audio only) the giving of the warnings and any waiver of rights to eliminate any question concerning whether the warnings were given and whether coercion was used to gain a waiver.

Section 13.1(a.5) Waiver

A defendant may waive the right to have the assistance of counsel and/or to remain silent. The waiver must be made voluntarily and knowingly. In *Miranda* the Supreme Court said that "heavy burden" of proving that a defendant made a knowing and voluntary waiver rests with the prosecution; courts are to presume no waiver.

In determining whether there has been a waiver, the totality of the circumstances is considered. The actions of the police, as well as the defendant's age, intelligence, and experience are all relevant to this inquiry.

An express waiver, preferably written, is best for the prosecution. However, a defendant's waiver does not have to be express to be valid. In *North Carolina v. Butler*, 441 U.S. 369 (1962), the Court held that "[I]n at least some cases waiver can be clearly inferred from the actions and words of the person interrogated." However, silence on the part of a defendant never amounts to a waiver. So, if a defendant refuses to state, or otherwise indicate, that he understands a right and wishes to waive it, the police should not conduct an interrogation.

Section 13.1(a.6) Violating Miranda

Any statement obtained in violation of *Miranda* is inadmissible at trial to prove guilt. Further, any other evidence that is the fruit of such a statement must also be excluded from trial. The defendant ordinarily raises the issue prior to trial through a motion to suppress.

Although statements that are illegally obtained may not be admitted to prove a defendant's guilt, the Supreme Court has said that statements that violate *Miranda* may be admitted, under certain circumstances, to impeach the defendant.[5]

Section 13.1(b) Sixth Amendment

Miranda has effect as soon as a person is in custody and is subject to interrogation. This can occur long before or directly prior to the filing of a formal charge. Once the adversary judicial proceeding has begun, the source of protection changes from the Fifth Amendment (*Miranda*) to the Sixth Amendment.

In *Michigan v. Jackson*, 475 U.S. 625 (1986), the Supreme Court held that the Sixth Amendment provides the same protections as *Miranda*, *Edwards*, and similar cases. The Court reasoned that interrogations by the government of a defendant after criminal charges have been filed are a critical stage, at which counsel is necessary to protect the defendant's rights.

Section 13.1(c) Voluntariness Requirement

As was true under the common law, all confessions must be made voluntarily. This is required by the Due Process Clauses of the Fifth and Fourteenth Amendments. The "totality of the circumstances" must be examined when making the voluntariness determination.

Police officers do not have to physically coerce a confession for it to be involuntary. Mental or emotional coercion by law enforcement also violates a defendant's due process rights.

Involuntary confessions are to be excluded at trial. For years, the admission of a coerced confession resulted in an automatic reversal of conviction. This was changed in *Arizona v. Fulminante*, No. 89–839, slip op. (U.S. 1991), where the United States Supreme Court decided that a conviction is not to be automatically reversed because a coerced confession was admitted at trial. Rather, the Court held that if the prosecution can show beyond a reasonable doubt that the trial court error was harmless, the conviction is to be affirmed. That is, if there was sufficient other evidence to sustain the conviction, then it stands.

SECTION 13.2   ELECTRONIC SURVEILLANCE

Many forms of electronic surveillance are used by law-enforcement agencies. Wiretaps and highly sensitive microphones are examples. When the Supreme Court first addressed the issue of wiretapping, it concluded that there was no Fourth Amendment protection because there was no trespass into a constitutionally protected area. This changed when the Court issued the *Katz* decision, which advanced the idea that the Fourth Amendment protects people, not places. Now, if a person has a justifiable expectation of privacy, the Fourth Amendment applies.

Despite the constitutional aspect of using such devices, this is an area of law that is highly regulated by a federal statute: Title III of the Omnibus Crime Control Act and Safe Streets Act of 1968.

Section 13.2(a)   Title III of the Omnibus Crime Control Act

Title III of the Omnibus Crime Control Act and Safe Streets Act of 1968[6] is a federal statute that regulates the use of electronic surveillance. It is also known as the Federal Wiretap Act.

The act prohibits wiretapping, bugging, or other electronic surveillance of a conversation when the parties to that conversation have a reasonable expectation of privacy. Violation of the act may result in civil and criminal penalties. Evidence obtained in violation of the act is excluded at trial.

The statute permits states to enact their own electronic surveillance laws; however, those laws cannot provide less protection of individual rights than the federal statute. A state may, however, provide greater protection of individual rights through its surveillance law than does the federal statute.

Section 13.2(a.1)   Court-Ordered Surveillance

Law-enforcement officers may not intercept telephone conversations or other electronic messages without first obtaining court approval. The act permits court approval only for certain crimes. Espionage, treason, murder, kidnapping, robbery, extortion, drug crimes, and bribery of public officials are included in that list.

To obtain a court order for the interception of electronic communications an officer must present an application supported by oath or affirmation to a court. The requirements for obtaining such a court order are similar to those for obtaining a warrant. The application must contain the following:[7]

1. The identity of the official applying for the order and the official authorizing the application;
2. Evidence establishing probable cause to believe that the person whose communication is to be intercepted has committed, is committing, or is about to commit one of the named crimes;
3. Evidence establishing probable cause to believe that the communication to be intercepted concerns the crime;
4. A statement that other normal investigative procedures have been tried and failed, or that no other procedure is available;
5. The time period during which the interception will occur;
6. A full description of the location where the interception will take place;
7. A statement reflecting all prior attempts to obtain a similar order for any of the same places or persons.

If the judge grants the application, the order must specify the person whose communication is to be intercepted, the location of the interception, the nature of the communication to be intercepted, the crime involved, and the duration of the interception. In all cases, the surveillance is to cease once the desired information has been seized (recorded). After the interception has ended the recording is to be given to the judge who issued the order for safe-keeping.

Implicit in court orders under this statute is the authority to enter premises to install listening devices. Courts have held that it would be nonsensical to give an officer the authority to conduct surveillience, but not to enter the premises of the defendant to install the necessary device. The court order does not have to specifically give this authority; it is implicit in the order itself. Of course, where an officer may go depends on the facts of each case.

The statute authorizes judges to order third parties, such as phone company personnel, to assist law-enforcement officers in executing an electronic surveillance order. Third parties must be compensated for their assistance.

Section 13.2(a.2) Exceptions to Title III

In a number of situations a court order is not required to intercept an electronic communication. Eight exceptions are discussed here.

First, be aware that the act tracks the privacy aspect of the *Katz* decision; that is, only communications where a person has a reasonable expectation of privacy are protected. Since Title III does not expand the privacy protection aspect of the Fourth Amendment, decisions concerning whether a person has a reasonable expectation of privacy under the Fourth Amendment are applicable to Title III.

One party to a communication has no reasonable expectation that the other party will not record the conversation or permit others to listen. So, no court order has to be obtained for a law-enforcement officer to listen in on an extension (or later listen to a recording), as long as one party to the conversation consents. The Federal Wiretap Act has a provision that reflects this position.

It has also been held that a person has no reasonable expectation of privacy when using a cordless telephone. Because cordless phones use radio waves, which are broadcast in all directions and are subject to being received by countless people, courts have reasoned that a person cannot have a reasonable expectation of privacy when using one.[8] However, whenever one party is using a cordless phone and the other a traditional line phone, it is likely, unless the second party knows that the other is using a cordless phone, that the second party has a reasonable expectation of privacy.

Critics of this position charge that whenever a person places a call to a particular person, whether on a cordless phone or a traditional phone, it is reasonable to expect the conversation to be private. Another view contends that such hair-splitting is confusing to the average person. As the quote that opened this chapter states, it may be true that the professional criminal knows that he has no reasonable expectation of privacy on a cordless phone, but the average citizen does not.

Second, any employee of a communications company who intercepts an incriminating communication while engaged in ordinary duties (i.e., maintenance) may disclose such information to the authorities, and it may be used at trial.

Third, officers need not obtain a court order when engaged in certain national security investigations.

Fourth, in emergency situations, where an officer does not have time to obtain a court order, the interception may begin immediately, but an application must be made within forty-eight hours. If the judge determines that there was no emergency justifying a warrantless tap, then any evidence obtained must be suppressed.

Finally, electronic beepers and transmitters used to track a person or thing are governed by normal search and seizure law. Additionally, the Supreme Court has held that pen registers and similar devices that make a record of telephone numbers called do not implicate the Fourth Amendment because there is no search when they are used.[9]

SECTION 13.3 PRETRIAL IDENTIFICATION PROCEDURES

Law-enforcement officers use a variety of techniques to identify a person as a criminal, such as eyewitness identifications, fingerprinting, blood tests, and, recently, deoxyribonucleic acid (DNA) tests.

The use of any of these procedures raises certain constitutional issues, such as the right to be free from self-incrimination and the right to counsel.

There is also another concern: reliability. Eyewitness identification, while powerful, has a few inherent problems. First, each person will testify to his or her perception of an event, and people often perceive the same event differently. Second, not every person will use the same language to decribe what was witnessed. Third, a witness may simply have a faulty memory and unintentionally testify to an untruth. Fourth, for a variety of reasons, a witness may intentionally lie.

Scientific testing may also prove to be invalid or unreliable. How accurate is the test when performed properly? Was the test performed properly in this case? Is the evidence tested actually the defendant's? These are the types of questions that are asked of expert witnesses who testify as to the results of scientific testing This discussion will begin with eyewitness identification procedures.

Section 13.3(a) Lineups and One-Man Showups

A **lineup** is where the police exhibit a group of people, among which is the suspect, to a witness or victim for identification as the criminal. A **one-man showup** is an exhibition of one person to a witness or victim for identification as the criminal.

In practice, police conduct a lineup and, if the suspect is identified, the witness is asked at trial to testify that he or she identified the perpetrator of the crime at the lineup . Therefore, if the initial identification is faulty, the subsequent in-court identification is also faulty. Even if the witness is asked to identify anew the perpetrator of the crime, such an identification is tainted by the witness's earlier identification. In the following landmark case the Supreme Court addressed the problems inherent in pretrial identification procedures.

UNITED STATES
V.
WADE

338 U.S. 218 (1967)

The question here is whether courtroom identifications of an accused at trial are to be excluded from evidence because the accused was exhibited to the witness before trial at a post-indictment lineup conducted for identification purposes without notice to and in the absence of the accused's appointed counsel.

The federally insured bank in Eustace, Texas, was robbed on September 21, 1964. A man with a small strip of tape on each side of his face entered the bank, pointed a pistol at the female cashier and the vice president, the only persons in the bank at the time, and forced them to fill a pillowcase with the bank's money. The man then drove away with an accomplice who had been waiting in a stolen car outside the bank. On March 23, 1965, an indictment was returned against respondent, Wade, and two others for conspiring to rob the bank, and against Wade and accomplice for the robbery itself. Wade was arrested on April 2, and counsel was appointed to represent him on April 26. Fifteen days later an FBI agent, without notice to Wade's lawyer, arranged to have the two bank employees observe a lineup made up of Wade and five or six other prisoners and conducted in a courtroom of the local county courthouse. Each person in the line wore strips of tape such as allegedly worn by the robber and upon direction each said something like "put the money in the bag," the words allegedly uttered by the robber. Both bank employees identified Wade in the lineup as the bank robber.

At trial, the two employees, when asked on direct examination if the robber was in the courtroom, pointed to Wade.

LEGAL TERMS

lineup
Where the police exhibit a group of people, among whom is the suspect, to a witness or victim for identification as the criminal.

one-man showup
Where the police exhibit one person to a witness or victim for identification as the criminal.

The prior lineup identification was then elicited from both employees on cross examination. . . . But the confrontation compelled by the State between the accused and the victim or witnesses to a crime to elicit identification evidence is peculiarly riddled with innumerable dangers and variable factors which might seriously, even crucially, derogate from a fair trial. The vagaries of eyewitness identification are well-known; the annals of criminal law are rife with instances of mistaken identification. . . . The identification of strangers is proverbially untrustworthy. . . . A major factor contributing to the high incidence of miscarriage of justice from mistaken identification has been the degree of suggestion inherent in the manner in which the prosecution presents the suspect to witness for pretrial identification. A commentator has observed that "[t]he influence of improper suggestion upon identifying witnesses probably accounts for more miscarriages of justice than any other single factor—perhaps it is responsible for more such errors than all other factors combined." . . . Suggestion can be created intentionally or unintentionally in many subtle ways. And the dangers for the suspect are particularly grave when the witness' opportunity for observation was insubstantial, and thus his susceptibility to suggestion the greatest.

> Moreover, "[i]t is a matter of common experience that, once a witness has picked out the accused at the line-up, he is not likely to go back on his word later on, so that in practice the issue of identity may (in the absence of other relevant evidence) for all practical purposes be determined there and then, before the trial." . . .

What facts have been disclosed in specific cases about the conduct of pretrial confrontations for identification illustrate both the potential for substantial prejudice to the accused at that stage and the need for its revelation at trial. A commentator provides some striking examples:

> In a Canadian case . . . the defendant had been picked out of a line-up of six men, of which he was the only Oriental. In other cases, a black-haired suspect was placed among a group of light-haired persons, tall suspects have been made to stand with short non-suspects, and, in a case where the

perpetrator of the crime was known to be a youth, a suspect under twenty was placed in a line-up with five other persons, all of whom were forty or over.

Similarly, state reports, in the course of describing prior identifications admitted as evidence of guilt, reveal numerous instances of suggestive procedures, for example, that all in the lineup but the suspect were known to the identifying witness, that the other participants in a lineup were grossly dissimilar in appearance to the suspect, that only the suspect was required to wear distinctive clothing which the culprit allegedly wore. . . .

Since it appears that there is grave potential for prejudice, intentional or not, in the pretrial lineup, which may not be capable of reconstruction at trial, and since presence of counsel can often avert prejudice and assure a meaningful confrontation at trial, there can be little doubt that for Wade the post-indictment lineup was a critical stage of the prosecution at which was [entitled to counsel]. . . .

[The Court then concluded that in-court identifications must be excluded if they follow a lineup at which a defendant is not permitted counsel, unless the in-court identification has an independent origin.]

Section 13.3(a.1) The Right to Counsel

What *Wade* mandates is that counsel be provided at pretrial lineups and showups. For years it was unknown whether this meant all pretrial lineups and showups or just those after the Sixth Amendment attaches. *Kirby v. Illinois*, 406 U.S. 682 (1972), resolved this dispute by requiring counsel only after initiation of "adversary judicial proceedings—whether by way of formal charge, preliminary hearing, indictment, information, or arraignment."

Section 13.3(b) The Fairness Right

In addition to having a right to counsel at post-indictment lineups, an accused is entitled to a fair lineup; one that is not unnecessarily suggestive of guilt. In *Stoval v. Denno*, 388 U.S. 293 (1967), the Supreme Court found that the Due Process Clauses of the Fifth and Fourteenth Amendments prohibit identifications that are so unnecessarily suggestive that there is real chance of misidentification. In addition to being impermissibly suggestive, an identification must be unreliable to be excluded.[10] When making the determination of whether an identification violates due process, a court is to examine the "totality of the circumstances" surrounding the identification. Examples of impermissibly suggestive were mentioned in the *Wade* opinion. For example, if a witness states that a white male committed a crime, it would be an improper to exhibit four black men and one white man in a lineup.

One-man showups, obviously, are more suggestive of guilt than lineups. As such, they should be used with caution. Generally, a one-man showup should occur within a short period of time after the crime (minutes or hours). If there is time to organize a lineup, this is the preferable method of identification procedure.

Section 13.3(b.1) Self-Incrimination

It is not violative of the Fifth Amendment's privilege against self-incrimination for a defendant to be compelled to appear in a lineup. The privilege against self-incrimination applies to "testimony" and not to physical acts, such as walking, gesturing, measuring, or speaking certain words for identification purposes.[11] If a defendant has changed in appearance, he or she may be made to shave, to don a wig or hairpiece, or wear a certain article of clothing.

The question under the Fifth Amendment is whether the act requested is "communicative." If so, then the defendant may not be compelled to engage in the act. If not, the opposite is true.

Section 13.3(c) Photographs

Police may show a witness photos to gain an identification. The due process test discussed above applies to the use of photos; that is, the event must not be impermissibly suggestive and unreliable. The showing of one picture is likely to be determined improper, absent an emergency. As is true of lineups, the people in the photos should be similar in appearance. Also, a "mugshot" (a picture taken by law-enforcement agencies after arrest) of the accused should not be mixed with ordinary photos of non-suspects. Nor should the photos be presented in such a manner that the defendant's picture stands out.

The Supreme Court has determined that there is no right to counsel at a photo identification session, either before the initiation of the adversary judicial proceeding or thereafter.

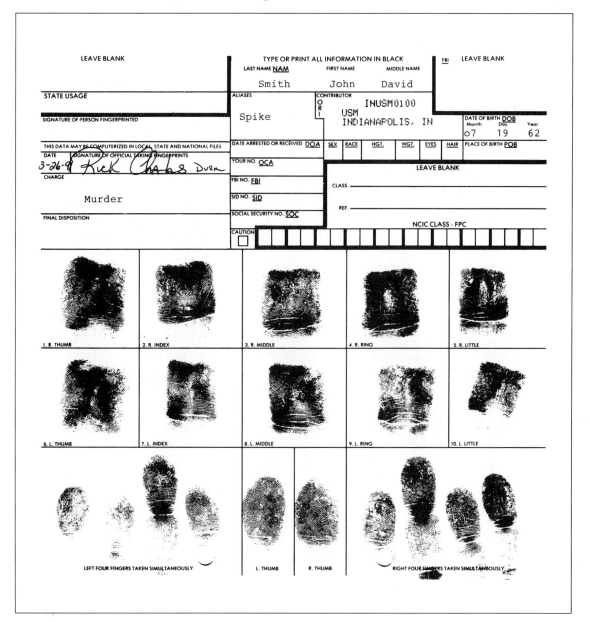

Fingerprint Card

Section 13.3(d) Scientific Identification Procedures

Law enforcement may use scientific methods of identification to prove that a defendant committed a crime. Fingerprinting, blood tests, genetic tests (deoxyribonucleic acid, or DNA, testing), voice tests, and handwriting samples are examples of such techniques.

Such tests are not critical stages of the criminal proceedings, and, accordingly, there is no right to counsel. There is also no right to refuse to cooperate with such testing on Fifth Amendment grounds, since the defendant is not being required to give testimony. However, if a test involves an invasion of privacy, then the Fourth Amendment requires probable cause before the procedure may be forced on an unwilling defendant.

SCHMERBER
V.
CALIFORNIA

384 U.S. 757 (1966)

Petitioner was convicted in Los Angeles Municipal Court of the criminal offense of driving an automobile while under the influence of intoxicating liquor. He has been arrested at a hospital while receiving treatment for injuries suffered in an accident involving the automobile that he was apparently driving. At the direction of a police officer, a blood sample was then withdrawn from petitioner's body by a physician at the hospital. The chemical analysis of this sample revealed a percent by weight of alcohol in his blood at the time of the offense which indicated intoxication, and the report of this analysis was admitted in evidence at trial. . . .

II. The Privilege Against Self-Incrimination Claim

. . . We . . . must now decide whether the withdrawal of the blood and admission in evidence of the analysis involved in this case violated petitioner's privilege. We hold that the privilege protects an accused only from being compelled to testify against himself, or otherwise provide the State with evidence of a testimonial or communicative nature, and that the withdrawal of blood and use of the analysis in question in this case did not involve compulsion to these ends. . . .

IV. The Search and Seizure Claim

The overriding function of the Fourth Amendment is to protect personal privacy and dignity against unwarranted intrusion by the State. . . .

The values protected by the Fourth Amendment thus substantially overlap those the Fifth Amendment helps to protect. . . .

Because we are dealing with intrusions into the human body rather than with state interferences with property relationships or private papers—"house, papers, and effect"—we write on a clean slate. . . .

In this case, as will often be true when charges of driving under the influence of alcohol are pressed, these questions arise in the context of an arrest made by an officer without a warrant. Here, there was plainly probable cause for the officer to arrest petitioner and charge him with driving an automobile while under the influence of intoxicating liquor. The police officer who arrived at the scene shortly after the accident smelled liquor on petitioner's breath, and testified that petitioner's eyes were "bloodshot, watery, sort of a glassy appearance." The officer saw petitioner again at the hospital, within two hours of the accident. There he noticed similar symptoms of drunkenness. He thereupon informed petitioner "that he was under arrest and that he was entitled to the services of an attorney, and that he could remain silent, and that anything he told me would be used against him in evidence." . . .

Although the facts which established probable cause to arrest in this case also suggested the required relevance and likely success of a test of petitioner's blood for alcohol, the question remains whether the arresting officer was permitted to draw these inferences himself, or was required instead to procure a warrant before proceeding with the test. Search warrants are ordinarily required for searches of dwellings, and, absent an emergency, no less could be required where intrusions of the human body are concerned. . . . The importance of informed, detached and deliberate determinations of the issue whether or not to invade another's body in search of evidence of guilt is indisputable and great.

The officer in the present case, however, might reasonably have believed that he was confronted with an emergency, in which the delay necessary to obtain a warrant, under the circumstances, threatened "the destruction of evidence," . . . . We are told that the percentage of alcohol in the blood begins to diminish shortly after drinking stops, as the body functions to eliminate it from the system. Particularly in a case such as this, where time had to be taken to bring the accused to a hospital and to investigate the scene of the accident, there was no time to seek out a magistrate and secure a warrant. . . .

Finally, the records show that the test was performed in a reasonable manner. Petitioner's blood was taken by physician in a hospital environment according to accepted medical practices. We are thus not presented with the serious questions which would arise if a search involving use of a medical technique, even of the most rudimentary sort, were made by other than medical personnel or in other than a medical environment—for example, if it were administered by police in the privacy of the stationhouse. To tolerate searches under these conditions might be to invite an unjustified element of personal risk of infection and pain. . . .

To assure that physical evidence discovered during an investigation remains unchanged and is not confused with evidence from other investigations, police must maintain chain of custody.

The officer who discovered the evidence must mark the evidence, and then subsequent contacts with the evidence, such as by forensics officers, must be recorded. This creates a record of who had possession of the evidence, known as chain of custody. A record of chain of custody must be precisely kept from the time the evidence is seized until it is introduced at trial.

Section 13.3(e) Exclusion of Improper Identifications

The consequences of not providing counsel during an identification procedure after the adversary judicial proceeding has begun were discussed in *Wade.* First, testimony about an illegal identification must be excluded at trial. Second, in-court identifications may be excluded if tainted by the pretrial identification. However, if the government can show, by clear and convincing evidence, that an in-court identification has a source independent of the illegal pretrial identification, then it is to be allowed. The *Wade*

Court said the following factors are to be considered when making the taint or no taint determination:

1. The prior opportunity to observe the criminal act;
2. The difference between a witness' pre-lineup description and actual description of an accused;
3. Whether the witness identified another person as the criminal before the lineup;
4. Whether the witness identified the accused by photo prior to the lineup;
5. Whether the witness was unable to identify the accused on a previous occasion;
6. The lapse of time between the crime and the identification.

In most cases, a court will find an independent source for an in-court identification and will allow a witness to identify the defendant during trial while prohibiting mention of the pretrial identification.

The same rules apply to identifications that are impermissibly suggestive and unreliable. They must be excluded, as must the fruits thereof, unless an independent basis for an in-court identification can be shown.

REVIEW QUESTIONS

1. List the rights included in the *Miranda* warnings. When must they be read to a defendant?
2. What happens if an officer fails to read a defendant his rights prior to obtaining a confession?
3. Is it a violation of the Federal Wiretap Law (Title III of the Omnibus Crime Control and Safe Streets Act) for Gary to allow law-enforcement officers to listen to a phone conversation between himself and Terry without Terry's knowledge? If so, what happens if Terry makes incriminating statements?
4. Does a defendant have a right to counsel at a lineup? If so, what is the source of that right?
5. Does a defendant have a right to counsel at a photo identification session? If so, what is the source of that right.
6. Why must law-enforcement officers obtain a court order to intercept a telephone conversation using traditional line phones and not a conversation using a cordless phone?

7. What is chain of custody?

8. Assume that a prosecutor wants a defendant to submit to genetic testing (deoxyribonucleic acid, or DNA) in order to compare his DNA with that of hair found on a victim. Does he have a Fourth Amendment challenge? A Fifth?

REVIEW PROBLEMS

1. While on patrol officer Norman heard a scream from the backyard of a house. The officer proceeded to the back of the house where he observed two people; a badly beaten victim and a young man (Tom) standing over her. Shocked by the sight of the victim the officer exclaimed "What happened here?" Tom responded, "I killed her and threw the baseball bat over the fence." Officer Norman restrained the young man, called for an ambulance, and retrieved the bat. While waiting for the ambulance to arrive officer Norman asked the young man what his motive was for injuring the woman. Tom explained his motive to the officer. The officer never mirandized Tom. A motion to suppress the statement, "I killed her and threw the baseball bat over the fence," as well as the statement explaining his motive has been filed. Additionally, Tom claims that the bat should be excluded because it is a fruit of an illegal interrogation. What should be the outcome? Explain your answer.

2. An officer has made application for a court order approving electronic survellience of Defendant. The order is granted, stating: "From June 1 to June 7, Officer X, having established probable cause, is granted the authority to intercept the wire communications of Defendant." The officer proceeded to enter Defendant's house, without a warrant, to install the listening device. Eventually, a recording is made of the defendant discussing his illegal activities with a friend. Defendant is arrested, charged, and has filed a motion to suppress the interception. Defendant asserts that the entry into his house was illegal. Discuss.

3. Why are the rules concerning the admissibility of confessions more stringent than for other forms of evidence?

4. Do you believe that it is self-incrimination to give blood, hair, etc., which proves one's guilt?

5. Describe a pretrial identification which you believe is unduly suggestive. Explain why it is too suggestive of guilt.

NOTES

[1] Laurence H. Tribe is professor of constitutional law at Harvard University School of Law. Mr. Tribe has taught at Harvard since 1968.

[2] *Brown v. Mississippi*, 295 U.S. 278 (1936).

[3] *New York v. Quarles*, 467 U.S. 649 (1984).

[4] *Michigan v. Mosley*, 423 U.S. 96 (1975).

[5] *Oregon v. Hass*, 420 U.S. 714 (1975).

[6] 18 U.S.C. §2510, et seq.

[7] 18 U.S.C. §2518.

[8] *Tyler v. Berodt*, 877 F.2d 705 (8th Cir. 1989).

[9] *Smith v. Maryland*, 442 U.S. 735 (1979).

[10] *Manson v. Braithwaite*, 432 U.S. 98 (1977).

[11] *Schmerber v. California*, 384 U.S. 757 (1966).

APPENDIX A

The Constitution of the United States of America

We the People of the United States, in Order to form a more perfect Union, establish Justice, insure domestic Tranquility, provide for the common defence, promote the general Welfare, and secure the Blessings of Liberty to ourselves and our Posterity, do ordain and establish this Constitution for the United States of America.

ARTICLE I

Section 1 All legislative Powers herein granted shall be vested in a Congress of the United States, which shall consist of a Senate and House of Representatives.

Section 2 (1) The House of Representatives shall be composed of Members chosen every second Year by the People of the several States, and the Electors in each State shall have the Qualifications requisite for Electors of the most numerous Branch of the State Legislature.

(2) No Person shall be a Representative who shall not have attained to the age of twenty-five Years, and been seven Years a Citizen of the United States, and who shall not, when elected, be an Inhabitant of that State in which he shall be chosen.

(3) Representatives and direct Taxes shall be apportioned among the several States which may be included within this Union, according to their respective Numbers, which shall be determined by adding to the whole Number of free Persons, including those bound to Service for a Term of Years, and excluding Indians not taxed, three fifths of all other Persons. The actual Enumeration shall be made within three Years after the first Meeting of the Congress of the United States, and within every subsequent Term of ten Years, in such Manner as they shall by Law direct. The Number of Representatives shall not exceed one for every thirty Thousand, but each State shall have at Least one Representative; and until such enumeration shall be made, the State of New Hampshire shall be entitled to chuse three, Massachusetts eight, Rhode Island and Providence Plantations one, Connecticut five, New York six, New Jersey four, Pennsylvania eight, Delaware one, Maryland six, Virginia ten, North Carolina five, South Carolina five, and Georgia three.

(4) When vacancies happen in the Representation from any State, the Executive Authority thereof shall issue Writs of Election to fill such Vacancies.

(5) The House of Representatives shall chuse their Speaker and other Officers; and shall have the sole Power of Impeachment.

Section 3 (1) The Senate of the United States shall be composed of two Senators from each State, chosen by the Legislature thereof, for six Years; and each Senator shall have one Vote.

(2) Immediately after they shall be assembled in Consequence of the first Election, they shall be divided as equally as may be into three Classes. The Seats of the Senators of the first Class shall be vacated at the Expiration of the second Year, of the second Class at the Expiration of the fourth Year, and of the third Class at the Expiration of the sixth Year, so that one third may be chosen every second Year; and if Vacancies happen by Resignation, or otherwise, during the Recess of the Legislature of any State, the Executive thereof may make temporary Appointments until the next Meeting of the Legislature, which shall then fill such Vacancies.

(3) No Person shall be a Senator who shall not have attained to the Age of thirty Years, and been nine Years a Citizen of the United States,

and who shall not, when elected, be an Inhabitant of that State for which he shall be chosen.

(4) The Vice President of the United States shall be President of the Senate, but shall have no Vote, unless they be equally divided.

(5) The Senate shall chuse their other Officers, and also a President pro tempore, in the Absence of the Vice President, or when he shall exercise the Office of the President of the United States.

(6) The Senate shall have the sole Power to try all Impeachments. When sitting for that Purpose, they shall be on Oath or Affirmation. When the President of the United States is tried, the Chief Justice shall preside: And no Person shall be convicted without the Concurrence of two thirds of the Members present.

(7) Judgment in Cases of Impeachment shall not extend further than to removal from Office, and disqualification to hold and enjoy any Office of honor, Trust or Profit under the United States: but the Party convicted shall nevertheless be liable and subject to Indictment, Trial, Judgment and Punishment, according to Law.

Section 4 (1) The Times, Places and Manner of holding Elections for Senators and Representatives, shall be prescribed in each State by the Legislature thereof; but the Congress may at any time by Law make or alter such Regulations, except as to the Places of chusing Senators.

(2) The Congress shall assemble at least once in every Year, and such Meeting shall be on the first Monday in December, unless they shall by Law appoint a different Day.

Section 5 (1) Each House shall be the Judge of the Elections, Returns and Qualifications of its own Members, and a Majority of each shall constitute a Quorum to do Business; but a smaller Number may adjourn from day to day, and may be authorized to compel the Attendance of absent Members, in such Manner, and under such Penalties as each House may provide.

(2) Each House may determine the Rules of its Proceedings, punish its Members for disorderly Behaviour, and, with the Concurrence of two thirds, expel a Member.

(3) Each House shall keep a Journal of its Proceedings, and from time to time publish the same, excepting such Parts as may in their Judgment require Secrecy; and the Yeas and Nays of the Members of either House on any question shall, at the Desire of one fifth of those Present, be entered on the Journal.

(4) Neither House, during the Session of Congress, shall, without the Consent of the other, adjourn for more than three days, nor to any other Place than that in which the two Houses shall be sitting.

Section 6 (1) The Senators and Representatives shall receive a Compensation for their Services, to be ascertained by Law, and paid out of the Treasury of the United States. They shall in all Cases, except Treason, Felony and Breach of the Peace, be privileged from Arrest during their Attendance at the Session of their respective Houses, and in going to and returning from the same; and for any Speech or Debate in either House, they shall not be questioned in any other Place.

(2) No Senator or Representative shall, during the Time for which he was elected, be appointed to any civil Office under the Authority of the United States, which shall have been created, or the Emoluments whereof shall have been encreased during such time; and no Person holding any Office under the United States, shall be a Member of either House during his Continuance in Office.

Section 7 (1) All Bills for raising Revenue shall originate in the House of Representatives; but the Senate may propose or concur with Amendments as on other Bills.

(2) Every Bill which shall have passed the House of Representatives and the Senate, shall, before it become a Law, be presented to the President of the United States; If he approve he shall sign it, but if not he shall return it, with his Objections to that House in which it shall have originated, who shall enter the Objections at large on their Journal, and proceed to reconsider it. If after such Reconsideration two thirds of that House shall agree to pass the Bill, it shall be sent, together with the Objections, to the other House, by which it shall likewise be reconsidered, and if approved by two thirds of that House, it shall become a law. But in all such Cases the Votes of both Houses shall be determined by Yeas and Nays, and the Names of the Persons voting for and against the Bill shall be entered on the Journal of each House respectively. If any Bill shall not be returned by the President within ten Days (Sunday excepted) after it shall have been presented to him, the Same shall be a Law, in like Manner as if he had signed it, unless the Congress by their Adjournment prevent its Return, in which Case it shall not be a Law.

(3) Every Order, Resolution, or Vote to which the Concurrence of the Senate and House of Representatives may be necessary (except on a question of Adjournment) shall be presented to the President of the United States; and before

the Same shall take Effect, shall be approved by him, or being disapproved by him, shall be repassed by two thirds of the Senate and House of Representatives, according to the Rules and Limitations prescribed in the Case of a Bill.

Section 8 (1) The Congress shall have Power To lay and collect Taxes, Duties, Imposts and Excises, to pay the Debts and provide for the common Defence and general Welfare of the United States; but all Duties, Imposts and Excises shall be uniform throughout the United States;

(2) To borrow Money on the credit of the United States;

(3) To regulate Commerce with foreign Nations, and among the several States, and with the Indian Tribes;

(4) To establish an uniform Rule of Naturalization, and uniform Laws on the subject of Bankruptcies throughout the United States;

(5) To coin Money, regulate the Value thereof, and of foreign Coin, and to fix the Standard of Weights and Measures;

(6) To provide for the Punishment of counterfeiting the Securities and current Coin of the United States;

(7) To establish Post Offices and post Roads;

(8) To promote the Progress of Science and useful Arts, by securing for limited Times to Authors and Inventors the exclusive Right to their respective Writings and Discoveries;

(9) To constitute Tribunals inferior to the supreme Court;

(10) To define and punish Piracies and Felonies committed on the high Seas, and Offenses against the Law of Nations;

(11) To declare War, grant Letters of Marque and Reprisal, and make Rules concerning Captures on Land and Water;

(12) To raise and support Armies, but no Appropriation of Money to that Use shall be for a longer Term than two Years;

(13) To provide and maintain a Navy;

(14) To make Rules for the Government and Regulation of the land and naval Forces;

(15) To provide for calling forth the Militia to execute the Laws of the Union, suppress Insurrections and repel Invasions;

(16) To provide for organizing, arming, and disciplining, the Militia, and for governing such Part of them as may be employed in the Service of the United States, reserving to the States respectively, the Appointment of the Officers, and the Authority of training the Militia according to the discipline prescribed by Congress;

(17) To exercise exclusive Legislation in all Cases whatsoever, over such District (not exceed-

ing ten Miles square) as may, by Cession of particular States, and the Acceptance of Congress, become the Seat of the Government of the United States, and to exercise like Authority over all Places purchased by the Consent of the Legislature of the State in which the Same shall be, for the Erection of Forts, Magazines, Arsenals, dock-Yards, and other needful Buildings;—And

(18) To make all Laws which shall be necessary and proper for carrying into Execution the foregoing Powers, and all other Powers vested by this Constitution in the Government of the United States, or in any Department or Officer thereof.

Section 9 (1) The Migration or Importation of such Persons as any of the States now existing shall think proper to admit, shall not be prohibited by the Congress prior to the Year one thousand eight hundred and eight, but a Tax or Duty may be imposed on such Importation, not exceeding ten dollars for each Person.

(2) The Privilege of the Writ of Habeas Corpus shall not be suspended unless when in Cases of Rebellion or Invasion the public Safety may require it.

(3) No Bill of Attainder or ex post facto Law shall be passed.

(4) No Capitation, or other direct, Tax shall be laid, unless in Proportion to the Census or Enumeration herein before directed to be taken.

(5) No Tax or Duty shall be laid on Articles exported from any State.

(6) No Preference shall be given by any Regulation of Commerce or Revenue to the Ports of one State over those of another; nor shall Vessels bound to, or from, one State, be obliged to enter, clear or pay Duties in another.

(7) No Money shall be drawn from the Treasury, but in Consequence of Appropriations made by Law; and a regular Statement and Account of the Receipts and Expenditures of all public Money shall be published from time to time.

(8) No Title of Nobility shall be granted by the United States: And no Person holding any Office of Profit or Trust under them, shall, without the Consent of the Congress, accept of any present, Emolument, Office, or Title, of any kind whatever, from any King, Prince or foreign State.

Section 10 (1) No State shall enter into any Treaty, Alliance, or Confederation; grant Letters of Marque and Reprisal; coin Money; emit Bills of Credit; make any Thing but gold and silver Coin a Tender in Payment of Debts; pass any Bill of Attainder, ex post facto Law, or Law impairing the Obligation of Contracts, or grant any Title of Nobility.

(2) No State shall, without the Consent of Congress, lay any Imposts or Duties on Imports or Exports, except what may be absolutely necessary for executing its inspection Laws: and the net Produce of all Duties and Imposts, laid by any State on Imports or Exports, shall be for the Use of the Treasury of the United States; and all such Laws shall be subject to the Revision and Controul of the Congress.

(3) No State shall, without the Consent of Congress, lay any Duty of Tonnage, keep Troops, or Ships of War in time of Peace, enter into any Agreement or Compact with another State, or with a foreign Power, or engage in War, unless actually invaded, or in such imminent Danger as will not admit of Delay.

ARTICLE II

Section 1 (1) The executive Power shall be vested in a President of the United States of America. He shall hold his Office during the Term of four Years, and, together with the Vice President, chosen for the same Term, be elected, as follows:

(2) Each State shall appoint, in such Manner as the Legislature thereof may direct, a Number of Electors, equal to the whole Number of Senators and Representatives to which the State may be entitled in the Congress: but no Senator or Representative, or Person holding an Office of Trust or Profit under the United States, shall be appointed an Elector.

The Electors shall meet in their respective States, and vote by Ballot for two Persons, of whom one at least shall not be an Inhabitant of the same State with themselves. And they shall make a List of all the Persons voted for, and of the Number of Votes for each; which List they shall sign and certify, and transmit sealed to the Seat of the Government of the United States, directed to the President of the Senate. The President of the Senate shall, in the presence of the Senate and House of Representatives, open all the Certificates, and the Votes shall then be counted. The Person having the greatest Number of Votes shall be the President, if such Number be a Majority of the whole Number of Electors appointed; and if there be more than one who have such Majority, and have an equal Number of Votes, then the House of Representatives shall immediately chuse by Ballot one of them for President; and if no Person have a Majority, then from the five highest on the List the said House shall in like Manner chuse the President. But in chusing the President, the Votes shall be taken by States, the Representation from each State having one Vote; a quorum for this Purpose shall consist of a Member or Members from two thirds of the States, and a Majority of all the States shall be necessary to a Choice. In every Case, after the Choice of the President, the Person having the greatest Number of Votes of the Electors shall be the Vice President. But if there should remain two or more who have equal Votes, the Senate shall chuse from them by Ballot the Vice President.

(3) The Congress may determine the Time of chusing the Electors, and the Day on which they shall give their Votes; which Day shall be the same throughout the United States.

(4) No Person except a natural born Citizen, or a Citizen of the United States, at the time of the Adoption of this Constitution, shall be eligible to the Office of President; neither shall any Person be eligible to that Office who shall not have attained to the Age of thirty five Years, and been fourteen Years a Resident within the United States.

(5) In Case of the Removal of the President from Office, or of his Death, Resignation, or Inability to discharge the Powers and Duties of the said Office, the Same shall devolve on the Vice President, and the Congress may by Law provide for the Case of Removal, Death, Resignation or Inability, both of the President and Vice President, declaring what Officer shall then act as President, and such Officer shall act accordingly, until the Disability be removed, or a President shall be elected.

(6) The President shall, at stated Times, receive for his Services, a Compensation, which shall neither be increased nor diminished during the Period for which he shall have been elected, and he shall not receive within that Period any other Emolument from the United States, or any of them.

(7) Before he enter on the Execution of his Office, he shall take the following Oath or Affirmation:—"I do solemnly swear (or affirm) that I will faithfully execute the Office of President of the United States, and will to the best of my Ability, preserve, protect and defend the Constitution of the United States."

Section 2 (1) The President shall be Commander in Chief of the Army and Navy of the United States, and of the Militia of the several States, when called into the actual Service of the United States; he may require the Opinion, in writing, of the principal Officer in each of the executive Departments, upon any Subject relating to the Duties of their respective Offices, and he shall have Power to grant Reprieves and Pardons for Offenses against the United States, except in Cases of Impeachment.

(2) He shall have Power, by and with the Advice and Consent of the Senate, to make Treaties, provided two thirds of the Senators present concur; and he shall nominate, and by and with the Advice and Consent of the Senate, shall appoint Ambassadors, other public Ministers and Consuls, Judges of the supreme Court, and all other Officers of the United States, whose Appointments are not herein otherwise provided for, and which shall be established by Law: but the Congress may by Law vest the Appointment of such inferior Officers, as they think proper, in the President alone, in the Courts of Law, or in the Heads of Departments.

(3) The President shall have Power to fill up all Vacancies that may happen during the Recess of the Senate, by granting Commissions which shall expire at the End of their next Session.

Section 3 He shall from time to time give to the Congress Information of the State of the Union, and recommend to their Consideration such Measures as he shall judge necessary and expedient; he may, on extraordinary Occasions, convene both Houses, or either of them, and in Case of Disagreement between them, with Respect to the Time of Adjournment, he may adjourn them to such Time as he shall think proper; he shall receive Ambassadors and other public Ministers; he shall take Care that the Laws be faithfully executed, and shall Commission all the Officers of the United States.

Section 4 The President, Vice President and all Civil Officers of the United States, shall be removed from Office on Impeachment for, and Conviction of, Treason, Bribery, or other high Crimes and Misdemeanors.

ARTICLE III

Section 1 The judicial Power of the United States, shall be vested in one supreme Court, and in such inferior Courts as the Congress may from time to time ordain and establish. The Judges, both of the supreme and inferior Courts, shall hold their Offices during good Behaviour, and shall, at stated Times, receive for their Services, a Compensation, which shall not be diminished during their Continuance in Office.

Section 2 (1) The judicial Power shall extend to all Cases, in Law and Equity, arising under this Constitution, the Laws of the United States, and Treaties made, or which shall be made, under their Authority;—to all Cases affecting Ambassadors, other public Ministers and Consuls;—to all Cases of admiralty and maritime Jurisdiction;—to Controversies to which the United States shall be a party;—to Controversies

between two or more States;—between a State and Citizens of another State;—between Citizens of different States;—between Citizens of the same State claiming Lands under Grants of different States, and between a State, or the Citizens thereof, and foreign States, Citizens or Subjects.

(2) In all Cases affecting Ambassadors, other public Ministers and Consuls, and those in which a State shall be Party, the supreme Court shall have original Jurisdiction. In all the other Cases before mentioned, the supreme Court shall have appellate Jurisdiction, both as to Law and Fact, with such Exceptions, and under such Regulations as the Congress shall make.

(3) The Trial of all Crimes, except in Cases of Impeachment, shall be by Jury; and such Trial shall be held in the State where the said Crimes shall have been committed; but when not committed within any State, the Trial shall be at such Place or Places as the Congress may by Law have directed.

Section 3 (1) Treason against the United States, shall consist only in levying War against them, or in adhering to their Enemies, giving them Aid and Comfort. No Person shall be convicted of Treason unless on the Testimony of two Witnesses to the same overt Act, or on Confession in open Court.

(2) The Congress shall have Power to declare the Punishment of Treason, but no Attainder of Treason shall work Corruption of Blood, or Forfeiture except during the Life of the Person attainted.

ARTICLE IV

Section 1 Full Faith and Credit shall be given in each State to the public Acts, Records, and judicial Proceedings of every other State. And the Congress may by general Laws prescribe the Manner in which such Acts, Records and Proceedings shall be proved, and the Effect thereof.

Section 2 (1) The Citizens of each State shall be entitled to all privileges and Immunities of Citizens in the several States.

(2) A Person charged in any State with Treason, Felony, or other Crime, who shall flee from Justice, and be found in another State, shall on Demand of the executive Authority of the State from which he fled, be delivered up, to be removed to the State having Jurisdiction of the Crime.

(3) No Person held to Service of Labour in one State, under the Laws thereof, escaping into another, shall, in Consequence of any Law or Regulation therein, be discharged from such Service or Labour, but shall be delivered up on

Claim of the Party to whom such Service or Labour may be due.

Section 3 (1) New States may be admitted by the Congress into this Union; but no new State shall be formed or erected within the Jurisdiction of any other State; nor any State be formed by the Junction of two or more States, or Parts of States, without the Consent of the Legislatures of the States concerned as well as of the Congress.

(2) The Congress shall have power to dispose of and make all needful Rules and Regulations respecting the Territory or other Property belonging to the United States; and nothing in this Constitution shall be so construed as to Prejudice any Claims of the United States, or of any particular State.

Section 4 The United States shall guarantee to every State in this Union a Republican Form of Government, and shall protect each of them against Invasion; and on Application of the Legislature, or of the Executive (when the Legislature cannot be convened) against domestic Violence.

ARTICLE V

The Congress, whenever two thirds of both Houses shall deem it necessary, shall propose Amendments to this Constitution, or, on the Application of the Legislatures of two thirds of the several States, shall call a Convention for proposing Amendments, which, in either Case, shall be valid to all Intents and Purposes, as Part of this Constitution, when ratified by the Legislatures of three fourths of the several States, or by Conventions in three fourths thereof, as the one or the other Mode of Ratification may be proposed by the Congress; Provided that no Amendment which may be made prior to the Year One thousand eight hundred and eight shall in any Manner affect the first and fourth Clauses in the Ninth Section of the first Article; and that no State, without its Consent, shall be deprived of its equal Suffrage in the Senate.

ARTICLE VI

(1) All Debts contracted and Engagements entered into, before the Adoption of this Constitution, shall be as valid against the United States under this Constitution, as under the Confederation.

(2) This Constitution, and the Laws of the United States which shall be made in Pursuance thereof; and all Treaties made, or which shall be made, under the Authority of the United States, shall be the supreme Law of the Land; and the Judges in every State shall be bound thereby,

any Thing in the Constitution or Laws of any State to the Contrary notwithstanding.

(3) The Senators and Representatives before mentioned, and the Members of the several State Legislatures, and all executive and judicial Officers, both of the United States and of the several States, shall be bound by Oath or Affirmation, to support this Constitution; but no religious Test shall ever be required as a Qualification to any Office or public Trust under the United States.

ARTICLE VII

The Ratification of the Conventions of nine States, shall be sufficient for the Establishment of this Constitution between the States so ratifying the Same.

ARTICLES IN ADDITION TO, AND AMENDMENT OF, THE CONSTITUTION OF THE UNITED STATES OF AMERICA, PROPOSED BY CONGRESS, AND RATIFIED BY THE SEVERAL STATES, PURSUANT TO THE FIFTH ARTICLE OF THE ORIGINAL CONSTITUTION

AMENDMENT I (1791)

Congress shall make no law respecting an establishment of religion, or prohibiting the free exercise thereof; or abridging the freedom of speech, or of the press; or the right of the people peaceably to assemble, and to petition the Government for a redress of grievances.

AMENDMENT II (1791)

A well regulated Militia, being necessary to the security of a free state, the right of the people to keep and bear Arms, shall not be infringed.

AMENDMENT III (1791)

No Soldier shall, in time of peace be quartered in any house, without the consent of the Owner, nor in time of war, but in a manner to be prescribed by law.

AMENDMENT IV (1791)

The right of the people to be secure in their persons, houses, papers, and effects, against unreasonable searches and seizures, shall not be violated, and no Warrants shall issue, but upon probable cause, supported by Oath or affirmation, and particularly describing the place to be searched, and the persons or things to be seized.

AMENDMENT V (1791)

No person shall be held to answer for a capital, or otherwise infamous crime, unless on a presentment or indictment of a Grand Jury, except in cases arising in the land or naval forces, or in the Militia, when in actual service in time of War or public danger; nor shall any person be subject for the same offence to be twice put in jeopardy of life or limb; nor shall be compelled in any criminal case to be a witness against himself, nor be deprived of life, liberty, or property, without due process of law; nor shall private property be taken for public use, without just compensation.

AMENDMENT VI (1791)

In all criminal prosecutions, the accused shall enjoy the right to a speedy and public trial, by an impartial jury of the State and district wherein the crime shall have been committed, which district shall have been previously ascertained by law, and to be informed of the nature and cause of the accusation; to be confronted with the witnesses against him; to have compulsory process for obtaining witnesses in his favor, and to have the Assistance of Counsel for his defence.

AMENDMENT VII (1791)

In Suits at common law, where the value in controversy shall exceed twenty dollars, the right of trial by jury shall be preserved, and no fact tried by a jury, shall be otherwise re-examined in any Court of the United States, than according to the rules of the common law.

AMENDMENT VIII (1791)

Excessive bail shall not be required, nor excessive fines imposed, nor cruel and unusual punishments inflicted.

AMENDMENT IX (1791)

The enumeration in the Constitution, of certain rights, shall not be construed to deny or disparage others retained by the people.

AMENDMENT X (1791)

The powers not delegated to the United States by the Constitution, nor prohibited by it to the States, are reserved to the States respectively, or to the people.

AMENDMENT XI (1798)

The Judicial power of the United States shall not be construed to extend to any suit in law or equity, commenced or prosecuted against one of the United States by Citizens of another State, or by Citizens or Subjects of any Foreign State.

AMENDMENT XII (1804)

The Electors shall meet in their respective states and vote by ballot for President and Vice-President, one of whom, at least, shall not be an inhabitant of the same state with themselves; they shall name in their ballots the person voted for as President, and in distinct ballots the person voted for as Vice-President, and they shall make distinct lists of all persons voted for as President, and of all persons voted for as Vice-President, and of the number of votes for each, which lists they shall sign and certify, and transmit sealed to the seat of the government of the United States, directed to the President of the Senate;—The President of the Senate shall, in the presence of the Senate and House of Representatives, open all the certificates and the votes shall then be counted;—The person having the greatest number of votes for President, shall be the President, if such number be a majority of the whole number of Electors appointed; and if no person have such majority, then from the persons having the highest numbers not exceeding three on the list of those voted for as President, the House of Representatives shall choose immediately, by ballot, the President. But in choosing the President, the votes shall be taken by states, the representation from each state having one vote; a quorum for this purpose shall consist of a member or members from two-thirds of the states, and a majority of all the states shall be necessary to a choice. And if the House of Representatives shall not choose a President whenever the right of choice shall devolve upon them, before the fourth day of March next following, then the Vice-President shall act as President, as in the case of the death or other constitutional disability of the President—The person having the greatest number of votes as Vice-President, shall be the Vice-President, if such number be a majority of the whole number of Electors appointed, and if no person have a majority, then from the two highest numbers on the list, the Senate shall choose the Vice-President; A quorum for the purpose shall consist of two-thirds of the whole number of Senators, and a majority of the whole number shall be necessary to a choice. But no person constitutionally ineligible to the office of President shall be eligible to that of Vice-President of the United States.

AMENDMENT XIII (1865)

Section 1 Neither slavery nor involuntary servitude, except as a punishment for crime whereof the party shall have been duly convicted, shall exist within the United States, or any place subject to their jurisdiction.

Section 2 Congress shall have power to enforce this article by appropriate legislation.

AMENDMENT XIV (1868)

Section 1 All persons born or naturalized in the United States and subject to the jurisdiction thereof, are citizens of the United States and of the State wherein they reside. No State shall make or enforce any law which shall abridge the privileges or immunities of citizens of the United States; nor shall any State deprive any person of life, liberty, or property, without due process of law; nor deny to any person within its jurisdiction the equal protection of the laws.

Section 2 Representatives shall be apportioned among the several States according to their respective numbers, counting the whole number of persons in each State, excluding Indians not taxed. But when the right to vote at any election for the choice of electors for President and Vice-President of the United States, Representatives in Congress, the Executive and Judicial officers of a State, or the members of the Legislature thereof, is denied to any of the male inhabitants of such State, being twenty-one years of age, and citizens of the United States, or in any way abridged, except for participation in rebellion, or other crime, the basis of representation therein shall be reduced in the proportion which the number of such male citizens shall bear to the whole number of male citizens twenty-one years of age in such State.

Section 3 No person shall be a Senator or Representative in Congress, or elector of President and Vice-President, or hold any office, civil or military, under the United States, or under any State, who, having previously taken an oath, as a member of Congress, or as an officer of the United States, or as a member of any State legislature, or as an executive or judicial officer of any State, to support the Constitution of the United States, shall have engaged in insurrection or rebellion against the same, or given aid or comfort to the enemies thereof. But Congress may by a vote of two-thirds of each House, remove such disability.

Section 4 The validity of the public debt of the United States, authorized by law, including debts incurred for payment of pensions and bounties for services in suppressing insurrection or rebellion, shall not be questioned. But neither the United States nor any State shall assume or pay any debt or obligation incurred in aid of insurrection or rebellion against the United States, or any claim for the loss or emancipation of any slave; but all such debts, obligations and claims shall be held illegal and void.

Section 5 The Congress shall have power to enforce, by appropriate legislation, the provisions of this article.

AMENDMENT XV (1870)

Section 1 The right of citizens of the United States to vote shall not be denied or abridged by the United States or by any State on account of race, color, or previous condition of servitude.

Section 2 The Congress shall have power to enforce this article by appropriate legislation.

AMENDMENT XVI (1913)

The Congress shall have power to lay and collect taxes on incomes, from whatever source derived, without apportionment among the several States, and without regard to any census or enumeration.

AMENDMENT XVII (1913)

The Senate of the United States shall be composed of two Senators from each State, elected by the people thereof, for six years; and each Senator shall have one vote. The electors in each State shall have the qualifications requisite for electors of the most numerous branch of the State legislatures.

When vacancies happen in the representation of any State in the Senate, the executive authority of such State shall issue writs of election to fill such vacancies: *Provided,* That the legislature of any State may empower the executive thereof to make temporary appointments until the people fill the vacancies by election as the legislature may direct.

This amendment shall not be so construed as to affect the election or term of any Senator chosen before it becomes valid as part of the Constitution.

AMENDMENT XVIII (1919)

Section 1 After one year from the ratification of this article the manufacture, sale, or transportation of intoxicating liquors within, the importation thereof into, or the exportation thereof from the United States and all territory subject to the jurisdiction thereof for beverage purposes is hereby prohibited.

Section 2 The Congress and the several States shall have concurrent power to enforce this article by appropriate legislation.

Section 3 This article shall be inoperative unless it shall have been ratified as an amendment to the Constitution by the legislatures of the several States, as provided in the Constitution, within seven years from the date of the submission hereof to the States by the Congress.

AMENDMENT XIX (1920)

The right of citizens of the United States to vote shall not be denied or abridged by the United States or by any State on account of sex.

Congress shall have power to enforce this article by appropriate legislation.

AMENDMENT XX (1933)

Section 1 The terms of the President and Vice President shall end at noon on the 20th day of January, and the terms of Senators and Representatives at noon on the 3d day of January, of the years in which such terms would have ended if this article had not been ratified; and the terms of their successors shall then begin.

Section 2 The Congress shall assemble at least once in every year, and such meeting shall begin at noon on the 3d day of January, unless they shall by law appoint a different day.

Section 3 If, at the time fixed for the beginning of the term of the President, the President elect shall have died, the Vice President elect shall become President. If a President shall not have been chosen before the time fixed for the beginning of his term, or if the President elect shall have failed to qualify, then the Vice President elect shall act as President until a President shall have qualified; and the Congress may by law provide for the case wherein neither a President elect nor a Vice President elect shall have qualified, declaring who shall then act as President, or the manner in which one who is to act shall be selected, and such person shall act accordingly until a President or Vice President shall have qualified.

Section 4 The Congress may by law provide for the case of the death of any of the persons from whom the House of Representatives may choose a President whenever the right of choice shall have devolved upon them, and for the case of the death of any of the persons from whom the Senate may choose a Vice President whenever the right of choice shall have devolved upon them.

Section 5 Sections 1 and 2 shall take effect on the 15th day of October following the ratification of this article.

Section 6 This article shall be inoperative unless it shall have been ratified as an amendment to the Constitution by the legislatures of three-fourths of the several States within seven years from the date of its submission.

AMENDMENT XXI (1933)

Section 1 The eighteenth article of amendment to the Constitution of the United States is hereby repealed.

Section 2 The transportation or importation into any State, Territory or possession of the United States for delivery or use therein of intoxicating liquors, in violation of the laws thereof, is hereby prohibited.

Section 3 This article shall be inoperative unless it shall have been ratified as an amendment to the Constitution by conventions in the several States, as provided in the Constitution, within seven years from the date of the submission hereof to the States by the Congress.

AMENDMENT XXII (1951)

Section 1 No person shall be elected to the office of the President more than twice, and no person who has held the office of President, or acted as President, for more than two years of a term to which some other person was elected President shall be elected to the office of the President more than once. But this Article shall not apply to any person holding the office of President when this Article was proposed by the Congress, and shall not prevent any person who may be holding the office of President, or acting as President, during the term within which this Article becomes operative from holding the office of President or acting as President during the remainder of such term.

Section 2 This Article shall be inoperative unless it shall have been ratified as an amendment to the Constitution by the legislatures of three-fourths of the several States within seven years from the date of its submission to the States by the Congress.

AMENDMENT XXIII (1961)

Section 1 The District constituting the seat of Government of the United States shall appoint in such manner as the Congress may direct:

A number of electors of President and Vice President equal to the whole number of Senators and Representatives in Congress to which the District would be entitled if it were a State, but in no event more than the least populous State; they shall be in addition to those appointed by the States, but they shall be considered, for the purposes of the election of President and Vice President, to be electors appointed by a State; and they shall meet in the District and perform such duties as provided by the twelfth article of amendment.

Section 2 The Congress shall have power to enforce this article by appropriate legislation.

AMENDMENT XXIV (1964)

Section 1 The right of citizens of the United States to vote in any primary or other election for President or Vice President, for electors for President or Vice President, or for Senator or Representative in Congress, shall not be denied or abridged by the United States or any State by reason of failure to pay any poll tax or other tax.

Section 2 The Congress shall have power to enforce this article by appropriate legislation.

AMENDMENT XXV (1967)

Section 1 In case of the removal of the President from office or of his death or resignation, the Vice President shall become President.

Section 2 Whenever there is a vacancy in the office of the Vice President, the President shall nominate a Vice President who shall take office upon confirmation by a majority vote of both Houses of Congress.

Section 3 Whenever the President transmits to the President pro tempore of the Senate and the Speaker of the House of Representatives his written declaration that he is unable to discharge the powers and duties of his office, and until he transmits to them a written declaration to the contrary, such powers and duties shall be discharged by the Vice President as Acting President.

Section 4 Whenever the Vice President and a majority of either the principal officers of the executive departments or of such other body as Congress may by law provide, transmit to the President pro tempore of the Senate and the Speaker of the House of Representatives their written declaration that the President is unable to discharge the powers and duties of his office, the Vice President shall immediately assume the powers and duties of the office as Acting President.

Thereafter, when the President transmits to the President pro tempore of the Senate and the Speaker of the House of Representatives his written declaration that no inability exists, he shall resume the powers and duties of his office unless the Vice President and a majority of either the principal officers of the executive department or of such other body as Congress may by law provide, transmit within four days to the President pro tempore of the Senate and the Speaker of the House of Representatives their written declaration that the President is unable to discharge the powers and duties of his office. Thereupon Congress shall decide the issue, assembling within forty-eight hours for that purpose if not in session. If the Congress, within twenty-one days after receipt of the latter written declaration, or, if Congress is not in session, within twenty-one days after Congress is required to assemble, determines by two-thirds vote of both Houses that the President is unable to discharge the powers and duties of his office, the Vice President shall continue to discharge the same as Acting President; otherwise, the President shall resume the powers and duties of his office.

AMENDMENT XXVI (1971)

Section 1 The right of citizens of the United States, who are eighteen years of age or older, to vote shall not be denied or abridged by the United States or by any State on account of age.

Section 2 The Congress shall have power to enforce this article by appropriate legislation.

APPENDIX B

Excerpts of the Model Penal Code

PART I. GENERAL PROVISIONS

Article 1. Preliminary

Section 1.04. Classes of Crimes; Violations.

(1) An offense defined by this Code or by any other statute of this State, for which a sentence of [death or of] imprisonment is authorized, constitutes a crime. Crimes are classified as felonies, misdemeanors or petty misdemeanors.

(2) A crime is a felony if it is so designated in this Code or if persons convicted thereof may be sentenced [to death or] to imprisonment for a term which, apart from an extended term, is in excess of one year.

(3) A crime is a misdemeanor if it is so designated in this Code or in a statute other than this Code enacted subsequent thereto.

(4) A crime is a petty misdemeanor if it so designated in this Code or in a statute other than this Code enacted subsequent thereto or if it is defined by a statute other than this Code which now provides that persons convicted thereof may be sentenced to imprisonment for a term of which the maximum is less than one year.

(5) An offense defined by this Code or by any other statute of this State constitutes a violation if it is so designated in this Code or in the law defining the offense or if no other sentence than a fine, or fine and forfeiture or other civil penalty is authorized upon conviction or if it is defined by a statute other than this Code which now provides that the offense shall not constitute a crime. A violation does not constitute a crime and conviction of a violation shall not give rise to any disability or legal disadvantage based on conviction of a criminal offense.

(6) Any offense declared by law to constitute a crime, without specification of the grade thereof or of the sentence authorized upon conviction, is a misdemeanor.

(7) An offense defined by any statute of this State other than this Code shall be classified as provided in this Section and the sentence that may be imposed upon conviction thereof shall hereafter be governed by this Code.

Section 1.05. All Offenses Defined by Statue; Application of General Provisions of the Code.

(1) No conduct constitutes an offense unless it is a crime or violation under this Code or another statute of this State.

(2) The provisions of Part I of the Code are applicable to offenses defined by other statutes, unless the Code otherwise provides.

(3) This Section does not affect the power of a court to punish for contempt or to employ any sanction authorized by law for the enforcement of an order or a civil judgment or decree.

Section 1.12. Proof Beyond a Reasonable Doubt; Affirmative Defenses; Burden of Proving Fact When Not an Element of an Offense; Presumptions.

(1) No person may be convicted of an offense unless each element of such offense is proved beyond a reasonable doubt. In the absence of such proof, the innocence of the defendant is assumed.

(2) Subsection (1) of this Section does not:

(a) require the disproof of an affirmative defense unless and until there is evidence supporting such defense; or

(b) apply to any defense which the Code or another statute plainly requires the defendant to prove by a preponderance of evidence.

(3) A ground of defense is affirmative, within the meaning of Subsection (2)(a) of this Section, when:

(a) it arises under a section of the Code which so provides; or

(b) it relates to an offense defined by a statute other than the Code and such statute so provides; or

(c) it involves a matter of excuse or justification peculiarly within the knowledge of the defendant on which he can fairly be required to adduce supporting evidence.

(4) When the application of the Code depends upon the finding of a fact which is not an element of an offense, unless the Code otherwise provides:

(a) the burden of proving the fact is on the prosecution or defendant, depending on whose interest or contention will be furthered if the finding should be made; and

(b) the fact must be proved to the satisfaction of the Court or jury, as the case may be.

(5) When the Code establishes a presumption with respect to any fact which is an element of an offense, it has the following consequences:

(a) when there is evidence of the facts which give rise to the presumption, the issue of the existence of the presumed fact must be submitted to the jury, unless the Court is satisfied that the evidence as a whole clearly negatives the presumed fact; and

(b) when the issue of the existence of the presumed fact is submitted to the jury, the Court shall charge that while the presumed fact must, on all the evidence, be proved beyond a reasonable doubt, the law declares that the jury may regard the facts giving rise to the presumption as sufficient evidence of the presumed fact.

(6) A presumption not established by the Code or inconsistent with it has the consequences otherwise accorded it by law.

Section 1.13. General Definitions.

In this Code, unless a different meaning plainly is required:

(1) "statute" includes the Constitution and a local law or ordinance of a political subdivision of the State;

(2) "act" or "action" means a bodily movement whether voluntary or involuntary;

(3) "voluntary" has the meaning specified in Section 2.01;

(4) "omission" means a failure to act;

(5) "conduct" means an action or omission and its accompanying state of mind, or, where relevant, a series of acts and omissions;

(6) "actor" includes, where relevant, a person guilty of an omission;

(7) "acted" includes, where relevant, "omitted to act";

(8) "person," "he" and "actor" include any natural person and, where relevant, a corporation or an unincorporated association;

(9) "element of an offense" means (i) such conduct or (ii) such attendant circumstances or (iii) such a result of conduct as

(a) is included in the description of the forbidden conduct in the definition of the offense; or

(b) establishes the required kind of culpability; or

(c) negatives an excuse or justification for such conduct; or

(d) negatives a defense under the statute of limitations; or

(e) establishes jurisdiction or venue;

(10) "material element of an offense" means an element that does not relate exclusively to the statute of limitations, jurisdiction, venue or to any other matter similarly unconnected with (i) the harm or evil, incident to conduct, sought to be prevented by the law defining the offense, or (ii) the existence of a justification or excuse for such conduct;

(11) "purposely" has the meaning specified in Section 2.02 and equivalent terms such as "with purpose," "designed" or "with design" have the same meaning;

(12) "intentionally" or "with intent" means purposely;

(13) "knowingly" has the meaning specified in Section 2.02 and equivalent terms such as "knowing" or "with knowledge" have the same meaning;

(14) "recklessly" has the meaning specified in Section 2.02 and equivalent terms such as "recklessness" or "with recklessness" have the same meaning;

(15) "negligently" has the meaning specified in Section 2.02 and equivalent terms such as "negligence" or "with negligence" have the same meaning;

(16) "reasonably believes" or "reasonable belief" designates a belief which the actor is not reckless or negligent in holding.

Article 2. General Principles of Liability

Section 2.01. Requirement of Voluntary Act; Omission as Basis of Liability; Possession as an Act.

(1) A person is not guilty of an offense unless his liability is based on conduct which includes a voluntary act or the omission to perform an act of which he is physically capable.

(2) The following are not voluntary acts within the meaning of this Section:

(a) a reflex or convulsion;

(b) a bodily movement during unconsciousness or sleep;

(c) conduct during hypnosis or resulting from hypnotic suggestion;

(d) a bodily movement that otherwise is not a product of the effort or determination of the actor, either conscious or habitual.

(3) Liability for the commission of an offense may not be based on an omission unaccompanied by action unless:

(a) the omission is expressly made sufficient by the law defining the offense; or

(b) a duty to perform the omitted act is otherwise imposed by law.

(4) Possession is an act, within the meaning of this Section, if the possessor knowingly procured or received the thing possessed or was aware of his control thereof for a sufficient period to have been able to terminate his possession.

Section 2.02. General Requirements of Culpability.

(1) *Minimum Requirements of Culpability.* Except as provided in Section 2.05, a person is not guilty of an offense unless he acted purposely, knowingly, recklessly or negligently, as the law may require, with respect to each material element of the offense.

(2) *Kinds of Culpability Defined.*

(a) *Purposely.*

A person acts purposely with respect to a material element of an offense when:

(i) if the element involves the nature of his conduct or a result thereof, it is his conscious object to engage in conduct of that nature or to cause such a result; and

(ii) if the element involves the attendant circumstances, he is aware of the existence of such circumstances or he believes or hopes that they exist.

(b) *Knowingly.*

A person acts knowingly with respect to a material element of an offense when:

(i) if the element involves the nature of his conduct or the attendant circumstances, he is aware that his conduct is of that nature or that such circumstances exist; and

(ii) if the element involves a result of his conduct, he is aware that it is practically certain that his conduct will cause such a result.

(c) *Recklessly.*

A person acts recklessly with respect to a material element of an offense when he consciously disregards a substantial and unjustifiable risk that the material element exists or will result from his conduct. The risk must be of such a nature and degree that, considering the nature and purpose of the actor's conduct and the circumstances known to him, its disregard involves a gross deviation from the standard of conduct that a law-abiding person would observe in the actor's situation.

(d) *Negligently.*

A person acts negligently with respect to a material element of an offense when he should be aware of a substantial and unjustifiable risk that the material element exists or will result from his conduct. The risk must be of such a nature and degree that the actor's failure to perceive it, considering the nature and purpose of his conduct and the circumstances known to him, involves a gross deviation from the standard of care that a reasonable person would observe in the actor's situation.

(3) *Culpability Required Unless Otherwise Provided.* When the culpability sufficient to establish a material element of an offense is not prescribed by law, such element is established if a person acts purposely, knowingly or recklessly with respect thereto.

(4) *Prescribed Culpability Requirement Applies to All Material Elements.* When the law defining an offense prescribes the kind of culpability that is sufficient for the commission of an offense, without distinguishing among the material elements thereof, such provision shall apply

to all the material elements of the offense, unless a contrary purpose plainly appears.

(5) *Substitutes for Negligence, Recklessness and Knowledge.* When the law provides that negligence suffices to establish an element of an offense, such element also is established if a person acts purposely, knowingly or recklessly. When recklessness suffices to establish an element, such element also is established if a person acts purposely or knowingly. When acting knowingly suffices to establish an element, such element also is established if a person acts purposely.

(6) *Requirement of Purpose Satisfied if Purpose Is Conditional.* When a particular purpose is an element of an offense, the element is established although such purpose is conditional, unless the condition negatives the harm or evil sought to be prevented by the law defining the offense.

(7) *Requirement of Knowledge Satisfied by Knowledge of High Probability.* When knowledge of the existence of a particular fact is an element of an offense, such knowledge is established if a person is aware of a high probability of its existence, unless he actually believes that it does not exist.

(8) *Requirement of Wilfulness Satisfied by Acting Knowingly.* A requirement that an offense be committed wilfully is satisfied if a person acts knowingly with respect to the material elements of the offense, unless a purpose to impose further requirements appears.

(9) *Culpability as to Illegality of Conduct.* Neither knowledge nor recklessness or negligence as to whether conduct constitutes an offense or as to the existence, meaning or application of the law determining the elements of an offense is an element of such offense, unless the definition of the offense or the Code so provides.

(10) *Culpability as Determinant of Grade of Offense.* When the grade or degree of an offense depends on whether the offense is committed purposely, knowingly, recklessly or negligently, its grade or degree shall be the lowest for which the determinative kind of culpability is established with respect to any material element of the offense.

Section 2.03. Causal Relationship Between Conduct and Result; Divergence Between Result Designed or Contemplated and Actual Result or Between Probable and Actual Result.

(1) Conduct is the cause of a result when:

(a) it is an antecedent but for which the result in question would not have occurred; and

(b) the relationship between the conduct and result satisfies any additional causal requirements imposed by the Code or by the law defining the offense.

(2) When purposely or knowingly causing a particular result is an element of an offense, the element is not established if the actual result is not within the purpose or the contemplation of the actor unless:

(a) the actual result differs from that designed or contemplated, as the case may be, only in the respect that a different person or different property is injured or affected or that the injury or harm designed or contemplated would have been more serious or more extensive than that caused; or

(b) the actual result involves the same kind of injury or harm as that designed or contemplated and is not too remote or accidental in its occurrence to have a [just] bearing on the actor's liability or on the gravity of his offense.

(3) When recklessly or negligently causing a particular result is an element of an offense, the element is not established if the actual result is not within the risk of which the actor is aware or, in the case of negligence, of which he should be aware unless:

(a) the actual result differs from the probable result only in the respect that a different person or different property is injured or affected or that the probable injury or harm would have been more serious or more extensive than that caused; or

(b) the actual result involves the same kind of injury or harm as the probable result and is not too remote or accidental in its occurrence to have a [just] bearing on the actor's liability or on the gravity of his offense.

(4) When causing a particular result is a material element of an offense for which absolute liability is imposed by law, the element is not established unless the actual result is a probable consequence of the actor's conduct.

Section 2.04. Ignorance or Mistake.

(1) Ignorance or mistake as to a matter of fact or law is a defense if:

(a) the ignorance or mistake negatives the purpose, knowledge, belief, recklessness or negligence required to establish a material element of the offense; or

(b) the law provides that the state of mind established by such ignorance or mistake constitutes a defense.

(2) Although ignorance or mistake would otherwise afford a defense to the offense charged, the defense is not available if the defendant would be guilty of another offense had the situation been as he supposed. In such case, however, the ignorance or mistake of the defendant shall reduce the grade and degree of the offense of which he may be convicted to those of the offense of which he would be guilty had the situation been as he supposed.

(3) A belief that conduct does not legally constitute an offense is a defense to a prosecution for that offense based upon such conduct when:

(a) the statute or other enactment defining the offense is not known to the actor and has not been published or otherwise reasonably made available prior to the conduct alleged; or

(b) he acts in reasonable reliance upon an official statement of the law, afterward determined to be invalid or erroneous, contained in (i) a statute or other enactment; (ii) a judicial decision, opinion or judgment; (iii) an administrative order or grant of permission; or (iv) an official interpretation of the public officer or body charged by law with responsibility for the interpretation, administration or enforcement of the law defining the offense.

(4) The defendant must prove a defense arising under Subsection (3) of this Section by a preponderance of evidence.

Section 2.05. When Culpability Requirements Are Inapplicable to Violations and to Offenses Defined by Other Statutes; Effect of Absolute Liability in Reducing Grade of Offense to Violation.

(1) The requirements of culpability prescribed by Sections 2.01 and 2.02 do not apply to:

(a) offenses which constitute violations, unless the requirement involved is included in the definition of the offense or the Court determines that its application is consistent with effective enforcement of the law defining the offense; or

(b) offenses defined by statutes other than the Code, insofar as a legislative purpose to impose absolute liability for such offenses or with respect to any material element thereof plainly appears.

(2) Notwithstanding any other provision of existing law and unless a subsequent statute otherwise provides:

(a) when absolute liability is imposed with respect to any material element of an offense defined by a statute other than the Code and a conviction is based upon such liability, the offense constitutes a violation; and

(b) although absolute liability is imposed by law with respect to one or more of the material elements of an offense defined by a statute other than the Code, the culpable commission of the offense may be charged and proved, in which event negligence with respect to such elements constitutes sufficient culpability and the classification of the offense and the sentence that may be imposed therefor upon conviction are determined by Section 1.04 and Article 6 of the Code.

Section 2.06. Liability for Conduct of Another; Complicity.

(1) A person is guilty of an offense if it is committed by his own conduct or by the conduct of another person for which he is legally accountable, or both.

(2) A person is legally accountable for the conduct of another person when:

(a) acting with the kind of culpability that is sufficient for the commission of the offense, he causes an innocent or irresponsible person to engage in such conduct; or

(b) he is made accountable for the conduct of such other person by the Code or by the law defining the offense; or

(c) he is an accomplice of such other person in the commission of the offense.

(3) A person is an accomplice of another person in the commission of an offense if:

(a) with the purpose of promoting or facilitating the commission of the offense, he

(i) solicits such other person to commit it; or

(ii) aids or agrees or attempts to aid such other person in planning or committing it; or

(iii) having a legal duty to prevent the commission of the offense, fails to make proper effect so to do; or

(b) his conduct is expressly declared by law to establish his complicity.

(4) When causing a particular result is an element of an offense, an accomplice in the conduct causing such result is an accomplice in the commission of that offense, if he acts with the kind of culpability, if any, with respect to that result that is sufficient for the commission of the offense.

(5) A person who is legally incapable of committing a particular offense himself may be guilty thereof, if it is committed by the conduct of another person for which he is legally accountable, unless such liability is inconsistent with the purpose of the provision establishing his incapacity.

(6) Unless otherwise provided by the Code or by the law defining the offense, a person is not an accomplice in an offense committed by another person if:

    (a) he is a victim of that offense; or

    (b) the offense is so defined that his conduct is inevitably incident to its commission; or

    (c) he terminates his complicity prior to the commission of the offense and

        (i) wholly deprives it of effectiveness in the commission of the offense; or

        (ii) gives timely warning to the law enforcement authorities or otherwise makes proper effort to prevent the commission of the offense.

(7) An accomplice may be convicted on proof of the commission of the offense and of his complicity therein, though the person claimed to have committed the offense has not been prosecuted or convicted or has been convicted of a different offense or degree of offense or has an immunity to prosecution or conviction or has been acquitted.

Section 2.07. Liability of Corporations, Unincorporated Associations and Persons Acting, or Under a Duty to Act, in Their Behalf.

(1) A corporation may be convicted of the commission of an offense if:

    (a) the offense is a violation or the offense is defined by a statute other than the Code in which a legislative purpose to impose liability on corporations plainly appears and the conduct is performed by an agent of the corporation acting in behalf of the corporation within the scope of his office or employment, except that if the law defining the offense designates the agents for whose conduct the corporation is accountable or the circumstances under which it is accountable, such provisions shall apply; or

    (b) the offense consists of an omission to discharge a specific duty of affirmative performance imposed on corporations by law; or

    (c) the commission of the offense was authorized, requested, commanded, performed or recklessly tolerated by the board of directors or by a high managerial agent acting in behalf of the corporation within the scope of his office or employment.

(2) When absolute liability is imposed for the commission of an offense, a legislative purpose to impose liability on a corporation shall be assumed, unless the contrary plainly appears.

(3) An unincorporated association may be convicted of the commission of an offense if:

    (a) the offense is defined by a statute other than the Code which expressly provides for the liability of such an association and the conduct is performed by an agent of the association acting in behalf of the association within the scope of his office or employment, except that if the law defining the offense designates the agents for whose conduct the association is accountable or the circumstances under which it is accountable, such provisions shall apply; or

    (b) the offense consists of an omission to discharge a specific duty of affirmative performance imposed on associations by law.

(4) As used in this Section:

    (a) "corporation" does not include an entity organized as or by a governmental agency for the execution of a governmental program;

    (b) "agent" means any director, officer, servant, employee or other person authorized to act in behalf of the corporation or association and, in the case of an unincorporated association, a member of such association;

    (c) "high managerial agent" means an officer of a corporation or an unincorporated association, or, in the case of a partnership, a partner, or any other agent of a corporation or association having duties of such responsibilities that his conduct may fairly be assumed to represent the policy of the corporation or association.

(5) In any prosecution of a corporation or an unincorporated association for the commission of an offense included within the terms of Subsection (1)(a) or Subsection (3)(a) of this Section, other than an offense for which absolute liability has been imposed, it shall be a defense if the defendant proves by a preponderance of evidence that the high managerial agent having

supervisory responsibility over the subject matter of the offense employed due diligence to prevent its commission. This paragraph shall not apply if it is plainly inconsistent with the legislative purpose in defining the particular offense.

(6) (a) A person is legally accountable for any conduct he performs or causes to be performed in the name of the corporation or an unincorporated association or in its behalf to the same extent as if it were performed in his own name or behalf.

(b) Whenever a duty to act is imposed by law upon a corporation or an unincorporated association, any agent of the corporation or association having primary responsibility for the discharge of the duty is legally accountable for a reckless omission to perform the required act to the same extent as if the duty were imposed by law directly upon himself.

(c) When a person is convicted of an offense by reason of his legal accountability for the conduct of a corporation or an unincorporated association, he is subject to the sentence authorized by law when a natural person is convicted of an offense of the grade and the degree involved.

Section 2.08 Intoxication.

(1) Except as provided in Subsection (4) of this Section, intoxication of the actor is not a defense unless it negatives an element of the offense.

(2) When recklessness establishes an element of the offense, if the actor, due to self-induced intoxication, is unaware of a risk of which he would have been aware had he been sober, such unawareness is immaterial.

(3) Intoxication does not, in itself, constitute mental disease within the meaning of Section 4.01.

(4) Intoxication which (a) is not self-induced or (b) is pathological is an affirmative defense if by reason of such intoxication the actor at the time of his conduct lacks substantial capacity either to appreciate its criminality [wrongfulness] or to conform his conduct to the requirements of law.

(5) *Definitions.* In this Section unless a different meaning plainly is required:

(a) "intoxication" means a disturbance of mental or physical capacities resulting from the introduction of substances into the body;

(b) "self-induced intoxication" means intoxication caused by substances which the actor knowingly introduces into his body, the tendency of which to cause intoxication

he knows or ought to know, unless he introduces them pursuant to medical advice or under such circumstances as would afford a defense to a charge of crime;

(c) "pathological intoxication" means intoxication grossly excessive in degree, given the amount of the intoxicant, to which the actor does not know he is susceptible.

Section 2.09 Duress.

(1) It is an affirmative defense that the actor engaged in the conduct charged to constitute an offense because he was coerced to do so by the use of, or a threat to use, unlawful force against his person or the person of another, which a person of reasonable firmness in his situation would have been unable to resist.

(2) The defense provided by this Section is unavailable if the actor recklessly placed himself in a situation in which it was probable that he would be subjected to duress. The defense is also unavailable if he was negligent in placing himself in such a situation, whenever negligence suffices to establish culpability for the offense charged.

(3) It is not a defense that a woman acted on the command of her husband, unless she acted under such coercion as would establish a defense under this Section. [The presumption that a woman, acting in the presence of her husband, is coerced is abolished.]

(4) When the conduct of the actor would otherwise be justifiable under Section 3.02, this Section does not preclude such defense.

Section 2.10. Military Orders.

It is an affirmative defense that the actor, in engaging in the conduct charged to constitute an offense, does no more than execute an order of his superior in the armed services which he does not know to be unlawful.

Section 2.11. Consent.

(1) *In General.* The consent of the victim to conduct charged to constitute an offense or to the result thereof is a defense if such consent negatives an element of the offense or precludes the infliction of the harm or evil sought to be prevented by the law defining the offense.

(2) *Consent to Bodily Harm.* When conduct is charged to constitute an offense because it causes or threatens bodily harm, consent to such conduct or to the infliction of such harm is a defense if:

(a) the bodily harm consented to or threatened by the conduct consented to is not serious; or

(b) the conduct and the harm are reasonably foreseeable hazards of joint participation in a lawful athletic contest or competitive sport; or

(c) the consent establishes a justification for the conduct under Article 3 of the Code.

(3) *Ineffective Consent.* Unless otherwise provided by the Code or by the law defining the offense, assent does not constitute consent if:

(a) it is given by a person who is legally incompetent to authorize the conduct charged to constitute the offense; or

(b) it is given by a person who by reason of youth, mental disease or defect or intoxication is manifestly unable or known by the actor to be unable to make a reasonable judgment as to the nature or harmfulness of the conduct charged to constitute the offense; or

(c) it is given by a person whose improvident consent is sought to be prevented by the law defining the offense; or

(d) it is induced by force, duress or deception of a kind sought to be prevented by the law defining the offense.

Section 2.12. *De Minimis Infractions.*

The Court shall dismiss a prosecution if, having regard to the nature of the conduct charged to constitute an offense and the nature of the attendant circumstances, it finds that the defendant's conduct:

(1) was within a customary license of tolerance, neither expressly negatived by the person whose interest was infringed nor inconsistent with the purpose of the law defining the offense; or

(2) did not actually cause or threaten the harm or evil sought to be prevented by the law defining the offense or did so only to an extent too trivial to warrant the condemnation of conviction; or

(3) presents such other extenuations that it cannot reasonably be regarded as envisaged by the legislature in forbidding the offense.

The Court shall not dismiss a prosecution under Subsection (3) of this Section without filing a written statement of its reasons.

Section 2.13. *Entrapment.*

(1) A public law enforcement official or a person acting in cooperation with such an official perpetrates an entrapment if for the purpose of obtaining evidence of the commission of an offense, he induces or encourages another person to engage in conduct constituting such offense by either:

(a) making knowingly false representations designed to induce the belief that such conduct is not prohibited; or

(b) employing methods of persuasion or inducement which create a substantial risk that such an offense will be committed by persons other than those who are ready to commit it.

(2) Except as provided in Subsection (3) of this Section, a person prosecuted for an offense shall be acquitted if he proves by a preponderance of evidence that his conduct occurred in response to an entrapment. The issue of entrapment shall be tried by the Court in the absence of the jury.

(3) The defense afforded by this Section is unavailable when causing or threatening bodily injury is an element of the offense charged and the prosecution is based on conduct causing or threatening such injury to a person other than the person perpetrating the entrapment.

Article 3. General Principles of Justification

Section 3.01. *Justification an Affirmative Defense; Civil Remedies Unaffected.*

(1) In any prosecution based on conduct which is justifiable under this Article, justification is an affirmative defense.

(2) The fact that conduct is justifiable under this Article does not abolish or impair any remedy for such conduct which is available in any civil action.

Section 3.02. *Justification Generally: Choice of Evils.*

(1) Conduct which the actor believes to be necessary to avoid harm or evil to himself or to another is justifiable, provided that:

(a) the harm or evil sought to be avoided by such conduct is greater than that sought to be prevented by the law defining the offense charged; and

(b) neither the Code nor other law defining the offense provides exceptions or defenses dealing with the specific situation involved; and

(c) a legislative purpose to exclude the justification claimed does not otherwise plainly appear.

(2) When the actor was reckless or negligent in bringing about the situation requiring a choice

of harms or evils or in appraising the necessity for his conduct, the justification afforded by this Section is unavailable in a prosecution for any offense for which recklessness or negligence, as the case may be, suffices to establish culpability.

Section 3.03. Execution of Public Duty.

(1) Except as provided in Subsection (2) of this Section, conduct is justifiable when it is required or authorized by:

(a) the law defining the duties or functions of a public officer or the assistance to be rendered to such officer in the performance of his duties; or

(b) the law governing the execution of legal process; or

(c) the judgment or order of a competent court or tribunal; or

(d) the law governing the armed services or the lawful conduct of war; or

(e) any other provision of law imposing a public duty.

(2) The other sections of this Article apply to:

(a) the use of force upon or toward the person of another for any of the purposes dealt with in such sections; and

(b) the use of deadly force for any purpose, unless the use of such force is otherwise expressly authorized by law or occurs in the lawful conduct of war.

(3) The justification afforded by Subsection (1) of this Section applies:

(a) when the actor believes his conduct to be required or authorized by the judgment or direction of a competent court or tribunal or in the lawful execution of legal process, notwithstanding lack of jurisdiction of the court or defect in the legal process; and

(b) when the actor believes his conduct to be required or authorized to assist a public officer in the performance of his duties, notwithstanding that the officer exceeded his legal authority.

Section 3.04. Use of Force in Self-Protection.

(1) *Use of Force Justifiable for Protection of the Person.* Subject to the provisions of this Section and of Section 3.09, the use of force upon or toward another person is justifiable when the actor believes that such force is immediately necessary for the purpose of protecting himself against the use of unlawful force by such other person on the present occasion.

(2) *Limitations on Justifying Necessity for Use of Force.*

(a) The use of force is not justifiable under this Section:

(i) to resist arrest which the actor knows is being made by a peace officer, although the arrest is unlawful; or

(ii) to resist force used by the occupier or possessor of property or by another person on his behalf, where the actor knows that the person using the force is doing so under a claim of right to protect the property, except that this limitation shall not apply if:

(1) the actor is a public officer acting in the performance of his duties or a person lawfully assisting him therein or a person making or assisting in a lawful arrest; or

(2) the actor has been unlawfully dispossessed of the property and is making a re-entry or recaption justified by Section 3.06; or

(3) the actor believes that such force is necessary to protect himself against death or serious bodily harm.

(b) The use of deadly force is not justifiable under this Section unless the actor believes that such force is necessary to protect himself against death, serious bodily harm, kidnapping or sexual intercourse compelled by force or threat; nor is it justifiable if:

(i) the actor, with the purpose of causing death or serious bodily harm, provoked the use of force against himself in the same encounter; or

(ii) the actor knows that he can avoid the necessity of using such force with complete safety by retreating or by surrendering possession of a thing to a person asserting a claim of right thereto or by complying with a demand that he abstain from any action which he has no duty to take, except that:

(1) the actor is not obliged to retreat from his dwelling of place or work, unless he was the initial aggressor or is assailed in his place of work by another person whose place of work the actor knows it to be; and

(2) a public officer justified in using force in the performance of his duties or a person justified in using force in his assistance or a person

justified in using force in making an arrest or preventing an escape is not obliged to desist from efforts to perform such duty, effect such arrest or prevent such escape because of resistance or threatened resistance by or on behalf of the person against whom such action is directed.

(c) Except as required by paragraphs (a) and (b) of this Subsection, a person employing protective force may estimate the necessity thereof under the circumstances as he believes them to be when the force is used, without retreating, surrendering possession, doing any other act which he has no legal duty to do or abstaining from any lawful action.

(3) *Use of Confinement as Protective Force.* The justification afforded by this Section extends to the use of confinement as protective force only if the actor takes all reasonable measures to terminate the confinement as soon as he knows that he safely can, unless the person confined has been arrested on a charge of crime.

Section 3.05. *Use of Force for the Protection of Other Persons.*

(1) Subject to the provisions of this Section and of Section 3.09, the use of force upon or toward the person of another is justifiable to protect a third person when:

(a) the actor would be justified under Section 3.04 in using such force to protect himself against the injury he believes to be threatened to the person whom he seeks to protect; and

(b) under the circumstances as the actor believes them to be, the person whom he seeks to protect would be justified in using such protective force; and

(c) the actor believes that his intervention is necessary for the protection of such other person.

(2) Notwithstanding Subsection (1) of this Section:

(a) when the actor would be obliged under Section 3.04 to retreat, to surrender the possession of a thing or to comply with a demand before using force in self-protection, he is not obliged to do so before using force for the protection of another person, unless he knows that he can thereby secure the complete safety of such other person; and

(b) when the person whom the actor seeks to protect would be obliged under Section 3.04 to retreat, to surrender the possession of a thing or to comply with a demand if he knew that he could obtain complete safety by so doing, the actor is obliged to try to cause him to do so before using force in his protection if the actor knows that he can obtain complete safety in that way; and

(c) neither the actor nor the person whom he seeks to protect is obliged to retreat when in the other's dwelling or place of work to any greater extent than in his own.

Section 3.06. *Use of Force for the Protection of Property.*

(1) *Use of Force Justifiable for Protection of Property.* Subject to the provisions of this Section and of Section 3.09, the use of force upon or toward the person of another is justifiable when the actor believes that such force is immediately necessary:

(a) to prevent or terminate an unlawful entry or other trespass upon land or a trespass against or the unlawful carrying away of tangible, movable property, provided that such land or movable property is, or is believed by the actor to be, in his possession or in the possession of another person for whose protection he acts; or

(b) to effect an entry or re-entry upon land or to retake tangible movable property, provided that the actor believes that he or the person by whose authority he acts or a person from whom he or such other person derives title was unlawfully dispossessed of such land or movable property and is entitled to possession, and provided, further, that:

(i) the force is used immediately or on fresh pursuit after such dispossession; or

(ii) the actor believes that the person against whom he uses force has no claim of right to the possession of the property and, in the case of land, the circumstances, as the actor believes them to be, are of such urgency that it would be an exceptional hardship to postpone the entry or re-entry until a court order is obtained.

(2) *Meaning of Possession.* For the purposes of Subsection (1) of this Section:

(a) a person who has parted with the custody of property to another who refuses to restore it to him is no longer in possession, unless the property is movable and was and still is located on land in his possession;

(b) a person who has been dispossessed of land does not regain possession thereof merely by setting foot thereon;

(c) a person who has a license to use or occupy real property is deemed to be in possession thereof except against the licensor acting under claim of right.

(3) *Limitations on Justifiable Use of Force.*

(a) *Request to Desist.* The use of force is justifiable under this Section only if the actor first requests the person against whom such force is used to desist from his interference with the property, unless the actor believes that:

(i) such request would be useless; or

(ii) it would be dangerous to himself or another person to make the request; or

(iii) substantial harm will be done to the physical condition of the property which is sought to be protected before the request can effectively be made.

(b) *Exclusion of Trespasser.* The use of force to prevent or terminate a trespass is not justifiable under this Section if the actor knows that the exclusion of the trespasser will expose him to substantial danger of serious bodily harm.

(c) *Resistance of Lawful Re-entry or Recaption.* The use of force to prevent an entry or re-entry upon land or the recaption of movable property is not justifiable under this Section, although the actor believes that such re-entry or recaption is unlawful, if:

(i) the re-entry or recaption is made by or on behalf of a person who was actually dispossessed of the property; and

(ii) it is otherwise justifiable under paragraph (1)(b) of this Section.

(d) *Use of Deadly Force.* The use of deadly force is not justifiable under this Section unless the actor believes that:

(i) the person against whom the force is used is attempting to dispossess him of his dwelling otherwise than under a claim of right to its possession; or

(ii) the person against whom the force is used is attempting to commit or consummate arson, burglary, robbery or other felonious theft or property destruction and either:

(1) has employed or threatened deadly force against or in the presence of the actor; or

(2) the use of force other than deadly force to prevent the commission or the consummation of the crime would expose the actor or another in his presence to substantial danger of serious bodily harm.

(4) *Use of Confinement as Protective Force.* The justification afforded by this Section extends to the use of confinement as protective force only if the actor takes all reasonable measures to terminate the confinement as soon as he knows that he can do so with safety to the property, unless the person confined has been arrested on a charge of crime.

(5) *Use of Device to Protect Property.* The justification afforded by this Section extends to the use of a device for the purpose of protecting property only if:

(a) the device is not designed to cause or known to create a substantial risk of causing death or serious bodily harm; and

(b) the use of the particular device to protect the property from entry or trespass is reasonable under the circumstances, as the actor believes them to be; and

(c) the device is one customarily used for such a purpose or reasonable care is taken to make known to probable intruders the fact that it is used.

(6) *Use of Force to Pass Wrongful Obstructor.* The use of force to pass a person whom the actor believes to be purposely or knowingly and unjustifiably obstructing the actor from going to a place to which he may lawfully go is justifiable, provided that:

(a) the actor believes that the person against whom he uses force has no claim of right to obstruct the actor; and

(b) the actor is not being obstructed from entry or movement on land which he knows to be in the possession or custody of the person obstructing him, or in the possession or custody of another person by whose authority the obstructor acts, unless the circumstances, as the actor believes them to be, are of such urgency that it would not be reasonable to postpone the entry or movement on such land until a court order is obtained; and

(c) the force used is not greater than would be justifiable if the person obstructing the actor were using force against him to prevent his passage.

Section 3.07. Use of Force in Law Enforcement.

(1) *Use of Force Justifiable to Effect an Arrest.* Subject to the provisions of this Section and of Section 3.09, the use of force upon or toward the person of another is justifiable when the actor is making or assisting in making an arrest and the actor believes that such force is immediately necessary to effect a lawful arrest.

(2) *Limitations on the Use of Force.*

(a) The use of force is not justifiable under this Section unless:

(i) the actor makes known the purpose of the arrest or believes that it is otherwise known by or cannot reasonably be made known to the person to be arrested; and

(ii) when the arrest is made under a warrant, the warrant is valid or believed by the actor to be valid.

(b) The use of deadly force is not justifiable under this Section unless:

(i) the arrest is for a felony; and

(ii) the person effecting the arrest is authorized to act as a peace officer or is assisting a person whom he believes to be authorized to act as a peace officer; and

(iii) the actor believes that the force employed creates no substantial risk of injury to innocent persons; and

(iv) the actor believes that:

(1) the crime for which the arrest is made involved conduct including the use or threatened use of deadly force; or

(2) there is a substantial risk that the person to be arrested will cause death or serious bodily harm if his apprehension is delayed.

(3) *Use of Force to Prevent Escape from Custody.* The use of force to prevent the escape of an arrested person from custody is justifiable when the force could justifiably have been employed to effect the arrest under which the person is in custody, except that a guard or other person authorized to act as a peace officer is justified in using any force, including deadly force, which he believes to be immediately necessary to prevent the escape of a person from a jail, prison, or other institution for the detention of persons charged with or convicted of a crime.

(4) *Use of Force by Private Person Assisting an Unlawful Arrest.*

(a) A private person who is summoned by a peace officer to assist in effecting an unlawful arrest, is justified in using any force which he would be justified in using if the arrest were lawful, provided that he does not believe the arrest is unlawful.

(b) A private person who assists another private person in effecting an unlawful arrest, or who, not being summoned, assists a peace officer in effecting an unlawful arrest, is justified in using any force which he would be justified in using if the arrest were lawful, provided that (i) he believes the arrest is lawful, and (ii) the arrest would be lawful if the facts were as he believes them to be.

(5) *Use of Force to Prevent Suicide or the Commission of a Crime.*

(a) The use of force upon or toward the person of another is justifiable when the actor believes that such force is immediately necessary to prevent such other person from committing suicide, inflicting serious bodily harm upon himself, committing or consummating the commission of a crime involving or threatening bodily harm, damage to or loss of property or a breach of the peace, except that:

(i) any limitations imposed by the other provisions of this Article on the justifiable use of force in self-protection, for the protection of others, the protection of property, the effectuation of an arrest or the prevention of an escape from custody shall apply notwithstanding the criminality of the conduct against which such force is used; and

(ii) the use of deadly force is not in any event justifiable under this Subsection unless:

(1) the actor believes that there is a substantial risk that the person whom he seeks to prevent from committing a crime will cause death or serious bodily harm to another unless the commission or the consummation of the crime is prevented and that the use of such force presents no substantial risk of injury to innocent persons; or

(2) the actor believes that the use of such force is necessary to suppress a riot or mutiny after the rioters or mutineers have been ordered to disperse and warned, in any particular manner that the law may require, that such force will be used if they do not obey.

(b) The justification afforded by this Subsection extends to the use of confinement as preventive force only if the actor takes all reasonable measures to terminate the confinement as soon as he knows that he safely can, unless the person confined has been arrested on a charge of crime.

Section 3.08. Use of Force by Persons with Special Responsibility for Care, Discipline or Safety of Others.

The use of force upon or toward the person of another is justifiable if:

(1) The actor is the parent or guardian or other person similarly responsible for the general care and supervision of a minor or a person acting at the request of such parent, guardian or other responsible person and:

(a) the force is used for the purpose of safeguarding or promoting the welfare of the minor, including the prevention or punishment of his misconduct; and

(b) the force used is not designed to cause or known to create a substantial risk of causing death, serious bodily harm, disfigurement, extreme pain or mental distress or gross degradation; or

(2) the actor is a teacher or a person otherwise entrusted with the care or supervision for a special purpose of a minor and:

(a) the actor believes that the force used is necessary to further such special purpose, including the maintenance of reasonable discipline in a school, class or other group, and that the use of such force is consistent with the welfare of the minor; and

(b) the degree of force, if it had been used by the parent or guardian of the minor, would not be unjustifiable under Subsection (1)(b) of this Section; or

(3) the actor is the guardian or other person similarly responsible for the general care and supervision of an incompetent person; and:

(a) the force is used for the purpose of safeguarding or promoting the welfare of the incompetent person, including the prevention of his misconduct, or, when such incompetent person is in a hospital or other institution for his care and custody, for the maintenance of reasonable discipline in such institution; and

(b) the force used is not designed to cause or known to create a substantial risk of causing death, serious bodily harm, disfigurement, extreme or unnecessary pain, mental distress, or humiliation; or

(4) the actor is a doctor or other therapist or a person assisting him at his direction, and:

(a) the force is used for the purpose of administering a recognized form of treatment which the actor believes to be adapted to promoting the physical or mental health of the patient; and

(b) the treatment is administered with the consent of the patient or, if the patient is a minor or an incompetent person, with the consent of his parent or guardian or other person legally competent to consent in his behalf, or the treatment is administered in an emergency when the actor believes that no one competent to consent can be consulted and that a reasonable person, wishing to safeguard the welfare of the patient, would consent; or

(5) the actor is a warden or other authorized official of a correctional institution, and:

(a) he believes that the force used is necessary for the purpose of enforcing the lawful rules or procedures of the institution, unless his belief in the lawfulness of the rule or procedure sought to be enforced is erroneous and his error is due to ignorance or mistake as to the provisions of the Code, any other provision of the criminal law or the law governing the administration of the institution; and

(b) the nature or degree of force used is not forbidden by Article 303 or 304 of the Code; and

(c) if deadly force is used, its use is otherwise justifiable under this Article; or

(6) the actor is a person responsible for the safety of a vessel or an aircraft or a person acting at his direction, and

(a) he believes that the force used is necessary to prevent interference with the operation of the vessel or aircraft or obstruction of the execution of a lawful order, unless his belief in the lawfulness of the order is erroneous and his error is due to ignorance or mistake as to the law defining his authority; and

(b) if deadly force is used, its use is otherwise justifiable under this Article; or

(7) the actor is a person who is authorized or required by law to maintain order or decorum in a vehicle, train or other carrier or in a place where others are assembled, and:

(a) he believes that the force used is necessary for such purpose; and

(b) the force used is not designed to cause or known to create a substantial risk of causing death, bodily harm, or extreme mental distress.

Section 3.09. Mistake of Law as to Unlawfulness of Force or Legality of Arrest; Reckless or Negligent Use of Otherwise Justifiable Force; Reckless or Negligent Injury or Risk of Injury to Innocent Persons.

(1) The justification afforded by Sections 3.04 to 3.07, inclusive, is unavailable when:

(a) the actor's belief in the unlawfulness of the force or conduct against which he employs protective force or his belief in the lawfulness of an arrest which he endeavors to effect by force is erroneous; and

(b) his error is due to ignorance or mistake as to the provisions of the Code, any other provision of the criminal law or the law governing the legality of an arrest or search.

(2) When the actor believes that the use of force upon or toward the person of another is necessary for any of the purposes for which such belief would establish a justification under Section 3.03 to 3.08 but the actor is reckless or negligent in having such belief or in acquiring or failing to acquire any knowledge or belief which is material to the justifiability of his use of force, the justification afforded by those Sections is unavailable in a prosecution for an offense for which recklessness or negligence, as the case may be, suffices to establish culpability.

(3) When the actor is justified under Sections 3.03 to 3.08 in using force upon or toward the person of another but he recklessly or negligently injures or creates a risk of injury to innocent persons, the justification afforded by those Sections is unavailable in a prosecution for such recklessness or negligence toward innocent persons.

Section 3.10 Justification in Property Crimes.

Conduct involving the appropriation, seizure or destruction of, damage to, intrusion on or interference with property is justifiable under circumstances which would establish a defense of privilege in a civil action based thereon unless:

(1) the Code or the law defining the offense deals with the specific situation involved; or

(2) a legislative purpose to exclude the justification claimed otherwise plainly appears.

Section 3.11 Definitions.

In this Article, unless a different meaning plainly is required:

(1) "unlawful force" means force, including confinement, which is employed without the consent of the person against whom it is directed and the employment of which constitutes an offense or actionable tort or would constitute such offense or tort except for a defense (such as the absence of intent, negligence, or mental capacity; duress; youth; or diplomatic status) not amounting to a privilege to use the force. Assent constitutes consent, within the meaning of this Section, whether or not it otherwise is legally effective, except assent to the infliction of death or serious bodily harm.

(2) "deadly force" means force which the actor uses with the purpose of causing or which he knows to create a substantial risk of causing death or serious bodily harm. Purposely firing a firearm in the direction of another person or at a vehicle in which another person is believed to be constitutes deadly force. A threat to cause death or serious bodily harm, by the production of a weapon or otherwise, so long as the actor's purpose is limited to creating an apprehension that he will use deadly force if necessary, does not constitute deadly force;

(3) "dwelling" means any building or structure, though movable or temporary, or a portion thereof, which is for the time being the actor's home or place of lodging.

Article 4. Responsibility

Section 4.01. Mental Disease or Defect Excluding Responsibility.

(1) A person is not responsible for criminal conduct if at the time of such conduct as a result of mental disease or defect he lacks substantial capacity either to appreciate the criminality [wrongfulness] of his conduct or to conform his conduct to the requirements of law.

(2) As used in this Article, the terms "mental disease or defect" do not include an abnormality manifested only by repeated criminal or otherwise anti-social conduct.

Section 4.02. Evidence of Mental Disease or Defect Admissible When Relevant to Element of the Offense; [Mental Disease or Defect Impairing Capacity as Ground for Mitigation of Punishment in Capital Cases].

(1) Evidence that the defendant suffered from a mental disease or defect is admissible whenever it is relevant to prove that the defendant did or did not have a state of mind which is an element of the offense.

[(2) Whenever the jury or the Court is authorized to determine or to recommend whether or not the defendant shall be sentenced to death or imprisonment upon conviction, evidence that the capacity of the defendant to appreciate the criminality [wrongfulness] of his conduct or to conform his conduct to the requirements of law was impaired as a result of mental disease or defect is admissible in favor of sentence of imprisonment.]

Section 4.03 Mental Disease or Defect Excluding Responsibility Is Affirmative Defense; Requirement of Notice; Form of Verdict and Judgment When Finding of Irresponsibility Is Made.

(1) Mental disease or defect excluding responsibility is an affirmative defense.

(2) Evidence of mental disease or defect excluding responsibility is not admissible unless the defendant, at the time of entering his plea of not guilty or within ten days thereafter or at such later time as the Court may for good cause permit, files a written notice of his purpose to rely on such defense.

(3) When the defendant is acquitted on the ground of mental disease or defect excluding responsibility, the verdict and the judgment shall so state.

Section 4.04. Mental Disease or Defect Excluding Fitness to Proceed.

No person who as a result of mental disease or defect lacks capacity to understand the proceedings against him or to assist in his own defense shall be tried, convicted or sentenced for the commission of an offense so long as such incapacity endures.

Section 4.05. Psychiatric Examination of Defendant with Respect to Mental Disease or Defect.

(1) Whenever the defendant has filed a notice of intention to rely on the defense of mental disease or defect excluding responsibility, or there is reason to doubt his fitness to proceed, or reason to believe that mental disease or defect of the defendant will otherwise become an issue in the cause, the Court shall appoint at least one qualified psychiatrist or shall request the Superintendent of the _____ Hospital to designate at least one qualified psychiatrist, which designation may be or include himself, to examine and report upon the mental condition of the defendant. The Court may order the defendant to be committed to a hospital or other suitable facility for the purpose of the examination for a period of not exceeding sixty days or such longer period as the Court determines to be necessary for the purpose and may direct that a qualified psychiatrist retained by the defendant be permitted to witness and participate in the examination.

(2) In such examination any method may be employed which is accepted by the medical profession for the examination of those alleged to be suffering from mental disease or defect.

(3) The report of the examination shall include the following: (a) a description of the nature of the examination; (b) a diagnosis of the mental condition of the defendant; (c) if the defendant suffers from a mental disease or defect, an opinion as to his capacity to understand the proceedings against him and to assist in his own defense; (d) when a notice of intention to rely on the defense of irresponsibility has been filed, an opinion as to the extent, if any, to which the capacity of the defendant to appreciate the criminality [wrongfulness] of his conduct or to conform his conduct to the requirements of law was impaired at the time of the criminal conduct charged; and (e) when directed by the Court, an opinion as to the capacity of the defendant to have a particular state of mind which is an element of the offense charged.

If the examination can not be conducted by reason of the unwillingness of the defendant to participate therein, the report shall so state and shall include, if possible, an opinion as to whether such unwillingness of the defendant was the result of mental disease or defect.

The report of the examination shall be filed [in triplicate] with the clerk of the Court, who shall cause copies to be delivered to the district attorney and to counsel for the defendant.

Section 4.08. Legal Effect of Acquittal on the Ground of Mental Disease or Defect Excluding Responsibility; Commitment; Release or Discharge.

(1) When a defendant is acquitted on the ground of mental disease or defect excluding responsibility, the Court shall order him to be committed to the custody of the Commissioner of Mental Hygiene [Public Health] to be placed in an appropriate institution for custody, care and treatment.

(2) If the Commissioner of Mental Hygiene [Public Health] is of the view that a person committed to his custody, pursuant to paragraph (1) of this Section, may be discharged or released on condition without danger to himself or to others, he shall make application for the discharge or release of such person in a report to the Court

by which such person was committed and shall transmit a copy of such application and report to the prosecuting attorney of the county [parish] from which the defendant was committed. The Court shall thereupon appoint at least two qualified psychiatrists to examine such person and to report within sixty days, or such longer period as the Court determines to be necessary for the purpose, their opinion as to his mental condition. To facilitate such examination and the proceedings thereon, the Court may cause such person to be confined in any institution located near the place where the Court sits, which may hereafter be designated by the Commissioner of Mental Hygiene [Public Health] as suitable for the temporary detention of irresponsible persons.

(3) If the Court is satisfied by the report filed pursuant to paragraph (2) of this Section and such testimony of the reporting psychiatrists as the Court deems necessary that the committed person may be discharged or released on condition without danger to himself or others, the Court shall order his discharge or his release on such conditions as the Court determines to be necessary. If the Court is not so satisfied, it shall promptly order a hearing to determine whether such person may safely be discharged or released. Any such hearing shall be deemed a civil proceeding and the burden shall be upon the committed person to prove that he may safely be discharged or released. According to the determination of the Court upon the hearing, the committed person shall thereupon be discharged or released on such conditions as the Court determines to be necessary, or shall be recommitted to the custody of the Commissioner of Mental Hygiene [Public Health], subject to discharge or release only in accordance with the procedure prescribed above for a first hearing.

(4) If, within [five] years after the conditional release of a committed person, the Court shall determine, after hearing evidence, that the conditions of release have not been fulfilled and that for the safety of such person or for the safety of others his conditional release should be revoked, the Court shall forthwith order him to be recommitted to the Commissioner of Mental Hygiene [Public Health], subject to discharge or release only in accordance with the procedure prescribed above for a first hearing.

(5) A committed person may make application for his discharge or release to the Court by which he was committed, and the procedure to be followed upon such application shall be the same as that prescribed above in the case of an application by the Commissioner of Mental Hygiene [Public Health]. However, no such application by a committed person need be considered until he has been confined for a period of not less than [six months] from the date of the order of commitment, and if the determination of the Court be adverse to the application, such person shall not be permitted to file a further application until [one year] has elapsed from the date of any preceding hearing on an application for his release or discharge.

Section 4.09. Statements for Purposes of Examination or Treatment Inadmissible Except on Issue of Mental Condition.

A statement made by a person subjected to psychiatric examination or treatment pursuant to Sections 4.05, 4.06 or 4.08 for purposes of such examination or treatment shall not be admissible in evidence against him in any criminal proceeding on any issue other than that of his mental condition but it shall be admissible upon that issue, whether or not it would otherwise be deemed a privileged communication [, unless such statement constitutes an admission of guilt of the crime charged].

Section 4.10. Immaturity Excluding Criminal Conviction; Transfer of Proceedings to Juvenile Court.

(1) A person shall not be tried for or convicted of an offense if:

(a) at the time of the conduct charged to constitute the offense he was less than sixteen years of age [, in which case the Juvenile Court shall have exclusive jurisdiction]; or

(b) at the time of the conduct charged to constitute the offense he was sixteen or seventeen years of age, unless:

(i) the Juvenile Court has no jurisdiction over him, or,

(ii) the Juvenile Court has entered an order waiving jurisdiction and consenting to the institution of criminal proceedings against him.

(2) No court shall have jurisdiction to try or convict a person of an offense if criminal proceedings against him are barred by Subsection (1) of this Section. When it appears that a person charged with the commission of an offense may be of such an age that criminal proceedings may be barred under Subsection (1) of this Section, the Court shall hold a hearing thereon, and the burden shall be on the prosecution to establish to the satisfaction of the Court that the criminal proceeding is not barred upon such grounds. If the Court determines that the proceeding is barred, custody of the person charged shall be

surrendered to the Juvenile Court, and the case, including all papers and processes relating thereto, shall be transferred.

Article 5. Inchoate Crimes

Section 5.01. Criminal Attempt.

(1) *Definition of Attempt.* A person is guilty of an attempt to commit a crime if, acting with the kind of culpability otherwise required for commission of the crime, he:

(a) purposely engages in conduct which would constitute the crime if the attendant circumstances were as he believes them to be; or

(b) when causing a particular result is an element of the crime, does or omits to do anything with the purpose of causing or with the belief that it will cause such result without further conduct on his part; or

(c) purposely does or omits to do anything which, under the circumstances as he believes them to be, is an act or omission constituting a substantial step in a course of conduct planned to culminate in his commission of the crime.

(2) *Conduct Which May Be Held Substantial Step Under Subsection (1)(c).* Conduct shall not be held to constitute a substantial step under Subsection (1)(c) of this Section unless it is strongly corroborative of the actor's criminal purpose. Without negativing the sufficiency of other conduct, the following, if strongly corroborative of the actor's criminal purpose, shall not be held insufficient as a matter of law:

(a) lying in wait, searching for or following the contemplated victim of the crime;

(b) enticing or seeking to entice the contemplated victim of the crime to go to the place contemplated for its commission;

(c) reconnoitering the place contemplated for the commission of the crime;

(d) unlawful entry of a structure, vehicle or enclosure in which it is contemplated that the crime will be committed;

(e) possession of materials to be employed in the commission of the crime, which are specially designed for such unlawful use or which can serve no lawful purpose of the actor under the circumstances;

(f) possession, collection or fabrication of materials to be employed in the commission of the crime, at or near the place contemplated for its commission, where such possession, collection or fabrication serves no lawful purpose of the actor under the circumstances;

(g) soliciting an innocent agent to engage in conduct constituting an element of the crime.

(3) *Conduct Designed to Aid Another in Commission of a Crime.* A person who engages in conduct designed to aid another to commit a crime which would establish his complicity under Section 2.06 if the crime were committed by such other person, is guilty of an attempt to commit the crime, although the crime is not committed or attempted by such other person.

(4) *Renunciation of Criminal Purpose.* When the actor's conduct would otherwise constitute an attempt under Subsection (1)(b) or (1)(c) of this Section, it is an affirmative defense that he abandoned his effort to commit the crime or otherwise prevented its commission, under circumstances manifesting a complete and voluntary renunciation of his criminal purpose. The establishment of such defense does not, however, affect the liability of an accomplice who did not join in such abandonment or prevention.

Within the meaning of this Article, renunciation of criminal purpose is not voluntary if it is motivated, in whole or in part, by circumstances, not present or apparent at the inception of the actor's course of conduct, which increase the probability of detection or apprehension or which make more difficult the accomplishment of the criminal purpose. Renunciation is not complete if it is motivated by a decision to postpone the criminal conduct until a more advantageous time or to transfer the criminal effort to another but similar objective or victim.

Section 5.02. Criminal Solicitation.

(1) *Definition of Solicitation.* A person is guilty of solicitation to commit a crime if with the purpose of promoting or facilitating its commission he commands, encourages or requests another person to engage in specific conduct which would constitute such crime or an attempt to commit such crime or which would establish his complicity in its commission or attempted commission.

(2) *Uncommunicated Solicitation.* It is immaterial under Subsection (1) of this Section that the actor fails to communicate with the person he solicits to commit a crime if his conduct was designed to effect such communication.

(3) *Renunciation of Criminal Purpose.* It is an affirmative defense that the actor, after soliciting another person to commit a crime, persuaded him not to do so or otherwise prevented the commission of the crime, under circumstances

manifesting a complete and voluntary renunciation of his criminal purpose.

Section 5.03. Criminal Conspiracy.

(1) *Definition of Conspiracy.* A person is guilty of conspiracy with another person or persons to commit a crime if with the purpose of promoting or facilitating its commission he:

(a) agrees with such other person or persons that they or one or more of them will engage in conduct which constitutes such crime or an attempt or solicitation to commit such crime; or

(b) agrees to aid such other person or persons in the planning or commission of such crime or of an attempt or solicitation to commit such crime.

(2) *Scope of Conspiratorial Relationship.* If a person guilty of conspiracy, as defined by Subsection (1) of this Section, knows that a person with whom he conspires to commit a crime has conspired with another person or persons to commit the same crime, he is guilty of conspiring with such other person or persons, whether or not he knows their identity, to commit such crime.

(3) *Conspiracy With Multiple Criminal Objectives.* If a person conspires to commit a number of crimes, he is guilty of only one conspiracy so long as such multiple crimes are the object of the same agreement or continuous conspiratorial relationship.

(4) *Joinder and Venue in Conspiracy Prosecutions.*

(a) Subject to the provisions of paragraph (b) of this Subsection, two or more persons charged with criminal conspiracy may be prosecuted jointly if:

(i) they are charged with conspiring with one another; or

(ii) the conspiracies alleged, whether they have the same or different parties, are so related that they constitute different aspects of a scheme of organized criminal conduct.

(b) In any joint prosecution under paragraph (a) of this Subsection:

(i) no defendant shall be charged with a conspiracy in any county [parish or district] other than one in which he entered into such conspiracy or in which an overt act pursuant to such conspiracy was done by him or by a person with whom he conspired; and

(ii) neither the liability of any defendant nor the admissibility against him of evidence of acts or declarations of another shall be enlarged by such joinder; and

(iii) the Court shall order a severance or take a special verdict as to any defendant who so requests, if it deems it necessary or appropriate to promote the fair determination of his guilt or innocence, and shall take any other proper measures to protect the fairness of the trial.

(5) *Overt Act.* No person may be convicted of conspiracy to commit a crime, other than a felony of the first or second degree, unless an overt act in pursuance of such conspiracy is alleged and proved to have been done by him or by a person with whom he conspired.

(6) *Renunciation of Criminal Purpose.* It is an affirmative defense that the actor, after conspiring to commit a crime, thwarted the success of the conspiracy, under circumstances manifesting a complete and voluntary renunciation of his criminal purpose.

(7) *Duration of Conspiracy.* For purposes of Section 1.06(4):

(a) conspiracy is a continuing course of conduct which terminates when the crime or crimes which are its object are committed or the agreement that they be committed is abandoned by the defendant and by those with whom he conspired; and

(b) such abandonment is presumed if neither the defendant nor anyone with whom he conspired does any overt act in pursuance of the conspiracy during the applicable period of limitation; and

(c) if an individual abandons the agreement, the conspiracy is terminated as to him only if and when he advises those with whom he conspired of his abandonment or he informs the law enforcement authorities of the existence of the conspiracy and of his participation therein.

Section 5.04. Incapacity, Irresponsibility or Immunity of Party to Solicitation or Conspiracy.

(1) Except as provided in Subsection (2) of this Section, it is immaterial to the liability of a person who solicits or conspires with another to commit a crime that:

(a) he or the person whom he solicits or with whom he conspires does not occupy a particular position or have a particular characteristic which is an element of such crime, if he believes that one of them does; or

(b) the person whom he solicits or with whom he conspires is irresponsible or has an immunity to prosecution or conviction for the commission of the crime.

(2) It is a defense to a charge of solicitation or conspiracy to commit a crime that if the criminal object were achieved, the actor would not be guilty of a crime under the law defining the offense or as an accomplice under Section 2.06(5) or 2.06(6)(a) or (b).

Section 5.05. Grading of Criminal Attempt, Solicitation and Conspiracy; Mitigation in Cases of Lesser Danger; Multiple Convictions Barred.

(1) *Grading.* Except as otherwise provided in this Section, attempt, solicitation and conspiracy are crimes of the same grade and degree as the most serious offense which is attempted or solicited or is an object of the conspiracy. An attempt, solicitation or conspiracy to commit a [capital crime or a] felony of the first degree is a felony of the second degree.

(2) *Mitigation.* If the particular conduct charged to constitute a criminal attempt, solicitation or conspiracy is so inherently unlikely to result or culminate in the commission of a crime that neither such conduct nor the actor presents a public danger warranting the grading of such offense under this Section, the Court shall exercise its power under Section 6.12 to enter judgment and impose sentence for a crime of lower grade or degree or, in extreme cases, may dismiss the prosecution.

(3) *Multiple Convictions.* A person may not be convicted of more than one offense defined by this Article for conduct designed to commit or to culminate in the commission of the same crime.

Section 5.06. Possessing Instruments of Crime; Weapons.

(1) *Criminal Instruments Generally.* A person commits a misdemeanor if he possesses any instrument of crime with purpose to employ it criminally. "Instrument of crime" means:

(a) anything specially made or specially adapted [sic] for criminal use; or

(b) anything commonly used for criminal purposes and possessed by the actor under circumstances which do not negative unlawful purpose.

(2) *Presumption of Criminal Purpose from Possession of Weapon.* If a person possesses a firearm or other weapon on or about his person,

in a vehicle occupied by him, or otherwise readily available for use, it shall be presumed that he had the purpose to employ it criminally, unless:

(a) the weapon is possessed in the actor's home or place of business;

(b) the actor is licensed or otherwise authorized by law to possess such weapon; or

(c) the weapon is of a type commonly used in lawful sport.

"Weapon" means anything readily capable of lethal use and possessed under circumstances not manifestly appropriate for lawful uses which it may have; the term includes a firearm which is not loaded or lacks a clip or other component to render it immediately operable, and components which can readily be assembled into a weapon.

(3) *Presumptions as to Possession of Criminal Instruments in Automobiles.* Where a weapon or other instrument of crime is found in an automobile, it is presumed to be in the possession of the occupant if there is but one. If there is more than one occupant, it shall be presumed to be in the possession of all, except under the following circumstances:

(a) where it is found upon the person of one of the occupants;

(b) where the automobile is not a stolen one and the weapon or instrument is found out of view in a glove compartment, car trunk, or other enclosed customary depository, in which case it shall be presumed to be in the possession of the occupant or occupants who own or have authority to operate the automobile;

(c) in the case of a taxicab, a weapon or instrument found in the passenger's portion of the vehicle shall be presumed to be in the possession of all the passengers, if there are any, and, if not, in the possession of the driver.

Section 5.07. Prohibited Offensive Weapons.

A person commits a misdemeanor if, except as authorized by law, he makes, repairs, sells, or otherwise deals in, uses or possesses any offensive weapon. "Offensive weapon" means any bomb, machine gun, sawed-off shotgun, firearm specially made or specially adapted for concealment or silent discharge, any blackjack, sand bag, metal knuckles, dagger, or other implement for the infliction of serious bodily injury which serves no common lawful purpose. It is a defense under this Section for the defendant to prove by a preponderance of evidence that he possessed or dealt with the weapon solely as a curio or in a dramatic performance, or that he possessed it briefly in consequence of having found it or taken it from an aggressor, or under circumstances similarly negativing any purpose or likelihood that the weapon would be used unlawfully. The presumptions provided in Section 5.06(3) are applicable to prosecutions under this Section.

Article 6. Authorized Disposition of Offenders

Section 6.01. Degrees of Felonies.

(1) Felonies defined by this Code are classified, for the purpose of sentence, into three degrees, as follows:

(a) felonies of the first degree;

(b) felonies of the second degree;

(c) felonies of the third degree.

A felony is of the first or second degree when it is so designated by the Code. A crime declared to be a felony, without specification of degree, is of the third degree.

(2) Notwithstanding any other provision of law, a felony defined by any statute of this State other that this Code shall constitute for the purpose of sentence a felony of the third degree.

Section 6.04. Penalties Against Corporations and Unincorporated Associations; Forfeiture of Corporate Charter or Revocation of Certificate Authorizing Foreign Corporation to Do Business in the State.

(1) The Court may suspend the sentence of a corporation or an unincorporated association which has been convicted of an offense or may sentence it to pay a fine authorized by Section 6.03.

(2) (a) The [prosecuting attorney] is authorized to institute civil proceedings in the appropriate court of general jurisdiction to forfeit the charter of a corporation organized under the laws of this State or to revoke the certificate authorizing a foreign corporation to conduct business in this State. The Court may order the charter forfeited or the certificate revoked upon finding (i) that the board of directors or a high managerial agent acting in behalf of the corporation has, in conducting the corporation's affairs, purposely engaged in a persistent course of criminal conduct and (ii) that for the prevention of future criminal conduct of the same character, the public interest requires the charter of the corporation to be forfeited and the corporation to be dissolved or the certificate to be revoked.

(b) When a corporation is convicted of a crime or a high managerial agent of a corpo-

ration, as defined in Section 2.07, is convicted of a crime committed in the conduct of the affairs of the corporation, the Court, in sentencing the corporation or the agent, may direct the [prosecuting attorney] to institute proceedings authorized by paragraph (a) of this Subsection.

(c) The proceedings authorized by paragraph (a) of this Subsection shall be conducted in accordance with the procedures authorized by law for the involuntary dissolution of a corporation or the revocation of the certificate authorizing a foreign corporation to conduct business in this State. Such proceedings shall be deemed additional to any other proceedings authorized by law for the purpose of forfeiting the charter of a corporation or revoking the certificate of a foreign corporation.

Section 6.06. Sentence of Imprisonment for Felony; Ordinary Terms.

A person who has been convicted of a felony may be sentenced to imprisonment, as follows:

(1) in the case of a felony of the first degree, for a term the minimum of which shall be fixed by the Court at not less than one year nor more than ten years, and the maximum of which shall be life imprisonment;

(2) in the case of a felony of the second degree, for a term the minimum of which shall be fixed by the Court at not less than one year nor more than three years, and the maximum of which shall be ten years;

(3) in the case of a felony of the third degree, for a term the minimum of which shall be fixed by the Court at not less than one year nor more than two years, and the maximum of which shall be five years.

Alternate Section 6.06. Sentence of Imprisonment for Felony; Ordinary Terms.

A person who has been convicted of a felony may be sentenced to imprisonment, as follows:

(1) in the case of a felony of the first degree, for a term the minimum of which shall be fixed by the Court at not less than one year nor more than ten years, and the maximum at not more than twenty years or at life imprisonment;

(2) in the case of a felony of the second degree, for a term the minimum of which shall be fixed by the Court at not less than one year nor more than three years, and the maximum at not more than ten years;

(3) in the case of a felony of the third degree, for a term the minimum of which shall be fixed

by the Court at not less than one year nor more than two years, and the maximum at not more than five years.

No sentence shall be imposed under this Section of which the minimum is longer than one-half the maximum, or, when the maximum is life imprisonment, longer than ten years.

Section 6.07. Sentence of Imprisonment for Felony; Extended Terms.

In the cases designated in Section 7.03, a person who has been convicted of a felony may be sentenced to an extended term of imprisonment, as follows:

(1) in the case of a felony of the first degree, for a term the minimum of which shall be fixed by the Court at not less than five years nor more than ten years, and the maximum of which shall be life imprisonment;

(2) in the case of a felony of the second degree, for a term the minimum of which shall be fixed by the Court at not less than one year nor more than five years, and the maximum of which shall be fixed by the Court at not less than ten nor more than twenty years;

(3) in the case of a felony of the third degree, for a term the minimum of which shall be fixed by the Court at not less than one year nor more than three years, and the maximum of which shall be fixed by the Court at not less than five nor more than ten years.

Section 6.08 Sentence of Imprisonment for Misdemeanors and Petty Misdemeanors; Ordinary Terms.

A person who has been convicted of a misdemeanor or a petty misdemeanor may be sentenced to imprisonment for a definite term which shall be fixed by the Court and shall not exceed one year in the case of a misdemeanor or thirty days in the case of a petty misdemeanor.

Section 6.09. Sentence of Imprisonment for Misdemeanors and Petty Misdemeanors; Extended Terms.

(1) In the cases designated in Section 7.04, a person who has been convicted of a misdemeanor or a petty misdemeanor may be sentenced to an extended term of imprisonment, as follows:

(a) in the case of a misdemeanor, for a term the minimum of which shall be fixed by the Court at not more than one year and the maximum of which shall be three years;

(b) in the case of a petty misdemeanor, for a term the minimum of which shall be fixed by the Court at not more than six months and the maximum of which shall be two years.

(2) No such sentence for an extended term shall be imposed unless:

(a) the Director of Correction has certified that there is an institution in the Department of Correction, or in a county, city [or other appropriate political subdivision of the State] which is appropriate for the detention and correctional treatment of such misdemeanants or petty misdemeanants, and that such institution is available to receive such commitments; and

(b) the [Board of Parole] [Parole Administrator] has certified that the Board of Parole is able to visit such institution and to assume responsibility for the release of such prisoners on parole and for their parole supervision. . . .

PART II. DEFINITION OF SPECIFIC CRIMES

Offenses Involving Danger to the Person

Article 210. Criminal Homicide

Section 210.0. Definitions.

In Articles 210–213, unless a different meaning plainly is required:

(1) "human being" means a person who has been born and is alive;

(2) "bodily injury" means physical pain, illness or any impairment of physical condition;

(3) "serious bodily injury" means bodily injury which creates a substantial risk of death or which causes serious, permanent disfigurement, or protracted loss or impairment of the function of any bodily member or organ;

(4) "deadly weapon" means any firearm, or other weapon, device, instrument, material or substance, whether animate or inanimate, which in the manner it is used or is intended to be used is known to be capable of producing death or serious bodily injury.

Section 210.1 Criminal Homicide.

(1) A person is guilty of criminal homicide if he purposely, knowingly, recklessly or negligently causes the death of another human being.

(2) Criminal homicide is murder, manslaughter or negligent homicide.

Section 210.2. Murder.

(1) Except as provided in Section 210.3(1)(b), criminal homicide constitutes murder when:

(a) it is committed purposely or knowingly; or

(b) it is committed recklessly under circumstances manifesting extreme indifference to the value of human life. Such recklessness and indifference are presumed if the actor is engaged or is an accomplice in the commission of, or an attempt to commit, or flight after committing or attempting to commit robbery, rape or deviate sexual intercourse by force or threat of force, arson, burglary, kidnapping or felonious escape.

(2) Murder is a felony of the first degree [but a person convicted of murder may be sentenced to death, as provided in Section 210.6].[1]

Section 210.3. Manslaughter.

(1) Criminal homicide constitutes manslaughter when:

(a) it is committed recklessly; or

(b) a homicide which would otherwise be murder is committed under the influence of extreme mental or emotional disturbance for which there is reasonable explanation or excuse. The reasonableness of such explanation or excuse shall be determined from the viewpoint of a person in the actor's situation under the circumstances as he believes them to be.

(2) Manslaughter is a felony of the second degree.

Section 210.4. Negligent Homicide.

(1) Criminal homicide constitutes negligent homicide when it is committed negligently.

(2) Negligent homicide is a felony of the third degree.

Section 210.5. Causing or Aiding Suicide.

(1) *Causing Suicide as Criminal Homicide.* A person may be convicted of criminal homicide for causing another to commit suicide only if he purposely causes such suicide by force, duress or deception.

(2) *Aiding or Soliciting Suicide as an Independent Offense.* A person who purposely aids or solicits another to commit suicide is guilty of a felony of the second degree if his conduct causes such suicide or an attempted suicide, and otherwise of a misdemeanor.

Section 210.6. Sentence of Death for Murder; Further Proceedings to Determine Sentence.

(1) *Death Sentence Excluded.* When a defendant is found guilty of murder, the Court shall impose sentence for a felony of the first degree if it is satisfied that:

(a) none of the aggravating circumstances enumerated in Subsection (3) of this Section was established by the evidence at the trial or will be established if further proceedings are initiated under Subsection (2) of this Section; or

(b) substantial mitigating circumstances, established by the evidence at the trial, call for leniency; or

(c) the defendant, with the consent of the prosecuting attorney and the approval of the Court, pleaded guilty to murder as a felony of the first degree; or

(d) the defendant was under 18 years of age at the time of the commission of the crime; or

(e) the defendant's physical or mental condition calls for leniency; or

(f) although the evidence suffices to sustain the verdict, it does not foreclose all doubt respecting the defendant's guilt.

(2) *Determination by Court or by Court and Jury.* Unless the Court imposes sentence under Subsection (1) of this Section, it shall conduct a separate proceeding to determine whether the defendant should be sentenced for a felony of the first degree or sentenced to death. The proceeding shall be conducted before the Court alone if the defendant was convicted by a Court sitting without a jury or upon his plea of guilty or if the prosecuting attorney and the defendant waive a jury with respect to sentence. In other cases it shall be conducted before the Court sitting with the jury which determined the defendant's guilt or, if the Court for good cause shown discharges that jury, with a new jury empanelled for the purpose.

In the proceeding, evidence may be presented as to any matter that the Court deems relevant to sentence, including but not limited to the nature and circumstances of the crime, the

---

[1] . . . . The brackets are meant to reflect the fact that the Institute took no position on the desirability of the death penalty. . . .

defendant's character, background, history, mental and physical condition and any of the aggravating or mitigating circumstances enumerated in Subsections (3) and (4) of this Section. Any such evidence not legally privileged, which the Court deems to have probative force, may be received, regardless of its admissibility under the exclusionary rules of evidence, provided that the defendant's counsel is accorded a fair opportunity to rebut any hearsay statements. The prosecuting attorney and the defendant or his counsel shall be permitted to present argument for or against sentence of death.

The determination whether sentence of death shall be imposed shall be in the discretion of the Court, except that when the proceeding is conducted before the Court sitting with a jury, the Court shall not impose sentence of death unless it submits to the jury the issue whether the defendant should be sentenced to death or to imprisonment and the jury returns a verdict that the sentence should be death. If the jury is unable to reach a unanimous verdict, the Court shall dismiss the jury and impose sentence for a felony of the first degree.

The Court, in exercising its discretion as to sentence, and the jury, in determining upon its verdict, shall take into account the aggravating and mitigating circumstances enumerated in Subsections (3) and (4) and any other facts that it deems relevant, but it shall not impose or recommend sentence of death unless it finds one of the aggravating circumstances enumerated in Subsection (3) and further finds that there are no mitigating circumstances sufficiently substantial to call for leniency. When the issue is submitted to the jury, the Court shall so instruct and also shall inform the jury of the nature of the sentence of imprisonment that may be imposed, including its implication with respect to possible release upon parole, if the jury verdict is against sentence of death.

Alternative formulation of Subsection (2):

(2) *Determination by Court.* Unless the Court imposes sentence under Subsection (1) of this Section, it shall conduct a separate proceeding to determine whether the defendant should be sentenced for a felony of the first degree or sentenced to death. In the proceeding, the Court, in accordance with Section 7.07, shall consider the report of the presentence investigation and, if a psychiatric examination has been ordered, the report of such examination. In addition, evidence may be presented as to any matter that the Court deems relevant to sentence, including but not limited to the nature and circumstances of the crime, the defendant's character, background,

history, mental and physical condition and any of the aggravating or mitigating circumstances enumerated in Subsections (3) and (4) of this Section. Any such evidence not legally privileged, which the Court deems to have probative force, may be received, regardless of its admissibility under the exclusionary rules of evidence, provided that the defendant's counsel is accorded a fair opportunity to rebut any hearsay statements. The prosecuting attorney and the defendant or his counsel shall be permitted to present argument for or against sentence of death.

The determination whether sentence of death shall be imposed shall be in the discretion of the Court. In exercising such discretion, the Court shall take into account the aggravating and mitigating circumstances enumerated in Subsections (3) and (4) and any other facts that it deems relevant but shall not impose sentence of death unless it finds one of the aggravating circumstances enumerated in Subsection (3) and further finds that there are no mitigating circumstances sufficiently substantial to call for leniency.

(3) *Aggravating Circumstances.*

(a) The murder was committed by a convict under sentence of imprisonment.

(b) The defendant was previously convicted of another murder or of a felony involving the use or threat of violence to the person.

(c) At the time the murder was committed the defendant also committed another murder.

(d) The defendant knowingly created a great risk of death to many persons.

(e) The murder was committed while the defendant was engaged or was an accomplice in the commission of, or an attempt to commit, or flight after committing or attempting to commit robbery, rape or deviate sexual intercourse by force or threat of force, arson, burglary or kidnapping.

(f) The murder was committed for the purpose of avoiding or preventing a lawful arrest or effecting an escape from lawful custody.

(g) The murder was committed for pecuniary gain.

(h) The murder was especially heinous, atrocious or cruel, manifesting exceptional depravity.

(4) *Mitigating Circumstances.*

(a) The defendant has no significant history of prior criminal activity.

(b) The murder was committed while the defendant was under the influence of extreme mental or emotional disturbance.

(c) The victim was a participant in the defendant's homicidal conduct or consented to the homicidal act.

(d) The murder was committed under circumstances which the defendant believed to provide a moral justification or extenuation for his conduct.

(e) The defendant was an accomplice in a murder committed by another person and his participation in the homicidal act was relatively minor.

(f) The defendant acted under duress or under the domination of another person.

(g) At the time of the murder, the capacity of the defendant to appreciate the criminality [wrongfulness] of his conduct or to conform his conduct to the requirements of law was impaired as a result of mental disease or defect or intoxication.

(h) The youth of the defendant at the time of the crime.

Article 211. Assault; Reckless Endangering; Threats

Section 211.0. Definitions.

In this Article, the definitions given in Section 210.0 apply unless a different meaning plainly is required.

Section 211.1 Assault.

(1) *Simple Assault.* A person is guilty of assault if he:

(a) attempts to cause or purposely, knowingly or recklessly causes bodily injury to another; or

(b) negligently causes bodily injury to another with a deadly weapon; or

(c) attempts by physical menace to put another in fear of imminent serious bodily injury.

Simple assault is a misdemeanor unless committed in a fight or scuffle entered into by mutual consent, in which case it is a petty misdemeanor.

(2) *Aggravated Assault.* A person is guilty of aggravated assault if he:

(a) attempts to cause serious bodily injury to another, or causes such injury purposely, knowingly or recklessly under circumstances manifesting extreme indifference to the value of human life; or

(b) attempts to cause or purposely or knowingly causes bodily injury to another with a deadly weapon.

Aggravated assault under paragraph (a) is a felony of the second degree; aggravated assault under paragraph (b) is a felony of the third degree.

Section 211.2. Recklessly Endangering Another Person.

A person commits a misdemeanor if he recklessly engages in conduct which places or may place another person in danger of death or serious bodily injury. Recklessness and danger shall be presumed where a person knowingly points a firearm at or in the direction of another, whether or not the actor believed the firearm to be loaded.

Section 211.3. Terroristic Threats.

A person is guilty of a felony of the third degree if he threatens to commit any crime of violence with purpose to terrorize another or to cause evacuation of a building, place of assembly, or facility of public transportation, or otherwise to cause serious public inconvenience, or in reckless disregard of the risk of causing such terror or inconvenience.

Article 212. Kidnapping and Related Offenses; Coercion

Section 212.0. Definitions.

In this Article, the definitions given in section 210.0 apply unless a different meaning plainly is required.

Section 212.1. Kidnapping.

A person is guilty of kidnapping if he unlawfully removes another from his place of residence or business, or a substantial distance from the vicinity where he is found, or if he unlawfully confines another for a substantial period in a place of isolation, with any of the following purposes:

(a) to hold for ransom or reward, or as a shield or hostage; or

(b) to facilitate commission of any felony or flight thereafter; or

(c) to inflict bodily injury on or to terrorize the victim or another; or

(d) to interfere with the performance of any governmental or political function.

Kidnapping is a felony of the first degree unless the actor voluntarily releases the victim alive and in a safe place prior to trial, in which case it is a felony of the second degree. A removal or confinement is unlawful within the meaning of this Section if it is accomplished by force, threat or deception, or, in the case of a person who is under the age of 14 or incompetent, if it is accomplished without the consent of a parent, guardian or other person responsible for general supervision of his welfare.

Section 212.2. Felonious Restraint.

A person commits a felony of the third degree if he knowingly:

(a) restrains another unlawfully in circumstances exposing him to risk of serious bodily injury; or

(b) holds another in a condition of involuntary servitude.

Section 212.3 False Imprisonment.

A person commits a misdemeanor if he knowingly restrains another unlawfully so as to interfere substantially with his liberty.

Section 212.4 Interference with Custody.

(1) *Custody of Children.* A person commits an offense if he knowingly or recklessly takes or entices any child under the age of 18 from the custody of its parent, guardian or other lawful custodian, when he has no privilege to do so. It is an affirmative defense that:

(a) the actor believed that his action was necessary to preserve the child from danger to its welfare; or

(b) the child, being at the time not less than 14 years old, was taken away at its own instigation without enticement and without purpose to commit a criminal offense with or against the child.

Proof that the child was below the critical age gives rise to a presumption that the actor knew the child's age or acted in reckless disregard thereof. The offense is a misdemeanor unless the actor, not being a parent or person in equivalent relation to the child, acted with knowledge that his conduct would cause serious alarm for the child's safety, or in reckless disregard of a likelihood of causing such alarm, in which case the offense is a felony of the third degree.

(2) *Custody of Committed Persons.* A person is guilty of a misdemeanor if he knowingly or recklessly takes or entices any committed person away from lawful custody when he is not privileged to do so. "Committed person" means, in addition to anyone committed under judicial warrant, any orphan, neglected or delinquent child, mentally defective or insane person, or other dependent or incompetent

person entrusted to another's custody by or through a recognized social agency or otherwise by authority of law.

Section 212.5. Criminal Coercion.

(1) *Offense Defined.* A person is guilty of criminal coercion if, with purpose unlawfully to restrict another's freedom of action to his detriment, he threatens to:

(a) commit any criminal offense; or

(b) accuse anyone of a criminal offense; or

(c) expose any secret tending to subject any person to hatred, contempt or ridicule, or to impair his credit or business repute; or

(d) take or withhold action as an official, or cause an official to take or withhold action.

It is an affirmative defense to prosecution based on paragraphs (b), (c) or (d) that the actor believed the accusation or secret to be true or the proposed official action justified and that his purpose was limited to compelling the other to behave in a way reasonably related to the circumstances which were the subject of the accusation, exposure or proposed official action, as by desisting from further misbehavior, making good a wrong done, refraining from taking any action or responsibility for which the actor believes the other disqualified.

(2) *Grading.* Criminal coercion is a misdemeanor unless the threat is to commit a felony or the actor's purpose is felonious, in which cases the offense is a felony of the third degree.

Article 213. Sexual Offenses

Section 213.0. Definitions.

In this Article, unless a different meaning plainly is required:

(1) the definitions given in Section 210.0 apply;

(2) "Sexual intercourse" includes intercourse per os or per anum, with some penetration however slight; emission is not required;

(3) "deviate sexual intercourse" means sexual intercourse per os or per anum between human beings who are not husband and wife, and any form of sexual intercourse with an animal.

Section 213.1. Rape and Related Offenses.

(1) *Rape.* A male who has sexual intercourse with a female not his wife is guilty of rape if:

(a) he compels her to submit by force or by threat of imminent death, serious bodily injury, extreme pain or kidnapping, to be inflicted on anyone; or

(b) he has substantially impaired her power to appraise or control her conduct by administering or employing without her knowledge drugs, intoxicants or other means for the purpose of preventing resistance; or

(c) the female is unconscious; or

(d) the female is less than 10 years old.

Rape is a felony of the second degree unless (i) in the course thereof the actor inflicts serious bodily injury upon anyone, or (ii) the victim was not a voluntary social companion of the actor upon the occasion of the crime and had not previously permitted him sexual liberties, in which cases the offense is a felony of the first degree.

(2) *Gross Sexual Imposition.* A male who has sexual intercourse with a female not his wife commits a felony of the third degree if:

(a) he compels her to submit by any threat that would prevent resistance by a woman of ordinary resolution; or

(b) he knows that she suffers from a mental disease or defect which renders her incapable of appraising the nature of her conduct; or

(c) he knows that she is unaware that a sexual act is being committed upon her or that she submits because she mistakenly supposes that he is her husband.

Section 213.2. Deviate Sexual Intercourse by Force or Imposition.

(1) *By Force or Its Equivalent.* A person who engages in deviate sexual intercourse with another person, or who causes another to engage in deviate sexual intercourse, commits a felony of the second degree if:

(a) he compels the other person to participate by force or by threat of imminent death, serious bodily injury, extreme pain or kidnapping, to be inflicted on anyone; or

(b) he has substantially impaired the other person's power to appraise or control his conduct, by administering or employing without the knowledge of the other person drugs, intoxicants or other means for the purpose of preventing resistance; or

(c) the other person is unconscious; or

(d) the other person is less than 10 years old.

(2) *By Other Imposition.* A person who engages in deviate sexual intercourse with another person, or who causes another to engage in deviate sexual intercourse, commits a felony of the third degree if:

(a) he compels the other person to participate by any threat that would prevent resistance by a person of ordinary resolution; or

(b) he knows that the other person suffers from a mental disease or defect which renders him incapable of appraising the nature of his conduct; or

(c) he knows that the other person submits because he is unaware that a sexual act is being committed upon him.

Section 213.3. Corruption of Minors and Seduction.

(1) *Offense Defined.* A male who has sexual intercourse with a female not his wife, or any person who engages in deviate sexual intercourse or causes another to engage in deviate sexual intercourse, is guilty of an offense if:

(a) the other person is less than [16] years old and the actor is at least [4] years older than the other person; or

(b) the other person is less than 21 years old and the actor is his guardian or otherwise responsible for general supervision of his welfare; or

(c) the other person is in custody of law or detained in a hospital or other institution and the actor has supervisory or disciplinary authority over him; or

(d) the other person is a female who is induced to participate by a promise of marriage which the actor does not mean to perform.

(2) *Grading.* An offense under paragraph (a) of Subsection (1) is a felony of the third degree. Otherwise an offense under this section is a misdemeanor.

Section 213.4 Sexual Assault.

A person who has sexual contact with another not his spouse, or causes such other to have sexual conduct with him, is guilty of sexual assault, a misdemeanor, if:

(1) he knows that the conduct is offensive to the other person; or

(2) he knows that the other person suffers from a mental disease or defect which renders him or her incapable of appraising the nature of his or her conduct; or

(3) he knows that the other person is unaware that a sexual act is being committed; or

(4) the other person is less than 10 years old; or

(5) he has substantially impaired the other person's power to appraise or control his or her conduct, by administering or employing without the other's knowledge drugs, intoxicants or other means for the purpose of preventing resistance; or

(6) the other person is less than [16] years old and the actor is at least [four] years older than the other person; or

(7) the other person is less than 21 years old and the actor is his guardian or otherwise responsible for general supervision of his welfare; or

(8) the other person is in custody of law or detained in a hospital or other institution and the actor has supervisory or disciplinary authority over him.

Sexual contact is any touching of the sexual or other intimate parts of the person for the purpose of arousing or gratifying sexual desire.

Section 213.5. Indecent Exposure.

A person commits a misdemeanor if, for the purpose of arousing or gratifying sexual desire of himself or of any person other than his spouse, he exposes his genitals under circumstances in which he knows his conduct is likely to cause affront or alarm.

Section 213.6 Provisions Generally Applicable to Article 213.

(1) *Mistake as to Age.* Whenever in this Article the criminality of conduct depends on a child's being below the age of 10, it is no defense that the actor did not know the child's age, or reasonably believed the child to be older than 10. When criminality depends on the child's being below a critical age other than 10, it is a defense for the actor to prove by a preponderance of the evidence that he reasonably believed the child to be above the critical age.

(2) *Spouse Relationships.* Whenever in this Article the definition of an offense excludes conduct with a spouse, the exclusion shall be deemed to extend to persons living as man and wife, regardless of the legal status of their relationship. The exclusion shall be inoperative as respects spouses living apart under a decree of judicial separation. Where the definition of an offense excludes conduct with a spouse or conduct by a woman, this shall not preclude conviction of a spouse or woman as accomplice in a sexual act which he or she causes another person, not within the exclusion, to perform.

(3) *Sexually Promiscuous Complainants.* It is a defense to prosecution under Section 213.3, and paragraphs (6), (7) and (8) of Section 213.4 for the actor to prove by a preponderance of the evidence that the alleged victim had, prior to the time of the offense charged, engaged promiscuously in sexual relations with others.

(4) *Prompt Complaint.* No prosecution may be instituted or maintained under this Article unless the alleged offense was brought to the notice of public authority within [3] months of its occurrence or, where the alleged victim was less than [16] years old or otherwise incompetent to make complaint, within [3] months after a parent, guardian or other competent person specially interested in the victim learns of the offense.

(5) *Testimony of Complainants.* No person shall be convicted of any felony under this Article upon the uncorroborated testimony of the alleged victim. Corroboration may be circumstantial. In any prosecution before a jury for an offense under this Article, the jury shall be instructed to evaluate the testimony of a victim or complaining witness with special care in view of the emotional involvement of the witness and the difficulty of determining the truth with respect to alleged sexual activities carried out in private.

Offenses Against Property

Article 220. Arson, Criminal Mischief, and Other Property Destruction

Section 220.1. Arson and Related Offenses.

(1) *Arson.* A person is guilty of arson, a felony of the second degree, if he starts a fire or causes an explosion with the purpose of:

(a) destroying a building or occupied structure of another; or

(b) destroying or damaging any property, whether his own or another's, to collect insurance for such loss. It shall be an affirmative defense to prosecution under this paragraph that the actor's conduct did not recklessly endanger any building or occupied structure of another or place any other person in danger of death or bodily injury.

(2) *Reckless Burning or Exploding.* A person commits a felony of the third degree if he purposely starts a fire or causes an explosion, whether on his own property or another's, and thereby recklessly:

(a) places another person in danger of death or bodily injury; or

(b) places a building or occupied structure of another in danger of damage or destruction.

(3) *Failure to Control or Report Dangerous Fire.* A person who knows that a fire is endangering life or a substantial amount of property of another and fails to take reasonable measures to put out or control the fire, when he can do so without substantial risk to himself, or to give a prompt fire alarm, commits a misdemeanor if:

    (a) he knows that he is under an official, contractual, or other legal duty to prevent or combat the fire; or

    (b) the fire was started, albeit lawfully, by him or with his assent, or on property in his custody or control.

(4) *Definitions.* "Occupied structure" means any structure, vehicle or place adapted for overnight accommodation of persons, or for carrying on business therein, whether or not a person is actually present. Property is that of another, for the purposes of this section, if anyone other than the actor has a possessory or proprietory interest therein. If a building or structure is divided into separately occupied units, any unit not occupied by the actor is an occupied structure of another.

Section 220.2. Causing or Risking Catastrophe.

(1) *Causing Catastrophe.* A person who causes a catastrophe by explosion, fire, flood, avalanche, collapse of building, release of poison gas, radioactive material or other harmful or destructive force or substance, or by any other means of causing potentially widespread injury or damage, commits a felony of the second degree if he does so purposely or knowingly, or a felony of the third degree if he does so recklessly.

(2) *Risking Catastrophe.* A person is guilty of a misdemeanor if he recklessly creates a risk of catastrophe in the employment of fire, explosives or other dangerous means listed in Subsection (1).

(3) *Failure to Prevent Catastrophe.* A person who knowingly or recklessly fails to take reasonable measures to prevent or mitigate a catastrophe commits a misdemeanor if:

    (a) he knows that he is under an official, contractual or other legal duty to take such measures; or

    (b) he did or assented to the act causing or threatening the catastrophe.

Section 220.3. Criminal Mischief.

(1) *Offense Defined.* A person is guilty of criminal mischief if he:

    (a) damages tangible property of another purposely, recklessly, or by negligence in the employment of fire, explosives, or other dangerous means listed in Section 220.2(1); or

    (b) purposely or recklessly tampers with tangible property of another so as to endanger person or property; or

    (c) purposely or recklessly causes another to suffer pecuniary loss by deception or threat.

(2) *Grading.* Criminal mischief is a felony of the third degree if the actor purposely causes pecuniary loss in excess of $5,000 or a substantial interruption or impairment of public communication, transportation, supply of water, gas or power, or other public service. It is a misdemeanor if the actor purposely causes pecuniary loss in excess of $100, or a petty misdemeanor if he purposely or recklessly causes pecuniary loss in excess of $25. Otherwise criminal mischief is a violation.

Article 221. Burglary and Other Criminal Intrusion

Section 221.0. Definitions.

In this Article, unless a different meaning plainly is required:

(1) "occupied structure" means any structure, vehicle or place adapted for overnight accommodation of persons, or for carrying on business therein, whether or not a person is actually present.

(2) "night" means the period between thirty minutes past sunset and thirty minutes before sunrise.

Section 221.1. Burglary.

(1) *Burglary Defined.* A person is guilty of burglary if he enters a building or occupied structure, or separately secured or occupied portion thereof, with purpose to commit a crime therein, unless the premises are at the time open to the public or the actor is licensed or privileged to enter. It is an affirmative defense to prosecution for burglary that the building or structure was abandoned.

(2) *Grading.* Burglary is a felony of the second degree if it is perpetrated in the dwelling of another at night, or if, in the course of committing the offense, the actor:

    (a) purposely, knowingly or recklessly inflicts or attempts to inflict bodily injury on anyone; or

    (b) is armed with explosives or a deadly weapon.

Otherwise, burglary is a felony of the third degree. An act shall be deemed "in the course of committing" an offense if it occurs in an attempt to commit the offense or in flight after the attempt or commission.

(3) *Multiple Convictions.* A person may not be convicted both for burglary and for the offense which it was his purpose to commit after the burglarious entry or for an attempt to commit that offense, unless the additional offense constitutes a felony of the first or second degree.

Section 221.2. Criminal Trespass.

(1) *Buildings and Occupied Structures.* A person commits an offense if, knowing that he is not licensed or privileged to do so, he enters or surreptitiously remains in any building or occupied structure, or separately secured or occupied portion thereof. An offense under this Subsection is a misdemeanor if it is committed in a dwelling at night. Otherwise it is a petty misdemeanor.

(2) *Defiant Trespasser.* A person commits an offense if, knowing that he is not licensed or privileged to do so, he enters or remains in any place as to which notice against trespass is given by:

(a) actual communication to the actor; or

(b) posting in a manner prescribed by law or reasonably likely to come to the attention of intruders; or

(c) fencing or other enclosure manifestly designed to exclude intruders.

An offense under this Subsection constitutes a petty misdemeanor if the offender defies an order to leave personally communicated to him by the owner of the premises or other authorized person. Otherwise it is a violation.

(3) *Defenses.* It is an affirmative defense to prosecution under this Section that:

(a) a building or occupied structure involved in an offense under Subsection (1) was abandoned; or

(b) the premises were at the time open to members of the public and the actor complied with all lawful conditions imposed on access to or remaining in the premises; or

(c) the actor reasonably believed that the owner of the premises, or other person empowered to license access thereto, would have licensed him to enter or remain.

Article 222. Robbery

Section 222.1 Robbery.

(1) *Robbery Defined.* A person is guilty of robbery if, in the course of committing a theft, he:

(a) inflicts serious bodily injury upon another; or

(b) threatens another with or purposely puts him in fear of immediate serious bodily injury; or

(c) commits or threatens immediately to commit any felony of the first or second degree.

An act shall be deemed "in the course of committing a theft" if it occurs in an attempt to commit theft or in flight after the attempt or commission.

(2) *Grading.* Robbery is a felony of the second degree, except that it is a felony of the first degree if in the course of committing the theft the actor attempts to kill anyone, or purposely inflicts or attempts in inflict serious bodily injury.

Article 223. Theft and Related Offenses

Section 223.0 Definitions.

In this Article, unless a different meaning plainly is required:

(1) "deprive" means: (a) to withhold property of another permanently or for so extended a period as to appropriate a major portion of its economic value, or with intent to restore only upon payment of reward or other compensation; or (b) to dispose of the property so as to make it unlikely that the owner will recover it.

(2) "financial institution" means a bank, insurance company, credit union, building and loan association, investment trust or other organization held out to the public as a place of deposit of funds or medium of savings or collective investment.

(3) "government" means the United States, any State, county, municipality, or other political unit, or any department, agency or subdivision of any of the foregoing, or any corporation or other association carrying out the functions of government.

(4) "movable property" means property the location of which can be changed, including things growing on, affixed to, or found in land, and documents although the rights represented thereby have no physical location. "Immovable property" is all other property.

(5) "obtain" means: (a) in relation to property, to bring about a transfer or purported transfer of a legal interest in the property, whether to the obtainer or another; or (b) in relation to labor or service, to secure performance thereof.

(6) "property" means anything of value, including real estate, tangible and intangible personal property, contract rights, choses-in-action and other interests in or claims to wealth, admission or transportation tickets, captured or domestic animals, food and drink, electric or other power.

(7) "property of another" includes property in which any person other than the actor has an interest which the actor is not privileged to infringe, regardless of the fact that the actor also has an interest in the property and regardless of the fact that the other person might be precluded from civil recovery because the property was used in an unlawful transaction or was subject to forfeiture as contraband. Property in possession of the actor shall not be deemed property of another who has only a security interest therein, even if legal title is in the creditor pursuant to a conditional sales contract or other security agreement.

Section 223.1 Consolidation of Theft Offenses; Grading; Provisions Applicable to Theft Generally.

(1) *Consolidation of Theft Offenses.* Conduct denominated theft in this Article constitutes a single offense. An accusation of theft may be supported by evidence that it was committed in any manner that would be theft under this Article, notwithstanding the specification of a different manner in the indictment or information, subject only to the power of the Court to ensure fair trial by granting a continuance or other appropriate relief where the conduct of the defense would be prejudiced by lack of fair notice or by surprise.

(2) *Grading of Theft Offenses.*

    (a) Theft constitutes a felony of the third degree if the amount involved exceeds $500, or if the property stolen is a firearm, automobile, airplane, motorcycle, motorboat or other motor-propelled vehicle, or in the case of theft by receiving stolen property, if the receiver is in the business of buying or selling stolen property.

    (b) Theft not within the preceding paragraph constitutes a misdemeanor, except that if the property was not taken from the person or by threat, or in breach of a fiduciary obligation, and the actor proves by a preponderance of the evidence that the amount involved was less than $50, the offense constitutes a petty misdemeanor.

    (c) The amount involved in a theft shall be deemed to be the highest value, by any reasonable standard, of the property or services which the actor stole or attempted to steal. Amounts involved in thefts committed pursuant to one scheme or course of conduct, whether from the same person or several persons, may be aggregated in determining the grade or the offense.

(3) *Claim of Right.* It is an affirmative defense to prosecution for theft that the actor:

    (a) was unaware that the property or service was that of another; or

    (b) acted under an honest claim of right to the property or service involved or that he had a right to acquire or dispose of it as he did; or

    (c) took property exposed for sale, intending to purchase and pay for it promptly, or reasonably believing that the owner, if present, would have consented.

(4) *Theft from Spouse.* It is no defense that theft was from the actor's spouse, except that misappropriation of household and personal effects, or other property normally accessible to both spouses, is theft only if it occurs after the parties have ceased living together.

Section 223.3. Theft by Unlawful Taking or Disposition.

(1) *Movable Property.* A person is guilty of theft if he unlawfully takes, or exercises unlawful control over, movable property of another with purpose to deprive him thereof.

(2) *Immovable Property.* A person is guilty of theft if he unlawfully transfers immovable property of another or any interest therein with purpose to benefit himself or another not entitled thereto.

Section 223.3. Theft by Deception.

A person is guilty of theft if he purposely obtains property of another by deception. A person deceives if he purposely:

(1) creates or reinforces a false impression, including false impressions as to law, value, intention or other state of mind; but deception as to a person's intention to perform a promise shall not be inferred from the fact alone that he did not subsequently perform the promise; or

(2) prevents another from acquiring information which would affect his judgment of a transaction; or

(3) fails to correct a false impression which the deceiver previously created or reinforced, or which the deceiver knows to be influencing another to whom he stands in a fiduciary or confidential relationship; or

(4) fails to disclose a known lien, adverse claim or other legal impediment to the enjoyment of property which he transfers or encumbers in consideration for the property obtained, whether such impediment is or is not valid, or is or is not a matter of official record.

The term "deceive" does not, however, include falsity as to matters having no pecuniary significance, or puffing by statements unlikely to deceive ordinary persons in the group addressed.

Section 223.4. Theft by Extortion.

A person is guilty of theft if he obtains property of another by threatening to:

(1) inflict bodily injury on anyone or commit any other criminal offense; or

(2) accuse anyone of a criminal offense; or

(3) expose any secret tending to subject any person to hatred, contempt or ridicule, or to impair his credit or business repute; or

(4) take or withhold action as an official, or cause an official to take or withhold action; or

(5) bring about or continue a strike, boycott or other collective unofficial action, if the property is not demanded or received for the benefit of the group in whose interest the actor purports to act; or

(6) testify or provide information or withhold testimony or information with respect to another's legal claim or defense; or

(7) inflict any other harm which would not benefit the actor.

It is an affirmative defense to prosecution based on paragraphs (2), (3) or (4) that the property obtained by threat of accusation, exposure, lawsuit or other invocation of official action was honestly claimed as restitution or indemnification for harm done in the circumstances to which such accusation, exposure, lawsuit or other official action relates, or as compensation for property or lawful services.

Section 223.5. Theft of Property Lost, Mislaid, or Delivered by Mistake.

A person who comes into control of property of another that he knows to have been lost, mislaid, or delivered under a mistake as to the nature or amount of the property or the identity of the recipient is guilty of theft if, with purpose to deprive the owner thereof, he fails to take reasonable measures to restore the property to a person entitled to have it.

Section 223.6. Receiving Stolen Property.

(1) *Receiving.* A person is guilty of theft if he purposely receives, retains, or disposes of movable property of another knowing that it has been stolen, or believing that it has probably been stolen, unless the property is received, retained, or disposed with purpose to restore it to the owner. "Receiving" means acquiring possession, control or title, or lending on the security of the property.

(2) *Presumption of Knowledge.* The requisite knowledge or belief is presumed in the case of a dealer who:

(a) is found in possession or control of property stolen from two or more persons on separate occasions; or

(b) has received stolen property in another transaction within the year preceding the transaction charged; or

(c) being a dealer in property of the sort received, acquires it for a consideration which he knows is far below its reasonable value.

"Dealer" means a person in the business of buying or selling goods including a pawnbroker.

Section 223.7. Theft of Services.

(1) A person is guilty of theft if he purposely obtains services which he knows are available only for compensation, by deception or threat, or by false token or other means to avoid payment for the service. "Services" includes labor, professional service, transportation, telephone or other public service, accommodation in hotels, restaurants or elsewhere, admission to exhibitions, use of vehicles or other movable property. Where compensation for service is ordinarily paid immediately upon the rendering for such service, as is the case of hotels and restaurants, refusal to pay or absconding without payment or offer to pay gives rise to a presumption that the service was obtained by deception as to intention to pay.

(2) A person commits theft if, having control over the disposition of services of others, to which he is not entitled, he knowingly diverts such services to his own benefit or to the benefit of another not entitled thereto.

Section 223.8. Theft by Failure to Make Required Disposition of Funds Received.

A person who purposely obtains property upon agreement, or subject to a known legal obligation, to make specified payment or other disposition, whether from such property or its proceeds or from his own property to be reserved in equivalent amount, is guilty of theft if he deals with the property obtained as his own and fails to make the required payment or disposition. The foregoing applies notwithstanding that it may be impossible to identify particular property as belonging to the victim at the time of the actor's failure to make the required payment or disposition. An officer or employee of the government or of a financial institution is presumed: (i) to know any legal obligation relevant to his criminal liability under this Section, and (ii) to have dealt with the property as his own if he fails to pay or account upon lawful demand, or if an audit reveals a shortage or falsification of accounts.

Section 223.9. Unauthorized Use of Automobiles and Other Vehicles.

A person commits a misdemeanor if he operates another's automobile, airplane, motorcycle, motorboat, or other motor-propelled vehicle without consent of the owner. It is an affirmative defense to prosecution under this Section that the actor reasonably believed that the owner would have consented to the operation had he known of it.

Article 224.   Forgery and Fraudulent Practices

Section 224.0.   Definitions.

In this Article, the definitions given in Section 223.0 apply unless a different meaning plainly is required.

Section 224.1.   Forgery.

(1) *Definition.* A person is guilty of forgery if, with purpose to defraud or injure anyone, or with knowledge that he is facilitating a fraud or injury to be perpetrated by anyone, the actor:

    (a) alters any writing of another without his authority; or

    (b) makes, completes, executes, authenticates, issues or transfers any writing so that it purports to be the act of another who did not authorize that act, or to have been executed at a time or place or in a numbered sequence other than was in fact the case, or to be a copy of an original when no such original existed; or

    (c) utters any writing which he knows to be forged in a manner specified in paragraphs (a) or (b).

"Writing" includes printing or any other method of recording information, money, coins, tokens, stamps, seals, credit cards, badges, trade-marks, and other symbols of value, right, privilege, or identification.

(2) *Grading.* Forgery is a felony of the second degree if the writing is or purports to be part of an issue of money, securities, postage or revenue stamps, or other instruments issued by the government, or part of an issue of stock, bonds or other instruments representing interests in or claims against any property or enterprise. Forgery is a felony of the third degree if the writing is or purports to be a will, deed, contract, release, commercial instrument, or other document evidencing, creating, transferring, altering, terminating, or otherwise affecting legal relations. Otherwise forgery is a misdemeanor.

Section 224.5.   Bad Checks.

A person who issues or passes a check or similar sight order for the payment of money, knowing that it will not be honored by the drawee, commits a misdemeanor. For the purposes of this Section as well as in any prosecution for theft committed by means of a bad check, an issuer is presumed to know that the check or order (other than a postdated check or order) would not be paid, if:

    (1) the issuer had no account with the drawee at the time the check or order was issued; or

    (2) payment was refused by the drawee for lack of funds, upon presentation within 30 days after issue, and the issuer failed to make good within 10 days after receiving notice of that refusal.

Section 224.8.   Commercial Bribery and Breach of Duty to Act Disinterestedly.

(1) A person commits a misdemeanor if he solicits, accepts or agrees to accept any benefit as consideration for knowingly violating or agreeing to violate a duty of fidelity to which he is subject as:

    (a) partner, agent or employee of another;

    (b) trustee, guardian, or other fiduciary;

    (c) lawyer, physician, accountant, appraiser, or other professional adviser or informant;

    (d) officer, director, manager or other participant in the direction of the affairs of an incorporated or unincorporated association; or

    (e) arbitrator or other purportedly disinterested adjudicator or referee.

(2) A person who holds himself out to the public as being engaged in the business of making disinterested selection, appraisal, or criticism of commodities or services commits a

misdemeanor if he solicits, accepts or agrees to accept any benefit to influence his selection, appraisal or criticism.

(3) A person commits a misdemeanor if he confers, or offers or agrees to confer, any benefit the acceptance of which would be criminal under this Section.

Offenses Against the Family

Article 230. Offenses Against the Family

Section 230.1. Bigamy and Polygamy.

(1) *Bigamy.* A married person is guilty of bigamy, a misdemeanor, if he contracts or purports to contract another marriage, unless at the time of the subsequent marriage:

(a) the actor believes that the prior spouse is dead; or

(b) the actor and the prior spouse have been living apart for five consecutive years throughout which the prior spouse was not known by the actor to be alive; or

(c) a Court has entered a judgment purporting to terminate or annul any prior disqualifying marriage, and the actor does not know that judgment to be invalid; or

(d) the actor reasonably believes that he is legally eligible to remarry.

(2) *Polygamy.* A person is guilty of polygamy, a felony of the third degree, if he marries or cohabits with more than one spouse at a time in purported exercise of the right of plural marriage. The offense is a continuing one until all cohabitation and claim of marriage with more than one spouse terminates. This section does not apply to parties to a polygamous marriage, lawful in the country of which they are residents or nationals, while they are in transit through or temporarily visiting this State.

(3) *Other Party to Bigamous or Polygamous Marriage.* A person is guilty of bigamy or polygamy, as the case may be, if he contracts or purports to contract marriage with another knowing that the other is thereby committing bigamy or polygamy.

Section 230.2. Incest.

A person is guilty of incest, a felony of the third degree, if he knowingly marries or cohabits or has sexual intercourse with an ancestor or descendant, a brother or sister of the whole or half blood [or an uncle, aunt, nephew or niece of the whole blood]. "Cohabit" means to live together under the representation or appearance of being married. The relationships referred to herein include blood relationships without regard to legitimacy, and relationship of parent and child by adoption.

Section 230.4. Endangering Welfare of Children.

A parent, guardian, or other person supervising the welfare of a child under 18 commits a misdemeanor if he knowingly endangers the child's welfare by violating a duty of care, protection or support.

Section 230.5. Persistent Non-Support.

A person commits a misdemeanor if he persistently fails to provide support which he can provide and which he knows he is legally obliged to provide to a spouse, child or other dependent.

Offenses Against Public Administration

Article 240. Bribery and Corrupt Influence

Section 240.0. Definitions.

In Articles 240–243, unless a different meaning plainly is required:

(1) "benefit" means gain or advantage, or anything regarded by the beneficiary as gain or advantage, including benefit to any other person or entity in whose welfare he is interested, but not an advantage promised generally to a group or class of voters as a consequence of public measures which a candidate engages to support or oppose;

(2) "government" includes any branch, subdivision or agency of the government of the State or any locality within it;

(3) "harm" means loss, disadvantage or injury, or anything so regarded by the person affected, including loss, disadvantage or injury to any other person or entity in whose welfare he is interested;

(4) "official proceeding" means a proceeding heard or which may be heard before any legislative, judicial, administrative or other governmental agency or official authorized to take evidence under oath, including any referee, hearing examiner, commissioner, notary or other person taking testimony or deposition in connection with any such proceeding;

(5) "party official" means a person who holds an elective or appointive post in a political party in the United States by virtue of which he directs or conducts, or participates in directing or conducting party affairs at any level of responsibility;

(6) "pecuniary benefit" is benefit in the form of money, property, commercial interests or anything else the primary significance of which is economic gain;

(7) "public servant" means any officer or employee of government, including legislators and judges, and any person participating as juror, advisor, consultant or otherwise, in performing a governmental function; but the term does not include witnesses;

(8) "administrative proceeding" means any proceeding, other than a judicial proceeding, the outcome of which is required to be based on a record or documentation prescribed by law, or in which law or regulation is particularized in application to individuals.

Section 240.1. Bribery in Official and Political Matters.

A person is guilty of bribery, a felony of the third degree, if he offers, confers or agrees to confer upon another, or solicits, accepts or agrees to accept from another:

(1) any pecuniary benefit as consideration for the recipient's decision, opinion, recommendation, vote or other exercise of discretion as a public servant, party official or voter; or

(2) any benefit as consideration for the recipient's decision, vote, recommendation or other exercise of official discretion in a judicial or administrative proceeding; or

(3) any benefit as consideration for a violation of a known legal duty as public servant or party official.

It is no defense to prosecution under this section that a person whom the actor sought to influence was not qualified to act in the desired way whether because he had not yet assumed office, or lacked jurisdiction, or for any other reason.

Section 240.2. Threats and Other Improper Influence in Official and Political Matters.

(1) *Offenses Defined.* A person commits an offense if he:

(a) threatens unlawful harm to any person with purpose to influence his decision, opinion, recommendation, vote or other exercise of discretion as a public servant, party official or voter; or

(b) threatens harm to any public servant with purpose to influence his decision, opinion, recommendation, vote or pecuniary

benefit as consideration for exerting special influence upon a public servant or procuring another to do so. "Special influence" means power to influence through kinship, friendship or other relationship, apart from the merits of the transaction.

(3) *Paying for Endorsement or Special Influence.* A person commits a misdemeanor if he offers, confers or agrees to confer any pecuniary benefit receipt of which is prohibited by this Section.

Article 241. Perjury and Other Falsification in Official Matters

Section 241.0. Definitions.

In this Article, unless a different meaning plainly is required:

(1) the definitions given in Section 240.0 apply; and

(2) "statement" means any representation, but includes a representation of opinion, belief or other state of mind only if the representation clearly relates to state of mind apart from or in addition to any facts which are the subject of the representation.

Section 241.1. Perjury.

(1) *Offense Defined.* A person is guilty of perjury, a felony of the third degree, if in any official proceeding he makes a false statement under oath or equivalent affirmation, or swears or affirms the truth of a statement previously made, when the statement is material and he does not believe it to be true.

(2) *Materiality.* Falsification is material, regardless of the admissibility of the statement under rules of evidence, if it could have affected the course or outcome of the proceeding. It is no defense that the declarant mistakenly believed the falsification to be immaterial. Whether a falsification is material in a given factual situation is a question of law.

(3) *Irregularities No Defense.* It is not a defense to prosecution under this Section that the oath or affirmation was administered or taken in an irregular manner or that the declarant was not competent to make the statement. A document purporting to be made upon oath or affirmation at any time when the actor presents it as being so verified shall be deemed to have been duly sworn or affirmed.

(4) *Retraction.* No person shall be guilty of an offense under this Section if he retracted the falsification in the course of the proceeding in which it was made before it became manifest that

the falsification was or would be exposed and before the falsification substantially affected the proceeding.

(5) *Inconsistent Statements.* Where the defendant made inconsistent statements under oath or equivalent affirmation, both having been made within the period of the statute of limitations, the prosecution may proceed by setting forth the inconsistent statements in a single count alleging in the alternative that one or the other was false and not believed by the defendant. In such case it shall not be necessary for the prosecution to prove which statement was false but only that one or the other was false and not believed by the defendant to be true.

(6) *Corroboration.* No person shall be convicted of an offense under this Section where proof of falsity rests solely upon contradiction by testimony of a single person other than the defendant.

Section 241.2. False Swearing.

(1) *False Swearing in Official Matters.* A person who makes a false statement under oath or equivalent affirmation, or swears or affirms the truth of such a statement previously made, when he does not believe the statement to be true, is guilty of a misdemeanor if:

(a) the falsification occurs in an official proceeding; or

(b) the falsification is intended to mislead a public servant in performing his official function.

Section 241.9. Impersonating a Public Servant.

A person commits a misdemeanor if he falsely pretends to hold a position in the public service with purpose to induce another to submit to such pretended official authority or otherwise to act in reliance upon that pretense to his prejudice.

Offenses Against Public Order and Decency

Article 250. Riot, Disorderly Conduct, and Related Offenses

Section 250.1 Riot; Failure to Disperse.

(1) *Riot.* A person is guilty of riot, a felony of the third degree, if he participates with [two] or more others in a course of disorderly conduct:

(a) with purpose to commit or facilitate the commission of a felony or misdemeanor;

(b) with purpose to prevent or coerce official action; or

(c) when the actor or any other participant to the knowledge of the actor uses or plans to use a firearm or other deadly weapon.

(2) *Failure of Disorderly Persons to Disperse Upon Official Order.* Where [three] or more persons are participating in a course of disorderly conduct likely to cause substantial harm or serious inconvenience, annoyance or alarm, a peace officer or other public servant engaged in executing or enforcing the law may order the participants and others in the immediate vicinity to disperse. A person who refuses or knowingly fails to obey such an order commits a misdemeanor.

Section 250.2 Disorderly Conduct.

(1) *Offense Defined.* A person is guilty of disorderly conduct if, with purpose to cause public inconvenience, annoyance or alarm, or recklessly creating a risk thereof, he:

(a) engages in fighting or threatening, or in violent or tumultuous behavior; or

(b) makes unreasonable noise or offensively coarse utterance, gesture or display, or addresses abusive language to any person present; or

(c) creates a hazardous or physically offensive condition by any act which serves no legitimate purpose of the actor.

"Public" means affecting or likely to affect persons in a place to which the public or a substantial group has access; among the places included are highways, transport facilities, schools, prisons, apartment houses, places of business or amusement, or any neighborhood.

(2) *Grading.* An offense under this section is a petty misdemeanor if the actor's purpose is to cause substantial harm or serious inconvenience, or if he persists in disorderly conduct after reasonable warning or request to desist. Otherwise disorderly conduct is a violation.

Section 250.3 False Public Alarms.

A person is guilty of a misdemeanor if he initiates or circulates a report or warning of an impending bombing or other crime or catastrophe, knowing that the report or warning is false or baseless and that it is likely to cause evacuation of a building, place of assembly, or facility of public transport, or to cause public inconvenience or alarm.

Section 250.4. Harassment.

A person commits a petty misdemeanor if, with purpose to harass another, he:

(1) makes a telephone call without purpose of legitimate communication; or

(2) insults, taunts or challenges another in a manner likely to provoke violent or disorderly response; or

(3) makes repeated communications anonymously or at extremely inconvenient hours, or in offensively coarse language; or

(4) subjects another to an offensive touching; or

(5) engages in any other course of alarming conduct serving no legitimate purpose of the actor.

Section 250.5. Public Drunkenness; Drug Incapacitation.

A person is guilty of an offense if he appears in any public place manifestly under the influence of alcohol, narcotics or other drugs, not therapeutically administered, to the degree that he may endanger himself or other persons or property, or annoy persons in his vicinity. An offense under this Section constitutes a petty misdemeanor if the actor has been convicted hereunder twice before within a period of one year. Otherwise the offense constitutes a violation.

Section 250.6. Loitering or Prowling.

A person commits a violation if he loiters or prowls in a place, at a time, or in a manner not usual for lawabiding individuals under circumstances that warrant alarm for the safety of persons or property in the vicinity. Among the circumstances which may be considered in determining whether such alarm is warranted is the fact that the actor takes flight upon appearance of a peace officer, refuses to identify himself, or manifestly endeavors to conceal himself or any object. Unless flight by the actor or other circumstances makes it impracticable, a peace officer shall prior to any arrest for an offense under this section afford the actor an opportunity to dispel any alarm which would otherwise be warranted, by requesting him to identify himself and explain his presence and conduct. No person shall be convicted of an offense under this Section if the peace officer did not comply with the preceding sentence, or if it appears at trial that the explanation given by the actor was true and, if believed by the peace officer at the time, would have dispelled the alarm.

Article 251. Public Indecency

Section 251.1. Open Lewdness.

A person commits a petty misdemeanor if he does any lewd act which he knows is likely to be observed by others who would be affronted or alarmed.

(1) *Prostitution.* A person is guilty of prostitution, a petty misdemeanor, if he or she:

(a) is an inmate of a house of prostitution or otherwise engages in sexual activity as a business; or

(b) loiters in or within view of any public place for the purpose of being hired to engage in sexual activity.

"Sexual activity" includes homosexual and other deviate sexual relations. A "house of prostitution" is any place where prostitution or promotion of prostitution is regularly carried on by one person under the control, management or supervision of another. An "inmate" is a person who engages in prostitution in or through the agency of a house of prostitution. "Public place" means any place to which the public or any substantial group thereof has access.

(2) *Promoting Prostitution.* A person who knowingly promotes prostitution of another commits a misdemeanor or felony as provided in Subsection (3). The following acts shall, without limitation of the foregoing, constitute promoting prostitution:

(a) owning, controlling, managing, supervising or otherwise keeping, alone or in association with others, a house of prostitution or a prostitution business; or

(b) procuring an inmate for a house of prostitution or a place in a house of prostitution for one who would be an inmate; or

(c) encouraging, inducing, or otherwise purposely causing another to become or remain a prostitute; or

(d) soliciting a person to patronize a prostitute; or

(e) procuring a prostitute for a patron; or

(f) transporting a person into or within this state with purpose to promote that person's engaging in prostitution, or procuring or paying for transportation with that purpose; or

(g) leasing or otherwise permitting a place controlled by the actor, alone or in association with others, to be regularly used for prostitution or the promotion of prostitution, or failure to make reasonable effort to abate such use by ejecting the tenant, notifying law enforcement authorities, or other legally available means; or

(h) soliciting, receiving, or agreeing to receive any benefit for doing or agreeing to do anything forbidden by this Subsection.

(3) *Grading of Offenses Under Subsection (2).* An offense under Subsection (2) constitutes a felony of the third degree if:

(a) the offense falls within paragraph (a), (b) or (c) of Subsection (2); or

(b) the actor compels another to engage in or promote prostitution; or

(c) the actor promotes prostitution of a child under 16, whether or not he is aware of the child's age; or

(d) the actor promotes prostitution of his wife, child, ward or any person for whose care, protection or support he is responsible.

Otherwise the offense is a misdemeanor.

(4) *Presumption from Living off Prostitutes.* A person, other than the prostitute or the prostitute's minor child or other legal dependent incapable of self-support, who is supported in whole or substantial part by the proceeds of prostitution is presumed to be knowingly promoting prostitution in violation of Subsection (2).

(5) *Patronizing Prostitutes.* A person commits a violation if he hires a prostitute to engage in sexual activity with him, or if he enters or remains in a house of prostitution for the purpose of engaging in sexual activity.

(6) *Evidence.* On the issue whether a place is a house of prostitution the following shall be admissible evidence: its general repute; the repute of the persons who reside in or frequent the place; the frequency, timing and duration of visits by non-residents. Testimony of a person against his spouse shall be admissible to prove offenses under this Section.

Section 251.3. Loitering to Solicit Deviate Sexual Relations.

A person is guilty of a petty misdemeanor if he loiters in or near any public place for the purpose of soliciting or being solicited to engage in deviate sexual relations.

Section 251.4. Obscenity.

(1) *Obscene Defined.* Material is obscene if, considered as a whole, its predominant appeal is to prurient interest, that is, a shameful or morbid interest, in nudity, sex or excretion, and if in addition it goes substantially beyond customary limits of candor in describing or representing such matters. Predominant appeal shall be judged with reference to ordinary adults unless it

appears from the character of the material or the circumstances of its dissemination to be designed for children or other specially susceptible audience. Undeveloped photographs, molds, printing plates, and the like, shall be deemed obscene notwithstanding that processing or other acts may be required to make the obscenity patent or to disseminate it.

(2) *Offenses.* Subject to the affirmative defense provided in Subsection (3), a person commits a misdemeanor if he knowingly or recklessly:

(a) sells, delivers or provides, or offers or agrees to sell, deliver or provide, any obscene writing, picture, record or other representation or embodiment of the obscene; or

(b) presents or directs an obscene play, dance or performance, or participates in that portion thereof which makes it obscene; or

(c) publishes, exhibits or otherwise makes available any obscene material; or

(d) possesses any obscene material for purposes of sale or other commercial dissemination; or

(e) sells, advertises or otherwise commercially disseminates material, whether or not obscene, by representing or suggesting that it is obscene.

A person who disseminates or possesses obscene material in the course of his business is presumed to do so knowingly or recklessly.

(3) *Justifiable and Non-Commercial Private Dissemination.* It is an affirmative defense to prosecution under this Section that dissemination was restricted to:

(a) institutions or persons having scientific, educational, governmental or other similar justification for possessing obscene material; or

(b) non-commercial dissemination to personal associates of the actor.

(4) *Evidence; Adjudication of Obscenity.* In any prosecution under this Section, evidence shall be admissible to show:

(a) the character of the audience for which the material was designed or to which it was directed;

(b) what the predominant appeal of the material would be for ordinary adults or any special audience to which it was directed, and what effect, if any, it would probably have on conduct of such people;

(c) artistic, literary, scientific, educational or other merits or the material;

(d) the degree of public acceptance of the material in the United States;

(e) appeal to prurient interest, or absence thereof, in advertising or other promotion of the material; and

(f) the good repute of the author, creator, publisher or other person from whom the material originated.

Expert testimony and testimony of the author, creator, publisher or other person from whom the material originated, relating to factors entering into the determination of the issue of obscenity, shall be admissible. The Court shall dismiss a prosecution for obscenity if it is satisfied that the material is not obscene.

GLOSSARY

accessories Parties who are not present during a crime, but who assist the principals in some manner. An accessory before the fact aids, counsels, assists, or encourages before the act takes place, and accessories after the fact assist the criminal in avoiding arrest or prosecution after the crime.

actus reus One of two essential elements of crimes. It is the physical part, the act engaged in by the accused. Mens rea is the other essential element.

admission A statement which is inculpatory, but not a confession.

affirmative defenses A special defense, such as insanity or self-defense. Contrary to the general rule, defendants have the burden of production concerning affirmative defenses in all jurisdictions, as well as the burden of persuasion in many.

aggravating circumstance A factual reason justifying sentencing a defendant more harshly than the applicable presumptive sentence.

alibi A defense. A claim by a defendant that she was not present at the scene of a crime at the time it was committed.

appellate courts Courts that review the record from lower courts for error. The federal system and most state systems have two levels of appellate courts, an intermediate and highest level. The intermediate level is commonly known as a court of appeals and the high court as a supreme court.

arraignment The hearing at which the formal charge is read to the defendant and he is required to enter a plea.

arson In the common law arson was the 1. malicious 2. burning 3. of a dwelling 4. of another person. Most states have expanded the definition of arson by statute to include the burning of one's own property and to include any property.

assault 1. To put another in fear or apprehension of an imminent battery. 2. An attempted battery.

assumption of duty When a person begins a rescue attempt, that rescuer has a duty to complete the rescue, if possible. The rescuer is said to have assumed the duty of rescuing the person in danger.

attempt When a person 1. has an intent to commit some crime 2. takes some act beyond mere preparation in furtherance of that crime 3. but the crime is not completed, attempt has been committed.

battery An intentional (or reckless) touching of another that is harmful or offensive.

beyond a reasonable doubt The standard of proof in criminal cases. The prosecution must prove every element of the

495

charged offense beyond a reasonable doubt to obtain a conviction.

bill of attainder An act of a legislature punishing a person without the benefit of a judicial trial. Article I of the Constitution prohibits both the federal and state governments from enacting bills of attainder.

bill of particulars A document filed by prosecutors that provides details concerning the charges against a defendant.

Bill of Rights The first ten amendments to the United States Constitution. It contains certain rights that are guaranteed to the people, such as the freedom from unreasonable searches and seizures.

breaches of the peace Crimes that involve disturbing the tranquility or order of society. Disturbing the peace, rioting, inciting violence, and vagrancy are examples of crimes that are categorized as breaches of the peace.

bribery 1. Soliciting or accepting 2. anything of value 3. with the purpose of violating a duty or trust. Common classifications of bribery are commercial and of a public official.

burden of persuasion The duty of a party to convince the factfinder that something is true.

burden of production The duty of a party to raise an issue and introduce some evidence in its support. It is unnecessary to convince the factfinder that the contention is true.

burden of proof The duty of a party to raise legal issues or introduce facts to support a position. Burden of proof involves two concepts: burden of production and burden of persuasion.

burglary In the common law the elements of burglary were: 1. the breaking and entering 2. of another's dwelling 3. at night 4. with the intent of committing a felony. By statute, burglaries now include most

structures and can be committed at either day or night.

Canons of Statutory Construction Rules that must be followed by courts when interpreting statutes. One such rule is that statutes that can be interpreted as constitutional or violative of the Constitution must be read as constitutional.

cause in fact To prove some crimes, particularly those that require behavior amounting to purposeful under the Model Penal Code, it must be shown that the defendant's behavior was the cause of the resulting harm. This is also known as the "but for" or *sine qua non* test. This is because "but for" the defendant's behavior the harm would not have happened.

challenge for cause To request that a potential juror be removed because the juror has exhibited an inability to be fair and impartial.

civil liberties Also known as civil rights. Individual, personal rights. In the United States many of these rights are protected by the constitutions of the national government and the many state governments. The freedoms of speech and religion are examples of civil rights.

clear and present danger doctrine Words that create a clear and present danger are not protected by the First Amendment and may be regulated by government.

co-conspirator hearsay rule An exception to the hearsay rule, which permits the hearsay statements of co-conspirators to be admitted at trial, provided such statements are made during the conspiracy.

common law A body of unwritten law that develops from the customs, principles, and practices of a nation as recognized in judicial decisions. Although the common law can be found in written caselaw, it is often referred to as unwritten in the sense that the legislature has not created a written statute.

compensatory damages Damages that equal the amount of loss and nothing more.

complaint A written statement containing the essential facts and law under which a defendant is charged. Used to obtain an arrest warrant (or summons) or to establish probable cause at a preliminary hearing.

concurrence For those crimes that consist of both a mental and physical part it must be shown that the mens rea and the act were joined to cause the result.

concurrent jurisdiction When two or more governmental units share authority over a policy area, person, or thing.

concurrent sentence Whenever two sentences run together, so that the actual sentence time equals the greater of the two sentences, they are concurrent.

confession A statement claiming that one has committed a crime.

consecutive sentence Whenever one sentence follows another it is consecutive. The actual sentence time equals the sum of the two sentences.

consent A claim by a defendant that a victim agreed to the acts. A defense to some crimes, such as larceny and rape. Consent, even if true, is not a defense to some crimes, such as statutory rape and murder.

consent searches A person may waive her Fourth Amendment right to a search warrant. The consent must be voluntary, and the person consenting must have an interest in the property for the consent to be valid. There must be more than a mere property interest; the consenting party must have rights of control and use of the property.

conspiracy A crime. The elements are 1. an agreement 2. between two or more people 3. to do something unlawful or to do something lawful in an unlawful manner.

constructive intent Intent to cause the result of an action which is imputed to a defendant even though the defendant had no desire to cause the result. The intent may only be attributed to the defendant if the act had a substantial likelihood of causing the outcome.

contempt Failing to comply with a court order or interfering with the administration of a court is contemptuous. Contempt has many forms. Civil contempt is used to coerce persons into complying with court orders. Criminal contempt is levied as a punishment for violating court orders. Violations that occur in the presence of a court are referred to as direct, and those outside the presence of a court are indirect. Legislative bodies also possess contempt power.

continuing criminal enterprise (CCE) A federal statute, commonly known as the "Drug Kingpin Statute," because its aim is at high-level drug dealers and smugglers. To prove a CCE violation it must be shown that 1. the defendant was an administrator, organizer or other leader 2. of a group of five or more people 3. who have engaged in a series of drug violations.

contract law A branch of civil law concerned with written agreements between two or more persons. These written agreements are called contracts. A violation of a contract is known as a breach of contract.

conversion An unauthorized control over property intending to permanently deprive the owner of its possession.

corporate liability A form of vicarious liability. Corporations, partnerships, and other organizations may be liable for the acts of their agents when those agents are acting within the scope of employment.

corpus delicti Latin phrase meaning "the body of the crime." Refers to the substance of the crime. In murder, the corpus delicti is the death of the victim and the act of the defendant which caused the death. A burned structure and the act that caused the fire are the corpus delicti of arson.

court rules   Rules of civil and criminal procedure established by courts. Generally these rules supplement codes of civil and criminal procedure.

courts of general jurisdiction   are courts that have the authority to hear a wide variety of cases, both civil and criminal. Most state trial courts are general jurisdiction courts.

courts of limited jurisdiction   are courts that have the authority to hear only specific classes of cases. Some states have family law, criminal law, probate and juvenile courts, all of which are limited jurisdiction courts.

courts of record   are courts which maintain a verbatim record of the trials and hearings it conducts.

criminal law   The substantive law of crimes and punishment. Defines what conduct is criminal and what punishment may be imposed for such conduct.

criminal mischief   The destruction or damaging of another's property is commonly known as mischief.

criminal procedure   The law that establishes processes for putting substantive criminal law into action.

culpability   Blameworthiness; guilt.

damages   1. The loss suffered by an individual due to the wrongful act of another. 2. Money received from a lawsuit to compensate for loss to property, person, or rights.

deadly weapon   Any item, which from the manner used is calculated or likely to cause death or serious bodily injury.

Deadly Weapon Doctrine   A rule that states that juries may infer that a defendant intended to murder if a deadly weapon was used to kill the victim.

derivative use immunity   A witness's compelled testimony may not be used against him, nor may any fruits of that testimony. However, the immunity is not complete. If the government obtains independent evidence it may be used against the witness.

diminished capacity   A defense. Whenever a defendant's mental condition does not meet the test of insanity, but the defendant's mental state prevented the forming of the requisite mens rea, most states allow the defendant to introduce evidence of her mental state in an attempt to be convicted of a lesser crime. Some states do not permit this, as they treat the defense of insanity as "all or nothing."

discovery   The pretrial process whereby the defense and prosecution exchange information about a case.

Double Jeopardy Clause   The Fifth Amendment to the United States Constitution prohibits prosecuting or punishing a person twice for the same act. The double jeopardy clause does not prohibit two sovereign entities from punishing a person for the same act.

due process   A concept embodied in the Fifth and Fourteenth Amendments to the United States Constitution. Also contained in all state constitutions. Generally held to mean that no person shall be deprived of life, liberty, or property without first being provided notice of an impending government action against the individual, the opportunity to be heard, and often the right to a jury trial. Generally, a provision requiring that individuals be given their day in court before their government can act against them.

duress   A defense applicable when a person commits a crime under threat of serious bodily harm or death.

Durham test   A test used for determining insanity. Under Durham a person is not guilty because of insanity if the unlawful act was the product of mental disease or defect. The test is no longer used by any jurisdiction.

element Each crime consists of many parts. Each part of a crime is known as an element. Each element must be proven beyond a reasonable doubt by the prosecution to support a conviction.

elements The parts of a crime. The prosecution must prove all the elements of a crime to gain a conviction.

embezzlement The 1. conversion of 2. personal property of 3. another 4. after acquiring lawful acquisition 5. with an intent to defraud the owner.

entrapment A defense. Under some circumstances it is entrapment for law enforcement officers to encourage a person to engage in criminal conduct for the purpose of arresting and prosecuting that person for committing the crime encouraged. There are two tests used to determine if entrapment exists. One test focuses on whether defendants are predisposed to engage in criminal behavior (subjective), and the other focuses on the propriety of the police conduct (objective).

ex post facto law A law that declares an act illegal after it has been taken, increases the punishment or severity of a crime after it has occurred, or changes the procedural rules of a case to a defendant's detriment after the defendant has committed the illegal act. Article I of the Constitution prohibits both the federal and state governments from enacting ex post facto laws.

exclusionary rule Evidence that is obtained by law enforcement in an unconstitutional manner may not be used at trial to prove a defendant's guilt.

factual basis Before a court may accept a plea of guilty a factual basis to believe the defendant committed the crime must be established.

factual impossibility It is not a defense to a criminal accusation for a person to claim that it was impossible for the crime to be completed.

failure to file Failing to file a required return, or other information, is a crime of omission.

false imprisonment The 1. intentional 2. interference with 3. another person's liberty 4. by use of threat or force 5. without authority.

false pretenses 1. False representations 2. of material present or past fact 3. made with knowledge that the fact is false 4. and an intent to defraud the owner of property 5. thereby causing the owner to transfer title to the actor.

federalism A system of government with two or more levels of government where each maintains a certain amount of independence over a policy area from the other levels of government.

felony-murder doctrine If one causes the unintended death of another during the commission, or attempted commission, of a felony, that person is guilty of murder. The rule imputes the mens rea required to establish murder to the defendant.

Fighting Words Doctrine Words that cause injury or tend to cause immediate breaches of the peace are fighting words. Such expression is not protected by the First Amendment to the United States Constitution.

final order The order or judgment ending the case. Generally, no part of a case may be appealed until a final order is issued.

first-degree murder A homicide that is willful, premeditated, and deliberate. Generally, a purposeful murder under the Model Penal Code. The highest form of murder and is punished the most severely.

foreseeability A causation concept, specifically a test to determine proximate cause. People are liable for their actions if the consequences are foreseeable. Results are foreseeable if a reasonable person would have known that the result was probable.

forfeiture In criminal law forfeiture refers to the loss of property or money due to a violation of law. Forfeitures are not fines, as fines take money from a person regardless of where the money came from. Forfeiture is concerned with money and property related to the crime. If one violates RICO that person may lose any profits from the enterprise, as well as the enterprise itself.

forgery The 1. making of 2. false documents (or the alteration of existing documents making them false) 3. and passing those documents 4. to another 5. with an intent to defraud. In many states this constitutes two crimes: forgery and uttering. In those jurisdictions, one need only make the false document with an intent to defraud to commit forgery. To commit uttering one must pass the document with an intent to defraud; there is no requirement that one make the document for the crime of uttering.

fruit of the poisonous tree Evidence that is derivative or tainted by a prior unconstitutional search, seizure, or arrest is inadmissible at trial.

general deterrent A theory of punishment that states that by punishing individuals for offenses all members of a society are deterred from committing future offenses.

general intent The intent to take an act, but not necessarily to cause the results of that action.

grand jury A body of citizens numbering from twelve to twenty-three that investigates alleged criminal conduct and issues indictments.

habitual offender law A statute which imposes a penalty for multiple violations of criminal laws.

harmless error Not all errors at the trial level justify a reversal. If an error is harmless, the judgment is affirmed.

hearsay An out-of-court statement. The general rule of evidence makes hearsay inadmissible. There are many exceptions to this rule.

incapacitation A theory of punishment where removal of an individual from society is sought so as to eliminate the danger that individual poses to other members of society. Incarceration and capital punishment are two types of incapacitation.

independent source An exception to the Fruit of the Poisonous Tree Doctrine. Evidence that is obtained unlawfully, but is also obtained from an independent source, is admissible at trial.

indictment One of two formal methods of charging a person with a crime. Indictments are issued by grand juries.

inevitable discovery doctrine An exception to the Fruit of the Poisonous Tree Doctrine. Evidence that is obtained unlawfully, but would be inevitably discovered by the police, is admissible at trial.

inference A conclusion that a judge or jury is permitted to reach after considering the facts of a case.

inferior courts Courts with limited jurisdiction. Usually not courts of record and fall under trial courts in the hierarchy of the court system.

information One of two formal methods of charging a person with a crime. Informations are filed by prosecutors.

injunctions Orders issued by courts directing someone to take an act or to refrain from acting.

intentional torts A branch of tort law that deals with compensating individuals for the intended acts of others that cause injury to property, person, or rights.

interlocutory appeal An exception to the final judgment rule. Appeal of an order taken prior to final judgment, and, accordingly, running concurrently with the ongoing litigation.

interpret   Whenever a court reads statutes or other law and determines the meaning of that law, the court is interpreting law.

interrogation   The questioning of a person suspected of committing a crime by the police.

intervening cause   An independent happening that occurs after an act and affects the outcome of an act. Intervening causes can act to lower or eliminate criminal liability as to a particular result.

irrebuttable presumption   A conclusion that the judge or jury must make and that cannot be disproved.

irresistible impulse   A test used to determine insanity. The elements of the test are the same as the M'Naghten test, except it is broader. Even if a person does know the nature and quality of an act, the person may be not guilty because of insanity if the mental disease prevented the defendant from controlling her conduct.

judicial review   The power of the judicial branch to review the acts of the executive and legislative branches and declare any action that is in violation of the Constitution void.

jurisdiction   1. Authority of a governmental unit over a policy area, person, or thing. 2. Authority of a court to hear a case. 3. Location where a governmental unit resides.

kidnapping   The 1. unlawful 2. taking and confinement and 3. asportation (carrying away) of 4. another person 5. by force, threat, fraud, or deception. All kidnappings involve a false imprisonment.

knowingly   Under the Model Penal Code an act is taken knowingly when the result is practically certain to occur, although causing that result is not the purpose for taking the act.

larceny   The 1. trespassory taking and 2. carrying away (asportation) 3. of personal property 4. of another 5. with an intent to permanently deprive the owner of possession.

legal cause   In addition to proving cause in fact, it must also be shown that defendant's actions were the legal cause or proximate cause of the harm. To do this it must be shown that the harm that resulted was similar to the harm intended by the defendant.

legal impossibility   A defense to criminal accusations. A person who takes an act, believing it illegal when it is not, is not liable for attempt.

legislative history   The statements of members of Congress, reports of committees, and other similar information concerning a statute before it became law are known as legislative history. Legislative history often will help judges determine what legislatures intended to accomplish by enacting the statute.

lineup   Where the police exhibit a group of people, among whom is the suspect, to a witness or victim for identification as the criminal.

M'Naghten test   A test used to determine insanity. Generally, it must be shown that a disease of the mind caused the defendant to not know either the nature and quality of the act or that the act was wrong.

manslaughter   An unlawful homicide that is punished less severely than murder. Manslaughter is commonly divided into voluntary and involuntary, the former being the higher crime. Manslaughter is often distinguished from murder by the absence of culpable mens rea.

marital rape exception   A common-law rule that held that a husband could not be charged with the rape of his wife. The rule no longer exists, in its original form, in any state.

mayhem   The crime of intentionally dismembering or disfiguring another.

mens rea   Guilty mind; the state of mind required to be held criminally liable for an act.

mitigating circumstance   A factual reason justifying sentencing a defendant below the applicable presumptive sentence.

Model Penal Code   A criminal code written by criminal law scholars for the American Law Institute. The Model Penal Code has greatly influenced modern criminal law.

motion   A formal request made to a court that it do something, usually to issue an order.

necessity   A defense applicable when a person commits a crime in order to avoid a more serious harm from happening.

negligent torts   A branch of tort law that deals with compensating individuals for the unreasonable acts of others that cause injury to property, person, or rights.

negligently   Under the Model Penal Code an act is negligent when a person takes the act and fails to perceive the substantial risk of harm that may result from the act.

objective intent   A legal determination of what a defendant should have known or believed at the time he or she acted, regardless of the defendant's actual intent.

omission   A failure to act when required to do so by a criminal law. Failing to file a tax return is an example of an omission.

one-man showup   Where the police exhibit one person to a witness or victim for identification as the criminal.

ordinance   The written law of a municipality. Ordinances are enacted by city councils and can be civil or criminal in nature. Ordinances must be consistent with state and federal law, and in the criminal law context deal with minor offenses.

overbreadth   A statute is overbroad and invalid if it includes within its prohibition protected activity, as well as unprotected activity.

parole   An early release from prison. An offender must comply with a number of conditions while on parole. Violation of a condition of parole may result in recommitment to prison.

peremptory challenge   When a party removes a juror without giving a reason. Both the defendant and the government are given a stated number of peremptory challenges.

perjury   The 1. making of a 2. false statement 3. with knowledge of its falsity 4. while under oath.

plain view   An officer, who is in a location where he has a right to be, may seize evidence which falls into his plain view.

plea   The defendant's response to the formal charge. There are three pleas: guilty; not guilty; and nolo contendere.

plea agreement   An agreement reached between the prosecution and defense concerning the disposition of the case. It is common for the prosecution to dismiss or reduce charges in exchange for a plea of guilty.

precedent   A decision or order of a court that is binding on other courts in the future. Generally, a decision of a court is binding only on itself and its lower courts. However, other courts may look to its opinion for guidance.

preliminary hearing   A defendant's second appearance before a court. The purpose of the preliminary hearing is to have a neutral party review the evidence to be sure probable cause exists.

preservation   Some legal issues must be raised at the trial level, or they may not be raised on appeal.

presumption A conclusion that a judge or jury is required to make.

presumptive sentence A precise sentence within a range of possible penalties that must be the sentence imposed by a court in the absence of aggravating or mitigating circumstances.

principals Participants in a crime who are present during the criminal act. A principal in the first degree is the party who actually takes the prohibited act, while a principal in the second degree aids, counsels, assists, or encourages the principal in the first degree.

principle of legality A legal maxim that requires criminal laws to be written, such as statutes and administrative regulations. Additionally, the principle requires that criminal laws be more precise than civil and must have been enacted before the alleged criminal act took place.

probable cause The Fourth Amendment requires the existence of probable cause before a warrant for a search, seizure, or arrest may be issued. Warrantless arrests must also be supported by probable cause. Probable cause is a phrase describing a quantity of evidence greater than mere suspicion, but less than beyond a reasonable doubt.

probable desistance A third test that states that if the defendant had passed the point in preparation where he is unlikely to quit, he is guilty of attempt.

prostitution The crime of 1. providing 2. sexual services 3. in exchange for compensation.

provocation A defense that does not excuse a crime, but causes it to be reduced to a lesser crime. If a reasonable person would have been so enraged by the acts of the victim that the act of the defendant is not beyond what a reasonable person would consider normal, then the defendant may have the defense of provocation. In cases of homicide a legitimate defense of provocation reduces the crime from murder to manslaughter.

proximate cause Nearness; closeness. In criminal law the prohibited result must be proximately caused by criminal act. That is, the result must be a consequence of the act, not coincidence.

proximity A test used to determine if a person's actions rise to the level of attempting a crime. Proximity focuses on the acts taken in furtherance of the intended crime and what acts remain to be taken to complete the crime.

punitive damages Damages that exceed the amount of actual loss and are intended to prevent future misconduct.

purposeful Under the Model Penal Code an act is purposeful when taken with an intent to cause a particular result.

rape Sexual intercourse with another without that person's consent. Additionally, it is sometimes unlawful to engage in sexual relations with consenting parties, such as minors and incompetents.

rape shield laws Statutes that prohibit evidence concerning a victim's sexual history and reputation in the community to be admitted at trial. However, evidence of a sexual history with the defendant is admitted.

reasonable expectation of privacy The legal standard for determining whether the Fourth Amendment comes into play. Government action that encroaches upon a person's reasonable expectation of privacy amounts to a search under the Fourth Amendment.

reasonableness The standard of care expected of all people in tort law.

rebuttable presumption A conclusion that the judge or jury must make until disproved.

receiving stolen property 1. Receiving property 2. that has been stolen 3. with knowledge of its stolen character 4. with an intent to deprive the owner of the property.

recklessly Under the Model Penal Code an act is reckless when it is taken in disregard of substantial risk.

record The entire file, including a transcript of the trial and other hearings, of a case.

regulations Rules, which have the effect of law, created by administrative agencies. To be valid the legislature must have granted the agency the power to make the rule, provided at least minimal guidance and limits to the agency's authority to make law, and the agency must not have exceeded its grant of authority.

rehabilitation A theory of punishment where society attempts to alter the criminal's behavior to conform to social norms. Education, training, and therapy are among the methods used to rehabilitate or correct the violator.

res ipsa loquitor A second test that looks to crimes individually for a specific act that indicates that the defendant has no other purpose than the commission of some specific crime.

retreat doctrine If it is possible to safely do so, one must retreat before using deadly force to repel an attack.

retribution A theory of punishment that asserts that a social benefit is derived when society takes revenge on those who violate criminal laws.

revocation hearing A court proceeding wherein it is determined if a defendant violated a condition of probation and, if so, whether the defendant should be incarcerated.

RICO An acronym for Racketeer Influenced and Corrupt Organizations Act, which is a federal criminal statute concerned with organized crime. To prove a RICO violation it must be shown that the defendant 1. received money or income 2. from a pattern of racketeering activity 3. and

invested that money in any enterprise that is in interstate commerce or affects interstate commerce. Violation of RICO can lead to both civil and criminal actions. There are also state versions of RICO.

robbery The 1. trespassory taking 2. and carrying away (asportation) 3. of personal property 4. from another's person or presence 5. using force or threats 6. with an intent to deprive the owner of the property.

scienter A mens rea concept that requires that a defendant knew, or should have known, that the act taken was prohibited by law.

second-degree murder All homicides that are murder, not manslaughter, but do not rise to the level of first-degree murder. Punished less severely than first-degree murder, but more than manslaughter.

selective incorporation doctrine Those rights contained in the Bill of Rights that are both fundamental and essential to an ordered liberty are incorporated by the Fourteenth Amendment and applied against the states. Nearly all of the Bill of Rights has been incorporated.

self-defense A defense that justifies the use of force against another to avoid personal injury or death. The defense is extended to defending others.

separation of powers The division of governmental power into the legislative, executive, and judicial branches.

sodomy A sexual act against nature. A prohibited sex act. Fellatio, cunnilingus, bestiality, homosexual behavior, and anal sex are commonly included in sodomy statutes.

solicitation The crime of 1. encouraging, requesting, or commanding 2. another 3. to commit a crime.

specific deterrent A theory of punishment that states that by punishing an individual for one offense society is deterring that individual from committing future offenses.

specific intent The intent not only to act, but to cause the precise harm that results from that act; the intent not only to act, but to cause a consequence beyond what occurred; intent to cause a result that is imputed to a defendant when the act taken is substantially likely to cause the result, even though the defendant did not possess a true desire to cause the result.

standing Without standing, a person may not assert a constitutional right. There are two aspects of standing. First, a person must have an interest in a proceeding before he may assert a consitutional privilege therein. Second, the defendant's right must be asserted. For Fourth Amendment issues this means that the defendant must have a privacy interest in the place searched or thing seized.

stare decisis Latin for "Let the decision stand." Legal principle that requires courts to respect the previous opinions of other courts (precedent) if the facts and law are the same in both the new case and old case.

statute of limitation Legislative enactments that establish a time limit for the prosecution of certain offenses.

statutes The written law created by a legislature. A subject matter compilation of statutes is known as a code.

statutory rape The act of sexual intercourse with another who is under a specified age. Whether the victim consented is not relevant. In most states the crime is one of strict liability. There are a few states that recognize an exception in those instances where the defendant possessed a "good faith" or reasonable belief that the victim was of lawful age to engage in sexual activity.

strict liability A type of criminal offense that requires no showing of mens rea.

One is liable for such crimes merely by committing the prohibited act.

strict liability torts A branch of tort law wherein liability exists for injuries caused by certain acts even though no intent to injure exists, and the party being sued exercised extreme care.

subjective intent The desires, motives, and intentions in a defendant's mind when he or she acts. The actual intent of a defendant.

subornation of perjury The 1. act of convincing or procuring another 2. to commit perjury.

substantial capacity test The test for determining insanity found in the Model Penal Code. Similar to, but broader than, the M'Naghten test, a person is not guilty because of insanity if because of mental disease or defect he lacks substantial capacity either to appreciate the criminality (wrongfulness) of his conduct or to conform his conduct to the requirements of the law.

substantial steps A fourth test, from the Model Penal Code. If a defendant has taken substantial steps toward completion of a crime, and the steps strongly corroborate her intent to commit the crime, then he or she is guilty of attempt.

tax evasion The 1. willful 2. underpaying (or under-reporting) 3. of a tax.

tax fraud The use of fraud or false documents to avoid a tax obligation.

tort law A branch of civil law concerned with compensating individuals for personal injury, property damage, and other losses. The duty to not injure another in tort law is created by the law, in contrast with contract law where the duty is created by the parties themselves. Many crimes are also torts. To commit such a civil wrong is to commit a tort.

transactional immunity This occurs whenever a witness is given full immunity from prosecution on all charges that were testified to.

transferred intent A legal doctrine that holds that if a defendant intends to harm A, but unintentionally harms B using the means intended to harm A, the intent to harm A is transferred to B. This allows defendant to be prosecuted as if there was an intent to harm B.

trial courts Usually the first court to hear a case, except in those instances when an inferior court has previously heard the case. Usually a court of general jurisdiction. Known by various names in state systems, such as district, circuit, and county. District court in the federal system.

unlawful disclosure Information contained in tax returns is confidential. Any revenue official or employee who discloses such information, even to law enforcement, is guilty of unlawful disclosure.

vagueness A statute is void if it is so vague that a person of common intelligence can not determine what conduct is proscribed.

vicarious liability Whenever a person can be held criminally liable for the actions of another, that person is vicariously liable. No showing of mens rea has to be shown for either the person who acted or the person liable. Further, the person liable does not have to take any action to be criminally liable.

voir dire French. Translates "to speak the truth." The stage of trial also known as jury selection.

Wharton's Rule A legal doctrine that prohibits cumulative punishment in cases where two parties are necessary for the underlying offense, such as bigamy, gambling, and bribery.

INDEX

NOTE: Italicized page numbers refer to non-text material. Italicized page numbers following the word "defined" refer to definitions placed in the margins of the pages referred.